Pursuits of Happiness

Pursuits

OF

Happiness

ON BEING INTERESTED

Eva Brann

PAUL DRY BOOKS

Philadelphia 2020

First Paul Dry Books Edition, 2020

Paul Dry Books, Inc.
Philadelphia, Pennsylvania
www.pauldrybooks.com

Printed in the United States of America

Library of Congress Control Number: 2020937410

ISBN 978-1-58988-147-1

To Heather Latham
A friend in need . . .
Spring 2020

Contents

Preface

Two things of opposite natures seem to depend
On one another, as a man depends
On a woman, day on night, the imagined

On the real . . .

   (Wallace Stevens, *Notes Toward a Supreme Fiction*,
   "It Must Change," IV)

"Pursuits" of Happiness: "the pursuit of happiness," mentioned in our Declaration of Independence as an "unalienable right," doesn't, it appears, mean "the endless chase" but "the actual practice" of happiness, as in "the pursuit of a vocation" (Arthur Schlesinger, 1964).

I can't think of a single essay in this collection that isn't at bottom about this "vocational" happiness (what elsewhere I call "ontological optimism"), to be maintained in the face of reality's recalcitrance.

Subtitle: see the central essay "On Being Interested," where are considered the plying of happiness, the habit of interestedness, the interdependence of opposites, and the self-inclusion of dualities—my notion of the way things are.

Stevens's quotation: I was led to this very long poem, of which I understand about five stanzas, by Jesse Edward John-

son's *Yearbook*, a "young adult" fiction (hence *very* sophisticated). He quotes this pertinent passage:

> He had to choose. But it was not a choice
> Between excluding things. It was not a choice
>
> Between, but of. He chose to include the things
> That in each other are included, the whole,
> The complicate, the amassing harmony.

> ("It Must Give Pleasure," VI)

Since the poem is in free verse, I feel entitled to mend
the willful line breaks and engage with the prosaic wisdom
so recovered. In the opening quotation, all three dependencies are to be reversed, especially this one: the real actually
depends, in crucial contexts, on the imagined. But in the second quotation, the clause "that in each other are included"
especially gets to me. I know a luminous example of self-
inclusion: Thomas Aquinas's understanding of human will
as being at once deliberating desire and longing reason (for
example, *Summa Theologiae*, First Part of the Second Part,
Question 82, Article 4, Reply to Objection 1). More on self-
inclusion below.

Here, taking the second set of lines first, are thoughtful
wanting and longing mindfulness, each involving two very
diverse, even antithetical, psychic powers, reason and passion, both together, tightly clutched—proof of the soul's, of
our, unity-in-diversity. And, moreover, Thomas has got it
absolutely right, in exact concordance with innermost experience, mine, at least: the parts, the powers of our soul, are
indeed among "the things that in each other are included."

What really are, in general, "the things / That in each other
are included"? Here's an example of things that can't be: geometric figures. Let a triangle have been shown to be congruent with another, that is to say, angle by angle and side by side
equal and positioned the same. To be sure, there's no way to

prove that this produces congruence except to slide the one figure onto the other—but this Euclidean geometry eschews motion! Do it anyhow, as Euclid daringly does (*Elements* I 4). Now the figures coincide. And immediately Leibniz's Law of the Identity of Indiscernibles (not yet promulgated but nevertheless in force) kicks in; it says that items which differ in no discernible property are identical, one and the same. So the two figures are now one. Well might we ask: Has anything been proved about the *two* triangles by making them vanish into *one*? But let that be. Consider instead a human counterpart. Our students often seek to find and, unless they lose interest, finally do find, themselves. At that moment seeker and sought rush into each other's arms and become identical, and this establishes the youngster's "identity" and with it maturity. The whole agony is now in the past and a little jejune; its sufferer is no longer discernible from the persona found. Behold a grown-up!

But the enigma of the transition from merely mutual to accomplished self-inclusion continues into adulthood.

So it's on to love. Love is one of the few desires—perhaps the other is learning—that we don't want to assuage by excess, such "That, surfeiting, / The appetite may sicken and so die." In fact, I think, like the Duke of Illyria, that there is a simulacrum of love, more superficial, gustatory lust than deep, cordial passion:

No motion of the liver [seat of passion] but the palate,
That suffer surfeit, cloyment, and revolt;

but he's stupidly wrong in attributing it to women as opposed to men: "they lack retention."

Well, that's Orsino in *Twelfth Night*. Suppose we agree that love longs to be fulfilled rather than satiated, is it, or how is it, mutual and so, finally, self-inclusive? Again a poet answers, Donne in "The Ecstasy" (the ecstasy is literally the "standing out" of the soul from the body).

So two sit on a swelling bank, and wish for perfect union. But this is the lovers' insuperable impediment: They, being embodied souls, are not immaterial triangles and thus unable, though congruent, to become coincident. Both soul and body strive to meld, but the bodies "intergraft" only at their extremities, hands, skin:

> So t'intergraft our hands, as yet
> Was all the means to make us one;

As yet! Poor man, who is hoping for an ultimate but impossible consummation. Meanwhile,

> When love, with one another so
> Interanimates two souls,

an "abler," "new" soul issues, truly one from two, the unity that controls "defects of loneliness."

Thus bodily intergrafting is less efficacious than psychic interanimation. But then, the poet asks, why do we put up with, "forbear," that is, tolerate, our bodies "so long, so far"? It's because

1. "They're ours, though they are not we"
2. "We owe them thanks because they thus/
   Did us to us at first convey"

Heaven does not influence man directly, in its own spiritual mode, but indirectly, somatically:

> So soul into the soul may flow,
> Though it to body first repair
> . . .
> So must pure lovers' souls descend
> T'affections, and to faculties
> Which sense may reach and apprehend. . . .

It all appeals to me: the application of poetry to philosophy that is a figure for the body's service to the soul, the glad acceptance of our aboriginally compromised being, the close-thinking picking apart—and putting together of what is interesting, leaving the topic the better for it in sum, the double thinking that issues in more clarity and distinctness than does univocal doctrine, and yet underwrites single-minded faith. The essays to follow were written in this spirit.

Now to the first lines, that arouse my impulse to knowing better: "The imagined [depends] on the real." Just as self-inclusion in its various appearances will be a theme ghosting through these essays, so will be the imagination in its many operations. A hard-nosed, plausible interpretation of the poet's dictum might go like this: No matter how fantastical, how fanciful a mental image or a verbal or pictorial fiction is, its basic elements are borrowed from reality. Take the simplest case, a unicorn, a young horned mare, such as is depicted in the Unicorn Tapestry up in the Cloisters of New York. There are people who make the—contestable—claim that these images have no "real" originals, but that the creature is "just"—"just" is another contestable claim—a paste job: Take a narwhal's horn and affix it to a mare's forehead; you've "created" a mythological rather than a biological animal. (I doubt that this contrived critter would project virginality.)

The problem here is: Whence is reality itself borrowed? Kant, whom no one would call a fantasist, speaks of a "productive imagination" as "a hidden art in the depths of the human soul" (*Critique of Pure Reason* B 180), one that brings together our radically diverse faculties for thinking and sensing, and this imagination-mediated union first makes possible any and all cognizable existence of things, of "reality."

But if you're averse to the critical philosopher, believe the writer of fiction, Delmore Schwartz. He entitles a story "In Dreams Begin Responsibilities"—he might have written "Realities." In brief: Was anything ever artfully made that did not begin in a meticulous dream or a punctilious image? The young man of the story actually dreams a movie. *Watching* movies isn't, I think, up to reading books, because in their photographic precision movies forestall our imagination: Every visual detail is pre-defined; we only re-produce. But cinematic *dreaming* is imagining on the brink of producing thinghood

Well, this picking on some lines isn't quite fair, though poets think gnomically and such condensed speech wants picking apart, unpacking. Yet after all, though he instantiates only one dependent side, Stevens does say that they "depend/ On one another." And his final word is

> We say God and the imagination are one . . .
> ("Final Soliloquy of the Interior Paramour")

What he actually meant, I do not know, but what it might mean pervades the ensuing attempts, see the final essay, "[The Idea of] the Good."

I considered alternative titles. One was "Essays Old and New." This really unimaginative title had the homely virtue of correctness. Some of the older essays were published in those obscure and soon defunct venues I'm so fond of. The pieces are all right, at least I'm not in a revisionist mode— on the trouble-forfending mantra of my old age: "Been there, done that." Others were written recently, as I began going to thought-places I hadn't sufficiently been to—or at all, and taking up readings I hadn't properly done—or at all.

The other title was "Ways of Engagement." It was to have had the subtitle "With, Among, Beyond," three prepositions respectively descriptive of the involvements I muse about in the first, the middle, and the final essay of this book. This somewhat obvious title had the irking vice of cuteness.

In these writings I've used my happy device of putting the notes, containing contributing but collateral thoughts, right in the text, indented and in a different font. (Quotations are indented but in the text font.) These notes are where I have my fun, which not all, even well-disposed, readers, might find so funny or so pertinent. So they're easy to take in and easy to leave out (whereas footnotes and endnotes are distracting impositions on a dutiful reader and ignorable nothings to casual readers). As for references and credits, I've given the former only where their absence would mildly infuriate me as a reader, and supplied the latter where I've simply swiped* a

> I've allowed myself all the words to be found in some dictionary or other, even if marked "informal"—my preferred mode, not, I pray, to be taken for "undignified." And, very occasionally, when a micromotion of the soul or a minimotion of the mind had no established name, I've made one up. Let it be, as the Greeks say so nicely, a *hapax legomenon*, "a thing said but once."

distinctly identifiable thought-packet.

E. B.
Annapolis, 2018

1

Thing-Love*
Do Cars Die?

I would like to follow my guru-ess, Mary Norris of *Between You & Me*, on the matter of the hyphen. I think she's against it here, but it would take an afternoon to get that clear. So I'll do it my way.

Is there a love of things—of objects not having souls even in part like mine?* The answer is unequivocal: yes and no.

> "In part": as do animals. By and large I'm not fond of slobbery, smelly other species. If I was rich, however, and it wasn't illegal, I'd keep several bottle-nosed dolphins in a large seaside reservation and learn to talk to them. One day I'd offer to open the gates to the ocean. Now it becomes sheer fantasy: They'd say, "No, don't; we'd rather stay. You're more interesting than those clicking boors out there." Then I'd come in with them. This is the oceanic dream alternative to my galactic fantasy of going off with the spaceship that has made its delivery at Devil's Tower, Wyoming (I've been there), of disappeared WWII aviators. These aliens are nice people and would make do with getting me in exchange for that most enchanting little boy they've borrowed (*Close Encounters of the Third Kind*, 1977).

Yes, there is such a love, but no, it's doubtfully reciprocal. So that's the real question: Do beloved things respond—*themselves* respond? Who can doubt it? Don't we use the locution, "This thing—landscape or painting, fiction or poem, cantata or symphony—speaks to me, gets to me"?

1

Most people are not as dull as they make out, so, I imagine, thing-love, a sensibility alive to appealing things, is pretty general.* I mean the real thing: admiration up to adoration,

> The Economist's obituary (August 2018) for Mary Ellis, a ferry pilot in WWII, who had just died, aged 101, is headed "In love with Spitfires"; she climbed into the plane she was delivering made up as for an assignation. So there.
>
> Other thing-lovers: Robinson Crusoe among his companionable contrivances (see Essay 25, "The Unexpurgated Robinson"); children with their ratty teddy bears—there were times as a little girl when I cried more for my big doll Peter than for my little brother Wolfgang.

arousal into ardor, and, finally, fixation on acquisition.

Yet what real counter-love* can there be from those most

> I'm translating Greek ant-eros (Plato, Phaedrus 225d). Aristotle makes the following distinction in the Nicomachean Ethics (Bk. VIII, 2 and 5): For inanimate objects, since they neither reciprocate feeling (anti-philesis), nor do we wish their good, we don't feel fixed "friendship" (philia) but passing "liking" (philesis). To me it is heartening that Aristotle, who isn't given to oddity, has our affective relation to things in his purview.

acceptable of first responders to the fires they've lit? If they seem to address us, a doubter will say: "That's just you; you're discerning facets, glossing subtleties, reflecting rhythms, inspiriting matter—this thing's your golem." Yet my former colleagues, the true-born archaeologists, seemed able to maintain some mutuality of response with their artifacts.* So the

> I had no real talent for archaeology, for life among these things, august in their antiquity and almost unfailing elegance; I was a mere sojourner (it came to me) among the greats of my trade. They could get immersed in the contemplation of a pot sherd or a sculptural fragment and resonate to it: the more intensely transporting the viewing the more prosaically technical was the report thereof.
>
> One time my pots did take on life. I was sitting in my office, also a store room—shelves and shelves of archaic pottery—at the American excavation of the Athenian Agora (Marketplace). A minor earthquake: all the pots came tottering toward me. I thought: We dug you up and glued you together; now you'll come

apart again and bury me. (I didn't really think that till later; I was scared stiff.) The tremor stopped before they went over the cliff.

doubter says: "It's just you, endowing the object of your keen attention with responsive receptivity." Just?! Of course, it's my doing, my roused sensibility, my focused attention. But I'm not contriving, I'm finding. I'm one who, like most of us, "Finds tongues in trees, books in the running brooks, sermons in stones . . ." (*As You Like It* II i).

The thing has that in it which elicits my desirous mindfulness and excites my perception. Can one really say that it's not *doing* something, doing it to me, even seeking my reciprocating response? Or is that merely a cute conceit?

Before figuring that out, a parenthesis: There is a love of things, the materialism of the soul, that is plain base, though not for all that uninteresting—the love for power, money, trophy-partners, sex objects. The Christian Bible proclaims: "For the love of money is the root of all evil" (1 Timothy 6:10). Actually it's not the "love of money"; it's *philarguria*, more like "money-regard." These things are coveted; the desire is for possession, it's greed. My dictionary says of both covetousness and greed that they are "excessive desire." That doesn't seem to reach their essence. Isn't it less that the desire is immoderate than that it's desire for possession?*

> This thought is borrowed from Kant: the pleasure in beauty is "disinterested," meaning non-possessive. For "disinterested" means disjoined from all care for the object's existence, since such care is always desirous. So beauty is best loved unpossessively (*Critique of Judgment* §2).

But is a miser's fondling his gold or his greenbacks love at all? Is desire for possession ever really love? Isn't the sound desire that usually accompanies love simply desire for what we call, bureaucratically, "access"? The desirous facet of love wants welcomed togetherness. But that's not the love itself.

It sounds a little bizarre even to me, who's writing it, but it's so: Love is *not* desire (see Essay 33, "Difficult Desire"). Love is fulfillment, not lack, and thing-love is the exemplary case: lackless love.

For the situation is somewhat different when the *object* of love is a fellow *subject*. It, he, she can, as can I, withdraw, elude, alter. But: ". . . Love is not love/Which alters when it alteration finds" (Sonnet 116). I'm used to thinking that he knows everything about it, but here Shakespeare might be wrong. Of course, he means that love doesn't bend "with the remover to remove," but who can carry on forever in the absence of hope? Moreover, what if the lines were read as saying that love outlasts *any* change in the object? How can it, if the love was for *this* being *here*, precisely as I've*

Which happens to be what Aristotle means by a "Being, simply" (*tode ti*, *Metaphysics* 1030a19).

known it?*

Of course, not all changes are alterations, "becoming other." Some are self-completions and perfect one's reciprocal love.

At this point I must say what I mean here by a thing: whatever is recognizable as an entity but (probably) without a self- and other-communicating soul, so: 1) natural discrete units like mountains; 2) inarticulate animals without prejudice to those embattled parrots, dolphins, and chimps; 3) surd artifacts like pots and paintings and speaking ones like books and music.

Let me address pots as exemplary objects of thing-love, both because they're so very thingy and because a batch of them was once under my very absorbed care.* These objects,

Late Geometric and Protoattic Pottery, The Athenian Agora, vol. VIII (1962). Archaeologists are, it must be told, inveterate anthropomorphizers. A wine jar has a neck, shoulders, belly, foot, even hand[le]s in our catalogue descriptions.

essentially shaped and baked earth, had the following features: 1) If long lasting is an approach to immortality, they exceed my mortality by far: 2700 years and running, to my 90 and slowing down. 2) If maintaining shape and resisting ravage is a sign of dependability, they are more steadfast than even my most solid friends. 3) If being a demanding lover is an equivocal virtue—either nerve-racking or exhilarating; the artifacts I've known longest and best, novels, are models of the latter sort—the investment of attentive realization required by a text, be it in cluing out the subtext or in calling up the imagery, might be called, were it not so enjoyable, arduous.*

4) If expressing a state of mind is trustworthy evidence of inwardness, it's even possible that things have souls. This is in a note because it borders on kooky, but it happened: An alumnus came in from D.C. to go to lunch and had clearly lost my house number. I saw his car pass down the road and roll to a stop. I could swear *it* looked puzzled.

Apropos of my four If's: Touchstone, that incarnate test of sense, says: "Your 'if' is the only peacemaker, much virtue in 'if'" (*As You Like It* V iv); I'm all for de-polemicizing hypotheses, for iffing, Socrates' way, for which he was willing to die. (See Essay 18, "Carryover.")

Better late than never: I should say that those pot-ponderings are *not* about aesthetics, the study of beauty as we respond to it with our sense organs and our psychic sensibility; some of these round-bellied pots* aren't even that beauteous,

Archaeologists use "vase" only reluctantly, for the crème de la crème, finely figured vessels.

are certainly not "vases." My perplexity is about thinghood as attaching. So then, is it possible to fall in love with, to be enchanted by, captivated by, a thing—with a love that is at least kindred with human-to-human love? The answer is plain: *yes*, articulably. And is it possible that such love is not only unidirectional? Can a thing be both beloved and lover? The answer is, once again, also plain: *No and yes.* No, because it's just a thing, after all. But yes, because these are things that "exercise" attraction,* and that's the perpetual

> "Who, moving others, are themselves as stone" (Sonnet 94). Here's a new mode of hybrid love, thing- and person-love intertwined, frequently to be observed these days: A couple walks along, holding hands in the middle, but outside each holding a cell phone to his/her ear.

puzzle. Things, and not just artifacts, which might be regarded as "objectifications"* of the maker's subject-imbued

> Hegel's coinage, I think: *"Objektivierung."* In his *Philosophy of Nature* he dwells on my experiential question on a deeper conceptual level: How does spirit close in on Nature?

visions, and so messages, even love-letters, to readers and viewers, aren't they dynamic?* Mountains and wide rivers

> Even the "ideas" of the Platonic dialogues turn out to be not just knowable but affected by being known; they are said to have *dynamis*, a power, a potency for being "moved," by being "intellected," recognized (*Sophist* 248c–e).

(especially the Mississippi) do sometimes speak to us, as we discover when we are moved to reply. And so of course do statues and vases; thus a fragmented Apollo silently says to his viewer: *"Du musst dein Leben ändern*, You must change your life" (Rilke, "Archaic Torso of Apollo"), or a vase finally utters: "Beauty is truth, truth beauty" (Keats, "Ode on a Grecian Urn"). This admonition and this pronouncement, did they come from our parents or our professor of aesthetics, would have no heft at all; here that's derived from their poetic provenance.

So poets make marbles talk* as well as pots, and composers

> As epigraphists do stones: *Saxa loquuntur,* "The stones speak," they say.

make singers talk and novelists do nothing but talk. To be sure, these works of art always say the same thing (Plato, *Phaedrus* 215d), but in that they don't much differ from us live speakers, and what they do say is sometimes more worth hearing—and perhaps needs that much repetition to be understood.*

> Some of the books I own are falling apart, so repetition can't be the problem. And commentaries, which try to say the same thing *otherwise*, can be treacherous. For why would "otherwise" be 1) easier, but 2) the same?

Well, I take it as proved that it is feasible to love soul-curtailed and soul-less beings, that is, animals and natural or made things. The salient question was all along: Do they love us back?* This is a deep question, not to be answered by

> My friend, Ray Coppinger, a dog-evolutionist, breeder, and owner, once told me: "Don't you believe that about man's best friend. They're in it for themselves." I thought: "Like us?"

experience, because our all-too-eager imagination can supply a deceptive affirmation. It is, like all that goes deep, in the end an ontological question, a question concerning the (true) account of Being and beings. Are *mere* beings, things, so made as to have some responsive commonality with us?* In

> Lest even a well-disposed reader now suspect me of veering toward the Christian Fundamentalists' "intelligent design" argument—not so. If anything, it's the Aristotelian Divine Mind (*Nous*, *Metaphysics* XII 7), who governs the world by moving, himself unmoved, *all* beings, namely by the power of his attractive—self-sufficient, un-thing-like, immaterial, fully actual—life, moving them in the same way in which we speak of "being moved," impassioned, by an object. Yet the *Nous* has no personal relations.

other words, is our world, be it ever-existent or, once made, so constituted that all discernible entities within it have some reciprocal relation, which can be singularly activated by one being's initiative? Of course, I don't know the answer, beyond that hopefully expectant construal which is not to be taken for belief but precludes doctrinal skepticism.* Here is how I

> No one is more unbudgingly self-certain than the theoretical knowledge-denier.

live with this unanswered question: To love things is like living with a terminally reserved person who's full of inhibited
love.*

> Answer to the question in the title, "Do cars die?" They die on you,
> all right, and it's pure malignancy.

All that said, I can't imagine that any thing, any material
entity, can ever evoke that degree of ardent love in which the
soul threatens to burst into starry fragments and to diffuse
itself through the universe. That takes a fellow human—little
or grown-up, manly or womanly, sound or suffering, translucent or opaque—and alive or dead.

2

Secular Original Sin
Aboriginal Wrongness

There's no doubt about it: Theological original sin is a vivid, highly concrete conception, at least as set out by Thomas Aquinas in thirteen articles (through three Questions, 81–83, of *Summa Theologiae*, First Part of the Second Part, On Habits, Vices, Virtues). Nonetheless I can't feel myself afflicted by this evil, for specific reasons. Since not every reader will find the features and my objections as engrossing as I do, I'll put them in a note.* But this belongs in the text: Some version of

Question 81 on the transmission of original sin from the First Parent, Adam: This sin is transmitted through the semen; thus Mother Eve, I'm glad to read, is not responsible, though she is plainly the originator of the Fall. Through this genetic inheritance the theological sin afflicts all men. None of this is plausible to me: not the tricky business (which Thomas is brilliant at) of biological transmission of a psychical condition, nor the innocence of that part of the paradisical pair mentally acute enough to do the evil that really hurts Heaven (see Essay 24, "Eve Separate"), nor the present universality of this deep-seated sin, when I know people too innocently light-minded to have a sense of it in themselves. In brief, my sin assuredly does not come to me from my father (or from my paternal grandmother whom alone I resemble, in my once-blue eyes), from whom I think I have a very welcome trait, that of an occasional inner conclusiveness without loss of ambivalence.

Question 82 on the essence of original sin: Thomas's circumscriptive terms are entirely recognizable to me. It belongs to this kind of sin to be a habit, an ingrained mode, to be at least a second, if not a first nature. It is, centrally and negatively, the "absence of original justice," that is, the failure of the soul's parts to be well adjusted to each other. It is an "inordinate disposition," that is, a disordered temperament, expressed as "concupiscence," that is, the greedy desire for admiration and gratification—bottomless assertions of self-esteem such as the current purveyors of that therapeuticized term haven't the slightest notion of, combined with the incapability of self-removal from temptation. I'm saved from perdition only by what Thomas calls the "languor of nature," my torpidity and inertia. It's an exploitable vice: too lazy to be very malignant. For all its particular psychological familiarity, this original sin is alien to me as a generality. Not only don't I see, as I said, any universality, but some people seem to me pretty good by nature and some are even, as I said, ignorantly innocent, too dopey for well-specified guilt. But above all, there's no god in my aboriginal sin, which isn't a rebellion against a lord but a way of being a subject, in the sense of being a self, namely selfishness. But above all, I'm all against imputing faults to anyone other than the immediate perpetrator, against assigning generic or individual blame for others' ill-being or wrong-doing.

To be sure, it is an act of grace when offspring feel burdened by their progenitors' evil deeds, such as some Nazis' children were. Or when descendants take on the sins of their country's history—that's a sign of decency. On the other hand, it then becomes the victim-by-inheritance's duty to dissuade these guilt-arrogators *not* from acts of restitution but from feelings of contrition. The children of victims and of perpetrators are equally innocent, namely totally. This discussion is one way to defeat history—a humanity-enhancing, very private, activity of real consequence.

Question 83 on the seat of original sin: That is the soul, of course. In spite of the carnal transmission of sin, flesh cannot be sinful; it's just stuff, even if organic. And sin belongs to the soul essentially, not accidentally because it is, as has been said, a corruption of its very being, its well-adjusted powers. That's how it feels—a deep-seated, ineradicable proneness to being wrong, to being in the wrong. Where, then, is it seated in the soul? Thomas says, in the will. The will is a psychical faculty not of mere appetite, such as is immediately expressed in the body, but of rational desire, the longing not for a merely apparent but a true good, thought-informed desire or desire-infused thinking, deliberated longing and desirous planning. Here Thomas is the master of the phenomena of human being. And my secular sense of inborn sin, if a world away from the theology and its rebellion, yet lives in the same universe of discourse; the seat of original sin is that perversion of the will called willfulness—the will coopted to the service of the self rather than of an other, be it a person, an object, a world.

original sin, sin from way back, even preceding any deed, is very familiar to me. Moreover, I'm pretty sure that I wouldn't relish getting into a moral hassle with a fellow human who was entirely devoid of this sense of unconditioned wrongdoing. I mean more than the obvious fact that I'm apt to be mistaken as to circumstance and defective in judgment, having scrambled, or even forgotten, relevant dates, events, concepts, principles. Being in error like that leaves me relatively sanguine. You're just as likely as I am to be thus secularly wrong, and if you're not, you're a terminally annoying person. I mean sinfulness as *evil*, as different from normal human baseness as gin is from ginger ale—spicy badness.* Such as: successful

It's a difference analogous to Nietzsche's between *schlecht*, mingily "base," and *böse*, juicily "evil" (for example, *Beyond Good and Evil* no. 260).

diddling of the truth, effective one-upmanship, enjoying of others' come-uppance, relishing favorable comparison to a denigrated world, rehearsing with gusto others' misdeeds toward me and devising elegant vengeances for them—in sum, inflicting preventive suffering to secure my safe superiority—self-righteousness, the enjoyment of my own goodness.*

On the edge of sin: Our—my—large appetite for admiration and its silly complexities: I am praised and my bosom swells; I'm in my element. And yet—I could slip under the table with ambivalent embarrassment: how excessive in amplitude—and how deficient in discernment!

And the ignoble protestantism of it all: its vast overestimation of deedless subjectivity and its self-elevating conviction that sins contemplated are "as good as" sins committed, with the

sneaky conviction that evil articulated is evil secularly confessed and that this confession too entails absolution.*

> The arch-Protestant in these complexifications: Kierkegaard. The
> plain truth is that what you didn't *do*, you *didn't do*. Thinking is an
> activity but not an action. It may, on the contrary, be the case that
> an inner relish for evil is Nature's or Nature's God's safety valve:
> harmlessly inactive satisfaction. Though immediately a danger
> arises: When is it explosively pathological? For sure, when there is
> the proclamation of a planned action.
> My parents had a Yiddish word for such Kierkegaardian sub-
> tlety: *überkandidelt*, "too clever by half"—a little mad.

Is there real internal self-harm with worldly consequences?
Of course, there's the one that is, to my mind, most dangerous: being bored by the normality of decent, peaceable dailiness, seeing honesty as naïvety, quietude as dullness, dailiness
as routine, especially the last. Focused souls find in just such
repetitiveness the continuo, the thorough bass, that seconds
soaring melody or, if you like, the cantus firmus that supports
multiple voices.*

> Unfortunately there's a consortium of quixotic disenchanters, who
> desiccate and dispirit the ordinary: functionaries, experts, educa-
> tionists, intellectuals. They make young lives violence-prone. But
> enough said elsewhere.

What deeds go with being *soundly* light-minded about secular original sin, living right not in spite but because of it?
Here are my maxims—politically so incorrect that one of the
morality preceptors would turn the set red with ink edits.

1) Be especially *nice* to people you don't like, on the—at
bottom implausible—hypothesis that it's not their fault but
yours.

2) Don't lose your temper except when it would denigrate
the world not to; in other words, never lose it, but sometimes
let it *loose*.

3) Stay *focused*, affirm the meaning of a holiday, a holy day,
and subvert that of a vacation, a vacant time; marshal every
day under the matter at hand, so that if any thought grist to

the speculative mill turns up, you're ready to grind. But no, unseemly simile. What's a better self-precept? I've got it: alert letting-be.

4) Nourish your natural aversion to current moralisms, not because something doesn't need fixing but because the self-righteous fixers make it worse. Activate the virtue of *butting-out*; allow others their prejudices:

> The enumeration in the Constitution, of certain rights, shall not be construed to deny or disparage others retained by the people (Eighth Amendment).

I construe this article to mean that we retain the undisparaged right to be idiots, each in his/her own way, even anti-Semites.

5) Let others say their say and *hear* it. Stay on the case. Care can't be a one-off.*

> It doesn't quite work practically. One of my freshmen, after talking: "Is this the last time?" Me: "Why on earth?" She: "Because soon I'll be a sophomore." Me: "Once your tutor, always your tutor." I meant it, but there's new students every year.

6) I'm beyond such action now, but when I was in the thick of it, I favored swift and *conclusive punishment* for provable misbehavior: "Out!" Yet the ejection from our community of what in our South they call "bad cess" was questionable as a purification, since it was now splashed all over the environing world. Still, be sometimes conclusive.

7) Swim *upstream*. The so-called "movement" currently agitating women's issues is moving the wrong way, though perhaps about the right thing—the wrong way in unwoman-ing us: self-esteem is the undoing of self-respect, self-asser-tion the corruption of self-confidence, and the disparaging of maleness the confounding of womanliness. For it's char-acteristic of a woman to have a soft spot especially for young males, because of their awkward charm and their breakable pride. (Every female, twelve and up, is my age.) The sum total of my iffy wisdom: men and women feel in different ways and

think in the same way—a notion that develops subtleties not suitable for social thinking. So do it yourself. Wanting indiscriminately to "belong" is aboriginally sinful.

8) *Never* try, or hope, to *say anything new*—just say what you think. By the articles our alumni send me to mend my supposed disjunction from the world, *homo sapiens* came into it ever earlier, now 300,000 years ago. In my experience, *sapientia*, "wisdom," is not circumstantial, it precedes and outstays any current condition. So how could there be anything sensible that remains unsaid in those three thousand centuries gone by since we first became sapient, wise? To be sure, there are many things, most things, new to *me*, but never to the *world*; at least, it's unlikely. So it's probably part of my sort of original sin to wish to be original, in the basest of its several senses: novel. Self-admonition: Be grateful it isn't even in you actually to be innovative.

Annapolis, 2018

3

Immediacy
The Ways of Humanity

I want to steal four minutes of my talking time to speak of the role that the Santa Fe campus has played in my life. I remember vividly the atmosphere around its founding in the years before 1964, but only confusedly the arguments pro and con—though among the latter one worry was predominant: Were we overextending ourselves? It was a reasonable worry because of our president's plan, reported on page 6 of his book *The Colonization of a College* (1985). Here is what Dick Weigle said:

> I elaborated a quixotic plan for six St. John's Colleges strategically located throughout the United States.

It was a vision in equal parts exhilarating and terrifying. When I used to bowl across the continent in my little blue bug to assume my teaching duties in the early Graduate Institute at Santa Fe, I would sometimes take the northern, sometimes the southern route and imagine three colleges of a Johnnie

A presentation to a conference on the Liberal Arts in honor of the fiftieth anniversary of the founding of the Santa Fe campus of St. John's College, October 2014.

empire strung across the top, three across the bottom of these United States, or even six lined up diagonally along the legendary Route 66. Yet the question was, were six St. John's four or five too many for this world?

Doubt about the feasibility of many colleges turned into delight with the actuality of one, as the colony turned into a sister-college. Siamese sisters as it seemed to me, two bodies with one soul, separate existences with one essence, separable only on pain of death for one or the other.

As time went on, the myth-making that arises in real communities proceeded. Annapolis, locked in by its east-coast creeks, was over-intense and hyper-intellectual, Santa Fe, expansive under southwestern skies, was laid-back and loose-minded, in touch with Native American wisdom, while Annapolis was dominated by a bunch of stuffy Teutons. I was one of them, a latecomer. Quite a few of these central Europeans had in fact found a refugee's welcome in Maryland. It was the kind of spirited nonsense by which incipient communities develop what's called their identities. The wonderful truth was that the Program had traveled so well, had shown itself so safely beyond a time or a place, that the conversation was just the same in the wide Southwest as in the constricted mid-Atlantic—not a boring same but an exhilarating same, like Cleopatra, of whom it is said that

> Age cannot wither her, nor custom stale
> Her infinite variety
>
> (*Anthony and Cleopatra* II ii 240).

Meanwhile I had my private mythology, since every place that has some atmosphere resonates with cognate visions. From my balcony on the lower campus I could see the then more magically defined Cerillos in the distance and, close up, the Territorial architecture of the campus. To my Aegean imagination, in its light columns and bright courtyards, it bore a resemblance to King Minos's palace in Cretan Knossos, which harbored the thrilling mystery of the Labyrinth and its Minotaur. That's how your campus felt to a visitor from summer-soggy Annapolis.

So now from autobiography to my real matter: *immediacy*. Sometimes I think that this quality, which I'm about to delineate, is our deepest, most defining characteristic. I imagine that we could remain ourselves although we lost in turn every element of our program of learning, if only we saved that mode of being. But then again, it seems to me that this directness of ours is best, perhaps even exclusively, served by the pedagogic practices and the programmatic materials we do, in fact, employ. So I'm in this respect in my most frequent state—that of thinking out of both sides of my mind, so to speak (not of my brain, I hasten to say, because that's an improbable activity). This is how I frame the question for myself: What is our central good, and are there alternative ways of achieving it? The second part of the question is open in theory, though in practice, who would want to jettison so well-working a way of teaching and so coherent a plan of learning?

As for the first part—what is our central virtue?—I think the history of the St. John's Program gives a clue. Like any maturing community, we have accumulated, and are bound by, masses of customs, practices, rules. But we're very unlike most institutions in having divested ourselves of more and more intellectual inhibitions as we went. You might say we have become more radical as we aged—not in the sense of "more incendiary" but of "closer to the roots," in my terms, more *immediate*.

Here's an example. In the first, the 1937–1938 Bulletin of the Program, written by its intellectual founder, Scott Buchanan, the Great Books list was, as is academic convention, ranged under rubrics. Thus Homer and the Old Testament came under the rubric of "Language and Literature." Now, if you think about it, this classification intervenes between the book and the reader with a strong dose of meddling opinion: It shields the student from the fact that Homer was thought of by the Greeks as their prime theologian and that the Hebrew Bible presents itself as the history of a people and their God. I don't mean to disparage Scott Buchanan, whose educational originality is beyond dispute. But we've eradicated the vestiges of conventional intermediation which were, I imagine, under his radar in those exciting days.

There are any number of small ways in which we've become more immediate. I'll give one more example. In the early days a historical significance was often attached to the fact that our seminar list is largely ordered chronologically; terms such as "medieval," "Renaissance," "the modern mind" were still used. For most of us this temporal order is now simply a practical device: Later books often refer to preceding ones, as Newton uses Euclidean propositions. We don't put a scholar-devised designation on books but read them directly. Our context is not interpretative back-grounding and scholarly introduction but what you might call the quarreling, contemporaneous brotherhood of Great Books.

Let me take a moment here for a word on Great Books, a term our clueless advisors tell us to jettison. To my mind it is a true category whose members are truly discontinuous with other, perfectly good, books. There is no ultimate difficulty about listing the criteria, which require, however, not so much discernment as longevity to discern, since the chief characteristics take a lifetime to become evident. Opposition to greatness comes, I'm convinced, from the kind of irrational irritation that made the Athenians ostracize Aristides because they were tired of hearing him called "the Just," or from egalitarian resentment, or—this one I have real sympathy for—from fear of the demands things of quality make on us.

Back to context. It is an academic habit to insulate works of stature from students and the students from them by packing them in this cotton wool of back-grounding lectures and introductory readings. And since the students' valuable time has been thus preempted, teachers then make up for that by reducing original texts to selected snippets or reproducing them as travesties by paraphrased abstracts. Add to this the emergence of theories of interpretation so sophisticated as to make an innocent approach to these books seem simple-minded.

Well, we do not occupy students' time or prevent access to books by delivering premasticated versions of their settings or meanings. As far as I can tell we have only one interpretational maxim: *A cat may look at a king* (from an old adage, dating to 1562). Our royal texts can be confronted by any considering intelligence, feline or fellow-human.

I think most members of this college community—students, tutors, alumni, friends—will readily recognize this immediate relation to books as our very particular way. It carries with it certain opportunities, even obligations, that less direct approaches forego, even forbid. Chief of these is the question practically proscribed in most classrooms: Is this treatise of reasonings *true* in the existent world? Is this work of fictions *true* in the imaginative realm?

Now in educating our students and ourselves in this so natural and yet so misprized way we actually do, I think, tiny as we are, help to repair a more global loss. To explain that, allow me to return for a moment to autobiography.

When I came to this college in 1957, Jacob Klein was its dean, its third dean in the New Program. In Winfree Smith's *A Search for the Liberal College* (1983), a fine history of the beginning of the New Program, you will find a letter Jasha wrote to his future wife, Dodo, in 1938 after a few weeks at the college:

> . . . it is exciting to see how over centuries and oceans unspoiled boys (most of them are) are impressed by Plato. They read with a *directness* [my italics] that is sometimes frightening . . . I walked around the first days drunk with happiness (p. 105).

I know all about this blissful inebriation; it was the same when I came, something short of a score of years later. Eventually I sobered up into the stable state that Aristotle would recognize as happiness: an activity of the soul in accordance with virtue. In short, I did some real work.

But my point here is the "directness" Mr. Klein mentions.

There is a long and deep story behind this directness, and it is, in fact, the history behind this talk on immediacy. Generally speaking, I'm not much for hanging on to your teachers for too long; our students should take off on their own: "I was never anyone's teacher" says the greatest of them with teacherly irony as a lesson to us tutors (Socrates in the *Apology* 33a). But let this be one of those permissible moments of grateful memory.

Jacob Klein wrote a book that was eventually republished by Dover as a classic. Its subject was the origin of Western algebra in a great mathematical revolution at the beginning of modernity. The work was quite specifically technical but it could be interpreted to have a very wide resonance: the loss of immediacy that made modern times so superlatively efficient in some respects and so sadly soul-deficient in others. I will try to say in a word what this indirectness, this loss of immediacy that has captured us moderns, consists of: We tend to see and approach our lives and the world through a screen of concepts, techniques, and symbols. We focus on means rather than ends, formalisms rather than substance, media rather than content. This last displacement is having its era of frenzy at the moment, when the interest in speed and variety of delivery is no longer in finite proportion to the quality and interest of the message.

So you can see that my view of the college is indebted to this book, or rather to my appropriation of it. Now it happens to belong to the human condition to be born as frighteningly direct babies and to be capable of retaining this immediacy, or to recover it through boy- and girlhood—and even in old age. To me our college is one agent in this recovery, this renaissance of immediacy. Let me race, then, through other elements of reborn immediacy that seem to me to characterize us, to the benefit of our humanity.

My first item was that we, tutors and students, do not, prematurely, let opined interpretations intervene between us and the books we've chosen to study. There is a second kind of intervention we cancel: time. The past we admit into our Program has *not* passed; it is now, an ingredient in our being, our ground. Human beings who live only in the latest Now, in the *modo*, meaning "just now," the adverb from which "modernity" is made, are ungrounded, racing headless and footloose through nonlife, mistaking excitation for happiness and quantity for reality. So, inversely, have the folk on the other side, the reactionaries who are stuck in the sort of past that *has* passed, that is truly dead and gone, turned a ground into a grave.

Our study, then, is that living past which reaches right into the present. It lives in what may be called the Tradition, the works, the Great Books, that are both inexhaustibly interesting in themselves and the explanatory ground of our present. Not to know the Tradition is to become the helpless victim of circumstance, while to have some familiarity with it is to gain awareness. And to be aware is to abrogate tyrannical time and to master dominating circumstance, by living in the world immediately, not divided from it by opaquely unassimilated inheritances and pointlessly smart innovations.

Now I think that to those who inspect us through conventional categories we appear to have a powerful institutional method and strong implicit presuppositions. For to an ideology-ridden world, what is really natural appears very contrived. To my mind, we have the most minimal preconceptions, and are therefore as simple—you might say as deliberately naïve—in our ways as can be. I mean institutionally—most of my colleagues, and students as well, are replete with ingenious takes on who we are.

It seems to me that our direct and time-subverting approach to the works of civilization implies, besides the *A cat may look at a king* maxim, just one more precept: *Origins are significant*. Here we call to our aid a Greek word, *arché*. It turns up in slews of English words from archangel to archfiend, from archaeology to archetype, from archaeopteryx to matriarch: chief angel, principal devil, antiquarian study, original model, old wing, ruling mother. So *arché* means what is first, old, original, chief, and governing; an *arché* is a beginning that rules. That there are such beginnings is a faith that our Program expresses; it betokens our replacement of chronological history. That is, to be sure, a potent opinion ever in need of intelligent defense. But it is not an ideology in the current understanding, meaning a body of theory implying a political agenda. We keep our classrooms free of current politics not only to protect our students from their teachers' private preoccupations, but even more to provide them with one venue where they can think about personal and political problems deeply and directly, unobstructed by foggy drifts of current passion.

I've just used the word "teacher." In his last public appearance Socrates, one of the Program's master teachers, tells his Athenians a semi-truth I've already cited: "I was never ever (*popote*) anyone's teacher" (*Apology* 33 a). We tutors might say the same, and it would not be just a pretty pretense. Institutions of higher learning are staffed by professors who are distanced from their students by the authority of their expertise. The faculty of this college cannot pretend to such authority; we are intentionally and irremediably out of our depth. That is not only because our program of studies requires us to teach outside of our graduate training and professional competence—that's the least of it—but because we require ourselves and our students to delve into depths that are beyond most of us much of the time. That's because we demand seriousness of them as of ourselves, and in the realm of learning (as distinct from performance) seriousness begins just where competence ends.

This kind of non-professional pedagogy, which engages more in eliciting thinking than delivering answers, which regards the expression "I don't know" more as a sign of intellectual virtue than an admission of deficiency, which respects a well-framed question more than a facile answer, draws tutors and students together.* There is a genuine equality in

> Students preserve affection particularly for tutors who, setting aside self-esteem, address their self-respect. High point for me, from a student to whom I'd imparted some difficult truths along the lines of: "You're too good to think you're best." He said, "You're for real, aren't you." Well, when I've got the moral energy.

the face of great matter, which we express in the formality of our mutual address. Our classrooms are venues for conversation, a Latin word that, as I construe it, means "turn and turn about": All take their turn when the spirit is upon them; we do not stand on academic ceremony such as hand-raising protocol or professional primacy. We all participate spontaneously, and what matters is what is said, not who says it. And behold, in thus addressing ourselves to the matter, the individual humanity of the participants in the inquiry begins really to shine forth.

These four are probably our chief immediacies: unmediated reading of texts, time-disencumbered absorption of the tradition, theoretically unobstructed approaches, and unembarrassed relations between tutors and students. They imply all sorts of pedagogic ways—their direct fall-out. So there's a slew of other immediacies, some of which I'll now race through. They're all involved with each other.

To value utility is to raise means over ends; it is the antithesis of *im-mediacy*. Aristotle first defined liberal learning as something done, at least in part, for its own sake rather than as a means for use (*Politics* VIII 2, *Metaphysics* I 2). Its opposite is what is termed "vocationalism," the degradation of a beautiful word, for "vocation" means a "calling," a summons to a mission.

Our Program of learning is unabashedly non-vocational, non-instrumental—though that is a toxic admission under present conditions. That much the louder should we proclaim our educational radicalism. Vocationalism turns joyful learning into toilsome training, and relocates the pleasure of the college years from study to extracurricular activity. Thus it puts an intervening preparatory period between young adults and the reality of life—four years of deflected seriousness and deferred fulfillment, when the strenuous leisure of higher education ought to be as immediately real as anything in later life. We do mitigate the off-putting radicalism of an education that is its own end by pointing out that, as in much of real life, so also for our Program, the unintended consequences work their effects. In our case, these incidental outcomes are serendipitous: Our students are particularly well prepared to navigate the knowledge-economy of our time and to protect their happiness in a world fixated on means to the detriment of ends—and, I might add, on the dilution of tautly passionate engagement into slackly preferential liking.

An acute critic of the Program might object: "But in having revived, as you do, the medieval trivium and quadrivium, in organizing liberal education by means of the liberal arts, which are skills, haven't you actually committed yourself to a training in means, since such know-how seem to be not an end but a means to an end?" We would answer that we never teach mere skills or methods. We have no courses in the "scientific method" or in "mathematical thinking" or in the "writing process." We exemplify each approach by its finest destination, each process by its most elegant product, each skill by its most beautiful result. We keep doing and deed immediately together—study the ways of physical science through their most crucial theories, the ways of mathematics through their most elegant theorems, the ways of expression through their most moving products. In short, we rarely engage in mere training exercises but keep "how" and "what" in close connection. Our concomitant immediacy implies that we rarely require our students to collect published information or compile secondary opinions. Be it in speaking or writing, we want them to approach some important matters directly—as the cat looks consideringly at a king. That means that we expect them to be independently critical—but not so much in the mode of "questioning everything" as of asking questions. Thus it is not a standoffish, corrosive critiquing we look for but a reverent and often corroborative criticality— the sort that expresses close, respectful engagement.

Finally, in general we try to forgo mere formalisms. Instead we direct all our customs and rules to some articulable good end. In that spirit our "administrative" offices and officers stay true to their designation: they "minister to" our Program. We have only minimal bureaucracy; it is a word that literally means the "might of offices," a domination that separates a community from its purpose by introducing the notion of power. As competition is only marginal to our learning, so power is not a mode of our governance. For as competition in learning displaces attention to the actual object, so power in governance usurps compliance with trusted authority.

I could make a long list of other immediacies and take a long time to report them, so I'll put an end to it now. There's one addendum, however: In reading over what I've written I see what I really mean by "immediacy." I mean humanity. So now I'll put it to myself and to you not very humbly, but, I think, truly: It is the care of our college to maintain the ways of humanity.

4

The Tradition
Its Timelessness

It is both an honor and a pleasure to be among you. I don't know if I can show my appreciation by my talk. I can't quite believe that normal people want to hear composed speeches for breakfast. Most of us want to read our newspapers and drink our morning coffee in peace and quiet and don't want to be talked to even by their nearest and dearest. And now you have to listen to an alien from the northerly east coast.

Well, the ancient rhetoricians, who knew their business, taught that the way to begin a speech, the more so a breakfast talk, was with what they called a *captatio benevolentiae*, a "capturing of goodwill." I'll try that on you—I'll try to snaffle your benevolence by claiming that we are likely to have this in common: a great respect for tradition.

"Tradition" is a broad term. I think we commonly understand by a tradition a practice we repeat, say every week or every year, just because we've always done it. Part of its meaning comes precisely from its age, which makes it venerable, worthy of reverence.

For example, just two weeks ago I was in the American city so wonderfully called Athens, in Georgia, to lecture at the university there. The professor who had invited me, an orthodox Jew, asked me to dinner at his house. It was a Friday, *erev shabbat*, Sabbath evening, and though I was brought up in an assimilated household without Jewish ritual, this celebration of the seventh day, when God finished his creation and saw it was very good, was very familiar and poignant to me. But a good Jew can't stop himself from waxing witty even in sacred matters. And so I learned something hilarious: It is evidently a matter of competition what father of the house can say the shabbat blessing, the *bracha*, and other preliminary prayers at the fastest clip—in consideration of the hungry family that's drawing in delicious aromas from the kitchen. And so my professional host outdid any auctioneer in addressing our Lord, who is, presumably, also pressed for earthly time. It was purely wonderful because 1) I too was hungry and tired, having passed an afternoon trying to deal with the clever questions of a bunch of terrific graduate students in philosophy, and because 2) I've often observed that true reverence is full of puckish laughter, and here was corroboration from a genuine practitioner of Judaism.

What I've been describing, then, is tradition as ritual, which gains a certain patina, as copper grows green, from mere age. There's nothing in our Constitution that keeps damn fools from doing their thing, just as, for example, in the book of ritual for Passover, the Haggadah, in which one of those stupidly smart kids we've all run into is allowed to sit at the seder table and ask aggressively contemptuous questions. For my part, I don't think you ought to do everything you have a constitutionally protected right or your family's forbearing permission to do. But there's no question about the right—as long as you are willing to put up with the retaliation in which the offended side is, under the same Constitution, entitled to engage.

I've referenced a recent event* to make the point that

I have in mind a recent to-do brought on by a football player who refused to stand up for the national anthem to protest social injustice.

traditions that are venerable as settled ritual are vulnerable to disruptions: In fact, they are easy pickings for rebellious spirits in the demonstrative mode. Indeed, it is an urgent question how to protect our shrinking public forms and rituals without becoming reactionary about them; by "reactionary" I mean a mode that concentrates all feelings on defense, with little left over for the positive love of old forms, whose age is often a part of their beauty.

But I want to talk to you this morning of tradition in another sense, a sense that is the opposite of old. To be sure, the word "tradition" itself means "that which is handed over" or "handed down," and so by its very meaning tradition comes from the past. Now "past" too has two meanings. One, probably the more common sense, is "passed away, bygone, finished and done with"—as when we sometimes say "It's history," meaning that an event has seen its moment and no longer counts.

I'll tell you my favorite example of what ought to be past in that sense. If somebody has done you a bad turn, he might ask you to forgive him, and you might give him what he's asked for because he's said that he's sorry. Or you might even relieve him without his asking, because you—rightly, I think—don't believe that it's in our human power to forgive, that is, to declare someone else's wrongdoing all right, to undo a bad deed. You can't reach into the past and tweak it by making what's packed away there un-happen. "What's done cannot be undone," says that once-intrepid evildoer, Shakespeare's Lady Macbeth (V i 76), who goes mad through that knowledge.

And you probably know it from your own experience—you feel practically forever in debt to people who've forgiven you, and they feel it too, so your offense is alive in you both.

On the other hand, there's forgetting. If you've suffered a wrong, forget it in due time, not for the sake of the perpetrator who can justifiably be left to dangle awhile, but for your own sake, to nullify the whole sorry business. Forgetting, however, isn't really discretionary; you can try, but trying really hard is counterproductive. So even a suppressed fact will rise up, unbidden, from memory. But what *is* in your power is to suppress this feeling of having been wronged, to re-focus, re-position your awareness so that your sense of insult or victimhood is displaced because you're otherwise occupied. And behold, the incident is truly past where alone its presence matters: in yourself. Moreover, a forgotten wrong is a much truer blessing for the sorry perpetrator as well. He'll say, ages after, "I'm so sorry for what I did," and you'll say, "Jeez, I can't even recall what you did do." It might even induce a slight and well-deserved feeling of neglect on the part of the forgotten sinner.

All this was to set me up for that meaning of tradition which has, most rigorously, nothing to do with being past. That is the tradition, for us in America, the Western Tradition, most ours because it has given us the two notions and their realizations which we live by in much of our private and civic life. I'm speaking of mathematical science and of representative democracy, both of which are first set out in the philosophical books of which this tradition is partly composed. Add to this the texts, novels and poetry, musical compositions and works of visual art that have shaped our sensibility, our taste. This tradition, the elements of which used to be taught in public school and the masterworks of which made up the college curriculum, has only a circumstantial relation to the past: Its works were largely made there, but they themselves are in no way history, in no way by-gone, in no way passed away. Perhaps "in no way" is overstating it; I should say "in no essential way." For some of these texts employ languages no longer spoken and notations no longer in use and examples no longer familiar. That used to be a minor part of education: to catch you up on that left-behind information.

The books themselves, however, mostly don't even pretend to contain primarily information but rather thinking and imagining. And since little in them is intended to be data for us, nothing essential in there is dated. The best I can do so early in the day is to give the example that I imagine is most familiar and closest to many to you, the book of books, the Bible—as you probably know, from the Greek word *biblos*, "book"—*The* Book.

This book comes in two parts, the Hebrew Bible or Old Testament and the Christian Bible or New Testament. The Hebrew Bible, my book, with which in all candor, I'm woefully ill-acquainted, gives an account—it is not clear what its origin is—of the coming-into-being, by Creation, of our universe and of the story of a people: the Hebrews, who think of themselves as chosen by their divinity to carry on his business on earth, which they do very defectively in the short run and quite undeflectedly in the long run. It also contains the basic imperatives, namely ten, of their ethical life and the numerous rules, namely five hundred plus, of their daily observance. The second part of this dual book contains the personal accounts of witnesses to a new beginning in which God, in ways its interpreters think are foreshadowed in the Old Testament, empties himself of his divinity to take on human form, and a new law is instituted around his incarnation.

Post-Biblically, the Hebrews are dispersed out of the land they occupy in the Bible until the nation is reconstituted in Israel in the last century; the Christians as a community of faith spread over the West but face the threat of decline in recent times.

Now while the two communities, Jews and Christians, that live by these Bibles are, for all the dangers that dog them, still vitally alive, the books themselves seem vulnerable to aging, to being passé. Some Israelis I know think of the older Bible as simply a history book, venerable but subject to revision by archaeological research. Some American students I've had in class have never read either Testament at all, because faith was to their enlightened parents an antiquated mode, and its laws for living seemed to be an antiquated imposition.

To me these attitudes seem nonsensical. Neither failure of faith or of ethical adequacy is relevant to the reading, the keeping alive, of this first book of one of the two parts of our Tradition. (The second part of the Western Tradition is Greek: Jerusalem and Athens together are our ancestral cities, our spiritual hometowns. If you ask me to breakfast again, I'll talk about our Greek origin, to which I'm actually closer.)

Here is what I think counts. First, an unsquashable sense of the craggy grandeur of Volume I and of the stupendous novelty of Volume II of our Book, a sense that can come, to be sure, only to those who've been made, by their elders or their own curiosity, to open it.

But second, and far more to the point, is the objective content that arouses such veneration. Is there anything in the stories, songs, sayings, teachings, and revelations that does not move to thought a human being who is all there?—I mean one who doesn't live in the infinitesimally brief now, but whose soul is extended forward into expectation and backward into memory?

Take *Genesis*, whoever its author. Our personal memory does not reach to the universal beginning, the genesis of our world, but our imagination surely does. And then arises the question, an unavoidable question to an untruncated human being: Is that beginning self-constituting from a few elements and a few rules of combination, or is it from the first the institution of an intelligent design? Which one is more compatible with thinking, which more in accord with evidence?

Or take the end, John's Revelation, which is a wild prophecy of the way our world will end. What thoughtful person is not, now and then, overcome by the question *how* it will end or *whether* it will end, and if the end comes, whether it will come with a bang or a whimper, a bang being nuclear explosions (first strike and retaliation) and a whimper being the final taking down of the internet by cyber terror (be it by a government or a lone wolf)? Will Armageddon, if it comes, happen literally, at Megiddo in Israel? Or will we possibly have a chance to muddle through and go on, and John's vision will prove to be a fantasy?

So present faith is not necessary to declaring the Bible as unaffected by time. Nor is practical applicability to current conditions needed. For what comes first is non-practical thinking-out of "should" and "shouldn't" quite aside from "could" and "couldn't." For example, I start to read Leviticus; I can't pretend to get through it. But I take in enough to see that to live by it as an American is to draw large drafts on my account of others' tolerance, to cut myself off from most of my contemporaries—which was, I'm told, the actual intention of this rule-enclosed way of life. But all that's got nothing to do with the actuality of this priestly book. Who can live in this land of the free without wondering whether life without the constraints of obedience, obedience not to a person but to a law from on high, does not make us miserably shapeless, and where we should look for our rules, at what level or realm they should operate, and how much self-forgiving transgression is permissible?

So let me sum up what I'm trying to say. The Bible is not passé, not of the past, in the sense of "bygone" insofar as faith may be failing, because its depths are thought-inducing for the faithful as well as the faithless—perhaps they ought to be even more so for the latter. And similarly the Bible is not out of fashion insofar as its prescriptions may be inapplicable to contemporary life, because it is the very lesson book for thinking about what it means to duck out from under obedience to a divinity and to be driven only by the necessities of the world.

The Bible is just a best example for my claim: None of the works of the Tradition are to be considered old, except insofar as in human works—not so much in human beings—old age often brings beauty. These works are hardly ever doctrinal catechisms or operating manuals but something in-between:

places where incitements to ever-active questions and treasures of attempted answers are recorded.

Here I'll end. I think I may have been preaching to the choir, but I don't think I need to apologize. Since I agreed to make a speech, it was my duty to say something I believe in. And since I knew I was going to be addressing friends, I also knew that you might have had such thoughts before I came along. Well, so much the better—as Socrates says in his prayer at the end of Plato's grandest dialogue: "Friends have things in common" (*Phaedrus*).

Houston, October 6, 2016

5

On Compromise

Using Imagination

I am not a great believer in philosophizing—by which I mean trying to get to the bottom of things—concerning current affairs. That's because I think there has to be some calming distance and some extended thinking for unsettling events to reveal their stable shape. So I would like you to take me at my word when I say that my topic, compromise, is only coincidentally relevant to a contemporary condition of our civic life, which is generally agreed to have lost the will and the art necessary for compromise.

Compromise, as a term of speech and as a mode of conduct, has long interested me. I ask myself: Is compromise an act of prudence, and so a virtue, or a decision of the will, and so a trait of temperament? Does its framing require far-seeing wisdom or tricky calculation? Is it the condition for a prosperous life or the diagnostic of corrupt morality? Are these the right terms to ask about?

Well, the last either-or question is certainly suggestive. Consider the two opposite meanings of the verb "to compromise." We say, on the one hand: "After an all-night negotiation, both sides agreed to make some sacrifices; they found a way to compromise, and so they avoided a financial earth-quake. Thank heavens for such sensible leadership!"

But we also say: "He engaged in money laundering and other illegal practices and totally compromised himself and all the companies in which he had a stake. Lock him up!"

Or on a smaller, more personal scale: "I told a real whopper, but it was a white lie to save feelings and family peace. Now I feel compromised because I don't really like to lie, and yet I'm glad I made a compromise with the bald and hurtful truth."

The duality in the meaning of the term and its action poses a deep problem, or better a question. I am calling here on a distinction I came on long ago and have found really illuminating: A problem is a difficulty that goes away and becomes toothless history when you've solved it. A question is an incitement to wonder; it is never really resolved but only clarified, and a fairly lucid life is based on such clarifications. They are the purpose of education.

In fact, I'm hoping to contribute a little bit to yours with this clarification I'm proposing. It is, as I just said, not the sort of intellectual work that talking heads opining about current events, off the cuff and in a sound-bitten mode, can do. Let me put it this way: genuine insights, to be sure, come suddenly and out of the blue, but only after long futzing around in a wilderness of confusion.

How shall I frame the question? The practical problem is how to calibrate the prevalence of the evil of a sacrifice, which is often a loss of principle, over the good of a profit, which is often the gain of liveableness. It's a here-and-now calculation, and once you've made it, it's too late; you may have to live with the consequences, but the problem itself has been outlived.

It's the philosophical question that remains alive. And that's what the rest of my assigned half-hour will be about: the theory of compromise, who we are such that the quandary of making a practical compromise and being morally compromised can arise.

First let me be literal. What does the term com-promise literally mean? *Com* is Latin for "together," as in "common," and the second part, "promise," means just what we hear, "pledge." When two together mutually pledge to be or do something, it's a compromise, with the connotation, the implied meaning, that each must give something to get the other's promise. And "giving something" usually means giving it up. So the willingness to give in on, give up on, something is a natural connotation, a related meaning of making mutual promises.

That transaction involves, as I said, a calculation. And again, it can be a very worldly, a practical calculation, based above all on my desires. What do I want more, to shut up my vegetable stand with my lettuce wilting in the heat or to come down on my price, even if I lose my margin of profit, so as to get rid of my produce for at least something? One might even say that every exchange of commodities involves a compromise. I give up my handiwork to get hold of yours, which you're willing to alienate.

I'll interject an opinion here that you may not often have heard. Whatever you may think of Marx's effect on our world, he is, in his masterwork, *Capital*, the most enchanting expositor of what he calls "the fetishism of commodities." If you haven't read this brilliantly obnoxious exposition of what it means to be a made thing functioning in that community of things called the market, you haven't given thought to the "thinghood," that surrounds you and on which you spend much of your money. (See Essay 1, "Thing-Love.")

But sometimes the calculation involved in the mutual promise, in the compromise, is not about worldly possessions but about transcendent goods, and then you stop calculating and begin to think, to contemplate, to theorize, to philosophize, and sometimes to pray. That's because this non-practical thinking is deep and difficult. You can't do it only here and now, when the occasion arises. You really have to have done it long and extendedly, and in that sense you do have to do it here and now: *here* at the school you've chosen for the long haul, *now* in the classes that you attend on schedule, and in the corridors of your dorms where you meet friends casually.

This might be a first question: It arises in most do-or-die moral situations. Wasn't there a way to avoid the stand-off, especially when it involves more than bragging rights or material goods? Well-instituted institutions have all sorts of clever devices to avoid those compromising situations that involve the compromise of a sense of rightness. In families, for example, a large éclair is to be divided between two siblings; how to avoid complaints based on a compromised sense of fairness? Well, the mother says to elder: "You divide it," and to the other: "You choose first." And behold, you never saw such an effort to achieve a minutely equal division from an older sister and such a sense of uncompromised equality from the kid brother.

Or in the nation, imagine a Representative of our House who feels driven, for the sake of party unity, to vote for a bill he considers morally wrong. The Speaker can take him aside: "Vote your conscience; we've got the numbers." Neither the Speaker nor the Congressman is compromised; it's a system that's procedurally problem-solving—more squishily reasonable than rigorously rational.

Our Constitution was meant, I might argue, to do just that—to take the moral agony out of compromise, to make its extremities unnecessary. Its classical defense, the *Federalist*, which functions in the realm firmly fixed in the middle of down-and-dirty politicking and high-and-pure political theorizing, is, to my mind, simply the greatest text on de-fanged compromise, compromise freed from moral principle.

It abounds in inventions of prudence, which do just that—by-pass pure morals, for the sake of prosperous peaceableness.

Having got this far in my meditations, I searched for a model case of political compromise in the absence of a device-rich constitution. I found it in Lincoln's speech of 1854, given in Peoria, Illinois, on the Missouri Compromise. The speech consists of forty pages of closely reasoned lawyerly argumentation backed by detailed reference to historical fact. Lincoln says at the beginning that he will not question anyone's motives, fraught though the issue may be; yet he objects to the introduction of moral right on the pro-slavery side later on. It's exhilarating reading. But imagine a contemporary audience standing or sprawling for the hours it took to deliver. An aside: truly these Peorians had not only attention spans but also intellectual discernment no orator dares to impute to us nowadays.

The Missouri Compromise, you may recall, was an agreement that territories seeking to become states of the Union were to be matched, a free for a slave state, so as to preserve the balance of 1820. Its repeal induced a crisis, and Lincoln argues for its restoration. But, although he himself explicitly finds slavery morally repugnant, he sticks with a morally neutral prudential argument. Indeed, this is the very heart of Lincoln's political thinking: Give practical priority not to your most passionately held moral principles but to the grounds, the conditions on which these principles might be realized. Thus for him the Civil War was fought first for the preservation of the Union, because that was the condition for the abolition of slavery—a compromise of principle for the sake of the principle.

I am still in the realm of worldly practicality here, but I want to lay before you the inner, the psychic ways of compromising. That kind of inquiry has a name that may be unfamiliar to some of you: phenomenology. It means attending

closely to the description and meaning of the way our experiences appear in, are phenomena of, our soul. Look within
yourself and ask: What happens when I engage attentively in
the mutual promise that is a compromise of the sort which
involves more than material tit-for-tat?

Let me take a minute to introduce a helpful distinction.
I've used the word "principle" a number of times. I'll give you
a formula; it doesn't always work but it has much clarifying
force.

Some people live by explicitly formulated rules. The most
famous ten, formulated in Exodus and Deuteronomy of the
Bible, are mostly prohibitions: "Thou shalt not . . ." Or a
company commands its workforce "Don't be evil"—a formula, I'll say, whose moral matter is clearly zilch. But the rule
can be a positive principle: "Do unto others as you would
have them do unto you." This one isn't so different from the
éclair principle—practical mutuality. One name among philosophers—Kant—stands out for devising a sort of hyper-
principle, the notorious "categorical imperative," the absolute
commandment that tells you how to frame moral principles
for yourself. They must be such that if everyone were to act
in accordance with them it would continue to be a livable
world. The set of such principles, articulated universal rules
of conduct, may be called a *morality*. Its enforcer is the will, a
rational capacity that understands the content of commands.
There is an alternative conception which goes by the name of
ethics. Instead of principles it follows the desire for certain
elevated goods, and its directors are the virtues, individual
traits of character. It seems fair to say that those who betray
their goods feel *ashamed*, while those who breach their principles feel *self-compromised*.

I think these two reactions, being ashamed and being compromised, have a different feel, so to speak. Shame colors
our whole inner being and then appears externally as a facial
flush; it feels like a taint on our essence. Being compromised

feels more like an imputation on one's cleverness, a failure of the ignoble acuteness needed to get away with it. A compromised person is apt to ask himself: How'd I get into this? And the answer is: You weren't thinking straight. But that fatuous kind of self-compromise is not yet really interesting. What is interesting, at least to me, is the ultimate human predicament, when serious principles, serious commitments are at odds, and there is no readily apparent way to compose them, except for giving something up, or giving in— that will be a surrender of self.

Why are we in these predicaments to begin with? Well, it seems to be because of the really astounding, the mystifying duality of our being. Regarded as a class or a species, we have what matters in common, we have commonality. As a class we have a common *humanity*—man the humane or merciful; as a species we are all genetically *homo sapiens*—man the sapient or wise. But see us one by one, as a least element of the class or a specimen of the species, "no [longer] dividable," as an *in-dividual*. Then we differ in a myriad of ways; we are very particular, even hopelessly peculiar. Our commonality has receded in favor of our idiosyncrasy. That we should be so much the same conceptually and so much apart concretely, so uniform taken together and so distinct taken separately— is it by a malice of Nature or by the benefaction of the Creator? Who knows? But it has one pertinent consequence. It is surely the reason why compromise is necessary to us. As we are ultimately individual, in the sense of being the least, the atomic element of the human race, so we are individuals in the sense of being incomparably ourselves, like none other. That means that each of us has ultimately disparate beliefs and desires, incomposably antithetical, not capable of being melded or merged as is. For some beliefs seem, by their very essence, *absolute*—be they faithful or damnable. And some desires are, by their nature, *insuppressible*—be they satisfiable or ravaging.

Thus it seems to me that in the cases that really matter, compromise is really compromising. One might, consequently, claim that in countries like the United States, where religions by and large coexist peacefully, it's because their adherents care, when push comes to shove, more for peace and prosperity than they do for doctrine and orthodoxy. That's clearly thought-provoking.

Or maybe we are so made as to have another way to let others be, besides flabby concession. Let me give it a try.

In the last half century we've all heard a lot of criticism of individualism as the cause of lonely selfishness. It comes largely from the social philosophers of continental Europe and is aped by our intellectuals. I'm writing this page of my talk during Hurricane Harvey, while the floodwaters are rising in Corpus Christi, Texas, and people, in a pinch, are proving the attribution to Americans of social atomicism and psychic selfishness spectacularly wrong. So I am encouraged to try laying out a vision of sound individualism that makes compromise possible.

You've probably all heard of a description of such individualism by Alexis de Tocqueville in his *Democracy in America*. He says that it's "self-interest rightly understood," that is, intelligent selfishness, the sort that foresees long-term, and so forestalls unintended, consequences. It is the aptest imaginable description of sound worldly self-regard, but it probably falls short when the needs of the soul are taken into account. A closer look at the individualistic soul is needed.

Let me collect what I've said so far as it bears on healthy individualism. I've distinguished the ethics of virtuous character from the morality of firm principles. I think principles don't bear up under compromise. If you adhere, as morality requires, to universal and clear principles, then it's all or nothing; the universality admits no exception and the clarity exposes them. So compromise is better underwritten by personal virtue, which is a little bit fungible, flexible. There are several such ethics to choose from. A good example is Aristotelian, where a virtue is, as it were, captured between its opposing vices. Thus courage, for Aristotle the most virtuous virtue, is caught between craven cowardice and rambunctious boldness. This way of finding goodness as a middle ground underwritten by sound-mindedness clearly has some give in it, such as rigorous principles enforced by an iron will don't have.

Thus the ethics of virtue allows for saving tricks, for clever devices that allow a moral stand-off to turn into a soluble problem. If you follow Aristotle, you can navigate the moral spectrum and find the livable middle—but there are other non-rigid theories. One way to put this view of human well-doing is that it relies on prudence, the virtue of looking around, that is, on circumspection, and of "looking ahead," that is, on prudence, pro-vidence.*

> Some Greeks seem to have had a special talent for eating their cake and having it too—the ultimately practical compromise. Two examples: Odysseus tarries ten years with magical women, to bed down joyfully with his ever-recalled wife; Socrates lives a suspect life to be rewarded with the consummation of an execution—at seventy.

But perhaps the observation most relevant to my question is the one I made before about our curious double nature, as members of one common race, the human race with its sapient humanity, *and* also as ultimately incomparable individuals, locked into the idiosyncrasies of being the least entities with the most differences.

I think that to recognize this duality in us, to be puzzled by it, to wonder whether we should try to limit our individuality in favor of our commonality or cultivate it in favor of our sovereignty—that is the beginning. What are we like such that self-knowledge can make us amenable to uncompromised compromise?

Again let me recur to an easy way out, one that large swaths of Americans do in fact take. It might be called "religion-lite."

To me it seems better than heavy-handed rectitude, but not really good. It depends on intellectual vagueness and emotional woolliness. People firm in faith don't give in. They may save their life, they think, but they'll have lost themselves. There can, however, be two opinions about this. I'm Jewish myself, and I've read somewhere that our Talmud advises compromise and cunning in forced conversions: Pretend to be converted and practice your true faith surreptitiously, because Jews need to live—hence the Marranos, underground Jews for generations. It is the uneasy way out.

So here's *the* question, baldly stated: What are the capabilities of our souls, given to each of us by nature and realized by our efforts, that make it possible to live with each other as equally self-interested individuals?

I imagine you've all observed this weather phenomenon: The wind is making the withy branches of a willow stream in one direction, while the clouds high above are chasing across the sky in another. The winds tend to be roiled and short-lived down below, close to the earth's surface, but steady and long-breathed high up. Aren't you aware of similar phenomena within yourself, except that it's inverted? There's the surface turmoil, close to the top of your consciousness, that dies down before long, but there are also deep streams of calm but enduring awareness way down, deep in your being.

The most emotionally significant example is being "in love," a surface phenomenon which can be both tempestuous and short-lived, versus "love," a deep experience which is even-tempered and for good.

So I am implying that our psychic motions have something in common with our terrestrial weather: different levels, differently directed, with different tempos. The soul has been figured in multifarious ways. For example: by Plato, as a chariot that is drawn by a wild and a mild horse which stand for recalcitrant passion and persuadable reasonableness, respectively. Or by Freud, as a depth topography of different degrees of consciousness, from perception up front, through recallable memory, the Preconscious, down to an inaccessible hell of turmoil, the Unconscious that only an expert, a psychoanalyst, can approach. Or by cognitive scientists, who debate whether our mind is modular and has specific capacities for specific activities or whether mentation is always global so that the whole mind is involved.

Now I owe you a bit of phenomenology, an account of the inner appearances that I think I've observed. It seems to me that we do stream our inner experience on different levels, levels both of closeness to consciousness and of gravity in our life. Close to personal awareness, we are sometimes rather excitedly but really lightly, even shallowly, engaged. We intend and feel decent interest, sincere concern, and mild affection; we are mindful of and sympathetic toward extended family and friends, colleagues and coworkers, acquaintances and fellow citizens, and, on occasion, we flare up quite passionately about some particular object of attraction.

But the candid truth is that many of these psychic engagements are casual. We disengage easily and aren't deeply preoccupied by the happiness or unhappiness of the life, the salvation or damnation of the spirit, experienced by these fellow humans. We are sympathetic and helpful but within limits. We are friendly and considerate but without urgency. This lightness of touch, which expresses, to be sure, shallowness of engagement, also betokens a readiness to respect others' antithetical individuality, by not being intrusively involved. Put it this way: We are morally compromised from the get-go by our all-too-muted care, but we are also socially vindicated by our leave-people-be tolerance. It is the stream in which compromise wafts by smoothly and is not very compromising. The thing is to know it, admit it, accept it. I think it is a very characteristically American way of being together.

But then there is the deeper current that flows gravely rather than lightly and where compromise is ineluctably compromising. The First Amendment of our Constitution, in guaranteeing our public psychic freedoms, protects us from the occasion for serious compromises, like forced conversions, ideological or religious. But it is in this deep stream of our private psychic life that compromise is devastatingly compromising. I think our multi-streamed soul gives us a chance to frame most compromises so that they float harmlessly on the surface, on the superficially roiled surface waters of normal life, where our flexible virtues and goods-directed ethics are at home.

This busy, distracted, semi-engaged life protects us from the knowledge, borne along in the deep flux of our souls, that our compromises of convenience practically always compromise us in our principles—a condition best described as a secular original sin. (See Essay 2, "Secular Original Sin.") Our serious undercurrent in its submersion masks for us our ever-in-the-wrong condition. Social critics will regard this depth-displacement as our national sin: We are shallow. I think it's an American blessing: We are un-mired.

So much for the vicissitudes of practical life. But higher education isn't and oughtn't to be that life. Now is the time to go deep, to think about such appositions as the two I've delineated: our human commonality and our ultimate singularity, our light-living surface and our tenacious depths. Now is the time to descend—or maybe ascend—to those realms where the very compromises that make life livable leave the soul compromised.

Ashbrook Center, October 2017

6

Sacred Scripture
In Secular Settings

Our country's three major religions, in order of their entry into time, Judaism, Christianity, Islam, are scriptural. To adhere to one of them is to believe its Book, be it the Hebrew Bible (retrospectively the Old Testament, the "Covenant," anciently referred to as *ta biblia*, "The Books"), the New Testament, or the Quran ("Reading").

My reflections will concern the study only of the Judeo-Christian Bible in a classroom. I am not competent to opine about the study of the Quran, though I know that the works of a major Islamic writer, Al-Ghazali, are centered on the same questions about authority that underlie my own, much less learned or intense, thoughts.

The dual Bible became available to a select larger public in antiquity in the Latin Vulgate, and in modernity it became accessible to an essentially uncontrollable public through the invention of printing, which evoked translation into every vernacular. Thus it entered "world literature," the canon of "great books," on a par with them.

Reprinted with revisions from *Renovatio*, The Journal of Zaytuna College (Spring 2018).

Acquaintance with some items of this canon is now an ever less obvious requirement for students in the humanities. Moreover, the mode of reading its constituent books varies widely, from irritatedly reluctant glancings by students who regard the assignment as a jumping-through-hoops imposition, to keen, even gimlet-eyed, inspection by professionals with a fancy vocabulary, or from mildly appreciative engagement to deeply attentive delight. All the great books must suffer quite supinely being disregarded, assaulted, or embraced; were we to hear them thinking, we might hear a murmur: "We asked for it when we assumed that stature of *publications*."

Sacred scripture is less permissive, less tolerant of being ranged among literary works as "world literature"—of being read "*as literature*." These Books know themselves to be neutralized, castrated, cut down to size, adulterated, by being forced into this company, house-trained, so to speak. What is being done here, and why does it want doing?

So first, what does it mean to read a book "as literature"? For something to be taken *as* something, it seems to be a minimal condition that it should be in some aspects *like* that something. So the Bible must be in some aspect like literature.

What is "literature"? It is a term of unmeaning vastness that includes not only deliberate fictions and personal poetry, but also commentary and factual explanatory writings, like the technical disclosures that nowadays accompany one's bottle of pills—indeed anything composed of letters (Latin *litera*).

But in the humanities faculty of a modern university, a work is, so I've observed, usually identified as "literature" by having several features characteristic of humanism. Humanism is the ideological ground, going back to the Renaissance, of the humanities. It is the doctrinal commitment that puts humanity and its values in the place of divinity and its doxology. Thus, the humanistic *humanities* replace *theology*, which makes an account of God and humanity's relation to the divine the central concern. Eventually the humanities were themselves edged out by the *sciences*, by the mathematical study of nature.

Consequently, there is a much deplored, though circumstantially encouraged, *indifferentism* in the educational space. Literature is "elective," choice being more than occasionally a matter of practical convenience, passing preference or mere availability. Accordingly, the academic defense of reading works of quality is flabby, perhaps deliberately banal and un-deep.

Moreover, *criticism* is accorded more respect than appreciation. It is a professional pursuit, carried on by diplomaed practitioners who teach students abstract categories which are hard to regard as anything but diversions, as distractions from really reading. A novel, say, is thus dispersed into its psycho-socio-economic-political background. Furthermore, what was conceived as a mode of universal access and individual authority becomes a form of exclusionary expertise. It is indicative how often the terms of late humanism, intended to recognize natural rights, like "empowering" and "giving dignity," have a tone of bestowal from the powers that be. Therefore, in the humanities of higher education, certain preconceptions govern the classroom teaching of literature. These are so much taken for granted as to be rarely overtly acknowledged. With respect to literature, I'll try to develop them below.

The next question seems to be: What measures will keep the secular institutions of higher education free from sectarian doctrine in the classroom?* It was in consequence of this

> Oddly, there is little similar anxiety about other ideologies. While religious sectarianism is taboo in secular institutions, social and political ideologies creep readily into the classroom.

scrupulousness that the category of "scripture as literature" was devised. What is, as far as I can tell, not often sufficiently considered with the students corralled in a classroom is this question: Does the removal of sectarianism, that is, of preaching or teaching sacred doctrines, result in a preconception-free intellectual space? The assumed answer is often in the replacement of belief, the stabilization of the soul, by rationalism, the processes of the reason.* A feature, generally thought

> It is a preoccupation of mine how ultra- or sub-rational those processes, such as positing and inference, really are; I might, in a hyperbolic mood, argue that rationality is the ultimate mysticism.

to be inherent in rationality—I'm not sure it really needs to be assumed—is objectivity. This is a term that took, under the modern emergence of the human subject and its subjectivity as primary, a hundred-and-eighty-degree turn from the medieval usage. Then *subjectum* named the concrete reference that "underlies" thought, while *objectum* was an item merely represented, and so as "lying over against" the mental faculty. The question not sufficiently raised is whether our going notion of objectivity, as a capacity for focusing on the object of inquiry without interference from our late-discovered individual subjectivity, is viable. To me, the antithesis seems misconceived. It should not be "objective vs. subjective" but "truth-seeking vs. truth-aversive." Of course, I'm not implying that professors and their assistants are not perfectly honest people. I think, rather, that they themselves have devised, or have submitted to others' excogitation of, so sophisticated a conception of truth or its impossibility that undergraduates are not up to it. And indeed, the question "Is it true?" is generally taboo in university classrooms, especially for sacred books.

Next, what consequences follow from the underlying humanism of the curricular humanities, insofar as it requires that the only acknowledged authority be the human author? An author (from Latin *auctor*, "creator"), in a setting in which the "creativity" of humanity but not of divinity is accepted, is indeed a more reliable creator than a Creator. In fact, human authors are so cherished that their circumstances are of an interest often overshadowing the text itself. Moreover, their biography is regarded as explaining their work—and occasionally as nullifying it. Hence even the authors themselves are overridden by their secular, their worldly setting, by that tempo-psycho-religio-socio-economic-political complex which is as unmeaning, as devoid of imaginative particularity, as is the term literature. As my students and I think out why a terrifyingly resolute woman goes crazy from guilt while her initially hesitant husband becomes a boldly illusionless tyrant, how does it help us to know that their author was born in 1564, that his father was a glover, and that he was suspected of Catholic sympathies (Shakespeare, *Macbeth*)?

These devices, this importation of scholarly modes into the classroom, has, I think, the intention, if only implicit, of erecting a bulwark between the book and the students, partly to protect their so-called "sensitivities," lest they be "made uncomfortable" (*the* social sin of our day, albeit one of a teacher's duties), partly to deliver the teachers themselves from the difficult business of being thoughtful in the world of imagination, of applying the intellect non-lethally to fiction.

Thus it seems to me that the "as literature" rubric is compensatory. Having expurgated the Bible's sacredness, something both timelessly fine and temporally engrossing about it has to be substituted. And indeed the King James version is superlatively beautiful in diction, and the biblical narratives are full of down-to-earth human problems.

To give a well-known example: Abraham's sacrifice of his son, Isaac, first demanded by God and then effectively interdicted. Kierkegaard, in *Fear and Trembling*, offers four interpretations of this world-changing event, and they might be called to aid in a secular discussion of Genesis 22. Here, however, is the difficulty: Kierkegaard himself writes as a believer, albeit in the mode of agonized perplexity. So he is not the specific guide for faithless readers—nor would any illuminating exegete be.

Those readers have what I call a "problem of position." It is the perplexity that non-believers face in according due diligence to the works of authors whose relation to the text is simply not within the realm of acceptability for them. I don't mean differences in interpretation of the text itself—such variations energize the intellect in favor of the book—but disagreement concerning its very origin, the authority due to its author, and the requirements of trust put upon its readers: how to discount the divine origin, annul the credit of the source, and refuse the call to faith—in short, from what possible position to approach sacred scripture, when to read it as a book like any other is a sort of travesty.

To be sure, as an object, the Bibles are not distinguishable—the leather-bound and onion-skinned format of mine is surely a human embellishment—from ordinary works of literature.* So whence are we made aware of the claim that

> One set of sacred scriptures, the Homeric and Hesiodic epics, are indeed primarily works of poetry—of human making (from Greek *poiein*, "to make") within whose context the pagan gods are said by Herodotus (II 53) to have first been definitively delineated. However, in accordance with the primacy of poetry, even these authors are inspired by Olympian Muses, divine patronesses of the arts, especially of verbal and tonal music, who speak directly to the poets. Why is it that the pagan Muses pose so much less of a problem than the Christian angels who perform a similar annunciatory function (Greek *angelos*, "messenger")? The answer is: We moderns tend to regard the Muses themselves as poetic inventions. Not so Homer, I think. And so the question "Whence come the beings of poetry?" should remain *wide* open. (See Essay 17, "The Actuality of Fictions.")

scriptures come more directly from the deity than any other knowledgeable writing? Well, they present themselves as reaching us through a direct conduit from God. That intermediary is an *angel* from heaven's side but on the human side a *prophet*, a "speaker-out," who communicates divine revelations, "unveilings," to the people, sometimes injunctions of things to do, often predictions of things to come. Thus the perplexity is pinpointed in prophecy, whether it proclaims or predicts.

Now to the point of this attempt at clarification: What is to be done by teachers so as to read sacred scripture with their undergraduate students in a secular setting without imposition on them either of dogma or of the deconsecration of the text?*

> One such attempt at desacralizing the Old Testament by proving it a fiction through the negative finding of archaeology seems to me, a former archaeologist, simply absurd. The *New York Times* of March 9, 2002 reports that archaeologists digging in the Sinai have "found no trace of the tribes of Israel, not one shard of pottery"—thus no Exodus. What if my ancestors were not such butterfingers as to drop their pots all over the peninsula?

In institutions, be they sectarian or secular, that have wholistically conceived programs of instruction—examples of each are Zaytuna and St. John's College—it would be possible to prepare these readings by a careful, text-based discussion of the problem of prophetic authority, as is indeed done at Zaytuna.* But certain pedagogic commitments prevent this

Al-Ghazali is a main author.

at my own secular college, St. John's. We value our students' innocently immediate relation to books, what might be called their original, we hope indefeasible, naïvety. It makes each of the great books a novel adventure, never subject to learned canons of interpretation, though always to be read in the light of personal experience and sometimes with reference to preceding books. Four academic years are a short time to confirm or revise the teachings of our upbringing, and so we decline to spend even a fraction of those thirty-six months on a somewhat dubious intervention between book and reader.

How, then, can we incite in our students a position, or at least an approach—a way that might serve also in the even less leisurely and more professionally led classrooms of the ordinary elective-driven curriculum—to works that present themselves, or have been presented to readers, as sacred?

Here is my suggestion: Have recourse to one of our most remarkable capacities. Its terrific power is explained neither by the therapeutic approach of analytic psychology, which regards the human being as essentially in need of a physician, nor of neuroscientific laboratory science, which postulates an explanation of humanity as emerging from matter and its motions. This is our power of *at once* being and not being in a certain condition. It gives us a way to do justice both to self-avowed fictions and to other people's truths.

This capability is called the *imagination*. It practically defines our inwardness, what used to be called the soul. It can serve that function because it brings into awareness an aspect of inner life that is at once pervasive and inexplicable: internal images. These visions before the inner eye are *immaterial shapes*. If they image external objects, they leave outside, leave behind, their "reality," meaning their immattered being, their "thinghood." If they are internally produced, it is without our having *any* knowledge of their origin, or our part in it, and without their shape settling in some graspable material, unless they are externalized by some art, say poetry or painting.* Though they are without matter, they can be more

_____

Or by drinking blood as do the vaporous dead of Hades, so that Odysseus may hold onto them for talk (*Odyssey* XI 146 ff.).

potent than the material objects that matter to us: The dead beloved whom we summon and who is not embraceable matters maybe more to us than seven billion contemporarily live human bodies.

This, then, is our capacity for harboring entities within that are not what they are, or are what they are not, just as an external image, say a statue, is rightly said *to be*, say, a lion and equally truly *not to be* a lion. (I'll show you my granddaughter, says a colleague, and after lots of swiping produces a lovable kid on the screen of his iPhone.) This capacity empowers us to be what we need to be for the present case: We can be *at once heart-whole and soul-divided.*

By "heart-whole" I mean that we feel entirely undriven to give up our deeply lodged and well-thought-out beliefs; by "soul-divided," I mean that we can faithfully imagine, envision, even enter into, others' worlds without in the least losing the intellectual ground on which we stand—that we can at once experience along with others *imaginatively* and stand apart from situations wholly diverse from our own *intellectually*. For intellect and imagination are diverse but entangled within the soul.

The same in other words: The capacity called imagination is the power of image-making, of having or producing mental images, of inner perceptions: immaterial scenery, bodiless people, canvasless pictures, soundless songs—which are sometimes even more poignant than embodied tones:

> Heard melodies are sweet, but those unheard
> Are sweeter: . . .
>
> (Keats, "Ode on a Grecian Urn")

Such images both are and are not what they "re-present," what they make to be "again (*re*) present"—that is, derivatively, not originally. Our ability to harbor such duplicities within us enables us to be in several conditions at once: to remain, if we wish, wholly unaffected by the book's designs on our committed love, and yet to engage the text unreservedly both with the critically appreciative intellect and with the world-representing imagination. Thus our heart and our apprehending soul are together engaged in reading the Book somewhat as those closest to it might wish.

So a non-subverting reading of sacred scripture in secular institution seems to me to demand an assiduous exercise of the imagination: a deliberate, detailed visual realization of the verbal setting, an acute listening to the voices that ring through in these settings, and finally the imaginative super-position of these situations on the real, current world they are meant to inform: the application of an old text to a current context. It is also the non-believer's way of experiencing the world as it looks and feels to someone who sees it in the light of the Word, while the intellect is at work apprehending.

This image-enlivened, intellect-grounded reading is not, as I mean it, *em*pathy—as the Germans say *Einfühlung*, feeling our way into others' hearts and souls. I think that we cannot truly enter feelingly *into* the affects of those who believe as we do not.* Imagining, on the other hand, implies that distance

Though we can, if our hearts are large enough, feel in our way along *with* them, which is called *sym*pathy.

which attaches to vision, since vision is the distance sense, the very opposite of touch. Thus apprehension by images is at once closely regardful and retiringly discreet, a psychically courteous mode of interest, in sync with heart and thought, both.

I will end with an anecdote. I once had a fine colleague; he left my college to pursue therapeutic psychology. We had just finished an oral examination on the New Testament of a student who, it turned out, was a Fundamentalist. My colleague expressed amazement at the phenomenon of one of ours being of that persuasion. I said: "Maybe he knows something we don't know." My friend again looked astonished: "Eva, you can't mean it!" I thought, but didn't say: "There are more things in heaven and earth"—here I deviated from Hamlet's words—"friend Gary / Than are thought of in your philosophy."

Final thought: How should an engaged seeker regard committed believers? I think we should honor them for their generosity of soul that delights in worship and the largesse of heart that rejoices in reverence.

7

The Empires of the Sun
Encounter the West

I shall begin with two sets of facts and dates. On or about August 8 of 1519 Hernán Cortés, a hidalgo, a knight, from Medellín in the Estremadura region of Spain, having sailed his expeditionary fleet from Cuba to win "vast and wealthy lands," set out from a city he called Villa Rica de la Vera Cruz on the Gulf of Mexico to march inland, west toward the capital of Anahuac, the empire of the Nahuatl-speaking Aztecs. The city was called Tenochtitlán and its lord, the emperor, was Montezuma II. Cortés knew of the place from the emperor's coastal vassals and from delegations Montezuma had sent loaded with presents to welcome—and to forestall—the invaders. The presents included many works of well-crafted gold.

This extended and revised lecture is dedicated to my friend and fellow tutor William Darkey (d. 2009), who first introduced me to the book behind this lecture, William Prescott's *History of the Conquest of Mexico*. Reprinted from *The St. John's Review* vol. 47, no. 1 (2003); scholarly bibliography omitted. A version of this essay also appeared in *Homage to Americans* (Paul Dry Books, 2010).

Cortés had with him about three hundred Spaniards, including about forty crossbowmen and twenty *arquebusiers*, that is, men carrying heavy matchlock rifles. He probably had three front-loading cannons. His officers wore metal armor. There were fifteen horses for the captains and a pack of hunting dogs. (I might mention here that the Aztec dogs were a hairless type bred for food.) The band was accompanied by Indian porters and allies, a group that grew to about a thousand as they marched inland. Early in November they passed at 13,000 feet between the two volcanoes that guard the high Valley of Mexico. Some Spanish captains astounded the Indians by venturing to climb to the crater rim of the ominously smoking Popocatépetl. On November 8, Cortés was on the causeway to Tenochtitlán. On November 14, Montezuma, the ruler of a realm of 125,000 square miles, capable of putting in the field an army of 200,000 men with a highly trained officer corps, quietly surrendered his person to the custody of Cortés, declared himself a vassal of Emperor Charles V, and transferred his administration to the palace assigned to the Spaniards. He soon made them a present of the state treasure which they had discovered behind a plastered-over door in the palace aviary. Cortés's surmise that just to enter Tenochtitlán was to take Anahuac captive seemed to be justified.

On June 30, 1520, Cortés being absent, Montezuma was either murdered by the Spaniards or stoned to death by his own people as he appeared on the palace wall attempting to contain a rebellion. The latter account seems more plausible, since he appears to have been shielded by Spaniards to whom he was a valuable pawn and since some of his nobles were growing disgusted with his submissiveness. The uprising had been induced by the young captain whom Cortés had left in charge, who had massacred unarmed celebrants of the feast of Huitzilopóchtli, the city's chief god; this god both was and stood for the Sun.

The Mexican uprising culminated in the *noche triste*, the

Sad Night, when the Spaniards were driven from the city with enormous loss of life.* In June 1521 the Spanish situation

> At age sixteen, Robert Frost wrote a long poem, "La Noche Triste" (his greatness yet in bud), which responds to the terrific romance of it all—so far in time, so near in place.

looked desperate to them, as a vigorous, indomitable, eighteen-year-old emperor, Cuauhtémoc, Montezuma's second successor (the first having died of smallpox), assumed the leadership of an Aztec army now better acquainted with these once apparently invincible invaders.

On August 15, 1521, just two years after his landing, Cortés's band, augmented by some new arrivals and an allied Indian army from Tenochtitlán's old enemy, Tlaxcála, fought its way, foot by foot, back into the city, with frightful losses on both sides. The Spaniards were supported by a flotilla of forty brigantines, light square-rigged sailing vessels that Cortés had ordered built and dragged overland to Lake Texcoco, the complex shallow water on which Tenochtitlán stood. It was the first fleet of sailing ships to float on the lake.

I am still in the realm of fact when I say that within a few days this city, surpassing all cities then on earth in the beauty of its situation and the magic of its aspect, was completely razed. Within four years it was overlaid, under Cortés's supervision, by a complete Spanish city, whose cathedral, the Cathedral of Mexico City, was eventually built hard by the Great Temple of Tenochtitlán. In this total catastrophe the Spaniards had lost fewer than a hundred men, the Aztecs or México about 100,000.

I have, of course, omitted myriads of gripping details, such as a novelist might hesitate to invent. But I shall now abbreviate an abbreviation: In August 1519 there was a large, powerful, highly civilized empire called Anahuac. By August 1521 it was gone; instead there was a new realm, a colony called New Spain; Spanish was replacing the native Nahuatl.

Now the second set of facts, even more curtailed. On May 13, 1532, Francisco Pizarro (like Cortés from the Estremadura and his distant relation) arrived at Tumbez, a port at the northern end of the Inca empire and of modern Peru. This empire was called by its people Tahuantinsúyu, meaning the Realm of the Four Quarters. Pizarro had 130 troopers, 40 cavalry and one small cannon. The Inca Atahualpa—Inca means Lord—had an army of 50,000 men. On November 16, 1533, the Inca came, at Pizarro's invitation, to meet him in the town plaza of Cajamara. There he was unintelligibly harangued by the chaplain of the expedition and given a breviary: the Inca scornfully threw the scribbles to the ground. Within thirty-three minutes, he having been seized, 4,000 of his men had been massacred. Resistance and the empire itself fell apart with his capture. Atahualpa offered to fill his prison, a cell 22 x 10 feet, with gold to the height of his reach in exchange for his freedom. While the temples which were encrusted with gold were being denuded and the condition was being fulfilled, the Inca was condemned to death by burning. This sentence was commuted to strangulation when he agreed to be baptized. Pizarro soon took Cuzco, the capital, and installed a puppet Inca, Mánco Cápac, who mounted a rebellion; it was put down with great loss of life on the Inca's side in 1534. There followed a period of civil war among the conquerors. Again to summarize the summary: A tiny band of Spanish ruffians brought down, within two years, the most efficiently administered polity of its time. Quechua, the native language, was replaced by Spanish as the chief language.

It is thought that this second scenario was, on Pizarro's part, a reprise of Cortés's conquest. If so, it is a demonstration of the inferiority of imitations.

The kind of facts I have listed here are spectacular yet uncontested discontinuities in the stream of life. The dates, which tell us both the temporal order of these facts and their distance from us, serve to dramatize the discontinuity: About half a millennium ago there occurred, not very far south of us and close to each other in space and time, two mind-boggling events—the destruction by a very few Spaniards of two great civilizations.

We at this college have read or will read in Herodotus's *Persian Wars* how in July of 480 B.C. a band of 299 Spartans, the same in number as Cortés's original companions, died in holding the pass of Thermopylae against an Asian army of who knows how many hundreds of thousands, led by Xerxes, king of Persia. Their object was to give the Greeks time and courage to repel the invader. But the Spartans were defending their own land from a self-debilitating behemoth. The Spaniards' situation in Mesoamerica is just the inverse, except that in each case the few were the free. What, we may wonder, would our world be like if the Asians had prevailed in 480 B.C. or the Nahua in 1519 A.D.?

How could it happen? How did these American empires fall? Just as Herodotus drew conclusions about the nature of the Greeks from the Persian defeat, so one might wonder if illumination about the nature of our West might not be found in these catastrophes that mark the beginning of modem life. To put it straightforwardly: In reading about Mexico and Peru I began to wonder if there might be a clue in these events to the apparently irresistible potency of the West when *it* touches, be it insidiously or catastrophically, other worlds, be *they* receptive or resistant.

Let me explain the not altogether appropriate use of the term "the West" in my title, "The Empires of the Sun encounter the West." Our tradition—I mean the one whose works we study at this college—is usually called the Western tradition. It is thereby revealed as defining itself against the East, Near and Far, the Orient, the place where the sun rises. Our North American republic is in this sense the West's very West and its currently culminating expression. But, of course, the Aztecs—let me interrupt myself to say that the people of the

imperial city of México-Tenochtitlán did not call themselves
Aztecs but México and that they called those who spoke
their language the Nahua and that the term Aztec was introduced to the English-speaking world by the aforementioned
Prescott—these México, then, of course thought of the invaders as being *from* the quarter of the rising sun, from the east.
This turns out to be a significant fact. Columbus thought that
he was "sailing not the usual way" but west—sailing west to
reach the East, Japan, China, India. It was for quite a while
a very unwelcome discovery that the people whom the adventurers so hopefully called Indians (as I will continue to do
here) inhabited a long continent which, although it contracted
into a narrow isthmus in the middle, blocked the ocean route
to the fabulous Orient. Thus Prescott calls Tenochtitlán "the
great capital of the western world." So "West" is, strictly
speaking, nonsense as used in this context, but I cling to it
because it is the available shorthand for ourselves, for those
living in the tradition that has its roots in Jerusalem and Athens, achieves its modernity in Europe, has come to its current
culmination on this continent, and is spreading its effects all
over the globe. What can be more necessary at this moment
than to grapple with the being of this West?

As I read on it seemed to me often that the reasons given
by historians for Anahuac's sudden collapse before the Spaniards might well be cumulatively necessary but could not
be sufficient conditions. I mean that without their operation the Empires could not have fallen so quickly, but that
altogether they did not so completely account for the fall as
to make it seem unavoidable. It is true that the Spaniards
brought horses into a land without draft animals, and so the
cavaliers could run down the pedestrian Aztec warriors and
frighten the Indians into seeing the Europeans as centaurs,
four-footed monstrous men-horses. But these Indians soon
learned that man and horse were separable and mortal; during their desperate and bloody defense of Tenochtitlán there

appeared on the skull rack of a local temple, beneath fifty-three heads of Spaniards, the heads of a number of horses, of "Spanish deer," as they were now called. The crossbows and cannons may have delivered more swift and terrifying destruction than the Aztec javelin-throwers, the metal armor deflected the cuts of obsidian-studded wooden swords; the driving greed for gold, which, as Cortés ironically represented to an Indian official, was the specific remedy for a disease that troubled the Spaniards, may have disoriented the people; the physical disease brought by the Spaniards, the smallpox, did more than decimate the uninoculated natives; Spanish luck at crucial junctures may have demoralized the caciques, the Indian chieftains; the harsh exactions and suppression of Montezuma's empire did indeed provide Cortés with Indian allies (though the 150,000 Indians that came with the now 900 Spaniards to retake Tenochtitlán were by their very numbers an encumbrance on the heavily defended causeways into the island city and by their excited hatred for their México oppressors a danger to Cortés's prudent intentions); the crucifix may well, in Carlos Fuentes's words, "have made their minds collapse," as they saw how their own numerous gods demanded numerous sacrifices of *them*, while this one Christian god sacrificed one man, himself. Such factors or forces are called, in the categories in which history is conceptualized, technological, demographic, epidemiological, political, psychological, or what have you. Perhaps they were necessary to Spanish success. But a number of contemporaries thought that at various junctures it might well have gone otherwise. For example, the strong-minded king of Texcoco, Cacáma, said that all the Spaniards within Tenochtitlán could be killed in an hour; Cortés himself thought so. To me historical inevitability seems an *ex post facto* cause. It is the way a *fait accompli* presents itself, when passage has turned into past. I cannot quite tell whether my rejection of historical determinism should be reinforced or thrown into doubt by the fact that the México themselves had given themselves over to fate, as I will tell. Perhaps that very self-surrender was a sufficient *condition*, the factor that made the outcome practically certain. But that would only be half the *explanation*; for the other half one would have to look in the nature of the Europeans as well.

Before doing that, let me complete the apology for my title. In it I mention the two empires, though I will speak of one only, Anahuac. I mean no reflection on the Inca realm, that marvel of social administration and public works built with the most astounding masonry I've ever seen. But both of the Peruvian protagonists were like deteriorated copies of their Aztec templates. Pizarro was an intrepid thug, by all accounts, and Atahualpa a culpably and carelessly arrogant man with a violent history. Since it seemed to me that the pairs of chief actors in this drama not only were the main factors because both empires were autocracies, but were also in their very distinctive ways personally emblematic of their worlds, I chose the more humanly accessible, the more expressive duo.

Finally, I refer to the Sun because the solar domination under which both these Precolumbian empires labored seemed to me more and more significant. The Incas called themselves the Children of the Sun; their great Sun Temple at Cuzco, the Coricáncha, was studded with gold, "the tears wept by the sun." So too the Mexicans, who called their generals "the Lords of the Sun," had come into the marshes of Lake Texcoco, their place of destiny, led by priests who bore on their backs a twittering medicine bundle. It was Huitzilopóchtli, who was reborn on the way at Teotihuacán, the birthplace of the gods, and later installed in Tenochtitlán's Great Temple. There he was incessantly nourished with human blood. Of course, when I use the indicative mood in speaking of the Aztec gods, I am not reporting fact—I am telling what the Aztecs said and are thought to have believed. The most difficult thing, I have discovered, is for historians to find the right voice in speaking of alien gods, especially when they are many in number, fluid in function, and visible in many forms.

The Indians' relation to the sun I have come to think of as symbolic of the whole debacle and even its proximate cause. To anticipate my version of a common idea: The daily, annual, and epochal returns of the heavenly body were to the Aztecs so fearsomely antic, so uncertain, that they burdened themselves, as their traditions taught them, with rituals and sacrifices. These were so demanding that they enfeebled both the Nahua empire and the Nahua's souls. The West's relation to the Sun was just the opposite.

In 1506, just about the time young Cortés came to the Indies, Copernicus was beginning to write *On the Revolutions of the Heavenly Spheres*. It is one of Western modernity's seminal works, which our sophomores study. In it he shows that the mathematical rationalization of the heavens is more economically accomplished and the celestial phenomena are better "saved" if the sun stands stably at the center of the world. But his motive is not only mathematical economy. "For who," he says, "would place this lamp of a very beautiful temple in another place than this, wherefrom it can illuminate everything at the same time?" Cortés was surely not a premature Copernican, but he acted out of a tradition in which one God controls the cosmos through the laws of nature. Since the deity is not capricious, celestial nature is ever-reliable, well-illuminated and confidence-inspiring. Nature's sun does not, in any case, respond to human propitiation, and Nature's god prefers costless prayers to human sacrifices.

Let me append here a poignant incident told by Cortés. In the final days of the investment of Tenochtitlán, a delegation of parched and starving Méxica came to the barricades. They said that they held Cortés to be a child of the Sun, who could perform a circuit of the earth in a day and a night. Why would he not slay them in that time to end their suffering?

Let me hold off yet one more minute from my main task, to tell you what motives drew me into a study so far from our Program. To begin with, there was the sheer enchantment of what proved to be a fragile civilization and the unburdened romance of comfortably un-current drama. All that romance I got from reading William Hickling Prescott's *Conquest of Mexico* of 1843, and his *Conquest of Peru* of 1847. Of the first book he himself wrote that it was conceived "not as a philosophical theme but as an epic in *prose*, a romance of chivalry." For this approach later historians, for whom demythification, deromanticization, and the dispersal of human deeds into forces and patterns is a professional requirement, despise him somewhat, and it took me a while to see what valuable lesson could be drawn from his telling. Prescott has it right; first the great tale, then the critical theory.

Great tales usually have a theme, which to discern and formulate is the engaged reader's privilege. I would say that this story's deep driving sense is: "Fateful Complementarities."

From the first I knew I was reading the American Gibbon. We at St. John's used to read parts, particularly the notorious fifteenth chapter, of that English historian's monumental *Decline and Fall of the Roman Empire*, completed in 1788. To my taste the American is the finer of the two. Gibbon conceals in the magnificently Latinate periods of his style the universal irony of the ultimately enlightened man. I do not fault him for sitting in judgment, for a non-judgmental historian is an incarnate contradiction and produces only an armature of facts without the musculature that gives it human shape. But I am put off by his judging as an Olympian enthroned on Olympus. In that fifteenth chapter, which treats the question "by what means the Christian faith obtained so remarkable a victory over the established religions of this earth?" (a question of the kind I am asking), he reflects with raised eyebrows in turn on the mortification of the flesh, pious chastity, and divine providence, so as to come to a pretty secular answer, just as if Christianity were not first and last a faith. Surely when a faith conquers, its substance must be given some credit.

Prescott, on the other hand, who had in his youth privately critiqued Gibbon's style for its "tumid grandeur," writes with deliberate American plainness, though, to this twenty-first-century ear, with a dignified elegance. What matters more to me is that he does his level best to enter into the feelings and thoughts of his alien world, finding much to admire in the Aztecs and much to blame in the Spaniards; for example, he calls the massacre of the Indians in fateful Cholula a "dark stain" on Cortés's record. But for all his romantic pleasure in new marvels he never condescends to accept the horrifying elements of Aztec civilization. He recognizes that these are not individual crimes but systemic evils that his Western liberal conscience cannot condone. One might say that he dignifies his subjects with his condemnation. For this candor he is, as you can imagine, belittled these days as naïve, culture-bound, and ethnocentric. I shall have a word to say on the sophisticated reverse bigotry of his belittlers.

His style, to add one more feature, is extraordinarily vivid; it compares to Gibbon's as a classical statue in all its original bright encaustic colors to one that has been dug up, now only bare white marble. This visual aliveness may be a "blind Homer" effect. When Prescott was a young student dining at the Harvard Commons, he was hit in the eye by a hard piece of bread during a food fight and was half-blind for the rest of his life. It is characteristic of this man that, although he knew whose missile had hit him, he never told the name. His enormous collection of sources was read to him and evidently richly illustrated in his imagination.

I might mention the other chief (early) sources I read. First for anyone interested in the actual course of the Conquest is Bernal Díaz del Castillo's *True History of New Spain* of 1555. This simply told, incident-rich account of the march on

Tenochtitlán and what happened afterwards gains credence
from the fact that the old trooper was disgruntled with his
captain's assignment of rewards—the common condition of
the Conquistador ranks; the poor devils got little for their
endless exertions and wounds. In spite of his grievances,
Díaz's love and admiration for Cortés unsuppressably dominates his story.

The Conquistadores are sometimes represented as having
had eyes for nothing not made of gold. Here is the old soldier's recall of Tenochtitlán as he first glimpsed it, thirty-six
years before, on a causeway leading toward the island city:

> We were amazed and said that it was like the enchantments they
> tell of Amadis, on account of the great towers and *cues* (temples)
> rising from the water, and all built of masonry. And some of our
> soldiers even asked whether the things we saw were not a dream.
> It is not to be wondered that I here write it down in this man-
> ner, for there is so much to think over that I do not know how to
> describe it, seeing things, as we did, that have never been heard
> of or seen or even dreamed.

These men, some of them ruffians, but with medieval
romances behind their eyes to help them see alien beauty,
were evidently not altogether sick with gold greed. But those
later writers who don't blame them for the one, accuse them
of the other: they're either merely medieval knight errants or
merely mercantile expeditionaries. In fact, they seem to have
been poignantly aware that they were seeing sights no European had ever seen before or could ever see after.

Here is what they saw: A city edged by flowering "floating
gardens," the mud-anchored *chinampas*, lying on the shining
flat waters of a shallow, irregular lake collected in a high valley guarded by the snowy peaks—even in August—of the two
volcanoes; straight broad causeways connecting the city to the
shore giving into straight broad avenues leading from the four
directions of the winds to its sacred center, the center of the

world, with its great, gleaming, colorfully decorated temple pyramid; a grid of smaller streets edged with bridged canals; a myriad of lesser temple pyramids, some smoking with sacrifices; palaces with stuccoed walls and patios polished to gleam like silver; sparkling pools; crowds of clean, orderly people going about their business, especially in the great market of Tlatelolco; gardens everywhere; and the white houses of the city's quarter million inhabitants with their flat roofs, the *azoteas* from which two years hence such a deadly shower of missiles would rain down on the returning Spaniards that the dwellings were demolished one by one.—All these features of the vision have been, incidentally, described with a poet's relish by William Carlos Williams:

> [T]he city spread its dark life upon the earth of a new world, sensitive to its richest beauty, but so completely removed from those foreign contacts that harden and protect, that at the very breath of conquest it vanished.

Our tutor Jorge Aigla in Santa Fe has made a verse translation of an anonymous transcript of Tlatelolco, written only seven years after the starved and sick México, who had defended their city foot by foot, finally surrendered its devastated remains. Here are a few stanzas:

And all of this happened to us.
We saw it all
We watched it happen
With this sad and mournful fortune
We saw each other's anguish.

On the road lay broken arrows;
Hairs are scattered
The houses unroofed
Their walls red, blackened.

* * *

A price was set upon us.
A price for the young man, the priest,
The child, the virgin maiden.

Enough! The price of a poor man
was two handfuls of corn,
only ten insect cakes;
Our price was only
twenty cakes of salty gruel.

Gold, jades, rich embroidery,
Quetzal plumages,
All that was precious
Was valued not at all . . .

The mutual admiration of Indians and Spaniards was great—in the beginning. True, the Spaniards, whom Cortés's vigilance kept sleeping in their armor, stank in the nostrils of the much-bathing Indians, and the priests with their long, blood-matted hair in their gore-bespattered sanctuaries nauseated the Spaniards. (I omit here, for the moment, the Spaniards' response to the sacrifices themselves, which marked, on the Christians' side, the beginning of the end of amity.) The Spaniards were astonished by Indian craftsmanship. Díaz describes after decades a necklace made of golden crabs (others say crayfish) that Montezuma placed around Cortés's neck. Of course, Díaz described the golden gifts more often in terms of the pesos they weighed when melted down into bullion. I note here that the Aztecs did not, evidently, have scales and did not reduce objects to their universal stuff, ponderable mass (thus the Mexicans used natural items, quills of gold dust and cocoa beans, for currency, while the Spanish had the *peso d'oro*, the "gold weight," calibrated in fact to silver, to 42.29 grams of the pure substance); this intellectual device of universal quantification even those critics of the West who deplore it can hardly forego in the business of life. The Spaniards were astounded by, and perhaps a little envious of, the stately splendor of the cacique's accoutrements. The Indians, on their part, were amazed by the invaders' daring, tenacity, and endurance. They called them, as the Spanish heard it, *teules*, *téotl* being the Nahuatl word for god. The term seems to have been used somewhat as Homer uses *dios*, indicating sometimes just excellence and sometimes divinity. As we shall see, the Aztecs had a serious reason to call Cortés and his people gods. The Spanish, on their side, in their very horror of the frightful-looking Aztec god-images, paid them a certain respect in regarding them not as mere idols, deaf and dumb objects of stupid worship, but much as the México themselves did: Sahagún, of whom I will shortly tell, records an Aztec ruler's admonitory speech in which he says: "For our lord seeth, heareth within wood, within stone." The god-representations were not masks of nothing to the Christians, but they were images of demons, of the Devil in various shapes. Thus in looking at the Nahuatl side in Sahagún's dual language text, I noticed that Spanish *diablo*, Devil, had become a loan word in Nahuatl—*one* new name for all the old divinities, to be abominated but also acknowledged.

The second eyewitness source is Cortés himself, who wrote to his sovereign, Charles V, five letters reporting on his activities. Of these *cartas de relación*, letters of report, all but one are extant in copies. They are not notes but voluminous, detailed accounts beginning with the first, pre-Cortés exploration of the Gulf Coast and ending with Cortés's own post-Conquest explorations; the second and third letter contain the material for this lecture. The English version conveys a flavor of studiedly plain elegance. These clearly literary works are charged by historians with being both subtly self-aggrandizing and consciously myth-making. To me it would seem strange if Cortés, in writing to his sovereign, on whom depended acknowledgements and rewards, did not portray his exertions most favorably. It might be said—I don't know whether in mitigation or exacerbation—that he was also willing to suppress a brave but irrepressible compañero's guilt: Nowhere have I found even a mention of Alvarado's culpability in the events leading to the *noche triste*. It is also said that Cortés invented the myth of an Aztec empire which rivaled Charles's own, to whet the Spanish emperor's interest in his new dominion. To me, the account itself, telling of tributes owed by the subject cities and of their chiefs obliged to be in attendance in Tenochtitlán, sounds more like information he was in fact given by proud México officials or disaffected dependents.

Above all, Cortés fills his letters with myriads of meticulously noted detail—too thick and too vivid to be attributed to mere mendacious fantasizing. He would have had to have been a veritable Gabriel García Márquez to invent so magical a reality. For, he says, "we saw things so remarkable as not to be believed. We who saw them with our own eyes could not grasp them with our understanding." Cortés himself will appear in a moment.

The third source, the most exhaustive in scope and remarkable in method, is *The History of the Things of New Spain* by the before-mentioned Friar Bernadino de Sahagún. He had arrived as the forty-third of the religious that Cortés had requested in one of his letters to the emperor. The Conquistador needed them to carry on the task of conversion, because, as he said, the Indians had a great natural attraction to Christianity; indeed, in the early post-Conquest years, Indians were baptized by the thousands a day. (The reasons that Cortés's observation is not implausible will be mentioned below.)

The name *New Spain* in Sahagún's title is, incidentally, Cortés's own for conquered Anahuac: "New Spain of the Ocean Sea." For the Conquistador it betokens a great colonial accession to old peninsular Spain and the emphasis is on "Spain." But later the accent shifts to "New," as the criollos, the Mexican-born Spaniards, rebel against the old country's domination. Eventually a nativist revival and a growing sense of nationhood leads to a rejection by the native-born Spaniards themselves of their Conquistador heritage, and when in 1821 the country achieves independence, it will be called by the old Nahua name for Tenochtitlán, *México* (now pronounced in the Spanish way, *Mehico*). Nativist Mexico's tutelary deity will be Quetzalcóatl, the dominating god of this lecture, of whom more in a moment.

Back to Sahagún. He learned Nahuatl himself and spent the rest of his life, with much untoward clerical interference, compiling the world's first great inside ethnographic account. In his college he trained his own informants, Indian boys, often of noble descent, who could interview their living elders and obtain the information that Sahagún presented in parallel columns, Spanish and Nahuatl. The work, in twelve volumes, is known as the *Florentine Corpus*. Lisa Richmond, our librarian, fulfilled my unexpectant hopes by buying the very expensive English edition for our library, and if one reader a decade finds the delight and illumination in it that I did, the investment will be well justified.

Sahagún begins with the gods and their births—for like Greek gods, these gods were *born*, at Teotihuacán, thirty-three miles northeast of Tenochtitlán. This sacred city was well over a millennium old when Anahuac was established, and in ruins. But there the Méxica came to worship, particularly at the great temple pyramid dedicated to Quetzalcóatl. What bound new Anahuac to old Teotihuaca—the name means City of the Gods—was their common era, that of the Fifth Sun, upon whose destruction the world would end.

Sahagún then records everything from the sacred rituals and binding omens to the set moral speeches (much more charming without failing to be scary than similar speeches made by our elders) down to the riddles people asked, such as "What drags its entrails through a gorge?" Answer: "A needle." The next-to-last book is an inventory of the "Earthly Things" of New Spain, its flora, fauna, and minerals; the chapter on herbs begins with the plants "that perturb one, madden one," the hallucinogens. The twelfth book is Sahagún's own history of the Conquest.

Some say that the first bishop of New Spain, Zumárraga, conducted a huge *auto-da-fe*, a book burning of Aztec codices, those books folded like screens, composed in glyphs (stylized figures with fixed meanings) combined with lively pictures. Others say that those codices that weren't destroyed by the hostile Tlaxcalans or in the great conflagration of Tenochtitlán were spirited away by Indians. In any case, the art of illustration was still alive, and Sahagún used the talents of Indian painters to supplement his records in this visually delightful pre-alphabetic way.

Finally I want to mention the *History of the Indians of New Spain* by another Franciscan, affectionately named by his Indian parishioners *Motolinía*, Nahuatl for "Little Poor One," since he took his vow of poverty seriously. He reports the terrible post-Conquest sufferings undergone by the Indian population; worse than their cruel exploitation by the disappointed Conquistadores and colonists was the succession of European plagues (smallpox, bubonic plague, measles, for which the Indians reciprocated only with syphilis). I am impressed, over and over, with this pattern: that the inoculated West does most of its harm to other civilizations unintentionally, and I mean not only through their physical susceptibility but even more through their spiritual and intellectual vulnerability. The reason we can cope with our dangerously developed, potent tradition is that we know how to fight back, how to subject our powers to constraining criticism and how to correct our aberrations by returns to sounder beginnings. *Critique* and *Renaissance* are the continual evidence of our self-inoculation, and we see right now the dangerous consequences of the Western invasion of souls not so protected.

But Motolinía also reports successes, not only in conversions, which were too stupendous in number and abrupt in spiritual terms to be always quite real. What is lovely to read about is not only his affection for the gentleness and dignified reticence of his boys but their quick intelligence and general talentedness; some learned enough Latin in a few years to correct the grammar—a tense but triumphant moment for their teacher—of a visiting dignitary. They sang liturgies like angels and easily learned to play European instruments. No wonder Mexico City was to become, in the eighteenth century, this hemisphere's greatest center of baroque music; its chief composer, Manuel de Zumaya, Chapel Master at the very Cathedral of Mexico City which replaced Huitzilopóchtli's temple, was part-Indian.

I should also mention two more works written with great sympathy for the Indians: Bishop las Casas's *Short Account of the Destruction of the Indies* of 1542, a book of passionate accusation against the Spanish conquerors and colonists, and Cabesa de Vaca's *Relación*, the story of the tribulations of a discoverer of Florida, who was himself for a while enslaved by Indians.

By contemporary historians the Aztecs are treated in almost comically opposite ways. Jacques Soustelle paints their daily life as an idyll of gentle, flower-loving, orderly culture, made poignant on occasion by the necessities of the ritual care and feeding of the gods. It is the myth of harmony and happiness the México themselves encouraged in the revisionist accounts that succeeded the "book burning" by Itzcóatl, their first emperor. Inga Clendinnen, on the other hand, depicts a somberly severe, fear-ridden, God-encumbered society, whose sacrificial rituals, coruscating with dizzyingly whirling visions and penetrating musical stridor, were, she helpfully says, "infused with the transcendent reality of the aesthetic." Hugh Thomas, the most recent historian of the

Conquest, a sensible and thorough marshaller of thousands of facts, speaks similarly of "the astounding, often splendid, and sometimes beautiful barbarities" of Aztec ritual practice.

What astounds me is not the antithetical views of Aztec life, for these polarities seem to have been of the Aztec essence. What takes me aback is that my contemporaries seem to wish to appear as knowing what is beautiful but not what is wrong. There are of course exceptions, writers who feel insuperable moral unease over these alien customs they are by their professional bias bound to honor. The imaginary experiment that I, as an outsider and amateur, have devised for myself to put the profession in general to the test is this: When the Spaniards first came on the remains of ritual killings— later they saw the rituals themselves and eventually found the body parts of their own comrades—they broke into the holding pens where prisoners were being fattened and stormed the temples. Would the professors have done the same or would they have regarded the practice as protected by the mantra of "otherness"? I am assuming here that they do disapprove of human sacrifice in their own culture. For my part, I cannot tell what I would have had the courage to do, but I would have been forever ashamed if I had not shared in the revulsion, the reversal of an original appreciation that, for all their rapaciousness, the Christians had for the Indians—and I might add, for certain remarkable Indian women.

I have thus evolved for myself two categories of historians: non-condoners and condoners. The older writers tend to be non-condoners; they are not careful to cloak themselves in moral opacity; what they abhor at home they will not condone abroad, be it ever so indigenous and ever so splendid. One remarkable exception is the before-mentioned Bartolomé de Las Casas, who lays out the case for human sacrifice as being both natural—since men offer their god what they hold most excellent, their own kind—and also as being within our tradition—since Abraham was ready to sacrifice his son Isaac at God's bidding, and God himself sacrificed *his* son. The difficulty with this latter argument would seem to be that Abraham's sacrifice was called off, and God's sacrifice was unique, while Indian sacrifices were multitudinous.

Las Casas is the preceptor of Tzetan Todorov, a European intellectual who, in his book *Conquest*, tries hard to come to grips with "the Other," with the Aztec non-West. He finally elevates the Other over his own: The Aztecs made sacrifices, the Spaniards committed massacres. And here the rational difficulty is that Aztec religion commanded these deaths and Christian religion forbade them, so that Todorov is comparing customs with crimes.

This enterprise of restricting universal morality in the interests of empathy with otherness puzzles me a lot. For if we are really and radically each other's Other, then those who leave their own side to enter into the Other will thereby also lose their footing as open-eyed contemplators. In any case, it seems to me that the non-condoning Prescott's grand narrative has done more for the memory of this bygone civilization than have the condoning contemporaries. For he induces what Virgil calls *lacrimae rerum,* tears for lost things—while they invite, in me at least, contrariness, resistance to their sanctimonious self-denial.

You can see that as I read on I developed an interest in historiography, the reflective study of historical accounting itself. For it seems to me of great current importance to consider a propensity of Western intellectuals, particularly pronounced in the social studies and expressive of a strength and its complementary weaknesses native to this tradition: knowledgeable self-criticism flipping into unthinking self-abasement before the non-West. I say this mindful of the moral quandary of pitting the humanly unacceptable, but, so to speak, innocent evils, the traditional practices of a whole civilization, against the crimes of individuals transgressing the laws of their own, crimes magnified by its superior power.

And now a final motive for this, my aberrant interest: We here on the Annapolis campus are only 200 miles further from Mexico City than from our other half in New Mexico; Incan Cuzco is nearly on our longitude of 76° W. Yet these Precolumbian empires are hardly ever in our common consciousness, even less now than in the decades after Prescott's very popular book appeared. True, some of the skyscrapers of the twenties and thirties intentionally recalled Mesoamerican pyramids. True, the Nahuatl words *chocolátl* and *tamálli* are in our daily vocabulary, as is Nahua cooking, that is, Mexican food, in our diets. The Aztecs had in fact a high cuisine; the description of the emperor's daily service with its hundreds of dishes—among which (lest we be tempted too much) there *may* have been, as Díaz reports, the meat of little children—is staggering in its variety; indeed there cannot ever have been a potentate more luxuriously or elaborately served. Of all this we've adopted, through modern Mexico, the low end, but where else do the Empires of the Sun figure in our lives? This surprised sense of their missing influence made me engage in another one of those imagination-experiments by which we see the world anew: What if, as King Cacáma of Texcoco and some later historians thought possible, the México had just killed Cortés and his band, so that the Westernization of Anahuac had been held off for some centuries?—for it is not within my imagination that the West was forever to be resisted. Suppose the unwitting extermination of the Indians by disease had thus been prevented. (I might say here that this huge demographic disaster, possibly among the worst in history,* is numerically unfixed. Some say Anahuac had a

Except perhaps for the Black Death of 1348 and the flu epidemic of 1918.

population of thirty million, some say it had four before Cortés. Some say by the mid-fifteenth century this population had been reduced to 2.6 or 1.2 million, to be fully restored only much later.) Suppose, then, that the ravaged generation of the Conquest and post-Conquest era had instead been preserved, and Nahua civilization with it. Suppose eventually North American jeans and technology had drifted down and Aztec gorgeousness and craftsmanship up the latitudes.— I might inject here that the Peruvian novelist Mario Vargas Llosa, who has grappled seriously with such dreams, comes to the sad but realistic conclusion that the loss of native culture is worth the benefit to ordinary people that these imports bring.—Suppose moreover that our American English had absorbed some of the suavely dignified classical Nahuatl, its urbane address, its poetic rephrasings, its expressive word agglutinations; suppose as well that the speech of the Nahua had accepted some of our flamboyant informality. Suppose our clothing had been restyled by Aztec orchidaciousness and our manners had been a little improved by Aztec ceremoniousness. Suppose our political discourse had been informed by a neighboring monarchy against which we had never had to rebel. We can learn in our imagination whether such fine acquisitions could have come into our way of life without losing their hieratic heart. Would not one of the parties in this cultural exchange eventually turn out to contribute the core and the other the decoration? My provisional answer is that the West would assert itself as the substructure and the Empire of the Sun would become part of its recreation—they would be the pilgrims and we the tourists.

The Mexican writer Carlos Fuentes tells of a similar imagined reversal of history in the semi-historical story "The Two Shores." Here Aguilar, Cortés's first interpreter, who had long lived with the Maya, speaks from the grave. He tells how even while in Cortés's employ he held with the Indians and, by always translating not what Cortés said but what he thought, caused trouble. He confesses that he was jealous of Malinche, the Nahuatl- and Mayan-speaking woman, whose Mayan Aguilar translated into Spanish. She soon became Cortés's

mistress and learned Spanish; she was one of the central figures of the conquest, present and mediating on every great
occasion; Aguilar was made redundant. But revenge is not his
final passion. It is rather a plan to mount with his Mayans
a reverse conquest, a successful invasion of Spain, and there
to recall the defeated Moors and the expelled Jews, to inau-
gurate a darker-skinned, better melded Europe, "a universe
simultaneously new and recovered, permeable, complex, fer-
tile," where "[s]weet Mayan songs joined those of the Proven-
cal troubadours. . . ." But Aguilar, as he dreams his impossible
dream, is dead of the bubonic plague that did not attack only
Indians.

So these imagination-experiments endorse the question
raised by the facts with which I began: How can we understand what happened here, on this American continent,
between 1519 and 1534? Can we compel the fortunes of war
and the forces of history to show their human motive power?

To get at some sort of answer, I shall take up the four factors in the conquest of Mexico that seem to me most revealing: One is a god, Quetzalcóatl; one is a practice, human
sacrifice; two are men, Montezuma and Cortés.

1) *Quetzalcóatl*, the most appealing of the Mesoamerican
gods, is also most deeply implicated in the Mexican debacle.
This is a complex figure, a god of human interiority and of
the works of civilization, a searcher into the depth of hell and
the guardian of terrestrial idylls, a priest king of Tula and the
deus absconditus of Anahuac, an Indian Prometheus.

He was not the tribal god of the México, having been in
the country long before they arrived. Their god was Huitzilopóchtli, the god of war and of the sun, or rather the Sun itself,
who shared the great temple pyramid of Mexico-Tenochtitlán, the scene of so much of the drama in this tale, with
Tlaloc, the god of rain—the god who floods the heavens in
light with the god who drenches the earth in water. When the
Mexica were still Chichimeca (as the Nahua called the wan-

dering semi-savages of the north), coming down from their
mythical city of origin Aztlan* (whence the name Aztec) in

I suspect that some of the nomenclature of C. S. Lewis's Nar-
nia series, such as the lion-god's name, Aslan, is adapted from
Prescott.

search of their appointed home, their priests carried on their
backs, as I mentioned before, a twittering medicine bundle.
This was Huitzilopóchtli, reborn at Teotihuacán, the birthplace of the gods, as the Fifth Sun. His name means "Hummingbird On the Left" or "On the South," perhaps because he
and his people went southwest to find their marshland home
on Lake Texcoco, perhaps because the god-figure was half-
bird, having a thin, feathered left leg. In effect their god was
crippled. Cripples, dwarves, hunchbacks, albinos play a great
role in Nahua history, partly because the valley people had
an inexhaustible interest in the sports and varieties of nature:
Montezuma's palace complex included, besides an aviary, a
zoo, an arboretum, a gallery of anomalous humans; but there
may be something deeper to it, some sense of awe before the
exceptional—I don't know.

The war god was a hummingbird because Aztec warriors
who died in battle went not to the murky Hades of Mictlán
but to a sunny Elysium where they flitted about feeding on
flowery nectar—perfect examples of a dominant Aztec characteristic, the abrupt juxtaposing of or transiting from the
brutal to the delicate.

Most of the Aztec gods seem to have had frightful aspects.
There is a statue of Huitzilopóchtli's mother Coatlicúe, a
chunky monster with a necklace of human parts and a head
like an oblong package made up from two compressed snakes
springing from her neck. The tribal god himself must have
looked inhumanly terrifying. Not so Quetzalcóatl. The Aztecs were very sensitive to human beauty—the ugliness of the
gods is clearly deliberate—and this god was represented as

beautiful, albeit in a way which, although not unique to him, is yet most remarkable.

Quetzalcóatl's name combines the word *quétzal*, a Meso-american bird that has precious green tailfeathers (the green of quetzal feathers and of jade was the color of the Mexica nobility), with *coatl*, meaning snake. So he is the bird-snake, or the Plumed Serpent, belonging both to the sky and the earth. And thus he is shown in some sculptures with coils, whose scales are lengthened into feathers, neatly piled into a spiral. The fanged jaws are wide open and frame a hand-some, spare young male face, with high-bridged nose, well-shaped eyes, thin-lipped mouth—the face, I imagine, of a young Aztec noble.

Is this face that of the god within a serpentine integument, or is the creature as a whole the god, or is it the god's priest in his ritual costume? It is not clear that it is even a permissi-ble question. The Aztecs appear to have had the most flexible notions of their divinities. The gods amalgamate compe-tences, share names, identify with their victims, and merge with their priests. As far as I can tell, this mode is neither confusion nor indeterminacy. It is rather a kind of concep-tual fluidity which does become fixed in the very precisely promulgated rituals. The graphic art of the Aztecs expresses this multifarious melding by its complexly intertwined figures with their attributes all drawn indistinguishably on one plane and discriminable only to an expert in Aztec divinity.

But of Quetzalcóatl we know that he was indeed both god and man (a duplex being, not beyond comparison with Jesus). As man he was then lord of Tula, and as the Toltec lord he became fateful to the México.

To me the most appealing characteristic of these newcom-ers, these recent Chichimeca, was their longing deference to a city of the past, Tula, a city forty miles north of their lake and overthrown more than 300 years before Montezuma's day. Tula was to Tenochtitlán what Athens has been to Europe and still is to us in Maryland and New Mexico: the source of wisdom, art, and ideals of life. The Toltecs were to the México like gods, walking swiftly everywhere on blue sandals, wrapped in flowery fragrance. For them corn sprouted in enormous ears, precious cocoa beans—one of the Mexican currencies—were found in plenty, and cotton grew already dyed in rich colors. They made works of art so exemplary that the Aztecs gave their own craftsmen the generic name of *toltéca*, Tulans.

Over this earthly idyll Quetzalcóatl Topíltzin, Our Dear Lord Quetzalcóatl, ruled as priest and king, godlike but also all too human. I cannot tell you what then happened in all its tragicomic detail. But in brief, Huitzilopóchtli and other gods arrived in the guise of mischief-making wizards. Never mind the disparity in dates. This is the story of a newer god of war undoing an older god of civilization, and, I suspect, the story of how Huitzilopóchtli's people betrayed their assumed Toltec heritage. These wizards assaulted the Toltec lord, who had grown in some way neglectful, with portents and temptations. They tempted him with pulque, the wine made from the maguey cactus, the American aloe, whose consumption was fiercely regulated in Tenochtitlán. They raised indecent passions in princesses and induced civil wars that Quetzalcóatl had to win with his army of dwarves and cripples. They caused the Tolteca to sing and dance themselves to death. To these temptations the lord of Tula succumbed as a participant. Finally, however, they tried to force him to make human sacrifices. Here he balked and refused and was for that steadfastness driven from Tula. All this is told by Sahagún and other Indian sources. This is the moment to say once more what needs saying just because it seems too naïve for words: To report that Huitzilopóchtli did this and Quetzalcóatl that is not to confer the status of existence on these divine figures. Indeed, they became fateful to their people precisely because they were so vulnerable to non-existence proofs.

There is a stone head that shows the Dear Lord weeping, long clublike tears issuing straight from the god's eyes, probably those he wept as he went into exile. The same head shows him heavily bearded, an unusual feature in a young god, and among the Indians in general. He is also supposed to have been light-skinned.

Quetzalcóatl flees toward the east. He crosses, in space not time, the path of the México's god going southwest, and he makes his way toward the east coast, there to embark with his loyal band on a raft of serpents and to drift into the rising sun—the very way Cortés, a white, bearded man, took in reverse going west and inland. Cortés comes this way in 1519, just as the year that in the Aztec calendrical cycle is Quetzalcóatl's birth and death year, *ce ácatl*, One Reed, had come round again. In this year the Dear Lord was destined to return by boat from his transoceanic exile. You can see the tragedy taking shape.

The biggest pyramid in America rose at Cholula to mark one of the god-man's stations of flight. There the god failed his people when, on his way to Tenochtitlán, Cortés massacred more than a hundred unarmed Cholulan nobles in his temple precinct. Cortés thought he had uncovered a plot to betray his band to the México. Perhaps he had, and perhaps the planned ambush would have been the end of him if he had not prevented it with his characteristic merciless decisiveness. That we shall never know, but we do know this: The Cholulans remembered an old prophecy that the god who had rested from his flight in their city would protect them, and that if they pulled a stone out of his pyramid, a flood of water would sweep the enemy away. With panicky energy they succeeded in wrenching out a stone—and got a cloud of dust.

The Plumed Serpent, briefly to finish his tale, was not permanently discredited, nor did he cease to occupy imaginations. He became the savior god of a resurrected Mexico. The friars who came at Cortés's request wanted a warrant for treating the Indians as aboriginal Christians; they saw in the wandering god not Jesus but St. Thomas, one of Jesus's twelve disciples who was his missionary to India. Quetzalcóatl was also the guardian god of the nativist movement in New Spain and Mexico, celebrated in murals and hymns by Mexican painters and intellectuals and even by that wandering Englishman D. H. Lawrence. His novel of 1926, *The Plumed Serpent*, is a repulsively fascinating, garishly proto-Nazi fantasy of the god's return in provincial Mexico, complete with the paraphernalia of Nuremberg: a charismatic god-representing leader, choreographed soldiery, Nazi-like salutes, and finally human sacrifice—all this so that the heroine, a manless ageing Irishwoman, might find a man who *is* a man, that is, who hardly ever talks. It is a travesty of the sorrowful Toltec mandivinity of civilization.

2) *Human sacrifice* was, I have learned to think, not really just a Mexican custom ascribable to "otherness." The México knew the story just told of Quetzalcóatl. I cannot believe that some of them, especially their last emperor, did not reflect that they were co-opting the god into a practice he abhorred and over which he went into exile. Perhaps those priests of Huitzilopóchtli, with their skull-decorated black gowns and blood-matted hair, were fanatics totally absorbed in their cultic task, but the educated nobles, admirers of Tula, so refined in their intimate habits and their social life, must have had qualms and doubts—unless there is *no* way to infer from ourselves to others.

The numbers are staggering. It is reported that at the inauguration of Huitzilopóchtli's Great Temple in 1487, 20,000—by some readings 80,000—victims were lined up four abreast in queues stretching from the temple onto the city's causeways. (Is it altogether an ironical coincidence that these were about the numbers of Indians said to have presented themselves for conversion on certain days after the conquest?) And this killing went on, in smaller numbers, in the numerous minor temples of the city. Every twenty days, by the ritual calendar, there was a god's feast, requiring sometimes quite a few children, sometimes a woman, sometimes a specially prepared youth. The operation itself is often shown in the codices. The victims march, mostly unassisted, to the top of the pyramid; there they are laid on a convex sacrificial stone, their limbs are held by four priests while a fifth chokes off their screams with a wooden yoke, the obsidian knife rips into the chest, the heart, still beating, is held up to the Sun and put in a wooden bowl, the "eagle dish." The victim is rolled down the steps to be dismembered and distributed for feasting according to a strict protocol. The victims are children bought from the poor, the pick of slaves for sale in the market (who are ritually bathed), beautiful young nobles prepared in a year of splendid living for their role as *ixíptlas*, god-impersonators. Evidently certain divinities, like the ever-present Tezcatlipóca, Lord of the Near and Nigh, who shared functions with the city god, were not only recipients of victims but were themselves sacrificed, albeit through their human incarnations—one more noteworthy parallel to Christianity.

It seems to be true that these ritual killings were not sadistic in intention or demeaning to the victims. While there are reports of weeping family and frightened victims, the sacrificial human was evidently well co-opted into the performance. Moreover, the cactus button *péyotl* and the mushroom *teonanácatl*, "Flesh of the Gods," both hallucinogens, and the alcoholic pulque seem to have been administered to the sacrifices, who were, in any case, intoxicated with the ritual swirl and the musical stridor around them. For the prepared chosen, at least, this passage into a flowery next world was perhaps a high point of this life—though who knows how many victims, particularly the children, died experiencing extreme fear.

These frightful, somber, and splendid festivals were evidently thought to be truly necessary to the survival of the city and the continuing existence of its world. Yet, as I said, the Aztec nobility, who were so finely attuned to right and wrong conduct (as their stock homilies, preserved by Sahagún, show), must have felt themselves to be living over a moral abyss, doing a balancing act in a threatening and fragile sacred world, which doomed them in their hearts for what they did and through their sacred duties for what they might omit to do.

I have neglected to mention the largest and most steady supply of victims, the prisoners. The highest calling of Huitzilopóchtli's people, the soldiers of the Sun, was war, and the object of war was to take captives, an even higher object than the subjugation of Anahuac's cities. Promotion in the army was strictly according to the number of prisoners taken. The warriors needed to take prisoners to rise in rank; the city needed prisoners for their flesh and blood, the sacrifices that would feed and maintain the good will of the gods. It was a tight circle of necessities.

This religious trap—I will call it that—had three devastating secular consequences. First, the Mexican army never learned, until it was too late, to fight to kill, to fight a war for survival in realest earnest. Second, Tenochtitlán trained up a deadly enemy for itself, the city of Tlaxcála, seated between itself and the eastern coast. There was a bizarre but logical institution in Anahuac, the so-called "flowery war," *xochiyaóyotl*. The Triple Alliance of Anahuac, eventually dominated by Tenochtitlán and including Texcoco, had a mutual arrangement with three cities across the mountains, of which the aristocratic republic of Tlaxcála was the most independent. The agreement was to stage battles regularly for the sole purpose of obtaining from each other prisoners for sacrifice. This was a strange kind of ceremonious warfare, which required the highborn warriors skillfully to take their enemies alive, only to bring them back home to their delayed warriors' death. Meanwhile the Tlaxcalans remained free, in training, and full of hatred, and they became Cortés's most effective allies, while the cities lost some of their finest.

And third, the evidence and actual sight of human sacrifice turned the Spaniards' stomachs—as powerful a revulsion as the moral one, I imagine. So when, as I said, they saw the remains of their own people, an ineradicable repugnance seems to have turned their hearts, a disgust which became the pretext for much savagery of their own.

3) *Montezuma* was installed as *tlatoáni* of Mexico-Tenochtitlán in 1502. *Tlatoáni* means "He Who Speaks," who has authority. Since Tenochtitlán was the secular and sacred center of the Aztec world, he was the speaker over the universe, the *úei-tlatoáni*—usually rendered as "emperor." When he was killed in 1520 he was fifty-two. His lineage was even shorter than the city's existence, whose founding date is 1345. The Anahuac empire was put together during the next century; Axayacatl, Montezuma's father, who died in 1481, was only the third emperor. As was the custom, the council that chose the new lord did not go to the son but first to Axayacatl's two brothers. When Montezuma became the sixth emperor, Anahuac was less than seventy years old. Historians disagree whether objectively the empire was in a state of youthful vigor or in the course of rigidified decline when Cortés came. But there can be no doubt that Montezuma was a monarch who personally felt doom coming. Motolinia says (probably incorrectly) that his very name—*nomen omen*—meant one who is sad and serious, as well as one who inspires fear and respect.

As was necessary for the *tlatoáni*, he had proved himself as warrior and officer, but he was also a highly educated man. The México, like most high civilizations, were committed to a well-defined and diversified plan of education for their young. The set speeches, the traditional admonitions, that the ruling nobles made to their boys and girls upon their having reached the age of discretion are loving, somber, straitlaced, meticulous—and full of Nahua charm. The one from which I will quote a sampling goes on for six of Sahagún's columns. It begins thus:

> Here art thou, thou who art my child, thou who art my precious necklace, thou who art my precious feather, thou who art my creation, my offspring, my blood, my image.

And then the child is inducted into Aztec pessimism:

> Hear well, O my daughter, O my child. The earth is not a good place. It is not a place of joy; it is not a place of contentment.

Then the little girl is given rules of conduct, for example:

> At night hold vigil, arise promptly. Extend thy arms promptly, quickly leave thy soft bed, wash thy face, wash thy hands, wash thy mouth, seize the broom; be diligent with the sweeping; be not tepid, be not lukewarm.
>
> What wilt thou seize upon as thy womanly labors? . . . Look well to the drink, the food; how it is prepared, how it is made. . . .

Then the speech touches deep moral matters:

> May thou not covet carnal things. May thou not wish for experience, as is said, in the excrement, in the refuse. And if thou truly art to change thyself, would thou become a goddess?

But there was also public education, a dual system. The Young Men's (and Women's) House, the *telpochcálli*, was open to the lower nobility and even to commoners. The boys' house had features of our prep school. The emphasis was on physical hardening and the performance of rough public service. A lot of rowdy fun was overlooked; some of the older boys even took mistresses, and, Sahagún reports, "they presumed to utter light and ironic words and spoke with pride and temerity."

The second institution, the famous *calmécac*, was part seminary, part cadet corps. Here went the high nobility and commoners destined by talent to be priests. The daily routine was punishing; for example, sleep was often interrupted when the boys were called to draw blood from their earlobes and ankles with maguey spines. This self-sacrifice was said to have been instituted by Quetzalcóatl, who was in fact the tutelary divinity, the super-tutor, of the *calmécac*. Discipline was fierce. There were constant humiliations, and if a noble's son was found even a little drunk on pulque he was secretly strangled; a commoner was beaten to death.

The curriculum was rigid and rigorous. The boys learned the revisionist Méxica version of Nahua history from painted books that were expounded to them. They learned to speak ceremoniously and to perform ritual songs and dances accurately. They learned, besides the signs and number count of the 360-day solar calendar with its five unfortunate "hollow" intercalary days, the divinatory calendar. This was the "Sacred Book of Days" by which the priest told the feast days of the gods, the personal destiny of a baby, and the epochs of the world. This study was evidently the most effective initiation into the Aztec way of seeing the world. That is the reason why the friars, trying to extirpate Aztec worship, denounced this sacred calendar with particular vehemence as having cast loose from the natural heavenly revolutions and being an evil convention—as they said: "the fruit of a compact with the Devil."

The two calendars came together every fifty-two years, an era called the Bundling of the Years. Ominously, such an epoch evidently occurred in 1506, "One Rabbit," when just as many year-bundles had gone by as would make the setting of the fifth Sun imminent, and with it the final destruction by earthquakes of Huitzilopóchtli, his city, and the world whose center was Tenochtitlán. The year of 1519, moreover, was, as I said, *ce ácatl*, "One Reed," the name of the year of Quetzalcóatl's birth, exile and prophesied return. A student of the calendar presumably knew himself to be living at once near doomsday and near delivery.

From this schooling and his experience in the field, Montezuma emerged as high priest, warrior and *tlatoáni*: spiritually austere for all his palatial luxury, a severe father to his México, rigidly religious, and, for all the self-abasement his set accession speech required, an autocratic and aristocratic ruler, the first to restrict high office to the nobility. He was inaccessible to the populace, stately and ceremonious with his nobles, reserved as to his person (much like the English queen): When Cortés, as he himself tells, tried to hug him "in Spanish fashion," Montezuma's attendants stopped him; this was court etiquette but presumably also personal preference. But above all he was a burdened man, doom-ridden, half hopeful, self-doubtful. "What shall I do, where shall I hide? If only I could turn into stone, wood or some other earthly matter rather than suffer that which I dread!" he cried out, this victor of nine pitched battles, to his magicians who could not turn to good the omens of evil to come (and got severely punished for it). This was no coward's funk but a pious man's terror of a probably inevitable future.

There was a city across the lake, the aforementioned Texcoco, a member of Tenochtitlán's Triple Alliance. It paralleled the Italian cities of the Renaissance in high culture; it was a Tula revived. In the fifteenth century it had a poet-king, Nezahualcóyotl, whose poetry has the fragrance that arises when the melancholy of existence melds with soundness of heart. Like a Nahua Lucretius he offers his bitter cup with the rim sweetened by honey. He speaks:

I, Nezahualcóyotl, ask this:
Is it true one really lives on the earth?
Not forever on earth,
only a little while here.
Though it be jade it falls apart,

though it be gold it wears away,
though it be quetzal plumage it is torn asunder.
Not forever on earth,
only a little while here.

This is beauty to console for the brevity of being, but in
the Texcocan Renaissance prince it is without the panicky
gloom of the Mexican Emperor of the late Fifth Sun. Nezahualcóyotl's underlying sense of life's inconstancy is the same,
but Montezuma's was infected by the consciousness of a more
starkly immediate doom.

I think that Montezuma was probably an overwrought exemplar of a México noble: devout witness of constant bloody
brutality; refined connoisseur of jade and feather work;
watcher for imminent death and destruction; avid collector of
fleeting things like birds and flowers; cruel lord and ever-cour-
teous prince; liar of great ability and treacherous too, as the
Tlaxcalans believed; high noble of candid and simple bearing:
Witness the poignant speech of submission he appears to have
made to Cortés when he was still in his own palace, when he
still believed in the Spanish savior. He said with a smile:

> You too have been told perhaps that I am a god, and dwell in
> palaces of gold and silver. But you see it is false. My houses,
> though large, are of stone and wood like those of others. And
> as to my body [here he threw open his cloak]—you see it is flesh
> and blood like yours.

Some see delicate irony in his words, particularly in the reference to the absence of gold. But to me his speech sounds
heartfelt, and he was in fact submitting to men he thought
might be *teules*, gods; Cortés's band, the *santa compañia*, the
Holy Company, might indeed be bringing back Quetzalcóatl-
Cortés, "the white hero of the break of day."

He had had some cause to be thus receptive, for in the
decade before Cortés's arrival the omens had multiplied: the
spontaneous combustion of Huitzilopóchtli's temple, tongues

of celestial fire, finally a bird found in Lake Texcoco bearing a black mirror in its head in which the emperor briefly glimpsed the strangers landing—Sahagún catalogues eight serious omens.

I think Montezuma became heartsick and started vacillating, now welcoming the Spaniard from afar with golden gifts, now holding him off or even arranging his ambush. In the end he was transfixed like a rabbit by a snake, truly a snake since Cortés played the role of the Plumed Serpent. So he sent the Spaniard Quetzalcóatl's regalia, since it was the year *ce ácatl*, One Reed. Not all his nobles were pleased at the emperor's submissiveness; they wept when not much later they attended his litter to his place of custody, his father's palace.

Some historians think the omens were an *ex post facto* invention to make the catastrophe more palatable to simple people. But they sound very plausible; ominous events do occur in clusters before disasters (as Machiavelli observes in his *Discourses*), at least for those who have prophetic souls. The omens help explain Montezuma's fragility before the crisis. It was, I want to say, a type of fragility almost designed to highlight Cortés's robustness, as if Montezuma had found his fated match, the better to reveal the West to itself.

Once he had made his submission to the Spanish emperor and been taken into Spanish custody, another side of his character came out: He became receptive to new experiences, learned to shoot the crossbow, sailed Lake Texcoco on a brigantine, the first wind-driven vessel on those waters.—It is always the West's inventions, especially those that shoot far and go fast, that first beguile the non-West. He retained his exquisite courtesy and generosity; he became sociable and even affectionate with the Spaniards. It has been suggested that he was displaying the pathological bonding of a victim to his kidnappers. But by a concord with Cortés Montezuma was running his empire from Axayacatl's palace where he and the Spaniards were quartered, and he was free to indulge in his old pleasures like hunting. It is reported that if there was fun afoot he could dissolve in giggles.

But this priest-emperor never converted or gave up human sacrifice, although frequently subjected to Cortés's passionate theological harangues against the ritual on the grounds of human brotherhood. As Fuentes says, it was simply a more urgent question to him whether the sun would rise and the world go on than what the Spaniards did to him or his empire.

Nevertheless, I wonder if it ever came to him that his religious practices were, in the nature of things, futile, that the Christians had a sun that moved reliably and stably (and would even stand still) precisely because it was not a god and therefore not amenable to human exertion and sacrifice. Octavio Paz says in his *Labyrinth of Solitude* that the Aztecs committed suicide because they were betrayed by their gods. *I think they were, speaking more precisely, betrayed by their trust in their visible and palpable gods, who did nothing and were nothing and absconded more crassly than could an invisible deity or one less abjectly served—a truth I have, strangely enough, never found enunciated by the historians I have read.*

I should add that the conquering generation, far from discounting the defeated gods, accorded them stature by transforming them into devils. The pre-Conquest gods had proved impotent; their post-Conquest transfigurations were evil—a wily, yet genuine, avowal of the power of faith.

4) *Cortés*, finally, the Conquistador, seems to me a man as emblematic of the conquering West as Montezuma was of the empire of the doomed Sun. Cortés was a hidalgo from an old, turbulent, moderately situated family. Having gotten into various scrapes he chose to come to the Indies in 1504 when he was nineteen—an age more often given over to wanderlust than to acquisitiveness. In 1519 he began to subdue Anahuac, whose chiefs became, as he put it to his sovereign, "Your Majesty's vassals, and obey my commands." No sooner had he

conquered Mexico for Spain than he was beset by endless *audiencias* and *residencias*, tribunals and inquiries, conducted by officials whose rectitude was apparently not much greater than his own and whose daring was considerably less. Nevertheless, by 1529 he was Marquess of the Oaxaca Valley and Captain-General of New Spain, empowered to discover further lands and to colonize them. (In fact, following Mexico he discovered and named California after a queen in one of those medieval romances.) He died in 1547, and his bones have undergone grotesque removals paralleling his downward course in Mexican history, during which Quetzalcóatl was raised to a national hero while his unwitting impersonator was suppressed by the descendants of the Conquest.

The story of his and his Holy Company's march toward Tenochtitlán in 1519, his first peaceful entrance into the sacred and magical city, his expulsion, near-annihilation and devastating re-entry have lately been retold in all its fiction-defying detail by Hugh Thomas in *Conquest*. (Gary Jennings's blockbuster novel, *Aztec*, 1980, is a fictionalization of these events—a page turner.) He lands on Anahuac's eastern shore with his little fleet of "water houses," as the natives described his three-masted square-riggers, of the type called *naos*. When they first saw them, they reported on them as "mountain ranges floating on water." His boldest first stroke is to dismantle his ships before he marches inland. Now the thirty-four-year-old sailor emerges as a man of many devices and deceits, a bold man of faith—and greed-inspired audacity—albeit *somewhat* more devoted to the salvation of his soul than to the amassing of gold; a resilient man well acquainted with suffering and depression; a man of self- and other-punishing endurance and scary tenacity, who seems to live on little sleep; cruel and charming, careful of his companions and demanding their utmost; prudent and daring; circumspect and lightning-quick; generous and grasping; kind and manipulative; and always an adventurer and a wanderer—as complex a man in his way as Montezuma. Prescott says in his personal memoranda, in which he details for himself the oppositions of Cortés's character:

> The great feature of his character was constancy of purpose. . . . He was inexhaustible in resources, and when all outward means were withdrawn, seemed to find sufficient to sustain him, in his own bosom.

Now listen to the beginning of Homer's *Odyssey*:

> Tell me, O Muse, of the man of many twists (or "roles"—*polytropos*) who wandered so much when he had sacked the sacred city of Troy. He saw the towns of many men and knew their mind, and suffered much on the sea, seeking to save his soul and the return of his companions.

No two men could be more alike; if I were to inventory the characters of the two adventurers nearly every feature in one list would turn up quite recognizably in the other, beginning with "constancy of purpose"—Odysseus is *polytlas*, the "much enduring"—including the occasional bouts of depression. And this happy circumstance tells me that Cortés was *not* primarily a man of his time: not just a medieval knight-errant or a mercantile-minded gold prospector, or a hard-to-control vassal of the Spanish crown, or a fierce competitor for the rights of first conquest. He was certainly all these, and it was because he returned to the Gulf Coast to intercept his Spanish pursuers that he first lost Tenochtitlán. But before these and more fundamentally, he was a man who in his intense individuality expressed an ancient type of the West, Odysseus the self-sufficient, who talks to his own heart, who has many twists, roles, and devices, who is blunt and tactful, who can be driven to extreme cruelty and engage in gratuitous acts of kindness, who lies but not ignobly, and above all, who can, in a pinch, rely on his virgin goddess, Athena, *because he relies on his many-featured self.*

In Cortés that ancient pagan character type seems to have comfortably accommodated, or better, absorbed the God from the other root of the Western tradition, though Cortés was particularly devoted to the Virgin, as Odysseus was to Athena. Hugh Thomas says that he became more God-fearing as the expedition went on—who wouldn't? His flagship sailed under a banner he had inscribed with the saying: "Friends, let us follow the Cross, and if we only have faith, in this sign we shall conquer." He was citing the legend under which the Emperor Constantine fought the battle that in 312 turned the Roman Empire Christian. Cortés's Christianity is a debated subject, but to me it seems unquestionable. One kind of evidence is that this prudent commander several times put his expedition at risk because of his religious impetuousness and had to be restrained by Bartolomé de Olmeda, the wise and patient friar with the expedition, a man who while practicing prudence also thought of the Indians' feelings—so unlike Pizarro's fatal chaplain. On one memorable occasion, the emperor, at Cortés's request, invited him with some of his captains to come up the Great Pyramid of Huitzilopóchtli. Montezuma himself was, as usual, carried to the top, but Cortés insisted on marching up all 113 steep narrow steps and declared to the solicitous emperor waiting for him that "Spaniards are never weary"; indeed, as I mentioned, Cortés slept little when on campaign. Montezuma then obtained permission from the priests for Cortés, who was clearly already in the Christian conqueror mode, to enter the sanctuary. This reeking place so disgusted him that he asked Montezuma with a smile—not a charming one, I imagine—how so wise a prince could put his faith in a representation of the Devil. He offered to install in this temple, as he had on other pyramids, a cross and an image of the Virgin, before which the false gods would shrink into oblivion. Montezuma was deeply shocked and said—here is irony—that these were the gods that had ever led the México to victory. Cortés, perhaps nudged by Friar

Olmeda, apologized. But it was a dangerous moment. Montezuma stayed behind to expiate the sacrilege. This action, which could have meant the early end of Montezuma's policy of submission, was certainly impolitic and clearly inspired by pure if untimely Christian fervor. In his own account Cortés naturally suppresses this incident in favor of what must have been a later occasion, when he did actually topple the idol down the pyramid steps, and, as he claims, stop the sacrifices.

Cortés became de facto emperor of Anahuac close to the time, namely 1513, that Machiavelli's *Prince* appeared. So I looked Cortés up, as it were. I have often wondered for whom this manual on rulership is meant, since natural princes already know it all and untalented rulers will simply use it as permission for misconduct. Cortés, it turns out, knows most of Machiavelli's lessons: how to fight both like a fox and a lion, for he was proud of his "cunning stratagems" and fierce even when wounded and unarmed; how not to be good on occasion, for he could be brutal; how to get credit for every exploit, for his letters take care that he should; how to rule more by love than fear, as his trooper Díaz attests; how, finally, to be lucky, and—a Machiavellian or Odyssean trait of his own—how to lie royally without being commonly dishonest. But there were many more things that he did not do by this book but did rather against its explicit advice: he relied heavily on auxiliaries, fought with an amateur's improvisation, and did not study eminent predecessors—for there were none. But above all, Machiavelli doesn't seem to know, or at least to enunciate, the one thing most needful to an imperial conquistador: faith—in Cortés's case, Christian faith, but faith also in a more expansive sense, as I will try to show.

Both rulers made mistakes. Montezuma should not have sent gold to greet the "Holy Company," though how was he to know? He should not have quartered the Spaniards in Axayacatl's palace where the state treasure was hidden—and so on. But the chief mistake was to believe the prophecies and to submit to the omens, and so to the bearded white men coming over the water. Some of his nobles seem to have realized this, but they were themselves used to submitting to their lord, and so they wept silently.

Cortés's errors were those of a nervous yet decisive aggressor. At Cholula he stained his name with a possibly preventable massacre. At Tenochtitlán, when he hastened to the coast to repel his Spanish pursuers, he left in charge a valorous young brute, Pedro d'Alvarado, whom the Indians called *Tonatíuh*, the Sun, because he was blond and beautiful. He proved worse to them than their own doomed Fifth Sun, for as he was edgy, eager, and without judgment, he unleashed a massacre on the unarmed celebrants of Huitzilopóchtli's festival which ended every chance of peaceful dominion and brought on that Sad Night. This was the night when the Spaniards, their Indian allies, and the several women, both native and Spanish, fighting desperately alongside their men, were driven from the city and nearly exterminated.

Above all, on his return, he razed Tenochtitlán, the finest city in the world. Was it a mistake, a crime? Here is what he himself says in his account of the recapture of the city from the México, who under the young Emperor Cuauhtémoc, Montezuma's nephew, had learned the Spanish skills: to fight to kill, to fight at night, to fight from the water. The passage is from the third letter to Emperor Charles V:

> All I had seen forced me to two conclusions, the one that we should regain little of the treasure the Mexicans had taken from us; the other that they would force us to destroy and kill them all and this last weighed on my soul. I began to wonder how I could terrify them and bring them to a sense of their error. It could only be done by burning and destroying their houses and towers of the idols. . . .

Of course, the letter explains first things first: why the Emperor isn't getting his customary fifth of treasure. Of course, it assumes that the México are legally in rebellion. But it also reveals a certain travail of spirit, a conscience, a care for a people whose intelligence Cortés admired and whose fate he pitied, albeit he was its cause. On Cortés's premise the destruction was a necessity, but was the premise itself necessary? For my part, I simply cannot judge. It is true, however, that once he was master of Anahuac he looked carefully after his realm and probably did it more good in the long run than it ever was in Montezuma's power to do: He spent his own resources in rebuilding the country, introduced new plants and draught animals, condemned the enslavement of the Indians and recorded in his will his deep misgivings of conscience about the institution itself, and tried to mitigate the treatment of the natives by the colonists. And, of course, he abolished human sacrifice. All in all, his dubious deeds had the effect of relegating Anahuac to the past; his good deeds gave Mexico a future. And, pressed to think in these terms about the Conquest itself, I suppose with the Peruvian writer Mario Llosa that it belongs in the long run to the credit side of something, call it human welfare.

But the question I proposed was how and why it could happen. So let me try to come to some sort of conclusion. Two worlds clashed (here the cliché tells the simple truth), and the leaders happened to be emblematic of their worlds. Let me first compare the divinities that led the leaders.

We have an alumnus, Peter Nabokov, the stepson of the man to whom this lecture is dedicated, William Darkey. He is an expert on Indian sacred life and its sacred space. When he heard that I was reading on this subject he sent me a large box of books from his private library. In one of these books I found an article containing an antithetical listing of Aztec and Christian religiosity.

On the left, the Nahua side, are listed (I select for brevity's sake) Symmetry, Autonomy, Interchangeability, and Cyclicality. On the right, the Spanish side, are listed Hierarchy, Centralization, Fixity, and Linearity. This right side is in fact recognizable as a checklist of features condemned *in* the West as evils *of* the West, a compendium of the self-critique of the West such as was current in the later part of the last century, and still is.

I also recognize the left side of the list, and it does appear to me to be descriptive of Aztec religion. But notice this strange effect: how each characteristic of that religion induced an *opposite effect* on the Aztec polity. The complexly related Symmetries of divine functions make for a draining tangle of rituals; the Autonomy of the deities—as many as 1600—leads to a burdensome multiplicity of services; the Interchangeability of identities leads to dependence on priestly interpreters; and the Cyclicality leads to a sense of inescapable doom. In fact it was Anahuac that most tended toward social Hierarchy, administrative Centralization, and rigid Fixity of protocol. The Spanish side, on the other hand, gave its real-life practitioners one supreme God, reliable in his operations, author of a stable creation, progressing hopefully into a new day. And so it was the Spaniards who could afford to be free, flexible, energetic, and self-reliant—especially when separated by an ocean from their emperor. When God permits them to be defeated it is, Cortés says, on account of their own sins, a deserved punishment, not a divine antic. Thus his world is hospitable to boldness, while Montezuma's compels constriction.*

> This view implies that the gods of Anahuac were perhaps creatures of Aztecan imagination, thus reflections of an ethnic disposition. Thus is raised the existence question for all divinities. That's a perplexity I'll shun here.

But, a student of Aztec religion might argue, its similarities to Christianity are also remarkably exact and numerous, so why would religion make the difference? To give a sampling of the parallelisms: The Indians had the symbol of the cross, a Maltese type, that turns up frequently in their visual art. They had absolution by confession, though it could be undergone only once in a lifetime. They had a form of baptism, of ritual fasting, even an invisible god. Above all, they had the ritual ingestion of their god's blood: the victim's or their own blood was kneaded into loaves of amaranth seeds that were god-images and were then eaten. This last practice, the analogue of Christian communion, is most interesting to me, because some scholars represent this Christian sacrament as a form of cannibalism that brings Christianity closer to the Aztec feasting on flesh. But, of course, the blood partaken of during the Christian Eucharist is precisely not the blood of a living human being. Even a very untheoretical Christian knows that it is a mystery which is accompanied by a complex rational theology. Communicants know, if vaguely, that the wafer and wine are neither merely symbolic nor brutely real—the nature of their transformation is open to rational questioning: For example, have they undergone *transubstantiation*, so that the substance itself, the bread and the wine, are to be regarded as now the body and blood of Christ, or have they achieved *consubstantiation*, such that they present a duality of visible properties and invisible essence?

I may be allowed to dismiss the beguiling but bizarre notion of the friars that the Indians were lapsed Christians, baptized a millennium and a half ago by Quetzalcóatl-St. Thomas; at any rate, they themselves were always afraid that the willing conversions of the Indians were perhaps rather shallow and masked the survival of the old similar-seeming worship. It remains a problem, requiring really deep investigation by people who know *not only* the methods of comparative ethnography but the ways of faith, whether such similarities betoken pure coincidence, or are features belonging to some general human religiosity, and whether such all-human phenomena have a deep or shallow common root. To me it seems, judging only at first glance, that a religion supported by many disparate narratives, whose meaning, being a matter of memory, is uncircumventably in the hands of trained priests, is simply incommensurable with a religion that has one simply told "Good News" (*Evangelium*), one master story whose ever-new interpretations, carried on by priests, theologians, and laymen alike, strive for coherence. Let me make my point brusquely and minimally: Such a religion, Christianity in the present case, seems to me, as I said, simply more energizing. To wit: Cortés liked to read, as he said, when he had time, and he knew some theology which, in turn, gave him the self-confidence to harangue an emperor. He went to mass in the morning without fail and was ready for the day. In defense, Montezuma could only tell divine stories—myths to us—and insist on his gods' past services, which he had to keep securing by spending every day much time and many resources on arduous cultic performances.

Moreover, Cortés's Holy Company could rely on their God, who, being invisible—though having one and only one human incarnation—was therefore impervious to sudden toppling. This God, a god mysterious but not capricious, made nature according to laws and left it largely alone. Thus, once more, God's created nature was open to the self-reliant inventiveness of human beings. This natural realm, being amenable to human rationality, invited initiative, for its God had himself engaged in radical innovation once when he created the world and again when he irrupted into history in human form.

I have been engaged by this puzzle: We know that the Indians had wheeled toys; why did Anahuac wait for Cortés to introduce wagons? It seems to me that it is not generally true that necessity is the mother of invention, but rather that inventions develop necessities: We see a convenience and we need it. Anahuac, to be sure, had enough slaves and commoners with tumplines to drag its building stones anywhere. But why didn't someone think of the splendor of rolling in stately carriages over the waiting causeways of Tenochtitlán? By my premise it was not lack of need but something else, at which I am guessing: the Aztecs were close and loving onlookers and clever users of nature, but they were not on the lookout to go her one better, to whirl rather than to walk over her terrain. Perhaps the wheel isn't the most convincing general example, since it seems to have come to the Western world not as an original invention but by diffusion, probably from Mesopotamia. But to me its absence in Anahuac does seem telling for Aztec invention-inertia. Why did they not lever their simple tools into machines, those devices for compelling nature to outdo herself? Why did they refrain from enlarging their bare-eyed observation through those instruments that bring close things that are beyond and below human vision? Why had they, as gifted a people as ever was, no interest in seizing the mechanical advantage or extending sensory acuity? Well, as for the latter, they had no glass for lenses (which is why Cortés's glass baubles were acceptable gifts). But then—why not?

Theology, the laws of nature, interpretative accessibility, and inventiveness—these are the great but not the only advantages that these Westerners who came out of the East carried with them. Others have been intimated: the fraternal equality of human beings insofar as they are ensouled creatures that Cortés preached to the Aztec nobles, to a caste-ridden Anahuac; the ensuing closeness of the leader to his men that made Cortés listen to the complaints and sometimes—never at crucial moments—heed the advice of his companions, whereas Montezuma was deliberately remote; he was autocratic, the *tlatoáni*, the Speaker, *not* the spoken-to, whose subjects had to avert their eyes when he passed. Then there was the project of propagating to all the world a truth felt to be universal that unquestionably drove Cortés if not the "Holy Company" (the name was first given ironically), namely monotheism, whereas the México, though they imposed Huitzilopóchtli on the cities they conquered, then collected their gods in turn, ever more of them, for whom Montezuma even established a sort of all-Anahuac pantheon. But above all, there was the tenacity of the Christians in holding on to life, whereas the Aztecs of all castes seemed somehow—I'm far from understanding it—to surrender themselves more readily to the thought of death and to death itself.

Of course, the Conquistadores' Christianity was intertwined with that other root of our West, pagan Greco-Roman antiquity, of which I mention now only the intellectual taproot, the Greek one. From this dual root more particularly stems that faith in a more comprehensive sense which I mentioned before, the faith that underlies a daily life free for confident projects: the trust in the stable motions of nature combined with a contemplative care for transcendence, the faith in "the Laws of Nature *and* of Nature's God," to cite our founding charter with a special emphasis.

All of us here know—or will learn in the next four years—how much the Christian and post-Christian West owes to the Greek science of celestial nature and the rational account of divinity. But I want to recur to the human model that is exemplified with such spectacular accuracy by Cortés, the Homeric Odysseus, the first mature Western man (for Achilles, though in years the same age in the *Iliad* as was Cortés in 1519, is constitutionally a youth). This man, a soldier and sailor too, is free, self-reliant, inventive, a discoverer of new lands, be it of the world or the soul, and, I nearly omitted to say, the lover of women of stature: Like Odysseus, who had his semi-goddesses abroad and his Penelope at home, Cortés had in his life two royal daughters of Montezuma and two Spanish wives, but above all his comrade, his advisor and interpreter, Malinali or Malinche, the Mexican princess christened Doña Marina. It was his partnership with her that gave him his Nahuatl nickname—the Indians addressed him as "Malinche"; if it was meant in derision, it was a misplaced scorn. She and Cortés were, like Odysseus and Penelope, one in their wily works, and they had a son, the Conquistador's heir Don Martin Cortés (named after the Conquistador's father), a son to whom he was as attached as Odysseus was to his Telemachus.*

> By way of last names, Greeks were called by their patronymics, that is, *sons* of their father. Only Odysseus, as far as I know, refers to himself as "Called the father of Telemachus" (*Iliad* II 260, also IV 354).

I cannot pretend to understand how this distinctive species of Odyssean individualists is propagated down the ages, nor can I quite figure out whether this self-reliant, energetic type produces the tradition of trust in nature's manageableness or whether the tradition of inquisitiveness generates the type of the man of many devices, the *polymechanos*, the polyman incarnate. Yet, to me this question seems askable and therefore pursuable: Whatever may be the case for the rest of the human world, is our West ultimately more a civilization or a kind of human being? I tend toward the latter, but for the moment I will take the safe though weasly way and say that the two together, type and tradition in tangled reciprocity, are responsible for the West's apparently irresistible expansiveness. The Empires of the Sun, on the other hand, fell so fast into ruin because they and their leaders displayed in their high-bred, melancholic rigidity, their mono-mold, and their fearful care for the courses of their Sun, characteristics that were, so to speak, the matched antithesis of the confident and focused daring of the Western invaders—a fateful complementarity.

The lessons learned in thinking about a problem amount more often to collateral insights than direct solutions. So I want to end with two such lessons I believe I learned: First, that we really must come to grips with our West in its apparently irresistible expansiveness and if, on thoughtful consideration, it proves necessary, acknowledge candidly its superiority—superiority, that is, in the scope it gives, remarkably enough, to individual human nature by the very universality of its conceptions. And two, that we, as conscious representatives of that tradition, owe those overrun and extinguished civilizations, with all their irreplaceable strange beauty, a remembrance—not merely as projects for research but as objects of human regard.

Addendum: In the question period at the Santa Fe campus on September 13, 2002, a deeper issue than is broached above was raised. I have presented Cortés as the apt heir of a European tradition of ever-hopeful receptivity to, and invention of, machines and devices (one such, not mentioned above, is the huge—and ludicrously failed—catapult employed in the retaking of Tenochtitlán). Now the question was asked whether, aside from being a more freeing and invigorating faith than was the service of the Aztec pantheon, Christianity also provided the conditions for the transformation of the ancient *"theoria* of natures" into the modern "science of Nature" and the project of its mastery. In other words: was Christianity implicated in technology? I have come upon this claim in an article by M.B. Foster in *Mind* of 1935–36. Its main point is this: Natural science presupposes that nature must embody an intelligible mathematical scheme, but which of the possible laws it realizes is left to experimental observation. These conditions imply that the world was *created* (not generated) by a God who wills it—hence its contingency—but whose will is constrained by his *understanding*—hence its intelligible lawfulness. This, Foster argues, is basic Christian theology. So this Aztecan excursion issued in a deeply interesting and very contemporary question.

8

Patriotism
Large Love, Less Liking

It's been one of the multitudinous puzzles of my life that I can love so expansively* what I like so choosily—mostly not. Real

> With sympathetic friends (not in public) I'll allow as the U.S. is the New Jerusalem (*my* Jerusalem, without forgetting the Old Jerusalem of my forbears and the awe that came over me whenever I looked up to the Temple Mount) and my "shining city on a hill"— just a better land than any of the others I've been to (eleven, now no longer counting), heard of, or read about.

Americans like or, as we say, love (in the weakest of senses*)

> Examples: I *love* caerphilly or your kid's drawing as I *hate* okra or the latest bureaucratic directive.

entertainment and sports watching: late night talk shows, stand-up comics, musicals, nights out, and football or hockey—baseball less. Now, I'm a great believer in my new adage, "People who play together, stay together."* So I'm

> Old one: "People who pray . . ."

really bothered by the fact that I just don't like much of pop culture,* the tastes popular with the very people I respect and

> There are exceptions, above all the likable impersonal, routine politeness that greases public life—as distinct from the lovable

109

uninhibited, natural friendliness of Americans when they're not
harried. Not to mention fast food, which is plain tasty; I mean it
appeals to one's gross gusto as distinct from one's discerning taste.
There's also baseball, baby pictures, casual dress, Dutch apple pie
with thick icing on the top crust and what down south they call
"shit on a shingle"—creamed chipped beef on toast.

love insofar as love en masse can be actual. Which it can be
when one human being seems for one moment to contain multitudes,* to be, lovably, both this one and everyone else, so

> A Whitmanesque occasion, for sure.

that instance and kind coalesce and bring about a lofting moment.

I should expand a little on the difference between liking
and loving. Liking seems to me to be a superficial but steady
occasional attachment, "occasional" here meaning "out of
sight, out of mind." When the occasion offers, I like being
together, and occasionally I think of the object of that liking,
human, or otherwise, auto-special or hetero-special.* Love,

> Belonging to my own kind or another species.

on the other hand, is, once installed, be it by slow growth or
a *coup de foudre*, never out of mind nor sight, since it is *the*
inciter of mental imaging.

Liking feels like contentment, comfortable pleasure in
being together, once-in-a-while reminiscence of a good time
had, really mildly gilded indifference. Loving is the ultimate
differentiator; it differentiates *this* being from the whole world
of not-this-beings; it fills the soul with alternations of mood-
weather—black despair, grey dreariness, golden glory:

> Kind is my love to-day, to-morrow kind,
> Still constant in a wondrous excellence;
> Therefore my verse, to constancy confined,
> One thing expressing, leaves out difference.

(Sonnet 105)

You can tell that that's sheer laughter in the dark and intentional self-delusion.

Likes are fairly persistent, though often by reason of shallowness. Love is simply ineradicable, not to be erased by distance, death, or even indefensible conduct.

Liking, then, is shallow, and shallowness enables tolerance; the defects in our likes are easily discerned, easily borne with, and easily escaped. In love there may be no-fault collisions that break a too-close embroilment, and clear apprehensions of defects that only serve to highlight the other's essential virtues—or one's own failings. But for real deficiencies, above all, smallness of soul, love has no easy tolerance,* only the

Like love and compromise, "tolerance" has a taut and a lax meaning: Literally it means "bearing it" (Latin: *tolerare*), but one sort of putting up with is done indulgently because it's tolerable, and the other aversively, because it's inescapable.

deeply compromised resignation of hard bondage.

Back to patriotism. So I have deep affection for this U.S., affection sometimes without much empathy. Like some native-born Americans I've run into abroad, I feel this waffly empathy for my country most palpably when I'm out of it, that is, by contrast with other lands; there is no civic aphrodisiac like the leaving of one's love—much like personal love.* Once

Re the love of non-persons, see Essay 1, "Thing-Love."

back, there it is, my litany, with another center every decade, while long usage has brought some liking for the old squawks. I still *don't like* the big-time violent national game—but baseball is plain lovable, with its languorous tempo interspersed with sudden glory and its pastoral atmosphere roiled by the stadium erupting in ritual waves. Nor its music, country, pop, or academic—but I sort of enjoy its stylistic antics, meant to be so distinctive but, to me, willful non-aficionado, so tellingly generic. I'll add: Nor its shopping malls in their arid homogeneity—that are nonetheless venues of prosperity geared to the easy satisfaction of our natural acquisitiveness, our self-expansion by the accumulation of accoutrements, be they wearables or equipment. Nor, sometimes, our warriors, a little rigid and single-visioned—yet evidently brave as well as decent, and within their world, reflective and, yes, peaceable.* But here respect really preponderates.

> As I know from having been in seminars with officers, at my college and at our neighbor, the Naval Academy in Annapolis, MD; at the Army War College in Carlisle, PA, where general officers are trained; and at the Air Force Academy in Colorado Springs, CO, for the fledgling fliers. Their undergraduates, too, midshipmen and cadets, were willingly thoughtful.

My aversion for this particular decade (it's 2018) is the demand to be made comfortable and the consequent eclipse of individual courage. But is "individual courage" not a redundancy? Isn't courage always a, perhaps *the*, attribute of individuality? To be sure, one person's leadership may be infectious, but is caught courage real courage, the kind that is high-heartedness (Latin *cor*, "heart") such as follows on thought-prepared decision? Shouldn't *my* intellect infuse the heart rather than *another's* example? Isn't this derivative courage, a *hysteron proteron*, as the Greeks say, "the latter [ahead of] the prior," the loaded cart of high spirits put before the pulling horse of full awareness?*

> Thus a movement meant to empower women and highlight their civil courage shouldn't call itself "Me too," the language of dependency. And shouldn't wear black, the dress of funerals. I can't think of a virtue that is more intimately tied to the pronoun "I," first person singular, than courage. Hence its fitting situation is loneliness, aloneness (etymology: "all one"), not "me *along* with you." Anyone who's ever taken a courageous stance knows the scary exhilaration of this solitariness.

So these locutions, the obligatory anxious inquiry "Are you comfortable with this?" (where the question should be "What do you think?") and the cravenly flabby "You're making me uncomfortable" (where a skewering gimlet glance would likely settle the matter) are plain unlikeable. The mindset*

> In fact, we should not permit ourselves a set mind. This bed, arm-chair, and running shoes should, of course, be comfortably worn in, just not the alert soul.

behind them calls, on me, at least, for overt opposition. In particular, students who demand that a topic should not be broached because it makes them uncomfortable should be told by their teacher: "You're here to be made uncomfortable, and I'm here to do you that service."*

> I'll pass over the two conditions that support comfort-demanding frames of mind: the professionalization of human relations and the bureaucratization of institutional life. These are ways of diminishing personal agency (by encasing it in punitively pro-tective rules) and ways of depressing communal distinctiveness (by regularizing it through technology-driven standardization). Some of these modes might, in fact, be welcomed as useful and even necessary, were it not for the insidious cart-before-the-horse effect which creeps in quickly, so it goes unnoticed while it grows entrenched.

But love is deeper and wins out. We all know that looking askance at our country is our way of looking with love. Com-plaininess is our way of keeping patriotism unchauvinistic—provided it isn't just knee-jerking.

Tolstoy famously began *Anna Karenina* with this obser-vation: "All happy families are alike; each unhappy family is unhappy in its own way"; Aristotle, however, preceded him. In the *Nicomachean Ethics* (II 6) he cited an anonymous verse: "Bad men have many ways, good men but one." So it's true that, badness being multifarious, the limits to liking are terminally diverse while, goodness being singular, the cause of my love for America can be gathered into this trinitarian unity: 1) Who's going to hang me for writing what I think? 2) What better, more lovable and more decent fellow-citizens could I ask for? 3) What continent, from sea to shining sea, is more hospitable and, in the great spaces not given to utility, more gently or grandly beautiful? Oh well, a fourth: Where else can a college like mine, dedicated to self-knowledge and reflective learning, come into and stay in being?*

Albeit forever on the brink.

Annapolis, 2018

9

Liberal Education
Inefficient Efficacy

I. A UNIVERSITY EDUCATION THROUGH A SIMILE

Imagine the brute nuttiness of a bunch of big fellows playing a highly scripted game of violent collisions. They are bulked up and suited in all manner of protective gear (which proves, however, ineffective against brain damage). They have undergone arduous training in following signals; for breakfast they eat steaks together at training tables and perform at scheduled times on marked fields before multitudes of electronically distracted holders of expensive tickets, who roar their approval or displeasure.

Now behold a faculty of professors concentrated on publishing competitive polemics. On occasion they assume the dignity of gaudy robes, betokening a common, laborious, intellectually constricting training in academic protocols. They eat salads together at the faculty club, and perform on a designated campus before halls of tuition-paying audiences texting on their iPhones; from time to time these vent their resentment by filling out multiple-choice forms evaluating the professorial performance.

It shouldn't be that way.

II. A PRELIMINARY CONTRASTING DESCRIPTION OF
   A LIBERAL EDUCATION, IN POWER POINTS

I'll preface my exposition of a more civilizedly sane education with a half dozen somewhat extended bullet points that set out the gist of my conception, to form a contrast with the admittedly satirical, but also unhappily accurate, picture I've just delineated.

• 1) Liberal education is not a professional performance of authorities highly trained in graduate or professional school before a but slightly engaged spectatorship. It is rather a *participatory activity* in which learners on various levels, made effectively equal under the aspect of the magnitude of the task, together achieve a sort of intimate distance with each other—intimate in the closeness of the cooperation, distant by the exclusion of improper invasions of privacy (see Essay 10, "Teachers and Students."); teaching affects the intellect, it does not finger the soul. (On the day of graduation this student-tutor connection may become a lifelong friendship.) In this relation of student to student, student to teacher, teacher to teacher, the permissible competition is self-competition. It follows that schools should be small; bigness draws down quantification, and this measuring disfigures the soul.

• 2) The characteristic frame of mind befitting liberal education is *reverent radicality*—deep respect and penetrating questions. It is a serious mistake to present liberal education as preoccupied with "questioning," a surreptitiously skewering aggression on the way things are. Questions may indeed sometimes dissipate prejudices, but they are as likely to clarify and so to confirm a heritage. A real radical is one who goes to the roots, digs them up, often for more secure reburial, having examined them in the light of reason rather than the murk of rationalization. Parents who fund their children's liberal interlude may indeed get them back alienated, but, if it was a genuine education, they will find them more sympathetic in the long run.

• 3) Liberal education is costly. It requires leisure. (Here's a fact to make you smile: the word that gives us "school," *scholé*, signifies "leisure" in Greek.) It requires tutors, the guardians of this learning, to whom their vocation is not only their life but also a living. Consequently the night of a child's conception should be followed that morning with the first small investment in this *guarded leisure activity*.

• 4) *The prime object*, its be-all and end-all, is *happiness*. All else is unintended though hoped-for consequence—the less intended, the more likely to eventuate. It is emphatically neither to teach students to think—a patent impossibility—nor to make them "productive citizens"—a dangerous wish until you know what they'll produce. Much righteous defense of non-vocational education is drivel, and people who have its future at heart should come clean. So once more: the four years conventionally assigned to such education should themselves be gloriously happy—always remembering that true happiness requires the heightening delimitation of occasional agony, confusion, and even despair. In fact, happiness as a "pursuit" is specifically American, an unalienable right (meaning not an anxious chase but a steadily pursued activity)—so says our Declaration, Public Law Number One. Other ways to put this view of the aim of Liberal Education is that it is not a utility, a means, whose satisfaction might be called *check-off contentment*: Did the reading, handed in the paper, prepared for the test—done, done with. *No, liberal learning should be done for its own sake, since it is the present experience of an arduous fulfillment, and the acquisition for the future of the unwearying habit of thoughtful happiness.*

• 5) This mode of life needs *concreteness*; it is inherently non-virtual. ("Virtual," recall, now means "inactual." It used to be closer to its noun, virtue.) It requires a fixed place, the location, call it the crystal bubble, in which its participants readily meet face-to-face. In fact the "decoding" of human expression, the reading of faces and bodily gestures, is part of a liberal education. Hence "distance learning" is not compatible with the close-up, experiential setting of a liberal education. The mode of togetherness fitting this education is *conversation*—not argument, debate, or even discussion but "talking together, taking turns" (con-versa-tion), speaking and then listening. Domination, winning, does not fit, but there is room for self-respect and pride such as comes from mutual attention and admiration. "Excellence" can mean "being very good" or "standing out"; the way of liberal education is to emphasize inherent worth over comparative valuation. (Thus grading on any kind of curve is a clanging corruption of teacherly judgment.)

• 6) Some human works are best learned by doing. Improving worldly conditions is not among these. A time of receptive learning should precede active intervention; *first shape yourself*, then *society*; in particular, form views about what makes for human contentment, then interfere judiciously. The necessary acquisition of technical know-how should follow the stocking of the human soul's treasury with desirable goods. ("Soul" is largely a proscribed term currently; say subjectivity, consciousness, etc., if you must, and let those who don't want a soul do without it.) In brief: the learning matter of liberal education should be *the lovable per se*.

• 7) It is an immediate consequence that education should *not be preoccupied with current evils* and their eradication. That project requires political engagement and usually involves ideology. Ideology, pre-packaged thinking, does not belong in a community of learning: political philosophy, yes; politics, no. The sure test is this: If people get hot under the collar it's politics; if they become deeply interested, it's philosophy. The program of a liberal education should concentrate on works of *great quality rather than of so-called "relevance,"* with its thoughtlessly complicit instrument, "information." Information is purest relativity; it gains its standing as knowledge relative to a pre-judgment of purpose, and it preempts mentation by dislodging reflection.

The works of highest worth used to be called classics, after a Roman ranking of social classes, the highest of which was called "classic" simply. I prefer the adjective "great," used with articulable specificity (see V below). The chief reason for adhering to atemporal greatness of quality over relevance to current conditions is that liberal learning should raise us out of ourselves. The Greek word for that condition is *ekstasis*. Such learning should be, on occasion, a *soberly ecstatic experience.*

III. RESPECTABLE ALTERNATIVES TO LIBERAL EDUCATION THAT HELP TO DELINEATE ITS PROPER CONCEPTION

It cannot be a grab bag of choosable commodities, consumer-oriented knowledge produce (like a supermarket, many of whose advertised items are, however, out of stock). It is rather a coherent plan designed and maintained by a collegial faculty in devoted service not to its own several careers but to the program's survival. New members sign voluntarily on to a plan they have not themselves originated but in which they have some faith. The faculty's attentive devotion, its ever-critical faith, is the essential human ground of such a program's maintenance—that and the backing of the administration, the agency that "ministers to" the plan; beyond them stands the governing and supporting agency, the Board.

The broader requirement is that the plan should be neither too confiningly ideal for actual implementation nor too permissively chaotic for holding its shape. In other words, what's wanted is sensible practicality in the service of high reaching; people have to combine high purpose with common sense. As my numismatics professor at Yale taught me: "Pure principles and corrupt administration"—the mantra of my deanship.

There are, I think, quite a few possible patterns for programs of liberal education, but once adopted, the roiling distraction of curricular revision, driven largely by faculty members tired of actual learning and real teaching, is destructive. Let a plan, once instituted, gain some venerability from endurance and gather the gravity of accumulated experience.

Some of these alternative plans are educational but really illiberal, that is, they are intentionally doctrinaire; some are liberal but not very educational, that is, they are excessively permissive. But, so as not to befuddle my account with refined combinations, let me offer four common variants which clarify the conception of true liberal education when distinguished from it. They are:

Training—coaching for competent know-how,
Indoctrination—inculcation of an ideology,
Formation—molding of the soul to faith,
Cultivation—acquisition of the Liberal Arts.

This is the moment, not to "define my terms," a vocabulary exercise with little intellectual resonance, but to sketch out the meaning of the phrase "liberal education."

Education, it is a commonplace to point out, is derived from the Latin "continuative" (duration-indicating) verb *educare*, "to keep on leading out," presumably from the dark cave of ignorance. It is indeed an extended activity, four years in this country, devoted to learning by means of the texts, traditions, and conceptions, years of absorbing systematically the treasures—and tragedies—of one's civilization.

"Liberal" qualifies this arduously exhilarating effort as being free-spirited. It is Aristotle's term. He writes (*Politics* VII, 3) not "free" (*eleutheron*, Latin *liber*), meaning education for the sons of non-slaves, but "in a free mode," (*eleutherion*, Latin *liberalis*). The difference is but an iota, a jot, but it is full of meaning. This education—the education, not its beneficiary—is adjectivally free, it is carried on in a free spirit, constrained neither by utility nor by ideology.

So liberal education is inherently *not* a kind of *training* for practical use, which results in competent know-how and is best done by apprenticeship and practical application. Indeed, competence, qualified capability, is not a remarkably frequent result of being liberally educated. A friend of our college, Tom West, whose admiration for our ways was not whole-hearted, used to say that Johnnies come knowing nothing and leave knowing that they know nothing. It was a huge compliment, though not so intended: A clear apprehension of our limits is a very acute sort of knowledge. *Such self-knowledge* is surely one aim of liberal education.

Nor is liberal education *indoctrination* with a set of opinions, because that is the very opposite of free-spiritedness, of flexibility with respect to our own opinions. Free-spiritedly educated people do not have a "mind-set" but *mind-mobility*: Re-examination is ever possible. However, as I said before, this freedom of mental motion does not mean that nothing is ever to be unreservedly approved. What Auden demands of a poet we may expect from good schooling:

> In the prison of his days
> Teach the free man how to praise.
>
> ("In Memory of W. B. Yeats")

The notion that liberal education is necessarily subversive is not only false but somewhat dangerous, because it divorces what should be acknowledged as everyone's good from popular feeling. Moreover, it is best, I think, to be baldly honest about our ignorance concerning the true causes of outcomes: Was it the four years of this schooling or mere life gone by that made one student this and the other that? On graduation day they gratefully claim we did it; I can but wish.

Then there is faith-based education, and it can be liberal. Colleges that are both *formative* in a faith and seriously liberal in the sense of free inquiry are probably rare, yet I know of some: fundamentalist "Christian" colleges, Catholic Thomas Aquinas College, and recently Islamic Zaytuna College. Such schools pose the most intellectually engaging questions for themselves and the sympathetic outsider: What does it mean for inquiry to start from a ground postulating truths of faith and to reach a ceiling on open question-asking? What or who bestows authority in doctrine, and how does a layperson discern it? What does it mean to believe in the divinity through a human intermediary, be it written scripture or human prophet? Not to be seized by these issues betokens a lack of seriousness about the question-asking that is the beating heart of liberal education. Thus the existence of faith-based schools, protected in America's Constitution, should be regarded as a blessing to the secular schools that deal with these particular problems of interpretation only occasionally, only when the reading assigned is the sacred book of any faith. Yet liberal education is *not*, properly speaking, *formative*.

Now, finally, to the distinction between liberal education and the liberal arts. Whereas liberal education is a *mode* of learning, the liberal arts are the *skills* of learning. Their comprehensive enumeration comes to us from Roman and medieval writers. The arts were regarded as the preparation for the study of philosophy and theology. The distinction between these two finalities diminishes when we consider that the grand philosophical conceptions—Plato's, Aristotle's, Kant's, and Hegel's—all culminate in some form of divinity, while the great theologies, such as Augustine's and Thomas's, affirm that faith seeks understanding.

In contemporary "liberal arts" colleges, the term is used loosely; it means mostly scholarship in the humanities. "Human" studies are, of course, what the liberal arts were precisely not, being in the service of divinity. Moreover, the humanities nowadays exclude mathematics and science, while these formed the major part of the medieval arts, so the term "liberal arts" is now untethered from its more cosmic origins. Still, be they strictly or loosely understood, the cultivation of the liberal arts is *not* the whole of *liberal education*. For the account of the liberal arts as a major part of liberal learning I shall draw on my own threescore plus years as a tutor at St. John's College, which has revived and adapted this learning matter.

IV. THE LIBERAL ARTS AS THE PROPER PREPARATION FOR LIBERAL LEARNING

The tradition counts seven liberal arts—"arts" because they are skills not to be entirely captured in formalisms, methods and "rules for the direction of the mind," but require spontaneity and ingenuity.

The first set of three, the *trivium*, consists of grammar, rhetoric, and logic. These arts are thus concerned with the skills of mentation and its language. Their unfortunate decline is captured in the current meaning of *trivial*—"insignificant."

Grammar includes everything from syntax, the correct connection of words into sentences that propose a thought, to the composition of sentences into paragraphs that connect thoughts and these into whole works that expound at large, back down to punctuation, which might be called the gestures of writing, plus etymology, which uncovers what a word meant before use rubbed out its origin.

Rhetoric is the art of using language seductively so as to persuade a listener that something, perhaps even something true, is being said, be it by means of an aggressively appealing style or of artful lying.

Logic, finally, is the art of apprehending and applying the rules by which we compel thinking into definite courses—

or perhaps by which thinking compels us to proceed in those courses. It is also the skill of dealing with symbols, signs stripped of natural verbal connotations, having bare functions and assigned meanings.

The trivium has its own pedagogy, more conventional than the ways of teaching that befit liberal education. It is pursued in the "language tutorial" ("tutorial" from our designation of ourselves as "tutors" or guardians of learning, in lieu of "professors," authoritative purveyors of knowledge).

In the language tutorial a certain learnedness on the part of the faculty comes into play, for we want to avoid reducing these arts to abstracted techniques and methods. That means that we must be rich in illustrative materials, in models, paradigms, exemplars—our own or those given us by colleagues. Here are some examples of such concreteness. Re punctuation: "The holiest hyphen in literature is the hyphen in *Moby-Dick*" (the title is hyphenated, not the whale himself: Mary Norris, *Between You & Me: Confessions of a Comma Queen*). What does the hyphen do to the Dick? Or re rhetoric: What would it do to America's greatest speech to substitute "eighty-seven" for "four score and seven" years ago? Or re logic: Is the fundamental law of assertoric speech, that "the same property cannot be asserted and denied of the same thing at the same time," valid when any child is both fully human and not yet quite so at any moment? Or re set theory: How does a non-dimensional thought morph into two-dimensional space, that is, how does the abstract thought of class inclusion become visible in a spatial picture, a Venn diagram?

In the language tutorial, in trivial circumstances, a tutor will intervene more, direct and correct more, demand rote learning, and even give quizzes. The chief exercise of this class is *translation*, best done from a dead language, because of its fixity. We therefore learn Greek, which also supports our freshman texts. But later on we learn French, in part because it is thought to refine the sensibility.

Plato's Socrates, who first (I think) enumerated the quadrivium in *Republic*, Book VII, refers earlier and briefly in Book II to the training of children's sensibility by poetry, which is to be well censored so as to suppress indecency and irreverence. It is the trivium for kindergarten. But for our freshmen, learning Greek allows us to raise such questions as this: The Greeks have a word, *areté*, which can be translated as goodness or as excellence. Is goodness, which seems to include reticent modesty, compatible with excellence, which betokens ambitious standing out? We read—uncensored—poetry, ancient and modern, and thus are able to ask: Is the poetry, say of Homer, the poetry *of Olympus*, different in kind from the poetry which Wallace Stevens delineates thus:

> The poem *of the mind* [my italics] in the act of finding
> What will suffice. It has not always had
> To find: the scene was set; it repeated what
> Was in the script.

("Of Modern Poetry")

What, we are able to inquire, is the difference between the poetry of antiquity, whose script was an inherited *myth* and whose figures were brought down by the Muses, and a poem of modern times which has no Olympic libretto but a *story* found, invented, in the poet's own mind, staffed by folk met with right down here in ordinary life.

The second set of four arts, the quadrivium, consists of arithmetic, plane geometry, solid geometry, and music. Arithmetic introduces number and calculation. Plane geometry measures flat surfaces such as earth presents locally, and solid geometry constructs matterless bodies, particularly the five regular solids. Thus a mathematical counterworld is generated, with which to give a rational account of the cosmos, of well-ordered nature. The culminating fourth art adds motion. It is called "music" because the most spectacular such motions, those seen in the heavens, were thought to move in systems (Greek: "harmonies") and to generate heavenly consonances. We call such systems of solids in motion and their powers "physics."

For music in the normal sense we do have its own tutorial, where, from the physical production of the diatonic scale and its consonances on to the elements of composition, students learn to listen knowledgeably, and to analyze scores, and even to compose on their own.

For the modern study of physics we have added an eighth skill—that of replicating experiments in which nature is forced, so Kant says, to answer our questions as a prisoner before an interrogating judge. It becomes one of our major questions whether the answers forced from nature in the laboratory, although they render her rational and operable, present her truly and wholly. The progressive skills of the quadrivium are represented in our curriculum by the mathematical sciences: kinematics, through classical dynamics, relativity theory and quantum mechanics. We complement these sciences of mere bodies with the sciences of living bodies: anatomy, genetics, and evolution.

The first of the quadrivial arts, arithmetic, has special standing, since it raises fundamental questions about counting and account-giving. Socrates thinks of it as the engine which first levers us into reflection: What is a number, say "two," such that, although it is made up of ones, it has no trace of oneness in it, while, say a pair of cherries, taken together, is as cherryish and as juicily red as was each single one? To be perplexed by the phrase "Each one, together two" is the mark of a willingness to wonder, that is, to be on the brink of philosophic reflection. We would like our students to have this experience.

Again the pedagogy of the quadrivium is fitted to the matter. There is the hands-on laboratory, and its novel *mathematics of motion*, developed after the quadrivium, the calculus. There are proofs to be put on the board, with help from the class; we wonder together why the proof of a theorem does not allow us as much discretion as the translation of a sentence.

Our characteristic teaching mode for the quadrivium, for mathematics and science, assumes that it is natural for human beings to understand them—that is the very meaning of the Greek word "mathematics": "what is learnable." So we go, here especially, slow and deep, slow enough to carry along everyone some of the way, deep enough to elicit the naïve and fundamental questions often most present to beginners. Thus the quadrivium leaves its mark even on those students who don't take in much detail. Perhaps the most basic perplexity associated with mathematical science is how our world, murky, variable, and aberrant, comes to be intelligible through that most crystalline, lucid, and definitive of mental activities which is mathematics: How does the messy world come to be rediscovered as a cosmos, a thing of ordered beauty—and by its very regularity amenable to practical exploitation?

V. GREAT BOOKS AS THE GIST AND ESSENCE OF LIBERAL EDUCATION

The arts, then, are ancillary to liberal learning, which has a matter of its own without which it would descend into that vacuous talk for which students have a term borrowed from bovine life processes. This matter is the "Great Books."

"Great" is, once more, a concretely and specifically signifying term for us. These works are *above us*; we couldn't write them. They are also *for us*; their authors meant for us to read them. Moreover, they affect us; they take us *out of ourselves* and return us to ourselves the better for it. That's their effect on us.

Here's their nature in themselves: They are *inexhaustible*. Every reading, after an often semi-stunned first time, reveals subtleties unnoticed before.

They are *beautiful*. It might be a crotchety or a canonical, a stylish or a crooked, a perfect or a blemished beauty, or—that's a possibility—the ugly beauty of mere sharp intelligence.

Great books are *original*; they go to the beginning of things. Great fictions give the lie to reality; they imagine worlds and figures with more actuality than mere facts possess. While it would be hyperbole to claim that they move the soul more boisterously than do real existences, it is fair to say that they move it more resonantly. I won't go on, though I could. (See Essay 11, "The Greatness of Great Books.")

Books with such and more features are the fitting study matter of a liberal education. They are, as I said before, better than "subjects" because they are not yet jigged into preordained categories; they are more initial and so more question-fecund. Once again, we arrange them in chronological order because that is—or can be thought of as—a meaninglessly mechanical ordering and so devoid of prejudgments about true priorities. Let students decide which is intellectually earlier, Einsteinian relativity or the Newtonian dynamics that turns out to be a local instance of the former, and which is simpler, the time of relativity that is nothing but what a clock tells or classical absolute time that is an elaborate mental construal requiring a divine mind, God's "sensorium," in which to take place.

The great books curriculum too has its proper pedagogy. We meet around a table in a class called the *seminar*, the "seedbed." Our seminars of twenty souls at the very most are normally led by two tutors who guard the conversation, among other ways by being two and so not easily addressed directly by students, who should be talking mostly to each other. Moreover, these two colleagues offer occasional demonstrations that well-read, rational adults can differ severely from each other. By and large, tutors are supposed to be very recessive in the conversation (pity the older tutor, stuffed with undelivered wisdoms), even judiciously allowing it occasionally to go off the rails or through the roof into the wild blue yonder. Yet its main focus should be the meaning of the book of the evening, followed by—and this is distinctive, since it is proscribed in most university classrooms—the bald question: Is it true? For our pedagogic aim is not to leave students indecisively befuddled among our circa one hundred and seventy-five texts, but to enable them to form opinions they can live with. Seminar takes place bi-weekly in the evenings when students grow loquacious. Tutors take turns asking "the opening question," an art which, together with its products, is a part of the college's teaching tradition. Although this question rarely directs the two whole hours of the seminar, it starts the conversation off—for well and ill. It should, of course, not be the sort of "teachers' question" that is done away with by a one-word answer, say, a fact.

This question might, surreptitiously, embody a tutor's theory of the work, or it might fix on a detail that contains a key to the whole. (Great authors love to lurk in little items.) Effective tutors spend time preparing their questions. Example: When Aristotle delineates the figure of a "natural slave," a defective human incapable of making decisions, is he rationalizing or delegitimizing actual Greek slavery, which was supplied by captured soldiery and defeated populations not fitting his definition?

Tutors' seminar anxiety derives from this situation: They feel, and indeed are, responsible for the students' experience without having the power really to direct it. Students' pressure, on the other hand, comes from having to prepare faithfully and participate regularly; they must control a tendency to supine marginality, such as deprives the class of their contribution, or a contrary impulse to answer every question first, producing subsequent silence.

There is *no* "seminar method." Our seminar is intended to do what professionals think is impossible: to conduct during a prepared, scheduled event a natural, spontaneous conversation. In fact there are only two rules: *civility*, to attain which we address each other as Ms., Mr., Miss, Mrs., whichever a student chooses (I balked at "Mx," but gave in), with last names. On graduation day, "Ms. Bennet" for four years becomes "Elizabeth" to me for life, a great moment for both of us.

The other rule is: be willing to *explain yourself* or at least to explain why you can't explain. That's it. Or perhaps a third rule: *listen with respect* and regard no expression of the human mind, especially no question, no matter how naïve, as uninteresting.

If you didn't prepare, come anyhow and acquire the art of winging it. It's always best to be there, since the school is a community of learning; we mean to have our studies and our talk in common. (But don't imagine tutors can't tell when you haven't read the book.)

A dean, long dead, used to describe the seminar experience by sweeping out a roller coaster in the air: miserable lows and exhilarating highs. We give up dismal currency, so-called "relevance," for perennial heights—truths too true to be squalid—and we avoid fixed subjects for inchoate originality—future topics taking shape. We eschew history insofar as it treats what came before us as by-gone—"it's history," people say, meaning it's gone inactive—because we think that greatness is timeless, ever-fresh.

As we disregard mere time if it stands in the way of living meaning, so we don't let the mediation of scholars and the opinings of intellectuals come between us and these Program books. Therefore we discourage our students from reading introductions and background essays—or, better, from referring to them in our conversations; let them read what they like. What they really like, it turns out, is fantasy literature, to relieve, I imagine, all the actuality we confront them with.

So, to sum up the spirit of the liberality in this education: We cherish directness, immediacy in closure with the text. We are convinced that minutely careful, laboriously analytic construal of passages, alternating with the comprehensively sweeping intake of wholes, far from killing texts, make them come alive. To have learned to read means being able to make much of little by apprehending significance in detail, but also to succeed in comprehending concisely, in epitomizing large designs with accurate brevity.

If that seems as if learning how to read were the practical purpose of liberal education, there is truth in it, providing reading is taken largely enough. It ought to be understood as knowing how to interpret everything from the secrets of the book of nature to the expressions of the human face, from the subtleties of poetry to the potencies of mathematical diagrams. What is the truest profit of learning literacy? It's simple: It eradicates boredom. And boredom is *the* most dangerous human condition; it breeds cleverly rationalized violence.

VI. STUDENTS' LIFE AND ITS ALTERNATIONS

As for the life rhythms of our students, we hope they will alternate studious solitude with communicative sociableness. We hope they will discover that close-to-the-book industry should alternate with gazing-into-space leisure, with putting the text off in order to look inward and reflect. For study is not yet thinking. Nor are the prepared conversations of the classroom more than preliminaries to the arduous candor of after-class self-expression by which students will form the lifelong friendships that they should take with them when they leave us.

We hope they will make peace with the fact that their educational program is one long required imposition, under-

standing that "electives" are human absurdities. Choosing
well is the consequence, not the condition, of education; first
learn, then elect.

Finally, students should bear in mind that we have two
coequal campuses, Annapolis and Santa Fe, the same in principle and Program, different in setting and atmosphere. This
duality was established in part so that if it gets to be too much
on one, there is the alternative other.

It goes without saying that the studies here presented have
a penumbra of extracurricular activities, from croquet, our
signature sport, to sailing away along "the gentle Severn's
sedgy bank," or setting off on the Atalaya trail for the mountain's glorious views.

In particular, the community is hugely musical, offering in
its biannual student concerts delicate solos on the Japanese
harp and roof-beam-shattering bands working every drum
the college owns plus two acoustic guitars. There are dramatic productions from Shakespeare to Beckett and beyond,
and all kinds of high jinks occur, sometimes tersely witty,
like the intact tire, found on the morning of a festivity called
Reality, encircling the base of our Annapolis flag pole. To be
sure, these activities are not so absolutely extra-curricular;
the Program is the ghost in the machine. In fact, we have no
extra-curricularity. Moreover, for us laughter, in and out of
the classroom, is the enabler of seriousness, the irruption of
"sudden glory," the recognition of an absurdity as confirming
the efficacy of liberal learning.

VII. HERE IS A TRUE IMAGE OF THE PROGRAM
      IN ITS HUMAN EFFECT

The iceberg cuts its facets from within.
Like jewelry from a grave
it saves itself perpetually and adorns
only itself, . . .

Icebergs behoove [befit] the soul
(both being self-made from elements least visible)
to see them so: fleshed, fair, erected indivisible.

(Elizabeth Bishop, "The Imaginary Iceberg")

The rest is consequence, the less intended, the more likely.

Annapolis, 2017

10

Teachers and Students
Intimate Distance

There's something strange about our world, about its things, events, people. They reach us in two ways: real and unreal, genuine and fake, true and false, actual and virtual. It's surely the point of a real "higher" education to help us make out which is which, how they get entangled, switch sides, complement each other and, last but not least, how to live in this dual world and even get a—livable—living out of it.

A witty colleague of mine used to say that at St. John's we're always hunting down the primal amoeba. It's quite true—a genuine education does a lot of tracking down and tracing back: delving deep into the hidden bases of things, following them back to their first beginnings. This passion for digging down and finding out holds us together. It shapes the relation between us teachers and our students. Succinctly put, we are all in it together—teachers, students, and a great third element: our Program. We form—all of us together—a "community of learning." Such a community *has* to be small, face-to-face, day-by-day. There are large, virtual connectivities in our world that do useful things (such as online courses with ten thousand takers), but as *communities of learning*, they are illusionistic irrealities.

So the three elements of our college, a real community of learning, are the Program, the teachers, the students—mentioned last, but really first, because they are the reason for our existence. Why? Because there can be students without teachers, but a studentless teacher? That would be like a mute singer—a pathetic urgency.

And yet I'll soon want to say that we really aren't teachers, and therefore call ourselves "tutors" (of which more below), and that our students don't just study. I mean that they aren't supposed to study in the sense of now and then, at examination time, "hitting the books" (as they used to say), which sounds like a deliberately caused traffic accident. We hope rather that they will read steadily, but put down the book often to look up and think by themselves, or find their friends to talk with about what they've absorbed—or, for that matter, take a tutor to lunch for conversation (which is free; no one ever went to this college dining hall for the gourmet experience, yet tutors are delighted to be asked).

Even the first element that makes us one, the Program, is not a rigid prescription but a way to freedom: the relief from blind choices and sign-up anxieties, the security in having the grounding to do anything whatsoever in life, and the comfort of having classmates with whom to share discoveries and work out problems. We are great believers in thinking *by oneself* and studying *together*—both in turn.

Notes are where writers park matter too close to their hearts to be left out, but perhaps for the moment skippable by the intended reader. I shall put in a text-note what I think of as the main characteristics (not the actual content) of the St. John's Program.*

I think four characteristics describe our Program: Greatness, Books, Tradition, Truth-Seeking, all closely interwoven.
    Experts tell us that they've all four gone out of style among the young; that is why I want to sketch them out here. The experts are the folks who suppose that you find out what human beings think by instructing them to fill out questionnaires. I think that

our students are practically defined by being unresponsive to jigged pseudo-questions, the kind that have numbered or yes/no answers, because for-real questions, which take time and human back-and-forth to produce a consummation, are the main way of our college. So if you believe that such results about contemporary late adolescents are true, you'll believe anything.

Greatness. We, the tutors, the faculty, think that human works, particularly the kind called "texts," tapestries (like in "textile") woven of words, notes, symbols, come in gradable degrees of fineness: low-grade junk, passable mediocrity, unsurpassable greatness—and lots of unplaceable stuff. All human words, like the beings that produce them, can be interesting—appealingly or repellently fascinating. Nonetheless, we think that it's our pedagogic responsibility 1. to make out, by reading and thinking together, which is which and 2. to put into our Program mostly the works we think are the finest, the greatest. We are convinced—and this is emphatically not what is practiced much in universities—that since the world is full of lowness, banality, mediocrity, badness, and even evil, our students will have ample time to study and grapple with these later on. We are persuaded that just as those children live most competently in the world who experienced goodness at home, so those students will do best later who are amply provided in college with ideas of what is genuinely desirable, great. For how can you "change" the world (the almost universal student desire except for the often misguided one of making a lot of money) if you don't know in what direction?

Books. Such matter is found in books, or as academics say, in texts of all sorts: verbal, musical, mathematical, even instructional (such as laboratory manuals). Great Books are not "delivery systems" for information (which is only informative when you already know what you're doing) but are brought about by a high art in which the how and the what are conjoined. They may come in any format—from real letters printed on solid paper to virtual texting on a translucent tablet (though, for all I care, a student may come to class, like Moses down from Mount Sinai, with engraved stone tablets)—as long as they have been well studied, have opened the mind for conversation, and are present on the table for ready reference.

Tradition. Who wants to live on the thin forefront of all that went into making the present, and so, ignorant of what's pushing from behind, be helplessly driven into a future not of their own making? We study "the tradition"—meaning the works that made modernity—not because they're old but because they're at work in our present. Not to experience the illumination to be gotten from this tradition is to live in the dullest and most dominating of all time-phases: the *mere* now.

Truth-Seeking. In most classrooms in our country (I'm pretty sure) there's "correct" and "incorrect" for the hard sciences but *not* "true" and "false" in the squishy humanities. In these, where are raised questions of moral right and wrong, of esthetic beauty and ugliness, of human power or impotence, of first and last things, people shy away from asking: "Is what this author says true or not really true, truly beautiful or just elaborate, really penetrating or ultimately evasive?" We pursue a middle course: We stay away equally from delivering dogmas and from wishy-washy disengagement. We ask our students (as ourselves) to *try* to answer, to form *their own* opinion, but also to *explain themselves to each other.*

You can see that I've mostly said what we are not; human ways that are seriously significant are often, to begin with, best described from the outside in, from what they avoid and resist, and so I'll go on like that for a little more.

We, the faculty, call ourselves "tutors" to avoid the appellation, standard for colleges, of "professors." Professors have certain properties we disown: They are trained in a profession, that of scholarship and research, and are expert in a subpart of it, their specialty. Their duty is to train their students in the methods, and to impart to them the material in which they are competent authorities. Oddly enough, they usually have no training in teaching, on the assumption (for which I actually have a lot of sympathy) that if you know "your subject" really well, are engaged in "original research" in it, and have some residual enthusiasm for it, you will infuse your expertise into your students.

As a result a professor's relation to undergraduate students labors under a certain built-in awkwardness and even liability. Professors are far more learned in their area than are their students and so, rightly, assume superior standing. But they are also teachers who, in order to be effective, need to be on a level, on a human equality, with their pupils. It is not easy to find the right tone between mature superiority and human togetherness. The danger of dominance is great; what's more, sometimes it is exactly what students want: to be told things, to be molded. But the more they want it, the more fraught with delicacy, even embarrassment, the relation must be.

A tutor has a different—I think a *very* different—relation to students. The word "tutor" is Latin and means a watcher-over, a guardian. At our college, the teachers are tutors who protect the students' learning—even from the tutors themselves. They try not to dominate the students' thinking but to elicit it by asking many pertinent questions and then really participating in the resulting dialogue—not *as if* the participants are equal but *because* they are equal—equal as thinking, feeling, bottomlessly mysterious and inexhaustibly interesting human beings.

Here are the two dominations from which we most strenuously abstain: *political* and *personal*. A teacher who perverts occasions for learning into opportunities for propaganda is either naïvely or cannily corrupt; a teacher who exploits a student's devotion for personal use is just plain iniquitous. It's not that students may not ask our advice or, in a limited way, regard us as models; in fact, no faculty could ask for more appreciative respect than we get from our students and alumni. (By "our" students I mean the students at our college.—I've rarely heard a colleague speak of the personal property called "my student.")

Not being professors makes all sorts of additional difference here: We are not professionals of knowledge but amateurs of learning: Amateur means "lover"—that is, a lover of learning who is on the way, not at the end. All of us have acquired a small file of information and a sufficient fund of knowledge—enough to help our students in the most empathetic way through a demanding Program (one that has in it not the ghost of a gut course). But much of what we learned in pursuit of our advanced degrees is out of commission here: We all begin at the beginning to learn the same material as the students. We, as they do, advance in the Program, but there is no such thing as mastering it; its matter is too deep and too inexhaustible. Thus we are, in some significant sense, viewed from the heights of real knowledge, always on a level with our students—and so the awkwardness of inequality ceases. It takes our freshmen a little while to be really persuaded that their tutors are waiting for them to articulate their own thoughts, the fruit of their studies (and their lives), and that when their teachers speak, they're not talking *at* them but *with* them.* One way to put this is as a paradox: We're non-

> Recently: a freshman in seminar asks: "Ms. Brann, can I ask you a question?" "Of course." Do you know the answer to the question you just asked us or is it for real?" I thank my lucky stars; it's for real. Great mutual satisfaction!

teaching teachers.

So now I'll try to delineate the relation of students and tutors from the inside out. But the more I think about it, the more it seems that this relation is really pervasively paradoxical (but then, so are all humanly significant matters). By "paradoxical" I don't mean evasively messy, or elusively murky. Not at all: paradoxes can state crisply the way things really are, which always includes a bit of their opposite: integral bipolarity. So here are five rubrics that seem to me to describe our tutors', our non-teaching teachers', relation to our students.

1) Unequal Equality
2) Formal Closeness
3) Intimate Distance
4) Reticent Accessibility
5) Respectful Love

1) *Unequal Equality:* I've already said a good deal about that, but it is basic: Our whole school is basically egalitarian. Tutors have no ranks, students are not ranked. Competition has its place—in the gym. Thinking well requires a lot of high spirits, and speaking well surely involves the desire to shine— but not at each others' expense. Students don't do each other

in so they can stand out; tutors don't out-do each other for academic bonuses (there aren't any). Students will have no success trying to impress the tutors; we have a good nose for pretense and don't like it.* Tutors don't squash students with

> On the other hand, we don't, I don't, pretend to know them. For example, when I'm about to be appalled at our kids' gullibility, they show themselves as accomplished scoffers, and when I despair at a text getting to them, they reveal themselves as true believers.

their magnificence; if ever they do, our upperclass students go to the dean and complain: He or she "dominates." Basically, students and tutors are *serious* with each other and that precludes personal pretensions. What makes us serious is our willingness to face the depths and abysses broached by the Program of study. (One proof of living seriousness is finding a lot to laugh about, such as all-too-consistent conformities and irresistibly comical incongruities.) We approach these problems *unequal* in maturity and with different levels of learning and experience, but *equal* in the desire to deal with the question at hand and on the same level in the face of its depth. At least, that's how it works when we're at our best; we aren't— here's a full disclosure—all the time.

2) *Formal Closeness:* This college observes a lot of customs, most for articulable reasons. One is that we call each other Ms. or Mr. or by a slew of new honorifics—no first names (except in circumstances where strict observance is ridiculous). The reason is that we often converse about matters that touch us deeply. Indeed, a true tutor knows this wonderful fact: Ontological and theological inquiries, questions about the way things are and what might be beyond our world, give rise to the most *intimate* conversations conceivable. Thus those formal observances are required; they are an important shield against becoming personal in the wrong way. They make possible what you might call a higher-level closeness: We can pierce surfaces without lacerating each other. Generally, tutors and students maintain these formal-

ities, through which they can touch each other inoffensively, until Commencement. On that day it's first names and, for some of us, friendship for life.

3) *Intimate Distance:* For while at the college, tutors and students are not friends in a genuine sense. The essence of true friendship—there are wonderful books about this on the Program's reading list—is real reciprocity (equal give and take) and true mutuality (simultaneous esteem). How can tutors expect real reciprocity in intellectual guidance or students true mutuality of esteem? Tutors do, in fact, tend to know a lot more than students, and what's more, tutors are obligated to evaluate students. So their equality in inquiry and their esteem for each other as human beings sometimes has to recede before a clear and candid assessment by tutors of students' efforts and performances, including some pretty strong tutorial words of what, by a euphemism, would be called encouragement. In other words, tutors must, on scheduled occasions, tell students what's what, which is not a mode of friendship.* So a distance opens up.

> For example, told before: The occasional student who "vaunts himself to be" (Homeric phrase) the best needs to be told: "You're too good to think you're best." I think that tutors in the admonishing mode are fully aware that the one condition reliably self-curing is young age.

And yet there remains a personal intimacy—that of watchful care, of having the students' interest at heart. But that—to repeat a deep and difficult claim—is not the only or chief sort of intimacy which a discreet distance makes permissible. The word intimacy comes from a Latin adjective, *intimus,* meaning "innermost," "most deeply within." What our books speak to us about is, as I've said, what is most internally ourselves. Especially when we are young, when we are most self-consciously involved with other people, we tend to think that we get really to know and be known by others from the inside through revealing exchanges of personal confidences and by daring disclosures of secrets. But the intimacies of our souls that are suitable to common learning leap past these privacies, such as should be reserved for particular friends, to a common humanity. But yet again: everything concerning the human soul—including the perfectly legitimate question whether we have one—is delicate and requires a certain careful distance from each other in order to be approached together.

4) *Reticent Accessibility:* We tutors don't keep posted office hours: "Tuesday and Thursday from 3–4 P.M. and by appointment." We are available when needed, and not only in an office (many of us don't have one), but wherever on campus we can sit and talk. Put it this way: People in offices are official, and while the relation of students and tutors sometimes has a semi-official aspect, as in scheduled oral examinations or "don rags" (our evaluations), for the most part even these are not so much bureaucratic or administrative (which are particularly powerful and, as it happens, unavoidable ways of being unreal) as genuinely human ways of guarding learning. So tutors and students get together in spontaneous ways, not hedged around with protocols of hierarchy and officialdom. On the other hand, there are restraints on these relations. We, the tutors, cannot function as personal trainers of students, riding herd on their indiscipline, and even if we would, we couldn't because of the demands on us. And in fact, students are respectful of our time, and we of theirs. Nor are we mom-and-dad substitutes; much as we may in our hearts sympathize with our students' griefs (which are much better known to us, even without telling, than they may know). We—students and teachers—contain our personal affairs below overt expression. Our students have a wonderful capacity, which has won my particular admiration, since it shows that the learning we do together has really taken: They exercise a thoughtful literacy in framing their most intimate feelings—of certainty or confusion, pride or guilt, triumph or grief; they communicate in those expressive terms, available

to the beneficiaries of a real education, which make it possible to talk about anything, poignantly and yet without unwanted psychic touching. So in brief: Tutors and students are mutually accessible—but under restraint. And here's a bonus: A little loss in laid-back self-expression leads to a great gain in psychic intensity.

5) *Respectful Love:* Everything I've said so far about the relation between tutors and students really comes to this: There's a sort of love between us, real enough but well hedged by the realities of the situation. The best name, I think, for that sort of love is *respect*. "Respect" is yet another significant Latin word. "To respect" means "to look back at"; respect is thus a kind of keenly responsive regard—not a bold and intrusive stare but a guarding *and* guarded glance, a careful *and* caring attention. Our regard for each other is reciprocal, but it cannot help but be somewhat different in kind. First, as far as mere ocular looking, seeing appearances, goes—and such physical eyeing is an unavoidable aspect of all "respect"—the young are just nicer to behold than their elders, and so far—this is a plain truth—we are in their debt (not to mention here the attendant dangers). But the young, our students, are works in progress while we, the tutors, are closer to works accomplished, and so they look up to us (and here too are dangers, already mentioned). Second, as far as genuine respect, the true regard we have for each other's being, is concerned, one difference is that each tutor knows quite a number of students while each student knows only a few tutors. So the tutors' loving regard is—perhaps—somewhat more distributed, the students' admiring respect somewhat more intense. On the other hand, we—perhaps—know better what to look for than they do and so our regard is more realistic. But when all is said and done, what is truly mutual is affectionate regard, respectful love, lasting a lifetime.

Annapolis, 2013

11

The Greatness of Great Books
A Determinate Meaning?

My subtitle is a question, and since I do not believe that one's answer, the thesis, should be withheld, like the solution of a mystery, until the page before the last, I shall give it up front.

Presumably, most people still know what a book is, so I assume that the difficulty I often hear about "Great Books" lies with the word "Great," an etymologically unpromising word. Does it denote a real, perhaps even a natural category and does it have legitimate arbiters?

I think that the answer to both parts of the question is definitively *yes* and that it is the business of those who use and propagate the phrase to articulate the answer, to say what it means to claim that some books are indeed great and that those who make this claim have not so much the right as the duty to articulate the meaning.

One word more about "I think," the beginning of my answer. This "I think" does not mean *I* think this and *you* think that, true for me and true for you, to each his own. I mean, on the contrary, I *think* this, and, since a thought is the weightiest object the world contains, what I really mean is: If I truly think so, that thought lends the gravity of truth, of being the truth-bearer, not to me but to my object. It also means that if we speak our thoughts out clearly enough they will turn out to be in many respects common. There will, of course, be opinions, yours and mine, about terminally particular things that are insuperably idiosyncratic. The standing of certain personally favorite books will probably be among these.

Someone might reasonably say that the adjective "great," in all its benign woolliness, such as in "Have a great day," is best off left alone. A program of learning, be its agent anything from a whole college to a small program at a university, may make its students read difficult, deep, and original books behind the scenes, but babble up front about teaching them to be independent thinkers and productive citizens. The former endeavor is assuredly an impossibility, in fact a self-contradiction, the latter effort is probably a dubious good, depending on what's being produced.

I am serious in my doubts about these two mantras of institutions defending liberal education. To me, liberal teaching is not about messing with students' minds but consists of putting before them examples, works of large intellect and fine sensibility, whose quality I'm about to delineate, while enforcing not moral but intellectual virtues, from listening first of all to oneself and next, with corresponding interest, to others, and then willingly responding, however, ineptly that may at first be, down to proofreading papers and putting commas in reasonable places, while (further to expand a too-long sentence) offering oneself as a model of abiding interest in such works of excellence.

And as for that productive citizenry—I'd go along, if we could agree that sometimes most eventuates when the least is produced, when human beings just *are*. Besides, not all products are so welcome; for example, lawyers refer to their briefs as work products—and charge accordingly.

One more preliminary, closer now to the Great Books question. Colleges in trouble—and which isn't?—with underpaid faculties and overwrought administrations accept money, hundreds of thousands of dollars, to call in consultants. We've had one who modestly expressed ignorance and set about learning. Others knew everything in general and nothing much in particular; they were sponge-like about current preoccupations and tin-eared about well-wearing traditions. Then they issued recommendations that might buy us a few years of existence and bring about the prompt demise of our essence. The Great Books were an attractive nuisance to them. They claimed to know from their research that, if books are toxic with prospective college students, Great Books are positively leprous.

It's nonsense, of course; teenagers come, as they always have, in all intellectual modes. Some are bookworms from way back and have gnawed their way into the center of the written world long ago; some have been snaffled later into reading by one particular book that got to them; and some have looked over the wall into an enticingly alien realm to which they felt ready to emigrate. All three modes have brought us our students.

Whence comes this animus against Great Books, that inept polling seems to confirm? But "inept" is the wrong word. This polling and questionnairing isn't incompetent; it's simply skewed. I raise the question because the detailed justification and implied praise of Great Books is involved with this false perception of what our young care about.

What, or rather who, skews the intellectual life? I want to say it is (using the term, disparagingly, as a type) the intellectual. In my sense an intellectual is a producer, one of those productive citizens, a producer of thought-packets, idea-bundles, called "concepts." Devising and employing concepts, cultivating a conceptualizing mind is, it seems to me, close cousin to being an ideologist. Ideology is a term with a respectable past. For instance, Thomas Jefferson was the American proponent of a French movement, a philosophy of mind, called Ideology. Marx evidently originated the seriously derogatory use of the term ideology as a false, self-serving class consciousness. In its current use, the one I mean, ideology is the thought-divorced indiscriminate application of certain conceptual bundles to all matters political, from far left to far right. I think that study by means of Great Books is a preventive of concept-mongering and ideology-adhering; it can deflect intellectualism into thoughtfulness. That's the broader setting.

Let me come to the end of these preliminaries to say as forthrightly as I can what more particular frame of mind is apt to want to quash Great Books as a learning matter. I can discern three main notions. One is a utilitarian propensity: Education is admitted to need an apology for existing. Reading old books of no easily discernible application to active life is not a preparation worth paying for. So an excuse must be offered, namely a vocational intention. "Vocational" is a degraded term; the pristine meaning of a vocation is a "calling," and one intention of liberal education is certainly that its students might find a vocation, a calling, a work that can preoccupy their hearts and souls.

The second notion inimical to Great Books is the current version into which that dreary old historicism has morphed, the confident attribution of agency to conceptions that are entirely incapable of any practical activity by reason of lacking personhood: time, society, culture. When the human condition as diagnosed in various disciplines is credited to, or blamed on, any of these three, books need not be read as communicating common truths in particular voices. These texts can then be superseded by textbookish abstraction-mush and trendy opinion-having, such as do indeed appear to have been indited by time, society, or culture. I hasten to say here that I'm an avid reader of anthropology, which seems to me to require a very specific talent for devotedly hoovering up pertinent detail and keenly discerning accurate generalities—temporal, social and cultural generalizations that have some hope of being convertible into human universals. My personal hero in this line is Herodotus, the founder of such inquiries, and one of his successors, Clifford Geertz.

The third notion unfriendly to Great Books is in what I think of as a megalomaniac morality, the indifference to small individual harm, like taking the contents out of a found wallet, in favor of demonstrating outrage at large social evils— replacing the self-repression of forgoing small loot by engaging the self-expansion of moral display in a crowd. In this frame of mind the charge of elitism is brought against Great Books. It is factually absurd, since the Anglo-Saxon Great Books movement originated in English workmen's institutes. And of course some of these books show more social sympathy than the critics have heart for.

In my experience the attacks on Great Books come not only from a source I haven't yet mentioned, a hyper-sophisticated view of writing, of reading, of authors, and of authority that bars the way to simply taking up and reading a text, the simple way necessary to an undergraduate Great Books program. The attacks also come from harried administrators worried about declining enrollment, from somewhat absent-minded professors who think that paraphrases are clearer, briefer, and more efficient than their originals, and from academics who long to be out in the so-called real world, read Plato's *Republic* under duress twenty years ago and came away with the demonstrably false notion that it is intended as a political blueprint for what is obviously a dystopia, saw *Pride and Prejudice* in several movie versions in which people, most inauthentically, kiss each other, and know of *The Brothers Karamazov* only from that infamous snippet "The Grand Inquisitor."

I am sure that it is necessary to summon very specific sorts of sympathy for people who opine about things they're pretty ignorant of and people who decide in a panic mode. The former deserve gentle nudging toward actual acquaintance, the latter advice with a backup of backbone. I've thought about this a lot and always come out with a similar sense: Don't give in to contingencies and conditions. True practicality is in jealously guarding carefully evolved settings, and that means in every significance-laden detail—or else it's not a world worth working in—for example, the exchange of a room with chairs around a table for a hall with chairs in rows.

In matters of learning, efficiency is ineffective. To me this means that some tweaking can usually be harmless, but it has to be done by those who have the experience, understanding, and above all love, to do it cannily. And that's the last thing I wanted to say about the maintenance of Great Book learning, which is to me the best instantiation of serious, liberal education: Don't give in, just do it better.

So now to a delineation of the greatness of Great Books. I have ten marks of the notion, but I will be concise to the point of being cursory.

1) I think that "great" is a discernible characteristic, distinct from "good." Setting out the marks of greatness discursively is an unending task, but there might be somatic indices that are more immediate. My teacher at Brooklyn College, who brought me to Homer, once revealed—to a largely unmoved class, as I recall—her unerring sign that a book was great: the hair on the back of your neck bristles.

Is "Great Books" then a natural category? Of course it is natural, insofar as it is natural to human beings to make artifacts, as anyone knows who has had, for example, the incomparable experience of seeing the original Paleolithic cave painting of Lascaux in the Dordogne, done some hundred and seventy centuries ago. And it's a category insofar as there is a simply unbridgeable chasm between the great and the many good and competently produced books fond readers like myself snuff up with appreciative pleasure. There is even a competence for mediocrity: books not deeply soul-satisfying but pleasingly time-killing, the traveler's solace, the airport book. How else, if Great Books weren't a given class, would it happen that people who have actually read such works will so often and so readily agree on the classification? After all, Great Books lists have been made, accepted, and revised since antiquity; for example, Quintilian, of the first century C.E., clearly had such a list. Our own Great Books list at St. John's is derivative, as I mentioned, from one devised in the late nineteenth century for the English Workers and Mechanics Institutes. Not exactly an elitist origin!

Whatever particular marks I'll now continue to propose, the main justification for the title "great" is our experience. Spend a weekend talking to friends about *Hamlet* and how weary, stale, flat, and unprofitable now seems ordinary, if worthy poetry—the kind I think of as musing in free verse.

Though that's not quite right. These books are not snobbish and abruptly discrete, though the experience of them is; they live in a comradely continuum with, they actually validate, the huge reservoir of respectable and the trash heap of rabble literature. I don't quite know how it works; I doubt that anyone does. But the fact that so many people of my acquaintance, for example, express the micromotions of their souls in that very forgiving free verse and evolve complex plots for far-fetched novels, that they respect superior models and readily read each others' work, functions somehow as the greenhouse in which a black orchid may someday flower among the bromeliads. Similarly for the concept-inventions of lesser philosophy. Though small in scope, yet they are on a spectrum with grand visions perhaps to come. An afterthought: Are there subject genres, excepting hard pornography, inherently incapable of greatness? Well, *The Brothers Karamazov* is a murder mystery, and some current mysteries, like Indriðason's *Jar City* and Walker's *Black Diamond*, are high on the spectrum of excellence. So almost no subject seems to me to carry inherent limitations on distinction.

2) The term "great" can, of course, apply to all kinds of human art, to all the style genres of writing: lyric poetry and long epics; drama, tragic and comic; and fiction, particularly that peculiarly modern kind, the "novel," that is to say, the narrative that is based more on new stories than on old myths. So also does it—of course—apply to visual works, two- and three-dimensional, that is, to painting and sculpture. And most particularly to musical compositions, be they "pure" or mated with liturgies like cantatas and with libretti like operas. Moreover, "great" most assuredly applies to works of the intellect directed to an essentially static field of non-sensory matter, that is, mathematics, or to mobile, immattered nature, that is, science. (I mean that terms of motion are metaphorical in mathematics and intrinsic to nature.) It is a point for special emphasis; accounts of mathematics, science, and their technological embodiments are among the Great Books. Mathematicized nature and the human devices for imposing our will on her should, in fact, be a normal part of Great Books learning.

Let me add, as a pertinent aside, that readers of history come on the term "great" often; Herodotus announces that his inquiry will preserve "the great and wondrous" deeds of Greeks and Barbarians from oblivion. And when history was still a curricular given in high school we learned of great kings—Alfred, Elizabeth, Peter, Frederick, "the Great"—inegalitarianism even among royals. Such greatness-assignments appear to be a human propensity, oddly enough particularly strong among Americans; although we are the aboriginal adherents to the gospel of equality by reason of a common creation, many of us have a keen sense of the difference between patented nobility and popular celebrity. My point is that, confronted with the experience of greatness, some of us feel a frisson of expectation while others sense a stiffening of their defenses—and that these temperamental differences may furnish a broad backdrop to this Battle of the Books.

3) It is a strong mark of a great book that it invites the questions: What is its subject? Who is its hero? What is its intention? Is Newton's *Mathematical Principles of Natural Philosophy* a book of theology, as the author clearly states, or a book of physics, as the reader working through the propositions laboriously discovers? Is the hero of Dostoievsky's *Brothers Karamazov* the angelic Alyosha or the demonic Smerdyakov, as an alert reader might suspect? Is the main intention of Kant's *Critique of Pure Reason* to set out the limiting conditions of cognition or to make room for morality? Great books are so inherently initial, so literally original, that they almost always precede compartmentalization. They engage the intellect not only by what they propose but even by what they are. And what they are is determined largely by the choice of persons, settings, embroilments. An adequate art of divining what complexities a character is capable of developing, what resonances a setting may be attuned to, and what confusions are worth unravelling, is surely necessary to engaging with greatness.

4) Great Books are inexhaustible. Every reading is a new reading, and that is not only because of the blessing of forgetfulness, which keeps life from becoming a well-worn routine, but because of the multitude of meanings missed at the last reading. Such missed valuables vary from tiny subtle detail to large imposing scope. For example, there is Homer, the most sophisticated poet I've ever read. He works with those infamous epithets, the "handles" as they say in the trucking world, that are as often ignored as misapplied. But look at them under the presupposition of Homer's incomparable greatness, and what seemed mechanical becomes cunning, for example, when the character's conduct countermands the epithet's meaning. Recall the occasion when Achilles is called by his epithet "swift-footed" while sitting, unbudgeably sulking, in his tent. Or consider the other end of the scale, when the

character and actions of the *Odyssey*'s Odysseus precisely and tellingly invert those of the *Iliad*'s Achilles. There's always more for the repeat reader, and when it's not seen as new it's seen to go deeper.

5) Such works entail their own modes of education, and one of these is the very liberalism of liberal education: The work is taken up for its own sake, freely not compulsively, not as a means to some material profit. Making such works mandatory reading, requirements rather than free choices, seems, at first sight, very much at odds with liberal learning. But it is an imposition on the student for the sake of a fuller freedom than that of abstaining, the freedom of talking together, albeit in class, about the experience of being encouraged to be all there, to ask questions, give opinions, even to resist. Besides, joining an all-required curriculum was a choice; we are not Rousseaus, *forcing* folks to be free. Indeed, for many students the path of seduction by books is via the route of, sometimes quite vehement, rejection. It's not the worst way to get hooked on philosophy to oppose Socrates as a great bully. Closer consideration of the dialogue will duly follow.

It is the teachers' duty to guard—we at St. John's call ourselves "tutors," guardians—the conversation, to prevent themselves from professing and students from dominating, to protect the conversation from fancy concepts only half-understood, yet proudly trotted out, and from current ideologies, the sort that make the non-compliant get hot under their collars. I've said before why I think Great Books aren't well approached with academic conceptualizations and current ideological preconceptions; an example of such a misdeed is to demand that readers of *Mansfield Park* should consider why the Bertram family refuses to talk about the slave trade in Antigua, whence Sir Thomas has just returned, or that they should believe slavery to be at the center of the novel. "Slave trade" is mentioned once in the book as a side issue in a tea-time conversation preceding a family blow-up, for Heaven's sake! And the delicious iniquities the female Bertrams practice toward prissy Fanny are the making of that novel.

In sum, it is the teacher's task to keep students from being talked at, introduced to, or prevented by a preface from confronting immediately a book after all written for them, literate people.

Teachers do, to be sure, face a problem, a perennial mystery to me. Even *our* students, who have often talked their parents into forgoing their own career ambitions for them and making financial sacrifices in their behalf—why do even they abstain from arousing interest in themselves—a perfectly viable effort? The answer seems to be that late adolescence is at once the best and the worst time for real learning, since then the passions are at once most adverse and most receptive to it. Well, sometimes the spontaneous frisson of greatness supervenes, while sometimes going off voluntarily and letting maturity have its way works, and sometimes just plain threats of ejection will do wonders.

To return to positives, however. Sometimes late in our life with a book, a lecture is welcome, but in the early stages students shouldn't, as I said, be talked *at* but should converse *with* each other. Great books are ingestible and testable sources of information only by-the-way and least-of-all. And finally, a seminar room really is the right and a lecture hall the wrong physical venue for Great Books learning.

6) The willingness to admit differential grading, that is, to do such grading at all, is constitutive of community, and so an adherence to Great Books is community-forming. Let me try here to formulate a thought which some listeners will find unacceptable or even repellent—perhaps both at once. A proper community requires individual dignity; to be properly together with others it is necessary to be self-respectingly alone with oneself, and, second, to be self-respecting

it is necessary to be open to reverence. By reverence I mean my capacity for rejoicing in things and beings greater than myself—a bit of the temperament for delighting in greatness mentioned before. Daily proximity to Great Books enhances that capacity.

This community of free fellow learners—for what self-respect plus reverence delineates is human freedom—this community of independent and receptive colleagues is the body that finds, adopts, and amends the reading list. For this band of tutors the term "great" does not meet with a resistant stare but with a sense of shared assumptions. After that come rousing arguments about ranking in quality and pedagogical fitness. By pedagogical fitness I mean that the students are always on the faculty's mind; it is fine that any selection the faculty has made might be somewhat beyond our students' preparation—isn't it apt to be above ours?—but not too much. For example, every year someone argues that we should get rid of Hegel's *Phenomenology of Spirit*, and every year it turns out that there were a sufficient number of seniors who were the better for having understood one third of it, better off than having missed out on it altogether.

7) The following may sound like self-contradiction, because I've inveighed against introductions and prefaces, be they printed or *viva voce*. But my idea of being properly prepared for getting hold of one great book is, if it's so-called literature, having learned to read and having lived at least a decade and a half; if it's philosophy, preparation comes from other Great Books. For example, having read some Aristotle and some Kant is preparation for reading Hegel—if anything is. So the context of a great book is life or another great book, not a Great Book derivative. And, of course, the liberal arts, the *trivium*, the triple arts of expressing *thought*, and the *quadrivium*, the quadruple arts of knowing *things*. (See Essay 9, "Liberal Education.")

The feature of greatness that underwrites this claim is the ultimate autonomy of a book so qualified. Nearly every book on our list—which, incidentally seems to contain a hundred plus works; I haven't counted and believe that if other than Western traditions are included (we have venues for them) there may be half a thousand—what's it matter?—so, nearly every book on our list is self-sufficient, meaning that it contains, at least for a student of liberal arts, pretty nearly all the terms, arguments, information, and citations needed to stand alone. Hence Comparative Literature seems to me an unilluminating study when it comes to works of the highest quality; it does better with run-of-the-mill books. For great treatments, from geometries to cosmologies, from epics to novels, build worlds of their own. Thus to root around in several for comparative motifs requires scouring away their subtle particularities to get gross outlines. And that's to fall between two stools. At any rate it's an exercise that should come not first but last for students—if at all.

8) Timelessness and beauty are readily conceded to be the marks of greatness, but they require some analysis. "Being of its time," "being required by the times," etc., are phrases with practically unassignable meanings. Is time some sort of a box in which happenings eventuate, or is it some rough beast slouching toward Silicon Valley to be born, or some force aligning our motions, as does an electromagnetic field? If, however, there is such a condition as being of one's time, then the great anthropological philosophers, who have unifying insights not into the light, loud, and self-assertive chatter of the day but into the deep, tacit, and common opinions of the era, will by that very fact be beyond their time, disembedded from it. And so the books most truly cognizant of present conditions are also most timeless. For example, Mann's *Doctor Faustus*, which contains clever simulacra of the philosophies ending up in National Socialism, is surely a period

piece, but by reason of its insight into the time it is a timeless masterpiece. Incidentally, not all fictionalized philosophy is mere deft semblance: George Eliot's *Middlemarch* is full of real philosophizing; this mixing of modes gives grief to some of my colleagues and joy to me.

Beauty is, I think, a practically fixed feature not only of literary but also of great expository works. Think of Augustine's Latin or Bacon's and Hobbes's English—often the harsher the message the handsomer its delivery. I might even claim—don't laugh—that Kant's works are beautiful, insofar as he presents world-inverting novelties in apt neologisms.

However, my most salient meaning of beauty comes from one of those fugitive passages in which brilliant notions often flash by in Platonic dialogues. In the *Phaedrus* Socrates says, in effect, that beauty is the "form" of visibility; beauty is what makes things shine out. And if shining out is the most immediate apprehension of Greatness, then beauty is built into its self-presentation, hence into its very notion.

Are there then any ugly great books? Well, Locke's prose is less than elegant, but his politics make up for this lack of shine by being proto-enlightened. No, there aren't.

9) A great book can be life-changing. So can any book, but the great ones have the staying power. How do they do it? By preoccupying the soul, mind, and affects, in a double way. Their message comes in this most captivating dual mode: "What an illumination," I say, and immediately add "but I've always known it!" We take the book's sayings in with a sense both of amazement and familiarity—ancient newness.

But more important than what we receive is what we invest. Every great book—I know of no exception in any genre; not even mathematical texts—offers a world bidding us to participate. It is a moral proving ground: Here is a great drama; what could Oedipus have done, what might I do, effectively to prevent the tragedy? Or is the prevention of a grand tragedy in fact a diminution of the human condition? Here is a great novel, to my mind the greatest of the last century, Paul Scott's *Raj Quartet*. Would I have overlooked my closest school friend Kumar, now a black face in a native crowd? Would I have broken through colonial taboos? What would it have taken?

Great fictions, epics and novels especially, are also the exercise fields of the imagination. Words have the—so far unexplained—ability to raise mental images, and many a great fiction hides its secrets in plain sight. To bring them forward you must develop the ability to form mental imagery, to visualize according to textual intimations that direct you to intercept looks, to see what is salient in a situation, to unveil the unsaid. Example: As you listen to the devil that visits Ivan Karamazov, look carefully at him: It's surely Smerdyakov's, the bastard half-brother's, look-alike, who's got into Ivan's head, hence onto this sofa—a brazen devil, goading a dithering intellectual.

Besides eliciting the exercise of the imagination while we're within the book, there are imaginative uses of Great Books once they're in us, once we've made them our own. They furnish models for how to be and how not to be. In youth good models invite imitation, in maturity interrogation. When I was dean and about to exert power simply because I had it, I would call up Lincoln and listen to him; it restored decency. (It helped to have a little bust of him in sight.)

Reading large fictions or systematic philosophy teaches world-expansion. Thus mundane dailiness sometimes resonates to scenic reminiscences from fiction and sometimes fits itself to framing visions from philosophy.

And, of course, much reading of intelligently beautiful prose will contribute to our linguistic alertness and expressive deftness; these are the safety valves for bad temper and the desire to hurt. Not to speak of our ability to do our own right retelling, to paraphrase justly, which is the best proof

that we've apprehended what we read or heard and that we've
let it work on us—maybe enhance, improve us.

10) Now, finally, the mark of a book's greatness that I regard as unfailing. Almost every great book has an unabashedly repellent anti-hero, meager, mean, malicious, evil.
Usually it's a human being, sometimes a doctrine, an institution, an empire—more rarely, a real devil. And every such vil-
lain in a great book *has a moment of grace, and with it the
work rises from great to sublime.* Thus even Satan (Milton's)
has such a moment; in sight of Eve:

> . . . the evil one abstracted stood
> From his own evil, and for the time remained
> Stupidly good (IX 463).

Morningside Institute, New York, 2019

12

Dangers to Liberal Education
Call to Resistance

Liberal education was born endangered: the dangers *of* such education have been, since ancient times, a source of dangers *to* it.

The tradition of educating the young that is the recognizable antecedent of what we still think we are doing in some enclaves of higher education began, as far as I know, in the Athens of the fifth century B.C.E. Philosophers, sophists, rhetoricians had their mutually embattled versions of it, while the solid citizens, the parents, looked on, suspicious and worried.

Herodotus tells how Persian boys were brought up; they learned just three things: to ride horses, use bow and arrow, and tell the truth. My guess is that many an Athenian father wanted just that—the antithesis of liberal learning—for his boy.

I won't bore you with a thumbnail history of liberal education, mostly because I think that, though history holds many lessons, they have that little drawback of being unlearnable. I will, however, have to try to say what this endangered liberal education is, and then I'll give a little list of those perennial putative dangers *of* liberal education which eventually turn into dangers *to* that education. But since the title of this talk, "Dangers to Liberal Education," ought really to have been "Current Dangers to Liberal Education," what I'll mostly do is to list and describe the present assaults which are mutations of the old dangers. I must tell you that when I first thought about this talk I had seventeen such headings within thirty-four seconds. My list for you will be more select, particularly since most of it won't be news to you, and because the possible profit of this talk will probably be less in its completeness and more in hearing some of your anxieties articulated—and perhaps in a few notions about what to do.

To start, then, with the perennial resistances. We've probably all heard ourselves say that *liberal education is intended to be freeing*. Its essence is *liberation*. Historically, however, that isn't quite right. When Aristotle speaks of such learning, he means the education *of the already free*, the freeborn young who are not bound to serve for money, who have the leisure to engage in learning for its own sake; for him the essence of liberal learning is *inutility*.

I want to say now that that second feature, *learning for its own sake*, seems to me still the essence of liberal learning. I do not mean that knowledge so acquired might not have useful applications, both for doing something for the world *and* for making a living. But that will be incidental; learning for its own sake is of the essence. More of this later.

Now by both these understandings, liberal learning has been felt to be dangerous. For if "liberal" means "liberating," the paying parent might well ask "from what?" "Do I want my children to lose their faith, to condemn their country, to critique me?" This worry goes way back. Such fathers turn up in Platonic dialogues and in the Athenian courtroom that condemned Socrates for corrupting the young. And we still hear about it, if in a muted and apologetic way, for example, on Parent's Day, when our president and dean meet with concerned fathers and mothers.

But if "liberal" means "at leisure" and "deliberately non-vocational," the resistance is even stronger. "What am I paying for, if it's all fun and games, and in the end my children won't realize my ambitions for them in the world or even get a good job?" This latter parental anxiety and the resulting drive for vocational education—incidentally the greatest misnomer imaginable, since a vocation is calling, and a calling is the most not-for-profit enterprise in this world—this rampant vocationalism is near the top of the current list of dangers to liberal education. It is the latest mutation of that old charge against leisured learning, that it is elitist, only for the upper classes, or, as we say in America, for the privileged.

But let me pass from these old resistances that are called out by the very nature of liberal education to some specific contemporary dangers to such learning that arise perhaps less from its very virtues and more from its own vices as well as from present conditions. I'll start with a numbered list of selected headings, then explain them a little more and, along with that, try my hand at formulating possible ways to face them.

Zero, as I'll number it, is nothing more nor less than our current atmosphere, those present conditions.

First is the internal degradation of the liberal arts.

Second is the professionalization of the tradition of liberal learning.

Third is the politicization of curricula.

Fourth is the expense of this education.

Fifth is the trendiness of education-talk.

Sixth is quantified accountability.

You'll see right away that some of these dangers seem to be internal, others external to learning itself, though they are all originally external. A better way to put it is: The current dangers liberal education is facing are all—or so I think—derived from the fact that its custodians have succumbed to external seductions and threats.

So to "zero." In a lecture given in 1979, Michael Oakeshott described our environment:

> The world in which many children now grow up is crowded, not necessarily with occupants and not at all with memorable experiences, but with happenings; it is a ceaseless flow of seductive trivialities which invoke neither reflection nor choice but instant participation. A child quickly becomes aware that he cannot too soon plunge into this flow or immerse himself in it too quickly; to pause is to be swept with the chilling fear of never having lived at all. There is little chance that his perceptions, his emotions, his admirations and his ready indignations might become learned responses or be even innocent fancies of his own; they come to him prefabricated, generalized and uniform . . . From an early age children now believe themselves to be well-informed about the world, but they know it only at second hand in the pictures and voices that surround them. It holds no puzzles or mysteries for them; it invites neither careful attention nor understanding.

A generation later this description is more intensely true, because the world is infinitely fuller of "seductive trivialities"—I don't need to mention them; they're largely electronically supplied. How to deal with this world? I have truly excellent advice: Ignore it. Act with students, while they're yours, as if nothing mattered but the object of learning before them and the motion of apprehending within them, as if there were no material to be covered by you, no performance expected from them, no ingenious devices brought to bear on their learning. Collect them out of the dispersion of their wits into "communication" (I've got that intentionally in quotations), information, and amusement by poring with them, slowly and face to face, over something of abiding interest—not by, the Lord save us, "covering material," but by penetrating it, not by being a star in class, but a fellow-inquirer, not by displaying so-called "creativity," but truth-seeking. I'm not doing a great job here of describing a mode of teaching close to my heart, but we've got a question period for doing better.

Next is the internal degradation of the liberal arts. By that I mean their simultaneous expansion and contraction, until they are quite thoroughly bent out of shape. On the one hand, almost any subject of research or field of interest can be taught in a liberal arts program, be it established by some genuine inquiry or some trendy ideology; all its practitioners advance claims to their specialty as being legitimate choices for students to elect, so that some common learning becomes practically impossible. On the other hand, the liberal arts, and liberal education with them, are now commonly equated with the humanities; my favorite dictionary, the *American Heritage*, defines the humanities as "those branches of knowledge, such as philosophy, literature, and art, that are concerned with human thought and culture, the liberal arts." That sounds as if mathematics and science were not activities of human thought and therefore excluded from the liberal arts, though they are arguably the most exemplary ones and thus half the mainstay of liberal education. This view of liberal arts as confined to the humanities is an enormous impoverishment.

You've probably noticed that I've slipped into an undefended identification, that of the liberal arts with liberal education. I do think they go together, the liberal arts being those skills that turn learning into liberal learning. This claim is much too cursory, and perhaps I'll have a chance to expand it in the question period. (See Essay 9, "Liberal Education.") Let me apply it here to the case at hand: Without some experience with mathematics, not as a problem-solving technique but as a basic capability of human thinking, as a liberal skill, it seems to me that liberal learning is going to be quite illiberal—undeep and inexpansive.

For how can one think, say, about poetry (whose formal structure, prosody, numbers what is said and what is silent) or music (which is numbered sound, symbolized horizontally as meter and melody, vertically as harmony, and in both dimensions a polyphony) without having thought about bare numbers? How can one think about moving through the world without having thought about the possible configurations of space in geometry and the formal expression of motion in the calculus? Some elementary mathematics seems to me a necessary part of liberal education.

Perhaps I should stop here for a moment in my recital of the dangers that beset liberal education to say what I think its identifying marks are.

First, as I said, I think Aristotle is right: Liberal education is essentially an activity engaged in for its own sake. I'll put that more palatably by saying that only if it is done in that spirit will it fulfill its purpose, that of bringing out our humanity and thus making us better at living with ourselves and others. (It would be a real pleasure to be asked later to specify just how liberal education does make our lives better; it is that sort of specificity which saves education talk from being drivel.) The world is full of ugly problems with contorted solutions; we can learn about those in graduate school or through apprenticeships or just by life. Liberal education is about ends, not means, and for my part, I'd rather see my world's problems taken on by those fellow-humans who've first thought about what it is to live well.

Second, it follows that the learning matter should be fine; I'll even use that currently proscribed word "beautiful": the bare beauty of mathematics, the embodied beauty of the arts, the ethereal beauty of theology and the lucid beauty of philosophy. Evil and ugliness certainly make their appearance in the world of liberal learning, but they are there transfigured— think of Milton's Satan, a figure of badness and splendor.

Third, in liberal learning the boundaries between learning matters are recognized as a source of interest rather than of mutual exclusion. To be in the course of being liberally educated means never saying "That's not my subject because I'm not (say) an anthropologist," but rather "I know too a little about being a human being, perhaps the science of humankind can help."

Fourth, such learning is done together—not by a professor expounding as an authority before students supinely taking notes, but as one—slightly more advanced—learner guiding participating students in an inquiry still alive for the teacher. This is the kind of teaching I was attempting to describe before.

Fifth—and this is the chief stumbling-block in our colleges and universities—if liberal learning is common to teachers and students, so much the more ought it to be at least a somewhat common enterprise for the teachers themselves. From this common learning there might then arise some agreement about the liberal curriculum—what basic skills and what first-rate matter all will have to educate themselves in and will consequently have in common.

Now I'll get back to those dangers. The first of these, already discussed, was the degradation of the liberal arts.

The second, then, is the professorialization of liberal arts teaching, whose consequences I've already taken up as well. The mental distance between the discipline-trained professor and the intellectually naïve freshman is too great, and the fiercer the specialization of graduate training gets the more difficult good teaching becomes.

What to do about this disproportion between what teachers know and what students should learn? My impossible dream is a concerted push for getting rid of the humanistic doctoral dissertation (that life-bending agony fought out against the chimerical demand for an "original contribution") and substituting for it an extended reflection on the human significance of some discipline. But since that's impossible, it seems to me that schools seriously concerned for liberal education can neutralize the deformations of graduate school by encouraging their young appointees to teach beyond their field and by rewarding their despecialization.

The third danger, the politicization of curricula and classrooms, has been too much discussed to need more explication. To me it seems scandalous that any teacher or group of teachers should constitute themselves an occupying army of the students' soul just because they themselves are preoccupied by some problem, that they should assault their students' preconceptions, "raise their sensitivities," force them into uncongenial "role-playing." *Because* the very liberality of liberal education consists in part of the free and leisurely consideration of the human condition—just because of that, it seems to me of the essence that the teacher's voice be very reticent, more questioning then opining, or at least more ruminating than ideologizing.

How to combat this misuse? Declare this professional arrogation of the social-reformer function unprofessional. To me it seems in fact on par with imposing personal intimacies on a student; it's a form of harassment. Thus, advocating specific acts of "social justice" is pedagogic malfeasance; inducing a freely searching conversation about it is good teaching.

Now, with the fourth danger, I come to external factors endangering liberal education. Since it is labor- or rather effort-intensive, it is almost prohibitively expensive. This fact gives it an entirely unwanted and undesirable aspect—an aspect of elitism. Yet no type of higher education is intrinsically more extendedly human—I would almost say populist—than liberal learning, which goes to our common human concerns—lowest to highest.

I wish I knew a way out that doesn't hurt. If the right principle is that any student who has even the glimmer of a desire for liberal learning should be able to work up a package of self-help and family contribution together with loans and grants, then clearly the realization depends on making student aid a very large part of the school's budget. My point here can only be that it's a matter that should concern a liberal arts faculty, even to the point of some sacrifice.

My fifth rubric is the tiresome trendiness of so much public speech about education. It's a current danger because of its present muscle-flexing tone and its illiberal sources. Education-talk in modern times and in this country has always been a little on the side of pious babble, but it's at least been edifying and friendly. Now, however, it has turned somewhat toward aggressive utilitarianism, as if the obligatory mission of schools were to turn out competitors in the global economy.

To me it seems that we teachers should take on more of the task of speaking to parents and to the general public about learning. Our advantage is what we are not: not research-publishing educationalists, not government-advising panelists, not lobby-beset legislators, not employee-seeking business people. So our vocabulary is not the jigged and jargonistic one favored by educationists and managers and administrators. Our explanations might have more of the freshness of first-hand accounts, and the vividness of concrete experience, so they might more convincingly bring home the life-shaping capacity of liberal learning to those whose friendly regard and financial support we need to win. We ought to know best how to speak the truth with convincing detail: that liberal education is a way to the good life, perhaps not the only way, but the most deliberate and reliable one.

Here is my sixth and last danger, the one most recent and most acute: quantified accountability. It has been decades in coming and has now become a preoccupation of the federal Department of Education. Since most of our colleges and universities depend heavily on federal funding, particularly for student aid, and since our accrediting agencies, without whose approval we can't get that funding, are in turn accredited in Washington, the government can, through them, lean heavily on institutions of higher education and reach deeply into their practices.

What I'm saying now may be very well known to you, but I'll enunciate it in my way; perhaps it can become a topic of discussion amongst us.

Let me say the obvious fact first: accountability is a perfectly reasonable demand. If you accept money you have to account for your use of it. An older notion was that you had to show that what was done at your institution was in accord with the mission you published and the promises that implied. The focus was on the programs and practices of the school. It made sense.

Now there is a new understanding abroad. It is called "outcomes assessment." Here the focus is on the student regarded as an analogue to an industrial product. The school works on this item and adds some value to it, value realizable in the workplace. Education is a value-adding process and the quantifiably assessable product is the student. The ideal instrument of assessment would be one test administered at the beginning and the same at the end of the usual four years; the difference in the score would be the value added. I've heard that such tests are in fact being developed or even marketed.

Where to begin with this deleteriously wrong-headed view of education? (I should mention here in all fairness that such hard-line intrusions are said to be primarily directed to delinquent for-profit proprietary schools. But bureaucracies find it constitutionally difficult to depart from the apparent equity of "one-size-fits-all" to make fine distinctions.)

First of all, such outcomes assessment makes an assumption false and fatal to students' self-responsibility: that the result of a student's learning is mostly the effect of the school's or the teacher's effort. This view of learning, at least in adults or near-adults, simply ignores that old and so very true saying "You can lead a horse to water but you can't make it drink." To be sure, you can do a lot toward persuading students to study, but in the end it's up to them. Assessing the school by students' success carries the risk of some future undesirable consequences, one of them being that institutions become preemptively even more selective than they strive to be now, so they'll look good. But selectivity in admission doesn't fit liberal education, which ought to be risk-prone and inclusive. One might say that *a selective admissions policy betokens a defective teaching faculty.* That's, however, peripheral. Here's what's centrally wrong. It's not the danger of a schools' being branded a failure, for the bar will of necessity be set so low that most of our liberal arts institutions will be fine. The danger is to the ideal of liberal education itself. For most institutions, just because they know they'll pass through the number ordeal safely, will feel disinclined to resist. And so without much reluctance or remonstration liberal education will top the slippery slope of yet another kind of degradation: the notion that measuring the immeasurable is an innocent concession.

Why is liberal learning not quantifiable? Well, first its effects don't necessarily show up right away; there's often a delayed reaction, sometimes as late as mid-life. Second, all quantification depends on homogeneity, and liberal learning is terminally individual, non-competitive, and incommensurable. Yet grades, especially percentage grades, even in the absence of that abomination of injustice, "grading on a curve," are implicitly comparative. In real learning, moreover, effort is far more valuable than outcome and the efforts of laborious seriousness are worthier than the accomplishments of facile talent. How are we going to express that numerically?

But above all, the evidence of thoughtfulness is just not numerable. Let me give an example: In my present freshman seminar we were discussing Plato's *Gorgias*, where Socrates makes the passionate claim that bad human beings cannot be happy. A young man, given to down-to-earth candor, took issue with Socrates. He said that when he was a child, his mother had put out a plate of cookies to cool off and told him and his little brother to stay away. Our student had eaten up all of the cookies and put the blame on the younger boy. It was wicked, he knew, but he had had great pleasure in eating the cookies and real happiness in getting away with it. All this he said in a clear public voice. And then he added, still audibly but under his breath, *sotto voce*, "But he didn't trust me again for a long time." It was, thinking back on it, a wonderful moment: spirited resistance to a text, and the supervening second thought. That is learning, and it is literally invaluable.

Of course students' effort and accomplishments must be evaluated; that's part of the duty of teaching. And grades must be given if only for external use, mostly for getting into graduate school. But those evaluations, given by teachers for the students' good, are not at issue in outcomes assessment.

Back home at my college we think a lot about how to meet this assault. There seem to be these three opinions: one is to go along, accommodate, and if need be, compromise our principles. One example of such a compromise would be to improve our retention and graduation rates by ceasing to send students away for not engaging with our demanding program. Or we could train ourselves to cease to regard our program of learning as successful when after a year or so it causes some students to find their way to other, more specialized studies, although some of these non-graduates are our most loyal alumni. Or we could, by subtle changes in our study plan, prepare students for outside tests, or compromise ourselves by testing them quantifiably in-house. None of these can we bring ourselves to do.

A second option is to resist on principle and to oppose such evaluation. That's impossible because our students would lose access to federal aid. We can't afford it.

A third possibility is pretending—to half-do, or to do with a wink, what we think is illiberal and educationally wrong. But the soul of our institution is intellectual propriety; we can't do that either.

So we must find other ways, and some of these ways out might be helpful to you. What I personally would love to do is to send the Department of Education a cartload of our annual papers, two per student, the freshman essay and the senior essay (our version of the masterpiece that guilds used to require on the road from journeyman to mastercraftsman). Then let *them* figure out whether value has accrued.

What we've more or less come down to is this principle: since we have a commendation-winning evaluation plan at work for our students, a plan that uses no number or letter grades but is all discursive speech, and since we want to impose nothing on them that betrays our vision of liberal learning, we'll hold on to that.

But we do have lots of statistics about our alumni's careers and lots of information concerning their estimation of the education they gave themselves at their college. These reports do contain much evidence that could be maneuvered into a quantifiable outcomes assessment. Yet these numbers are not such as would compel us to reshape our plan of liberal learning, and so we give up nothing in recording them; they don't endanger our sense that the human soul's learning can indeed be evaluated qualitatively but should not be misrepresented quantitatively.

As I said in the beginning, I think, as I also hope, I have not said anything that is very new to you, since the last thing an account of dangers needs is originality. But perhaps there was some value in articulating what we've all lived with or heard of.

Transylvania University, 2008

13

Seminar Questions
What Works?

I.

I'll begin by borrowing from my freshmen, some of whom have boundless faith in—no, flaccid reliance on—definitions. They've been traumatized by "Define your terms," the knock-down, drag-out defense against receptivity to meaning. They'll begin a paper on some topic (when it's for me, usually of their own devising; that's part of the task) by quoting their dictionary, usually Wikipedia; for me, that's an indictment of their high-school training. Yet, this time, I'll do the same.

So here's the *American Heritage Dictionary*, my favored recourse, on "sem·i·nar," from Latin *seminarium*, "seed plot," as in "semen" or "seed":

> A small group of advanced students in a college or graduate school engaged in original research or intensive study under the guidance of a professor who meets regularly with them to discuss their reports and findings.

Or:

> A meeting for exchange of ideas; a conference.

At my college "seminar," *the* seminar, the focus of our all-required program, meets none of these definitional elements, because:

175

1) Nobody is "advanced"; all of us, tutors and students, are always at the beginning: our quest is initial or even proto-initial.

2) "Original research" is a contradiction in terms; it is an inherently secondary activity. "Re-search" itself says so: the *re* is, to be sure, used intensively, but its basic meaning is "again," a "second time." In the humanities it is carried on by scholars, who, again by the dictionary, are learned specialists, largely engaged in collating and critiquing previous scholarship.*

> I should know. For a brief moment in my early life I was a genuine scholar, reporting my findings on the group of lovely Attic pots assigned to me, pots found in the American excavations of the Athenian Agora (Market Place). For an even briefer moment I probably knew more than anybody else then alive in the world about this specialty, the "Late Geometric" and "Protoattic" periods; that included a pretty complete command of its "literature," articles and books, with which I had to come to terms. In sum: I read and referenced as much—no, even more—than I looked at those pots. (It was the archaeologists' pretension never to say "vase.")

3) We produce no "findings," but, at our best, questions, conjectures, and clarifications, perhaps some—temporarily—mind-settling discoveries.

4) We don't "exchange ideas." An "idea," the modern degradation of a Platonic form (*idea, eidos*), is a thought-packet to be cashed in, acquired for possession and exchanged for reputation. Ideas have a shelf-life with an expiration date. We are devoted to thinking as a fluidly continuous activity with resting-places (as described by William James).—Besides, most bright ideas darken the world.

5) In our seminar the prevailing mode of communication is, I think, not discussion nor argument but conversation. (The word means "turn and turn about, together.") We talk to each other, each to all, tak-

ing turns, sometimes surmising, sometimes making points, sometimes asking, and always listening and responding.

II.

Thus our seminar is, as a conception, a sort of unicorn, definitionally fugitive because vagrantly potent, modally composite, inherently contradictory.

Here, in particular, are the self-contradictions, as I discern them, that the conception embraces and we actively embody:

1) Natural conversation directed by assigned readings: prepared spontaneity and preplanned open-endedness.
2) Students' independence and tutors' leadership: equality of unequals and non-teaching teachers.
3) Perfect freedom of expression constrained by rules of civility: intellectual permissiveness and controlled conduct.
4) Inconclusive sessions and life-changing outcomes: effective futzing around and long-term fruition.

III.

This version of a seminar begins with a start-up question asked by the tutor—"Tutor" instead of "Professor" to indicate guardianship without authoritative professing. Normally there are two of us; we intend bi-polarity.

What kind of question works best, best for engaging students and inciting thoughtful responses? There are several opinions; of course, our reasonable faculty tries them all at some point. Let me list a few.

Some think that our great-souled writers tend to secrete their dearest truths into tiny nooks, so they start off by quoting an apparently inconsiderable passage; others ask questions that are incitements: "Figure out what I'm thinking." Some tutors identify straightforwardly the text's grand theme and ask the members of the seminar to talk about that; others give up on guidance and just want to know what it all means.*

> In the old days, with a mostly male faculty and before the smoking ban, this hazy question was accompanied by meditative pipe-puffing.

Two apparently antithetical questions—"apparently" because they may actually be complementary—seem to me substantially interesting because they respond to a perpetual puzzle of the teaching life. This is the perplexity, memorably put in a phrase by Paul: "What I would, that I do not" (Romans 7:15; me too, it goes without saying). It goes especially for our students, readers from way back, who came to us to be absorbed in the literate thinking life. Why should there be a difficulty about engaging them so that they participate in this novel sort of conversation, one that is utterly free and yet disciplined at once? Yet there is such a difficulty, and the most satisfactory explanation I know comes from the text of one of my best loved, because, oh, so apt, Bach cantatas:

> *Es ist ein trotzig und verzagt Ding um aller Menschen Herzen.* "There is something recalcitrant *and* [my italics] timorous about the heart of all human beings" Cantata 176, text by Christiane von Ziegler; based on Jeremiah 17:9, taken as a commentary on John 3:2: Why does the well-connected Nicodemus come to Jesus only under cover of night?

So which opening way is better for a good seminar conversation? One side raises a monitory index finger and says: Before taking an attitude, read carefully and try to understand what an intellect surely ahead of yours is saying. First construe, then judge.*

> Here is a yet prior concern: Isn't there an impertinence in approaching grand works with such bold naïvety? It's not a difficulty I would have conceived had it not been for an illuminating day spent at Islamic Zaytuna College, whose faculty emphasizes

respectful reading. Well, most of our great authors, being deceased, are, probably, invulnerable to the depredations of our spirited young—or, perhaps, even pleased by their involvement.

The other, my side, says: Get the drift of the book and let it work on you. Does it induce obstinacy and despondency in you, or passion and longing for a truth possibly relevant to your life, and why either? Once so engaged, we'll figure out what it actually says: First feel, then think.

So: read—and talk—first with earnest but distanced discernment, or with passionate and so, involved, suspicion.*

Though it really may be, at least for some youngsters, a new emotional world somewhat startling to me: Ms. X, a student of wonderful insights, wants to have lunch once more. In the course of talk about something else entirely in her life as a freshman—but perhaps nothing in the ambience of liberal learning is ever entirely about anything else—this question: "Ms. Brann, have you ever been in love?" In the roughly eighteen hundred such lunches over the past sixty years, no one's ever had the gall? or the innocence? to ask that. I was befuddled for a moment and then said: "Ms. X, you've sat obliquely across from me for over six months; what do you think?" She had the grace not to ask "With *whom?*" and she lacked the sophistication to add "Or with *what?*" (a deeper but more permissible question of one's elders; see Essay 1, "Thing-Love"). She dwelt in a world with lax social bounds and with surprising experiential lacunae—considering all the "experimentation." Or maybe it's linguistic inexpressiveness induced by the word-indigence of texting? There's a slight resemblance to a Down's syndrome kid, Matthew, with whom I once spent an afternoon: a truly good and rather acute person, yet wanting.

Here's my trouble with putting the cluing-out of a text first, of getting it right, especially for books of the quality we put before our students: It takes long times of quiet solitude to work that out, and "getting it right" is not a reliable option. Of course, we can try to work it out together then and there. But not only are there too many of us for such close work but, since we believe (contrary to the education establishment) that students should often face books above their "grade level," many of the freshmen, at least, are probably not prepared to do much with little, to go deeply rather than widely. Moreover, the genuine hermeneutic impulse, be it charitable or suspicious, seems to me to be driven by the *desire* to discover truth—or falsity. For a great book—and why read others in dedicated learning time?—can, if rarely, be false, be it by reason of an unintentional mistake or of an intentional fraud. And then the how and why of it will at least be illuminating.*

> Take it on faith: I've got examples even among undeniably great texts, but I'll name a very fine book of a lesser kind mentioned before, a model of a true-to-type murder mystery, *Jar City*, by the Icelander Arnaldur Indriðason. (For a country of little more than a third of a million people, Iceland seems to have quite a few fine writers, particularly Halldór Laxness, the author of the masterpiece *Independent People*.) *Jar City* is full of horrible, often disgusting stuff, addiction, rape, genetic disease, sewers, grave robbing, organ canning ("jar city") and stealing, with moments (few) of pure sweetness, all melded into a distinctly hyper-realistic brew, intending brutal realism and producing surrealism, utterly involving *and quite unconvincing*. Now *that's* food for thought.

In sum, truth-indifference, be it juicy or dry, seems to me a deflating frame of mind, not conducive to meaning-extraction. First, let the book take hold of your soul, then let your mind grasp the text.*

> That can go too far. You wouldn't believe the things our alumni go through life thinking Plato told them.

Finally, a word about the soundness of conversations tethered to a text. This requirement, to engage in object-directed thought rather than in subjective revelation, felicitously inhibits self-expression, which diminishes inwardness: the more you ex-press to the outside, the less you've got left for yourself.

Annapolis, 2018

14

Self-Address
Silent Speech

"Speech is the body of thought."

S. W. Clark, *A Practical Grammar*, 1847

My first title for this little musing was "Silent Speech." That, however, turned out to be inaccurate. As I thought out what had set me wondering about this strange capacity that I, all of us human beings, possess for talking to ourselves and recalled that there is no source of the "love of wisdom" (*philosophia*) other than "the feeling of wondering" (Plato, *Theaetetus* 155d), I noticed that self-address is not always silently interior.

Some such speech is uttered (etymologically: "outered"). Yet, a further wrinkle, not all audible speech spoken to no discernible auditor is in fact addressed to oneself. For years there was a sad case haunting the streets of Annapolis: bent forward as if in urgent escape, this man strode along, talk-

Reprinted with revisions from *Renovatio*, The Journal of Zaytuna College (Fall 2018).

ing. To himself? I doubt it; he was probably addressing a deaf world or its divinity. Also I had a friend of three-quarters of a century who in her later years talked unstoppably. To me? No, it was addressless, interruptible speech, an urge, I think, to hear herself being still alive.

These idiosyncratic ways of speaking confirmed a belief of great significance to me: Ask anyone what speech "is for" and the answer will be "Speech is for communication." To be sure. But *not* primarily! *Speech is first for self-address.* Yet if you've ever been requested to send a self-addressed envelope, one intended to make its rounds and return to you, you'll have experienced the same slight shiver of weirdness that set off this inquiry.

This sort of musing has a name in professional philosophy: Phenomenology, the account of the *inner appearances* our consciousness produces. It is, as beginning in wonder, descriptive, but may lead to the deep principles of human being.*

"Phenomenology" was on the scene long before Edmund Husserl made it into a school pursuing the features of consciousness. Kant, in his *Metaphysical Foundations of Natural Science* (Ch. 4), calls the study of matter, insofar as it appears and is therefore an object of experience, "phenomenology."

Consciousness itself is not the object of this essay. It is a property of Mind (a heading dramatically but wisely absent from all my dictionaries of philosophy though philosophers are bold enough in defining it; for example, for Locke it is an empty box with operational capacities, for Hume a stream without unifying identity). Consciousness, be it a state inferred from external observations or an experience introspectively reported, be it epiphenomenal or causal, is terminally elusive. See Güven Güzeldere, "The Many Faces of Consciousness: A Field Guide" in *The Nature of Consciousness: Philosophical Debates*, The MIT Press (1998), p. 26 ff.

The engrossing question of inner speech is, as far as I can tell, not a developed topic of consciousness studies.

Can there be any doubt that we talk mostly internally (setting aside occasional bursts into utterance)? We address ourselves in all the moods of grammar: indicative (asserting), imperative (enjoining), optative or subjunctive (wishing or doubtful) and, above all, interrogative (asking).*

An odd fact: "interrogative" is not a grammatical mood, perhaps because it has no special morphology in the ancient languages but signifies by auxiliaries and word order or because it is too universal a propensity—adaptable to ordering, beseeching, expostulating, and so expressible in any mood. Question-asking is thus not a grammatical but a philosophical rubric.

Why can't I think of speech as *primarily* communicative? First, as I've said, copiousness; whether we live much with others or more alone, the number of words we say to or by ourselves must, I think, outdo the number said to others by a factor—I'm surmising wildly—of ten. Second, because children talk when alone, so possibly to or for themselves, quite a while before they engage in other-directed "conversation" (literally "turn and turn about, together"). Wake up very early, and there he is, about one year old, holding himself up by the railing of his crib and jabbering away in the sweetest, most persuasively human tones, albeit unintelligible to me. In inept child-development terminology it's called jargoning. Is he expressing thought? He *looks* full of meaning. And he stops as soon as this intrusively curious grown-up appears on the scene; he becomes the "infant," the "non-speaking" human we think he is. And third, how, if I did not converse with myself, would I have anything thoughtful to say to my friends? Everything would be deleteriously spontaneous and unthought-out.

But here's the puzzle, or better, enigma. Who is taking turns with whom? I ask myself: What does it, what does the Apostle John, mean: "In the beginning was the Word"? What beginning: in time or in being? What word: a name, a common noun? Spoken by whom: the Divinity, or was it not a spoken word at all? I'm reading it in the Gospel of John: is he speaking? But I'm saying it; am I speaking?
Here arises a sub-enigma, the aftermath of a great event in

internality, when Augustine observed that his beloved bishop, Ambrose, a man open to all, "retired himself from the clamor of other men's business" and read—something utterly new to Augustine—"silently to himself" (Augustine, *Confessions* VI iii). So this question is added: When I read, silently, and take in the words, either scanning them impressionistically (which is our modern mode) or perusing them alertly: does a second or a third speaker enter my consciousness? Is the silent inner rehearsal of written speech an alien supervenience or an assimilated reception? For example, when I, not being a Christian, take issue with John, such as: "No, Joshua of Nazareth was not a, or the, *Logos* but a Man, at once venerable and dangerous," am I talking to myself, to him, to whom? Whose is the voice of a text I've "internalized"? Surely mine, transmuted into *my* speech by that salubrious plagiarism called "learning."

That question returns me to the central issue. Who is that I, such that it appears to address itself? What is speech, that it can mediate between myself and me? Incidentally, "I" has a remarkable linguistic feature: *no* etymology, no aboriginal meaning whence it has evolved; hence it is a completely original word, without pre-history and thus without explanatory genesis.*

> It shares with the verb "to be" another etymological feature, namely different roots for different grammatical forms: "I" has my, me, we, ours, us in declensions; "to be" has am, are, is, was, were, for inflected forms. "Be," however, does have an illuminating etymology; from *phyo*, to make grow, an avatar on which Heidegger bases his very understanding of metaphysics, of first philosophy (*Introduction to Metaphysics*, para. 14 ff.).

Yet it will soon turn out that this I, an apparently analytically inaccessible term, acts self-diremptively, self-divisively. To me it feels like a sort of natural, sound schizophrenia, a split-mindedness, by which the I, taken as a person, a subject with its subjectivity, a consciousness with its self, is all but defined.* Note, however, that before long I'll want to reject

> All but defined in opposition to Descartes' understanding of mind as a "thinking thing" (*res cogitans, Meditations on First Philosophy* II).
> My colleague Louis Petrich reminded me of a case neatly interpretable as a third internal speaker, the one who decides "when the heart is divided twoways-through" (*diandicha, Iliad* I 189). Achilles ponders whether to kill his chief, Agamemnon, who has mistreated him. Athena, visible to no one, tells him to sheathe his already drawn sword. That's the third, audible, inner speaker: Achilles' embodied second thought.

the aforesaid version of the question concerning self-address: "What does it *feel* like?"

Note also that both subjectivity and self-consciousness have somewhat squishy secondary meanings: intense my-owness and embarrassed self-awareness. That's revealing because it distinguishes us human persons from thingly objects, as having what the Greeks call *pathe*, "affects," all too often sufferings, which we share with animals in broad kind though surely not in the subtle differentiations we can experience; those seem to require speech.

Perhaps, however, that notion of double-mindedness is not the ultimate description of the phenomenon of self-address. So let me get down to business with three negatives, with three, as I think, false approaches I want to forfend, in order of interiority.

First, I've tried talking to myself with utterance muted, with inner speech not involving the soundless excitation in the larynx, the organ enfolding the vocal cords. I can't do it: I literally can't hear myself; I seem to have a virtual inner ear that must be addressed by vocalization, albeit muted. If this observation is correct, it seems to me to imply a positive element: Speech, spoken aloud or silently, is an *embodiment*. It is thought made somatic, that is, physical. Inner speech is analogous to inner sight, to the imagination, which is visibility minus ponderable matter, as the former is audibility minus overt sound.

This glottal self-address is thus distinguished from "hearing voices." In its benign form this event usually occurs between sleep and wake, but if it takes over, it can be pathological and dangerous. It betokens that self-communion has yielded to other-possession.

Second, a way of inquiry that has gained much traction seems to me to be misleading because it predetermines an evasive answer. "What Is It Like to Be a Bat?" is the title of an article concerning the nature of consciousness by Thomas Nagel; he postulates:

> [F]undamentally an organism has conscious mental states if and only if there is something that it is like to *be* that organism— something it is like *for* that organism. (In *The Nature of Consciousness*, p. 519 ff. The article is very frequently cited.)

Surely that must mean something "that it *feels* like."

Now questions about self-speech are evidently questions about consciousness, which both involve self-consciousness and invoke it in the very asking.* If, however, I follow this

---

"Involve self-consciousness." Remarkably, Aristotle says definitively, long before self-consciousness was singled out as a topic, that, whether we be sensing or thinking, we are always aware that we are sensing and thinking, and then (spectacularly both anticipating and emending Descartes' "I think, therefore I am") that this secondary awareness means "that we exist" (*Nicomachean Ethics* 1170a 34): "I am aware that I think, and that is what it is to exist."

Both "subject" and "consciousness" are terms clearly involved in the issue of self-address, but too far-reaching for this essay. So I'll confine myself to elements immediately pertinent. *Subject*, "that which is cast beneath," is the support or bearer, which is the thing "underlying" (*hypokeimenon*) the defining and accidental properties of a being. When the subject is an *I*, the whole complex is a *person*. Kant, in the *Critique of Pure Reason* (for example, 350 A), most particularly insists on the ego-nature of the subject (I and ego are cognate, both without etymology).Our common understanding of "subjective" as being peculiarly *mine*, and probably *not* held in common with *you* or "shared," would, I think, have appalled Kant, the devotee of rationality, though he may be unwittingly responsible, either directly, or by having called down upon us the Romanticism that adheres to "personality," as distinct from "person." Consciousness is generally thought of as the property of mind that is the precondition, shared with animals, of self-communing; *self*-consciousness is the condition itself. Yet "self"-consciousness may be redundant. The *Oxford Dictionary of English Etymology* defines "conscious," from Latin *conscire*, "to be privy with [oneself]," as *conscius sibi de aliqua re*, "someone who is in the know with himself about something or other." Just as a "subject" has its subjectivity, its idiosyncrasy, so a consciousness has its conscience, its guilt-feelings.

I've preferred *soul* over mind and its consciousness, because the predominant meaning of mind is that it itself is, or is the seat of, thinking, whereas the soul almost always is regarded as including all inner motions, active and passive: rational, prideful, desirous, or, in later terms, spiritual, intellectual, willful, appetitive.

The predominant ancient tradition regards thinking, particularly rationality (*logos*), as definitive of humanity. Thus Aristotle (*Politics* I ii): A human alone of all living beings (*zoa*) has reason (*logos*). Or Lucan (*Bellum Civile* 21): "If it is a man (*homo*), it is a mortal animal partaking of reason (*ratio*)." Though this view is no longer a given, particularly in the post-Darwinian era, I've thought that, since speech is at issue in this essay, a major mode (although not a grammatical mood), that of searching, of inquiring speech, namely *question-asking*, should come forward; it may indeed be the most definitively human element of the humanly defining *logos*.

formulation and look for likeness, I am precisely evading the challenge of uniqueness. The positive lesson is: Be not beguiled by similes, by likenesses or likeness-feelings, but remain off-kilter. For either I end up with the mere "feels like an internal dialogue," which is, for all its vivid descriptiveness, just a figure of speech, or there's nothing like *self*-address because I and me are in fact split, schizoid. But in that case, I am not sane, so now thinking is a form of insanity! That's called being on the horn of a dilemma. I must resolve to try to reawaken not the feel but the condition itself of self-address and to avoid diversion into similitudes.

The third negative is deepest and least likely to win agreement: Neither when I seek, in general, to embody my mind's ideas in speech, nor, in particular, to frame a question and elicit an answer, is the framing or the filling of the frame my doing. *It comes to me*, whence is not a question to be shrugged off but to be pursued. The positive implication of these assumptions are two: one, that there is thinking which precedes speech. (A professional term of this preverbal mentation is "mentalese," but that presumes much, namely that this fullness of the mind is already speech-like.) And two, that I am in no way creative, that I don't invent and make up something from nowhere and from nothing. Instead, I *am* receptive. Thus arise two enigmas as inciting as any: one, the relation of mind to speech and, two, the source of ideas in general and of solutions in particular. To me it seems that these profundities must draw me into regions transcending the hither world of matter-in-motion, of physics, into thither realms of stable ideas, of metaphysics up to theology.

Thence arises also this positive aspect: There *is* something I am responsible, answerable, for, and that is my admitting of the question, my framing of it as a possibly soluble problem, my capture of it in my abiding attention and my spotlighting of it by my concentrated focus. But if I am now tempted to distribute question-focusing and framing between will and intellect, I should recall that in the great tradition will and intellect are mutually inclusive and essentially identical, the former being thoughtful desire and the latter appetitive thought.*

Thomas Aquinas, *Summa Theologiae* Pt. I of Pt. II Q. 82. To me it is remarkable that Socrates, the boldest psycho-analyst of the soul's *parts*, speaks so sparingly about their internal *operations*.

On, now, to the more directly positive phenomenology. Shakespeare speaks, wonderfully, of "the sessions of sweet silent thought" (Sonnet 30). "Sessions" invokes the sittings of courts of law, where judgments are rendered. "Of sweet silent thought"? How does sweet silence go with convicting verdicts (literally "truth-speakings")? It goes most excellently, since the feel of much self-address is judgmental: internal closing arguments convicting our opponents, grand orations expressing our judgmental natures—which current opinion bids us hide. "Don't be judgmental," we're told, when we were put on earth to render judgments—on ourselves first of all, to be sure.

But to my mind, our most specific function, most expressive of our species-nature, is the asking of a question. A question is not "questioning," a subliminally accusatory inquisition. It eventuates rather when, having awoken to the strangeness of familiar things, we outline the yet unknown so that in searching for an answer we can recognize it when we come on it. In this understanding, a question is a shaped vacancy, a void primed to accept a particular content: "Yes, that's what I was seeking." It is the wonder of the *recognition* of the hitherto unknown, an unexplained ability that turns inquiry into "recollection" (Plato, *Meno* 81d).

Hence the chief question of self-address: Who is asking whom? Is the reference made above to doublemindedness, to sage bipolarity and sane schizophrenia, right? Are we two when we ask ourselves or are we one and the same?

I used to think that twoness was the answer, led on by Socrates' claim that the capacity for "thinking-things-through," *dianoia* in Greek, is "the accounting (*logos*) that the soul goes through about the things it might be looking at." Then he says that which makes me trust him above all: "I'm not showing you something *as if I knew.*" With that caveat, he continues:

> This is the likeness that presents itself to me: the soul when it thinks-things-through (*dianooumene*) is doing nothing else but talking-through (*dialegesthai*) something and herself asking herself and answering, and both alleging and disclaiming (Plato, *Theaetetus* 189e, *Sophist* 264a).

Here Socrates is doing—very hesitantly—just what I've forsworn above: likeness-making. And, of course, in his likeness, the soul seems, while thinking-through and talking-through whatever she is attending to, also to double herself, as if there were two "herselves." Indeed, the crucial preposition here, the prefix *dia*, "through," is cognate with *duo*, "two." Thus the translation of "dialogue" into German is *Zwiesprache*, "two-speech," as opposed to "monologue," "one-speech." It seems confusing because it is confusing; it is the crux of the question of inner speech and of the soul and its self-communication, or of consciousness and its self. So seriously: are we two or one when we address ourselves?

I want to enter an answer that preserves the uniqueness of this event. I call it an event, on the hypothesis that it eventuated, that in the course of our species' evolution, there was a first time when a first primate was first fully human and said "I" and then "me" and soon "myself."

There is no simile or likeness that faithfully analogizes this perpetual event to anything.* Internal asking and answering

> Except perhaps the notion of the Trinity, a triune divinity in which each person is at once all the others and yet distinctly itself. The Trinity is accepted as a sacred mystery, and thus *the biune soul might be said to be a secular mystery*, meaning that, concerning it, surmises are not profanities.

is not role-playing in which I relocate myself on an internal stage to take the role of the other, be it the one who is nescient or the one who is in the know; both termini of the inquiry-spectrum are simultaneously for real. So I am both at once; this is neither a monologue nor a duologue (actually a dictionary word). I seem to be veering off into the *via negativa* of inquiry here, but I think these negative ascriptions have positive implications: This turn-and-turn-about dialogue is not a play *I* am staging. Whence then does it eventuate?

I think it is educed by the matter itself. We live in a world of unknowns, the more so the longer we live, because the world gets larger and we a little wiser. We become more knowledge-able by a very little, but we get a good deal more adroit at framing our ignorance.

A world presents itself to our inner being. Forget whether it comes as itself, or as a sensory appearance, or as a mental image, or as an impression—it comes. It comes as a matter for appreciative or deprecating reception, of marveling or skeptical wondering. I don't get it; I don't like it; it feels familiar, it's a mess, it's a blessing. So I'm invited by the event, to—apt slang—scope it. That means I survey it first so as to delimit its sprawling vagueness and collect it into an *object* of interest from the outside in; then, second, from the inside out, so as to find an outline, a frame that determines a question capable of receiving, that is, recognizing, an answer. I think this means that the questioner has some foreknowledge of the answer. Thus the prescient questioner and the providing answerer are to some degree in the same place, are one and the same.

We have the uncanny ability to push *in* speech *past* speech, to say more than we can understand. I surmise that this is because speech, although deforming thought by embodying and externalizing it, yet stays true to it, if imperfectly: There is an old saying: *Traduttore/traditore*, "A translator is a traitor." Yet he's also a renderer, a transmitter.

I can think of two elements in this dilemma. One is that the activity of thought* acting within its adequate habitat may

Activity of thought = thinking; *act* of thought = idea.

well be capable of conjoining, of co-thinking what in utterance is a paradox in the derogatory sense. I mean that what sounds like transgression in speech may be truth in transcendence.

The other element concerns object-making ("objectification" is the fancy term). By and in speech we put a fairly sharply outlined object before ourselves. That is to say, we capture in speech (by a process ill understood in cognitive studies) a thought, a thought-act, which is "about" the thing. Now, since the thought and the thinking that "attains" the thought are, the former, thought-out thinkings and, the latter, thinkings that pass into thought, both are of the same stuff, insofar as whatever thought be made of can be called stuff or even material. Yet, when I think a thought (*think* it, not intuit it*), the thought, the idea does not blend into the thinking,

> Aristotle says that in intuiting (*noesis*), which is the mode of contemplation (*theoria*), the mind (*nous*) becomes its object (*On the Soul* III iv).

the operation. Speech can mimic this state of affairs, albeit imperfectly; this capability is called *intentionality*, which somehow—it is not known how—intends, reaches, snaffles, what the word "is about" and conveys that captured content to us. Yet the word's intention does not merge with its intended meaning; they are distinguishable; reach and grasp stay distinct.

Note that this is *a* theory of speech; there are others, for example, that words are labels (mental nametags somehow affixed to things) or symbols (verbal signs signifying by convention or similarity what particular something is meant).* In

> The last two have a satisfying ring but suffer, as theories, from the little difficulty of being terminally metaphorical; thus they require a demythifying metatheory.

any case, it seems to me that the intentionality of words, their aboutness, images the relation of the containing aboutness of thinking as an operation to its thought-objects. Only human mentation seems to be capable of intentionality (which is why no material contrivance can ever be said to think in the experiential sense. It appears that "aboutness" cannot be immattered, except in that one case, audible speech—when it is inexplicable except by postulated formalisms).*

> I've dealt most insufficiently with intentionality, a modern revival of a medieval term by Franz Brentano. He argued that all and only mental phenomena have the capability of aboutness.

Speech is very likely to have many features particularly suitable to rendering what we think, at least on the now unseasonable notion that thought and thinking generates speaking and knowing. A prime example is the subject-predicate form of declarative sentences in the languages with which most of us are familiar: It may be that most identifiable objects which enter the mind in thoughts are in fact concretions, coalescences exhibiting properties, and it is of these that we speak.*

The more current notion is that we think of things as being the underlying bearer of properties because that's how our language is constituted. To me it seems implausible. Why should the human beings among whom language evolved have found it advantageous to make up a subject-predicate language *not* true to its world? Otherwise put: Don't most things actually appear to us as substances underlying accidents—the very object-structure reflected in the grammatical terms?

An astounding article by eight well-known students of language, including Noam Chomsky, appeared in 2014 and is accessible online on Harvard's DASH. These researchers from as many fields agree that we have in effect *no evidence for the evolution of language*. A sensible amateur will have conjectured as much, above all because it is not, so far (?), provable that brain activity is either coextensive or homologous with thinking thoughts, nor is the brain, soft tissue, a good candidate for evolution studies.

I'll close with a summary. First, however, I should make sure that I acknowledge the partial character of my considerations. I've left out, on the low side, the continuous insignificant inner chatter that accompanies our mundane moods. And on the high side I've passed by our high-strung moments, those in which we're painfully impassioned and driven to unremitting self-inspection and those when we're happily astir and reveling in pleasant bookkeeping: "How do I love thee? Let me count the ways" (Elizabeth Barrett Browning, "Sonnets from the Portuguese" 43). And perhaps above all, the triumphantly accusatory silent orations by means of which public whining is forfended.

As I said in the beginning, some of this self-address can border on the pathological. There are those people from whom issue unstoppable torrents of talk when there is a listening ear, though it is not to communicate that they flow. When these talkers are alone, I imagine, the river goes underground—silent speech, but probably, as I said, more in the service of evincing thereness to oneself, more a sort of self-stimulation, than actual self-address hoping for a reply. My catalogue of the modes of inner speech probably doesn't begin to exhaust this type; I've but begun to attend the sessions of sweet silent thought.

Following Socrates, I'll begin my summary by holding myself harmless; I'll admit that I don't know but only conjecture, only figure, to myself what I'm saying, well knowing that similitudes are in principle inadequate here. Moreover, a poem comes to mind, though it be both mawkish and brutal (properties frequently conjoined):

> Flower in the crannied wall,
> I pluck you out of the crannies,
> I hold you here, root and all, in my hand

—and, the poem goes on: If I could understand you, "I should know what God and man is" (Alfred, Lord Tennyson, "Flower in the Crannied Wall"). Read it and think: That little flower is done for; you may understand something high up and down home, but the thing's dried up and dead. So the poem is apt to my enterprise. These so-called second-order inquiries, self-self-consciousness, as it were, may, no, *will*, be destructive of their object; It is just not possible both to think about something and to think about that thinking; the one occults the other. And yet, we do it.

So I must retract some. It *is* possible, in an iffy, dodgy way, which way is, moreover, in itself illuminating: If we do in fact stand in our way in self-inspection, that does seem to be testimony to our unity, to our being all one.* So to the summary

---

*"All one" is the etymology of "alone." To me that is significant because it points to a close connection of privacy to selfhood. Privacy is undoubtedly one of the very urgent psychic issues of postmodernity: Does its loss entail the demise of personhood?

of self-address:

1) I have an intimation, a mental impending; something demands attention.* I neutralize my exterior as much as possible:

> Belatedly, I should credit William James with the thought that our very own chief contribution to productive mentation is actually attention, focus ("Attention," Ch. XIII in *Abbreviated Psychology*, 1892).

the body is to be in that parenthetical state in which it is ignorable, not so much comfortable as unregarded; intrusive devices are on "off"; there's time enough to seem like time without end, nullified time.

2) Then I attend wittingly, try to focus, on what is yet without silhouette, to frame the question without being fully in sight of its object.

3) Then I formulate and reformulate into the linguistic utterance of which I am generally capable by my human species-nature, but which I possess in particular by having learned the conventions, a possession to which someone for whom English is a language learned past infancy might be particularly alert. This is the moment when the inner duologic monologue appears in all its two main enigmatic features, its ambivalence with respect to number and identity of participants and the mysterious source of its, possibly fresh, content. I, my personal self, am emphatically not the author of the question, which comes from the way things are and address me, nor of the answer, which arrives I know not whence nor how. I contribute only the effort of formulation.

And here I enter my main conclusion: In inner self-speech I am not addressing *me*, signifying as grammatical form a direct object and as a psychological condition an objectified other. I am rather speaking to *myself*, grammatically a reflexive pronoun signifying, even in the oblique case (here dative), identity: In Greek, it might be in the "middle voice." This linguistically dyadic speaking is really a duologic monologue: *I'm two-in-one*—no subterfuge, no "so to speak."

4) Moreover, such inner speech is also—just about—
"outer," is *utterance*. This speaking mediates between private musing and public declaration; it commutes thinking,
an internal activity, into communicating; it's the outering. To
this mediating, commuting, conveying function *silent utterance* that is both unheard and yet vocalized is well adapted:
"Heard melodies are sweet, but those unheard / Are sweeter"
(John Keats, "Ode on a Grecian Urn"). Just so such inner
speech as sometimes survives in writing and is edited out by
responsible editors in the interests of linguistic normality, is
sweetest to its originator.

5) Finally, the defects of internal utterance, of this unedited
self-address. These consist of the contingent disappointments
in wait for the speaker gone colloquially public, and in the in-
principle incapacities of language itself. The disappointment
is in the ordinariness that ensues when the off-the-rack suit of
linguistic clothing now safely invests our newly housebroken
ideas and even presents these homeschooled thoughts in institutional uniform. The in-principle incapacity of speech, while
welcome testimony to the potency of pre-linguistic mentation—welcome because the aboutness of our speech is here
first engaged*—also severely inhibits the verisimilitude, the

> Some writers claim it as true that there is no thinking without
> speaking: Thinking requires speaking. (Everyone agrees that the
> converse, "speaking requires thinking," is quite false.) Thus Lud-
> wig Wittgenstein says (along with much else): "When I think in lan-
> guage, it is not the case that beside the linguistic expression some
> 'meanings' float before me; but rather the language itself is the vehi-
> cle of thinking" (*Philosophical Investigations* no. 327 ff., esp. 329). To
> me, Wittgenstein's vehicle metaphor countermands and displays
> the implausibility of the claim. In my life, a vehicle, say a pickup,
> carries loads that are different from the truck itself; thus language
> truly *conveys* meaning, which is distinct from the former and has in-
> deed, if not "floated before me," preceded speech, namely within me.

truth-likeness of our most determinate conscious mode; we
simply can't render our mind's apprehension accurately; we
are so made as to fall forever short of our own intimations.

A final thought: I am the firmest believer in the commonality of thoughts, the condition of their communicability. Now "common" and "shared" are often identified, which seems to me the loss of a valuable distinction. Bodily, material matter can be shared; that piece I twist off from your kindly-shared power bar leaves you with less.* Non-physical things,

There may be counterexamples, but I can't think of them. Time-sharing? But that means giving up our opportunity for some specific time. Room-sharing? Just try living higgledy-piggledy without assigned private places, inaccessible to the housemate.

however, are common in their very being. We participate in them not in the sense of *taking off a part* but of *taking our part in* being together by means of them.* Nor need we be

Here is a possible complication: I think that our soul comes to us clearly and distinctly only in an embodiment—like speech. Thus Aristotle calls the passions "immattered ratio-relations" (*enhyloi logoi, On the Soul* I i), pointing both to their vivid bodily presence within us and their proportionateness to an object without. In that sense it might be possible to "give," against a poet's advice, "your heart away" (A.E. Housman, "When I Was One-and-Twenty")—perhaps by collapsing the ratio relation?

actually together for this commonality. The best example I can think of is the silent reading that so impressed Augustine who is to me the finest of phenomenologists. Millions of us must have read his *Confessions*, by ourselves, alone. And yet we have it in common and, if quantity is pertinent in regard to the soul at all, we might say that our lonely reading amplified the book by a factor of a million or more. This is the consequent question: Can the eventuations in our soul, and above all, the address of herself to herself, be under a common description, or are we finally self-pleasingly idiosyncratic ("peculiarly blended") and incorrigibly eccentric ("off-center")? Is what I've figured out here a description of my particular case or a delineation of the common condition?

15

Tips on Reading Homer
And on Writing Yourself

For our graduate students.

I'm not sure that I have much faith in what I've agreed to do here: give advice on how to read Homer's two epics, the *Iliad* and the *Odyssey*. Actually, in my heart of hearts I think: Do it any way that suits you, as long as you do it. But occasionally I've had the experience of telling people how to do things, such as advising our undergraduate seniors on their essay-writing, and they've listened and done it, and even said they were the better for it. Those are triumphant moments for a teacher. So I'll barge ahead and give some tips that might help.

We call these two huge poems, and others that explicitly relate to them (such as Virgil's *Aeneid* and Milton's *Paradise Lost*), *epics*. The *Odyssey* begins with the words *Andra moi ennepe, Mousa, polytropon.* . . ." I'll translate like this: "The man—put him into words for me, O Muse, that man of many roles. . . ." The man is not named until later, but it is Odys-

---

A transcription of two talks with students of the Graduate Institute.

seus. Homer is preparing to be spoken to of a many-sided
man, a man of great virtuosity.*

> A recent translation by Emily Wilson renders *polytropos* as "com-
> plex." It's clever, but I have my doubts: My Odysseus can take many
> turns, assume many roles: warrior, pirate, skipper, craftsman,
> lover, leaver, liar—and poet. But he can go whole-heartedly simple
> when the moment demands it.

The *Iliad*, in contrast, begins thus: *Menin aeide, thea, Pele-
iadeo Achileos / oulomenen. . . .* "The anger sing, O Goddess, of Peleus' son Achilles / the fatal anger. . . ." Homer in
the *Odyssey* is asking the Muse (she is the same as the goddess, I think) to speak to him in *words* of Odysseus, a whole
man of many parts and much experience, but in the *Iliad* to
sing to him the *song* of Achilles, a man contracted into this
soul- and life-corroding wrath.

For both poems, Homer appeals to one of the nine Olympian divinities, the Muses, each of whom is in charge of one
of the arts. (Calliope is the muse who supervises epic, but
Homer does not name her in his invocations.) To repeat: He
asks her to *speak* to him, to put words in him: *en[n]epe.* So
epic, *epos* in Greek, "word," is here rightly named; for Odysseus, the Muse gives the poet *words*—puts them into him,
lets him in on the tale. But of Achilles, he asks to be sung to;
it's not as much a tale to be told as an event that reverberates.

Note: this poet does not believe he is being creative; he
thinks he needs to hear and to listen: Poetry comes *from* him
only because it came *to* him, both as narrative and as poetry.

We might ask a number of comparing questions: Why
must Achilles' anger be rendered as a *song* while Odysseus's
humanity is told in *speech*? Why are poetic figures of speech
rarer in the *Odyssey*? Why is the heavenly singer called a goddess and the same heavenly speaker a muse? Why does Homer
ask the muse to speak *to him* about Odysseus but doesn't
mention himself in his prayer about Achilles' anger? But once
again I'm going where I don't want to be: into comparison.

Comparative Literature is the very last thing I want to draw you into, because it should, in fact, come, if at all, *last* when each work has been read and reread and lived in as a world in itself. Premature comparison of works, or worse, whole "literatures" gives you mostly empty abstractions, skeleton stories without the flesh of particularity.

So let me extract from this comparison of first lines a first tip: We know from the *Odyssey* itself that palaces had a resident bard, a so-called rhapsode, which means a "stitcher-together of song"—their names were Demodocus, Phemius, and even Odysseus himself. They intoned the lines without script and accompanied themselves on the lyre. But at some point these song-medleys became written works and eventually ceased to be musical performances, becoming instead reading experiences, words altogether, certainly for us.

So we are readers, not, as were the ancients, hearers—they must have been stupendously acute auditors. From that follows the pertinence of Tip One. Whoever Homer was (we do not definitely know), whether you think of him as the redactor, the composer and overseer of the last oral composition as it went into the written mode or as the first literary poet, the first to have supervised a version using the recently introduced alphabet (a version which is actually said to have been prepared in Athens)—however you regard him, *expect the height of sophistication.* This man—in the nineteenth century Samuel Butler propagated the kooky notion that it was a woman, namely Princess Nausikaa of the phantasy-land Phaeacia, called "Scheria," the "Cut-off Land"—this Homer, the first and greatest of all poets, perhaps assisting his own hyper-acute memory with writing, that artificial external memory, and, armed with the keenest knowledge of humanity and the subtlest art of expression, transformed old lays into surely timeless epics. Here is what follows for us, his latest readers, my Tip Two: *Be kept continually off-kilter* by the recognition that you're missing a lot. It's a little like starving yourself in expectation of a feast; you become sharp-set, hungry for discoveries.

At the same time it's absolutely unnecessary to look up every unknown term or to recall every name. The ghost of a memory is enough to alert you if a thing or person suddenly acquires a new significance. In a word, my Tip Three: Rewardingly attentive reading is not stodgily pedantic trudging. Be alert, but *don't force it*.

So as not to be talking vacuously, let me give examples of micro-artistry. I mean small but wonderful detail, such as pervades Homer's poems. In the ninth book of the *Iliad*, Odysseus, the great diplomat among the Greeks, is sent by his king and commander, Agamemnon, on an embassy to Achilles, who sits sulking in his tent, nursing his wrath against this king who has taken away his prize of battle, a woman Achilles has grown fond of. His absence from the battle against the Trojans endangers the whole Greek expedition. Odysseus is instructed to bring him back into the fight by means of a list of gifts of restitution and Agamemnon's oath that he has never slept with Achilles' captive. This message Odysseus pretty much repeats: "I will swear an oath," he recites, "that I never went up into her bed or had intercourse with her as is usual. . . ." The king's message went: "as is usual among men and women." But Odysseus stops and adds both a word, and, I think, a bow. He says: "as is usual, *my lord*, among men and women." It is a grace note, which to miss deprives the reader of a pleasure. But noticing it requires some oral memory of what was said a hundred and forty-two lines earlier. So my tip here amounts to this: Have faith in Homer's artistry and you'll be more apt not to miss it, since it's everywhere—but don't be strenuous about it.

I said that I myself added the courteous inclination of the small, short-legged diplomat. Homer, incidentally, leaves hints of his favorite's, Odysseus's, looks all over; he says, for instance, that he appears larger sitting down than standing up. I meant to convey that I visualized the scene. The ancient report was, as we've all heard, that Homer was blind. No one knows whether the final artist of the epics was in fact sightless, but if he was, it wasn't from birth and, if he wasn't, it was a clever fabrication. For these poems are one long incitement to visualization, such as we can imagine takes place in the imagination of a man who, undistracted by casual gawking, sees what he is intoning to himself more intensely. Blind Milton, who wrote the only epic I know of that can vie with Homer's, corroborates the claim, since *Paradise Lost* is full of terrific spectacles. In fact the Homeric epics at times require listeners, be they an ancient audience at an oral recital or a modern solitary reader, to see what Homer doesn't explicitly say. I'll give you the most spectacular example I know of, in all my reading.

It is the climactic day of the *Iliad*, in the twenty-second book. Hector has killed Achilles' friend Patroclus. Here is a great passionate friendship, not erotic but that much the more fervent. Now Achilles is chasing his friend's killer around the citadel of Troy. Hector, the crown prince of Ilium, whose name means the "prop" or "stay" of Troy, turns around and falls. Achilles stands over him and sees him not face-to-face but concealed by his face-covering armor. This is the armor Hector had taken from dead Patroclus. But it is not Patroclus's own armor either. It is Achilles' armor that he had given to Patroclus, who had begged to enter the battle as Achilles' surrogate. (Recall that Achilles has angrily withdrawn from the war and refused even Odysseus's diplomatic peace-making.) Now Achilles is about to drive his spear into Hector's jugular. What is he looking at? He sees Patroclus in armor and behind Patroclus he sees himself. Homer does not say a word; he has barely reminded us of what Hector is wearing sometime earlier. When Achilles thrusts he kills both his friend and himself—for his mother has told him that he will die in the war he himself is now bringing to an end.

Here's my Tip Four: *Always visualize*, and the action will become more poignant.

And then turn your attention back to words, which will corroborate the vision: Five books earlier, when the news of Patroclus's death was first brought to him, Achilles had cried out, using a phrase that has a double meaning in Greek: "Him have I lost," but also "Him have I killed"—a truth, if we recall that Achilles has allowed Patroclus to go forth to battle in Achilles' armor, a tender man falsely emboldened and exposed beyond his warrior-abilities.

To be sure, translators don't notice or can't convey this double meaning, this example of Homer's verbal ingenuity. So my Tip Five here would have to be: *Learn Greek*. It is not an altogether silly notion, when we consider to what not so profitable discretionary activities we do in fact devote our free time.

Just as in order to get the most out of the poems that are full of sights, it helps to *see* what isn't straightforwardly *said*, so to get the most out of poems that are essentially made of words (recall: the epics are in both worlds), it helps to *hear* what is only implicitly said. Here's a fine example, which my favorite translator, the poet Robert Fitzgerald, does catch. It is from the *Odyssey*.

Penelope, the queenly wife, has been waiting for her husband's return from Troy for twenty years, keeping together their much exploited estate and bringing up their much endangered boy, Telemachus.

Let me interrupt myself here to point to another aspect of Homer's tale that deserves attention: names. We don't know how bound he was by his oral tradition ("Hector," for instance, was probably inherited), but my guess is that some of the name-felicities are his own. Thus Odysseus's son, a shy boy whom he left in Ithaca as an infant, is called Telemachus, which means "Far-from-Battle," while Achilles' fierce son, whom he left at home in Phthia, is called Neoptolemus, "New-to-War," which indeed he is when he comes to Troy after his father's death. And while I'm at it, *Phthia* has in it the sound of a verb that means dying. Achilles, full of wrath at the insult Agamemnon has put on him, has threatened to go home, to his "deathland." When he stabs the image of himself in the throat he is in fact, as I said, going to his death.

So my Tip Six for reading Homer is: Be aware that beneath your notice *the poem is boiling away with intimations.* That is, as I've suggested before, the root of a good reader's virtues: alertness.

To get back to Penelope and to listening for unspoken words. When you come to discuss the *Odyssey,* one lovely question might be: At what point does Penelope recognize the wrinkled beggar as the husband for whom she has been waiting for over two decades while stringing along by a strategem the suitors for her hand who have been besieging the palace? She tells them that when she has finished weaving the funeral cloth, the shroud for her retired father-in-law, Odysseus's father Laertes, she'll be ready to make a choice. So by day she weaves, and what she adds by day she undoes at night, thereby, I think we are to imagine, postponing Laertes' death indefinitely.

So Odysseus turns up, worn and wrinkled. It is part of his nature to undergo sudden transformations of appearance. I think of him as maybe forty-five or fifty (past middle age in Mediterranean climes), though sometimes he blooms into lusty youth. She hears his voice in her halls before she sees him. Then begins what I think of as a canny game between them: He pretends to be a vagabond but an old friend of her husband. She pretends that he is a news-bringing guest. When does she recognize him? I say: when she hears his voice, even before she sees him: How wouldn't she? They are, forever and always, the archetypal husband and wife, equal and coordinated. For example, he always speaks of her, his consort, in royal, kingly—not queenly—similes.

But in case you think it's not a cautious, cunning game, here's what happens, to prove it: She invites him to a private conference in the evening—very unconventional—and orders the old nurse of the house, Euryclea, to wash his feet, as is the hospitable custom. Here is what she says to the servant:

> But come, get up now, circumspect Euryclea,
> And wash your lord's—age-mate's feet.

The end of the line—she has forgotten herself for a brief moment, and is about to make a slip—was clearly to be "wash your lord's feet." She quickly recovers and substitutes "age-mate's." A moment later the foot clatters into the basin as his old nurse recognizes an old scar on his leg. Penelope doesn't notice—Athena has turned her mind away. Athena is the divinity of the quick mind; Penelope is alertly self-possessed, deliberately absent-minded. For everything depends on their common discretion, guarding the secrecy of his return; they know that to acknowledge each other even in private may lead to public self-betrayal.

Tip Seven here is: Be alert to *quick twists away from the expected*. Homer knows what he is doing.

Tip Eight: Homer is *the most subtle psychologist* you'll ever read, partly because he's not impeded by psychological type-jargon. The royal couple between them, with the aid of their son, now a young man, and a couple of faithful servants, have utterly defeated, in a blood-bath, the hundreds of suitors infesting the palace. But they have not yet had a moment of recognition. Penelope, whose very life was faithfulness, is strangely withheld, reluctant. She imposes a test. What actually *is* the test? Homer does not say overtly. She tells Odysseus that she has cut loose their marriage bed, built by him, which was literally rooted in a once-live olive tree. When he hears this, Odysseus, the unflappable, loses it, as we would say: he goes ballistic. And that, Homer intimates, is for Penelope the completely satisfactory passing of the test—the spontaneous emotional acknowledgement that his marriage has not lost its hold on him. Together they go to bed, where he tells her, in his bardic mode, all his adventures with witches and demi-goddesses. No, more: in effect, he is, as he was in Phaeacia, the poet of his own poem. And in this candid telling, mostly of female encounters, he wisely leaves out one: the youngest, the girl-woman, the Phaeacian princess who shyly fell in love with him and whom he promised never to forget. This man knows what's what.

Tip Nine: As always, *watch for what isn't said*, but, above all and again (perhaps all my tips are one) expect in Homeric epic a sophistication concerning the human soul as it was and is, and I hope ever will be, beyond what you're used to in contemporary novels. Poetry is not progressive.

Now finally, the poetic figure that particularly distinguishes Homeric poetry, the simile. Here's my favorite, from the *Iliad*, eighth book. An otherwise undistinguished young Trojan is shot to death by an arrow in the chest. Homer says:

And like a poppy he let fall his head to one side, a poppy that is
    in a garden
Laden with fruit and the showers of spring,
So he bowed to one side his head made heavy with helmet.

Formally a simile is a comparison of similars—here "as a poppy, so the head." Homer likes to put the imagined comparison first and that matters.

Thus the last, Tip Ten: I've talked about the importance of visualizing Homeric scenes. Similes require a *double visualization*. So, *first* see the poppy, blowy red flower, stem buckled just below the petals by the weight of the fruit capsule and the raindrops. Then lay over that backdrop as a transparency the picture of a young warrior, his head bent over his slim dead body by his heavy helmet. Hold both together in your inner eye, and ask yourself: What is Homer doing with this dual vision? Is it a message of despair—human violence outdoing nature? Or is it one of comfort—war as part of, and partaking of, nature? It will be a wonderful conversation. The gist of my Tip Ten is: *Take similes as incitements to seeing double and thinking that out.*

As you can imagine, this isn't the half of it. I could talk of Homer's descriptive genius for infusing places with atmospheres, of his artfully intimating modifications of the dactylic hexameter line, of his cleverly intricate interweaving of timelines, and on the grandest scale, of the very precise contrasts and comparisons delineating his two antithetical heroes: short-lived, swift-footed, blazing Achilles and long-lived, versatile, undercover Odysseus in their own and each other's poems. Instead I'll let you go to read them.

Now, briefly to your own writing, on writing yourself:

1) I can't resist this, though it is not to the point exactly. It's something more about how to read than how to write, though discovering such devices might embolden you as writers. How many of you have read Plato's *Republic*? If you have, or expect to, do the following. The numbers in the margin are called Stephanus pages. First calculate how many of them the *Republic* has, then find the middle page, which you can do by a little arithmetic. Then open to the middle page. Look at where you are—and marvel at how this book is written: You've landed on Socrates' introduction of the philosopher kings, its central notion. Try it yourself, but don't force it.

2) There is only one semi-moral injunction (one might say), one piece of advice concerning writing: Do it. The way to write a paper is to sit down and write it. (Or walk, stand, squat, lie—best in a warm tub.)

3) Don't drivel. What do I mean by driveling? Freshmen will write a paper that begins: "Euclid was the greatest mathe-

matician that ever was." That's drivel. If you've written a sentence that's bombastic or vacuous, don't use it. Cross it out.

4) Have a fellow student or friend read your paper. Let that person correct your spelling and your punctuation, as long as you do the following: Whether you accept the correction or not, know why. This is the honest way to learn to spell and punctuate correctly and hand in clean work.

5) Use the word "I." I used to startle students in paper conferences by saying, "Did you write this paper?" They'd look at me as if I were accusing them of something. I'd say, "It's all in the passive, there aren't any personal pronouns. You don't take charge." So use the word "I"—you're years beyond your self-love-suppressing high-school teacher. *You* are writing the paper, and its writing should engage you in a very immediate way. Your personal experience should turn up. You don't have to give it in personal terms. You could fictionalize it, or you can present it as an anecdote, but there's no reason why you and what you've learned in life shouldn't appear. In fact, it lends zest to a paper if it includes an account of the way your personal experience bears on what you are thinking about.

6) Here is a practical thing to do: Make an outline. An outline is good not because you're going to use it as a constraint—you can throw it out before you're finished—but because it means that when you get up in the morning or sit down in the evening or in the afternoon or whenever you have time to work, you know what to do next. And in writing a paper, it's very important to know that, to be in a revved-up midst rather than at a cold outset.

7) Therefore never finish writing completely. If you're working late at night, when you find that you're one paragraph before having said all you can think of, stop. Then when you next get to it, you're not starting cold. And you know how much more difficult starting is than going on.

8) When you've completed the paper, if you followed your outline, use its parts as subheadings. Papers with subheadings

are not just easier for others to read, but also easier for you to survey, so as to judge whether you've developed your line of thought clearly.

9) If you can, wait for the Muse to descend and welcome her eagerly. If she comes—and she will come—she'll give you the opening sentence. Recognize a really good opening, the harbinger of an engaging paper. An *unpromising* beginning: "Kant's *Prolegomenon* is very hard to understand but contains many important ideas"—not at all false but worse: banal. A promising beginning: "Kant's *Prolegomenon* claims credit for radical novelty, and is therefore both hard and engaging." However, consider that a captivating first sentence may also turn out to be the last to be written—a forerunner or summation.

10) Here is something I believe in, but this may not work for you. I think you should be absolutely preoccupied by the paper you're writing. Think about it wherever you happen to be. That way it attains a certain ripeness, and, once more, when you sit down you know what you're going to be doing. So it really makes sense to devote yourself to this task utterly, on the one hand. On the other hand, don't make too much of it. This is kind of tricky, and my advice has two sides to it. On the one hand, I've just said, "Really concentrate, spend the week devoted to this." On the other hand, here's the somewhat pusillanimous contrary side: "Don't let it overwhelm you or scare you. After all, it's only an exercise." Find some way to combine being involved and not being overwhelmed; say to yourself, a little flabbily: "I really want to do this well, but if it doesn't work out—next time." As ever, the sound solvent of these embroilments is *interest*; once you're interested, all paper-agonies disperse.

11) Start early. If the paper assignment was made today, start thinking about it tonight. Don't do anything at the last moment. Writing is not something you can do quickly. It takes time, it's got to ripen. So be finished sometime before

the thing is due, then let it stew in its own juice. Just before handing it in give it a last reading/tasting. Add some literary condiments and corrections, and make it perfect. Another way to put it: achievable perfection simply takes time, so give it time.

12) And now, the most important tip, implicit in those preceding, but countermanding the notion I voiced above, "It's only an exercise." It's never just an exercise: Write on something you care about. It could be a problem or a question. A problem is something you can solve; a question is something you can clarify. It could be a book you love; it could be a book you hate (for hate, too, is engagement); it could be a sentence that grips you; it could be a passage you don't understand. But whatever it is, try to find something that seizes you. Don't do it in a bureaucratic sort of way, a routine requirement to check off. Do it purposefully with passion. Most of you probably know this: Passion can be self-induced. You can rouse it in yourself: When something interests you, focus on it. And if you're not "into it" after dwelling on it for a while, chuck it out and switch topics. No doubt about it, the most efficacious advice I have to give you is: Love it or leave it.

Annapolis, 2017

16

Novels over Dramas
Command Performance

It's a personal taste. I'm a devoted reader of novels, but I go to plays only if one of my students is involved. Now our students think—not one and all, but by and large—that there's no accounting for tastes. But if you can't give an account for your attachments, what *can* you explain? Moreover, I was challenged by my esteemed publisher to defend my preference. So, by Paul's orders, I'll try.

"Drama" is Greek and means "Things Done," actions. "Novel" is Latin and means "Novelty," news.

Greek drama, tragedies, were mostly—modified—enactments of myths, old stories currently circulated by bards, singing poets. Many mythical plots were derived from an epic matrix (Aristotle, *Poetics*, Ch. 26).

Our novels are the fictional counterparts of the proto-newspapers of early modernity; these latter printed "ballads" were intended to be read more than sung and reported natural and social catastrophes (Lennard J. Davis, *Factual Fictions*, 1983; there were proto-novels in antiquity, post-classical prose-epics, romances of love and adventure, fairly light reading, see Tomas Hägg, *The Novel in Antiquity*, 1983).

Novels are *our* literature; in title-number they surely over-whelm the other going genres: plays, lyric poetry and certainly epic, and in word count, more so by a factor of thousands. Novels are, to be sure, outdone quantitatively in turn by peri-odical and documentary print, that is, non-literature. (I mean by non-literature, verbal productions in which fictionality is the result either of ignorance or ill intention.)

Novels are most neatly compared to epics, to which they seem to me close because both are long but unlike because they are in *prose*, while epics are in *verse*. "Verse," literally a turning (Latin *vertere*, "to turn"), gives epics the framing of rhythmic elevation and repetitive stability, while "prose," lit-erally a forward-turning, from *proversus* (past participle of *provertere*, "to turn forward"), gives novels a feel of entrepre-neurial business and ingenious novelty.

Let me admit right now that what—or whom—I really like best is epic Homer and late-found Milton—the latter espe-cially for my namesake, a far more modern woman than I can "boast myself to be" (Homeric diction). But "like" is the wrong word: I don't like their words enough to be read-ing them when not on assignment, but I *love* them for being lodged in my imagination so that their imagery, panoramic or local, steals, be it as overlay or background, into my daily scenes.

What I read uncommandeered and continuously is novels. Our epoch is not only thick with prose fiction but actually rich in fine novels. The present century is too young for a great one to have cast loose from the pack. (Perhaps the Fer-rante novels will survive re-readings.) But in the last century there were such, and they are close to my heart. Whenever I pull one off the shelf, from Thomas Mann's Joseph novels to Paul Scott's *Raj Quartet*, I'm at home and settle down.

So, with a few more preliminaries, I'll get to my question-able denigration of stageable plays in favor of book-length stories—"questionable" because of my high respect for classical tragedies. One of these, Aeschylus's *Eumenides*, speaks to me most intimately because it is the very model of perspicuously reverent patriotism, while in our early modernity there is Shakespeare's *Macbeth*, a similarly acute poem about personal and public tyranny, the political problem to which I'm most attuned. (See Essays 21 and 22, "*The Eumenides*" and "Lady Macbeth.") Nonetheless, I'll barge on, happily preceded in genre-choosiness by Aristotle, who says that tragedy is obviously superior to epic for its compression (*Poetics*, Ch. 26). Novels were as yet an uninvented genre, or Aristotle would, I think, have put them as most inferior because most distended, rarely grand, and thus least "poetic." Here, then, are some reasons for my preferences:

1) Life takes time. No, life *makes* time. By life I mean embodied awareness, some of it *below* present perception, or, as we say, *sub*conscious.* The chief subconscious power is our

As distinct from the incoherent notion of "unconscious," that is, mentation inaccessible to its enactor without expert mediation.

memory, the partly accurate, partly transformed store both of perceived and of imagined events; even its possibility is a, possibly ultimate, mystery. Time arises by the sequence-tagged laminations of memory. By going down into memory, by recalling internal or external perceptions, we produce times past; by going up, projecting ahead internal perceptions, that is, imagery, we generate times future. Thus aware living generates human time.

A good life is, in my experience, devoid of disruptively isolated incidents, be they wonderful or, more often, terrible. For these cast over the continually recurrent events of ordinary life the leaden light that surrounds extraordinary glare; they overshadow the glows of dailiness. Extraordinariness can be addictive and will call out in-between time-killing addictions; celebrities die young.

A great drama is a dense, compressed irruption into the

play-goer's day. It's finished in two and a half hours; you rub your eyes and issue into sallow daylight. Once, in London, I fell in love with the actor and the character of Thomas More in Robert Bolt's *Man for All Seasons*. I went three nights in a row. (My friends went elsewhere.) It closed out the budget but did not fulfill desire.

Novels, on the other hand, take their time; their temporal tempo is much more like actual living. To be sure, life has its meaning-devoid moments,* while novels are meaning-dense.

> Mostly during so-called "amusements" (cited before: from Old French for "stupid staring").

Read a little on many a busy day or read for long on a rare free day—a really big novel, and it's not coincidence that many great novels are also big,* will take weeks to live through. A

> Here's a sort of proof that, as is rarely the case for public speech, for novels, length is a positive attribute. Thus the lately invented genre-busting "flash fiction" is probably a fly-by-night novelty.

king, a queen, a prince, the chosen occupant of plays, "struts and frets his hour upon the stage," but the normal residents of a novel, a citizen, husband, wife, youngster, will, if all goes well, amble their decades through life.* The genre for this

> The poignant model of a modern, democratic, common man's counterpart to the ancient royal and very public tragedy is Arthur Miller's *Death of a Salesman*, tellingly subtitled "Certain *Private* [my italics] Conversations in Two Acts and a Requiem." It is nonetheless a corroboration of tragic exceptionalism. Biff, the son of Willy *Loman* [my italics], the tragedy's hero, speaks of him as "a fine troubled prince" (Act Two), and, while his wife calls him, lovingly, "a small man" to whom, however, "attention must be paid," his second son describes him as having had a dream: "To come out number-one man" (Requiem).

time-honored, life-supporting ordinariness is the novel— ongoing, full of incidents tethered to before and after, to circumstances happening and events eventuating, and ending, just as do good things in life, a little before "Tis not so sweet now as it was before." In short, novels abound in novel eventuations because they have the means to convey their ground: the ordinary. You can be with, live in, go through a novel in the temporal mode of real life: coherent duration. 2) But, on the other hand, you can get out at will. You buy a seat at a play, you're stuck, imprisoned.* Partly because, just

> You might say that watching together with others is, in fact, an enhancement. That was surely true in an ancient outdoor theater, nestled into the side of your acropolis, in seats without arms to lower and houselights to be dimmed, so as to fence you off from and render you blind to your rowmate. Moreover, those dramas were not primarily entertainments but civil solemnities and uncivil high jinks.

as in a respectably philistine household, like my childhood home, you eat what's on your plate, so, as a solid, thrifty adult, you consume what you've paid for. Besides, you came with someone who wants to stay—and is your ride. Once or twice we coincided. In Santa Fe's spectacular opera house, I found myself at Alban Berg's relentlessly murderous *Lulu*. My friend and I looked at each other, and we barged our way out, mercilessly climbing over the row of knees. I'd gone to train my naïvely baroque ear up to modern sophistication, but that project remained unmournedly incomplete.

3) A novel I read at home in my reading chair. If I want to do it to the—admittedly solecistic—accompaniment of my music, who's to say me nay? And that guy, who, albeit he has a perfect right to be four feet tall from the waist up so as to obscure my view—why must he be a beanpole in front of *my* seat? The creature comforts are all on the side of reading over spectating.

4) If I miss part of a show because I'm rooting around in my popcorn bucket, it's lost. A book is all there, always.

5) The greatest plays are in verse, novels are in prose. Verse, blank verse, by its very stable recurrence gets under your skin but also on your nerves: it's sacrosanct, while prose is permis-

sibly paraphrasable. The retelling of a novelistic plot is not necessarily travesty.

6) Since life takes time, and that time is only two-thirds waking hours, we are, at least I am, geared so as to come to slowly. Not all I take in comes immediately to reflective awareness, so I miss a lot, now not from distractions but from the fleetingness of occurrences on stage. But also from what you might call engaged distraction: our—my—apparently insuperable habit of internal comment is not conducive to total empathy.* When I watch a tragedy unfold on the stage, my

> Not that empathy seems to me an actual human possibility; sympathy, "feeling with," yes, but "feeling in," as in another soul—that's illusory. To be in one's own trouble is just insuperably different from being even the most involved attendant.

mind wanders pseudo-helpfully: what little bit of sanity-restoring sensibleness would prevent this from happening? In my spectator's seat I'm then nullifying the tragedian's intention.* In fact, in Greek drama there's evidence that the

> Example: If you've heard from an authoritative source that you'll kill your father and marry your mother, for heaven's sake don't lose your temper at any elderly man you come across and don't marry any woman with nearly grown-up children.

dramatist doesn't want me going off on my own: the customary Chorus of elderly persons anticipating my very exegesis. That's its proper business: to pre-think me and prevent my musing at the drama's expense.

In my reading chair, however, I will miss nothing by stopping the works; moreover, I'm probably fulfilling the writer's hopes, who may, in fact, wish to instigate my private thinking by his people's actions. So we may both decide that a fatal catastrophe is not in this world's best interest, and, not being a tragedian, my novelist may, with my glad approval, devise a wonderful novelty "to restore every body, not greatly in fault themselves, to tolerable comfort," as says the most perfect of them all (*Mansfield Park*).

7) The liberating simplicity of the productive process of writing is, I think, inversely mirrored in the enjoyable complexity of the work. To write a book, you need a writing tablet and a pencil (at best); to put on a play, you need a playwright, a playhouse, a producer, a director, actors, stagehands (boys, "monkeys," whatever), and loads of money. All these too many cooks roil the broth; a staged play, the actualized drama, is not always, maybe rarely, a realization of the dramatist's intention. It's an odd kind of artifact whose actualization may be its artist's despair.* And if it all comes together,

True of music too, of course, but there the constraints on miscontrual are stricter. To me it's a disconcerting perplexity: Teamwork, mutual submission to compromise, is the vital force of politics, but for great artistry it's the single soul in her sovereign discernment.

it's still a small venue of three walls (or "in the round," in which case you're treated to backsides three-quarters of the time). A novelist, on the other hand, can single-handedly deliver worlds—an authentic *author* (Latin: "creator").

That's for production. Something similar holds for consumption. Play-going is lots more expensive than book-buying, and then you have to find a parking place and eat out.

Now it gets serious.

8) Staged drama is seriously overdetermined; I'm shown too much, though the pretense is discombobulating, for the characters are real people, yet not the ones they pretend to be; the setting is a three-dimensional, materialized venue, though not actually inhabitable; everything that moves does so scriptedly, the same every performance—jigged spontaneity. In the cinematic genre the stuff, the matter, is gone, but now magical morphings become possible, preempting my fantasy. In short, *I'm relieved of imagining.* And that's just what the strictly verbal book requires: my exercise of our most mystifying capacity, that of turning words into images. Great novelists have just this art, that of painting with words, a deliberately paradoxical trope, but the very figure for catching the magical fact

that speech may intend to invoke sight. But it's left to me to produce this drama on the internal scene. I actualize the text, from battlefield scene to soirée, from the scoundrel's sour grin to the saint's sweet smile. I get to stay upright in one of those word slaloms over a page and a half on which Thomas Mann takes me, and to be bowled over by the moral boldness Charlotte Brontë insinuates into her Victorian proprieties. Once again, performed drama is of necessity overdetermined, too specific, while, for all their verbal copiousness, novels are imaginatively understated.

9) Drama queens or kings, or, for that matter, statesmen, live their stage lives in epitome; they have no time to round themselves out. So they are "abstractions," aspects "drawn off" from wholes. The immediate consequence is that they function as symbols; they *represent* the fates and the features that make them dramatic but are in other respects curtailed beings. Thus the tragic hero of heroes, Oedipus, smart and impulsive, caringly kingly and truth-seekingly blinkered, is the man for his oracle—and not much else.

But no grand novel I know is symbolic. Novels do signify universal truths, but if they do it directly they do it smilingly: "It is a truth universally acknowledged . . ."—which the novel indeed brings to particular fruition, for "the single man in possession of a good fortune" does find that he is "in want of a wife," who, in turn, whatever she may allow herself to think, is in need of getting away from her family and not averse to being the mistress of a fine estate like Pemberley.*

> The words above from *Pride and Prejudice* are (probably) the most famous opening of an English novel. Isn't it interesting that the American counterpart, by way of frequent citation, "Call me Ishmael" of *Moby-Dick*, is as darkly fraught as the former is brightly nimble: Ishmael, the wild man and outcast, is not-Isaac, is the less-loved half-brother of him whose name means "Laughter" (Genesis 21). Islands tend to affect supple lightness, continents go for bearing burdens.

The novelistic way to universals is that a portrait, be it of a person or a venue, is so replete with pertinent detail that its significance, its universal involvement in the scheme of things, emerges, albeit unelicited. It is an ever-perplexing question how concrete and ultimate individuality manages to bear the mark of ideality, but great novels prove that it does. It does so more densely, in fact, than does real life, because life has those dead times of total unmeaning, while an artifact—that's its magic—is everywhere replete with significance, often more so in its prosaic than its passionate passages.*

> Example: Jane Eyre's human type is more in evidence as a teacher of Mr. Rochester's little French ward, whom she only half likes, than in her moments of grand erotic drama, such as her facing down his impetuous pleas. At least, I think so.

That's my budget of positive arguments for novels over drama: 1. lifelike temporality, 2. free engagement, 3. creature comforts, 4. perpetual presence, 5. paraphrasable prose, 6. mental commentary, 7. liberating simplicity, 8. imaginative involvement, 9. human repleteness.

Finally: There were nine Muses in antiquity, among which were one each for epics, tragedies, lyrics, love songs, and comedies. But, of course, the latter-day novels missed out. So I'll supply a tenth Muse for them. Her name, a polysyllabic name for a multiverbal art, a name terminally prosaic, is "She Who Has the Art of Post-Mythic Writing": NEOMYTHOGRAPHIKE.

Annapolis, 2017

17

The Actuality of Fictions
Nonexistent Objects

The Being of Fictions is many-faceted. The philosophical version of the issue would be: What is the ontological status of fictions? What kind and degree of being do fictions have? The literary question would be: How does a fictional text convey the nature of its creature? What literary devices distinguish fictions from lies? The logical version would be: What is the logical quality of the existence operator that a fiction commands? Are statements about nonexistent beings somehow true or simply false? In psychology one might ask: What is the mental framework proper to the reception of fictions? Is a special psychological vulnerability involved? In ordinary experience the question is: Whence comes the power of the unreal? Is it to be accepted or discounted in ordinary life? And in cognitive science the most clearly defined problem was: Can one show experimentally that there are mental images? Could the

Talk delivered at the Seminar on Cognitive Theory and the Arts, Harvard Humanities Center, November 2002. Published in *Perspectives on Political Science* 46: 1–6 (2014) Routledge.

visual imagination, as a faculty for making canvasless and paintless pictures visible to none but the imaginer, be made to reveal its products to empirical science?

All the questions I have mentioned are, as a matter of course, about cognition and its theories: What is there of interest to us that isn't? But only the last is about cognitive science as an experimental study. Let me explain first why I put the question in the past, as a superseded problem, so to speak, and then why it once mattered to me and still does matter to the being of fictions.

Like many of us who spend a very lively part of our lives immersed in fiction, I live somewhat split-mindedly, schizophrenically. On the one hand I readily give in to the particular seduction of novels, not so much in the mental frame of suspended disbelief (which implies an initial vigilant skepticism) as in an unguarded readiness to be taken over, to believe. But of course I emerge from the realm of reading, and the question is: "Where have I been?", and the frame of mind is: "I believe; help thou my unbelief." Put more prosaically, a lover of fiction is likely to be driven to reflect about its status. For me, at least, such an inquiry has two aspects. There is a world to be penetrated, the world of the imagination as a natural *amateur's* realm of fiction—what goes on inside all of us (or at least most of us, because it seems to be true that there are some people, significantly enough, often people of very high logical purity and sensitive moral consciousness, whose imaginative inner realm is very narrow). And then, emerging from and distinct from this relatively inchoate space of fiction in general, there are the well-formed specific fictions of the *proficients*, the poets and the novelists. Their products particularly induce reflection on the controlled exploitation of the imagination, on the artificial modifications that lead to public fictions, and above all, on the warranties and certifications of existence with which fiction writers strive to supply their individual figures.

Let me begin again, with a particular incitement. John Fowles's *The French Lieutenant's Woman* is a very considerable novel, yet terminally indeterminate. Its Chapter 13 (the number may be intended to signify something hapless) begins with the sentence "I do not know." It is followed by a litany of un-knowing concerning the being of the novel's fictions. It's a ruse, of course. As an author mindful of the time-expired writer's notion that "the novelist stands next to God," he, although shamelessly disowning all responsibility for his creatures and their iffy being, yet assumes full credit for their existence. This author arrogates to himself all authority while investing himself with a veil of ignorance. It needs thinking out.

In looking for light on this question, I immersed myself a while ago in the literature of what was then the current research in cognitive science, the work on mental imagery. Before saying something brief about its history, its results, and its decline, let me tell you why it seemed pertinent at all. It seemed to me that writers of fiction, epic poets and novelists, evidently could not help but be guided by the world we inhabit into a dual configuration: background and foreground, scene settings and beings moving through them, backdrops and the shapes appearing against them, atmospheres and the figures emanating from them. Amateurs of the imagination are pretty good at unformulated atmosphere, but it takes a master to coagulate the figures:

As imagination bodies forth
The forms of things unknown, the poet's pen
Turns them to shapes, and gives to airy nothing
A local habitation and a name.

   (*Midsummer Night's Dream* V 1)

At any rate, Shakespeare intimates that poetry begins with internal visions, and so, I'm persuaded, does most prose fiction. And it takes a cognitive constitution able to re-envision the shapes to become a reader of the scripture that comes from the poet's pen, which, put technically, means that mental imagery is a *sine qua non*, an absolute necessity, for reading fiction.

Let me give you—a twice-told tale in this book—a magnificent example of this necessity, the most spectacular one I know, though I can think of scores of other good ones. It is from the *Iliad*. Having been insulted by the commander in chief, Achilles has withdrawn from the battle before Troy. Now, driven by the rout of the Greeks to fatal half-measures, he has dressed his bosom friend Patroclos in his own well-known armor, in the wrongheaded hope that the mere appearance of a figure looking like himself—recall that Greek armor covers the whole man, face included—will scare off the Trojans. Of course, Patroclos, who has been told to fight only defensively, loses control and charges ahead. Hector the Trojan kills him and strips off Achilles' armor, as is the custom. He proudly puts it on himself, and Zeus makes it fit. Achilles, in a blazing fury and with new armor, will rejoin the battle. On the next day Achilles' intended face off between him and Hector takes place. (It is, incidentally, the Homeric fighter's mode to become a *promachus*, a forefighter, who emerges from the background battle to stand out in a duel, somewhat as the scenic imagination bodies forth figures.) Hector takes to his heels and runs three times around Troy, chased but not caught by the man whose chief epithet is "swift-footed." They run as in a dream; Hector cannot get away and Achilles cannot catch up. They stop to catch their breath and to think. Athena, who is always there when people are thinking for their lives, brings about a confrontation. Achilles and Hector face each other. And now the mindful readers, those who see the moment, will feel the hair of their heads stand on end, for what is it that Achilles faces? His last glimpse of Patroclos as he had sent him to his death in his own armor, but also of himself as he was before his several fatal decisions. This is the apparition he will now transfix with his spear. Of this implied climactic vision Homer says only the briefest, most passing word, though it has been nearly three thousand lines since the last mention of that fatal armor.

So to come out of the poem, the ability to have mental imagery is of the essence in reading narrative, and to know something about its nature must be, I thought, helpful to understanding what a fiction (that is, a figure of fiction) might be.

Now just at that time in the late 1980s when I was reading around, very encouraging research on mental imagery was being done in cognitive science. The method peculiar to cognitive science was to force out into the empirical open, by cleverly designed experiments, aspects of cognition that had so far had to rely on introspection to appear, or, being unconscious, had not been available at all. The latter case was of most interest, because the science had as one of its assumptions that cognition has more to it than shows up in consciousness. And that in turn was connected with an even deeper assumption, that the mind is an epiphenomenon of the brain and that the unconscious phases of what ends up as a conscious cognition could be ultimately externalized as a neurophysiological event.

Mental imagery seemed to be a particularly rewarding small bailiwick within the cognitive psychology part of cognitive science. Roger Shepard had been first to devise a way to test one aspect of mental images: Subjects were shown two complicated shapes composed of cubes in different positions. The question to them was whether they were the same. The point was to determine from the time subjects took to answer whether something like a mental rotation was going on. The test results were convincingly positive. (I was put onto this research by Barry Mazur, who was in the audience when I delivered this talk.) Stephen Kosslyn, then of Harvard, took up and expanded these experiments in mental scannings and their latency times. I think the subject has since fallen into abeyance. I have not kept up with the research, but I do see why it could not go much further. To say why this is so, let me give the briefest background of the fate of mental imagery.

The behaviorists who dominated psychology earlier in the last century and philosophers of a positivist empirical cast of mind had been simply denying that we have such imagery: For the behaviorist psychologists it was a brute dislike of intro- spection that set them against so invisible and behaviorally elusive an item. For the philosophers the issues were, it seems to me, deeper and more perplexing. I think that Wittgenstein asked the most unsettling and seemingly unanswerable ques- tions, from which most later investigations derived, and the deepest of them, in his own words, is this: "What makes my image of him into an image of him?" In other words, is there a certifiable correspondence between an image, especially a mental image, and its original, wherever located?

In testable terms and for *mental* images, that question yielded this problem: Does the cognitive process of generat- ing a mental image give evidence of being analogous to seeing a real figure in real space? And, of course, if that question had a persuasively positive answer, then the prior question, "Do we have mental imagery to begin with?" would be answered. Kosslyn's school of research does seem to have shown that mental images behaved in many ways like spatial figures— you could scan them, zoom in on them, and rotate them.

Now, here are two interesting circumstances. One is that it all didn't do much good. Proofs were produced, which showed that the issue was formally undecidable, that every effect accounted for in quasi-spatial terms could also, if some- what more laboriously, be explained in verbal or digital terms. To be sure, the quasi-spatial account was more imme- diate. Moreover, it jibed with what everyone believes anyhow: that we have a mind's eye, so that to the question, "How do you know you are imagining *him*?", the answer is: "It's him all over; it *looks* like him." To be sure, scientists tend to have a low opinion of what they call folk-psychology, as do certain aestheticians who claim not to know what "looks like" might mean. But in the end what you know introspectively you know unfalsifiably; that is, after all, why introspection is the bugbear of cognitive science and a last resort of philosophy. But these undecidability proofs discouraged, I imagine, further research—they and a certain recalcitrance in the problem itself. If mind science was ultimately brain science, then to take seriously the notion that mental imagery was space-like would be to show that some imaging brain activity was observably, realistically space-like, which didn't seem to be in the cards.* But if there was some irreducible distinction

> Though I recall seeing the brain scan of a macaque monkey that fuzzily imaged a segment of concentric circles that it had been shown.

between spatial views and brain processes, then the epiphenomenon had some independence and introspection was the likely access to it, not to mention that the possibility of effective introspection is assumed anyhow in every such subject-response experiment.

And now the second curious thing. While many cognitive psychologists, methodological quandaries notwithstanding, had persuaded themselves that we do see images internally, the philosophers, especially the ones committed to scientific method, went right on rejecting this form of cognition. Why, incidentally, would one even call it a form of *cognition*? One question the investigators in fact asked is whether one can learn from one's mental imagery. They decided that there *could* be that in the imagination which the thinking mind had yet to know. I think that my Homeric example is proof positive because, as I mentioned, the verbal text says next to nothing at the event, so that in the absence of visualization, the reader is apt to miss the great moment. Homer is, incidentally, the most reader-participant poet I know, precisely because he relies on the reader not only to see more than he describes but to infer more than he states. For example, when Odysseus's son comes to the palace of Helen and Menelaus, he hears wedding music; it is Helen's daughter who is getting married, and before long Helen (!) will surely be a grandmother. The pathos of this dissonant fact will dominate Telemachus's visit, but Homer, again, says nothing out loud.

Nonetheless, philosophers continued to be strong defenders of the notion that imagery is illusionary and words are real, for a variety of interesting reasons, chief among which was a desire for univocity and explicitness. I think that those contemporary literary theorists who believe that meaning is entirely intratextual, that books have no outside reference, that mimesis is not involved in fiction, cannot help but belong to the same school of mental iconoclasts, though for different, one might say more frolicsome, reasons.

These mental imagery studies may later have run into a dead end for the researchers, but they were very profitable for me then. They made me ask what it might mean to believe in the reality of mental images in general. This was not the specific question I ultimately cared about, which was rather the ontological or existential status of the beings of fiction. But the cognitive researchers helped in thinking generally about what it means to have something in mind, before the mental eye, at all. They drew attention to the essential spatiality of images, to the character of closed configurations on a quasi-spatial background, to the nature of mental movement, and to the genesis of mental formations. But even the most ingenious detailing of the cognitive conditions of their possibility could not tell me whence the images came, what they meant, or whether these *beings* had real standing as *existences*, or were, perhaps, *in*existently actual.

I have produced on purpose a clause that displays four terms that are often used randomly as synonyms but that I want to distinguish: being, reality, existence, and actuality. I have a certain warrant for these distinctions in the philosophical tradition, but I will omit this background and hope you will go along anyhow.

Being means, from way back, whatever stable presence and intelligible nature anything has. It is the object of ontology, the study of Being, of which Aristotle says that it is what we search for of old, and now and forever. Being can be ideal or immattered.

Reality, from Latin *res*, means thinghood, and has come to signify what obdurately confronts the senses, particularly the material as opposed to the ideal grasp; reality is what is palpable.

Existence is being here and now; it is presence as time and space-affected; it is the being of facts, by which I mean objects that come to us as nodes of knowledge enmeshed in the fundamental modes of the world before us, in space and in time. Hence, reality and existence are indeed pretty much exchangeable. Most of what is here and now, or there and then, is also, or at least was once or will sometime be, palpable.

Actuality, the word in my essay title, I take to mean Being as it is fully at work being itself; when actuality descends into the existences of space and time, things are fully, potently, there—not mere subjectivities.

The cognitive scientists may be said to have concerned themselves implicitly with the existence of images, for they were teasing out their temporal and spatial features. But literary fiction is delivered primarily in words, and although someone without mental imagery will miss a lot (and ever since Galton made the earliest mental imagery experiments in the 1880s, it has been known that there are individual differences, that there are people who either don't have it or are somehow prevented from being aware of it), still words may convey plot and character, albeit too compactly and too generally at once for vivid fictional life.

So the question of fictional existence can be raised and, in fact, was first raised, in the verbal realm—and this will not surprise you—by logicians and logically minded philosophers. The issue was launched by Bertrand Russell and his highly respected—by him—antagonist Alexius Meinong at the turn into the century just gone by, and it has been periodically revived since then without any definite conclusion. I hope you will agree with me that while a good problem in mathematics and science may be one that has a hope of resolution, a worthwhile pursuit in human wisdom is one that has given us good cause for initial despair.

Here is how the problem, with which philosophers had so far only toyed, presented itself to Russell for serious solution: Suppose a teacher of Greek mythology asserts before a class as follows: "Pegasus is winged." What is he talking about? What is being referred to? The sentence seems true, but it is not about anything in existence; it denotes nothing; it has no real reference. You cannot find Pegasus grazing in the valleys of Montana with the wild horses or whisper him into gentleness. Moreover it is probably the case that horses that are real horses cannot, physiologically speaking, have wings, so Pegasus is not merely factually nonexistent; he is also physiologically impossible.

The trouble here, in Russell's view, is to be located in the sloppiness of ordinary speech that uses Pegasus as a proper name and thoughtlessly assumes that names have real references. Note, incidentally, that this low opinion of what we all say in ordinary life is an early parallel to the cognitive scientist's distrust of "folk-psychology," what we all believe about our minds in our time off. We should not talk this way, Russell thinks, and I quote:

> The sense of reality is vital in logic and whoever juggles with it by pretending that Hamlet has another kind of reality is doing a disservice to thought. A robust sense of reality is very

necessary in framing a correct analysis of propositions about unicorns, golden mountains, round squares, and other such pseudo-objects.

What we should do is not so much utter as symbolize, so as to get at the proposition in all its logical purity. And that involves following the unnatural but clean reconceiving of a sentence like "Pegasus is winged":

1) Get rid of the name Pegasus, which gives the false impression that some being is named thereby.

2) Then rethink the predicate "has wings" or "is winged" as a sort of function on a variable, $F(x)$, or $W(p)$ in this case. The predicate is now no longer a property inherent in the subject, as is sweetness in honey, but an operation assigned to a variable. It might be a unique one, a qualitative value, because here wingedness happens to be assigned to, or function over, a unique-valued variable, p.

3) Regard this x or p not as a thing rich in descriptive features but as a kind of nondescript prop to which functions can be applied. Oddly enough, the theory of propositions that I am describing is called "The Theory of Descriptions," but it should be called "The Theory of Nondescript Beings."

4) Now determine whether there is in fact an x in the domain of this function, and express this finding in terms of a so-called existence operator, the well-known reversed E.

5) In this case, if you have empirical evidence that there is one unique Pegasus, a fact among facts, you may read: There exists a p that is a winged horse and is the only winged horse and it is assigned to the domain of winged things.

6) And now it gets interesting: What if you have reason to think that no such creature ever lived through time or

occupied space? What if the one and only Pegasus or the scattered tribe of unicorns were, you are convinced, never a part of nature? Then you will put a symbol of negation in front of the existence-quantified prepositional function and read: "It is not the case that there exists an x that is . . ." and so on. Here is the spectacularly deflating result of one of the most successful logical theories of the last century: *All propositions about nonexistent objects are now simply false.* The assertion "Pegasus is winged," is not oddly and inexplicably but ineluctably somehow true; it is just false. The robust sense of reality requires that Pegasus and Hamlet have *no sort* of reality. And, *mutatis mutandis*, neither has mental imagery and its faculty, the imagination, since the scientific evidence for their existence is contestable.

But this is simply intolerable to anyone who loves and lives with fiction. Let me try to say how that point can be made. For Russell the status of things is exhaustively divided between existence and nonexistence, reality and unreality. But I have up my sleeve (and have already shaken out) yet another term which the dictionary once again insouciantly conflates with existence and reality, introduced above. That word is *actuality*, and traditionally it means, succinctly, Being insofar as it has potency. Pegasus, unicorns, and Hamlet all have actuality. The Russellian world is a world of existence, but there may be more modes of Being than are dreamed of in this philosophy. Here is how, in my experience, fictional beings are potently actual: They have more staying power than we do and are much longer-lived; in fact, they endure fresh and present through millennia, like Achilles, Hector, and Helen. They have powers of arousal, physical and mental, not the made-to-order goads of private daydreams but the objective attraction of autonomous beings. They are self-moving, like living things with a will, and poets record rather than invent their deeds; I cite the same beings in evidence. They have an inner logic and their own spontaneity of action, and they *surprise us*—here's the wonder—by doing exactly what they must. As models they instigate action in us, as Achilles incited Alexander to conquer the world. In sum, they have a good many of the indices of actuality, and so the mere fact of nonexistence should not make all speech about fiction simply false, if speech is to preserve its full human function.

Now Russell had a worthy opponent in his severe proscription of all nonexistence as unspeakable. This was the Austrian Alexius Meinong, a somewhat older contemporary. He came to the conclusion that there must be, as I have just intimated, other ways of being besides existence here and now. In working out these ways he produced what W. V. Quine, a Russellian in this matter, called "a slum of possibilities," "a breeding ground for disorderly elements," such as "offends the aesthetic sense of us who have a taste for desert landscapes." Now those of us who have plenty of occasions to visit desert landscapes (as I do because my college has a campus in New Mexico) know that the desert is in fact a veritable breeding ground for a wild profusion of flora and fauna and gods and ghosts, but let that be. The Meinongian slum contains at the least some very colorful additions to the gallery of linguistically possible, if existentially impossible, beings that it may be unwise to ignore if the human world is to flourish.

If the specific cognitive object of the cognitive scientists I have mentioned was the mental image and that of the logicians the negative existence-quantified proposition, the philosopher to be here considered, Meinong, begins with the cognitive object in general, with intentionality. Intentionality is a word used by its proponents to signify the essence of cognitive consciousness, that is to say, all consciousness simply (see Essay 14, "Self-Address"). To be conscious is to intend something, though not primarily in a purposive sense. It is always to be thinking a thought, to be mentally active about an object. All thinking is aboutness, all aboutness encompasses an object, and—here's the crux—no object of thought can be just nothing, a pseudobeing. Meinong begins by observing closely the varieties of consciousness, and in this observational mode he is a proto-phenomenologist, a precursor of the school of Phenomenology to whom the careful introspective description of intentional consciousness is a primary task. But the axiom that no object of consciousness can be flatly nothing—that is not merely descriptive but actually prescriptive, and it is undeniably metaphysics, to be precise, ontology. Meinong's own deliberately paradoxical formulation was: "There are objects of which it is true that there are no such objects." Now to say that a nonexistent object exists is rank self-contradiction, while to say that a nonbeing is, is mere paradox; I say "mere" because the statement can be made straight by proper qualification.

So the ensuing task was to distinguish as accurately and subtly as possible the types of intentional objects found in human consciousness. Of these there were broadly speaking three, and they make, I think, immediate sense. There are the perfectly palpable spatiotemporal existences as we receive them through the senses. Set these aside. There remains a pair of types to which Meinong applies a clever principle: the principle of the independence of "Being-thus" or "Being-so" from Being. In the traditional way of thinking this principle is phrased as the independence of whatness from thatness; in common language, it is the thought that there might be quite determinate and interesting natures that just don't and can't occur in the spatiotemporal world. Among these beings are the ideal objects of mathematics, which have, Meinong thinks, a being quite independent of our cognition, yet no existence. And then there is an infinite realm, Quine's overpopulated slum of quasi-beings, that is indifferent to, and outside of, both factual existence and the independent subsistence of ideal mathematical beings. These quasi-beings have articulable definite properties, both essential and accidental, but no genuine being at all. Among them the airy nothings of fiction find their habitation and their name.* Meinong gives

This assimilation of, say, geometric figures to fictional beings seems to me purely wonderful.

them the status of what he calls *Aussersein*, Beyond-being.

Though I admire Meinong's courageous intention to take on strange inquiries and by his meticulous distinctions to give the dignity of being acknowledged problems to elusive objects, it is not altogether easy to say what has been settled. To be beyond or outside Being is, to be sure, more than to be beneath it, to be the nonexistent value of a consequently false proposition. But it is not much more. For Beyond-being is a weasel term. It appears to grant fictions the ontological status of a determinate relation to Being while it takes away the actuality and autonomy that make being a being worthwhile. (Recall also that in Plato's *Republic*, the Good is said to be "beyond Being." But there that means: super-actual, the absolute ground; see the final essay, "[The Idea of] the Good.")

Meinong's kind of inquiry soon went into eclipse; people wanted results that were more spare and more punchy. Russellian minimalism won for most of the last century. But then, because these cognitive questions are unquenchable, in the latter part of the last century there came a revival.

In particular there was an attempt in 1980 by Terence Parsons to bring Meinongian notions into Russell territory—to reinterpret Meinong's Beyond-beings as nonexistent objects and to devise a theory that, though in content inconsistent with Russell's Theory of Descriptions (for recall that Russell denied to nonexistent objects the ability to enter into true propositions), would yet be symbolic and so, formal.

Parsons takes from Meinong the idea of a nuclear property, meaning all those predicates that make up the Being-so of an intended object. Now every existent object is conceived by Parsons as being *completely* describable by a unique set of nuclear properties. List them. This list exhausts all the objects that have proper existence, the kind of factual being that Russell and Quine find respectable.* This existence itself is not

Would it be a finite list?

one of the nuclear properties that the objects in the list have, but it is what Parsons calls an *extranuclear* property. It belongs to every member of the list by definition—this is the list of factually existent objects—but it is not a part of its description, of its Being-*so*.

Let me repeat that this list embodies one very important criterion of existence: Each object is *completely* described by its properties. It is a crucial characteristic of anything that factually exists that it has no indeterminacy about it: Any sensible question you ask of it, it will respond to, it will inform you about. If you ask any horse "Do you pasture in Montana?" it will say yes or no, as the case may be, and if you ask it "Are you winged?" it will say no.

Now go on to make up more sets of nuclear properties that are not in the list so far. Do it by dreaming up, in an orderly sequence, new combinations of nuclear properties, even properties never met with in this world. This list will be a lot longer, inexhaustible, in fact infinite. It will be a respectably defined list of nonexistent objects. But Parsons puts this in a clever way: All these new objects that do not exist empirically do not have extranuclear existence, but they do have nuclear existence. That is a way of saying that their existence is part of their description; it is ascribed to them as a property by the list-maker. If this reminds some of you of Anselm's famous argument for the existence of God, which crudely put, says that God's existence is included in his essence, you will be on the right track. Parsons makes the same connection. Fictions have existence as part of their Being-so.

Parsons's treatment is attractive to logicians because it can be almost completely formalized; what I like is the cunning solution he introduces, that of nuclear existence, existence not by fact but by description. But I like it more for its clarity than as a satisfying answer, because attributed existence just does not account for the actuality of fictional being. Reduced to its rock-bottom significance, to attach "nuclear" existence to a fiction is merely to reiterate that it is a fiction, a made-up being with a pretense of existence included in its makeup.

Moreover, Parsons had worked with an assumption that seems to me to be false, though it is a great help in thinking about fictions. He assumes first, as I've queried, that all individual objects in real existence can be listed—let the unlikely possibility pass—and then he assumes that every atomic existence is completely determined, that we can list all its properties. Now we know that real nature is, on the contrary, rife with indeterminacies. For example, if you ask a particle to give you both its position and its momentum at any instant, it cannot do it; this is the so-called indeterminacy principle of quantum physics. If you ask yourself whether you are usually in a completely determined state, the answer is apt to be no as well. So most real individuals are highly underdetermined, in principle or in fact.

But it is the opposed case, the case of nuclear existence, that includes beings of fiction, which is really interesting. Parsons supposes that, because real existences are determinate, nuclear or purely descriptive existences are constitutionally indeterminate. If you ask Pegasus where he grazes and whether he is winged, he might answer: On the Acropolis of Corinth, and yes, he has wings. But if you ask him about the musculature of those wings, he is silent, and there is no one who can tell and no way to determine what is inside that figure.

Now on the face of it, Parsons seems to be right. Books of fiction do not contain indefinitely long lists exhausting the properties of their fictional entities. They leave their characters highly incomplete. And yet, can't we answer far more questions about such beings than the explicit information would seem to warrant? And I don't mean just logical inferences of this boring type: If we meet Natasha Rostov, that apotheosis of girlhood, at the end of *War and Peace* in a married state, we may infer that the Russia of 1820 had an institution of marriage. What I do mean is that I could confidently fill in a checklist of the features, say, of Natasha Bezuhov's looks: I know in a general way what any dowdy, fussy mother, self-neglectfully and fanatically absorbed in her family, *looks* like, and also what she *is* like: how over the fundamentally contented continuo of her life there play descants of nagging complaininess and joyful resolutions. And I know, more particularly, what transformations the looks of that unique Natasha of the flashing black eyes, the slim figure, and the impetuous disposition have undergone to make her much less charming to the world and much more indispensable to her intimates. Some of it Tolstoy tells and the rest I make out by looking within. So at the least I can carry on a perfectly judicious conversation about it with my friends. No, it is surely not the case that fictions are ineradicably incomplete, at least not if they fall into friendly hands. But this means that the grounding distinction between existent and nonexistent objects either fails to do fictions justice or becomes too shaky for the clarity that was to be the bonus of the formal approach.

Where to go next, then, when all the cognitive approaches have been proved unsatisfactory through the very illumination they offered? The scannable quasi-space of mental imagery, the falsehood of existentially quantified propositions, the Beyond-being of intentional objects, the nuclear existence included among the properties of incomplete objects—all these help a lot in making more precise our reflections about the being of fictions. But the more accurately they define the problem, the more acutely they fail to save the phenomena in their actuality. If cognitive science, symbolic logic, phenomenological ontology, and finally the melding of these latter two do not give satisfaction, not to speak of the many other philosophical and literary inquiries that are, in my experience, less focused or less original, where to look next, besides of course, within? Well, there is one discipline left, and it offers strange and wonderful solutions: theology. I will leave for our discussion a further consideration of the possibility that the being of fictions is a matter for divine rather than secular science. One thing is certain: If it were so, if the being of fictions were properly a theological issue, there would ensue at least one unsettling consequence: The explanation that might be, to speak fancifully, most satisfactory to the fictional beings themselves might well be the one least acceptable to us who struggle not to be caught in the confusion between a wish and a warrant for belief. Anyhow, to make a beginning, here is one way a theological analogy might work.

I am thinking not only of the reference poets have traditionally made to divine inspiration, but of something much more specific: the remarkable similarity that the being of *angels*, as set out by medieval theologians, has to the being of fictions. Angels have life but do not age; they begin as creations but have no end; they do not change, being each its own intelligible species, meaning that they *are* a unique essence; yet they are not static but capable of crucial choices; to express their natures they assume bodies, which are, however, incorruptibly incorporeal; they do not live in passing time, yet they are compatible with its passage. They live instead in the *aevum*, a temporal mode between eternity and time, passageless time, the temporality of Paradise.

A short reflection will show that these features are exactly those of fictional beings, which also live without aging, which are made but not unmade, which are both once-and-for-all representations of their species and yet unique, autonomous

individuals, which have visualizable but incorruptibly immaterial bodies, which live alongside us but in their own passageless time. They too, like angels, live in the aeviternity of
Edenic space, namely their fiction, which is parallel to our
world, and, like angels, they are exempt from the human
injunction that the aspect of pain should not give pleasure.*

> With a slight twist: Angels in heaven live in apathic bliss enhanced
> by their contemplation of a much-suffering creation, while fic-
> tions in books suffer quasi-pains for the enjoyment of reading
> humanity.

The question is now raised: Does this comparative account
say to us that fictions are angels or that angels are fictions?
If the latter, the theologians, above all, Thomas Aquinas
(*Summa*, Q. 10, 50 ff.) had an insight into the being of fictions, which was at once quite devoid of intention at the time
and unmatched in depth thereafter.

18

Carryover

Influence and Hypothesis

"Carryover" is one literal translation of "metaphor"; another is "transfer," from the Greek preposition *meta*, "trans-, -over" and the verb *pherein*, to "bear, carry" a burden. Thus the word metaphor is itself a metaphor; it suggests the physical action of carrying something across.

I think that verbal metaphors primarily function to arouse overlays of mental images. The image of the subject has had drawn across it, carried over it (or behind it) a second image picturing this attributed likeness.*

> A quite different view of metaphorical functioning is semantic, that is, verbal. In I. A. Richards's terms, there is a *tenor*, the prosaic subject, and a *vehicle*, a verbal conveyance of a poetic likeness, to be attributed to that tenor, its literal "holder."

Metaphor is a so-called "figure of speech," usually thought of in tandem with simile ("similar"). Simile is simpler, more direct, more hard-hitting than metaphor; at its simplest it conflates likeness and identity: "You're an idiot."* But usually it

> That this is simile is shown by its use. It's indecent and senseless to say it to a real idiot to whom it applies literally. What's meant is: "You act enough like an idiot to be called one."

I've now used "literally" twice, one of those scintillating words like the bookmarks that show a dinosaur skeleton or a fully fleshed monster as you turn it. "Literal" literally means "by the letter" but it is used to mean "real." (For another such duplicity, see Essay 5, "On Compromise.")

Incidentally "idiot," from Greek *idiotes*, originally meant a private, unpolitical person or an unprofessional, amateurish one. Food for thought!

includes "like" or "as." Simile is Homer's forte, never banal and rarely ugly: As the Greek warriors withstood a Trojan onslaught, they didn't quail,

But stood their ground like clouds, that Zeus
Made stand in windlessness on mountain citadels,
Unruffled (*Iliad* V 522–524).

And for a moment, these warriors are transformed into— steadfast clouds. People using their visual imagination* will

> Our words call forth visions primarily, I think. But metaphor can also be auditory; there can be sound-similes, words, the tenors, "set to" the musical vehicle. Bach is full of them. (That's not to be confused with poetic diction having musical features, rhythm and melody.) The two noble senses, sight and hearing, are most apt, I think, to supply similes. The lower, up-close senses, touch and taste, for example, are more local and, it seems to me, less verbally accessible, and image-devoid. *Our words also conjoin the senses.*

see a two-in-one sight and think dislodging thoughts: the dark, bulky constancy of clouds?!

I might claim that simile is more poetic than metaphor because it focuses on the experience of the *substance* aligning the beings presented while metaphor attends only to the sameness of the *relation* among four items taken two by two. Thus Ayah, the rotund, sexually irresistible nanny in a Parsee family, is present to us very much in the flesh, as a universal source of excitement in others, but herself usually of "goddess-*like* calm."* This likening transforms Ayah, though for a

Chapter 9 in my current favorite: Bapsi Sidhwa's *Ice-Candy Man*. Here's an example of the book's attraction, at once totally Pakistani and absolutely English (though the author in fact lives in Texas), a sentence in its paradoxicality that is completely plausible to me: "Because theirs was an arranged marriage, they are now steamily in love" (Ch. 6).

moment herself in a dither, by means of an annealed transparent overlay, into a bebangled divinity of placidly self-contained sensuality, a being of a higher earthiness. It brings out the *essence* behind her accidents, and it works the same in a Punjabi folk-tale as in a Homeric epic.

Now consider metaphor, not imagistically, as an inner vision, but logically, as a thought structure of abstracted relations. First, it involves four terms, as does any analogy: This is to that as a third is to a fourth. Mathematical proportion provides the barest, most revealing case of metaphorical structure. For example: 1:2::3:6, "one is to two as three is to six." The relations of 1:2 and of 3:6 are each called a ratio.*

A mathematical ratio (Greek *logos*) is a precisely articulable relation of quantity. The Greek term for a quantitative proportion is *analogia*, "ratio carried over."

Just as it made sense to say that simile often turns *like* into *identical* by a pictorial overlay, so it is the case that the two ratios of a proportion are the *same*. The ratio of 1:2 is *one-half* and so is that of 3:6, for 1 is half of 2 as 3 is half of 6. This sameness is in fact a third relation, besides the two ratios, involved in a proportion, analogy, or metaphor.

Thus the fully stated formalism of a metaphor says that four items are identically related two by two: ratios, their articulated relations, are *not* equal, since a relation is not a quantity, but they are the *same*. Here is an example, not, to be sure, poetic but elegantly witty:

The force of his feelings is so much greater than his intellect that his mind serves his soul like a valet (John Chapman).*

My source is Ward Farnsworth's *Classical English Metaphor*, which offers an—entertaining—collection of metaphorical passages classified by topics. He regards metaphor, along with simile, as essentially "figurative comparison." (He must mean comparison as a result, not an activity such as that unprincipled teachers' practice of "comparative grading.") The metaphors here collected are inverted, abbreviated, assimilated to simile, so "comparison" is indeed the most you can say of the whole lot. My example is actually listed as a simile, but it can be unscrambled and analyzed as a four-term metaphor.

Analysis:

1) Force of feeling (passionateness)
                 is greater than (exceeds)
2) Intellect (intelligence);
4) Mind (thinking organ)
                 is in servitude to (valets)
3) Soul (animating organ).

Of the four terms, the first pair are *activities*, the second pair *actors*; this second pair is inverted. The relation connecting the first pair is quantitative: *greater than*; that of the second is instrumental: *in service to*. Reinverting 4 and 3 by turning the verb passive we get:

3) Soul (animating organ)
                 is served by (valeted by)
4) Mind (thinking organ)

Finally by identifying the quantitative "greater than" with the qualitative "served by" (that is, treating the latter as a simile for the former), what appears is, for all its complexity, a standard metaphor:

As his passionateness exceeds his intelligence, so his emotional soul uses his rational mind.

If you ponder this carryover, it reveals itself as a wonderful psychological portrait: an intellect overborne by feeling, a mind subservient to the affective psychic capacities: the *same* relation. In current terms, "his emotion governs his reason."

The above analysis shows, I think, that if simile is more punchy, metaphor is more precise in displaying likeness, namely as a *particular* relation of terms or appearances that is the *same* in two *different* subjects.

One more observation. If I seem fixated on etymology, the earliest meaning of a word discernible by linguists—that's true because the illuminations are wonderful, even hilarious. Here's my absolute favorite. Greek *nous* is our grandest capacity, Thought as Insight.* My etymological dictionary

> The English have adapted it to an English mode. Nous (rhymes with "house") is shrewdness and gumption (Norman Schur, *British English A to Zed*).

cites a derivation from nasal terms, nozzle, "s-nuffle, sniff" as in "sniff-out, track down by smell": The mind at its best is but nuzzling the Beyond.*

> Hjalmar Frisk, *Griechisches Etymologisches Wörterbuch* II 323; the derivation is cited as doubtful, but too jolly to set aside. Aristotle had, quite a bit earlier, considered the analogy between intellectual and sensory perception (*On the Soul* II 4).

Since I'm convinced that there is no aboriginal speech for non-perceptual mental activity, all such language is figuratively sensory, be it simile or metaphor, and be the sensory content internal or external. It means that philosophizing (which is what all of us should occasionally do) is an activity of understanding (itself a figure) the traditional figures and of trying one's hand (figure) at the discovery (figure) of, accurately descriptive (figure) figure for the pure mentation *within* (figure) and of the being (figure)* beyond the seeming *without*

> "Be" is related to Greek *phyein*, "to grow."

(figure).* Of course, if you didn't accept the evolution by

> It being clearly understood that an etymological figure *proves* nothing. It only *suggests*, for example, that "The mind is to the being which it is investigating as a pig is to the truffles for which it's rooting"—simply true to experience.

> Soul, *psyche*, mind, intellect, *logos*, ratio, *thymos*, spirit, affect, emotion—English or Greek, all have somatic origins.

abstraction from somatic conditions and the attendant reassignment to non-physical purposes of these terms, you'll drive yourself crazy. Thus when I say "psyche" (which is rarely), I don't mean "a cool breath," but an immaterial soul, as do all my fellow non-intellectuals.*

> What got into my trusty *American Heritage Dictionary*? "Mind . . . 1. The human consciousness that originates in the brain . . ." How would they know? Nobody does; it's a *postulate* of brain science, thus not decidable within the science.

This long prelude brings me to the point for sake of which I made metaphor my topic. There are two terms, clearly metaphor-words, that are full of puzzled fascination for me: 1) *influence*, whose physical origin betokens an "in-flowing" and 2) *hypothesis*, which means originally corporeal "placing-under." Yet neither can another's thought literally come to flood us as an influx from beyond nor can we literally put a supposition under our thinking.

So, first, what do we, what can I, mean, when I declare myself, gratefully or reluctantly, "under the influence of" not liquor, to be sure, but, say, a teacher or a book. And then, what am I signifying when I proclaim, as I do, that I would rather lengthily court a hypothesis than definitively possess a doctrine?

I'll take *influence* first. As do so many crucial words, it has opposite affects attached to it.* First, I was open to this influence

Such as "compromise," and "literal," already mentioned.

because in some part of my inwardness the sense with which it was awash was well, though inexplicitly, known to me. Thus I welcomed it as bringing me to myself. Or, alternatively, I was first beguiled by its novelty, but upon floating up through the flood I resented the alien inundation.

Hence there seem to me two options in dealing with influence. It goes without saying that before such dealing there must be recognition. Influence can be so subtle or so circumambient that coming to, becoming aware, is truly difficult, often only achieved through the lucky intervention of a counter-influence. It is the purpose of a real, a "liberal" education to rouse awareness of influence.*

> Never to preach its rejection, just to promote self-knowledge. Nonetheless, such education is by no means morally neutral: "Know thyself *and* thy tradition" is as serious a moral requirement as I can think of and more arduous than most other discretionary tasks.

So I'll concentrate on teachers and their principal teaching assistants, those masterful adjuncts, the works handed to them by a tradition that sifts "great" from "middling" over time.*

> Currency is no commendation for this activity; excellence can wait its turn and come to us as quite antique. I'm thinking of what's good for students; their teachers do have to keep—somewhat—current, because time can't do any sifting on its own.

Whence does influence actually come? From five venues, I think: persons, communities, workplaces, nature, things; or, alternatively put: individuals, cultures, employment, environment, artifacts. I'll pick out from these the first and last: teachers and books. I think that for the young influence will flow most naturally from a human being, a teacher, since the youthful imagination is too self-centered to be capacious and, in fact, not well enough stocked to be concretely detailed, and books tend to be sooner adopted than actually studied.*

> Thus, in my teens I lugged about Marxist screeds, obtained at the Worker's Bookstore in lower Manhattan—having them by on the off-chance that I might read them. I de-marxed myself long before I read that magnificent fantasy, *Capital*.

There seem to be two sorts of influencing teachers, the life-changing and the idea-instilling; of course they overlap.

Teachers of the first sort stand, like one of the two presences appearing to Heracles, Virtue and Debauchery, at the Forking of the Paths and influence students one way or another, of course not usually into the path of dissoluteness.*

My teacher rather drew me into Classics, away from my father's hope, Medicine—not really analogous to Heracles' Forking, though it was surely life-changing, this Ph.D. rather than an M.D.

The second sort of influencing, then, is idea-instilling rather than life-changing. You are told, hear, take to heart, certain interpretations—for once, the term "idea" fits—of world or book, notions that make for themselves a secure and permanent seat in the soul where guiding truths are lodged.*

Another influential teacher imbued me with the conviction that learning is not a noun, an acquisition, but a verb form, an activity, and thus that a Ph.D., a "Doctor of Philosophy," one learned in the love of wisdom, is an absurdity.

As for the influence of books, it can be so vast and multifarious that most attempts at "sourcing," at referencing a bit of influence, are doomed.* Since Bishop Ambrose, Augustine's

Though it's amazing how often a contribution is spatially located and sensorily marked: on this shelf, between these colored covers, the Critique of Pure Reason is a green, the Phenomenology of Spirit a maroon-tinted presence.

teacher, was first seen engaged in un-uttered, silent reading (Augustine, Confessions VI 3), books have been the companions of solitude. What is lost in human togetherness is gained (sometimes in exhilarating surplus, sometimes with a depressing deficit) in the self-sufficiency, in that incitement to doing it—cluing it out—by and for yourself which communion with artifacts brings with it. (See Essay 1, "Thing-Love.") Moreover, nobody interrupts.*

Especially these days when distraction isn't an interruption of concentration but the converse holds. The simile for our lives' tempo is: Little clots of being all there, dissolving in a sauce of being all over.

So now, second, *hypothesis.* I discern three types of knowing*: hypothesis, the tentative conjecturing which is attributable

Omitting Revelation by a divinity at the inception and Computing by a programmer at the conclusion of the calculational endeavor during which Information was transformed from the formation of internality to the providing of "bits" of fact.

to Plato's Socrates; doctrine, of which Aristotle, authority itself, is the chief proponent; and the conditions of possibility of physics, which are substituted by Kant for metaphysics as both the thinking and the thought that grounds Nature.

It's hypothesis I'm after. The word is frank about itself: a "putting beneath"; thus it is something done by the one who owns the hypothesis. Next I ask about hypothesis, doctrine, conditions of possibility, comparatively—which asserts actual knowledge? Certainly "doctrine," a "teaching," does so, as Aristotle explicitly says: philosophy starts in wonder but ends in its opposite; once you know, hypothesis ends.* The same

What one must know so as to understand beings—"this is not a hypothesis." (*Metaphysics* IV iii)

holds of "conditions of possibility"; Kant, their explicit formulator, calls the special "science" of these conditions, which he regards not as a doctrine but as a preparation for doctrine, "Critique." It sets the limits of understanding and enables such certain knowledge as is possible. He deprecates trifling about probability and conjecture (*Critique of Pure Reason* B XXXV, Part II; *Prolegomena to Any Future Metaphysics*, Scholia).

The hypothetical lover of wisdom, however, has no doctrines, no teachings. Socrates says emphatically: "I was never, ever, anyone's 'teacher'" (*Apology* 33a). Yet, although Socrates has appeared to me to differ from both Aristotle and Kant in being doctrineless, that's clearly not quite right. There was something he was willing to die for and in fact did. What could it have been but an opinion held ardently enough to be as a dogma? Moreover, Aristotle found plenty of teachings in the conversations Socrates had, as recalled or invented by Plato (no one knows which), enough to criticize them copiously.

Perhaps it helps to think of Socrates' hypothesizings, his supposings, on a level with Kant's conditions of possibility. But first, whence do I derive this association of Socrates with dependency on hypothesis (*Phaedo* 100a ff), suppositions that have a character not so remote from conjectures, best guesses?

During his last conversation in the flesh, on the day of his death, in the *Phaedo*, Socrates refers to his particular thought, that our souls are immortal, as a "first hypothesis" (107b). And already in his first dialogue, the *Parmenides*, when he was still almost a boy, he undergoes a kind of training session in dealing with antithetical hypotheses. But above all, hypotheses come into their own in the *Republic* (510–511), where they are at first, in mathematics, unquestioned starting points but morph into the questionable assumptions of dialectic, the highest thinking, which then in turn rises to an "anhypothetical," an absolute, beginning. Thus hypotheses are the means of reaching, by a kind of bootstrapping, *beyond themselves* to the ultimate *source* of being, truth, and good. This is the Idea of the Good itself. (See Essay 38, "[The Idea of] the Good.")

Therefore it makes sense to analogize Socratic hypotheses to the conditions of possibility, the critical assumptions that are *both* the grounds which enable what exists to exist, to be as it is, *and* the basis of the intelligibility that empowers us to discover the science of existences, namely physics.

And yet the two modes are a world—the world of nature—apart. For it is, as I just said, nature and its physics for which Kant is finding the conditions of possibility, with the consequence that, once they are shown to do their job, these conditions become themselves doctrinal.*

To me there has always seemed to be a missing step here: a uniqueness proof. Kant ought to show that these and only these condi-

tions would give us our world, and I can't see that he "deduces"
this uniqueness.

Socrates' hypothesizing is much more informal; it shapes
up as good guesses, happy intuitions, plausible analogies.*

Analogies: the metaphorically named sort of being that relates
ongoing thinking to seeing and a completed thought to an aspect
is an *eidos*, usually called "form," literally the *looks* of a thing. An
eidos is an "invisible (!) look." The metaphor implied in the Socratic
eidos as look, aspect, form, sight, is complex and asymmetrical: We
see with our eyes multitudes of appearances, most of which belong
to sets, insofar as they *look alike*, for example, the set of human
beings. Their aspect reveals the same *structural relations*, without
and within. Thus they are *analogical*, each with each, showing the
same visible ratios. Then we search *with our minds* for one originating look, that Socratic *eidos*, his chief *hypothesis*, the form itself,
the "supposition," that enables us to give the set a common name;
let it be "humanity." This one word can *intend*, "reach toward" (no
one knows how) the many analogous appearances *beneath* it. And,
as I've said, it can also reach *beyond* the visual appearances on
earth to name the one *eidos* in a "higher" realm.

This, then, is the metaphor, whose bare bones, once more, are:
As a first feature is to a second (in a subject-tenor), *so* is a third to
a fourth (in an attribute-vehicle). Thus, under the *as*, the likeness-
receptive part of the metaphor, we impute similarity to each other,
always with a, probably inexplicable, residue of ultimate individual
difference.

Then, under the *so*, we think ourselves into a realm where
resides the singular aspect from which originate (how is an
unsolved problem) the many earthly similars.

It is Socrates' hypothesis that this one look, the *form itself*, is
like the similarity of the appearances in being (figuratively) visible, yet *unlike* in *not* being a relation, articulable as a ratio (*logos*),
in *not* being many, in *not* being an appearance. Instead the *eidos* is
beyond rational speech, is singular, and is substantial. Through
this asymmetric metaphor Socrates' inquiry gains traction: As our
world exhibits visible and sayable similarities, so a realm beyond
harbors their quasi-visible and hyper-rational source.

They seem to do their work, to collect the world's infinite multiplicity into finite forms and to make speech possible by letting one word betoken many things.* Thus they are Socrates'

Else 1) language would need an infinite dictionary, a word for
every discernible appearance, and 2) spoken words could not

"intend," reach for, recognize, their particular thing. Of course, many criticisms have been mounted.

Swift offers one practical solution: Carry on your back a bundle of all the things you might wish to discourse on, and show them wordlessly (*Gulliver's Travels*, the Grand Academy of Lagado [Slow-in-deed], Laputa [Large-think], Ch. V).—Literally ostensive language, obviating the Logos and its perplexities!

faithful standbys. But I conjecture that, firm unto *death* as are these opinions sustained by thinking, Socrates loves a mite more the *life* they underlie, a life lived always, not anxiously but expectantly, on the cusp of a question, the quest for the *eidos*.

Annapolis, 2018

19

On Being Interested
The Central Essay

With a heavy Yiddish accent:
"We should be between each other"
(Paul's great-grandmother).

Is it permissible to say the same thing twice? That's the question, because at thrice no one's listening anymore—you could be mute, your every word surd. Yet, what can you do when something keeps coming to mind, something so significance-laden to you (that is, me) that it involves itself in ever-diverse relations and invests itself in ever-different verbiage? Here's what you can do: Barge on.

"Interested" is one of the best words I know:* *inter-esse*

Not the most beautiful. Someone—was it Mencken?—said that it was "cellar door." I think *cellier d'or*, the "golden storeroom," is prettier, though French; but most beautiful is "celadon," that greenish tinge which is as spring-like as "mauve," the grayish-violet hue of an old lady's dress, is depressing. I once saw, in a vitrine of the Metropolitan Museum, a small Chinese flask, colored celadon; it seemed to me to attract and contract into itself all the beauty collected in this vast New Yorkerish storeroom—far exceeding the magniloquence of the huge Baroque canvasses I'd been staring at.

In any case, the above shows me that the so-called music of words is—normally and legitimately—infused with their meaning. Pure word music is atonal nonsense—except for "Jabberwocky," which proves that intentional nonsense can't be total non-sense.

(Latin), "to be among and within" beings, to find them interesting, that is, worth being with.

"Being interested" is a kind of hold-all for me: summary and epitome, concise and compendious, a grab bag of what is on and in my mind.*

"On": a current preoccupation, to be taken care of, that is, thought out, and/or acted on. "In": seated in the soul as a hypothesis (see Essay 18, "Carryover"), both for steady support and occasional shakeup.

Is, I ask myself once again, the capacity for being interested a virtue of character* or a gift of nature? Why, oh why, is the

On the hypothesis that our "character," wonderfully cognate with onomatopoeic Greek *charassein*, "to scratch," is an *artifact*, inscribed upon our congenital nature, and thus, in part, a *product*, both of our upbringing and of our self-delineation—"in part" because our nature is, it seems, limitedly scratch-prone, in fact incision-resistant, from either hardness or softness.

arousal of *interest*, even of some of those students who willingly spend considerable time and a lot of money at places of learning, the teacher's most tricky task? It must be that its arousal is really intractable. If it's through character—attention-paying, attendance, industry, direction-following—it's a simulacrum of being all there, of being truly interested.* If

Or rather a diversion of interest into "doing well" quantitatively; thus a student asked me recently—it made my heart sink—"How many times should I enter the conversation in seminar?"—The right answer would have been: Whenever you've got something to say." But it wasn't—she always had something unexceptionally correct to say.

interest comes by nature, neither moral homilies nor good modeling will be effective. Natural indifference is obdurate, willfully deaf and blind.*

The German words for "interest," *Teilnahme, Anteilnehmen, Beteiligung*, "partaking, taking part in, participating," all have a tincture of human sympathy to them, as has our "taking an interest in." As always, there are also opposite meanings of "interest," strong and modified: proscribed usury and legitimate profit-taking.

Let me try to describe to myself the feel of being interested, interest as a way of being—interest in anything, be it tinkering or fixing, anything from a sticky door to a burnt-out clutch,* or figuring and thinking out, be it a formal argument

> Would that I could. Last time it cost me nearly $2,000; it appears I ride the clutch.

or the Idea of the Good. (See Essay 38, "[The Idea of] the Good," the last.)

Here's what interest is not: neither a pathological affectivity, a passion, nor—of course not—a pathological indifference, an apathy—in short, not an emotion.* One way to put it

> Any more than is happiness, at least in the ancient understanding: the soul well at work.

is that interest is not a flaring fire (an unavoidably destructive element for body and soul) but more a conserving power: banked ardor.

It is truly a way of being, namely of being all there, in the here and now (among each other and our things), in the there and then (among our images and memories), and with the above and beyond (our intimations and transcendings)— whatever venue befits us.

For me all that happens mostly in the company of books— of course neither primarily (that's with friends) nor exclusively (there's school), but most extendedly.

Books are dually interesting, interesting in two directions. One goes outward; it is the practical preparation for being with—not instructing but inciting—students. The other direction is inward; it is withdrawal from dutiful (albeit wellloved) action to not un-arduous but determinedly impractical contemplation.

So being interested "in"—I now add the essential prepositional *in* that indicates a destination—involves objects: babies, books, colleagues, cars. It comes to us possibly as a boon from a divinity (and thus as a cause of directed faith), or perhaps as a gift of nature (and thus as a reason for generalized gratitude). The cause, or, more so, its absence, could be multifarious: some people are a., born bored, some b., achieve boredom, and some c., have boredom thrust upon them.*

> *Twelfth Night* III iv 49 (tampered with): a. by nature; b. by their own inertia; c. by their sorry circumstances.

Boredom, the above implies, is the antithesis of interest. Who'll believe me?—but boredom is, assuredly, the most dangerous of all the normal states of being. Having nothing to do, nowhere to go, and above all, no good object to think about,* leaves a vacancy, a space where there is nothing to be

> Thinking as a steady state includes daydreaming.

"between" or "among," a void ready to receive the artificial paradise induced by soul-invading substances or by soul-stirring violence. In other words, being interested is salvific not only to those who are so, but to the world around them.

In imagining myself into the psychic state of those who are quotidianly uninterested, it seems to me that what they lack is a kind of mental music, the psychic symphony,* a faint human

> For me this interest-mood's music is in the minor mode. Curiously, the minor key is called *molle*, meaning "softly, gently, melancholily." To me it is tautly, gravely, perhaps somberly, exhilarating. That's why I engage in the malpractice of listening to real music while scribbling—to forestall the inner diminuendo.

strumming comparable to that cosmic background glimmering, the residue of an origin that underlies all thingly coagulations; in us it is a receptive arousal.*

> The work that depicts rising interest by an uninhibited simile—the phallus's going erect in the soul, betokening the soul's readi-

ness to be among beings—is Plato's *Phaedrus* (251b), the Socratic dialogue that is actual philosophy's *magna carta*.

The moment has come to detail, as concisely as I can, the elements I discern as associated with the state of being interested.* I have eight.

> Of course, by "state" I don't mean an inert condition but the mode of life that Aristotle terms *energeia*, "being-in-action," all there. He calls it happiness.

1) *Happiness*, above all. This happiness is spectacularly compatible with being *un*comfortable. In fact, should I be asked "Are you comfortable with it?,"* the answer would be

> One should be nicely polite and refrain from skewering with that augur-stare some of us can bring to bear—a Second Amendment right—on the pea brain that produces this query.

that edginess, uneasy excitation, is the antsily pushy part of the soul's arousal; call it curiosity, a less than noble novel-knowledge-greed, nosiness.* The interested soul is just not the

> Elsewhere I've cited an etymology of Greek *nous*, "insight," hilariously related to "nozzle."

abode of domestic comfort. In fact, the happiness of interest is girded by inner limitations, concentrated by worldly pressures, prompted by fleeing time—a happiness encompassed by its supporting negations of unrest and destabilization. In itself, I now see, it consists of that middle pursuit between internal clarification and its external production which my Greeks call *poetry*, "making"—here nothing to do with composing love ditties or heroic epics, but with the work of seizing hold of and compelling to stasis the motions of the soul. The demanding happiness of being interested, of being-there, has as its complement the antsy happiness of adequate recording.

2) *Self-inclusion* is a prominent aspect not of being interest-*ed* but of being interest-*ing*. "Self-inclusion" seems to work

as a term for this mutuality, since I mean that both aspects named are the *whole* subject. Here is an illustrative case of what I'm after. The soul is commonly said to be *in* the body, located in an invisible internality, for that's how it feels.* But

> "In": at least by those who have a soul and believe that their fellow humans do as well. "Feels": such reportable experience trumps demands for pointable-to evidence. So I think.

when we are with and among each other, there's no getting around it. We're betwixt and between *bodies.* And yet that's wrong; if it weren't, the interest in being together would be exclusively that proper to a natural scientist: a body "studying," that is, receptive to being impinged upon, by other bodies.*

> That's the reductionist's dilemma: Can matter (the scientist's) know matter (the world), unless "to know" becomes entirely a behavior? My blue armchair be my witness! I'm often totally supine, behaviorless, when most truly at work.

What seems to be true is that the human body, all of it, and the face particularly, "express" the soul, which is thus "pushed out," as it were, to be upon the surface of the body. Thus our soul is in our body, our body in our soul—self-inclusion, and that makes us interesting.*

> In Plato's *Timaeus*, a cosmological myth is told in which a cosmic soul, girding the cosmos *outside*, is constructed on a musical scale (35b); this soul is also woven *into* the whole (36e), binding all its beings together. Thus the world is full of music and is beautiful, organic and alive, knowable and known—aboriginally interesting. The Timaean soul is the this-worldly, the cosmic, counterpart of the Good in the *Republic*, I think. (See Essay 38, "[The Idea of] the Good.")

Here's another case of self-inclusion conducive to being both interested and interesting: I'm in my community, or better, communities—country, friends, college. But assuredly they are in me as well. They are interesting both because I am among them and yet am none of them: They're *mine* and yet *not me*—the perfect complementary conditions for being interesting. And I'm avidly interested, in my country's ways of being, its antic surface (at the moment) and sound base (in the long run), in my friends' ways of being, happy or troubled, in my college's fate, how to preserve its existence without losing its essence. A couple more; I've got a dozen*: Books well and

> I'll just mention one self-inclusion about which I've said more than enough elsewhere: Thomas Aquinas's wonderful exposition of the human will as both rational desire and desirous reason, thought and affect mutually inclusive—which makes the will the most interesting of human faculties—if not the most lovable.

truly read; they're all around me, shelves upon shelves, including and secluding me, and also they're within me—their thinghood surrounding me, their life dwelling within me. Or, one last: Some years ago I was driving around Taos with friends. Out of the windows I saw a scattering of luminous willows on a ground of golden straw; some horses were impersonating statues—or so I recall. I looked into the scene and for a magical flash it met and merged with my pre-memorial image of it—outside and inside in mutual embrace, and this was the perfection of *inter-esse*.

No, one more self-inclusion, at the other end of mental experience, not an aboriginal dream image but an ultimate ontological category: being each other's other—people, things, thoughts, one and the same *by reason of being opposites*.

3) *Opposition* is the splice, the binding energy, that holds individuals together in complementary antithesis, and the spice, the seasoning, that makes the identity interesting, mentally savory. An *other* is my antithesis, that is, the partner "set against" me, opposed merely by reason of being a not-me—whose not-me I am in turn: the sameness of otherness. Thus an other, particularly a friend, is my delineation and delimitation, and so my outline and definition.* Here I'm speaking in

> In Spinoza's famous formulation: Every negation is a determination. That is to say, every delimitation shapes the substance it

"de-fines," puts an end to it and so saves it from dispersion: a termination that is a determination.

dialectic terms,* non-sensory and un-particular.

> Socratic dialectic is thinking about and among the "forms" or "aspects" (*eide*), some of the greatest among which come in antithetical pairs: Being/Beyond-being, Rest/Motion, Same/Other, Great/Small. Savoring the power of such ideal concretions—*never* abstractions—*is* dialectical interest = philosophy.

This oppositionality can, however, be embodied and fleshed out. If I think of myself as a particular case of a particular other's other, I run, for example, into the condition of *similarity*, of semi-sameness. We're the same in our common humanity, but not identical, because we're different in our individuality. And again, the aforementioned condition: We're the same in both being individuals, and *that* is what makes us different. This is not verbal trickiness but rather one way into being truly interested. It leads to that double-mindedness, a truthful duplicity, a sound-minded schizophrenia ("split-mindedness") which brings us to attention, to taking in and appreciating others' particularities and peculiarities as viewed *against* an underlying commonality and its similarities. "Attending," as other words delineating human being, is a dual-purpose term; it connotes both "being interested in" and "being in service to." Love's a liege-lord.

But this dialectical approach doesn't only promote being interested in certain others.* It also induces "self-interest

> "*Certain* others" because friendship's interest is densest at that center of the world which is me and becomes more diffuse along the divergent radii of my circle of friends, until it dissipates entirely as the circle's circumference includes my town, state, country, continent, planet, galaxy, universe. Out there vivid particularized interest morphs into abstracted typological speculation—anthropology, cosmology.

rightly understood."* One such meditation on myself runs

Phrase retrieved from its political use by Tocqueville.

along these lines, an ethical dilemma we should, I think, all be plagued by: Everyone in my world opposes me by dint of mere not-me-ness. Fine; that's a dialectical problem; it can be phrased this way and so encapsulated, set aside: if I'm a convexity and my others are my concavity, who's defining whom? It's mutual because notional convexity/concavity is perspectival, depending on your position.

But some of my others oppose me *practically*, in my very being, my dearest opinions, my proposed actions. How do I deal with such, often serious, opposition, even antagonism? I cannot help but realize two circumstances: A. Such antagonism erects me, as it were; it makes me self-aware. It calls out my self-definition, brings out my articulatory competence— and exposes its timidities; it tries my temper—and finds it stickily aggrieved. B. On the other hand, unexpectedly respectable opposition teaches me—it needs doing over and over— that the other's side *always* has a point.* The fair-minded

No, not always. Sometimes even my antagonists are plain wrong— or me.

executive's quandary is how both to stick vigorously to your guns without disarming the opposition and to acknowledge the opponent's full force without going flabby in the face of it.*

This is a danger to us all, but a weakness especially of right-minded but weak-principled academics, administrations, and those rogue academics, the intellectuals.

4) *Choice* is surely involved in *becoming* interested. But do you choose the object or does it seize you? I like to think that becoming interested follows upon the display of the object's attractive power, as the peacock "displays" its fan. Our choice is to follow through, to get serious. For it's one thing to light up with the fire of fascination and another to bank that fire so that it becomes a steady heat, an ardor. The initial choice,

may, however, be very general—the interest may be, certainly often is for our students, just to learn.* We tell them what

I'm avoiding a bad locution: "to *get* an education"—can't be done.

they must read—though never, ever, what they should think.*

Though we do sometimes tell them, *briefly*, what we think— and are richly rewarded by uninhibited disagreement. Usually I'm a mite more right than they, sometimes spectacularly not— they glow.

The required study, whose particulars they have not chosen, poses an interesting perplexity: How to be interested in a work that has not chosen you but has been assigned to you? We ask, Hamlet-like, for an exercise of the will: "Assume a virtue if you have it not"—Pretend interest (though it is not exactly a virtue but a gift), as if fulfilling an obligation and keep up the pretense until the real thing befalls you, and you are unfeignedly interested, with the *dual* interest befitting studenthood: interested in the matter itself and interested in being interested, pride in being a proper student.

In fact, it is interesting how much duplicity there is, rightly, on the path to becoming interested. I am thinking of the mediations needed between choosing to be and effectively becoming interested, such as the above-mentioned pride in being a praiseworthy and well-praised minion, a condition absolutely ineradicable in good-natured young humans* and irrelevant

There are also the innocent natural mavericks and the slightly evil intentional rebels, whose interests are often clandestine. Then it is the teacher's problem to clue out whether these aberrant involvements are genuine convictions or cooked-up evasions of duty.

to genuine interest.

In my experience the most potent intermediary, or rather intermediator, is a sort of mundane—if I may dare to compare the sacred with the secular—John the Baptist,* who

For example, Luke 3. The comparison comes out curiously detailed when fed into the imagination.

functioned in the wilderness and whose baptism of water is the necessary preparation for the baptism of fire. The academic analogue is the teacher, love for whom precedes, as a catalyst, interest in a subject.

What's behind this human need for a forerunner, an intervener as advocate ("Paraclete," John 14:16) between us and our object, be it in matters of faith or of interest? I know that the latter, the interest, far outlasts, outweighs, outdoes the human conduit to it. Yet that human attachment is the often indispensable precipitator, even for interest-prone people.* It

As children they have a propensity for slightly manic pursuits, such as my sandbox cities with their flowing rivers (vainly sanctioned hydraulics; the garden hose was forbidden in the sandbox), my fiercely organized and reorganized stamp-collection, and my little phonograph (1934, pre-CD) clandestinely played under the blanket, my frisson-laden underworld.

must be that the soul's arousal is a pre-condition for objective care (one definition of interest). And that comes through human love—sometimes adoration—for the human intercessor and advocate for a subject matter.

What kind of love is it? First, in all candor, it's an exploitative love, for its human object serves as a medium, crudely put, a utility. Second, though of the spirit, it is intensely physical. For human peculiarities, physical and manneristic, are the potential learner's fixation, transmogrified into marks of uniquely poignant distinction, be the teacher female or male. One of the most wonderful, that is to say, remarkable, wondrous, human capacities is this one: the capability for passionate non-desirous somatic love, spiritual love fixed on appearance—the non-erotic* or only metaphorically

Meaning that it is passionate without being possessive, longing for closeness without desiring physical intimacy.

erotic arousal of the soul that almost any human being, from baby to elderly man, from youngish male assistant professor to dowdy middle-aged female full professor,* can induce.

> Professor: Brooklyn College, 1947 ff.: a roughish kind of wilderness wherein dwelt several of these prophets, the former preaching Goethe, the latter, far more life-changing, Homer.

5) *Stimulants* are a diurnal need, as love is an initiatory requirement. You have to get going; once started, mental motion is self-propelling. Is it the body, our inalienable abode, that causes initial mental indolence or the soul, our veritable self? Is the inertia of physics a drag on the soul? More than most human dispositions, the readiness to get down to it, or better, rise up to it, seems to me to be located in the intersection where the supposedly subservient body imposes on or resists the soul whilst the preferably receptive soul controls and commands the body.*

> I have a cartoon, entitled "The Mind-Body Problem," posted on my fridge: a man, planted potato-like on a couch, has a bubble coming out of his head (where the portion of matter particularly subservient to the rational will is located), saying "Get up," and another out of his torso, saying "No." The converse is also possible, especially when immersed in scribbling. Stomach: "I need cookies!" Me: "Later."
> Of course, the soul interferes with itself by self-distraction: angers, anxieties, hankerings. Even that vaunted serenity of old age has less to do with gathered wisdom than with waning energy.

What is more interesting than to observe the interactions of body and soul? That's because 1) their togetherness attests so uncontrovertibly to the separateness of the two; and 2) it is so revealing to learn which (or who) mostly wins and why and when.*

> I found astonishing testimony to the essential separability of soul and body in the oddest venue: cases where body and soul are congenitally and ineradicably mismatched, say the physiology is male but the psychology female. The modern mastery of nature has enabled the soul to make the body conform to its gender requirements, that is, sex to gender. Thus Aristotle's claim that the soul is an organic body's "actuality" (*On the Soul* 412a) and similar attributions are put in question. The classic on transsexuality is Jan Morris's *Conundrum* (1974).

How can it be, then, that lucid thoughts about their nature course through my consciousness merely because I've let a black brew run down my gullet? Or that I can't think my way from here to there, because I've pulled an all-nighter, and it's 5:30 A.M.?*

> Having read my way through a bit of brain and cognitive science, I know this: the answer is unknown, mere hopeful handwaving toward a mystery term: "emergence," meaning that from physical elements arise, emerge, conscious effects and affects.

Is there something wrong about stimulating the non-physical self by material intakes, even just coffee? Does it undermine being truly interested by circumventing or displacing the object of interest as the sole stimulant? Does it distract that inner ear, which hears me think, that my outer ear is currently infused with the agreeably inspiriting, even if half-heard, flow of a dozen recorder concertos—a not-so-minor abuse to which music, as the most immediate and most circumambient of arts, is subject?

But then are all stimulants somatically ingested?* Aren't

> Or worse, injected. I believe that all of us, not least those of us who believe ourselves to be fully in control, are on the brink of addiction. That is a condition which, I imagine, begins at the moment when desire casts off from and overwhelms reason. Recall that the classical understanding of the will is rational desire (see this essay, no. 2); so the beginning, at least, is a literal break-up of the will. Once that's happened it may well, as our mentors, the therapists, claim, morph into a disease, meaning it's no longer in our own power to cure by sheer intention.

books, for instance, stimulants? The more of them I've read, the more they play that role—occasions for casting off and taking off into my particular interests. (If there were a reader who did so with my scribbles, I'd feel well-used.) But the books we set for our students, and that I study as preparation for my time with them, deserve sticking with. And so I will stick with both students and books—even when now and then I have to *make* myself be interested artificially. And, of course, our books *are* great precisely for having and conveying plausible knowledge of what deserves our being-with, what is truly interesting.* So here's the answer, already intimated,

> Even if its articulation often is, and sometimes needs to be, repellently abstruse. *Chalepa ta kala* says Solon: "Hard are things beautiful." It's a fact, and I ask myself: Would life be better or worse if beautiful things—the Greek *kala* connotes fine and wise ones—were easy? Given we remained what we are, not gifted with the angels' tolerance for easy bliss, ennui would be our lifelong lot.

to the problem of stimulants: They're kick-starts; once begun, the object of interest, be it a question, problem, product, or practice, is itself stimulating. For being interested, being there, with the world, is its own *stimulus* (Latin for "goad"), an instrument of mental arousal, of the unrest and destabilizations that mobilize thinking.

6) *Reference* is the initial condition that fills the world with interest. It appears when you go utterly practical and just accept that the question "What's behind it all?" is not yours to the world but the world's to you—and that therefore all existences have *back-stories*, prequels. To those precedent stories all beings that are given to you make reference and from them they gain interest. There is, however, a next phase: See 8 (Afterthought).

7) *Singleness* is a condition of being interested in its most basic sense. For to be *with and among*, you first have to *be*, to exist as single, as a singular ultimacy,* as a veritable

> "Single" does not betoken "unique"; all these solitaries form classes: A bachelor of arts is as yet unattached and with a mind free to be at least interested in some matter and interesting to somebody. (But this is mostly verbal hijinks, since B.A.'s are no longer always single even at Commencement.) A monk is, in the original Greek, *monos*, "alone, single." (A nun, my *American Heritage Dictionary* derives from Latin, *nonna*, "nurse"; so also "tutor" derives from the Latin verb for "looking after"—pure serendipity, because "tutor" is my faculty's one and only title.) A clearly prospective spinster used to function as the family's learned member, for example, Mary Bennet of *Pride and Prejudice*. She, alas, "read[s] great books" (as do we at my college) and proses along at

every chance Miss Austen gives her; when we see her "adjusting her ideas" to her self-importance, she annoys her family and gives us wicked joy.

individual. If you don't go among others as a confirmed singleton, you'll be drawn into them as into a crowd—and you'll be humanly diminished: a human being in a crowd is not all there since "there's no there there."*

Is it Gertrude Stein? Los Angeles? My reader says yes, Oakland.

Animals such as corals and plants such as volvox can be crowd-beings, one organism, "colony individuals." But we, human beings, are, once our umbilical cord is cut, on our own—physically separate to signal our psychical singularity. That is, I believe, how we are meant to be, so that we may follow the counsel of Paul's great-grandmother (with a heavy Yiddish accent): "We should be between* each other"; put my

Lots even of native speakers don't distinguish "between," meaning "betwixt twain or two" from "among," akin to "mingle," that is, being in a crowd.

way (with a residual German accent): "We should be interested."

8) Afterthought: *Tenselessness* is what I take the Latin *inter-est* to signify, albeit it is syntactically in the present tense.* *Interfuit* is a simple past, and provides an illuminating

Interest: third person singular present, from *interesse*, "to be amongst"; our "interest" descends from this inflected form.

counterpart to our "interest." Roland Barthes says that "the founding order of photography" is *reference*. Look at an old photograph of a deceased person and say to yourself: "He was among us (*interfuit*)" (Barthes: in *Camera Lucida* [1980], ¶ 32).Without this pointer to a bygone reality, the photograph loses its interest—its very nature as a physically produced "light-writing," a semi-natural record of a past existent. Barthes is describing the very interest of my no. 6.

Genuine interest is not about what once was in, and has passed from, existence nor about what is not yet but may come to pass—or not. It is in the atemporal present; it is being amongst beings insofar as they are neither in nor out of existence, but are *actual*, effectively with us. (See Essay 17, "The Actuality of Fictions.")

Annapolis, 2019

20

Athens

The City Shining Under the Hill*

Jerusalem is the shining "city set *on* a hill" (Matthew 5:14), a place of salvation. My point will be that so is Athens, but its locus of salvation is *under* a hill, the Areopagus, the hill *on* which the Supreme Court of Athens met. In a cave below its seat were domiciled the Furies in their converted form as *metics*, the green-card holders, so to speak, of Athens. There they went, inducted by a procession of the Athenians, under a new name: "They of good mind; the kindly ones,"—the "Eumenides" (Aeschylus, *Eumenides* 916 ff.).

There are unanswerable questions—no one can think of a determinative answer—and insoluble problems—no one can think of truly dispositive construction. This is hard for Americans to believe, but it is the very element in which tragedy lives. One part of that which makes us solution-prone* is our

As ever, "us" means me included, which is not the common practice of social critics.

disposition to take a mitigating view of things done in ignorance of circumstances, a therapeutic view of knowing transgressions, a conventional view of bounds once regarded as natural.* To me it is an ever-revisited question whether this

Thus our students "tend" (meaning the most vocal ones) to think that only deeds knowingly done are imputable as misdeeds, that

the perpetrators are to undergo counseling rather than exile, and
that transgressing the bounds might be revisionist heroism rather
than sin.

way of thinking is ultimately a shallowfication of human
being or plain reasonableness*: everybody ends up somehow

They might be the same.

viable rather than dead.

There are, however, two Greek tragedies* that do solve the

Known to me; I haven't read them all.

insoluble and give—albeit mystifying—answers to *the* tragic
question: Where is guilt located when fate, delivered as an
explicit oracular prophecy foretelling the hero's actions, is
involved? The two plays are also two of the grandest, the *Eumenides* of Aeschylus and the *Oedipus at Colonus* of Sophocles.*

Aristotle in his *Poetics* writes of *Oedipus the King* (*Oedipus Tyrannos*) as *the* model tragedy. For a reason set out below, I would propose *Oedipus at Colonus* as the model of a different kind of tragedy.
Moreover, I think (a much inferior endorsement) of the *Eumenides* as the most wonderful of the tragedies known to me. (See
Essay 21, "*The Eumenides*.") Perhaps it needs saying that it is a
"tragedy" only by the genre name for these ritual performances.
Our understanding of "tragic" as grandly, awfully catastrophic
or plain miserable doesn't apply. The *Eumenides* is the glorious,
the triumphant, celebration of the solution of an insoluble problem: the viability in life of a matricide. It's done by the agency of
a divinity, Athena, who is willing not to cut a Gordian knot violently with a sword, but to unravel it cunningly with compromise
and by means of a place, Athens, receptive to the complex radicality of this solution. It is of this "happy" tragedy that the *Oedipus at Colonus* seems to me maybe not so much a model as a prime
manifestation.

I will suggest that the former illuminates the latter.* On

Although the dramatic date of the *Eumenides* is later, since no
intercausation is involved, that hardly matters. The royal houses
of Thebes and Athens are in no way connected, so there are no
direct generational involvements. But Oedipus's son Eteocles was

allied to Capaneus, one of the "Seven against Thebes," and Capaneus's son Sthenelus fought for Agamemnon before Troy. So Orestes, Agamemnon's son, belongs to the third generation after Oedipus:

Oedipus
↓
Eteocles = Capaneus
↓
Sthelenus = Agamemnon
↓
Orestes.

the face of it, that is a problematic claim, because it appears to be a good rule for reading works of stature,* be it a Platonic

And of attending to any non-utilitarian artifact.

dialogue or a Russian novel, *not* to read them comparatively, "comparative literature" being the intentional effort to fall between two stools by not being firmly placed (meaning detail-occupied) on either. However, in the case of these two plays, attending to Sophocles' Oedipus in the light of Aeschylus's Orestes does seem to induce dense specificity rather than vague generality.

Look at these parallelisms: In both plays a human being *in extremis*, hounded and in fear or expectation of death, comes to Athens in hope of some resolving finality. In both plays, the Furies are in attendance. In the *Eumenides* the Furies, the "Raging Ones" (*Erinyes*), are transformed by Athena's persuasion into the "Kindly-minded Ones" (*Eumenides*), and as such they, anachronistically, inhabit Colonus.* Both protagonists

A northern district of Athens (*Oedipus at Colonus* 42). At Thebes they were still Furies in Oedipus's day (*Antigone* 1075), since the transformation is yet to come.

come to the end of their travails. Orestes is pronounced free of blame for his mother's murder, though he has in fact killed her: He has not committed murder but has carried out a divinely commanded execution.

It is an ambivalent exoneration: Ten Athenians (the number is debated) had been sworn in as jurors and they produced a hung jury;* Athena casts the final vote for Orestes and placates

> Aristotle, in *The Athenian Constitution* (LXIX 1), says that if the votes are equal the defendant is acquitted. If this is applicable to Orestes' case, Athena's vote is legally redundant, but the more significant for proclaiming her partiality.

the Furies by offering them honor and a dwelling *under the Hill* of Ares. The Areopagus thus becomes the hill upon which meets the high court of Athens, of which these citizens, with their split verdict, are the instituting justices. The *Eumenides* is the account of the founding and first case of Athens's supreme court. In that drama the potentially endless retributive family killings are simply stopped dead by Athena; it is a precedent for the ages, under the maxim of *stare decisis.**

> Law talk: "to stand by decisions."

In both plays there is then finality, for similarly Oedipus's case is solved at *Colonus,* which means "Hill," and in a grove, as I said, anachronistically sacred to the Eumenides. But here the solution is—death? No, that would be an ordinary end to an extraordinary crime, not a commensurate solution. Oedipus does not die; he leaves no corpse; he has no grave. He is *annihilated* in a flash. His polluted body and his guiltless soul are, to coin a term, naughted.* There is no thunderbolt to

> Three of his four children are also dead by the end of the play *Antigone,* which is last in dramatic date though evidently first in composition. So the family pollution is done with, since Ismene, the weaker but more reasonable sister, disappears.

strike him; Theseus alone, the welcoming king, has seen, deep in the grove, something awesome and has been told a secret that, passed on only from king to king, would keep Athens safe forever.

Thus the place of Oedipus's annihilation will be a blessing to Athens. The end of this Oedipus play and the end of Oedipus are, I believe, Sophocles' incitement to our questions, which, I think, Aeschylus helps us to think out. I would begin this way: Is the doer of a specifically bad deed unavoidably also its perpetrator? Or is there guiltless guilt? Is the human being that is 1) "fated" to do some such thing and/or 2) doing it unknowingly, nonetheless culpable?* Are not facts, facts?

To "fated" I give a range of meaning from an oracle's prophecy of a suprahuman necessity to a human prognostication of great likelihood such as "he's an accident waiting to happen." By "doing it unknowingly" I mean that the doer can't know either the unintended consequences of the deed or what its proper denomination is; for example, is Oedipus's killing of his father "patricide" or "self-defense"? Does Clytemnestra "execute" or "assassinate" Agamemnon?

He killed his father, married his mother, and engendered four offspring in her. Thus he confused natural distinctions by melding mother with wife and offspring with siblings. Is that not a non-negotiable debt of conscience?

But why, an Oedipus might ask, why me? Is Oedipus, who finally denies his guilt and says of himself that his deeds "have been more a suffered sort than a done act" (*Oedipus at Colonus* 266), not the man for his curse—and only that? Of course, he is; he is the very venue for his fate. Like his father Laius and his daughter Antigone he has a terrible temper, a violent streak. I might even throw suspicion on his acuteness.* Was it wise to decide to circumvent the oracle to begin

His reputation for cleverness rested on his answering the riddle of the baleful Theban sphinx: What walks on four, two and three feet? Oedipus said "Man," as crawling baby, as erect adult, and as senior with a cane. Of course, *Oidipous*, "Swollen-foot" (because when his parents exposed him in fear of the oracle they riveted their baby's ankles with a metal pin) walked with a cane in robust manhood. Question: Is he a little obtuse in his cleverness here too? Should he have said: "Ha, you monster, look at me"?

Antigone is her father's daughter-and-sister also in having some of this slightly dubious cleverness. In a speech that critics, including Goethe (*Conversations with Eckermann*, March 28, 1827), have wished to prove spurious, she argues, sophistically, that brothers, siblings, alone deserve her ultimate sacrifice, since only they are irreplaceable (*Antigone* 904 ff.). It is absurd, but redeemed by the support of Jane Austen, who is often funny but never absurd: "[E]ven the conjugal tie is beneath the fraternal" (*Mansfield Park* II 6, speaking of Fanny and William Price's mutual love).

with and then to do it incompletely? I mean, without pledging himself never to kill an older man or to marry any woman clearly over thirty-five, such as Jocasta. Quick temper and half-baked resistance are the very disposition the oracle can invest to most dramatic effect. And spectacle is, together with—no, even more than—nourishing smoke from burnt offering and libations from spilled wine what the gods need to feed their insubstantiality and to relieve their immortality; no mortal can ever hope for an intervention from the theater-loving gods on Olympus if it means damping the action on earth.

More questions: Why does Jocasta hang herself, once her husband's murderer and her own incest is discovered,* while

> In *Oedipus the King*, which must be the first and most perfectly devised murder mystery of what will become a huge genre. Question: When does she first know who he is, even if only implicitly? I think: She always knew. How would a mother not intuit a son, especially if he is like his father? In Thomas Mann's medieval reprise of the Oedipus story, *The Holy Sinner*, the wife and mother of Pope Gregory confesses to him: "I always know you" ("The Audiences"), meaning "I knew all along."

he survives more than a decade? Could it be because she has no further function, certainly not as maternal spouse or wifely mother nor, perhaps more in accordance with her feeling, as sororal mother or maternal sister?* While he has not

> Lady Macbeth, too, commits suicide, while Macbeth lives on; she because she is sidelined, he because he has a world; she is fierce, he is tough. (See Essay 22, "Lady Macbeth.")

only an awful fate but also a solemn destiny, Queen Jocasta knows—knows who he is, knows he is doing what she knows men dream of (*Oedipus the King* 81). She knows and, whatever he may later say, he's still a man of action. She wants to stop the play's revelation; he drives it on. So she dies and he lives.

This Oedipus who is neither buried in earth nor (I think) received in Hades, this naughted, undone extra-human, is valuable to Athens, and the place of his disappearance is holy. Why, really? What secret has he bestowed on Athens's royal line?

I'll make a stab at it. He has given Athens the gift of a *real* future. A *real* future is an *empty* future, unburdened by oracular predetermination or natural determinacies. The secret the kings are to inherit is that there are sacred and secular places in Athens that have the power to undo past fact and to free the future. This is the reason, it turns out, why Oedipus was the right man for his fate: he was the man who would make the most of it; he was the man who could go to his quietus with a sense of glory, the recognition that he was about to be more in being annihilated than he had been in his lost absolute kingship, as *tyrannos.**

Tyrannos, "tyrant," is said to be used loosely for "king" in poetry, but a whiff of dominance must have kept clinging to it.

A last thought: One reason for studying the ancients is to put in relief what it means to be a modern. Here's a lesson, as it comes to me. The ancients consider great troubles as godsends for great souls, at once afflictions and distinctions. We are apt to turn our griefs into grievances, demanding therapy, both social and medical, and finding support in commonality. We elevate comfort widely spread above nobility narrowly concentrated; the tragedies of kings give way to the miseries of people. Who would choose splendid agony over a quick-acting pill?

One more contrast, now going inside, to our internality. Imagine an ancient reader, a resonating watcher of tragic performances, who somehow comes on this famous sentence:

It is impossible to think of anything at all in the world, or indeed even beyond it, that could be considered good without restriction [*Einschränkung*] except *a good will* (my italics; Kant, *Groundwork of the Metaphysics of Morals* I).

Allow this pre-Christian Greek anachronistically to understand what "will" here means. (See E.B., *Un-Willing* [2014], Ch. II 3.) This reader might well be appalled: The perfect good located in a human faculty?! The human subject exceeding all the world's goods by the mere quality of its choices?! Oedipus's intentions overriding the divine oracle's facticity in value?! Yes, it is a strain of modernity, this self-attribution of a limitless capacity for goodness that justifies us in imposing our will on the world, in subjugating the world's value-restricted objectivity to our well-intentioned subjectivity.

A good will puts paid to avenging Furies, for, once we empower it, they cannot gain traction on even the most horrific deeds. So also Athens's annihilating power over guilt then goes unemployed, since our exoneration comes from within.

Athens, oops!, Annapolis, 2018

21

The Eumenides *of Aeschylus*

The Grandeur of Reasonableness

Aeschylus's *Eumenides* is a play about an institutional innovation and a paean to the goddess of the city. It is an account of the origin of Athens' Supreme Court and a love poem to Athena and her people and places.

This poet, however, loves for cause and with a thoughtful passion. This people, the "Attic folk," schooled by their divinity, have the wisdom to *domesticate dread* and to *innovate moderately*. My aim will be to flesh out and give precision to these notions, in sum, to delineate the idea of a *reverent revolution*.

I ought to confess at the outset that I love this play, but that Greek tragedy as a genre is alien to me. In his youthful work, *The Birth of Tragedy from the Spirit of Music* (1872), Nietzsche propounds a stark opposition between Socratic

These reflections on the *Eumenides* originated in a seminar on board the *M/Y Callisto*, Captain Yannis Stupakis, sailing the Aegean Sea in October of 2006. Published in the *St. John's Review* Vol. 50, no. 2, 2008.

and tragic culture. He writes: "And now one must not hide from oneself what is hidden in the bosom of this Socratic culture: an optimism that deems itself limitless" (Ch. 18). I recognize myself as a minor instantiation of the Socratism that Nietzsche fears and despises, this—I might say, American— optimism that wants to nullify deep tragedy by the light of reason and neutralize fate by the devices of ingenuity. When I read a Greek drama I immediately fall to considering how its "tragedy" could have been forestalled. I think to myself: "What little bit of good sense could have circumvented this mess?" Moreover, I feel my way into the inwardness of the tragic heroines and heroes and find myself repelled by their super- and sub-human lack of what one might call life-intelligence. A few years ago I was having lunch with a colleague, Jonathan Badger, who had just lectured on Sophocles' *Antigone*, and expressing to him my view of that tragic heroine as a teenage monster. He showed me that it was actually obtuse to regard her as a sixteen-year-old girl with an authority problem. She is not a fiercely rebellious teenager but a human token designed to be caught in an ultimate, unresolvable clash of fearfully fundamental forces, a cosmic rift—here the one between family and city, between blood and politics. Tragedy, he was saying, is not about characters in situations but about catalysts of sub-rational and superhuman clefts in a world in which no man, woman, or girl can do the right, the saving thing. I saw his point.

One reason, then, that this drama, the *Eumenides*, speaks to me lies in what it is not. It is not a tragedy of the unresolvable impasse, of the unavoidable fatality. It is surely a drama, since *drama* is Greek for an eventful deed. But it is also a *pragma*, an affair practically handled, whose outcome is not all-round cleansing by devastation, but a future of good daily living, of mundane prosperity. At the same time it celebrates the *grandeur of reasonableness*; Athens's goddess endows diplomacy with splendor.

Socrates, who is, according to Nietzsche, the latecoming destroyer of deep-delving dark tragedy, was a boy of eleven when the *Eumenides* was first shown. Perhaps he was in the audience; I don't know if children were allowed in as spectators (they were indeed in the grand final procession of the play), but he was a great theater-goer in later life.[1] This much can be said: His severe critique in the *Republic* (383b) of the tragedians, including Aeschylus, can't stem from this play. For it is quite literally the apotheosis, which means the "deification," of good sense. As I said, Aeschylus invests this drama of sweet reason, of moderation triumphant, with exhilarating solemnity and participatory splendor. I mean that precisely. Whereas in most tragedies the audience looks on and reacts, perhaps recoils, at the fate of kings and heroes, in this play all Athens is on stage: The spectators see themselves as part of the play. And whereas in most Greek tragedy the audience faces fearful and pitiful depths, in this play it is carried to joyful heights by an act of prudence that subverts tragedy. The final tone of the play is that of a city led by a goddess whose wisdom is touched with glory. So I have broached the matter of my subtitle; now let me detail its parts.

I. WHOLE-HEARTED PATRIOTISM

Except for a brief prologue in Delphi, where lay the omphalos-stone, the navel of the world, the *Eumenides* is set in Athens, where, it will be shown, resides the world's wisdom. In Delphi the scene is the sacred enclosure of Apollo's temple; in Athens it is Athena's temple on the High City, the Acropolis, and then on the rock facing the Acropolis, Ares' Hill, the Areopagus.

This Athena, the Athena of the play, is Athena Polias, the City-Athena, the Democratic Athena. She is not, to be sure, the protagonist of the drama, that is a choral band; she is, however, its chief individual actor. I don't know if there are any other plays in which a divinity is the sole main character; it is, to say the least, a remarkable moment in stagecraft.

Athena is on stage together with her people, the "Attic folk," the Athenians, first with a few, then with the whole town. These people are named from their city, and their city is named from its goddess. But here is a wonderful fact: As in English, so in Greek, Athens is a plural: *Athenai*, "the Athenas." I will return to this name, but now I want to point out that no other great Greek city I can think of is thus named from the images of its divinity—not Sparta, nor Corinth, nor Argos at the center, not Syracuse in the west or Miletus in the east of Greater Greece.

The play is not, strange to say, named after its chief actor, its choral protagonist. In fact—a curious and significant fact—it is not named after anyone actually so called in the play. There are no "Eumenides" in the *Eumenides*.

Let me draw back here to place the play *Eumenides* in its trilogy, the *Oresteia*. The *Agamemnon* is the first of the three. It is a model tragedy in the familiar sense. The hero, just returned from the conquest of Troy, is killed by his wife Clytemnestra. She has her reasons; it is an open question whether she assassinates or executes him. I am reminded of that fine movie, *Witness for the Prosecution*, which ends with the wife stabbing her iniquitous husband in the courtroom; Charles Laughton, playing the winning but unwitting Queen's Counsel for the defense of the guilty husband, who will now defend the wife, terms that deed not a murder but an execution.

The second play, the *Libation Bearers*, is a bridge drama. The exiled son of Clytemnestra and Agamemnon, Orestes, returns clandestinely to kill his mother. Again it is an open question, the question for the final play, the *Eumenides*, whether his deed is polluting matricide or rectifying revenge.

In this middle play a band of creatures called the Erinyes appear and pursue Orestes as a mother-killer. Or rather they don't appear, for although they are on stage, they are visible only to Orestes, "dark-gowned and twisted round with swarming snakes," while to the women bearing the drink offerings they are mere "notions" (*doxai, Libation Bearers* 1049–51). Hence some interpreters have thought that they are extrusions of Orestes' guilty conscience.[2] If so, they are matricidal guilt phantasms only while the mother's blood is not yet dry. In the last play they have material lives and are plain to sight, to hearing and even to smell—they exhale stink (*Eumenides* 53).

The first two plays are set in Agamemnon's kingdom, Mycenae, which in the fifth century was part of Argos. Now, in the *Eumenides*, the scene shifts from Argos to Athens via Delphi.

I observe here that this final play of the trilogy will have none of the practically prescriptive features Aristotle ascribes in his *Poetics* to tragedy, the very features the *Agamemnon* has to perfection: no colorably good human being of high station with a tragic flaw, no so-called unity of time and place, no audience purification by pity and fear (Ch. 13, 5, 6). Instead, the play's occasion, Orestes, is a small-gauged victim of circumstance, the protagonist divinities are beyond human flaw, the play includes the world as its venue and covers months or years in its time.

It might even be said to qualify, before the event, Aristotle's claim that poetry is more serious than history because the historian only tells what did happen while the poet tells what might happen (Ch. 9). Now this poet so fuses, in his mythopoetic drama, what did and what might happen that the opposition between history and poetry is in effect canceled.

For the *Eumenides* is a revised story of an origin, of a founding, not a speculation about what might *in general* happen but a story about what might *in particular* have happened. So, indeed, is most imaginative writing, but this drama gives a mythopoetic account of the founding event of a *real* institution, the Areopagus, the High Court of Athens. It is intended to display the meaning of the Court's present. This is not factual history conjectured from evidence by research but the dateless past recovered through a vision of its present consequences—not fact but nonetheless, or better, *therefore*, truth. I shall try to explain myself later. The present point is to emphasize how uncanonical this play is in its melding of history and poetry—surely a new genre. And that brings me back to its name.

Eumenides was the title by which the play was known in antiquity; there is some agreement that it was Aeschylus' own.[3] I'll suppose that it was, since that leads to a thought-provoking and so perhaps intended consequence.

The play-going city, virtually every male citizen and resident, knew well who these Eumenides were. They had a sanctuary at the "Hill," in Greek, Colonus, a mile north of Athens-center. It was the place where in Sophocles' *Oedipus at Colonus* the patricide Oedipus will be said to have found refuge and release, as will the matricide Orestes on Ares' Rock, the Areopagus.[4] These divinities were also known to have a more central home, in the cleft beneath the Areopagus, facing northeast toward the Acropolis. And they were called variously the Awe-inspiring, the August Ones. People were evidently mindful of the literal meaning of *Eu-menides*, an adjective formed from *eu*, "well," and *menos*, "disposition." They were the Well-disposed Ones; as Sophocles will say: "because they receive the suppliant out of their well-disposed hearts" (*Oedipus at Colonus* 11, 39, 89, 486).

These gracious goddesses are thought of with respectful and even with affectionate trust. I will venture a comparison. Although refugees like Oedipus and Orestes aren't exactly "huddled masses," yet I am reminded of Emma Lazarus's poem inscribed on the main entrance of the Statue of Liberty, which announces that she receives those "huddled masses yearning to breathe free."[5] Just so the Eumenides represent the capacious, burden-removing, and, I might say, diversity-welcoming aspect of Athena's city—as we will see.

Now these well-disposed ones were on the playbill, or whatever apprised the theatergoer of the dramatic fare for the day. And behold! the creatures that form both the chorus and the character confronting the protagonist have the very opposite name. They are called the Erinyes, and sometimes speak as one in the first person singular through their leader, one Erinys (for example, 951). Moreover, they don't act as does the usual tragic chorus; thus, the old burghers of Argos in the *Agamemnon* are sidelined to ineffectual, mildly wise commentary. These are a fierce lot.

Everyone knew *them* as well. In English they are called the "Furies." Their Greek name may derive from *eris*, "strife,"[6] but the facts are lost in the mists of age. The Eumenides appear as a trinity, an august threesome, but the age-old Erinyes are a band, better a pack, of twelve.[7] They are horror incarnate, frightful and disgusting, dressed darkly in rags, with rheumy eyes, foul breath, and snakes through their hair. Apollo's Pythian priestess who opens the play is soon seen running out on all fours from their sight, which is Gorgonlike, but even more, bitch-like. When we first see them they are asleep, panting and slobbering in their dream of hunting their victim down:

Labe, labe, labe; phrazou!
Catch, catch, catch—mark him! (130).

The oldest manuscript of the play that we have, the Medicean Codex of the later tenth century, includes a life of Aeschylus which claims that he did yet another unheard-of thing: By letting the Erinyes "loose without order into the orchestra, he so scared the people that infants expired and women miscarried."[8] I don't think infants and pregnant women were in fact in the theater, but as I imagine it, the effect was—how shall I put it?—participatory.

The business of the Furies, the opposite of the releasing Eumenides, was to hold the world bound in the constraints of order and justice. In the *Iliad* they check Achilles' grieving horse when he bursts, unnaturally, into human speech (19.418). Heraclitus says that "the Sun will not overstep its measures; if he doesn't [control himself], the Erinyes, the helpers of justice, will rout him out" (Fr. 94). Clearly these dreaded beings guard the rightful courses of nature. Such natural order is called justice, *dikê*. These guardians of *dikê* are born of Earth in Hesiod's *Theogony* (184) and of Night in Aeschylus' *Eumenides*, of obscure darkness in either case.

As the action developed, the spectators began to understand that they were witnessing a terrific conversion: The Erinyes were turning before their eyes into Eumenides. They were transformed in bearing and garb—most significantly, as we will see—but also in number, although the play does not say so. Had I been the *choregos*, the producer, of the play, I would have had the transformation include the fading away of the twelve-pack Erinyes into the threesome Eumenides; the *Eumenides* would, in fact, make a terrific movie script. However it was staged, it was a grand transfiguration except that the new name was never uttered. Why not? Something near enough is said of them in the play: The reformed Erinyes are given the adjective *euphrones*, "well- (or kindly)-minded." These frightening faces, Athena says to her citizens, will be of great profit to you, if you, being kindly-minded, honor them, the Kindly-minded (*euphronas euphrones*, 992). As I imagine it, all of Athens, sitting there in enthralled solemnity, was meant to experience a dawning recognition: "But these transfigured horrors are *our* Kindly Ones, our Well-disposed deities, our Eumenides, that live on the other side of the hill not far from this theater!"

By the end of Aeschylus's century the name Eumenides is simply a euphemism for Erinyes[9]—very likely Aeschylus's doing, but not in his spirit. For in his play the Erinyes really do disappear, are transformed into the, yet unnamed, Eumenides. Athena and her people know how to turn the dreadful females into the Gracious Ladies, how to make the horrors holy. That is Aeschylus's trenchant patriotism: to see Athens as a sovereignly assimilative power, her goddess as supremely, grandly ingenious—and something else, something beyond that I will consider later; it has to do with the fact that the Eumenides, if no longer horrible, are terrible still: the frightening faces.

The learned term for any causal account, and thus for Aeschylus's mythical history, is aetiology, from *aitia*, a "reason or cause," and *logos*, a "rational account." Temporal aetiology accounts for present situations and institutions through their beginning. Primal times are explanatory times; to recall them is to recall the present to its sense of itself. Aeschylean aetiology, however, is not done by what we call archaeology or history, the unearthing of buried artifacts or the researching of old documents. It is rather the projection backward into the timeless past of an originary vision, of the origin as it appears *now* to the mythopoetic sight.

Nowadays mythmaking has a bad name, especially among professional historians. It is an accusation. For example, there is a well-known book by Garry Wills entitled *Inventing America*.[10] In its prologue, Wills analyzes Lincoln's "Gettysburg Address" of 1863. "Well, now," he says, "that is a very nice myth," a "useful falsehood," and a "dangerous thing." It is a reprehensible piece because, among other things, in the exalted biblical language of "four score and seven years ago" Lincoln traces the birth of the nation back to 1776 and so to the Declaration of Independence and to its self-evident truth "that all men are created equal." Wills, however, thinks he knows that this date of origin is deceitfully false. It was not until the final ratification of the Constitution in 1789 that we became a nation, and thus our conception was not in an idea but in all sorts of practical manipulations, messy and even unholy. What is more, Wills likes better that view of our country which sees it as the product of practical compromises than that which envisions its birth in a whole-hearted ideal, because such ideals are never "straight-minded," to borrow a word from the *Eumenides.* They always have, he thinks, a subtly pernicious hidden agenda, in Lincoln's case the establishment of a "civil religion," which made us falsely feel that we could save and redeem the world.

I cite this book only to sharpen by contrast the contours of both Aeschylus's and Lincoln's kind of patriotism, which does not consign its country's present to ever-disputable, secular historical fact but derives it from a primal act that contains timeless truth. Such origin-myths give a definite temporal dimension to presently active principles; mythopoetry is the art of putting a past event behind the present situation. This is truth-telling of a high order and has nothing in common with the falsification of facts—which Aeschylus did not have in any case. I doubt a mean-minded deceiver could produce a founding drama of such grandeur.

How to tell feckless disregard of facts and mendacious skewing of history from sound-minded *mythopoiesis?* Strangely enough, language tells. Aeschylus's Greek seems to me an essential element of his patriotic passion. It is as far as any diction can well be from what will one day be the crude formulas of propaganda. The marvel is that any of his Athenians understood him, for his language is so high *and* subtle, so grand *and* flexible, so archaic *and* neologistic, so bold *and* complex, that most of us who suppose that we knew at least a little Greek have to puzzle the text out laboriously with recourse to every aid available.

I will give a few examples of his word-making, poetry practiced on the very elements of language: *bdelýktropoi,* "a loathsome turn" (52); *palaiópaides*, "elderchildren" (69); *dysodopaípala*, a "rough-and-rocky" road (387); *brotoskópon*, "man-watching" (499). All these words are so new and sound so ancient; this diction is magnificent without being grandiloquent—though, to be sure, the reverently irreverent Aristophanes displays Aeschylus and Euripides in Hades hurling eleven-syllable masses of "tight-riveted words" at each other (*Frogs* 824). The Athenian audience, at any rate, loved it in all its stiffness and inventiveness, and they seem to have caught the hyper-intricate choral meters and savored the gorgeous staging.

For the *Oresteia* won first prize. Aeschylus wrote between seventy and ninety plays—we only have seven—and won first prize twenty-eight times; some of these awards were posthumous, since after his death the people of Athens decreed funds toward the revival of his plays.[11]

The *Eumenides* was first performed in 458 B.C.E., and it was rooted in the present of that year. There are at least four references to the current situation. To begin with, when Athena first appears she says that she has heard Orestes' call from far-off Troyland, where she had been taking control of territory assigned to her by the Greek victors. Not only is she presenting herself as a divinity with far-flung possessions, but to the Athenian audience she must have been heard, in these early days of the Delian League that would turn into Athens's empire, as asserting dominion over the cities of the Troad, a claim Athens was then in fact pursuing.[12]

Again, when the Erinyes finally accept Attic domicile they are re-robed onstage in "scarlet-dyed vestments" (*phoenikobaptois . . . esthemasi*, 1028). As they had been promised, they become "fellow-dwellers," *metoikoi* in Greek (869, 1011). These "metics," resident foreigners, something like our green-card holders, were just at this time being recognized as being of major importance to Attic prosperity. They participated in the great civic processions dressed in scarlet robes.[13] Aeschylus is expressing the inclusiveness of Athena Polias's city, or, put less amiably, he is endorsing the expansionism of post-Persian Athens.

A third topical reference lies in Orestes' grateful oath, pledging Argos to perpetual peace and alliance with Athens (764), a matter of considerable current importance to a city embarking on just that audaciously expansive foreign policy.

The fourth case I will mention concerns the Areopagus High Court, whose founding is the central event of the *Eumenides*. The old oligarchic Areopagus Council, the historical court, had recently been stripped of its expansive powers, powers of law enforcement, punishment, and censorship. In the democratic reform that occurred just a few years before the production of the play (463–61 B.C.E.), these had devolved on popular institutions. Aeschylus, evidently a moderate democrat, here appears to endorse this reduction of the court's brief to cases of murder, since he represents Athena as instituting it for just that purpose.

Aeschylus himself was deeply engaged in the city's life, and it was a factor in his fame. The year after winning first prize for the *Oresteia*, in his late sixties, he left Athens for Sicily, probably to execute dramatic commissions,[14] and died there soon after at seventy. The people of Gela, where he was buried, set him a grave marker with an inscription calling him Athens's pride and noting that he had fought at Marathon.[15] But he had fought also at Salamis, the other of Athens's two great single-handed battles against the Persian invaders. At Salamis the Athenians fought in ships under the view of Xerxes the King. Eight years later, in 472, a very young Pericles was the producer of Aeschylus's *Persians*, which takes place in Xerxes' court at Susa after the Salaminian defeat and is the grandest case of empathy for a vanquished enemy that I know of.

The time of his life as a whole and of this, his last recorded winning play, was altogether the high time of his city. When he was five years old, the Pisistratid tyranny was overthrown in favor of the Athenian democracy to which we might well be said ultimately to owe our own political being. When he wrote the *Oresteia* the Persians had been ejected from Greece for over two decades, and the perils of Attic imperialism were looming, though yet avoidable. When Aeschylus left Athens in 457 the rebuilding of the mighty old temple of Athena Parthenos, destroyed by the Persian occupiers of the Acropolis and rebuilt with tribute money paid by Athens' client states to the Delian League, money meant to protect them from the Persians, and in fact soon to be stolen by the Athenians—this ominous and glorious Periclean project was yet ten years off. So also was the restoration after the Persian sack of the Erechtheum, Athena Polias's house, being talked of but very far from even being begun.[16] This precinct, alluded to in the play (855), was Athena Polias's special seat, where was housed her primeval statue of olive wood, the one that will play a role in the drama, the bole that miraculously survived the Persian burning of the High City. And it was here that the testimonials of the contest between her and Poseidon for the possession of Athens were shown, a salt pool struck from the rock by the sea god and by it an olive tree sprung up from the rock at the behest of the city goddess.[17] It may be that the olive tree was a witness to Athena's trumping wit, which won her the city: A salt pool is put to real use as brine in which olives are marinated to make them edible.[18]

As I imagine it, Aeschylus felt his city to be at a cresting time, with some depths of danger and more heights of hope looming. 458 B.C.E. was a time of crisis for Athens—*krisis* in the Greek sense, a time for judgment when a provident poet-lover of his country would be inspired to foresee the glories and driven to forfend the disasters of the future.

Beside the astonishing language and the expansive spirit of the drama, the town folk who sat there took in astonishing new interpretations of the world they knew: the origin of the

Delphic oracle as well as of the names both of the Areopagus and of the Eumenides, the comparative stature of their goddess and Delphi's Apollo, the origin of their claims on Argos's loyalty.

But again and again and above all, these Athenians saw the magisterial management of their city's affairs by their goddess, the maternal virgin goddess, the peaceable warrior goddess, flexible and firm, the child close to her Father who is the highest, the universal divinity. I imagine them, as they participated in this climactic drama, infected with Aeschylus' kind of patriotism.

There are, as I said, different patriotisms, unsound and sound. There is "chauvinism," bigotry and exclusiveness, born of poverty of spirit and clumsy anger. And then there is a liberal patriotism based on moral consanguinity. Thus Lincoln says that those who adopt the moral principle of "that old Declaration of Independence" can claim to be "blood of the blood."[19] And there is also a community of customs and friendly feeling. And last but not least there is the land itself; the hills surrounding the city of Athens are sung as "violet-crowned" (iostephanoi) as the continent of America is sung for its "purple mountains' majesty." But first and above all there is a founding wisdom. Thus the third stanza of "America the Beautiful" qualifies patriotism:

> America, America, God mend thine every flaw,
> Confirm thy soul in self-control, thy liberty in law![20]

Thus, too, Aeschylus's patriotism is first and finally focused on his citizens' moral virtue: They are "sound-minded [or in the usual translation 'moderate'] in good time" (sophronountes en chronoi, 1000);[21] this is the most exalted praise their new co-dwellers know to give Athena's people.

With this quotation I come to the drama itself as an exemplar of my subtitle, The Grandeur of Reasonableness.

II. MODERATE MODERNITY

"Modernity" means literally "just-nowness," from Latin *modo*, "just now." This literal meaning suggests one defining aspect of modernity—there are others—that fits the Aeschylean revisioning of Athens's goddess. In this sense, modernity is an ever-recurrent moment in human history; it is the mode of rationality practically applied. A given situation goes from onerous to insupportable and human ingenuity finds a—usually radical—device for bettering man's estate in the here and now, an impatiently swift solution; this modernizing reason is bent on rectifying the condition just now. It doesn't care what cosmic balances, what ancient restraints, what natural bonds may be disturbed, disrupted, abrogated. Such enlightened reason is bright-eyed and lightheaded in its universalizing impulse and in its disrespect for the ancient obstacles. It is impatient with old naïve Nature and wants to supplant her with new, sophisticated Artifice. These abstractions are, I think, embodied in the two contending divinities of Aeschylus's play. The earlier part shows how Athena aids the new rationality, represented by Apollo, in winning its case against the old justice; the later part shows how Athena moderates this dangerous victory by inviting the old powers into her city and teaching her people how to be soundly rational by respecting the claims of a primeval cosmic equipoise, awful though it may be in aspect.

The *Eumenides*, being the last drama of a trilogy,[22] supervenes on a long chain of dramatic events. To recount it in skeletal form: Before the *Oresteia* begins, Atreus, Agamemnon's father, has killed Thyestes' sons and served their flesh to their father at a banquet. Agamemnon himself has sacrificed his and Clytemnestra's daughter to speed the Greek expedition on to Troy. In the *Agamemnon*, his wife, Clytemnestra, and Aegistheus, a surviving son of Thyestes, have killed Agamemnon on his victorious return from Troy, each for a

compelling reason. In the *Libation Bearers* Orestes, Clytemnestra's and Agamemnon's son, has killed her and Aegistheus
to avenge his father and preserve his own succession. Now in
the *Eumenides* Clytemnestra's ghost is clamoring for Orestes'
death as a matricide. That last killing would be the end of the
Atreides, the House of Atreus, and the vacating of the curse
on it for Atreus's deed. Thyestes' progeny had already been
erased. The two cursed lineages would have ceased. Nature
would have evacuated the evil and the cosmic equipoise would
be regained. This is natural justice, the justice of the Erinyes,
also called the "Curses" (*Arai*), who *are* naïvely furious justice: Why should a killer, especially a mother-killer, live? It is
against the logic, the measures, of nature.

Ordinary mortals, on the other hand, tend to be of two
minds. They have tit-for-tat justice in their bones, but they
also ask, as does the chorus at the end of the *Libation Bearers*: "When will there be rest from, when will there be a stop
to, the fury of this blind ruin (*ate*, 107 6)?" They long for an
imposed intervention, a forcible cut-off that ends the natural
course, the logical working out of the accursed drama.

This natural justice has the name *dikê*, or as its enforc-
ers sometimes say: *eutheia dikê*, "straight justice" (312, 436).
The Erinyes think of themselves as straight-justice-dispens-
ing. The word *dikê* with its derivatives is the dominating
sound of the play: *dikaios, endikos, dikastes, dikephoros,
orthodikaion, adikein*—the text bristles with it, and the ear
rings with it. This *dikê*, which the Erinyes claim as their own,
has a thoroughly practical, concrete use. It means old custom and usage; it will henceforth mean the actual lawsuit
brought and the effective judgment rendered; but above all, it
means the order and right of things. The noun *dikê* seems to
be anciently connected with the verb *deiknymi*, "show, indicate." The Erinyes say: "Come, let us join in the dance since
it *seems right to display* our hateful muse," for their office is
to do "straight justice," justice horrid but perspicuous (307).

The Erinyes' *dikê*, the justice of reciprocity, a life for a life, is *plainly* responsive to brute fact, particularly when blood relations are involved.

Dikê, the concrete justice of the Erinyes, is therefore not *dikaiosyne*, Just-ness, the thought-invoking object of inquiry mooted in Plato's *Republic*. The question behind the play is indeed "What is justice?," but it is here engaged by the parties to a trial and by judicial decisions. The accuser is dead Clytemnestra appearing as a specter (*eidolon*), the defendant her live son Orestes, the venue the Areopagus court of ten jurorjudges with Athena as arbiter; the advocate for Clytemnestra is the band of Erinyes, for Orestes, Delphic Apollo.

So the play begins in Delphi, and right away there is revisionist mythmaking, Aeschylean aetiology. The Pythia, the priestess of Apollo's oracle, comes out of the temple just to tell the story of Apollo's taking possession of Delphi. All the world knew that it had been a violent business,[23] but the Pythia paints the picture of a smooth, unforced inheritance. In this tale, Apollo is a welcome civilizing god, the "prophet" of Zeus. He appears as a divinity of easy—no, facile—dominion, a god whose people have been trained to suppress the darker circumstances of his installation in Delphi.

The priestess goes back in and soon runs out again, totally freaked out, as our students would say, by the creatures that sit inside on stools, asleep, slobbering and snoring. She exits. The temple doors are now open and we see them: the Erinyes. Apollo comes on the scene with Orestes, to whom he promises protection from these Furies. He tells him to flee from them over land, sea, and islands, but finally to go as a suppliant to Pallas Athena's city for "relief from his pains." He ends: "For *I* persuaded you to kill the mother-body" (84). Orestes sets out on his long expiatory flight.

Clytemnestra's specter appears and upbraids the sleeping Erinyes for neglecting their pursuit. They wake up to dance and sing the first of several choruses that have a terrible

kind of dignity and induce a repelled sort of pity. They sing
to Apollo: "You, the young male, have ridden down the old
female divinities" (*daimonas*, 150) by the respect you show
for a godless man. "This," they sing, "is what the younger
gods do who exercise power altogether beyond Justice" (162).
Apollo responds by reviling them. They then bandy words, a
foretaste of the arguments they will mount before the Areopagus, where both will claim to have justice on their side.

It is a long time later. We are now in Athens, on the Acropolis. Orestes has arrived to sit, as he had been ordered by
Apollo, as a suppliant with his arms around the old olive-
wood statue of Athena, the one kept in the Erechtheum. He
insists that he is no longer polluted because Apollo has purified him and that, moreover, his guilt has been blunted by
time and travel. But the Erinyes are still in hot pursuit. When
they see him clasping the statue they sing out a horrible song:
They will suck red clots of blood from his limbs in requital for
mother-blood, "Everyone receives the justice he deserves. . . ."
Hades "oversees all in his recording-tablet of a mind." What
they are saying is that some deeds are ineradicable, uneras-
able: "Mother's blood, once spilled on the ground, is scarcely
recoverable," even if retribution has been exacted (261 ff.).
Orestes claims, on the contrary, to have worked off his guilt
through travel and "time that, growing old along with everything, purifies it" (286).

And now the lead-Erinys announces the "Binding-Hymn."
It is a furious, long, stamping dance, an incantation for enchaining the mind (370, 332). It asserts the Furies' power and
right to pursue even into Hades those who commit inexpiable
crimes of blood.

Athena flies in, answering Orestes' call. Aeschylus was admired for his staging; she surely arrives, a *dea ex machina*,
by some cranelike device. But neither machines nor words
make the wonder of this moment; it is rather the spectacle
itself: Here is Athena's old *bretas*, the olive bole that Orestes

is embracing. Here is the possibly winged (1001) goddess herself, the divinity on which Orestes has called. He sees her, the spectators see her, the splendid deity vis-à-vis her presumably primitively carved, homely statue.[24] How could the sight of both together help but lead to reverent reflection? The city was full of statuary Athenas. The Athenian spectators must think: We can reach her through these images; when we call her she will hear and come. But they must, at the same time, feel reminded that their wooden board, their marble statues, and their clay statuettes are just that: images, not the goddess herself. And that is exactly what distinguishes their worship from idolatry. For an idol is to the worshipper *not* an image but the spirit itself, prayed *to*, not *through*. These Athenians, presented by their first playwright with the wooden token and the real goddess face to face, were being invited—whether they followed the call or not—to think about the patent defectiveness and the mysterious power of those increasingly perfect representational artifacts that their normally invisible goddess was eliciting from them.[25]

Athena descends and notices the Furies. Apollo had reviled them and driven them from his temple: "Out, I am ordering you. . . . You belong where there are judgments and butcheries of head-lopping and eye-gouging, and where the green youth of boys is ruined by destruction of seed" (186)—Aeschylean language for castration, high poetry to render the immoderate tone of the self-righteous young god.

Here is Athena's reception for them. She says that she is not afraid of, but she *is* amazed by, these creatures, which are unlike any other race, not seen among gods or comparable to humans in shape. Then she catches herself: "But to speak ill of someone close by us because he is misshaped does not approach what is just . . ." (413).

The Erinyes introduce themselves. They are called the "Curses," and are the children of Night who live beneath the earth. They begin the argument. Athena says: "I would understand [all this], if someone would give a perspicuous account" (420). Athena wants to hear from both sides in lucid speech. She admonishes the Furies not to insist on formalisms. The Furies begin to trust her and entrust their case to her decision. So does Orestes. The gist of the case is, on the Furies' side, a rationally connected double demand: that a mother-killer should be hunted down even into Hades and that their own just prerogative to execute this charge should not be abrogated. On Orestes' side, too, there is a double argument, which is not so rationally coherent, though Orestes has had a "smart teacher" (*sophos didaskalos*, 279) in Apollo. He admits to the deed but claims that he was justly requiting his father's murder, and he also offers the excuse that Apollo forced him to it with threats of "stinging pain to the heart" (466).

Once again something simply amazing happens. Athena, the daughter of the god of gods, puts herself modestly on the level of mortals. She says: "The affair is too great for some mortal to think he can adjudicate it,/Nor is it right for me to decide a judicial case concerned with a killing so acutely anger-filled." On the one hand there is before them a purified suppliant, on the other, the undeniable charge of the Furies who will, moreover, should they lose the case, poison the ground for ever. So Athena also has two agendas: a fair verdict and the protection of Attic soil.

She issues an ordinance "for all time" (484). Justice concerning killings will henceforth be turned over to *judges*. *Dikê* will go to *dikastai*; Justice is turned over to juries; the natural course of just requital is turned into a case-at-law, and the avenging Erinyes are to plead before a court. Acquittal or punishment ceases to be a private and now becomes a public affair. A British Lord Chief Justice said: "One . . . object of punishment is to prevent . . . the victims of crime from taking matters into their own hands."[26] Athena's institution of the high court of Athens is a revolution in human affairs, the kind of event I call modern, or, better, modernizing. It means the overthrow of ancient ways in the interest of a reasonable procedure, a crucial characteristic of which is the growth of public power, the expansion of what in our quintessentially "modern times," the times in which modernity becomes the established mode, is called the state.

But what if the accuser loses the case, if a guilty defendant escapes punishment on technicalities and the righteously aggrieved party is left helplessly furious? What if the humane, exculpatory rationality of the human court leaves the world out of kilter? We will see how Athena mitigates this inevitable consequence of institutional justice, the conversion of capital Justice as a power into lower-case justice as a process.

But first there is that initial, that mythic trial before the Areopagus. Athena goes off to select "the best [material, *ta beltata*] among my townspeople" (487). I don't think she means the aristocrats or oligarchs. Aeschylus' locution betokens that the juror-judges are just the fittest citizens. Aeschylus, recall, is a defender of Athenian democracy.

While she is gone, the Eumenides sing again, a song of despair and threatened withdrawal: "Now come the overturnings, the revolutions (*katastrophai*), wreaked by new ordinances—if the hurtful justice of this mother-killer is to dominate" (490). "I shall"—they sing as one—"permit every violent ruin (*moron*, 502)." "Let no one cry out 'O Justice! O thrones of the Erinyes!' . . . since the House of Justice has indeed collapsed" (511). And then in the middle of their lamenting threats they make a demand that justifies my picture of them as intended by Aeschylus to be the representatives of the aboriginal justice of equilibrium:

Approve neither the anarchic life
nor the tyrannized one . . .
God grants the power to everything middling.
I speak the proportionate word (*symmetron epos*, 531).

Athena, who was not there to hear them, will—wonder-fully—repeat their words.

But first the trial. The scene seems to have shifted to the chambers of the Areopagus court. Trumpets sound; the people stream in; the court sits. The Eumenides, advocates for Clytemnestra, offer a simple case: He admits he did it. The opposition's claim that Zeus, Zeus who overcame his own father, has more regard for a father's than a mother's death is implausible. Moreover, Clytemnestra, in killing her spouse, did not kill a blood relation, a mitigating circumstance for her. Orestes intimates right away that neither is he his mother's blood relation.

Apollo now speaks for Orestes. He again proceeds violently: "You altogether hateful beasts, hated by the gods . . ." (644). He follows Orestes' line: "The mother so-called is not the child's begetter" (658). He goes on to speak as a scientist to common folk, dispensing fancy then-modern biology, according to which the mother has no part in the embryo except that of a nurse.[27] So every mother is merely a foster mother. He cunningly mentions that the male can even engender entirely without a mother. He cites the daughter of Zeus, Athena herself, as a case. It is a smart lawyer's move, but once again, disregardful of the Erinyes. For Aeschylus has—against tradition—made them the children of Night, and she, Hesiod tells us, can bear "having slept with no one" (*Birth of the Gods*, 213); the Furies themselves (probably) have no father.

I interrupt the account here to point to a curious circumstance that must have crept into every spectator's mind: Apollo's argument, which in fact abolishes mothers insofar as they are nothing but carrying wombs, is cleverly made in a drama that is enacted, except for Clytemnestra appearing as a specter and the Amazons appearing in a story, mainly by childless females whose status is above, below, beyond natural womanhood: the Pythian priestesses who open the play, the Erinyes who are transformed in its course, the consecrated guardians of Athena's statue who lead the exit march. Above them all thrones Athena Parthenos, the Virgin (999). Why? Well, first this is a sacral drama, and the great Olympians are served by virgins. But more significantly, the two protagonists, female-gendered but non-bearing, are, on the one hand, male-like powers, the one of fiercely spirited engagement, the other of majestically large objectivity. Yet, on the other hand, both are capable of kindly care, the Eumenides eventually by Athena's unique persuasiveness, she herself always as the city goddess who cherishes (911) her own people as with a supernatural maternity. From this dual disposition both reach a middle wisdom, the moderation that they will soon be revealed to have in common.

The pleading is done. Athena addresses her citizens while the court deliberates. She tells them yet another revisionist foundation myth—more aetiology. The place where the court of juror-judges, a court that will exist forever, is deciding its first murder case, the kind for which she has instituted it, is called the Areopagus, "Ares' Rock," because there the army of Amazons from Asia that attacked Athens in the time of Theseus sacrificed to Ares (683). Again, all the world knew the current explanation of the name, which was that Ares, having killed a son of Poseidon for trying to rape his daughter, was tried on this hill for murder by a jury of gods. I assume that he was acquitted, as Orestes will be.

Why this new tale? One notion is that Aeschylus wants Orestes' trial to be the initial case of the new Areopagus court.[28] But if the earliest court consisted of the twelve Olympian gods, Athena's institution of a mortal court of ten would still be original enough, and if Ares had indeed been acquitted the precedent might be welcome. I think Aeschylus revises the naming event of this court's home to remind his audience of the more recent Asian army that had entered the city just over three decades ago, that of the Persians. Then Athens had ejected a male invasion—though they regarded the Persians as effeminate—as once before in mythical times it had defeated a female invasion. Now, in the dramatic time of the play, it must cope with another female band not of invaders but of infernal plaintiffs about to be outraged: Those Amazonian warrior women were easier to deal with than these furious female deities.

She uses the pause in the drama to make a consequent point: Reverence this Areopagus! Don't muck up—she uses strong language—your own bright water. Their own inborn fear and awe will keep the town's men from doing injustice, as long as "the citizens themselves don't make innovations in the laws" (*epikainonton nomous*, 693).[29] While in the course of instituting novelties she warns her people against innovation!

And then, in the most significant moment of the play, she goes on to say exactly what the Eumenides have said in her absence: "I counsel the caring townsmen to revere neither the anarchic nor the tyrannized way, and *not to throw all that is dreadful out of the city*. For who among mortals, fearing nothing, is yet imbued with justice?" (697).

She and the Furies together seem to be doing a long-term end-run around Apollo, although she is about to help him win his current case. Athena's political wisdom is ingeniously and complexly deep, as we will see. It is the art of compromise, raised to glory (see Essay 5, "On Compromise").

After the jurors have voted and before the votes are counted Athena makes a consequence-fraught announcement. If the vote is tied, Orestes will be acquitted, because her pebble is going into the urn for acquittal. Her reason is stupefyingly simple and unprincipled: "I support everything male—except for the matter of getting married [here speaks the virgin goddess], and I am very much my Father's child" (736).

This is another remarkable moment. Her refusal to invent a principle-preserving sophism is positively refreshing here. After all, she has a deeper reason that she is wise not to articulate before the Furies: to stop the descent of killing, to put an end to this murderous lineage without actually eradicating it. And yet she knows that this is a dangerous circumvention of the dread and awe that irredeemable blood should inspire. And that is, as ever, only one of two wise intentions. The other is to establish by precedence a permanent ordinance: the judicial compromise that will resolve an insoluble situation. The equality of votes, five to five, which she surely foresees— or so I imagine—betokens the inability of human beings to resolve this matter by themselves, to be of one dispositive mind, any more than the deity could deal with it alone. She knows that she is to be the tie-breaker; she must supply the casting vote, and it is for ever—and still for us—in favor of acquittal. When humans are equally divided in mind, civilization says: Let him go. Give him the benefit of the doubt. And ever after, in the goddess's absence, her tiebreaking vote, cast for clemency,[30] will be present in every court, and so will she.* (I don't say "cast for mercy" because this is pagan

> In Athenian law a tie vote effected acquittal (see Essay 20, "Athens"). This "benefit-of-the-doubt" rule could be interpreted as Athena's moderating presence in every court.

moderation, civilized leniency, not Christian forgiveness.) Furthermore, Athena's rule tends toward slowing innovation in deliberative assemblies: Positive action is defeated by a tie.[31]

So Orestes is acquitted, and he, full of gratitude and promises for an Argive alliance, quits the scene with his divine advocate.

Athena is left with her assembled people—and the absolutely infuriated Furies. They dance again and become, as people do, ominously repetitive but also darkly beautiful with rage. They again speak as one, fixated on the locution of being ridden down by the younger gods and iterating their lament:

I am she who is unhonored—she who is wretched, deeply angered

In this land—Oh!
I emit poison, my heart's poison in payment for pain,
In infertile drops on the ground. (780, 810)

And again the goddess does something astonishing, something no other divinity, I imagine, would or could attempt
and accomplish: She undertakes to calm the Furies, to gentle them. She speaks to them between their laments. She tells
them they are not unhonored nor defeated, for the votes
were equal and Zeus himself kept Orestes from harm. This
is tact—half the jurors, she points out, were for them; moreover, not their antagonist Apollo but the god of gods himself
ordered the outcome. Here she gently reminds all of her closeness to Zeus; she alone knows the keys to the chamber where
his thunderbolt is sealed (827). It is the subtlest of threats. But
above all she has begun to make her daring offer: Be "augustly
honored and be co-dweller (*synoikêtôr*) with me" (833). She
is inviting the Furies into her city!!
They still rage repetitively. "For me to bear this, oh!—for
me of such ancient good sense to dwell in this earth is a dis-
honoring defilement," they say twice over (838, 871).
Athena bears it patiently, though she tells them understat-
edly, "Zeus has not done badly by me either in giving me good
sense." She promises more, a place for them close to her own
Erechtheum, the prize of the country's first fruits, and honors
over any they might have from mortals elsewhere—if they will
not afflict her places with incitements to bloodshed, drunken
rages, fighting-cock hearts, and rash intractable aggression.
"Let our wars be external!," she says (861), since it is not war
she denounces but civil war. "I won't weary of telling you,"
she goes on, "so you can never say that by me, the younger,
and my city-holding mortals, you, the ancient deity, went unhonored and were made a stranger on this soil." If you have
reverence for the power of Persuasion, the honeyed soothing
and seduction of my tongue, you will stay (881, cf. 970).

Suddenly, as one, they cave in: "Queen Athena,"—now first they call her queen, as had Orestes before them (235)—"what settlement do you say you have for me?" (892). Why? Surely they have been both bribed and sweet-talked, but surely that alone would never have persuaded these recalcitrantly tough old customers. I think what gets to them is not only Athena's tactful rhetoric; she takes it so far as to incriminate herself as one of those hated younger gods, though one who is deferential to the ancient ones, whom she has begun to address in the singular as one deity (848). No, it is above all her genuine understanding of their indispensable function. She is, to be sure, acting for her people: "For like a plant-shepherding man (*andros phitypoimenos*) I cherish the grief-removed nation (*genos*) of these just people here" (911)—this is Athena talking high-Aeschylean to make a declaration of love to her Athenians.

But then, after she has already brought the corps of Furies over, after they have already accepted co-dwelling (*synoikia*, 916) with her, she says from kindly care for her citizens: I have finally fixed these great and hard-to-please spirits, "for it is *their* lot to manage what pertains to mankind" (927). This is powerful language, which shows that she is seriously acknowledging their dangerous potency, the risky blessing she is introducing into her city. Her wise management of these managers reminds me of what is perhaps the crucial line in Shakespeare's *Merchant of Venice*: Bassanio says to the vengeful Jew: "Can no prayers pierce thee?" and Shylock answers: "No, none that thou hast wit enough to make" (IV i 128). Athena *has* wit enough and wisdom to pierce the avenging Furies, and that is because she, unlike Apollo (or Bassanio), can summon a real, a reverential respect for them: "Great power has the Lady Erinys" (950).

They sing antiphonally, the Erinyes of blessings to be bestowed, Athena of the blessings to be received, telling her citizens to be ever well- (or kindly-) minded toward these Well-

(or Kindly-) minded ones, the *Euphrones*—which is as close as she seems to wish to come to naming the Eumenides. There is a great exit procession: the Areopagites, Athena's acolytes, her Athenians, and finally the goddess herself, conducting the Erinyes, now dressed in the scarlet of resident aliens, marching as metics (1028), to their permanent home beneath Ares' Rock. Here is the third strophe of the exit march, sung by the Erinyes, now, without need of naming, recognized by all the spectators as *their* Eumenides:

> *Chaīrĕtĕ chaīrĕt' ĕn aīsĭmĭaīsĭ ploūtoŭ,*
> Chaīrĕt', āstĭkōs lĕōs.
> īktăr hēmĕnoī Dĭōs
> Pārthĕnoū phĭlās phĭloī,
> sōphrŏnoūntĕs ēn chrŏnoī,
> Pāllădōs d'ŷpō ptĕroīs
> ōntăs āzĕtaī Pătēr.

> Rejoice and farewell[32] in the happiness of wealth,
> Rejoice, townspeople
> Seated close to Zeus
> Friends of the friendly Virgin
> Moderate in good time
> Under the wings of Pallas Athene
> As you are, the Father respects you (996–1002).

Of course, the whole theater was, though seated, marching, gliding along—after the parading epic dactyls (- ˘ ˘) of the first line, a light trochaic tread (- ˘), solemn but nimble, grave and exhilarated; the trochee is the metric foot for light steadiness. This was surely a high moment of sound-minded patriotism founded on whole-hearted trust in the wisely innovating goddess.[33]

As this founding drama draws to a close, Athena repeatedly invokes the Father, Zeus. Through her, her people are near to him. I think this means that though she acts locally, in this Attic land, on this Athenian High City, at this Rock of

Ares, she is instituting a larger way, she is thinking universal Zeus-like thoughts for other places and later times. *Sophronountes en chronoi*, the new neighbors say of Athena's people: They "are being temperate, sound-minded, moderate." All these terms are acceptable renditions of *sophronountes*, which is, moreover a present participle, a verbal form signifying a continuing action. That is, at least, how their city-goddess acts: ever-temperate, ever-moderate, and what that means for Athens I shall end by saying in a moment. But why *en chronoi*, "in time, just in time, in good time"—all of these are possible meanings? It has seemed to readers a puzzlingly reserved phrase, a note of restraint sounded among these transports of reconciliation.[34] Perhaps what the Erinyes mean is that moderation is neither inbred nor learned in a day, especially not in its ongoing realization, the very temporality suggested by the verbal form: *being actively* moderate—thinking *soundly over* time.

Under Athena's wings they keep learning. What is this— their, her—moderation in this forever critical situation, life lived literally with the Erinyes beneath?

Let me begin to answer by recapitulating Athena's acts of moderation and innovation: Apollo, to win his case, cites new science which in effect says, "There are no mothers"; Athena, ensuring the same outcome, refers instead to her unique case of motherlessness but abstains from inhumanly radical generalizations. Faced with repulsive creatures, Apollo insults and expels them. Athena rather controls her repugnance and accords them more courteous treatment than, I imagine, they have ever received since dark Night bore them; she soothes and invites them. Saddled with a case in which primevally simple and humanly compromised justice confront each other, she magisterially accepts the case but modestly recognizes that neither her people nor she can resolve the matter alone. Consequently, she founds a novel institution, a court for cases of killing, thus both making justice a public rather than a family responsibility and corroborating Athens as a place of refuge and resolution. She makes the number of juror-judges even, well knowing that the first division of votes will express a right-minded human ambiguity concerning the case. She assumes the office of tie-breaker to give this verdict to the god-driven killer who is the first to come before the Areopagus court, tacitly ordaining the rule that in subsequent cases, when the mortals decide in her absence, equal votes will moderate primitive severity by signifying acquittal. Having thus of necessity offended the Furies, she goes persuasively—and sincerely—far in acknowledging their priority and power, honoring them with titles: She names, or rather titles them, finally, the August Goddesses (*Semnai Theai*), and grants them prerogatives—in effect a share in the supervision of her city. Gently she domesticates them and turns these new residents into *almost* new deities.

And yet . . . She is a modernizing goddess who, as the Erinyes themselves say, has caused a revolution. But when she takes the tremendous risk of domesticating these justly vengeful deities (not so unlike Themistocles' patriotic treason, when he "betrays" the Athenian fleet at Salamis to the Persians, who close in on it—to their doom, Herodotus, *Histories* VIII 75), making them officially metics, that is, co-dwellers, it is their intention she converts, not their nature. They are, as everyone knew, now the Eumenides, the Well-Intentioned, the Kindly-Thinking Ones. But they are still angry Erinyes as well: Their dark character as children of Night is not canceled but preserved[35] in that cave in Ares' Rock, beneath the Areopagus Court.

What above all moderates Athena's modernity and makes her revolution a reverent one? It is that she knows and honors the ancient dread. When the Erinyes lament that the new young gods ride them down, she, though herself a member of the new generation of gods, knows what that means: The others, at least this Apollo, this avatar of a modern intellectual, are too brightly shallow to feel it, to feel the fear that the world will become unbalanced if holy terror fails.

Even as she is establishing that work of reason, the human jury sitting in judgment, where the public decides by the numbers and the perpetrator goes humanely free when there is doubt, even as she is freely innovating, she tells her Areopagites that "their reverence for the court and the inborn fear of the townspeople will keep them from doing injustice . . . as long as the citizens don't make innovations in the laws." And then, she gives her counsel, the gist of which I will quote once again: not to revere either anarchy or despotism,

> And not to throw all that is dreadful out of the city.
> For who among mortals, fearing nothing, is yet imbued with
>   justice? (698)

This dread, this fear that the citizens are bidden to preserve, is a deep awareness of—one might even call it a kind of trust in—the terrible consequences of lightly letting old laws lapse and forcibly bringing in a new rational relief that leaves the primal Justice of reprisal out of kilter.

A penultimate question: Are the Erinyes creatures of conscience? Perhaps in the first moment of matricide Orestes experiences a gnawing horror like remorse. For, recall, in the *Libation Bearers* only he sees the Furies. But they soon materialize, and in the *Eumenides* the whole city sees them. They are there *not* to express a haunting sense of guilt but to recall a world-dislodging deed, and they are *not* evocations of the perpetrator but emissaries of the victim. The Erinyes are, indeed, never renamed in the play, but at the very end the people in the procession give them one last fitting adjective: *euthyphrones*, "straight-thinking" (1040). They are also repeatedly called children: "elder children" (*palaiopaides*, 69), no-children children (*paides apaides*, 1034). There is in fact something naïvely, frighteningly, undeflectably direct about these ancient childless children; they demand straight simplicity like young children when they are in the holy terror mode, when they are fixed on the brute fact of an inequity: "Why is he allowed . . . ?" No, they are not extrusions of the perpetrator's conscience. But neither are they expressions of the victim's outrage. The Erinyes are rather exhibitions of a cosmic power. They are, by Aeschylus' fiat, daughters of Night. "Murky Night" has borne, as Hesiod tells in his *Birth of the Gods*, many daughters, among them Nemesis, Blame and Woe, Destiny and the Fates,

> Who pursue the transgressions (*paraibasias*) of men and gods,
> Nor ever do these goddesses cease their dread anger
> Before they have given evil attention to anyone who has gone
>   wrong (220).

The Erinyes belong among the divine powers who keep the world from going out of joint[36] by rectifying imbalances. Born from murky dark they bring a dreadfully simple clarity of accounting: Do and pay.

Such are these anciently young spirits, while Athena is the newly young deity, and yet they come together over cosmic and civic politics. Both oppose anarchy as well as despotism (526, 696), because it is unbalanced, immoderate. Yet Athena Polias is an altogether modern, modernizing goddess, a civic deity who innovates, makes political revolution in the modern mode still current with us: She transfers moral responsibility to public institutions, decides by the numbers, that is, by voting, resolves issues by rational fiat, encourages perspicuous speech in both parties: "Answer me with something intelligible" (442, 420). But she is in complete sympathy with the Furies' cry that precedes their proscription of political extremes:

> There is a place where the dreadful is well (*to deinon eu*),
> And, as overseer of the heart,
> It ought to stay seated there.
> It is of profit
> To be moderate in narrow straits (517).

So both connect moderation with the welcoming of dread. For certain blood spilled simply is irretrievable (1175), and some deeds are forever irredeemable. And the Apolline solution to "invent" what he calls "engines of relief" (82) racks up the debts in that economy of things which the Erinyes call Justice. What Athena understands is that this truth must be invited in and kept in mind: that continuous propitiating mindfulness by the beneficiaries of abrogated requital is required. This is not straight Justice but it *is* clement civilization. In that knowledge consists Athena's moderate modernity.

Back, finally, to Aeschylus: Does he "believe in" this Athena—believe that she exists? I answer abruptly, from the bafflement of a post-pagan and the enthrallment of an all-but-worshipper: He loves her as he loves his city, and love makes moot the question of existence—at certain high moments.

NOTES

1. There is even an old story that Socrates helped Euripides make his plays, who was consequently called by a later comic writer "Socrato-rivet-patched" (*sokratogomphos*, Diogenes Laertius, II 18).

2. Podlecki, p. 8.

3. Verrall, p. xxxvi.

4. It may be that the idea of bringing Orestes *to* Athens arose from the fact that in the Odyssey he comes *from* Athens to avenge his father (iii 307).

5. Emma Lazarus, "The New Colossus" (1883). ". . . 'Give me your tired, your poor, / Your huddled masses yearning to breathe free, / The wretched refuse of your teeming shore . . .'."

6. Podlecki, p. 7.

7. Sommerstein, p. 109, on 142.

8. Paley, p. xxxv.

9. E.g. Euripides, *Orestes*, 35 (408 B.C.E.); Sommerstein, pp. 11–12.

10. Garry Wills, *Inventing America: Jefferson's Declaration of Independence*, New York: Vintage Books (1978), p. xiv ff. A thorough rebuttal of Wills's facts: Harry V. Jaffa, "Inventing the Past: Garry

Wills's *Inventing America* and the Pathology of Ideological Scholarship," *The St. John's Review* XXX (Autumn 1981), p. 94 ff.

11. Paley, p. xxxvi; Sommerstein, p. 18.

12. Podlecki, p. 163, on 398.

13. Podlecki, p. 92, on 1028.

14. Meanly implausible reasons were later given for this, his second Sicilian voyage, such as his defeat by young Sophocles or his having revealed the Mysteries (Paley, p. xxv). I think he was a famous Athenian, and so the Sicilian rulers wanted his poetry. There is no reason to think he was an expatriate; it's hard to imagine after the *Eumenides*—but these Athenians were full of surprises.

15. Paley, p. xxxvi.

16. The Delian Treasure was seized and brought to Athens in 454 B.C.E.

17. Herodotus, *Persian Wars*, VIII 55.

18. This piece of Athenian wit was told me by Seth Bernardete over half a century ago. It seems mythopoetically true.

19. Abraham Lincoln, "Speech in Reply to Douglas at Chicago" (July 10, 1858).

20. Pindar, Fr. 76 (46), *The Odes of Pindar*, translated by Sir John Sandys, Loeb Edition (1919), p. 556, n. 1. Katharine Lee Bates, "America the Beautiful" (1893), in *The American Reader: Words that Moved a Nation*, edited by Diane Ravitch, New York: Harper-Collins (1990), p. 184.

21. Could it possibly be that this, the moral of the play, is not at the thousandth line by accident? To be sure, not all line counts agree. No, not likely.

22. In fact, the *Oresteia* is the only complete surviving trilogy.

23. Podlecki, p. 129, on 5–8.

24. I don't know whether such a scene is ever repeated. In Euripides' *Hippolytus*, for instance, where Aphrodite's and Artemis's statues seem both to be on stage, the deities themselves are not seen but only heard (86).

25. The all-time philosophical culmination of the reflection on image and original is in Plato's *Sophist* (240 ff.). Athena was the patroness of arts and crafts.

26. Lord Lane (1986), quoted as an epigraph in Sommerstein.

27. In the *Generation of Animals* Aristotle will elaborate this proto-thesis into a full-blown theory: The mother is an infertile male who contributes merely the receptive material to the embryo (I xix-xx, IV i).

28. Verrall, p. 126, on 686–93 with sources; Sommerstein, pp. 2–3; p. 273, on 685–90.

29. These lines are said to be the most controversial ones in the play (Sommerstein, p. 216). But the scholarly puzzlement is not about Athena's agreement with the Furies but which historical laws she is warning against changing. Is the passage attacking the democratic reform of the Areopagus? There are long discussions in Conacher (p. 199 ff.) and Sommerstein (p. 216 ff.). My notion is that Aeschylus's warning is not against a particular historical case but against an ever-recurrent human event: radically rational innovation.

30. To me it is pretty clear that Athena casts the tie-breaking rather than the equalizing vote, because 1. there are 10 complete exchanges between Apollo and the Erinyes, one speech for each act of voting (Verrall, p. 130, on 714–33), and 2. if Athena were evening the vote to bring about acquittal, the procedure for the court—that a tie acquits—would have had to precede its institution.

31. As it is in *Robert's Rules of Order* (1915), ¶ 46.

32. *Chaīrĕtĕ* means both "farewell" and "rejoice," but see Sommerstein, notes on 775, 996.

33. Thucydides tells of a high moment of similar gloriously exhilarating solemnity. It happens to be an actual celebration, the send-off that the Athenian people give their Sicilian expedition, also with trumpets, prayers, paeans. But as the Eumenidean exit is thoughtfully future-fraught, the Sicilian send-off is—to the reader who knows the end—fecklessly doom-inviting (*Peloponnesian War*, VI 32).

34. The commentators are stumped and so have a lot to say.

35. I would venture to say this only in a note: The Hegelian term *aufheben*, which means at once canceling, preserving, and raising up, fits this case.

36. Thus Heidegger translates *dikê* into German as *Fug*, "fit." It is that reciprocity which joins together a tight-fitting whole (*Introduction to Metaphysics*, IV 3). There is a German idiom: *mit Fug und Recht*, "with full right." Moreover, *Unfug* means "mischief."

REFERENCES

Conacher, D.J., *Aeschylus'* Oresteia: *A Literary Commentary*. Toronto: The University of Toronto Press (1987).

Lloyd-Jones, Hugh, *The* Eumenides *by Aeschylus: A Translation and Commentary*. Englewood Cliffs, N.J.: Prentice-Hill (1970).

Paley, F.A., *The Tragedies of Aeschylus* (Edition and Commentary). London: Whittaker and Co. (1879).

Podlecki, Anthony J., *Aeschylus'* Eumenides (edited with an Introduction, Translation, and Commentary). Warminster, England: Aris and Phillips Ltd. (1989).

Sommerstein, Alan H., Aeschylus, *Eumenides* (Edition and Commentary). Cambridge: Cambridge University Press (1989).

Verrall, A.W., *The 'Eumenides' of Aeschylus* (Introduction, Commentary, and Translation). London: Macmillan and Co. (1908).

22

Lady Macbeth
The Tyrant's Wife

In honor of Mera Flaumenhaft, who has a keen ear for a genre which I, resignedly, lack, I will try my hand at saying something, briefly, about a tragedy. If interpreters of texts have muses, she is mine.*

My warm thanks go to my colleague and friend Louis Petrich, who read this essay with gratifying attention and whose acute observations I've gratefully incorporated.

The only Shakespearean tragedy that really speaks to me is *Macbeth*.* Thus it was deeply gratifying to me to discover

And the early Greek tragedy, Aeschylus' *Eumenides*, which belongs to the tragic genre only because of its grandeur, not because of an ultimate calamity. It is the most magnificently jubilant play I know. Louis Petrich says that *Henry IV*, Pt. I should have that status. (See Essay 21, "*The Eumenides*.")

that *Macbeth* was also the play most highly regarded by Lincoln. Lincoln, that master of transatlantic English and father

---

First published in *Athens, Arden, Jerusalem: Essays in Honor of Mera Flaumenhaft*, edited by Paul T. Wilford and Kate Havard, Lexington Books, 2017. Bibliography omitted.

of noble populism, is the immigrant's best cause for a non-utilitarian patriotic fervor—not just the perfectly justifiable kind, whose motto is: *ubi bene, ibi patria* ("Where I'm well off, there's my country"), but something more high-hearted: an ardent faith that this country will not succumb to tyranny.

On August 17, 1863, the year that began, significantly, with the issuance of the Emancipation Proclamation, Lincoln wrote from the White House to the Shakespearean actor James H. Hackett, saying:

> Some of Shakespeare's plays I have never read; while others I have gone over perhaps as frequently as any unprofessional reader. Among the latter are Lear, Richard Third, Henry Eighth, Hamlet and especially Macbeth. I think nothing equals Macbeth. It is wonderful.

Why did the President think *Macbeth* unequalled and wonderful? I think one clue lies in his sense that, while comedies were more enjoyable seen on the stage—he loved, alas, going to the theater—the tragedies were better read at home. (Reported in Benjamin P. Thomas, *Abraham Lincoln: A Biography* [1957], p. 475.) *Macbeth* swarms with puns, equivocations, and ambivalences—with double meanings that are explicitly announced by the Weird ("wayward") Sisters' chant: "Double, double, Toil and Trouble" (IV i 10).* Such

> The Everyman Edition (1990), quoted in this piece, is only near-exhaustive in exposing puns on the facing page, thus leaving the satisfaction of "yet one more" to the reader.

wordplay reveals itself more surely to the reading eye that lingers on the page than to the listening ear that speeds after the performance.

A second clue is in Lincoln's "Address Before the Young Men's Lyceum of Springfield, Illinois" on "The Perpetuation of Our Political Institutions." This speech—I think it can be fairly called a twenty-nine-year-old's crypto-autobiography—projects to the world an inward apprehension of the dangers to political stability facing a polity of laws from the grand ambition of one who feels himself made for large action, an ambition that bears in itself the possibility of a terrible culmination in tyranny. My conjecture is that Lincoln was even then familiar with *Macbeth*. The Lyceum speech bears the signs in its allusive diction. Men of small ambition:

belong not to the family of the lion or the tribe of the eagle. . . . Towering genius disdains a beaten path. . . . It denies that it is glory enough to serve under a chief. . . . It thirsts and burns for distinction; . . . it will have it, whether at the expense of emancipating slaves, or enslaving freemen. . . . Is it unreasonable then to expect, that some man possessed of the loftiest genius, coupled with ambition sufficient to push it to its utmost stretch, will at some time, spring up among us? (In *The Language of Liberty: The Political Speeches and Writings of Abraham Lincoln.* Edited by Joseph Fornieri. Washington, D.C.: Regnery Publishing, 2009, 31–32.)

Here are passages from the play. Macbeth (my italics): "I have no Spur . . . but onely / *Vaulting Ambition*" (I vii 25 ff.); Old Man: "*A falcon to'wring* in her Pride o' Place . . ." (II iv 12); Macbeth: "under him / *My Genius* is rebuk'd, . . ." (III i 54); Apparition to Macbeth: "*Be Lion-mettled*, Proud . . ." (IV i 89).

In truth, young Lincoln's speech is self-admonition, a proactive renunciation of *tyranny* (although the word itself is suppressed*) by a statesman-to-be. Shakespeare's play, on the

An American subtlety: As Frederick Douglass points out, the Constitution deliberately suppresses the word "slavery" though the institution is intended, thus negatively highlighting the Founders' recognition of its badness ("The Constitution of the United States: Is It Pro-slavery or Anti-slavery?" March 26, 1860).

other hand, depicts the seduction by his "bold" and apparently remorseless wife (II i 1, I v 46) of a weakly, unstably

innocent man, "too full o' the milk of Human Kindness" (I
v 19), into a "bloody, bold, and resolute tyrant."* These last

> Though, to be sure, he is, early on, brutal in battle with a rebel
> (I ii 18 ff.), perhaps a presage of his conduct when he himself is
> the rebel. Moreover, Macbeth rather than Lady Macbeth could
> be regarded as the ultimate human cause of the dramatic action,
> since he is first to be seduced to high ambition by the witches on
> the heath (I ii 68 ff.) and then, in turn, tempts his wife (I v 1 ff.).
> This is a play of double interpretations.

words are those of that "apparition," a bloody child (IV i 78),
belonging to the company of the Weird Sisters. These "sisters" are, to my mind, avatars of Lady Macbeth, her famil-
iars on the heath (I i 6) or at the river of hell (III v 15), and
Macbeth's ladies away from his Lady, who imagines bloody-
ing her own baby (I vii 57), who mimics their chant, rhym-
ing with her husband's "Trouble": "All our Service/In every
Point twice done, and then done double" (I vi 15), who like
them, wearers of beards (I iii 44), is manly in her mettle (I vii
73), who calls on her "Spirits" to "unsex" her in her soul (I v
43)—and body ("my Milk for Gall," I v 50), and whose gross
language is of cats and swine, as is that of her Sisters (I vii
44, 67).

Macbeth seems to me to have both a public and private
theme: the transformation of a war hero into a regicidal tyrant
and the exchange of roles between husband and wife. From
Act III on, the nobility of Scotland in exile refers to Macbeth
as "Tyrant" (III vi 22, 25). By Act IV, in the long third scene
set in English exile, I count eight references to Macbeth as
tyrant and to his tyranny; in Act V, quite a few more,* until

> Human-, not machine-counted, thus approximate.

in the end, Malcolm, the new King, before calling home
the exiles "that fled the Snares of watchful Tyranny," pro-
nounces the obituary, "For this dead Butcher and his Fiend-
like Queen,/Who, *as 'tis thought*, by self and violent Hands/
Took off her life," (V vii 98 ff.).

I have italicized the clause regarding Lady Macbeth's death. This play of doublings and double talk* is also a drama of

> The bravura passage of puns occurs in a comic scene where the porter, as if to teach the audience how to hear this play's "Equivocators," produces four senses of the word "lye": lie, detumescence, sleep, urination (Everyman note to II iii 40).

silences, crucial ones. For example, right in the middle of the script by page count (II iii 19), Banquo is murdered by Macbeth's agents. But Fleance, his son, who by the Witches' prophecy (I iii 65) is destined to become king,* flees. We hear

> He or his offspring. We do not hear whether the new present king, Malcolm, Duncan's son, has or will have offspring.

no more of him, though his survival, as the placement of his escape shows, is *the* central political, that is, public event of the play.*

> We do not know whether he appears in the "Show of eight Kings" mounted by the witches (IV i 110 ff.).

So also to know how the "Fiend-like queen" really dies would be, I think, crucial to resolving the great puzzle of the play's private drama: How do these two partners in crime come to exchanges roles? How does the intrepidly resolute woman end up madly rubbing away at a spot of blood and dying unremarked—whether by inaction, accident, heart failure or her own hand we do not know for sure—while her husband, who seemed not man enough for her and who sees his hand turn a whole ocean red without being cleaned (II ii 52 ff.), survives into steady, coldly disillusioned desperation, to kill and be killed?

Macbeth has surely become butcher-like, but is Lady Macbeth fiend-like? A comparison with two close dramatic predecessors, two terrors-in-chief, both of sub- or super-human awfulness, springs to mind: Medea and Clytemnestra.

The former, to avenge her betrayal by her meanly unfaithful husband Jason, kills his superseding wife and her own two children, having previously dispatched sundry of her family members. About her children's murder she actually utters words not unlike Macbeth's upon hearing of his wife's death. He says, equivocatingly, "She should have died here-after" (V v 17). In Euripedes' *Medea*, she says, ambiguously, "In any case, they surely had to die" (1240). Both icy statements mean, I think, primarily: "Death is the common lot in any case."* Euripedes allows the filicide to fly off by a stage

> Or, for Macbeth, "She should have waited it out," and for Medea, "Jason's people would have killed them anyhow."

apotheosis in a stage contrivance, a dragon-chariot, evidently with the gods' complicity—a fiend, but god-approved. Medea is terrible, straight up, but she has old-fashioned right on her side: tit-for-tat—such as the Furies mete out. (See Essay 21, "*The Eumenides.*")

The Clytemnestra of Aeschylus' *Agamemnon* (a play named after the blustering Colonel Blimp of antiquity rather than after his more drastic wife simply because he dies in the play) is both grander and more complex. Whether she commits an assassination to save her own kingship (the right designation) and her weakish lover's life, or carries out an execution be-cause her returning husband had, ten years back, sacrificed their daughter in the interests of his expedition and has now come home with a woman in tow—that is an open question. But in both life and death, Clytemnestra is single- and sound-minded in her fury. She too is objectively terrifying and sub-jectively armor-plated—terrible termagants both—and both invulnerable in their transcendent awfulness; Medea is a fe-male fury, Clytemnestra a manly one. But both are just what they are throughout, while Macbeth's Lady is "fiendlike" in her early effect externally: the murder of King Duncan, and wraithlike in her subsequent affect internally: wracked with, but unready for, remorse. She is hopelessly repellent and yet sometimes pitiable, and in her pathos she is a puzzlement.

The enigma of Lady Macbeth presents itself to actresses as a practical problem of performance. Is she female only as withered witches are "she's"? Is she feminine only as she thinks of herself in self-pity: "this little hand" (V i 58)? Is she anywhere, in any way, womanly, or perhaps at least daughterly? She would herself have killed the king, "Had he not resembled/ My Father as he slept, I had done't—My Husband? (II ii 12)," a line too strange to go into very far.*

Duncan and the Macbeths may be kin in a way too tangled for comprehension, hence the resemblance (*New Variorum Edition*, p. 130). This is the only time his wife calls Macbeth "Husband"—*but* with a *question mark*; he may have to earn the address by announcing that he has, in fact, killed the father-lookalike (II ii 14).

I'll report two performers' solutions. The later of them is Ellen Terry's,* a nineteenth-century actress who was very

The Terry information comes from an online posting, "The Sheila Variations" (4/23/15); a print-out was kindly sent me by Kate Havard. Mrs. Siddons's "remarks on the character of the Lady Macbeth" are excerpted in the *Variorum Macbeth*, p. 472 ff.

popular but far from a natural tragedienne. For her 1888 performance, she very deliberately decided to exploit her own feminine beauty and to play Lady Macbeth as lovingly cajoling, magnificently dressed, "full of womanliness." (It is not, I think, an interpretation imaginable by a reader who sits at home with the bare text.)

Sarah Siddons, the great tragic actress born in the previous century (1755–1831), gave Ellen Terry her cue by delineating Lady Macbeth's beauty as "fair, feminine, nay, perhaps, even fragile." Mrs. Siddons played the part with overwhelming intensity, for she also saw Lady Macbeth as "having impiously delivered herself to the excitements of hell," incited thereto by Macbeth's letter reporting the prophesies on the heath (I v 1 ff.), and as given over to remorseless cruelty, a "daring fiend." Of Mrs. Siddons's many persuasive observations I shall cite the one with the greatest bearing on my inquiry. She had noted that, while *he* sometimes offers affection, *she* never reciprocates. I think that isn't in her nature. But she offers something of more consequence; she listens: "His heart has therefore been eased, from time to time, by unloading its weight of woe; while she, on the contrary, has perseveringly endured in silence the uttermost anguish of a wounded spirit." What has, principally, wounded her? They live in the same palace of Dunsinane but don't seem to see each other. And though Macbeth makes it clear that they might still have children (I vii 71), yet they don't seem to be procreating. Hearing of her sleep-walking, her husband does not go to her; he deputizes the doctor (V iii 39). He receives the news of her death with appalling dismissiveness, which-ever meaning it is given: "She should have died hereafter" (V v 17). And he follows up with a disquisition on the insignifi-cance of all life; a savage stoicism, perhaps of cruel comfort to his living self, but without remembrance for her lost soul.

This casting loose, this coming apart from her, had started way back. Early on, he had communicated the witches' prophecy, but by the third act he is, though joshingly, keep-ing her out of his plans except by aversive intimation: "Be innocent of Knowledge, dearest Chuck,/Till thou applaud the Deed" (III ii 46). What woman would not be irritated on the surface and frightened to the depths by this false famil-iarity and pretended protectiveness? She feels tremors from her ground. And yet she herself has invited this withdrawal. She had taunted him: What "beast," what *un*manly impulse, made him tell her a plan he was not man enough to execute (I vii 48)?

Once more: Of her earlier, heart-whole, almost insouciant amorality there is much evidence. To her husband's paralyz-ingly panicked conscience she has almost lightly dismissive responses: "A foolish thought to say 'a sorry sight'" (II ii 19); "Consider it not so deeply" (28); "These deeds must not be thought/After these ways: so, it will make us Mad" (30–

31); "us" here, once again, is—unintended—double talk; she means him but describes herself. More: "You do unbend your Noble Strength to think / So Brain-sickly of things. Go get some Water, / And wash this filthy Witness from your Hand" (41 ff.). He is inconsolable: "Will all great Neptune's Ocean wash this Blood / Clean from my Hand?" (55 ff.); how much more eerie is that single Hand, now and later, than would be a handwashing pair; it continues the action of his clutching the ghostly dagger, "The Handle toward my Hand" (II i 33).

Finally his Lady wants to abrogate his imaginative memory, his obsessively visualized guilt. She wants to nullify tragedy, which *is* the high concern with things without any remedy: "Things without all Remedy / Should be without Regard: What's done is done" (III ii 11). Moreover, she adroitly manages his mental aberration, his vision of Banquo's ghost at dinner (III iv 44 ff.); "real" ghosts, like Hamlet's father, are seen by others, not so this see-through guest.

And then, later, the reversal: there is a repetition of the heedless phrase, now spoken in prose and by a woman in a hopelessly altered state. She is sleepwalking: "To Bed, to Bed, There's Knocking at the Gate. Come, come, come, come, give me your hand. What's done cannot be undone. To Bed, to Bed, to Bed" (V i 74 ff.). Everything is revealed in that somnambulistic talk: He has not sought her bed, he has not come,* though he is right by, in Dunsinane; her ever-bloody

---

"Come" has been the call with which she invoked the "Spirits" (I v 42, 48); who knows what else is driving her.

---

hand remains ungrasped—and her insouciance is undone in the chill of the night: In the poetry of concerted and accomplished action the accent was on "done"—what's *done* is *done*; in the sobriety of lonely and comfortless hallucination, the stress is on *un*done—what's done can*not* be *un*done.

Is she haunted by her conscience, as he once was? Perhaps, but by a regret more bred of sidelined loneliness than, as the kindly doctor thinks, of theological compunction. He has it half right: "infected Minds/To their deaf Pillows will discharge their Secrets," but half wrong: "More needs she the Divine than the Physician" (V I 81 ff.). She needs neither, I think, as much as she needs her husband as bedmate and as advisee, a hearing, talking pillow—not as a comforter but as, so to speak, a colleague. This inciter of deeds in her husband, she who, childless, has raised him to manhood as if he were her child, will presently die of a cause that cannot be circumvented by the doctor's prescription: "Remove from her the means of all Annoyance" (V i 85; that is, of self-injury). Nor is the divinity to be invoked, since Lady Macbeth, in the very act of revealing their guilt to the people of the castle says: "What need we fear? Who knows it, when none can call our Powre to accompt?" (V i 42 ff.) I would read ambivalently, once with a new, notional punctuation: "What need we fear who knows it . . . ?," meaning that she doesn't care who knows of the murders since the Macbeths are all-powerful. And then again I would read it as printed, meaning that there is no god above to call them to account, and so again, it doesn't matter who knows on earth. She is just not much worried about the Hereafter; even "Hell is murky" to her (V i 41): She dies from inanition of purpose and from the forlornness of one who is proximate in body to another who is unreachable in soul.

One last corroboration of her sense of being left high and dry: She chants a creepy little ditty in her ambulation: "The Thane of Fife had a Wife."* The Thane of Fife is the very

> Printed as prose, but really:
> Thĕ Thāne ŏf Fīfe
> Hăd ă Wīfe:
> Whēre ĭs shĕ nōw? (V i 47).

Macduff whose knocking in Act II haunts both Macbeths, and the very husband who has left his wife and children exposed to Macbeth's murdering minions by fleeing to England—Lady Macduff says of him: "He loves us not,/He wants the Natural Touch" (IV ii 8, IV iii 28). He is the other husband that is "not," as we say, "there" for his wife. And the wife dies for it, as Lady Macbeth will. As she descends, he rises. From what, to what? It begins, as I said, with a small withdrawal from partnership, a slightly off jocularity, an incipient assertion of a manhood which she has, perhaps too often and too earnestly, impugned. Meanwhile she has all too well succeeded in damping his humane impulses. Although she gives in to her own recoil from killing Duncan just because he looks like her father, she will not allow her husband to spare the king just because he has honored Macbeth of late (I vii 32). So having once been pushed to murder, Macbeth grows into more perfect callousness, until he is ready for immediately executed "dread exploits": "From this Moment/The very Firstling of my Heart shall be/ The Firstlings of my hand" (IV i 145 ff.). "Firstlings" are firstborn children. This is what his wife knows without hearing it: His heart is not in procreating with his childless wife but in executing deeds upon others' progeny, deeds far beyond all humanity, acts of tyranny, of which the murder of Macduff's children is the most dire (IV i 151).

What is a tyrant's badness? Why did Lincoln, who had an imaginative intimation and a political horror of tyranny, think this play was wonderful?

Macbeth is bad with a specific tyrant's badness, and I imagine that this is what most particularly attracted Lincoln. Tolstoy says, in his most famous sentence, the first line of *Anna Karenina*: "All happy families are alike; each unhappy family is unhappy in its own way." Human goodness is always the same; badness comes in diverse types.* Iago, for example, a

---

The sententious novelist was anticipated by a more succinct poet: "Bad men have many ways, good men but one," quoted anonymously by Aristotle, *Nicomachean Ethics* (1106b 35; I think this maxim's truth depends on one's perspective; from the inside, nothing is more many-faceted than happiness).

mini-tyrant, is all meanly manipulative badness, arising from small resentments and low desires; his very candor is all ploy, and when the game is up he subsides into silence, since he has in him no generous last words (*Othello* V ii 371). He is a small, a "demi-devil" (V ii 368). Not so this tyrant.

Macbeth makes a nobler end. He is not a minor demon acting out his nature, but a great man gone unnatural. To Macduff he says: "But get thee back, my Soul is too much charg'd/With blood of thine already."* Then to himself: "And

> In Act I it was said of Cawdor, the traitor, that "Nothing in his Life/Became him like the leaving of it" (iv 7); in Act V it comes true again of the next Thane of Cawdor, Macbeth.

be these Juggling Fiends no more believed/That palter with us in a Double Sense" (V vii 34, 48).* Thus, toward his end,

> Prophecy has been double-tongued before this; for example, when Croesus, King of Lydia, asked the Delphic Oracle if he should wage war on the Persians, the response was that he would destroy a great empire if he did. It turned out to be his own (Herodotus, *Histories* I 53).

he recovers some of his humanity, and he discovers that he has been fooled by these "fiends."* He had, indeed, suspected

> The fiends had prophesied that "none of women borne" would harm him and that he would not be defeated until Byrnam Wood would come to Dunsinane. His killer Macduff was delivered by Cesarean, and the troops marching on Dunsinane were camouflaged by branches of trees (IV i 9 ff., 91 ff.; V v 33, vi 44).

it earlier: Their prophecy might be a trick, if so, "I'll pull in Resolution, and begin/To doubt th' Equivocation of the Fiend/That lies like Truth" (V v 41). So even before all is lost he is capable of coldly contemplating the worst and gathering resolution from his realism. This is the very scene in which he speaks to his reporting underlings with the contemptuously vulgar brutality that mark a type of tyrant: "cream-faced loon," "Lily-liver'd Boy," "Whey-face," accompanied by threats of hanging (V iii 12 ff., v 38). But it is not for his

brutalized manners that Macduff threatens to have him "as
our rarer Monsters are, / Painted upon a Pole, and under-writ /
'Here may you see the Tyrant'" (V vii 56). This threatened
fate immediately overturns Macbeth's reluctance to fight him,
for he is still proud. He's not some painted Tyrant but *himself*: "My name's Macbeth" (V vii 7).

For Macduff, Macbeth is the very type of a tyrant because
of the inhuman bloodiness, the boundless cruelty he has privately experienced. It falls to two minor characters, Scottish
nobles called Cathness and Angus, to summarize the public
aspect of tyranny. They are asked: "What does the Tyrant?"
Cathness answers: "Great Dunsinane he strongly fortifies. /
Some say he's Mad; others that lesser hate him, / Do call it Val-
iant Fury; but for certain / He cannot buckle his distemper'd
Cause / Within the Belt of Rule." Angus continues: "Now does
he feel / His secret Murthers sticking on his Hands; / Now
minutely Revolts upbraid his Faith-breach; / Those he commands move onely in Command, / Nothing in Love. . . ." (V
ii 12 ff.). In reciting his actions they slide into conjectures of
his situation: his crimes and the ambiance about him. Shakespeare reserves to the tyrant himself the first-person account
of the state of his soul. It is "direct discourse," if ever there
was, in the dumbfoundingly unreserved candor of its drearily
illimitable disillusionment.* I imagine that this aspect of the

Cathness' account of Commander Macbeth shut up in Dunsinane
castle sends memory to the Führer in his bunker and poses this
problem: How much do modern totalitarianisms have in common
with earlier tyrannies? More than you might think, is the answer
given by a Santa Fe colleague, David Levine, in his book *Profound
Ignorance: Plato's* Charmides *and the Saving of Wisdom* (2016). What
tyrants and "Leaders" both lack is *deep self-knowledge*. I think that
might be true of Macbeth as well, for all his lucid despair. He is too
blood-drenched in conscience and too vacated in soul to have a self
left for him to know. Doesn't self-knowledge require a reasonably
purged and well-furnished soul?

play most particularly engaged Lincoln.

In a short speech Macbeth confirms Angus' description of his situation and his frame of mind: "Hang those who talk of Fear" (V ii 19, 35). But it is the doctor's report of his wife's sickness of soul that brings out his nearly complete disengagement from her, his own lack of love. "Cure [her] of that" he says to the reporting doctor, with barely suppressed impatience. And then, with callous plain-speaking: "Canst thou not minister to a Mind diseas'd . . . ?" (V iii 39 ff.). And he turns, precipitately and prematurely, to his arming—instead of hastening to her.

But it is the report of her consequent death that elicits his deepest introspection. The early agitations of conscience have died away. He is lapped by a deadly indifference that at once *drags out*, day to day, a life devoid of significant *ends*:

> To morrow, and to morrow, and to morrow,
> Creeps in this petty Pace from Day to Day, . . .

and *compresses* it to an hour, into insignificant *duration*:

> Out, out, brief candle.
> Life's but a walking Shadow, a poor Player,
> That struts and frets his Hour upon the Stage
> And then is heard no more,

and *deprives* it of significant *meaning*:

> it is a Tale
> Told by an Idiot, full of Sound and Fury
> Signifying nothing (V v 19 ff.).*

> Macbeth is implicitly challenging his author, and behold: Shakespeare *can* turn an idiot's tale into a signifying drama.

If she was sick at soul, he is bereft of soul; finally worse off than she was. One might call it nihilistic stoicism, soldiering on in the absence of hope in this world or hereafter.

And now I want to try to determine the sense of the most shocking passage of the play, about which there seems to be no settled opinion. There is a "Cry within of Women" (V v 7 ff.). Macbeth reacts with irritation: "What is that Noise?" "It is the Cry of Women, my good Lord." He responds: "I have almost forgot the Taste of Fears." "Almost": He has not forgotten, though displaced, an earlier occasion, when he had asked: "And what Noise is this?" (IV i 104). Then what followed was a magical show of Banquo's royal line, apparently stretched out "to th' Crack of Doom." There was a time, he says, when his hair would have stood up at "a dismal Treatise . . . as Life were in it," when he could have summoned a response to a tragic tale—like his own; but now he is "supped full with horrors: / Direness familiar to my slaughterous thoughts / Cannot once start me. Wherefore was that cry?" (V v 15). "The Queen, my Lord, is dead." And he responds with these lines, which, did we hear them in real life, would be purely horrible: "She should have di'd hereafter; / There would have been a Time for such a Word:" There follows "To morrow, and to morrow, and to morrow."

He is so replete with blood that he is empty of all response. His inquiry is incurious, as of one more annoyance. The news of his wife's death is received with ultimate indifference. He is not yet cured of double talk: "She should have died hereafter" means both—"should," "would," what's the difference— "She would have died some time or other" or "She should have postponed her death." If the latter, he would have found "Time for such a Word." What word? A word of remembrance of her partnership? But he annihilates his helpmeet's service by his distraction. Uttering "hereafter" throws him off track; it recalls to him that unholy secular hereafter he faces: just an indifferent segment in a temporal procession from morrow to morrow to the last syllable of "Recorded Time," with no Hereafter, no resurrection following the Omega, the end-time—at least none that he believes in or, if he did, could hope for. Just "Dusty Death," now and when time ends in eternity.

Thus the colon after "such a Word" does not "deliver the goods"* of what precedes; don't we expect a word said of *her*?

Fowler's phrase in *Modern English Usage*; see "colon," under "Stops." The colon usually raises an expectation of a relevant completion.

But here the colon marks an abrupt thought-caesura: Her death is merely the occasion for his ultimate self-exploration, that of a man untethered from all attachment. For his Lady's five longing calls "To bed," he has three invocations of a hopeless "To morrow."* We would call it existential despair; he is

Similarly, his cool "hereafter" echoes, in a desperate tone, her glorious early vision of "The Future in an Instant": She somehow divined that the witches hailed Macbeth's future *thrice*, and so she speaks of his "all-hail hereafter" (I iii 60, v 57).

more desperate than she was forlorn; she hoped for him to come; he exists without hope of anything to come; "to morrow," the locus of hope, is just a dull "one more" to him. In fact, such hopelessness is his best hope, his escape from the fear of real hell.

The meditation on his existence, which is a diversion* from

An anti-Pascalian diversion: Pascal's *divertissement* (*Pensées* II 8) is *from* the conditions of existence *to* the contingencies of life; Macbeth flees *from* a hard fact of life *to* an existential state of mind.

his Lady's death, is to us who listen in, reading and rereading, hearing and meditating at home, a revealing insight into a tyrannical soul—revealing *and* distinctive—distinctive because I can think of three other types of tyrant besides the tyrant of desperate disillusionment.

Two of the types are antique, the third is contemporary. All four types exhibit the root characteristic of boundlessness, though in different psychical terrains.

One of the ancient types of tyrant, depicted in Plato's *Republic*, is modeled on a tyrant *boundless in his appetites*, beyond all moderating self-control and consequently self-enslaved. His enslavement of the world around him is but the external projection of the slavery within the soul (577d ff.). The other ancient type of tyrant, delineated in Plato's *Charmides*, is taken from a tyrant *boundless in his arrogance*. He has consigned himself to self-ignorance and intends to control the world by his hyper-knowledge (be that a mind-enslaving ideology or a body-manipulating technology). This ignorance is profound and boundless, because the tyrant himself has no notion of his own double ignorance; he knows nothing substantial and worse, doesn't know that he doesn't know.*

See the reference above to David Levine's *Profound Ignorance*.

The contemporary type is Iago-like. It is based on a tyrant who is constricted in scope of his soul,* though expansive in

Iago is ignorant of his own wife's truthfulness, which is his undoing (*Othello* V ii 170 ff.).

the assertion of power: He is *boundless in willfulness*, yet narrowly mean-minded: greedy for *abstract* accumulations such as power and popularity, but also insatiable for *showy* appurtenances, such as parades and mass-meetings, incoherent in his demagoguery yet cunning in his manipulations—and indefeasibly vulgar.* "Vulgarity" here is not to be construed

This description bears a relation to Hannah Arendt's characterization, over five issues of *The New Yorker*, of Nazi officialdom's evil as *banal* in "Eichmann in Jerusalem: A Report on the Banality of Evil" (1963). In *The Life of the Mind* (1971) she glosses this banality as "*thoughtlessness*," not stupidity, but cliché-governed functioning ("Thinking," Introduction). She is, however, speaking of the administering bureaucracy, not of the "Leader," whose evil was perhaps as shoddy but surely not as shallow.

as an esthetic quality of behavior, since the esthetic condemnation of evil-doing seems to me impermissible, at least as a principal objection. The totalitarian's vulgarity I mean is a quality of the soul that is willing to crush the delicacies of personhood into a mobilized mass,* to debase commonality

> In Iago's case, he sees, rather than individuals, a "kind" (*Othello* III iii 476 ff.).

into commonness and to degrade sensibility into sentimentality; for this type the Führer of my childhood is a paradigm.

Between the ancient and the recent tyrant types stands Macbeth's figure, somewhat closer to the antique depiction, from which it is, however, chronologically roughly six times as far removed as it is from ours. But then, time and essence are ever disjunct.

Macbeth belongs to a *noble type*, the tyranny of *boundless ambition* (I vii 27), and his meditations have a commensurate force.* I could, of course, not mean that his crimes have

> The first reader of this piece, our alumna Alexandra Wick, asked: "Does Lady Macbeth have a tyrannical soul?" She doesn't appear that way to me. She is altogether "The Tyrant's Wife," his bed-fellow and adjutant, the tyrant-*promoter*. That's in itself a fascinating soul type: Women were among the staunchest supporters of the Nazi *Führer*, from reactionary *Hausfrauen* ("*Kinder, Kirche, Küche*") to amoral film director (Leni Riefenstahl, *The Triumph of the Will*). What drove them? Are they bourgeois Lady Macbeths? Or is she *sui generis*, more fiend-like and less philistine?

grandeur or that he does not have outbursts of low vituperation. But his self-incrimination, his confession to having a "Soul too much charged with blood" (V vii 33), so dulled with excess of horror as to "have almost forgot the Taste of Fears" (V v 9), and his last reluctance to kill his most wronged victim, Macduff—these testify to a residual greatness.

Thus he manifests as well a contrary but complementary characteristic of boundlessness: "Our fears in Banquo" he says, "stick deep" (III i 46 ff.). Why? Because "He has a Wisdom that doth guide his Valour/To act in Safety . . . under him my Genius is rebuk'd." What is that genius, his inborn spirit, that is reprimanded by Banquo's "Royalty of Nature"?

Macduff formulates it: "Boundless Intemperance/In Nature is a Tyranny" (IV iii 67). Boundless intemperance equals evanescent moderation; I conjecture that this deficiency, his inner moral void, is the obverse, the inseparable backside of his outer boundlessness: He has schooled himself to elicit and live with the witty but negating devilry of duplicitous language and the insouciant but nullifying confounding of categories: "foul is fair and fair is foul" (Witches: I i 9; Macbeth: 39). And so he has achieved a perfection of sorts, perhaps the innermost desire driving his ambition: moral invulnerability, to be gained by deeds beyond all bounds. But then, to *do* anything and everything means to *be* no one and nothing. I imagine that what drew Lincoln to *Macbeth* was this self-exposure of a tyrant's soul.

A postlude to such "readings" of fiction, certainly mine: What am I doing? Am I reading the author's mind to fill in his incomplete telling? Safe enough, too safe, since authors are usually unavailable for corroboration, by reason of being elsewhere or dead. Am I fleshing out the characters' own speaking, helping them to make themselves more patent? Too easy, once again, for they cannot object, by reason of being fictional and inexistent—and tactlessly intrusive to boot, because latency may be essential to such negative existence. Am I making explicit the necessary nature of a fictional world? Yet again, too facile, because a fictional universe whose events were rationally necessary would exemplify not the artful spontaneity of humanly true drama but the abstracted constraints of a logical system.

And yet our dealings with the defunct, the nonexistent, the fictive are not without criteria, criteria not of bounden truth but of engaging plausibility. Readings that, in spite of all the above misgivings, discover inner coherencies in works and reveal them to be in touch with the actual world, whether as a revelatory overlay or an amending intervention, have some claim to legitimacy: The Tyrant's Lady appears to me to be coherent both as a spectacle, as a *dramatis persona* on stage, and as a real being, as a full-blooded participant in life.

23

Postmodern Don Quixote
Terminal Indeterminism

I'm living proof that what curmudgeons claim is impossible is in fact actual: high regard for a book to which I'm full of resistance. I readily admit that *Don Quixote* is a great book, but when I've had to read it as an assignment, it all but spoiled my summer. Why?

My fellow tutor and good friend in Santa Fe, David Carl, provided the answer: it's a *postmodern* novel. We were co-leaders of a seminar on *Don Quixote* in Madrid (where Cervantes is buried) and raising a slew of questions, all of which seemed, the more we talked, the less decidable. But how could an early seventeenth-century book, generally regarded as the first *modern* novel, belong to a literary type officially devised in the late twentieth century?

"Postmodernism" is a disparate category, first conceived as a reaction to architectural modernism regarded as an impersonal, ahistorical, functional style. Later, postmodernism opposed naïve realism in literature by endorsing a type of self-referential writing that attends continually to its own fictionality. And finally postmodernism attacked foundation-

First published in *Energeia* (a student journal) in 2014.

seeking philosophy and exploded into many sub-theories. Among these was deconstructionism, one of whose doctrines is the ultimate undecidability, the terminal indeterminism, of all truth-claims. So postmodernism as self-referential fictionality, deconstruction as terminal undecidability—that's what David meant.

Below I'll do only this: list questions about *Don Quixote* to which we in Madrid, twenty or so willing intellects, could find no determinate answer; what's more, we thought that the book *was meant* to stymie our efforts.

One: In the last, the one-hundred and twenty-sixth chapter of his Adventures, Don Quixote de la Mancha, the knight, is back to Don Alonso Quixano, the Good, a gentleman—his civilian name, as it were. He retracts his knight errant's persona and dies.

Readers may not know that Chaucer's *Canterbury Tales*, written two hundred years earlier, also ends with a renunciation of the Tales of Canterbury, *thilke that sounen into sinne*, "such as tend towards sin." (The Retraction follows the Parson's theological prose discourse.) But that's the author disowning his characters, be it for his own secular safety or his spiritual salvation—while his Wife of Bath herself carries on lustily and unrepentantly.

It's different for Cervantes' book. The Don himself, the hero of his book, recants his error, "that there were and still are knights errant in the world . . . I was mad and now I am sane" (II 74).

Does this recantation cancel the adventures by exposing them as acts of mere insanity or does it confirm them as the revelations of an illuminated imagination? Does it seriously consign the foregoing tales to fanciful drollery and picaresque extravagance or does it merely display the Don's last days as disillusionment, intended to be discounted, brought on by a lowering of zest in the face of death? Which?

Two: Who is the author of this book? The book itself gives the last word to one Sidi (Señor) Hamid Benengeli, who wrote it in Arabic (I 9) and who says: "And Don Quixote was born only for me, as I for him; he knew how to act and I how to write; only we two are a unity, in spite of that fake Tordesillan scribbler . . ." (II 74; that scribbler produced a spurious Second Part—anticipating its author—under the pseudonym of Avellaneda. A character out of this book turns up in the genuine Second Part, II 72). Sidi Hamid's Arabic text was translated by another Moor, who also acted as an editor, marking parts of the manuscript as apocryphal (II 5); who knows what else he did to the text? There is, furthermore, an "I" who writes Prologues, calls himself Don Quixote's "stepfather" (Prologue to I) and injects himself into the first line of the first chapter as the tale's teller. Later this "I" (Prologue to II) gives himself Cervantian autobiographical distinctions, such as the loss of the left hand in battle. But this "I" claims to be writing this history of a real Don Quixote (I 52), so he can't be all that real himself. The story this First Person reports is mutilated and leaves off just where Quixote and an inimical Basque are about to split each other's heads. Happily, "I" buys some old notebooks off a boy, and these are found to contain Sidi Hamid's whole composition, which now takes over. "I" is delighted, because Arabs, although liars, are hostile to Spaniards, and so Hamid won't have falsely embellished the tale. But there's also a Miguel de Cervantes Saavedra who, right in the middle of the work, signs a letter of dedication to his patron, which precedes the Prologue to the Second Part. And finally there's the knight himself, the character escaping from his false, and searching for his true, author. He is himself a keen critic of histories (though clearly not of chivalric romances) whom we see in the non-spurious Second Part avidly complaining about the author of the First telling so many irrelevant novellas rather than concentrating on him (II 3), and whom we hear even on his deathbed assuming responsibility for Avellaneda's "high flown non-sense" (II 74)—which is as much to say that he's the author of his fake adventures. Well then, in this spirit of confusion confounded, who *is* most truly the writer? I vote for the translating and editing Moor, since editors are well known to have primacy over authors; he certainly makes enough marginal comments (for example, II 61, 74).

Three: Is the ingenuous Gentleman of La Mancha really or disingenuously mad? When his squire or his friends try to bring him to his senses, he resists most strenuously—perhaps protests too much? But sometimes the cat gets simply let out of the bag: Sancho tells a tall tale, and "Don Quixote came over to his squire and bending low to his ear said: 'Sancho, if you want me to believe what you think you saw in the sky, you've got to believe what I think I saw in Montesinos's Cave. And that's all I have to say.'" Crazy as a fox!

This Cave of Montesinos is the most mystifyingly significant venue of the book (II 22). Whatever else it means, it tells what the knight knows when in a non-conscious state. Don Quixote is let deep down into the cave's abyss, falls asleep and awakes to a dreamscape. To make a long story short, he tells Sancho that in this place two companions of Dulcinea (the rough peasant girl the knight has chosen to transform, worship, and serve as his lady) come and ask him on her behalf to lend her six *reales* against her petticoat as security. He only has four, which he gives to one of the peasant friends, who receives it, ungraciously, and whirls away in cartwheels. (There exists an article giving an—unintendedly—hilarious psychoanalytic interpretation: Quixote's report is a protocol of Freudian dreamwork; Dulcinea is sexually needy; Quixote's being short two *reales* of the sum requested indicates his fear of impotence. To be precise—my addendum—he fears being one-third wanting!)

I think the dream shows that he knows that she's a vulgar girl who'll want money and that he has his hesitations about her and her entourage. He's at least one third more sane than deluded, deep down. But which more predominantly? And when?

Four: Is the world really enchanted for Don Quixote? In children's books an enchanted world is full of magical beings, in adult literature it is full of romantic feeling. Now take the early adventure of the windmills, which fixes the pattern: *Enchantment for the knight errant is disenchantment!* The windmills are giants, real beings in the true original world that have been transformed magically into workaday windmills in the false, secondary world, in order to spoil Quixote's adventures. He faces a whole world magicked into mundanity to spite his ardor for great deeds. His mission is to dis-disenchant the world, that is, to re-enchant it, to reveal its magic-occluded romance.

The chief case in need of such return from magicked ordinariness is Dulcinea; when he finally saw her in Toboso, Quixote beheld a coarse, ugly peasant (II 10). The condition of the retransformation is absurdly vicarious: Sancho has to agree to a self-flagellation of three thousand and three hundred strokes (II 35). What sort of inversion is Don Quixote forcing on the world? Surely a dreary one, because now, when much of the world is revealed as a false front, from which romantic reality has been leached, our workaday ordinariness stands degraded. No wonder his squire dubs him "The Knight of the Sad Face," a title Quixote accepts because the learned author "responsible for writing the history of my exploits, will have decided it would be good for me to take another name." He himself has no idea why he wears sadness on his face and shield, but it's surely because his errantry has made all that actually confronts him suspect—other than it seems to be, invalid in itself. What demons are these that strive to vitiate high romance by transforming it into low reality? Are they private to Quixote, a *folie à deux* with Sancho, or perhaps truths for us who are too sane to see it? Who is mad here and how?

Five: Who's the hero of this book? Is it actually the man in the title? In the First Part the knight predominates as he helpfully wreaks havoc on his beneficiaries, his so-far compliant squire, himself, and the world in general: Punished boys are rescued only to be beaten the worse by their masters; liberated criminals scatter over the countryside; property is damaged. It is amazing how much bodily mayhem is nonchalantly absorbed by all the folks; no one's pain is likely to elicit even an "ouch" from the reader—we laugh. In the Second Part, the knight gathers pathos and also acquires a socially useful role—so to speak. Don Antonio, Quixote's host in Barcelona, chides one of the knight's friends who is trying to bring him back to sanity: "May God forgive you for the damage you've done . . . in trying to cure the wittiest lunatic ever seen! . . . [W]hatever utility there might be in curing him, it would not match the pleasure he gives with his madness." So in the big city the Knight of the Sad Face serves the world as a kind of geek (II 65).

Meanwhile Squire Sancho proves to have the makings of a statesman. He's a practical man, full of those saws that encapsulate folk wisdom (like his successor in shrewd simplicity, Platon Karataev in *War and Peace*). But, it turns out, he also possesses a higher-order prudence. After waiting twenty years, he finally gets his wish—his own island to govern (courtesy of that Duke and Duchess whose castle is a major waystation for knight and squire and in whom generous hospitality and cruel cleverness appear in undecidable proportion). As governor, he shows Solomonic sagacity—practicality tinged with wit—in his judgments (II 45 ff.); he cuts through ensnaring logical conundrums with mercy, and his laws are wise and enduring. Being beset by the minders the ducal pair has imposed on him, he displays a last and rare wisdom. He leaves office.

Meanwhile Don Quixote endures mockeries that underscore his pathos for us, but begin subtly to undermine his own confident knight errantry. If the First Part had been subtitled "The Knight and His Squire," might the Second not have been called "The Squire and his Knight"? Well, yes and no. Sancho Panza has his own Cave Experience, but it is Don Quixote who brings deliverance from the pit, and the two go together, closer than ever, to their final adventures. But a reader—myself—might find the "Paunch" more substantial than his fey, skinny master.

Six: Is *Don Quixote* a Christian book or a travesty of faith and a take-off on Scripture? There's no denying the many religious references and no making out—I think—how they're meant. For example, Don Quixote proposes that "we can't all be friars . . . but knighthood too is a religion . . ." (II 8). No doubt there were religious knightly orders, but Quixote's is an order of one whose patent comes from his own imagination— and, of course, his deathbed retraction can be said to undermine his life's errantry.

There are allusions to the life of Jesus. The knight is paraded in Saragosa by his host Don Antonio, not wearing armor but street clothes, not riding Rocinante but a mule, with a sign affixed to his back "This is Don Quixote de la Mancha" (II 62), Who can help but think of Jesus' entry into Jerusalem on an ass, and the mocking sign nailed over his head at the Crucifixion: "This is Jesus the King of the Jews" (Matthew 27:2 ff., 27:37)? Is this pious allusion or blasphemous parody? But the main parallel comes from the false Don Quixote of Avellaneda, who precedes the knight's Second Coming and dogs him from first to last in the Second Part, more and more toward the end (for example, *Don Quixote* II Prologue, 62, 72, 74). Recall the New Testament: before the

Christ's return "false Christs and false prophets shall rise and shall shew signs and wonders to seduce, if it were possible, even the elect" (Mark 13:22). Is the Don a comic Christ, and is that a permissible or an impermissible distinction to accord him?—Unanswerable.

Seven: A small last open question. Is the book organic, in the sense that all its parts function for the sake of the whole? Do, for example, the set romances retailed in the Sierra Morena— delightful to somebody, perhaps, but boring to many of us— have a furthering purpose? Don Quixote himself complains of them as an irrelevant distraction from the telling of his own affairs (II 3). Is the multitude of adventures a purposeful series or just a vagrant redundancy—except for those who can't get enough of high jinks? And finally, the most puzzling fact: the "I"'s insistence, stated at the very beginning, that "the whole thing is an attack on romantic tales of chivalry" (First Part, Prologue) and Sidi Hamid's reiteration, at the very end, "that all I ever wanted was to make men loathe the concocted, wild-eyed stories told as tales of chivalry" (II 79). This intention, if one believed it, would obviate all attempts at finding more than topical meaning. So, are there depths beyond the novel's novelty? Can there ever be depth without a firm foundation? Is there delectation in the bottomless?

I think I've justified the appellation "postmodernist/decon-structionist" for the work: terminal indeterminism, self-involved fictionality, hovering undecidability. But it's a great book, doubtless.*

I've used the English translation by Burton Raffel (Miguel de Cer-vantes, *Don Quixote*, New York: W.W. Norton, 1999), except in one instance: In II 62, where Raffel says "beast," other translations say "mule."

24

Eve Separate
Mother of Modernity

In memory of John P. McNulty (1952–2005),
an acute and sensitive reader of great books
and a lovely partner in our New Jersey
seminar conversations, particularly about
Milton's *Paradise Lost*.

Contents by section:

First pubished in *The St. John's Review* XLIX 1 (2006).

1) IS THERE A SUBTEXT?

Milton's *Paradise Lost* is a poem of such panoramic grandeur and such human acuteness as may wean one—and has even weaned me—from a lifelong exclusive Homerophilia. Partly its attraction is that it is insinuatingly suspect. I keep having the sense that something is going on that runs right counter to the overt text. There seems to be a separate, opposed meaning. Should it be called a hidden agenda, a subtext? On the supposition of trust (to which I warmly subscribe) the words in a book say what the author means; it is simply the reasonable faith that the writer knows how to express himself. So if an attentive reader discerns an under-meaning, there is in fact a subtext, a second probably more seriously meant meaning. Such occulted meanings are associated with esotericism, "insiderism," the notion that the author speaks with a forked tongue—one text for the naïvely simpleminded, another for the initiable. The purpose is to protect the author from misapprehension by ungifted, and from persecution by orthodox, readers.

But I don't think great authors are often in that mode. The deep matters they raise are too well guarded from over-easy access by their inherent difficulty to want the shield of obscurantism, while from imputations of heterodoxy there is really no protection; its odor cannot be masked.

Consequently, I have a feeling, just a sense, that something much stranger than the double intention of a subtext runs through *Paradise Lost*: that Milton's judgments denigrate what his representations magnify, that his characters contradict his condemnations and justifications. I have no idea how much a close study of his published opinions or a deep penetration into his private thoughts could establish the truth; I feel terminally baffled by the points I'm about to make. I keep having the sense that some truth in this cosmic Christian drama keeps asserting itself to Milton as poet which, as a theologian, he suppresses. But that notion implies that the story of this temporal episode within eternity is not altogether a made fiction but has the power of unintended consequences that belongs to living truth; I just don't know. So I'll set out my sense, in brief.

2) SATAN'S EVE: THE SCHISMATIC PAIR

Satan lies in wait, hardly hoping that he "might find Eve separate." "Eve separate he spies" (9.422, 424). She has separated herself from her consort Adam—"split," as our young now say. It is a good word, the English for the Greek verb whence comes "schism," breaking away. Satan, in turn, addresses her as "sole wonder" and presents himself as "single" (9.532, 536). He often speaks of himself as "alone" (for example, 2.975, 3.441), but "single" had then as now another meaning as well: unmarried. And surely he woos her; he is the primal seducer. But it doesn't take much. Eve, that crooked bone, is a born schismatic, as Satan is a created one. Or it is at least a great question just how he and his host of fallen angels come to be heaven's splitters, the aboriginal protestants.

Here is how they are a pair, alike in features that bear the name of badness in Milton's book, but are attractive in description, and, what is more, have the stamp of approval in our day.

First then, Eve too wants to be alone. We respect that: "I need time to myself, I need space." She is indeed the instigator of her separation from a weakly reluctant Adam. "Eve first" speaks up: "Let us divide our labors"—she is the inventor if not of the division of labor then of separate work spaces! (2019: *WeWork*, a workspace-sharing company is deep in financial trouble.) "Sole Eve, associate sole" he answers, meaning more than he knows, the clueless man, but then he gets it: "but if much converse perhaps / Thee satiate, to short absence I should yield"—though she has pleaded efficiency rather than surfeit (9.205 ff.). He, the "patriarch of mankind," lectures her on free will: "O woman . . ." But "Eve/persisted, yet submiss." It is what we have learned to call the passive/aggressive mode, the underdog's determined self-defense.

She is, like Satan, a dissimulator who keeps some things private. For she has had a week to ponder Satan's night visitation in which, "Squat like a toad," he whispered suggestions in her ear. I imagine the left, for this is surely a parody of the impregnating Holy Spirit who comes to the Virgin by the right ear in many late Medieval paintings. There he manages to "raise/At least distempered, discontented thoughts" (4.806). Thus she has more in mind than mere efficiency in weeding Paradise as she separates from her husband. As she will later say: "Was I to have never parted from thy side?/As good to have grown still there a lifeless rib" (9.1153).

There is a whole list of similarities of situation and likenesses of character between the fallen angel and the woman, for which I could cite book and line: Both are kept at a remove from their God, he by the Son, she by her mate. His rebelliousness is proudly asserted, her resistance submissively masked, but both have that in them that is ready to abrogate obedience: "Our great Forbidder" she calls God, and Satan calls him "the Threat'ner" (9.815, 687). Satan is a brilliant sophist on the ancient model, but his clever proof to her that a God who inspires fear is no God, so that her "fear itself of death removes the fear" (9.702), is matched by her clever musings: "good unknown, sure is not had, or had/And yet unknown, is as not had at all./In plain then, what forbids he but to know,/Forbids us good, forbids us to be wise?/Such prohibitions bind not" (9.756).

She is willful, restless, venturesome, poignant in her lapse, proud as the mother of mankind. Satan is willfulness incarnate, a great engineer, the original Adventurer (10.440), both as explorer and in the older sense of undertaking grand ventures, such as the development of Hell, the colonizing of earth, and the sponsoring of the great highway that makes Hell and this world "one continent of easy thoroughfare" (10.392), he is the primal jet-setting globalizer. He is, in fact, a Promethean figure, a god at odds with his Chief; he is a patron of invention and, in his perverse way, a benefactor of mankind (Sec. 1). He is the instigating cause of the earth's obliquity, that skewing of the terrestrial pole which brings us seasonal variety and moral diversity; he is the ultimate reason for human mortality and the succession of generations (how on earth would Eden have held all the promised increase of immortals?), in short, of history. There is true pathos in the racking pain of his inability to love: About to spoil Paradise, he curses familiarly but eerily: "O hell!" he says, seeing the bright spirits, the humans, "whom my thoughts pursue with wonder and could love" (4.358). There is real candor in his confession of unwillingness to repent: He concludes a meditation on his certain relapse were he to submit with a chillingly final choice, "Evil be thou my good" (4.110). And there is residual receptivity to the influence of innocent grace: Seeing Eve, alone, "that space the Evil One abstracted stood / From his own evil, and for the time remained / *Stupidly* good" (9.463). My italics: surely Milton can't have thought that one can be good in a stupor!

Satan has been said to be modeled on Iago, literature's most notorious bad man. They are both, to be sure, racked with resentment for being passed over by their superiors, but there is an enormous difference in their stature: Iago suffers meanly and mutely, Satan grandly and candidly—at least by and to himself.

Eve cannot match his stature, but there are two capstone transgressions in which they are nearly equal. One is the drive to explore, experiment, experience—as he sails through the uncreated void to explore the created world, she dreams of flying with him to behold the earth in its immensity, the first human to ride the skies (somewhat like Superman and his girl). The second is the desire for godhead: He thinks himself God's equal, and she, eating, has Godhead in her thoughts (9.790).

3) EVE SEPARATE: THE MOTHER OF MODERNITY

In short, they are the original moderns, he in God's universe, she in our world. For there is a generic modernity: asserted individual will; unbounded experimental science (whose root meaning is, wonderfully, the same as that of schism: dividing, cutting off); chameleon-like adaptability (Lucifer-Satan is a master of transformations, willed and imposed: cherub, toad, serpent; Eve too undergoes some pretty dramatic changes: rib to woman, self-lover to partner, consort to runaway); future-oriented temporality (here Satan and the Son cooperate, one to make sin endemic, the other to make salvation attainable); and godlike creativity (such as is attributed to man by Pico della Mirandola in that manifesto of proto-modernity, the "Oration on the Dignity of Man" of the 1480s: Adam, man, has no fixed being; rather "our chameleon" assumes by his own free will whatever form he selects, and so he can be as God).

But this perennial set of possibilities is realized predominantly in historical modernity, our epoch, within which we are temporal compatriots. We are indeed the progeny of Eve, for with her the era's deeper characteristics originate, above all narcissistic individualism, the thirst for liberation, the lust for experience, a hunger for equality, and a drive to resolve all mysteries, "to leave no problem unsolved," as a founder of modernity puts it (Vieta, *Analytical Art*, 1591).

There is a startling story Eve tells Adam, a story of her first awakening into consciousness (4.449). "With unexperienced thought" she goes to a smooth lake, bends over it—and *falls in love* with what she sees, pining for her own image "with vain desire"; she is the first self- and image-worshipper, the first narcissist. When she first sees Adam she doesn't much like him; he is "less fair,/less winning soft, less amiably mild." She runs away; Adam tells her that she is part of him, body and soul, and she yields. Her first love is herself—even before Satan leaps into Paradise. Is self-love ever innocent? Now she gets what she is longing for, experience and experiences, discovery by trying things out and stimulation by affects deliberately aroused. She has eaten of the Tree of the Knowledge of Good and Evil, which the Tempter calls "Mother of science" (9.680). She has, instantly, grown "mature in knowledge." She knows what to call her fascination: "Experience, next to thee I owe,/Best guide;" "thou . . . givest access . . ." to secret wisdom (9.807). And in short order she invents novelties now well known to us; this wisdom of hers has in it much of applied science, particularly political and psychological know-how. She tells an outright, very politic lie, the original lie on earth: She figures first that she might keep the secret of the fruit so as to "render me more equal, and perhaps,/A thing not undesirable, sometime/Superior; for inferior who is free?" (9.823). After this very contemporary manifesto of family politics, she reconsiders to herself: What if I do die, as promised, and he takes on another Eve? Better to die together. But to him she cleverly claims that her "growing up to godhead" was all done for his sake, and that he must join her "lest thou not tasting, different degree/Disjoin us, and I then too late renounce/Duty for thee, when fate will not permit" (9. 883). A barefaced, self-serving lie!

Of course she has already invented drug-taking and having ecstatic experiences, and instant knowledge; experiential learning too will be her invention (10.967). Shortly she will propose birth-control—"willful barrenness"—and suicide to him (10.987, 1001, 1042). Ask where all the snares and escapes of our time come from, and the answer is: Eve. To him she calls herself the "weaker sex" (9.383), for that is what he thinks, but her submissiveness hides a huge ambition:

Satan gets to her by addressing her as Queen of the Universe, Empress of the World, "a goddess among gods, adored and served" (9.547). It cannot only be a really meek, dependent woman who glories in such appellations; it is, after all, what domineering men want as well. Recall that the primary, the horror-inspiring transgression of Mr. Kurtz in dark Africa is that he accepts worship and human sacrifice as a god, and he is a very demon of force. If anything, she's a born outlaw: To the Serpent she interprets paradisiacal life as bound by one prohibition, and for the rest "we live/Law to ourselves, our reason is our law" (9.653).

But from one perspective she's no outlaw nor a rebel either. Our political progenitor, Locke, points out that re*bellare* means "to go *back* to a state of war," and that the true *rebel* is the contract-breaking tyrant, not his imposed-on subjects; they are *revolutionaries* (*Second Treatise*, para. 226). Now Satan can claim that his monarch has in fact revoked, if not a social contract, then a heavenly understanding, and Eve does claim that the single prohibition is irrational in principle and defectively promulgated: She knows neither why the tree is forbidden, nor what the punishment means, nor when it will be imposed.

To return to my initial perplexity: There is no question that the above is a skewed version of these events, that Milton expresses more respect for Adam than for Eve, that he is not unsympathetic when he allows Adam to call her "that bad woman" (10.837), that Satan is the Evil One. There are formulaic explanations for my unhistoric perspective: Milton's poem sets out Christian doctrine, not necessarily orthodox but fervent; I am a post-Christian and quasi-Jewish modern who believes that the soundest part of modernity is rooted in Pagan philosophy. So what seems pernicious to him seems admirable to me. Or, alternately, Milton was in fact a revolutionary, a republican, a defender of regicide, so naturally he has some sympathy for the adverse party in heaven and on earth. Both explanations have plausibility, and neither resolves the perplexity: How do Satan and Eve come to be such exact types of modernity? Is our world Satanic or was Hell Luciferic, "light-bringing"? I mean: Is our present condition the consequence of a devilish seduction—as Goethe's Faust sells his soul to the devil for the boon of restless experience and grand enterprise—or is it really the other way round: that Hell was from its founding the place of enlightenment and progress—and we moderns found that out?

4) DOMESTIC ADAM: THE CLOD ERECT

And then, who is really dominant in the Original Pair? The splendor of Adam's looks is conveyed in sonorous lines. Satan sees the pair, distinguished from the other creatures by being "erect and tall,/God-like erect, with native honor clad/In naked majesty . . . though both/Not equal, as their sex not equal seemed;/For contemplation he and valor formed,/For softness she and sweet attractive grace,/He for God only, she for God in him:/His fair large front and eyes sublime declared/Absolute rule" (4.288).

Here is what is odd. That Adam is a well-made creature of fine bearing and natural dignity, a good man and loving husband, is unquestionable. But not contemplation, nor valor, nor absolute rule are in fact his forte. He is, to put it plainly, an upright klutz, one of those amiable, fine males a female might well cling to, well knowing she could run circles around him—and so Eve does.

As for contemplation: In that wonderful interlude, Books 5–7, the archangel Raphael is sent to Paradise to warn and instruct Adam—Adam, not Eve, who sits listening "retired in sight" (8.41), having served the angel a paradisiacal meal, which the angel, hilariously, falls to and begins "with keen dispatch/Of real hunger, and concoctive heat/To transubstantiate" (5.437). She listens on the sidelines to the story of

Satan's war and defeat. To be sure, it all comes too late; he has already leaped into Paradise and entered her imagination in a dream—part of Heaven's mismanagement I'll talk of below. But when Adam's "countenance seemed/Entering on studious thoughts abstruse" (8.39), that is, when the theological account of Heaven's battles and earth's creation are done and the astronomical part begins, she goes off to her gardening, and remains there, not "as not with such discourse/Delighted, or not capable her ear/Of what was high," but preferring to hear it from her husband; the angel, though gracious, is too stiff for her.

Here I must interject two observations: first, the question Adam asks that sets off Raphael's account of hypothetical rational astronomy is a cumbrous version of one asked him by Eve the night before, together with assurances of submission: "God is thy law, thou mine," she begins and then gives the loveliest speech of companionable conjugality imaginable: "With thee conversing I forget all time/All seasons and their change, all please alike" (4.637)—to end it all abruptly by posing the most embarrassing question of celestial mechanics: "But wherefore all night long shine these, for whom/This glorious sight, when sleep has shut all eyes?" She wants to know nature's purpose, and by implication, who's at the cosmic center. He gives a confidently ignorant answer, but knows enough to ask the angel: "Something yet of doubt remains. . . ." When he computes the world's magnitude (he actually can't), how is it that the firmament with its numberless stars seems to roll through spaces incomprehensible (he's a natural Ptolemaean, as are we all) "merely to officiate light/Round this opacous earth" (8.13)—same question, more Latinate vocabulary.

Second, Raphael gives, oddly, the Catholic answer. The preface by Bishop Osiander to Copernicus's *On the Revolutions of the Heavenly Spheres* (1543) tries to neutralize the heliocentric revolution by ranking it as merely an alternative hypothesis, a mathematical simplification devised, in Plato's phrase, "to save the appearances," that is, to mathematicize the phenomena. Raphael tells Adam, never mind fact, "rather admire." God has left his heavenly fabric to human conjecture and disputing, "perhaps to move/His laughter at their quaint opinions wide/Hereafter when they come to model heav'n/And calculate the stars . . . to save appearances" (8.75). Here's one of the Heavenly Host citing an Athenian Pagan! And so much for mankind's first and grandest and most theologically fraught science: "What if the sun/Be center of the world . . . ?" Of course the angel knows, as we know from Copernicus, that when astronomical—and moral—obliquity enters the world after the fall, when equator and ecliptic come apart at an angle, so that the sun appears to spiral up and down the earth making seasons, the more economical way to effect this phenomenon is to push the earth's pole askew. Yet even then Milton insists only that "Some say he bid the angels turn askance/The poles of earth twice ten degrees and more . . . some say the sun was bid turn reins" (10.668) on the now-skewed ecliptic—c. 23° 51', in fact—that very obliquity which produced corruption and pestilence and variety of season and weather for us.

And Adam, the biddable, is "fully" satisfied when enjoined to be "lowly wise," to descend to "speak of things at hand, useful." For him "experience," which widens Eve's horizon, teaches "not to know at large of things remote" (8.173); he is content to be temperate in knowledge. (So much for contemplation, which means, after all, taking a wide point of view, theorizing, transgressing conscientiously.) Eve is—until cowed by her lapse—more insatiable for wisdom than that, and a keener inquirer.

Now as for valor. We hear of his proneness to passion, which he is warned against by Raphael (8.635), and of his pusillanimity—he has to be told to have "self-esteem" (8.572), that contemporary buzzword—and he is, though inconsis-

tently, upbraided by Eve for his weakness in letting her separate from him (10.1155) and allowing Satan to prevail.
Michael, sent to comfort Adam, goes so far as to answer thus
his accusation that the beginning of man's woe is by women:
"From man's effeminate slackness it begins" (11.634). This
sedentary "domestic Adam" (9.315) has a stodgy but infirm
virtue that is no match for mobile, venturesome Eve's spirit
of independence. In the end it is he who cannot bear to be
without her; she is, after all, one of his bones. So much for
valor and for authority: "Was she thy God?" the "sovran Presence" asks him (10.145); the very thought had occurred to Eve
(9.790). Well, at the least she is used to having the final word,
one way or another: The "patriarch of mankind" has spoken,
"but Eve persisted, yet submiss, though last . . ." (9.376)—a
grimly hilarious line written by a two-timed husband.

And he's slow (though sweet) and inattentively clueless. Eve
has told him the tale of her self-love and how he at first repelled
her. When he regales Raphael, at the end of his visitation, with
the story of his own creation and of Eve's, it turns out he hasn't
listened at all: He thinks she ran from him out of coyness; she
"would be wooed, and not unsought be won" (8.503). And
when the great disaster has come, and Eve, doomed, offers
him the fruit, why does he not, simple man, think beyond
the two options of dying with her or getting a new Eve? Why
doesn't he refrain from eating and intercede for her?

Clearly "domestic" and "dominant" are at odds here—
maybe it is the reality of the Adamic character, that ensouled
clod of earth, that is prevailing.

5) POETIC MILTON: THE DEVIL'S PARTY

Much stranger things are to come, so this might be a moment
to consider theological poetry. Blake says that Milton wrote
in fetters of Heaven and at liberty of Hell because "he was a
true poet and of the Devil's party without knowing it" (*The*

Marriage of Heaven and Hell). I don't know what *he* meant, but I think I know what *it* means: The devil is—or wants to be—autonomous, a rule unto himself (as Eve thinks they are both in Paradise); he is literally a heretic—for "heresy" is a Greek word that means "choosing," or as we redundantly say, "choosing for oneself." In the realization of self-will and self-rule, he becomes innovative. Novelty is not new with him: Heaven starts it, knowing the possible consequences, which are therefore not wholly unintended. So also is this poet a maker of newness: Moses's Muse, Milton's first muse, is to sing "Things unattempted yet in prose or rhyme" (1.16; ironically, the line itself comes from Ariosto). His Raphael tells Adam "The secrets of another world, perhaps/Not lawful to reveal" (5.569). Milton writes a new epic, not "sedulous by nature to indite/Wars" and other old heroic and chivalric shenanigans (9.27), yet his great interlude, the "War in Heaven," is a magnificent war poem, though perhaps too embarrassing to Heaven to be decently revealed—yet Milton reveals it. We might well ask: Where does the poem leave Scripture? The poem is far more revealing; is it itself revealed? It is far more visible, a huge, magnificent moving picture, a blind poet's telling—and showing—"Of things invisible to mortal sight" (3.54), "lik'ning spiritual to corporeal forms" (5.573). Is the imaging of spirits permissible? It is "in nightly visitations unimplored" dictated to him by his second Muse, his "celestial patroness" Urania (9.21), though a heavenly, not, as far as I know, an orthodox source. To be sure, Milton denies that he means the pagan Muse of Astronomy: "The meaning, not the name I call, for thou/Nor of the muses nine" (7.5). But surely this is equivocation. The inspiration for his books on the cosmos comes from a Greek source, one "of the muses nine," though he disclaims her. And so this epic does not replace but absorbs pagan epic and pagan science, and puts Milton in a skewed position of accepting the splendor and deriding the culture of pagan hell (see Sec. 6).

To give a name to the poet's peculiar propensity: It is a form of Manichaeism, the teaching that evil is real and incarnable. In a long tradition, the Neoplatonists and their Christian partisans held that badness is nonbeing, defect of being. For example, Adam is, understandably, a confused Neoplatonist: When he loses his wonted composure, he nastily calls Eve in turn "serpent," and "this novelty on earth, this fair *defect*" (10.867), not sure whether a feminine being, that "rib/Crooked by nature" is lacking in something or oversupplied with "pride/And wand'ring vanity." Milton's Satan has no such doubts: To him his evil being is real and is accepted, no, vaunted as such, just as the darkness of hell is a paradoxical illumination. Surely the poet who produces a brilliant personification of evil is a perhaps unwitting, perhaps half self-admitted follower of Mani, not exactly of his doctrine but of the Manichaean propensity for the personification of the kingdom of darkness.

There is another huge work that makes a novel tale of a sacred story. As Milton had expanded the second and third chapters of Genesis, comprising that book's two alternative accounts of the creation of man, into a huge epic, so Thomas Mann developed his novel, *Joseph and His Brothers*, from twenty-six chapters in Genesis, telling the story of Jacob and his sons into nearly two thousand pages; he was executing a plan conceived by Goethe. But Mann has his "irony" to extenuate this dubious and so doubly engaging enterprise. He hovers above faith, and his ultimate belief is in the allusive imaging and reference-fraught story-telling itself.

Perhaps the poet's—and this poet's—indefeasible partisanship for the devil, that sets him "more at liberty" when writing of Hell, is in just this re-creative activity: Satan thinks he might not be a *creation* but an original, a *self-created* being (5.860). Poets too want to be original, themselves creators, if not of themselves, of their worlds. It makes them great iconodules (image-servers), for they love their creatures.

Iconodulia, a term from the old iconoclastic (image-breaking) battles culminating in the eighth and ninth centuries, was by the opponents understood as idolatry (idol-worship), praying *to*, not *through*, the icon. The charge goes way back, to that ancient quarrel between poetry and philosophy spoken of in Plato's *Republic*, where images are devices to distance us from Being by ensnaring us in the desire for sights (601 ff.), for appearances. Iconodulia is a sin of which Satan, the proudly unattached leader of that "atheist crew" (6.370), is not guilty, for he is his own original. But who can say that blind Milton did not love his invisible universe, made by him and made visible to himself, better than the real world made by God and made invisible to him, and, perhaps, better than the ultimately invisible God? He does not, in any case, succeed in making God lovable—or his Son interesting: "Hail Son of God, . . . thy name/Shall be the copious matter of my song/Henceforth . . ." (2.412), he says after two terrific books about Satan. But the "copious matter" of the remaining ten is not the Son either, but more Satan—and Eve.

I'll be concentrating on the problematic vision and thought-raising qualities of Milton's poetry, so I want to make here a declaration of love to the texture of words through which these are delivered: the steady English beat of the more than ten thousand iambic lines with their ever varied stresses in the hyper-English produced by the mixed Latinate and Anglo-Saxon diction—which with a little practice begins to read like mankind's original language.

6) INSIPID HEAVEN, SAPIENT HELL

The first two books of *Paradise Lost* are of paradise lost, of hell gained. Heaven itself comes on the scene only later, mostly at war. And this is well, because it is not attractive. I recall Bernard Williams saying in an encyclopedia article on death that Heaven's eternity must be boring—all that everlasting monotonic intoning. (In fact, in Milton's Paradise they play harps and occasionally sing in parts. Bach knew better; witness the glorious victory march-by in heaven on the words of Revelation 12:10, "Now is the salvation and the power and realm and the might" celebrating the Son's defeat of Satan in the "War in Heaven," Cantata fragment 50.) So the notion of celestial tedium is wrongheaded, for incorporeal substances don't experience the weariness of the bodily senses. What is offputting in the poetry of heaven is God's ultimate invisibility, for it is simply mystifying how formless light can by mere effulgence in fact produce any shaped copy, be it an ethereal image—the Son (6.680)—or an embodied one—man. I suppose there's plenty of theology about it. In any case, God is heard out of invisible obscurity: "Glorious brightness . . . / Throned inaccessible" (3.375); to Satan it looks like "Thick clouds and dark" (2.263), to Heaven it's a "golden cloud" (6.28); sometimes God speaks vengefully, from a "secret cloud" (10.32).

He often speaks peremptorily and on one occasion even with pointedly offensive vulgarity, when he promises to seal up hell: "See with what heat these dogs of hell advance"—as if they were bitches. He has suffered them to enter and possess earth, to puzzle his enemies "That laugh, as if transported with some fit / Of passion," thinking that it has not happened on purpose. No, they were called up on purpose, "My hell-hounds, to lick up the draff and filth" of man's polluting sin, so that gorged they might nigh burst "With sucked and glutted offal" (10.625)—infernal vacuum cleaners. In a human, that's surely gross talk.

But Heaven itself, with its unvarying obedience, is vapid—not surely to inhabit but, unavoidably, to read about. It is the poetic problem of goodness, which is, *ipso facto*, even-tenored, uneventful, not the stuff of intense drama or vivid imagery. It does not have the snags and hollows that throw shadows and catch our interest: Perfect globes are intellectually perfectly beautiful, but who wants to look at their image for long? It is why newspapers never report that three hundred and some million people went to do respectable work and came home to enjoy their families, but always that someone or other killed, raped, or stole. So Heaven is not interesting until there is civil war, and even then the so easily victorious Son fades against the brilliant, beaten Adversary, whose legions the heavenly general sweeps so easily over the brink into chaos, like Indians driving herds of buffalo over cliffs into canyons. Moreover, who can exonerate Heaven from the charge that in its war was born the notion that might makes right—and the hoary justification that right is in this case might?

As if to make up for its Chief's invisibility and its remaining inhabitants' spotlessness, Milton makes heaven and its furniture baroquely opulent. The Son's war chariot with its four Cherubic faces and eyes all over, made of beryl, crystal, sapphire, amber and all the colors of the rainbow, is extravagantly strange (6.753); there is no such vehicle even in Revelation, one of the Biblical sources for the war in Heaven (12:7). This is not the style of Hell.

It is, to begin with, a place of somber and restrained beauty. Opulence calls for Corinthian capitals, which are, as Palladio says, the most beautiful and elegant of the orders of columns. Pandemonium, however, rising "like an exhalation, with sound / Of dulcet symphonies and voices sweet / Built like a temple" (1.711)—a pagan temple, of course—employs the severe and chaste Doric order with a golden architrave, for gold is mined in hell. Mulciber, in Greek Hephaestus, the most gifted of the pagan gods, is the architect. The inside is illuminated by starry lamps.

It is a People's Palace, and there a consultative parliament is held, a large inclusive synod (6.156) such as is never called in monarchic heaven. Hell is a sort of democracy on the Athenian model, which had a presiding "first man." Its presid-

ing chief had once been Latin Lucifer, the "Light-bearer," so
called for his—former—brightness (7.131), but in my anachronistic ear there sounds also the word Enlightenment. Now
he is Hebrew Satan, *Shatan*, the "Adversary," and Greek
Devil, *diabolus*, the "Accuser." He is a revolutionary, a "Patron of Liberty," not only in seeming, as Abdiel, the coun-
terrevolutionary angel, claims (4.958), but in fact. For though
he had been *made* "free to fall" (3.99), he had, what is more,
claimed that right *for himself*. Moreover, he finds his companions worthy of liberty and honor (6.420). Thus he is
termed by his lieutenants "Deliverer from new lords, leader
to free/Enjoyment of our right as gods" (6.451). He has a bill
of accusations against his tyrant, not unlike the one found
in our Declaration of Independence; he accuses God of enforcing vassalage of demanding, "Forced hallelujahs" (2.243),
and, ironically but truly, of requiring image-worship (5.784)
in interposing the Son, his image, between himself and his angels. Interposition is indeed the sub-theme of Milton's justification—strange term—of the ways of God to man: the Son
as intermediary between God and the angels and as intercessor on man's behalf, Adam as God's representative to Eve
and interpreter to her of Heaven's messages, and even Satan
as Hell's emissary to earth. This God is a *deus absconditus*
whose ways are incessantly indirect.

Satan is, moreover, a real leader, intrepid, of unconquer-
able will (2.106). He heartens and rallies his troops, and they
respond to him with trusting enthusiasm (1.663), rejoicing in
their "matchless chief" (1.486). He is strangely like the Son in
being willing to volunteer for fatally dangerous service to his
people—to jet through Chaos where no devil wants to go, to
break out of by now homey hell to explore new lands for his
people's occupation (2.402); thus he is raised to "transcendent
glory" (2.427).

Proud, rebellious, and monarchical in his spirit though he
is, he knows how to assure his loyal band of their equality:

"O friends" (6.609) he addresses them at their great crisis, but even before his magnificent speeches to them were all about equality—their equality in freedom if not in power. For as Abdiel, the Tory, points out, Lucifer is himself a prince. But he presents himself as *primus inter pares*, first among equals: No one more often utters the word "equal" linked with "free": "or if not equal all, yet free,/Equally free; for orders and decrees/Jar not with liberty, but well consist./Who can in reason then or right assume/Monarchy over such as live by right/His equals, if in power and splendor less,/In freedom equal?" (5.791). And as he speaks, so, it appears, he rules in the spirit of our Declaration: that all angels are created equal, that they are endowed, Satan would say by their heavenly nativity, with certain unalienable rights, among which one is liberty—that is, their freedom derives from an equality of rights

From Satan's politics to his endowments: He sits exalted, "by merit raised/To that bad eminence" (2.5). He is a sublime psychologist and the only wit, a mordant one, in this high drama—except of course for Milton himself, whose wit, insinuated into the action through his whiplash enjambments and his fork-tongued puns, is borrowed by Satan, who can have no insight or wit but his maker's. In Satan's "Indeed," when Eve naïvely tells of their perfect freedom in heaven except for the forbidden tree (9.656), you can hear the supercilious Englishman. When he tells Hell how he seduced Man he adds, with a witty contempt: "with an apple;" it's a sheer, wickedly derogatory invention; I don't think it was just a juicy apple, but a fruit laden with drug-like magic—though Satan's put-down prevailed. Here is a pertinent ditty (see Sec. 11) from the early 15th century:

> And all was for an appil,
>   An appil that he tok.
> Ne hadde the appil taken ben,

The appil taken ben,
Ne hadde never our lady
A bene heven quene.
Blessed be the time
That appil taken was.
Therefore we moun singen
'*Deo gracias.*'

It announces the *fortunate fault*, Eve's guilty gift to mankind to come (Sec. 10). But Satan is more than smartly cynical; he is a great inventor and engineer. The manufacture of that tremendous contrivance, the cannon, which he builds in heaven, that devilish engine which nearly routs the heavenly host in the most tremendous cannonade I've ever read of, is vividly described by Raphael in Book 6. Like Persian Xerxes, who cut a mountain off from its mainland (Herodotus 7.22), he reconfigures nature: His offspring Sin and Death cut through Chaos "by wondrous art/Pontifical" (that is, bridge-building, 10.312) to join Hell to Paradise.

But back to Hell itself, a place of relative harmony: "O shame to men! Devil with devil damned/Firm concord holds, men only disagree" (1.496). It is a place of music, of "partial," that is, of complex polyphonic sound, as contrasted with the simple celestial unisons, I imagine. It is also "partial" as being of the devil's party, of inspiriting their heroic deeds, and it takes with "ravishment/The thronging audience" (1.552).

There is, above all, the sweetest soul-charming discourse: high reasoning "Of providence, foreknowledge, will and fate,/Fixed fate, free will, foreknowledge absolute." Round and round it goes as do conversations in a serious college: "And found no end" (1.560). They talk, as do we on earth, philosophy: of passion and apathy, of good and evil, of happiness and final misery. They have the experience for it; it is not talk abstracted from life but real inquiry.

"Vain wisdom all, and false philosophy," this passage concludes. That is Milton's way with Hell and the devils. It and they are depicted gloriously and dismissed ignominiously. It happens over and over. The representation raises what the judgment crushes.

Hell is altogether puzzling. Following an old Patristic tradition, Milton has all the fallen angels assume, as devils, the form of the pagan gods, some Levantine and horrible, some Greek and graceful, all vivid (1.375) and more distinctively individual than ever were the loyal archangels. All are beautiful, and though their looks deteriorate, as angels they can never be all bad in soul or all spoiled in form (1.483).

Satan, as I have imagined him, is the aboriginal modern, not only in his politics, but perhaps most of all when he is at home in hell where he asserts a modern hallmark: subjectivity, solipsistic ideation, inner-world creation: "The mind is its own place, and in itself / Can make a heav'n of hell, or hell of heav'n. / What matter where, if I be still the same . . . ?" (1.254). But he is not only a modern post-Christian, he is also a pagan pre-Christian; he encompasses the human salvational episode, coming before and after as it were. As G. K. Chesterton says: "It is profoundly true that the ancient world was more modern than the Christian" (*Orthodoxy*, Ch. 9).

As fallen Lucifer, in Hell Satan belongs to the Greek crew, though more as hero than god—albeit as god too. For like the Christian God he gives birth, though not to a Son but to a daughter, and like Zeus he gives birth through his head, not to wise Athena but to canny Sin. Yet primarily he is like the *Iliad*'s Achilles, first in battle, and offended by a sense of injured merit (1.98). The relation is, however, perverted for the occasion, as displayed in Satan's adaptation of Achilles' words in Hades: "I would wish rather to be a slave in service to another . . . than to be ruler over all the dead" (*Odyssey* 11.488). For Satan, at home in Hell, says instead: "Better to reign in Hell than serve in Heaven" (1.263); it is how he proudly counters good Abdiel's "Reign thou in Hell thy kingdom, let me serve / In heav'n God ever blest" (6.183).

Milton, to be sure, disowns Achilles: His is an "argument/ Not less but more Heroic than the wrath/Of stern Achilles" (9.13). And he most assuredly disowns the philosophizing of Hell. In *Paradise Regained* Satan advertises ancient wisdom as the final temptation of Jesus, sounding much like the catalogue of a Christian college trying to persuade applicants that a liberal education should include Greek philosophy: "All knowledge is not couch'd in Moses' law,/the Pentateuch or what the prophets wrote,/The Gentiles also know, and write, and teach/To admiration, led by Nature's light" (*Paradise Regained* 4.225). So "To sage philosophy next lend thine ear,/From Heaven descended to the low-rooft house/Of Socrates" (4.272). Jesus rejects it all, though, like Milton, he is an admirer of Plato and his Socrates. He says that Socrates "For truth's sake suffering death unjust, lives now/Equal in fame to proudest Conquerours" (3.96), but explains that this "first and wisest of them all profess'd/To know this only, that he nothing knew" (4.293). Even so Jesus rejects Satan's temptation. He neither knows nor doesn't know these things; his "light is from above;" any great reader must needs be "Deep verst in books and shallow in himself " (4.286). In this spirit Milton comments on the pair asleep in Paradise: "O yet happiest if ye seek/No happier state and know to know no more" (4.774).

So heroic poetry, philosophical inquiry, and book-learning appear to be rejected as Satanic. But that's the trouble; they flourish in or about Hell, which is a display case of antique lore and heroic character and liberal artistry and free inquiry and sophistic skill. Belial is Hell's most beautiful god "For dignity compos'd and high exploit"—here comes the customary whiplash—"But all was false and hollow," for "he could make the worse appear/The better reason" (2.110); this is verbatim the sophistry attributed to the Clouds in Aristophanes' play, those clouds that are parodies of Plato's Ideas and the sponsors of Socrates' Thinkery. In Hell is to be found all that was exciting in its splendor or rousing in its dubiousness in Paganism. In Hell as in life there is no escaping its attraction, and all the poet's damning postscripts cannot dim the glories of his "infernal pit." Milton's Satan speaks gallantly; Milton explicates: "Vaunting aloud—but wracked with deep despair" (1.126, my dash); it's still the gallantry that resonates.

"Insipid" means tasteless, savorless, as *sapor* means taste, savor: Milton's Adam, influenced by the taste of the forbidden fruit of knowledge, discovers its etymological connection with sapience, wisdom (9.1018). Hell is sapient as hell; is that an inherent truth asserting itself?

7) MISMANAGED MONARCHY

If Hell, when not racked with supererogatory spasms such as the yearly Hissing when all the devils turn into writhing snakes (10.508), is a well-run republic, Milton's Heaven can be said to be a mismanaged monarchy or firm. The archangels' inefficiency cries, so to speak, to high heaven. Set to watch out for escapees from Hell, Uriel, in his simplicity, is "for once beguiled" by Satan's cherubic disguise—though the heavenly gods are supposed to know good from evil (3.636)— and directs him straight to Eden, where he evades the angelic pickets posted at the gates by simply leaping over the wall of Paradise. God lets it go: "be not dismayed," he says to the unsuccessful sentinels; this intrusion "your sincerest care could not prevent" (10.37)—so what was the point of posting them? Raphael is sent too late to prevent the capture of Eve's imagination, and, by his own account, the heavenly army under Michael, outnumbering the forces under Lucifer's command two to one, are beaten; the Son alone saves Heaven (Book 6).

But that's the least of it. To take a coolly secular view, the ruler of this polity is either deliberately disruptive or disregards some prime rules of management: Don't add intermediate layers of authority; don't make yourself inaccessible; don't rebuff your insiders; if it ain't broke, don't fix it. Everyone knows what discontent the intromission of a provost between the president and a faculty induces in it, or the upset that bringing in a vice-president from the outside and disappointing fair expectations causes in companies. This is exactly what happens in Heaven. Once all worshiped and obeyed God alone, a God who, though inaccessible to sight, was equally so to all. Then one day there is a newcomer, a Son, born not created. Though it is not clear that he appears after the angelic creation, it is clear that he is one fine day proclaimed and anointed—and set over all the princely angels, God's loyal servants, as vice-regent, a head to be acknowledged Lord (5.609). It is a novelty, an innovation whose necessity is not apparent; God seems to be, in Caesar's words, simply *cupidus rerum novarum*, "avid for new things" (*Gallic Wars* 1.18). He does not need a Son. Indeed, when Adam, shortly after his creation, asks God for a mate, God slyly joshes him "as with a smile": "What think'st thou then of me . . . / Seem I to thee sufficiently possessed / Of happiness or not, who am alone / From all eternity, for none I know / Second to me or like, equal much less" (8.403). Either God has forgotten or is concealing that he too now has family, or he is signifying that he needs none. We do know that the Son was born—whenever it was in timeless time—before Adam was made, though, to be sure, the possibility of innovation in an atemporal realm is humanly incomprehensible. "When?" makes no sense in eternity. Of more human consequence is that Milton's God is playing a dangerous game with Adam: accustoming him to the sense that persisting in one's desire and opposing God's advice is permissible, even possibly successful. For Adam gets his consort.

Naturally some angels, created proud, are outraged at being set at a remove from the throne, at having their rights disrespected and expectations disappointed. Over and over Satan repeats that *this* is the cause—be it the mere occasion or the actual reason—of the rebellion, which is thus a revolution. The engaged reader (for irreverently deadpan literalism can be a way of respecting the story) has to ask: Is Heaven's action an incitement, an entrapment? God has given the angels free will. Has he made them dissimilar in nature, some more proud, more prone to apostasy, with more propensity to self-assertion and offense-taking? Is he calling these flawed ones out?

Here the question arises whether the angels, to whom God gave the knowledge of good and evil (11.85), know evil by their own experience or just by contrast to good. The latter *is* conceivable; Socrates in the *Republic* (409) demands that a judge should learn of badness by observation, not from within his own soul. Yet Satan says to Gabriel that he cannot know what it means to seek relief who "evil hast not tried" (4.896). But then, before the angelic uprising, what evil was there to observe? Do some, a third, have it in them? Is Heaven rife with potentiality for evil, waiting to be realized? Is God indeed planning a razzia, a raid on putative infidels?

God does have foreknowledge of the event. But his argument, that omniscience does not prove determinism, is persuasive. An atemporal Godhead oversees our entire temporal episode as a whole from its beginning to its end. Earth's history is not, after all, infinite in this story: Hell will be sealed and Heaven opened to man. *Sub specie aeternitatis*, under the perspective of eternity, foreknowledge is not foretelling, since to observe is not to interfere (at least not outside quantum theory). Since we see the past as fixed and conclude that because it is done it cannot be undone—which isn't even so very true—therefore we think, *a fortiori*, so much the more, that if it cannot be altered it must have been necessary— which is a plain paralogism. No more need God's sight, which includes the end, fix beforehand what happens; he is no cryptodeterminist. To foresee completely from a perspective outside time is not to predict certainly from causes within.

But it is an entirely different question whether Milton's God wishes that the catastrophe eventuate which he has made, at least and at most, possible. And everything points that way. He leaves Satan to his "dark designs" so that he might "Heap on himself damnation" (1.214). Indeed, the whole historical episode, from the angelic fall of one, Satan, who wants to rival God in power to the human fall of one, Eve, who wants to be like a god in experience, to its end in the re-opening of Paradise on earth and the first opening of Heaven to mankind, is an entertainment. It pleases the Godhead who watches it as a drama, just as it is an acute delight to the humans who read it as an epic. Yet while Aristotle allows that epics contain the *plots* for tragedies (*Poetics* 1459), Milton actually switches to the *tone* of tragedy within his epic: "I must now change/ Those notes to tragic" (9.5); thus a serene epic delight is, for us humans at least, converted into that notorious tragic pleasure whose well-known dubiousness lies in our enjoyment of the representation of excruciated bodies and souls. Is it so for God?

To rise from the aesthetic to the ethical: The poem abounds in conversions of good to bad and bad to good, in missed intentions and antithetical transformations. We must by our labor, says the Arch-Fiend, "Out of our evil seek to bring forth good . . . And out of good still to find means to evil" (1.163). Goethe's Mephistopheles is harmless in comparison: "I am a part of that power which ever wills evil and ever achieves good" (*Faust* I 1336). On the brink of Paradise, it is no longer transformation Satan intends but identification: "Evil be thou my good" (4.110); here the distinction between good and evil is not, as in Hell, perverted but simply obliterated. The angels, on the other hand, sing in unison: "his evil/ Thou usest, and from thence creat'st more good" (7.615), and God repeats it, his meaning just the opposite of Satan's. How is the human reader not to be absorbed into and confounded by all this relativistic confusion? And all this starts with the late fathering of a crown prince.

For there is no question that this is the cause of the revolt: being set aside, twice, once by the newly born Son, once by the newly made image, man. Over and over Satan expresses his sense of wrong, of merit unrecognized; in Hell he may sit "by merit raised/To that bad eminence" (2.5; note, as usual: first a term of praise, immediately undercut by censure). In heaven God excuses the Son's elevation: "By merit more than birthright son of God" (3.309). Lucifer, however—at Book 5, line 666, which is the number of the Beast, the Antichrist, in Revelation (13:18)—thinks "himself impaired." "Deep malice thence conceiving and disdain," he whispers conspiracy to his "companion dear," because he feels released from loyalty by the new laws God has imposed: "New laws from him who reigns, new minds may raise." Then next morning at his palace, he, "Affecting an equality with God," takes his royal seat to make that magnificent speech about the equal right to freedom. Injured merit, *ex post facto* laws, novel intervention, demeaning subjection, these are the griefs. The last is the most grievous: God has, "O indignity!/Subjected to his [man's] service angel wings" (9.154). Later the indignity is compounded by the replacement of his own contingent with newly created man. All this discontent is as foreseeable by us as it was foreseen by God: on earth a CEO would be asked to resign, and a monarch would have a revolution on his hands.

8) INFECTED PARADISE

Earthly Paradise is similarly questionable. How are we to go on with Milton's picture of terrestrial perfection? Do those who will one day fall never stumble, those who will soon need to be clothed—not just for shame but warmth (10.211)— never get nasty colds before the world is skewed? What happens if paradisiacal lushness gets out of control as Eve worries it will, when the leisurely gardeners can't keep up and growth goes rank? (10.205) Is Eve pregnant, and if not, why not, since passion is from the first practiced in Paradise (8.511)? Do they know death, with which they have been threatened, more distinctly than as something not-good, in some other way than as a blind, mystifying doom? More broadly, do they know some bad before they know evil, some harm before sin? Is Paradise already infected, as the serpent whose head is "well stored with subtle wiles" (9.184) seems to signify, who, though "not nocent yet," is physically "the fit vessel, fittest imp of fraud" (9.89), made in effect to perfectly incarnate Satan?

Kierkegaard, in his very pertinent meditation on Paradise, says that innocence is ignorance, it is the spirit yet asleep, dreaming. But the dream is infected with a presentiment of freedom, a "possibility of possibility," which makes the spirit anxious and, once awake, unresistant to sin (*The Concept of Anxiety* 1.¶6).

Eve conceives sin in her dreaming imagination, through Satan's insinuation; it is a realization of the philosophical Dane's potentiality for potency. Adam dreams soberly, merely of what is then actually happening and meant to be real: God—in what "shape divine," one wonders—guides him, gliding, through Paradise; shows him "the tree whose operation brings/Knowledge of good and ill" which God has set as the pledge of Adam's obedience by the Tree of Life, and warns: "The day thou eat'st thereof, my sole command/Transgressed, inevitably thou shalt die" (8.323); Adam demands a companion; falls into another sleep, really a half-conscious, waking anesthesia, while a "sinister," that is, a left rib is removed by God and shaped into Eve (8.460).

Eve dreams wildly, raptly, anxiously of what is to come, and her "organ of fancy" is receptive to evil. We already know that she, who falls in love with her own image, is image-prone, and now she is the first and prime instance for a long philosophical and theological tradition that sees in the human imagination the effective snare of evil: desire made visible and vivid.

One third of the inhabitants of Heaven were open to the suggestion of evil; in Paradise, it appears, one half of the rational beings is so—the imaginative half.

Adam delivers to Eve a well-meaning little lecture on our cognitive constitution. He inventories first judging reason, then "mimic fancy," and last the five senses. On the basis of these faculties, he trots out a soothing naturalistic explanation of the "wild work" the imaginative fancy produces in dreams from fragments of sensation, when judgment has retired into her private cell.

How wrong he is, the complacent man! He goes on to discourse comfortingly of evil: "Evil into the mind of god or man / May come and go, so unapproved, and leave / No spot or blame behind" (5.117). How would he know, not knowing evil—yet? But, I think, Eve does indeed now know, ahead of him—and how wrong the simpleton is. Thus Paradise is infected *before* the lapse. But it is not by the devil's temptation, it is by God's.

For what does the whole arboreal set-up betoken? Near the Tree of Knowledge is the Tree of Life. We learn that more such grow in Heaven, that after the fatal fall, man has to be moved from the proximity of the one in Paradise, for it can cure mortality (11.94). Why is one of these there at all? Surely the answer is ominous: Fallen humans who ate of it would be fallen immortals like the fallen angels (or those miserable immortals, Gulliver's struldbruggs), beyond salvation, incapable of participating in the redemptive history about to begin. Was the primal pair's ejection from Paradise an act of mercy—and if so because this irremediable catastrophe had crossed Heaven's mind? What a complexity of divine design!

But that's a side issue; it's the Tree of Knowledge that is at the problematic center of the Garden. Here is the question:

Is the fruit itself deleterious, some sort of spiritual poison, or is it a mere inert incitement to disobedience? Is the real evil ingestion or transgression? Is its intoxicating effect, which makes Eve so "jocund and boon," a "virtue" proceeding from the fruit itself and the tree's "operation" or from the sinner's mind? Moreover, when they have both eaten and love turns into lust, passion into concupiscence, nakedness into nudeness, candor into exposure, modesty into shame, harmony into hate, work into labor, what has changed? What is "the mortal sin/Original" (9.1003)? Of passion and of carnality there was plenty before: "Here passion first I felt,/Commotion strange" says Adam at the first sight of Eve (8.530). Or: "half her swelling breast/Naked met his under the flowing gold/Of her loose tresses," says Milton (4.495).

Is that very turn from love to lust the original sin, or is it its consequence? Or is the true primal sin indeed mere disobedience? This last thought is what Adam and Eve cannot entertain: that mere transgression will be punished. (Indeed, so far have we come in the way of Eve that "transgressive" is, for some postmoderns, a term of approval and a sign of sophistication.) They both think that the acquisition of knowledge and godlikeness is the virtue of the forbidden fruit. Adam, to be sure, first fixes on Eve's disobedience itself: "how hast thou yielded to transgress/The strict forbiddance" (9.902). But soon, he deprecates the danger that God, "Creator wise,/Though threatening, will in earnest so destroy/Us his prime creatures" (9.938), encouraged to think so by his previous experience with God's leniency. So he accepts the profit: a "Higher degree of life." Eve, a more subtle reasoner, goes even further: "What fear I then, rather what know to fear/Under this ignorance of good and evil,/Of God or death, of law or penalty?" (9.773). In other words, because she is ignorant of the terms she need not fear anything before partaking, since she doesn't even know what's to be feared; "Here grows the cure for all," she concludes, the cure, that is, for cluelessness.

The trouble seems to be, once more, the unintelligibility of the tree's operation (8.323, 9.796): Is it God's command that threatens or the tree's powers that are dangerous? Is it the fruit that imparts knowledge of good and evil or the fact of human transgression? Is that knowledge an experience or an understanding? Once again, the question is whether their novel unbowered daytime sex with its postcoital recriminations, whether love turned into lust, is the sin or its consequence? And over, and over, is God not only expecting but wishing the outcome?

This last question is perhaps answerable from Milton's perspective. He speaks in the *Areopagitica* of "the doom which Adam fell into of knowing good and evil—that is to say, of knowing good *by evil*" (my italics). So knowing evil takes precedence, and, accordingly, he, Milton, "cannot praise a fugitive and cloistered virtue unexercised and unbreathed [unexhausted], that never sallies out and seeks her adversary . . . Assuredly we bring not innocence into the world, we bring impurity much rather . . . That virtue therefore which . . . knows not the utmost that vice promises to her followers, and rejects it, is but a blank virtue." To me this signifies that the eating not only caused the world's obliquity but prepared the pair (and their progeny) to live in it, that is, to keep learning by experience and experimentation, as it had begun. But if that is so, then there is too fine a contrivance in it all not to be an intended or at least a wished-for consequence, a divine intention.

And altogether God's gift of free will, this is the occasion to observe, is a curiously strained thing. One of our students, Christopher Stuart, discussed in his junior essay, which I have before me, an apparently scandalously inconsistent line, spoken by Raphael to Adam. After telling him once more that his will was by nature ordained free, "not overruled by fate inextricable or strict necessity," the angel says, speaking of all created beings: "Our voluntary service he requires" (5.529).

How, the student asks, as we must do, do "voluntary" and
"require"—even "require" in the weaker sense of "ask"—
go together, when it is God who asks? Doesn't full freedom
extend beyond the liberty to choose between the allowed and
the forbidden to the determination of choices itself? Isn't the
deepest, innermost freedom the freedom to set one's own lawful limits? Isn't that what autonomy means? No wonder then
that Satan harps on his own kind of freedom even more than
on equality. He has fully felt that Heaven's gift of free will has
negating strings, limitations, attached.

These perplexities, however, the sequence to and significance of the will to disobedience and its punishment, the eating of the fruit and its effect, the skewing of the world and
the resulting diversity, all seem—at least seem to me—to converge in one archetype: the turning of love into lust.

When Adam shyly asks Raphael whether the angels have
intimate congress he gets a forthright answer delivered with
a "Celestial rosy red" smile. The angels "obstacle find none /
Of membrane" (8.625); their intercourse is "Easier than air
with air, if Spirits embrace, / Total they mix, union of pure
with pure / Desiring" (8.626). In Hell too there is passion:
Envious Satan sees the man and the woman "Imparadised in
one another's arms," and bemoans that in Hell there is only
"fierce desire, / Among our other torments not the least, / Still
unfulfilled with pain of longing" (4.506). In prelapsarian Paradise there is passionate desire and sexual congress, "preceded by love's embraces," "happy nuptial league."

Adam and Eve's love-making after the lapse when "in lust
they burn" inflamed with "carnal desire" is now carnal *knowledge*. Adam harps on Eve's sapience: "Eve, now I see thou art
exact of taste, / And elegant, of sapience no small part, / Since
to each meaning savor we apply" (9.1012). Now "that the false
fruit / Far other operation first" displays (note the fricatives),
we may ask: What is that operation which turns innocence
to lasciviousness and makes them, "as the force of that falla-

cious fruit" evaporates, wake up from "grosser sleep/Bred of unkindly fumes with conscious dreams/Encumbered." What has happened that when they rose, they "As from unrest, and each the other viewing,/Soon found their eyes how opened, and their minds how darkened" (9.1046)? The first instance of that darkening is that demeaning of Eve's intelligence, of her "sapience" (as in *homo sapiens*), into "savor," a cognate, meaning both the sense of taste and its relish for piquancy.

What the fruit has done is to make them sophisticated in sexual taste, *self*-conscious in their bodies, self-seeking in view of the other's otherness: This is schism all over, the renunciation of trusting obedience in favor of self-determination, self-will, and selfhood in desire and the advent of solipsistic separatism in body: They see each other as other, their bodies as obstacles to entire interpenetration, and they concentrate on parts that are therefore now become private, shameful and in want of hiding (9.1090). They have, to use Milton's word for the music of Hell, become "partial": particular in taste and partisan for themselves.

Now first Adam turns, in a bad moment, from an easy assumption of superiority to misogyny. He wishes that God had stopped his creating after the "Spirits masculine" of Heaven and before making "this novelty on earth" (10.890), a female; of course he doesn't know that angels are transsexual at pleasure (1.423); oddly enough, Hell proper, Sin excepted, really does seem exclusively masculine.

So there are these degrees, from love to lust: the total merging of angelic congress, the selfless closeness of the paradisiacal union, then the choosy separation of fallen sex—and a last grade, the unassuageable desire of loveless, lonely Hell, that seems to know no female but Sin.

Thus the eating and the fruit's operation are one: separation. The transgression and its punishment are one: schism. Their obliquity and the skewing of their world are one: sophistication—that is complex and varied knowledge in a world of polarities. At least, so it seems to me. What I wonder about is if it doesn't all start with Adam's little prelapsarian lapses: Does it begin when he asks God for a companion? When he fails to take Eve's Satan-inspired dream seriously? When he gives Eve—as God gave him—the freedom to disobey, although he has been warned? Were there Adamic falls before Eve's great Fall? Yes, though he doesn't have it in him to sin greatly.

But then arises a much more momentous question: Is the *original* sin that starts our way of being, Eve's Eating of the Fruit, a bad thing? This consideration is the crux of this piece. But first one more Miltonian intricacy.

9) ORIGINAL SIRING

There is no female birth-giving in this poem (excepting, if you like, Sin's, whose monster-children keep creeping back into her womb, 2.795). The birth of human children takes place out of Paradise. In Adam's last hours in Paradise Michael shows him the prospect of human history in ever more fore-shortened overview, up to the Second Coming (Books 11–12), while Eve, not only the "mother of mankind" by ordinary generation but also the bearer of the "Seed" by which the "greater deliverance" is to come (12.600), is sent to sleep and given a separate view, once again, in a dream—a remarkable locution, by the way, this recurrent reference to her remote progeny, Jesus, as "the Woman's Seed" (for example, 12.542, 601), for he is indeed begotten without male insemination.

So whatever is her condition when Paradise is lost, whether the first offspring is engendered on that racking last night in sin or before that, yet in innocence, or afterwards in their new world, there are no women's births before the fall: As he is henceforth to labor in the sweat of his brow in the fields, so she is to labor in unparadisiacal pain in childbirth (10.193).

But there are plenty of male sirings, firsts of their kind and strange, in Heaven, Hell, and Paradise. God *begets* a son

(5.603), having *made* the angels—geneses of which the human imagination cannot conceive. One angel—Satan—doubts his creation; he thinks he might be spontaneously generated, self-created, though he doesn't know how (6.853). As Zeus gives birth to Athena, so Satan gives birth to Sin from his head. She is his brain child, born from the seat of reason, in him a source of perversion. Soon he has congress with her, his daughter and wife, who bears Death, who in turn rapes his mother (2.747). Adam is formed from dust in God's image—who is however not an imageable original, being in his nature invisible. Eve is, not unlike Sin, born from her wombless progenitor's body, not from his head but from his sinister side (8.465, 10.885), as a body part; hence she is at once a part and, somehow, also a lesser image of his entirety and of God at a remove. She is—strictly speaking—at once Adam's offspring and his consort; like Oedipus's fratricidal sons (Eteocles, Polynices), one, though not both, of her children (Cain, Abel) will kill the other, earth's first murder (11.445; Aeschylus, *Seven Against Thebes*; Genesis 4:8).

Are these origins, these firsts of begetting, creating, imaging, producing, even intended to be closely inquired into? Are they just the hapless by-products of making theological mysteries into poetic pictures in which the *super*natural cannot help but appear as *un*natural? Or are they meant to be dangling perplexities, intended subtexts of questionableness, reflections on the consequences of entertaining nightly a Muse that tells of geneses beyond Nature?

10) EVE'S HAPPY FAULT AND SALUTARY FALL

Back to the great perplexity—the way the poem puts itself in question: The angelic crew falls into a hell that will at the end of time be sealed for eternity. The mortal pair wanders into a world that is "all before them," a world spaciously various in places, and eventfully progressive in time. Is man's fall and the sin that at once was and induced that fall a bad thing altogether?

The answer No is considered by Adam himself, when the Archangel Michael shows him the future and the Final Judgment. Then Christ will reward "his faithful and receive them into bliss,/Whether in Heaven or Earth, for then the Earth/ Shall all be Paradise, far happier place/Than this of Eden, and far happier days" (12.462).

To this astounding prophecy, astounding because it announces that mankind's posthistorical condition will exceed its prelapsarian state in happiness, Adam responds, with one last of those "good out of evil" turns: "O Goodness infinite, Goodness immense,/That all this good of evil shall produce,/ And evil turn to good . . . Full of doubt I stand,/Whether I should repent me now of sin/By me done or occasioned, or rejoice/Much more that much more good thereof shall spring" (12.469). A cunning inference such as issues from a stolid mind fussed by a novel idea!

This paradox of paradoxes, that one man's great Lapse, that his deliberate disobedience should send mankind on the way to the greatest bliss, so that repentance itself seems redundant, has a theological name: the *felix culpa*, "the fruitful, the fortunate fault." (*Felix*, related to "fecund," means, literally and significantly, "fruitful.") The long history of the thought and the phrase is traced in an article by Arthur O. Lovejoy, "Milton and the Paradox of the Fortunate Fall" (*Journal of English Literary History* 4.3, September 1937); it is referenced in Scott Elledge's marvelous edition of *Paradise Lost*. The precise phrase *felix culpa* seems to come from the "Exultet" of the Roman Liturgy, which also speaks of the "certainly necessary fault of Adam," giving a clear answer to the question of divine intention. The thought, however, goes back to the Church Fathers. Ambrose, Augustine's bishop, spoke of the *fructiosor culpa quam innocentia*, "the more fruit-bearing fault than innocence," and Augustine himself says straight out that God "wisely and exquisitely contrived" sinning so that the human creature, in doing what it itself wishes, also fulfills God's will—a generalization of the genetic original sin. Milton is said probably to have known this patristic tradition. It seems to me that his notion, to which I referred above, that the experience of vice is the necessary antecedent to fully operative virtue, is along the same lines.

Now here is something remarkable: In all of Lovejoy's quotations, including the little apple ditty copied above (Sec. 4), it is Adam's fault, Adam's apple. Milton himself begins *Paradise Regained*: "I who erewhile the happy Garden sung,/By one man's disobedience lost, now sing/Recover'd Paradise to all mankind."

But it's not one *man*'s disobedience. Though he is the apple taker, she is the apple giver, hers is the literal original sin—if priority now, under the *felix culpa* doctrine, bestows a certain credit. Hers is the first fault, for better or worse. Satan seduces her first, she Adam; his is a very secondary apostasy. Satan sins aboriginally as Hell's native; Eve sins by seduction, as Paradise's malcontent; Adam sins derivatively, as Eve's husband (10.2): "She gave me of the tree, and I did eat" (10.143). In fact for God this sinning at second hand is an extenuating circumstance for humans.

Indeed, Eve tries to accept full responsibility and all the punishment (10.934). Adam reproves her, God seems to agree: "Was she thy God . . . that to her/Thou didst resign thy manhood . . . ?" (10.145), but she is undeterred (12.619). And so is Milton, it seems, implicitly and explicitly: implicitly, in making *her* book, the book of her absconding from domestic Adam, the high point of the drama of the epic, with its modulation to tragedy, according to its own invocation (9.6); explicitly, when Michael, explaining why man is now in looks more Satan's image than God's likeness, terms the disfigurement "inductive mainly to the sin of Eve" (11.519).

So which is text, which subtext here? Eve is the original sinner, and her sin is fruitful; she is, in fact, the Mother of the
Seed. She is, moreover, much more disposed to disobedience
than he, so why isn't the Fall *her* drama? Isn't it indeed so in
this poem where the events are vividly enough seen to blanch
out an old tradition in Adam's favor—so to speak?

A disclaimer, lest these observations be imputed to me for
feminism. I'm not much for Eve. Her badness is bad: Her
adventurousness is feckless, her careless disobedience imma-
ture, her rebelliousness shallow, her susceptibility to flattery
foolish, her avidity for stimulation reckless, her appetite for
Godhead clueless, her lies to her husband ugly, and her argumentation too smart by half. It is not Eve I admire but Milton,
for his second sight in knowing how qualities connect, and
then, now, and always make up into a human type (of either
sex) which I think of as characteristically modern—vivid and
endangered and *very* familiar to a teacher.

Besides, it isn't even quite clear what she did for us. Under
the *felix culpa* doctrine Satan is an unwitting *agent provo-
cateur* for Heaven, but the Almighty in fact contradicts this
in a speech from the Throne: Let man, he says, "boast/His
knowledge of good lost, and evil got,/Happier, had it suf-
ficed him to have known/Good by itself, and evil not at all"
(11.86). This contrary doctrine jibes with a promise we have
heard earlier: Raphael, having transubstantiated a meal of
paradisical fruit, explains to Adam how this nourishment
"by gradual scale sublimed" can raise man's embodied soul
through degrees to full reason—"and reason is her being."
For the soul is the same in kind as the angels' though less in
degree, since man's reason is mostly discursive, the angels'
intuitive. So then, "time may come when men/With angels
may participate," and find that "from these corporal nutri-
ments perhaps/Your bodies may at last turn all to spirit . . .

and winged ascent/Ethereal, as we, or may at choice/Here or in heav'nly paradises dwell;/If ye be found obedient" (5.483). An amazing promise, though hedged: The route to Heaven is through diet and obedience! Thus the Fall achieved just a long detour to the same end: a choice of goods, either of a dwelling in Heaven or an etherealized life in Paradise. And Adam actually knew this before the Fall, as did Eve who had been listening in! We do not hear much more about it. Perhaps, we may surmise, the prospect of man etherealizing directly from Paradise to Heaven is embarrassing to the Father, for it leaves the Son without his salvific mission.

So has Eve, in causing history, launched mankind on its necessary road or on a futile byway? And did Milton intend to throw such doubt on the need for the Son's self-sacrifice, his entering history as a man?

11) WISDOM WITHOUT THEIR LEAVE

"The world was all before them, where to choose/Their place of rest, and Providence their guide:/They hand in hand with wand'ring steps and slow/Through Eden took their solitary way." With this solemn iambic saunter, sad but comforted, bereaved but hopeful, the divine epic ends and human history begins. Yet in the very last of these ten thousand five hundred and fifty-six lines there lurks still one more provocation to stimulate the intellectual sensibility like a dissonance in music: "solitary." Does it mean "alone"?—but they have a Guide. Does it mean "single"?—but they are a Pair. Does it mean "at one"?—but her "meek submission" (12.597) is dearly bought and perhaps not so very reliable or heritable (moreover it's not a meaning in the OED). Or could the word perhaps intimate that this same sole humanity is about to end, that in the poem Cain was perhaps conceived on that first and last night—or afternoon—the first given to the "contagious

fire" of "foul concupiscence" (9. 1035, 1078) and the last spent
on their "native soil" (11.269), in their Paradise—Cain, the
first man born out of Eden, at once the first murderer and the
first city-builder (Genesis 4:17).

If Milton's last lines intimate something obliquely but precisely, something beyond the general hopefulness of the opening of a wide land and a new era, namely the incipient first
natural birth on earth—a thing of course unprovable—then
not two only but a future three are leaving Paradise, and
history with its highway and so crucial byways has already
begun. For the Cainitic generation is a false yet necessary
start. While it is the main cause of the Flood in which it is
itself destroyed, it is also the indirect cause of God's covenant by which the earth is forever safely populated. For from
Noah's sons "was the whole Earth overspread" (Genesis 9:19).
Moreover, among their progeny was one Javan, the ancestor of the Ionian Athenians, our, at least my, Ancients. But
this is a fantasy in the spirit of the two new books (11–12) of
prospective history that Milton added to the second edition
of *Paradise Lost* (1674). My point is that here might be one
last exemplification of that derivation of good from bad that
informs the poem and makes one think.

And so we did, all of us, think about this question in the
seminars that incited these reflections, but perhaps the daughters of Eve in particular. One form of the recurrent question
was: What would we have done, what do we do and shall we
do, and, above all, let our young do, in the face of Satanic
temptation? By "Satanic temptation" I mean the Serpent's
promise of a riskless transgression, of acute experience, of our
equalization with the gods to attain "Wisdom without their
leave" (9.725). Do we owe it to ourselves to yield to temptation? The angels in Heaven evidently do know good from evil
without being affected by evil; they heard the report of man's
lapse "with pity" that "violated not their bliss" (9.25). The
angels in Hell know evil and violated bliss in its grand pathos

and deep misery. Recall what Milton preaches in the *Areo-pagitica*: We humans must know vice practically and previously to virtue to be capable of vital goodness.

If we permit, even encourage, the transgression of the intellect—Satan's temptation of Christ, resisted by him, to liberal learning and philosophy—and also of the senses—the "artificial paradises" of Baudelaire, drug-taking and similar stimulation, to put it plainly—are we realizing a plan inherent in our postlapsarian mortality? Unlike our Original Parents, we are born as babies and grow laboriously into our adult state, so we have no cause to be as cluelessly innocent as they were of the substance of sin and the meaning of the punishment. Moreover, on earth it is required not only that prohibitions be clearly promulgated but that they define an intelligible crime, and that the punishments be understandably formulated before we are answerable—the reverse of the order under which Eve commits the "mortal sin / Original" (9.1003). She knows what death, the punishment, is only after she has sinned: It is, as she puts it with brutal brevity, "I extinct" (9.829); before that it was "whatever thing death be," as Satan expresses for her the sum of her knowledge (9.695). And, I think, she never quite learns wherein the badness of the forbidden fruit lies beyond the fact that it is forbidden.

But perhaps that really is the meaning of the *felix culpa*, the fruitful fault: It is at once a first exercise of autonomy, expressed as mere disobedience, and a first lesson in its fruits, felt as potent wisdom. The poet of *Paradise Lost* seems to intimate that we might do well to opt for transforming experience over psychic intactness, to choose adventurous badness with Eve rather than stodgy goodness with the angels. But perhaps he would not want it said so baldly.

25

The Unexpurgated Robinson Crusoe

His God Daily

I imagine that many people think they have read Daniel Defoe's adventure novel, *Robinson Crusoe*, when they were children. They imagine that they know Robinson and "his man Friday." They don't really, for they read a heavily expurgated version. But it is the most curious clean-up imaginable. Usually it is sex that is censored. There is no sex whatsoever in the original book, though no one will think that the fact that Robinson was, for twenty-five of his twenty-eight years there, alone on his island and, as he says (102),[1] removed from the lusts of the flesh, is a sufficient explanation of the total absence of any thoughts of that sort. No, what children's versions subvert is Robinson Crusoe's frequent and prolonged struggles with sin and faith. What child not cowed by impositions of adult piety would put up with the dark nights of the soul, or, in contemporary terms, the existential crises, that Robinson Crusoe records? He tells us at the very beginning

---

First published in *American Dialectic* I 1, 2011; no subsequent issues.

that his last name, Crusoe, was a corruption of his German father's name *Kreutznaer* or Cross-ner, "Man of the Cross."

What children love in the book (and in its many knockoffs) is surely the other side of the intensely introspective Crusoe; it is Robinson's inventiveness, his survival skills, his endless practical ingenuity. This Robinson is the original do-it-yourselfer, the adult prolongation of the two-year-old's clamor: "I do it, I do it myself, I can do it." That's just what Robinson says: ". . . I found at last that I wanted nothing but I could have made it, especially if I had had tools . . ." (55). To him the world is a place of projects.

No wonder then that *Robinson Crusoe*, published in 1719, is not only among the first members of the novelistic genre, but also the oldest and longest lasting of all literary children's books. It was propagated as such by Jean-Jacques Rousseau in his huge educational romance *Émile* of 1762. Rousseau gives it to his pupil Émile as his first book, to teach him practical ingeniousness and self-sufficiency. I cannot help saying here, going off-topic, that *Émile* is as perverse pedagogically as can be; Jean-Jacques's charge is to be practically self-sufficient, but he is trained to be psychically dependent on his mentor for life.

Be that as it may, the project-magic worked on me. My European parents, obedient to Rousseauean tradition, gave me the children's book as the first I was to read to myself by myself. I was allowed to take it to the couch on which I, a wide-awake seven-year-old, endured an enforced afternoon nap-time. I employed myself by digging a hole in the plaster of the outside wall against which the napping-couch stood, and "if I had had tools" better than my poking index finger, I would in time have made my escape into the garden. As it was, I got as far out as my top joint when my parents gave up the nap-regime.

Besides the project-mindedness, what makes the book so inviting to children is the scarily exhilarating absence of supervision. Robinson is all by himself, as what child does not—for a limited time—long to be. One of the well-known bowdlerizations, *The Swiss Family Robinson*, spoils it all by bringing along the whole cozy clan.[2]

Robinson, however, is indeed all alone. I think his first name, Robinson, is also deliberately chosen; it signifies Everyman, an English Everyman. (One of the mutineers in the ship that finally takes Robinson off his island is named Robinson as if to say, that's what ordinary people are called, 210.) Now our Robinson is, on the face of it, as unlike every one else, as uncommon as can be, both in his strange fate and his extraordinary capabilities. Yet, I want to claim, Defoe presents him as an archetype, as a model of a new man, soon to be a predominant breed—a *modern* man. So it is his modernity that I will try to delineate—our modernity.

Robinson Crusoe is regarded not only as among the earliest of novels, but also as the first "realistic" novel. I would amend that: It is not really very realistic. In fact, it is perhaps quite implausible that anyone should live on a tropical island alone for a quarter of a century without succumbing to bugs or insanity. It is rather relentlessly factual, or full of facts, where by a fact I mean a processed piece of nature, an item of the world that has been entered into an accounting-scheme. This view of things comes over as thick, vivid detail, pleasing and edifying at once. Few who have a taste for things made and their handiness can resist Robinson's telling of his tale.

So *Robinson Crusoe* is perhaps the first fully realized specimen of this new and most copious literary genre, the novel. Everything about "the novel" betokens newness, not least the name itself. It refers to the *new*spaper-like reportage, a newsy fiction, full of novelties, not least of which are the themes. Think, in contrast, of ancient tragedy, which was almost always a version of a well-known story that had the standing of myth and its renowned hero. Robinson, the new protagonist, is given by his author, who was himself a journalist, the talent of a reporter and the occupation of a literal journal-ist, a journal-keeper (while the ink lasts). He, an obscure and private nonhero, is the on-site, first-person account-giver, the personal observer of factual situations and his subjective take on them. In fact, Defoe veils the fictional character of this fac-tual novel in every which way. Between him and Robinson he inserts a nameless editor who assures us that this story of a "private man's adventures in the world" is worth making pub-lic and that it is as I have described it, a "history of fact" (3). These tricks seem to work; I for one am persuaded that Rob-inson is candid, honest, and sincere, all words we have handy when we keep to the *intention* of the teller not to deceive so as to avoid reference to his *ability* to tell the truth. At any rate, this is an "I" book; one I is the teller, but to whom? I think first to himself. For that purpose he keeps that jour-nal, just as memory notes to himself. But this island account is later inserted into the middle of a, to some extent dupli-cating, narrative, evidently written after his rescue, and *this* story is written for the public. Crusoe becomes increasingly aware of the fact that he and his fate are interesting. I imag-ine that on the island, as ink gives out and his experiences deepen, he talks more and more to himself, silently, for his voice grows disused. But once off the island he tells his tale—we never hear how and when—to the paper or the editor or perhaps, who knows, to a now literate Friday. Crusoe knows himself to be interesting because he has two very disparate stories, and that is because he has two very different, but also complementary natures.

One side of him is, as I have intimated, absorbed in the world of facts, in putting nature to use, in fabricating con-trivances, in quickly passing beyond mere survival to civi-lized comfort, beyond necessities to conveniences. Thus he begins by building himself a secure fort and ends by design-ing a country house.

Is he really alone? Over the years he surrounds himself with possessions, the most remarkable of which to me is a folding umbrella (107) that he takes to England when he is finally rescued (218). He eventually presides over a dinner table with his "little family": an old dog, some cats, and his parrot, "the only person permitted to talk to me," as he says (118). This speaking bird too comes back to England. He frankly lords it over his domain; if he dines alone, it is "like a King" (118), though his reign is also his captivity (109).

Moreover, he remains enmeshed in the real chronology of the Christian world; he enters the melancholy "scene of silent life" on September 30, 1659 (52). As I said, he soon keeps a dated journal, and for much of his stay he hopes for earthly "redemption," that is, rescue from the island at a date expected though uncertain; in fact it will occur on December 19, 1686 (219). He preserves the mores of society with respect to going naked; he says that he "could not abide the thought of it, tho' I was all alone" (107), which is to say he continues to feel shame as does a social man.[3] Or, perhaps, more gravely, he is, even in his solitary semiparadise, an Adam after the Fall, who has grown forever ashamed of his nakedness.[4] He carries the inhibitions of his second nature right into nature, where clothes can serve neither sex nor status.

In fact, his being by himself gives scope to his most characteristic mode, which is his amateurishness. In the old days he never learned a trade; indeed, though the editor's title denominates him "Mariner," he prefers to take passage on his sea voyages so as not to have to work as a sailor (15). But he is curious, observant, and a quick study, for whom to have seen something done is to be able to do it: There is lodged in his memory some recollection of how to go about practically any process. Moreover, he has a great gift for figuring things out. As he puts it:

[A]s reason is the substance and original of the mathematicks, so by stating and squaring everything by reason, and by making

the most rational judgment of things, every man may be in time
master of every mechanic art (55).

This defines rationalized practicality; it shows Robinson as
the opposite of the medieval journeyman who ends up master
of one so-called "mystery;" he is every man in one and nothing is a mystery to him. All his productions are very imperfect,
as he honestly records, but they do just fine. He develops out
of his experience his own "best practices" for every need—the
aboriginal empirical rationalist.

Alone on the island he is altogether a man of projects, a
"projector" and "adventurer," as entrepreneurs used to be
called. He is a busy man, a man of business, labors, and accounts. Even on a deserted island he early on sets up a dou-
ble-entry balance sheet of his evils and goods "like a debtor
and creditor" (54). He establishes timetables and schedules
(58) and runs his island like a going concern of one. The ultimate individualist, he does everything by himself and for
himself and sets a world humming, a world that has only a
single human inhabitant, who is, however, all over it. He is indeed the true individualist, alone singled out by his God and
yet representing a paradoxical archetype: the *unique Everyman*. This society of one shows Robinson in a humanly novel
aspect: He gives meaning to the term "private enterprise."[5] He
is a culture of one.

Although he is "by himself," that is, his own companion,
indeed an internal chatterbox, there is in fact one other, pseu-
dohuman, voice on the island, a voice that does not disrupt
the anxious safety of his solitariness. It is the precursor of our
virtual connectedness. It belongs to that parrot of his, and
an uncanny episode involving his Poll brings us to Robinson's
other aspect, his Crusoe-nature.

After having put out to sea on a boat he has made and
very nearly being drowned in an eddy, Crusoe falls into an

exhausted sleep in his country house. He is frightened out of his oblivion by a human voice moaning at him: "Robin Crusoe, Robin Crusoe . . . *Poor* Robin Crusoe, Where are you? Where have you been? How come you here?" (113–114). His Poll has found him and is parroting his own questions, an eerie externalization of his existential ruminations, his nonhuman echo.

For Robinson, as I said, always talks to himself and, as time goes by, more and more to God—at first only in ejaculations such as, "Lord ha' mercy upon me," cries that cease when the particular disaster, be it earthquake, or danger of drowning, is past (65–70). Then his inner speech becomes mundane, deplorably so, as he thinks in bad moments. Usually, Robinson, even alone, is a temperate, receptive man with a wry sense of humor and some engaged kindness for the animal life that he observes around him (50). But there are times of deep depression following on sickness or on fright, when his isolation is borne in on him, and he is "wracked by terrible thoughts." His worst imaginations are those of being found by the cannibals, who, he discovers early in the second decade of his stay, visit the island for their horrid feasts (115, 122).

What is only at first a passing, merely occasional, turn to God becomes more significant when Robinson is beset by those bouts of loneliness. Then he takes refuge in a recognition that, as time goes on, becomes the focus of his inner life: a sense of having been singled out, saved time after time, as when, of three ships' companies whose loss he has witnessed, he alone survived (54, 178); he had in fact been shipwrecked once long before he was cast up on his island. Indeed, the chief events of his first eight adult years double, as if by a preparatory Providence, his castaway epoch: besides shipwreck and sole survivorship, there occurred captivity, loneliness, coping by amateur's wits, and the loyal friendship of a young heathen. Crusoe's retrospective sense of being watched over induces a progressive turn to, and incessant preoccupation with, God's Providence, but above all a consciousness of his unworthiness, his sinfulness, of a life so far spent "like a meer brute from principles of Nature, and by the dictates of common sense only, and indeed hardly that" (71).

This Providence appears, at least to this coolly distant reader, as the inner reflection of Crusoe's hedging about of his physical life with prudent arrangements of safety and comfort. Resourceful human prudence finds in him its counterpart in merciful divine Providence. Crusoe more than merely bears the cross of his marked solitariness; he turns it to his own profit. He finds increasing comfort in these reflections and even comes to wonder "whether thus conversing mutually with my own thoughts, and, as I hope I may say, with even God himself by ejaculations, was not better than the utmost enjoyment of human society in the world" (108).

Of course, the answer is ultimately "no," especially since his outcries go one way, and he is ever beset by loneliness. So when a ship is wrecked off his coast, he cries out,

> by every possible energy of words . . . O that there had been . . . but one soul sav'd out of this ship . . . that I might have but one companion, one fellow-creature to have spoken to me . . . (148).

And yet, it is simultaneously true that the "I" of Crusoe's tale is almost *too* omnipotent for company. As this individual of individuals makes a secular, physical world of contrivances *around* himself, so he calls up a God of comfort *within* himself. He is the objective and subjective master of his world; for all his expressions of subjection to his God, it is a deity *he* invokes when not occupied with fixing his island. In fact, he is and remains a man of dual motives: he refuses to go naked from shame *and* because he cannot bear the sun's heat (107); he longs both for a companion *and* a servant; he gives up his plan to exterminate the cannibals from "religion *joyn'd*" with prudence (137).

I want briefly to call attention here to a wonderfully revealing forerunner of *Robinson Crusoe*. It is the theological fantasy, *Hayy Ibn Yagzān*, written by the Muslim philosopher Ibn Tufayl in the twelfth century.[6] In this story Hayy is brought to an uninhabited island as a baby, is suckled by a doe, and grows up animal- and self-taught. But his interest in his external comforts and even in the sciences that he discovers diminishes to nothing as he becomes engrossed in evolving out of himself the complete theology of Sufism. That is another story, except to observe that, just like Crusoe, he is essentially self-sufficient in nature and self-constituted in soul, with this telling difference: the opposition of "objective" and "subjective," so crucially important to our modern life, is absent; it has no application to Hayy's divinity. But this very opposition is surely of the greatest significance for Robinson Crusoe, the Christian Everyman, the prototype modern, who needs both to tame (89) and modify the world and to record and rectify his soul.

Here is a revealing mistake Crusoe makes about himself. He is but shortly back home in England, both safe and rich. He accomplishes the transition, which we might imagine to be fraught with the anxiety of dislocation, in a few dry sentences: after having been thirty-five years absent he finds himself a perfect stranger, but his investments are secure. The first five pages of his return give a detailed account of his finances (219–225). His true home, we see, is the world of "business," first in the literal sense of the industry, the incessant busyness of his outward island life, and second in the usual sense of financial affairs.

After giving the bottom line of the wealth that has accrued in his absence, he likens himself to Job. He had found Bibles in a chest saved from the wreck of his ship—Bibles together with tobacco, heavenly and earthly comfort together—and had been reading assiduously. It is his sole book, though he has it in multiple copies meant for the conversion of the hea-

then slaves his ship, a slaver, was—irony of the ironies—
meant to take; he has it, as it were, in stock. It is *the* Book,
sufficient to the island. So he should know Job, his avatar.

The point of comparison is "that the latter end of *Job* was
better than the beginning" (224), certainly wealth-wise. But
beyond that, Crusoe and Job are each other's antithesis in
the two points that really count. Above all, and as a consequence of Job's unhumble recalcitrance, God is compelled to
speak to him audibly, to answer him out of that whirlwind.[7]
It is not merciful, but upbraiding speech: "Who is this . . ."
and "Where wert thou" he begins; it is the very question of
Crusoe's *parrot*. But, the point God makes and Job takes is:
I exist, I am potent, I am imponderably beyond you. That
is Job's real reward, God's objective being-there, and that
is what Crusoe's subjective God never evinces: independent
existence.

Here is the second great difference. Why does Job win out,
totally and completely? Because he will never capitulate to his
false friends' demands that he should admit to sin. Job knows
himself to be without great sin, and he, in turn, demands not
God's mercy but his justice, or if not justice, some objective
response, which he gets, as Crusoe never does.

The reason is that Crusoe is deeply and, I think, satisfy-
ingly absorbed in his rather vague sinfulness, which fascinates
his subjectivity, his self-devoted inner-life. It is not the sins
of the flesh that haunt him. As I have mentioned, the book
has simply no sex. Sometime after he returns to England, we
are told that he married "not either to my disadvantage," and
that just before the age of sixty-two (one may figure out) he
fathered three children and that his wife died to leave him
to pursue his former sinful ways (240)—all this in one short
paragraph. What these ways are I will say in a moment, but
comment here that he lives out what we call guilt-feelings.
Guilt-feelings are when you bemoan a fault you have no real
intention of amending.

Let me interject here a note on the remarkable sexual purity, so to speak, of this book. It was followed three years later, in 1722, by a thick novel called *Moll Flanders*, an exuberant account of the life of a lady who, and I quote portions of the subtitle:

Was Twelve Year a *Whore*, five times a *Wife* (whereof once to her own Brother), Twelve Year a Thief . . . at last grew *Rich*, liv'd *Honest*, and died a *Penitent*.[8]

So one could hardly claim that Defoe was ignorant of, or adverse to, that side of life. It is absent from *Robinson Crusoe* by the necessity of the hero's nature. I will venture an explanation: Between invention and introspection he is simply too busy for desire; he labors too hard. It is a recognizable feature of modern man: purity by preoccupation. What, then, is the sin, which he calls, in capitals, his ORIGINAL SIN? (154). It is dissatisfaction with the station wherein God and Nature have placed him, with that middling life which his father earnestly wishes for him (6). What is in Satan prideful rebellion against the Heavenly Father comes out in Crusoe as restless escape from his earthly father. Crusoe repents, but never for good; he even attributes his fault to Providence, which has not blessed him with "confin'd desires." Consider as well that "original" sin is also enabling sin, deeply ensconced. It is the first transgression that smoothes the path for subsequent ones, and as his gratitude to God's Providence abates as soon as a danger or difficulty is surmounted (64), so no sooner has a phase of life been concluded than Crusoe must crucify himself on new projects. In general, the more ardently he reads Scripture and thanks God for his safe solitude and repents of his "wicked, cursed, abominable" previous life, the more the reader is at a loss for its actual sins: he has never killed a man until he clubs a cannibal in clear self-defense. The more he blames himself for the hypocrisy of this thankfulness (90–91), the more this religiosity seems bound to mood-swings, humanly profound, but theologically shallow, deeply and familiarly egocentric. Sin seems a sort of luxury of solitude, the fascinated preoccupation of an expansive selfhood.

Then in the fifteenth year of his solitude, there is that sighting of the footprint, the presage of a new kind of life, and before long all the inner conversation turns into outer proselytizing.

This singular footprint is, again, eerie. In its singularity, it is a very literal refutation of his comforting conviction "that no human shape had ever *set foot* upon that place" (my italics, 79). Robinson first fears that it might be the Devil's imprint, who has only one human foot, and whom he takes quite seriously. (For him, remarkably, the Devil exists, externally visible as evil incarnate,[9] while God is wholly interior.) Then he argues himself out of that (123). In any case, his solitary paradise has been invaded, and soon he discovers to his horror that cannibals come here often from the continental side of the island to feast on their prisoners. There ensue some years of debilitating anxiety, which even reduces his inventive gusto, except that he focuses it on the destruction of these monsters.

Now appear some remarkable pages (133–37) in which he tells how he came to decide against murdering them all, remarkable because they delineate that most encompassing of modern virtues, tolerance. Briefly told, he decides that if God's Providence let them be, why shouldn't he, and that they really were not murderers in the strict sense; moreover, that they are not his business and that he would probably destroy himself in attempting to eradicate them. In short, "neither in principle or in policy" (137) should he concern himself, as long as he could keep safe. Here is our familiar mode of tolerance underwritten by the gospel of "none of my business." One might even call him an early cultural relativist.[10] He says of the cannibals that they were no more to be condemned as murderers than were those many Christians who kill captives of war (136).

Thus, as is so often the case with tolerance, it works only until things become up close and personal, as they do one day. The cannibals reappear. A young captive gets away from them and runs toward Robinson, who, though at first very frightened, finds himself "plainly called by Providence to save this poor creature" (160). To be sure, as I said, he hopes for a servant, but also for a companion. The rescue succeeds after a good deal of slaughter of the savages, and suddenly a quarter century of life alone is over: he has a human friend. And now the issues begin; although I've read very little of the secondary literature on the novel, I know that some contemporary critics would deny that to Robinson this primitive is either fully human—a *man*, or that he remains sexually unexploited— a *friend*. I want to show that both aspersions cast on Robinson's relations to Friday, slavery and sex, are false.

After feeding "his savage" (161), he describes him: a comely handsome fellow of twenty-six (about his own age when he came to the island), of great vivacity and with sparkling eyes, whose features are more European than Negroid, to be sure, but certainly not white. After delineating him, that is, taking full note of him, he Adamically (like the first man, who was charged with naming every living thing) calls him "Friday," because Friday is the day of his rescue according to Robinson's calendar, which we know by now is several days off, seventy-six days to be exact—he has after all, been on his island for over nine thousand days. But who can help thinking of Good Friday, the euphemistically named day of Crucifixion, Crusoe's day? Frankly, I do not understand what Defoe is signaling, but there is no getting around the central place of the Crucifixion in Christianity and the crucial place of Christianity for Crusoe. The day of the Cross is the day of his deliverance.

First "he falls to work for my man Friday," making him clothes (164)—not much like a slave-master. Then he teaches Friday, who is even quicker of comprehension than is Crusoe himself (and certainly better-looking in his young nakedness than his aging goat-skin-clad savior—is he attired as a scapegoat?), his own name for Friday's use, namely, "Master" (163).

Does this denominate Friday as his slave? Friday makes gestures of submission, Crusoe answers with marks of care. "Master" is used here more as an indication of earned rank. I know a pertinent case from the Naval Academy, my school's neighbor across the street in Annapolis. There I met a Colonel Hagee (I think it was) of the Marines, later on Commandant of the Marine Corps. He won my admiration for his disciplined openness and his junior officers' respect for his exemplary leadership. One of these told me that when they were all in the canteen exchanging nicknames, a cheeky youngster asked Hagee what *his* was. Without batting an eyelid he shot back "Colonel." These free young Americans found this naming by title totally in order; it was earned.

Robinson generally refers to Friday as "my man Friday" (171, for example) much as a latter-day Englishman would refer to his batman or butler. Crusoe's intention is not, I think, to patronize him (as it might sound to the currently correct ear); on the contrary, it is an explicit acknowledgment of Friday's *manhood*. For Robinson admires him, not only for his physical deftness, but for his intellectual quickness. Once it was: *his God daily*; now it is: *his man Friday*.

Robinson has cured Friday of his cannibalism by cooking him a savory goat stew, but Crusoe also wants to convert him to Christianity by administering true theology. There is a wonderful occasion when Friday simply floors Crusoe on these very theological grounds, no less. Friday has learned English very fast, and as soon as possible, Crusoe begins to convert him to his Protestant, anticlerical ways (171), using such doctrinal arguments as he knows. He has an easy time with the omnipotence of the Christian God and a devilishly hard one with the potency of the Devil. Friday wants to know *"if God much strong, much might as the devil, why God no kill the Devil, so make him no more do wicked?"* Crusoe is stumped, as aren't we all. "I therefore diverted the present discourse between me and my man;" he pretends to have some urgent business for gaining time to think of an answer, which turns out to be, by his own admission, more extensive than illuminating (173).

The three years they live together before their rescue is a time of perfect and complete happiness for Robinson *"if any such thing as compleat happiness can be form'd in a sublunary state"* (174). Are they lovers? Of course not. Part of the evidence is that "The savage was now a good Christian, a much better than I." Some literary critics, who never have enough to do, surmise that Achilles and Patroclus were lovers even though each of them goes to bed every night with his own captive woman and both have affectionate relations with them.[11] I mention this case, nearly three millennia earlier, to show that devoted friendships are always subject to this suspicion. But this is a book without sex, and so it remains to the end. Friday and Robinson are friends, the most loving friends, the latter says (168, 179), for Friday has a spontaneously loving nature (187). It is in evidence not only with Crusoe but when they rescue Friday's father (187), and there is no hint at all of anything more or, perhaps one should say, less. To be sure, Crusoe has a severe bout of jealousy when he suspects Friday of wanting to go home (217), but it is more the feeling of an adoptive father afraid of losing a son to his natural father, and he gets over it. This relation is part of what one might call, be it with smirk or smile, the purity of the book, which has turned it into *the* great children's book.

What makes this life possible for Friday, we are not asked to ponder, but what makes it plausible for Crusoe is implied in his nature. His maximum expenditure of inventive energy in the external world of objects together with his intense concentration on his inner being as a subject to himself, one subjected to his God, is what, as I have suggested, leaves no room for sex. Two centuries later this conversion of energy will get a name: "sublimation." I am not saying that I am convinced by Freud's hydraulic theory of the psyche, that there is really a steady flow of libidinous energy that can be converted, diverted, or dammed.[12] But I think that Defoe might have had some such notion of Crusoe's intimate life, or might have found it congenial if told of it. Crusoe is, after all, though an imagined being, yet endowed by his human creator with a character shaped by his maker's sense of the possible.

Defoe gives us plenty of evidence for this non-articulate aspect of Crusoe's inner life. As in the early years he suffers from bouts of deep existential depression during which he wrestles with sin and faith, later on he discovers a seer's sensibility in himself. Recall that his father had a turn for prophecy, foretelling Robinson's forlornness (7). He is given to "intuitions," as we would say, but which he calls "secret hints, or pressings of my mind," and to the "converse of spirits" (139, 197), which he learns to ignore at his peril. He is also visited by accurately prophetic dreams, the strangest of which is so precise a precursor-scenario of the cannibals' arrival and his rescue of Friday that when the event occurs, a year and half later, he actually plans his actions by making deliberate emendations to his dream (157, 162). I interpret these intuitions and dreams as the psychic work of his human prudence, the image of God's Foresight, His Providence.

Before long, after another bout with visiting cannibals, the island is well and variously peopled, by Crusoe's account: Friday, a Protestant; his father, a pagan; one rescued Spaniard, a Papist. But, as he says in the most suggestive and funny comment of the book:

> However, I allow'd liberty of conscience throughout my dominions. But this is by the way (190).

This is double-minded Robinson Crusoe, our forebear, at his most characteristic. Who could fail to recognize the simultaneous assertion of caretaking dominion and liberal intention, of management and tolerance?

To conclude, Robinson and Friday get off the island by helping the English captain of a mutinous crew recapture his ship; Robinson has got him to promise—hilariously—to carry him to England "passage-free" (201). The rest is somewhat forcedly farcical, a superfluous romp through Europe, the aftermath-doings of a man whose great tale has ended, but whose restlessness has in no wise abated; he cannot stop adventuring and he cannot stop telling. The book ends with a promise of more surprising incidents and further accounts.

Only one weighty thing happens back in Europe, and that is that account-giving I've mentioned, tale-telling at its most businesslike: Robinson Crusoe reports to us in exact numbers all the income accrued to him in his absence and all the goods dispatched to him from the plantation in Brazil he had co-owned. Indeed, his receipt of both letters of account and actual goods nearly make him die on the spot with joy (223–26, also 38).

No sooner has he made very generous disposition of this now considerable wealth than he is off again from Lisbon overland to London, then back to Lisbon, more accounting and disposing, and finally, in 1694 at sixty-two, back to his island to oversee affairs there. For it is now his "collony," as he calls it, and he has long thought of himself as its Proprietor (80, 240). Friday is always, daily, with him, but of God we hear less.

What has it all come to? No sooner off the island than he reverts to restlessness, his original sin. He is the most adaptable man, not much amenable to the "culture shock" Americans are expected by anthropologists to undergo when transiting to new environments (I know this from experience[13]), and like many flexible characters he is, at bottom, fixedly himself, incorrigible. Furthermore, as he expends himself in worldly affairs, his subjective life wanes, diffused into unanchored darting about. His subjectivity, always governed by tides of mood, becomes shallow.

So was his faith ever deep? Well, it has certain characteristics quite familiar to us. They may not betoken spiritual depth, but they are surely abidingly serviceable. This religiosity that I will briefly lay out is the coping stone of an arch of character whose one upright is inventive business, a conquering ingenuity, rebelliously rivaling within the world God's creative power beyond the world, while the other is a gnawing, conscientious inwardness, ever seeking and ever losing the repose of settled obedience.

Here are five features of Crusoe's religiosity, as they appear to me; they seem to make him the modern of moderns, in essence our paradigmatic contemporary.

First, there is that intense subjectivity I have been dwelling on, whose God is made in the individual's image, to be called up or relegated to oblivion as need and mood wax and wane. Crusoe is altogether a yes-and-no man, a man of two minds: utility and morality, cheer and melancholy, but above all, energetic enterprise and enervating sinfulness. As for that last, our expression for the correlative kind of conscience is, as I have noted, "guilt feelings," a talkative insistence on sins committed, accompanied by an unarticulated intention to remain as we were. Robinson's one expressively confessed sin is his unappeasable hunger for adventure, and, indeed, no sooner is he off the island than he's back at it, his outer drivenness being fully the match for his inner anxiety.

Second, there is that embarrassment of evil, the sense that its reality, for Crusoe personified in the Devil, cannot be squared with God's omnipotence, and that in the face of this dilemma it is safest to find some sudden business to do and later to engage in long, not entirely intelligible, bible-based discourses—as Crusoe indeed does.[14]

Third, there is Robinson's candor, or as we say, his sincerity. He is terminally honest and open in the account of his life. Whether he ever gets beyond sincerity to truth, beyond the frankness of his telling to searching into the way things are, is another question. He is, perhaps, too self-involved, too much an "I," to use his intellect for the discovery of truth rather than the allaying of anxiety—a familiarly modern subversion of thought.

Fourth, there is his inveterate busyness and his unselfconsciously proud success in business. He thinks of his enterprise, I have intimated, as the secular image of God's Providence; he is, in our favorite word "creative," arrogating God's prerogative. That busyness and business might be our life's center and "time off" a burden, or, at best, a relaxation of our proper efforts, is an eminently modern feeling. For previous ages, the human center lay in time free for noble pursuits.[15]

Fifth, there is Crusoe's most recognizably contemporary feature, one very agreeable to most of us, I would think, but also insidiously deleterious to his faith: his tolerance, what might fairly be called his cultural relativism. Cannibalism is a great issue in modern anthropology: Is our repulsion at the eating of our own species to be tempered when it is done in another culture's established setting, especially when scholars can find survival values for it (such as supplying protein otherwise lacking), motivations of which the culture in question may not even be conscious? Must what we judge abhorrent in ourselves be condoned in others? Crusoe had faced this problem and come to the tolerant conclusion that what God has allowed he must leave alone (135–37). But it returns to him again and again, especially after Friday's arrival, and in a last long meditation it leads close to doubting the chief attribute of his God, his Providence. Crusoe understands it as God's all-knowing, wisely-planning governance of *this* world. This is God as "the governour of nations" (74, 137), very much like the God of our Declaration of Independence. (Similarly, Crusoe dubs himself "commander and captain, generalissimo and governour" of his island, 193, 210.) Crusoe says that from his misgivings,

> ... I sometimes was led too far to invade the sovereignty of *Providence*, and as it were arraign the justice of so arbitrary a disposition of things, that should hide that light from some, and reveal it to others, and yet expect a like duty from both: But I shut it up and check'd my thoughts with this conclusion . . . (165–166).

The thought-blocking conclusion is that the savages must have sinned according to their own lights.[16] Anyhow, who are we to question the way God made us? What could be more contemporary than a taste for universal tolerance coming into conflict with the demands of a specific morality, and a resolution of this quandary by, as Crusoe says, shutting it up, that is, leaving it unresolved and turning to practical business?

So I might go so far as to say that this earliest of novels presents a first and near-complete portrait of a modern man, a new man in the new world inhabiting a new genre, a man engaged in hot pursuit of happiness rather than in quiet preparation for contentment, opting for a life of frights and highs (indeed whose fears are its euphorias), but, for all his edgy living, also the close record-keeper of concrete assets. In short, adventurer and accountant in the world, and within himself a man of developed subjectivity and opportunistic faith.

So it would not be surprising if many of us would find him in ourselves (is not America the most incessantly inventive and the most variously religious country on earth?), except that we have sustained one lamentable loss: Defoe's vividly concrete, succinctly expressive, simply delicious eighteenth-century prose.

P.S. Here is a neat fact, lately noticed. Robinson's chronology confirms his accountant's soul: Born in 1632 (5), washed up on his island in 1659 (52), taken off in 1686 (219), he had, at age 54, perfectly balanced his book of life.

NOTES

1. All page references to *Robinson Crusoe* are from the Penguin Classics edition: Daniel Defoe, *Robinson Crusoe* (New York: Penguin Putnam Inc., 2001).

2. The castaway children of William Golding's *Lord of the Flies*, on the other hand, are too long without grown-ups. The lord of their island is in fact the decaying corpse of an aviator—and the consequences are terrible.

3. Crusoe's aversion to going naked even in the solitude of his island contrasts revealingly with the way of the sailor who seems to have been his model, Alexander Selkirk. He spent four and a half years marooned on a small island in the Pacific. (Crusoe's is in the Atlantic, off Brazil's Orinoco River.) Selkirk reverted to the state of nature when his clothes wore out and went about in the nude.

4. Genesis 3:10.

5. The ship's company that mutinied in 1789 against the tyrannical officer (and terrific navigator) Captain Bligh sailed to the safety of self-exile under the leadership of the chief mutineer, Lieutenant Fletcher Christian. They took possession of the then deserted Pitcairn's Island. The third of Charles Nordhoff and James Norman Halls's *Bounty Trilogy*, *Pitcairn's Island* (1934), tells of their attempt to found a civil society, which only succeeded after the first, the mutineer generation, had practically exterminated itself. This story, which, to be sure, took place long after Robinson's landing on his island, makes plausible the hard-won precarious contentment of his life. He fears the hostility of fellow humans more than his own solitude—with good reason (129–30).

6. Ibn Tufayl's tale, translated by Simon Oakley, was published in England in 1710, nine years before *Robinson Crusoe*. Defoe might have known it. See Ibn Tufayl's *Hayy Ibn Yagzān: A Philosophical Tale*, translated by Lenn Evan Goodman (Chicago: University of Chicago Press, 2009).

7. *Book of Job*, 38:2 and 4.

8. Whoring Moll might appear to be blameless Crusoe's antithesis, but they have two deep characteristics in common. Both of them have an abiding interest in the bottom line and the business that produces

it, and both lead lives of stupefying variety, which are the expression of their constitutional restlessness. Both declare themselves the agents of their own miseries without much intention of amendment. Both are lucky, though as they are in effect asking for their own disasters, so they also maneuver their own fortunes. Both are outlaws, Moll achieving the status of gentlewoman by prostitution and thievery, Crusoe becoming the proprietor of a colony by being simply beyond the law, a law unto himself. Both are great record-keepers, though Moll mostly of her successful vices, Robinson of his effective virtues (which is why *Robinson Crusoe* could be transmogrified into a children's book, but never *Moll Flanders*). Both are interesting, though perhaps Moll, an accomplished crook and a beauty, is more scintillating. In a summer seminar on the two books, I asked the members which of the two characters they would rather have tea with. The vote was altogether for Moll, but the women made it clear that they'd invite her to a tea shop rather than to their home. "Moll," incidentally, is both the term for a prostitute and the nickname for Mary (!).

9. As it was for Defoe himself, which is clear from his *Political History of the Devil* (1726).

10. Though not the first; that was surely Herodotus: see *Persian Wars* III 38.

11. *Iliad* IX, 663.

12. Sigmund Freud, *General Introduction to Psychoanalysis* (1915–17), translated by Joan Riviere (Chicago: William Benton, 1988), Lecture 22; see also *Civilization and Its Discontents* (1929), translated by Joan Riviere (Chicago: William Benton, 1988), Section II.

13. My college was a Peace Corp training center and the expectation of culture shock was an obligatory anxiety. As far as I could tell from letters, the shock was more on the hosts' side.

14. The rigorously intellectual (Catholic) treatment of evil as absence of good, as nonbeing, is not available to Protestant Crusoe. Crusoe had professed himself a Papist from convenience in his pre-island time in Brazil, but he develops scruples about settling there and adopting that religion after his island stay, since it might not be "the best religion to die with." But that, it turns out, was not his main concern, which was: Who would take charge of his English fortune? (226).

Crusoe may have been made, in part, in the image of his creator, Defoe, who was a Dissenter, an inveterate protester, and so the protestant of Protestants: one who adheres to the spiritual life of the individual over the institutional rites of a church and its clergy.

15. Robinson might be said to be *diverting* himself with restless busyness. "Diversion" is Pascal's term for the dispersion of the soul in worldly activity. See *Pensées*, translated by A.J. Krailsheimer (New York: Penguin Books, 1987), pp. 66–71, Sec. VIII "Diversion." The ancients regarded leisure as the true center of life and its best activity as learning; hence our word for school, which derives from *schole*, Greek for "leisure." A parallel case is the Latin word for business, which is negative, *negotium*, from *nec otium*, "non-leisure." See Josef Pieper, *Leisure: The Basis of Culture* (New York: Mentor Book, 1952), p. 21. The modern mode turns this view of leisure around: Work is what we do; free time is carved out of the busy day—at least for movers and shakers.

16. Crusoe may be on the right track here for some cases. It appears from stories connected with the exile of the Aztec's god of civilization, Quetzalcoatl, the "Plumed Serpent," that he was driven out of Tula for refusing to accept the practice of human sacrifice and, presumably, the eating of the victim. See Miguel León-Portilla, *Native Mesoamerican Spirituality* (Mahwah, NJ: Paulist Press, 1980), pp. 169–170. (See Essay 7, "The Empires of the Sun.")

26

Persuasion

"The Most Beautiful of Her Works"[1]

A student at Cambridge, having announced to a Fellow of his college that he found Jane Austen's *Persuasion* "rather dull," received the reply that it was "the most beautiful of her works."[2]

My opinion is that it is the most wonderful of her six finished works, which makes it the finest novel in my reading of English fiction. Wonderful or beautiful—this question arises: Why should England's greatest novel seem dull to anybody, be it only a Cantabrigian smart-aleck?

The answer is: She so intended it. In her letter to Cassandra Austen of Friday, 29 January (1813) she breaks into pretty lame verse:

> I do not write for such dull elves
> As have not a great deal of ingenuity themselves.
>
> (A parody of Scott's *Marmion*, a poem Jane Austen hadn't learned to like [Letter to Cassandra Austen, June 20, 1808], and I've never read.)

On the tried and true rule that it's the dull who find stuff dull (the un-dull find it funny), we may conclude that Jane Austen expects two kinds of readers: those that don't get it and those that do. Well, that double possibility holds of every conceivable communication, be it intentional or accidental, so it doesn't mean much. There is also a seriously discriminatory distinction denominated "esotericism," "deep-insider-ism" (from Greek *esoterikos*), meaning one who is thought worthy of admission to certain insider's knowledge (*gnosis*) as distinct from the clueless ones, "more-on-the-outside," that is, the exoterics.

Of course I'm not silly enough to attribute something as fanciful as esotericism to Jane Austen, who wrote of herself, meaning, I think, to forfend such attributions, that she knows nothing of science and philosophy, and goes on:

> I think I may boast myself to be, with all possible vanity, the most unlearned and uninformed female who ever dared to be an authoress (Letter to J. S. Clarke, Dec. 11, 1815).

Yet, I think, she is up to something much more clever than willful exclusion: The "dull elves" who will find *Persuasion* dull and the possessors of "great ingenuity" are one and the same: the engaged and trusting readers whose first intention is to savor her lines.

What I'm about to name—imagining that readers of this little labor of encomiastic love will know all about it without terminology—is an Austenian sentence type I call a scorpion—or a whiplash-sentence. In the dull-elf mode it goes by prosaically, read over, stingless. But something tells you to call a halt, to re-read. And behold, it is a scorpion of a sentence! It runs by and turns out to have a back-bending tail with a stinger to inject a drop of poison as it goes by. Or alternately: You read and suddenly stop, jerked, taken aback by the delicious wickedness of it.

I think all six mature and finished novels have such sentences, but in *Persuasion* they come thicker and more effervescently, and this is one of the wonders of this book, the other wonders being its depth of feeling—and third, the coalescence of both. But before I come to that, I'll give some examples of scorpion-sentences, concluding with the funniest one I recall ever reading in English. (I'm not sure such a sentence could even survive in a German paragraph or so my sense of my native tongue tells me—except for the unlikely case of that Prussian Austenian, Fontane; see Essay 29, "Effi Briest.") Here, then, is one example of a scorpion-sentence, of the least poisonous type, but typical. The spendthrift Sir Walter Elliot is letting his estate as an economizing measure:

> [He was] prepared with condescending bows for all the afflicted tenantry and cottagers who might have had a hint to show themselves: . . . (Vol. I, Ch. 5).

Here's another, a little more acerbic; she says of young Captain Benwick:

> He was evidently a young man of considerable taste in reading, though principally in poetry; . . . (Vol. I, Ch. 12).

Of Mrs. Smith, who is, in misfortune, perversely cheerful by disposition, upon becoming well off:

> She might have been absolutely rich and perfectly healthy, and yet be happy (Vol. II, Ch. 12).

But this one, the last sentence of the book, exceeds them all. Read it as a culminating bit of pompous prose or as a concluding hilarity. I render it here with Jane Austen's capitalizations, which modern texts take down—and the fun with it. Wentworth and Anne are reunited at last:

> She gloried in being a Sailor's wife, but must pay the tax of quick alarm, for belonging to that Profession which is—if possible— more distinguished in it's [her spelling] Domestic Virtues, than in it's National Importance.[3]

This grandiloquent proposition asserts that the British navy's defense of the island and domination of the seas is outshone by its family values. I imagine that many a post-1818 ward-room rang with laughter. Read it once and find it prosily dull, read it twice and implode or explode—whatever your own mode of mirth may be.

That is one of the wonders of it, and its enabling genius is verbal virtuosity. The other depends on a different sort of linguistic magic, which I am simply unable to pin down: the delineation of deep feeling—I avoid the term "expression," which intimates that it is her own emotion that Jane Austen is "pushing out"—in few words and those devoid of melo-drama, sentimentality, or romanticism. Let me say up front that I think of this suffused glow as the overt reflection of her reticent devoutness.

I'll begin with three aspects of *Persuasion* that tether the book to sober reality. First is the age of the heroine, Anne Elliot, who, born in 1787, is twenty-seven at the date, 1814, at which the book begins. She is thus the oldest of all the Aus-tenian heroines, who are, insofar as I can figure it out, usually about the age that Anne was when Wentworth first came near Kellynch, namely nineteen. This heroine is fully mature and acquainted with grief. *Persuasion* is the account of a reprise: a second youth, a second chance at happiness.

The second aspect is evident in the previous paragraph. *Persuasion* is tethered to real time with dates actually given. Jane Austen was a stickler for correctness, be it about facts of nature or of society, but the other five novels live in their own time as they do in their own geography. There are rare refer-ences to datable events and only occasional excursions to real places. This novel is overtly fixed in public chronology and one real venue.

A third aspect I mention with much less assurance of its permissible pertinence. This book was written when she was increasingly ill and possibly—I can't imagine otherwise—beset by premonitions of death. I do think that this impend-ing ultimate reality cooperated in the shaping of *Persuasion*, albeit in a direction opposite of the one to be expected: It imbued the book with that positive intensity, both of fun and feeling, found in none of the others—of which more below. In any case, the meticulous, deliberate realism of the book is the ground for its unsentimental sentiment. Put another way: It is a story of love which is *not* a romance. Here is Jane Austen on romance-writing: An admirer advised her to write a historical romance that would be pleasing to his noble patron. She replied, with straight-faced courtesy, acknowledging that such a romance would be more popular than "such pictures of domestic life in country villages as I deal with":

> But I could no more write a romance than an epic poem. I could not sit seriously down to write a serious romance under any other motive than to save my life; and if it were indispensable for me to keep it up and never relax into laughing at myself or at other people, I am sure I would be hung before I had finished the first chapter (Letter to J. S. Clarke, Nov. 1815).

A romance is a love story beset by dramatic dangers and difficulties and carried on by a couple of highly romantic disposition. Charlotte Brontë wrote the romance of romances in this sense, *Jane Eyre*, and she defended fiercely her indefeasible propensity for melodrama, incidentally expressing her distaste for Jane Austen's venues and mores (Austen-Leigh, *Memoir*, Ch. VII). It is possible to love both books, but not equally.

Anyhow, Jane Austen clearly thought that her eschewing of romance and romanticism was due to an inability. If so, what a happy defect that made her capable of the tone that strums through *Persuasion*! To be sure, Anne Elliot herself uses the very vocabulary that Jane Austen abjures: she says, or rather Jane Austen says for her, falling into that famous "indirect discourse" she employs as the eloquent Author speaking for her creatures:

> She had been forced into prudence in her youth, she learned romance as she grew older—the natural sequence of an unnatural beginning (Vol. I, Ch. 4).

In light of the "handsome fortune" Wentworth now has from prize money, and with his apparently unmarried state to attest to his constancy, Anne reflects that she is now on the side of "early warm attachment against that over-anxious caution which seems to insult exertion and distrust Providence" (*ibid*). There isn't much melodrama in that depiction—of which her author seems to approve.

Another pertinent self-description appears in *Pride and Prejudice*, where Charlotte Lucas agrees to marry that most insufferable, delightfully absurd of all her awkward young clergyman, Mr. Collins, and explains to her friend Elizabeth Bennet, who is helplessly appalled:

> I am not romantic you know. I never was. I ask only a comfortable home. . . . (Vol. I, Ch. 22).

She means nothing much more than that she does not require being in love with her future husband—in this case anyhow an impossibility.

I should perhaps try to delineate the feeling that informs *Persuasion* and keeps the book taut. It is, to begin with, unexpressed, held in. That is not only because Anne has no suitable friend to confide in; even if she had, I doubt that Jane Austen would have had her speak of her suffering. It is incessant, ever-present as a background tremolo, sometimes out front as particular pain. (Note that the author's interest is, much like that of some divinities, at odds with that of her creatures. These would, no doubt, wish to be happy, but suffer they must, to give the work its interest.)

It is a pain at once in accord with a clear conscience and a great mistake (Vol. II, Ch. 11). However, these secondary sentiments have not done their usual work of overlaying the primary remembrance of love and its actual object; Anne is fully, and, to use a contrived and anachronistic term, self-accessibly, in love with Frederick. And this attachment has its basis in the real man, who is in every way worthy of her feeling for him. When reality underwrites feeling, then something of worldly significance is actually happening, be it in a book or in life.

This is a moment to dwell on a fact about *Persuasion* that is a complement to its anchorage in reality: It is a very bookish book, one in which literature is a major force, until, in a new eleventh chapter (see Note 2), Anne herself calls a halt. She has got into that all-determining friendly argument with one of those captains who are Wentworth's naval family, and of which Wentworth himself is the captive eavesdropper. The argument concerns the question which sex is more constant in love. Captain Harville claims to be able to cull from his reading fifty quotations on the side of manly constancy. Anne says:

> . . . if you please, no reference to examples in books. Men have had every advantage of us in telling their own story (Vol. II, Ch. 11).

The two friends come to an affectionate settlement, while Wentworth has been composing the letter that will close the fault between them. Anne, whose escape from sadness, whose comfort in despair, came from books, has renounced them, but her bridge to happiness is nonetheless to be a writing, Wentworth's letter.

Why a letter? Here gratitude to Edward Austen-Leigh is in order, for preserving the discarded chapter of the resolution, which throws light on this letter. In the old Chapter 10 this re-attachment of the early bond is brought about letterless, with a lack of drama that simply sucks the air out of the event. A device reveals to Wentworth Anne's non-attachment to her unsavory cousin, the heir of Kellynch. Thereupon he sits down and draws nearer to her:

> Her countenance did not discourage. It was a silent but very powerful dialogue; on his supplication, on hers acceptance.

The new letter preserves the reticence of the scene. Anne reads it, if not in private, at least not in view of her restored lover. Yet it allows him to be the passionate instigator of the reconciliation, its commander. After all, to Jane Austen he is always and to the end "Captain Wentworth," while she is simply "Anne."

But back to the quality of feeling—more intensely, if sadly, alive for being contained entirely within her heart, with a tinge of heroism for being converted into general usefulness. Here is what proves the sound realism of her feeling. It turns within the moment to "an overpowering happiness," a "revolution" made in "one instant," an agitation that could not be tranquilized in a social setting. In other words, Anne's feeling has not gone independently subjective; it has remained anchored to an objective condition and responsive to reality.

There follow her initial times alone and in society with him. If understated, parsimonious diction did wonders with suffering, the chapters of happiness, two out of twenty-four, have a particular glow. The author herself half-seriously criticized *Pride and Prejudice* for being "rather too light and bright, and sparkling: it wants shade; . . ." (Letter to Cassandra, Thursday, February 4, 1813). But that light sparkle is not the luminousness of *Persuasion*. She has managed to make perfect happiness plausible in words:

> All the surprise and suspense, and every other painful part of the morning dissipated by this conversation [with Wentworth], she re-entered the house so happy as to be obliged to find an alloy in some momentary apprehension of its being impossible to last. An interval of meditation, serious and grateful, was the best corrective of such high-wrought felicity . . .

"Meditation" is, I think, the author's reticent reference to prayer. The passage continues:

> The evening came, . . . It was but a card-party, . . . With the Musgroves, there was the happy chat of perfect ease; with Cap-

tain Harville, the kind-hearted intercourse of brother and sister; with Lady Russell, attempts at conversation, which delicious consciousness cut short; with Admiral and Mrs. Croft every thing of cordiality and fervent interest, which the same consciousness sought to conceal;—and with Captain Wentworth, some moments of communication continually occurring, and always the hope of more, and always the knowledge of his being there (Vol. II, Ch. 12).

It seems to me impossible to overemphasize Anne's deliberate, protective inhibitedness on this evening of bliss, a withholding in which Frederick is like-minded enough to collude. Explicitness, be it of expression or behavior, be it sophisticated or crude, is, after all, a diagnostic indicator of failing passion and deficient imagination.

Humanly grave matters demand physical containment. Thus music to which the body is thrown about declares its own psychic impotence. For example: I was listening with a group of friends to the fourth fugue (C♯ minor) of Bach's *Well-Tempered Clavier* (first series), which plays a thematic role in Daniel Mason's novel, *The Piano Tuner*, a book we'd just read together. All sat peacefully still. These musical formalisms are so feeling-fraught as to make one ashamed even of tears rising to the eyes: This music is not emotional but passionate. Jane Austen's reticence is enabled by her gift for linguistic transfiguration; she can convey vulgarity with elegance, clumsiness with deftness, iniquity with correctness, but, above all, as here, "highflown felicity" with verbal temperance, exemplified in the last clause with its held-in ardor. A way I put it to myself is that she manages in this work to redeem an ardent romanticism of the heart with a cool classicism of expression. Feel blue, flee to these pages.

Finally, I want to turn back to the time in which *Persuasion* was completed, 1816, the year at whose beginning "the symptoms of decay, deep and incurable" began to show themselves. She must have known that she was fatally ill, yet the effect on her was not that of depression but, as her brother Henry reports in his "Biographical Notice" prefixed to the posthumous publication of *Northanger Abbey* and *Persuasion* together, that of "a truly elastic cheerfulness."

Indeed, early in 1817, she began a new novel, *Sanditon*, of which Henry Austen gave excerpts and an account; to my mind, its humor is almost rambunctious. Something of the sort is evident in the more perfectly finished *Persuasion*; there is, on occasion, broad, even sharp, comedy. Substantial Mrs. Musgrove sits on a sofa so as to divide Anne from Wentworth, giving out "large, fat sighings over the destiny of a son, whom alive nobody had cared for":

> Personal size and mental sorrow have certainly no necessary proportion. A large bulky figure has as good a right to be in deep affliction, as the most graceful set of limbs in the world (Vol. I, Ch. 8).

But, the author adds, "fair or not fair, there are unbecoming conjunctions . . . which ridicule will seize." The fact is that the whole *dramatis personae* of *Persuasion* are, without exception, terminally humorless and artlessly self-same—which exposes them, one and all, heroine included, to Jane Austen's not always stingless ridicule. She wrote to her niece, Fanny Knight, that Anne, the "Heroine . . . is almost too good for me" (Sunday, March 23, 1817). Remember that it is the lack of a sense of humor that makes folks ridicule-prone; witty people are auto-immune to ridiculousness (not to ridicule).

Henry Austen, defending Jane Austen from reviewers who attempted to identify the real-life prototypes of her characters, said something really central:

> She drew from nature; but, whatever may have been surmised to the contrary, never from individuals (*Memoir*, Ch. X).

Consequently, although in a temporally realistic setting, the people of *Persuasion* have the universality of nature rather than the mere factuality of individuals. I think that this location of natural humanity in historical time is what generates the extraordinarily response-soliciting sensibility that is suffused over the book. And that feeling, in cooperation with its finely, even sharply honed wit, makes of the work a world that is laughable and lovable, wickedly comic and warmly affectionate—simply wonderful. Or beautiful, if beauty signifies a plenitude composed of complementarily opposed properties.

NOTES

1. With gratitude to the Piraeus Seminar of June 2017, a group of St. John's College alumni, their relations, and other friends of the College, for their enthusiastic engagement and its consequent insights, here freely adopted. The text used is: Jane Austen, *Persuasion*, edited by James Kinsley, with an Introduction and Notes by Deirdre Shauna Lynch and Appendices by Vivien Jones (Oxford World's Classics, Oxford University Press, 2004).

2. Quoted from Ch. IX of James Edward Austen-Leigh's *Memoir of Jane Austen* (1871). He was her nephew and himself knew her as a boy, as he knew her sister and closest friend Cassandra through her long life, as well as other members of the family.

Cassandra Austen was Jane Austen's chief correspondent. It is known that she destroyed "the greater part" of her younger sister's letters to her in order to keep private matters, such as personal attachments and family difficulties, from becoming public.

Since true lovers of great fiction are long and late in conceiving any desire for biographical background, they will thank her for her discretion (bemoaned by scholars) and try to countermand their own curiosity (prompted by shame). They will also be grateful to Edward Austen-Leigh for his straight-forward, sensible insights.

As an object of literary-critical scholarship, Jane Austen appears to have written her works in accordance with certain novel, even revolutionary, ideological preconceptions; her nephew tacitly consigns such interpretations to the *ex post facto* impositions of concept-mongering. He says of "the very deficiency" with which her novels "have been sometimes charged—namely that they make no attempt to raise the standard of human life, but merely represent it as it was" that:

> They certainly were not written to support any theory or inculcate any particular moral, except indeed the great moral which is to be equally gathered from observation of the course of actual

life—namely the superiority of high over low principles, and of greatness over littleness of mind (Ch. X).

Another example of the illuminations to be gotten from the *Memoir* is this report of a family saying:

> Cassandra had the *merit* of having her temper always under command, but that Jane had the *happiness* of a temper that never required to be commanded (Ch. I).

This observation jibes with the universal opinion of those who knew her: She attended to them and entered into their concerns and, as children, played with them so that they all felt well-loved by her. Moreover she was wittily funny—"conversible," as she would have said.

Similarly, her ironic view of her characters, even of her most admirable heroines, the fun she got out of their foibles, never stood in the way of her affection. On the contrary, she was, I think, grateful to them for being that way, for being reliably ridiculous in a way for which she had eye and ear. If any woman feels a pressing need for a model, she was it: the way to be. She would, however, have been appalled at this role, so it's not a recommendation.

Edward Austen-Leigh also deserves gratitude for publishing the canceled Chapter 10 of Volume II of *Persuasion*. Jane Austen had retired one night "to rest in very low spirits" because her first ending seemed to her "tame and flat." She awoke "to brighter inspirations" and replaced the first Chapter 10 with two new chapters, 10 and 11, and kept the old final Chapter 11, now Chapter 12. She wrote *Finis* on July 18, 1816 (actually a second time, since she had earlier added a paragraph to the final chapter). Three weeks later, in August 1816, she actually finished the novel.

Jane Austen died on July 18, 1817. Her favorite brother, Henry (not a paragon of "regular habits"), saw through the posthumous publication of *Persuasion*, and he gave the book its apt title. He too wrote a much shorter "Biographical Notice" (1817) as a preface to the dual publication of *Persuasion* with *Northanger Abbey* (also named by him). I have given the date of her death to emphasize what he asserts clearly: *Persuasion* was largely written when signs that her illness was terminal had begun to show themselves. I think, for once, biographical circumstance is significant—though in a contrarian way, as I shall try to show.

One more apparent fact: Her friends agreed that she was both devout and orthodox (Church of England) and that this fact outweighed everything—and, as I think, was *therefore* suppressed in her novels.

3. "Pay the tax": evidently an allusion to the British Crown's war taxes.

"Belonging to that Profession": one reading, which spoils the fun completely, is that it is the wife's wifely profession; I think it means her vicarious participation in Wentworth's naval career—though Admiral Croft's seagoing wife was probably the more actually competent sailor.

Annapolis, 2018

27

Clueless Wisdom

Captain Delano

This essay, about Melville's *Benito Cereno*, will be short because its thesis is compact. In 1799, Amasa Delano of Duxbury, Massachusetts, master of the merchantman *The Bachelor's Delight*, a sealer, boards a ship in distress. The ship is in fact a Spanish slaver that has been taken over by the slaves in a cleverly executed revolt. The Spanish captain, Benito Cereno, emaciated and helpless, has also been taken over—one might say, possessed—by his apparent body servant, a physically meager but hyper-intelligent negro, aged thirty, and called Babo. He is complemented by a huge sidekick, Atufal, who goes about in a parody of enchainment.

Everything on the *San Dominick* and every Spaniard sends signals to the American, who *sees everything and takes in nothing*. He has attacks of queasiness; he is "not unbewildered," but steadfastly obtuse in his innocence, "a man of such native simplicity as to be incapable of satire or irony." Thus an old sailor has knotted away at an exceedingly complex Gordian knot, which he tosses to the captain with the low words "Undo it, cut it, quick." He, puzzled, hands it over to an old negro who throws it overboard. Delano, filled with a "qualmish sort of emotion," apostrophizes himself:

". . . who would murder Amasa Delano? His conscience is clean. There is someone above . . . Fie, fie, . . . you are a child indeed."

Later he chides himself for his unease as "sappy Amasa."

My thesis is simply that Amasa Delano, in his indomitable good nature, his hopeless innocence, his blind confidence, achieves the clueless wisdom that averts catastrophe: his own murder and the capture of his ship. His antagonists are intensely self-aware in maintaining their assumed roles; his simplicity and unassumed benevolence defeats the revolted black's cunning and the enslaved Spaniard's collaboration. The episode ends when the *Bachelor's Delight*'s whaler arrives to pick up Captain Delano, Captain Cereno summons the energy to leap into the boat, and Delano's understanding is suddenly illumined. Soon the slaver is retaken and brought in to Lima, Peru, where the affair is officially investigated.

This simple thesis has a larger resonance. The American as perennial "innocent abroad" is an old rubric, begun (as far as I know) by Mark Twain's genially jocular *The Innocents Abroad* (1869) and culminating in Graham Greene's snobbishly sour *The Quiet American* (1955), an early Vietnam novel, in which American good nature is excoriated—the perfectly antithetical counterpart to *Benito Cereno*.

The quiet American, Alden—a New England name—Pyle, is, to the unbiased reader, a perfectly nice young man. Greene insinuates some holy and unholy attributes into his portrait. He is assassinated by an Englishman's agency when he is thirty-two, about the age when Jesus began his ministry. He owns and leads about on a leash a little black dog, a chow, which I think I recognize as akin to the black poodle in the form of which Goethe's Mephistopheles approaches Faust.

> Faust: Do you see the black dog, roaming through the crop and stubble?
>
> Wagner: I've seen him long since.—He didn't seem important to me. (*Faust* I, 1147 ff.)

The opium-smoking Englishman, Thomas—doubting Thomas—Fowler, says that he can sum up Pyle precisely: "A quiet American," as unlikely as "a white elephant." Fowler—his last name too is allusive—denounces Pyle for inciting terrorism, for acting on a dangerously innocent, book-learned theory, for being a rampaging child-man. At the end of the book, Fowler has recovered Phuong, the beautiful Vietnamese woman whom Pyle had won away, and has finally gained his English wife's promise for a divorce so he can now marry the girl. In short, he now has everything, and Pyle is on ice in the morgue. So he offers a flabby last thought for Pyle, who had once saved Fowler's life, as, indeed, he had Phuong's:

. . . how I wished there existed someone to whom I could say that I was sorry.

Meanwhile, he continually reinforces his derogatory view of Pyle's innocence. Here are supporting quotations:

1. God save us always . . . from the innocent and the good. (Pt. I, Ch. I)
2. Innocence is like a dumb leper who has lost his bell, wandering the world, meaning no harm. (Pt. I, Ch. III, 1)
3. I wish sometimes you had a few bad motives; you might understand a little more about human beings. And that applies to your country too, Pyle. (Pt. II, Ch. III, 3)
4. He'll always be innocent, you can't blame the innocent, they are always guiltless. All you can do is control them or eliminate them. Innocence is a kind of insanity. (Pt. III, Ch. II, 2)
5. He comes blundering in, and people . . . have to die for his mistakes. (Pt. IV, Ch. II, 1)

Fowler's conclusion is the opposite of Melville's, that Cereno, his Spaniards, and Delano himself are saved because the American is unsubtle in decoding evil. However, in the *Quiet American* the claim that innocence is dangerous runs into trouble with literary coherence. There is textually certifiable evidence that Alden Pyle of Boston is gutsy, kind, candid, loyal, generous, and modest. Yet Fowler says of him that, when Phuong is mentioned,

> His face lit up like one of those electric toys which respond to a particular sound. (Pt. III, Ch. II, 1)

In other words, to Fowler (the "hunter," the "trapper") he's inhuman. More seriously, is the man he is depicted as being capable, beyond Fowler's purview, of coolly backing the bombing of a civilian venue? Is this a novelistic paste job? For, if it is to be plausible, Pyle must be devilish, more leashed to black Duke, his dog, than the reverse. He must be Babolike, a sophisticated actor in both senses: an initiator of events and a hypocrite upon a stage. That description just does not match Greene's clues: Pyle is innocent and saves lives.

I might add here my personal experience, which leads me to think of Delano's way of being in the world as appearing paradigmatically among New Englanders. I had a university friend, my suite-mate in the graduate women's dorm at Yale (known as "Witches' Hollow"). She, a fellow archaeologist, had, like Captain Delano, acute powers of observation which, be it from a sense of propriety (leave people be) or from principled inertia (don't be a busybody) rarely rose to interpretative expression.

If I am right, and Captain Delano, with his republican sense of equality, his cheerful but well-controlled permissiveness, his "singularly undistrustful good nature"—note that Melville lets double negatives abound in describing Delano—if I'm right in regarding him as the quiet hero, the most significant of the three central characters of this tremendous story, then why is it entitled "Benito Cereno" rather than "Amasa Delano"?

Think of the story as a triptych, a triple-hinged panel, bearing three portraits, Benito Cereno, Amasa Delano, Babo. Who's central? Babo is the first candidate. He inserts himself as the uncircumventable mediator between the two captains. He is, without doubt, their superior in intellect, self-control, and wit—albeit of a Satanic sort. My colleague, John Verdi, discovered a grim example. Where the *San Dominick*'s figurehead would once have been, there is now a canvas wrapping and below it a chalked Spanish sentence: "Follow your leader." It turns out that the canvas hides the blanched skeleton of the passenger-owner of the slaves, Don Alexandro Aranda, who had been killed during the mutiny. Note also that Don Benito is observed by Delano to be

> like someone flayed alive, . . . where may one touch him without causing a shrink?

Here's the discovery: Babo is convicted and decapitated in Lima, and his head is mounted so as to look towards St. Bartholomew's church, where Aranda's bones are interred. St. Bartholomew was flayed alive and is portrayed as skinless, carrying his own skin as drapery. Cereno has in mind his friend and passenger's end. Babo, whom we must hold responsible for Aranda's fate, is making a sardonic comment on the skin-deep difference of black and white. In his deposition before the court in Lima, Cereno in fact recounts that Babo made each Spaniard look at Aranda's skeleton (which had been substituted for the figurehead of Columbus) and asked him "if from its whiteness he could not tell that it was a white's?"*

Though not really connectible to the story, a recent discovery, a first temple dedicated to the "Flayed Lord," whose worshippers were said to wear the flayed skins of human sacrificial victims, was found, to be sure, in Aztec Mexico rather than in Inca Peru—this find is too curious to subvert. Did Babo know of something not again seen until two hundred years later?

Melville's Babo is sometimes compared to Shakespeare's Iago, with whom he has this in common: resolute silence after arrest, but nothing else. Little, controlled Babo is a natural leader of men; loutish, lascivious Iago is a natural nothing. Is Babo a good man who has suffered evil or a bad man making the most of it? Is he righteous or malignant? Melville says nothing explicit. But Babo gets, to use an apt phrase, under, or onto, Cereno's skin, who dies of him, so to speak. For Cereno, though physically saved, is determined to die. To Delano's question, ". . . what has cast such a shadow upon you?" he replies "The negro." We know from the deposition that Cereno knew how Aranda's skeleton had been prepared: ". . . which he, so long as reason is left him, can never divulge."

Not only is Babo personally the most remarkable of the leading characters, he is also the most omnipotent, most minutely in control of his Noah's ark. What's in the way of Melville making him *the* hero, is, I think, that whatever the moral mitigation may be, he is, after all, a mutinied slave and a murderous conniver.

In this imagined triptych, Benito Cereno is the acknowledged central figure, insofar as his name figures in the title. Why does it? He's least of all three a hero: a twenty-nine-year-old, commanding by social position rather than experience, incompetent as regards seamanship, effete in his apparel, degenerate as an aristocrat, labile with respect to mood, and irresolute by temperament. To be sure, if this story were a classical tragedy and a tragic flaw were to be discerned, it would be in him, as the ship's master. But even that wouldn't quite work; he's more pitiful than tragic, I think.

Is Captain Delano, then, the rightful center figure, and if so, why isn't he the titular head of this gallery?

We do, in fact, just once see him placed at the center. When the two captains sit down to their frugal lunch, "like a childless married couple," Delano is taken aback by Babo's positioning himself not behind his—pretended—master but behind Delano, overlooking him so as to face Don Benito frontally. It is of course not, as the American imagines, in order to detect and serve Don Benito's desires, but so as to control him by observation. Usually, however, Babo is between the two captains, their intermediary.

And until the story concludes, Captain Delano's spontaneous as well as effortful misconstruals of all the deliberate and unintended signals sent him are insistently noted.

The fiction does not end with Cereno's physical and psychical collapse in Lima but continues for almost a quarter of the foregoing narration more, with depositions by the two captains before the authorities in Lima.

In 1928 the source of Melville's story (told in 1855)—and, I suppose, the very fact that it had a source—was discovered by Harold H. Scudder. It consists of the real Amasa Delano's *Narrative of Voyages and Travels* (1817), Chapter XVIII, together with official documents (See *A Benito Cereno Handbook*, edited by Seymour L. Gross (1965), p. 71 ff.). To me its interest lies in the modifications, the fictionalizations, Melville effected for his documentary coda. For example, the real Delano seems to have thought, falsely, that the Spaniard's name was "Bonito Sereno," which translates as "pretty" and "calm," and so is not suitable for the story. The real name, Benito Cereno, has been variously interpreted. I think that Melville may have heard in "Cereno," the Spanish word *cera*, "wax," that's something pale, soft, delicate, pliant, or even *cero*, "zero," something useless.

But Melville's main modification was to give the Spaniard, who does not come off well in Delano's *Narratives*, more plausibility and more pathos. Moreover, he picks up and elaborates on Delano's brief comment in four sentences:

> They all looked up to me as a benefactor, and as I was deceived in them, I did them every possible kindness. Had it been oth-

erwise there is no doubt I should have fallen a victim to their power. It was to my great advantage that, on this occasion, the temperament of my mind was unusually pleasant. The apparent sufferings of those about me softened my feelings into sympathy, or doubtless my interference with some of their transactions would have cost me my life.

So the fictional Delano's apparent secondariness may reflect the real-life Delano's unemphatic account. In all candor, I'm not sure Melville had worked himself into full awareness of the deep significance attaching to his portrait of an American type: the indomitable—yes—shallowness of the "pleasant temperament of mind" that secures a livable life, the practical wisdom of clueless innocence that defeats nocent connivance.

Annapolis, 2017

28

The Fourth Brother Karamazov
Pavel and His Brothers*

My colleague Peter Kalkavage suggested this sub-title when we'd just had a conversation about Thomas Mann's *Joseph and His Brothers*, which is inversely parallel to *The Brothers Karamazov*. I mean that Joseph is the chosen, not the despised brother, though the relation of the singular brothers to their fraternal clan is not dissimilar.

Fyodor Dostoevsky prefaces his novel *The Brothers Karamazov* with an author's note declaring that it is "the life story [biography] of my hero, Alexey Fyodorovich Karamazov." Alexey, affectionately known as Alyosha, is the youngest son of Fyodor Pavlovich Karamazov, the pater familias.*

Because I don't know Russian, I've used two translations comparatively: that of Constance Garnett, revised by Ralph E. Matlaw (1976) and that by Richard Pevear and Larissa Volokhonsky (1990); the latters' variants are in brackets.

My original manuscript was garnished with page references, but I removed them; so small an essay didn't need so much corroboration. The main chapters to which I might have referred are Bk. III 2, 6, 7; Bk. V 2, 7; Bk. XI 5–10; Bk. XII 8.

The second paragraph begins as follow: "He [Fyodor Pavlovich] was married twice and had three sons, the eldest, Dimitri, by his first wife, and two, Ivan and Alexey, by his second."

Both the author's note and the second paragraph proclaim falsehoods. I want to claim that the hero of the novel (if not "my" hero) is not Alyosha and that there is a fourth son, Pavel Fyodorovich, who is, whether the author likes it or not, the hero, the heroic anti-hero, if you like, of the book.*

> It could be that Pavel got away from his author. It is a favorite meditation of mine: How do fictions come to issue a declaration of independence, of separation from their author, to acquire their own principle of motion within (which for Aristotle is the trait that gives beings a nature)? It is as if a lowercase author in this world permitted, in analogy to the capital Author of all Creation, free will to his creatures. The little devil that will visit Ivan (see below)—who should know, since nothing gives his tribe more trouble than our free will—says that these freely acting imaginative creations are, as a subject, "a complete enigma." What is most wonderful here is that Ivan's devil cites Tolstoy by name as the ultimate maker of such creations, for that's as insightful a bit of literary criticism as I know of. Takes a devil, and a Dostoevsky, to put the rival's reputation in the keeping of this minor hellraiser.

Father Fyodor Pavlovich accepts without demurrer the name Pavel Fyodorovich, that is, the grandfather's Christian name and Karamazov patronymic, popularly assigned to this never explicitly acknowledged fourth son—*never*, by any brother, not even by Alyosha, who is, to be sure, at least polite to him.*

> To me, this thoughtlessness throws a doubt on the author's imputation of angelic loving-kindness to his favorite. What readers of this essay would do that to a half-brother, unlovable though he be, with whom they lived under their common father's roof?

Pavel has no respectable family name. He is called by father Karamazov, *Smerdyakov*, "Shit-son" (as in French *merde*), from his mother's epithet. She was a well-tolerated "holy fool," a dirty, speechless cretin, called Lisavetna Smerdyashkaya, who slept on the ground anywhere but returned to the Karamazov garden to deliver her son and to die in childbirth. Little Smerdyakov is informally adopted into the servants' hall of the Karamazov establishment by the couple Grigory and Martha. Only two people ever let on that he is a Karamazov. One is Marya Kondratyevna, Smerdyakov's mincingly graceful neighbor, later his landlady, who is making advances to him, which he, plunking away at a guitar, the pseudo-musician's instrument, turns off by mock-romancing her in the garden. He sings a silly ditty in a sugary "falsetto," the male's false hyper-tenor. For Smerdyakov is a psychic eunuch—a potent type, as any reader of harem literature will recall. The other admission is more an intimation. *The Brothers Karamazov* has many themes, among them God-seeking and God-denying, as well as carnal and romantic love. In its underlying structure, however, it is a murder mystery, or maybe not so much a mystery, since the actual killer, Smerdyakov, becomes evident early. Now the woman Ivan loves, Katerina Ivanovna, cries out to Ivan that he, Ivan, persuaded her of Smerdyakov's "patricide."* That's an incidental intimation to

Or whatever the Russian word is, perhaps parricide—"kin-killer."

Ivan's face of their fraternity.

Smerdyakov has two traits pointing both directly or inversely to his maternal parent, the open-handed, simple Lisavetna. He's naïvely, one might almost say, amorally, honest—and yet totally opaque. Twice he returns found or taken money, first, without a word, three hundred rubles to his father, who had dropped them while drunk. Late in the story he gives back to Ivan, without explanation, ten times that many rubles, the ones he'd stolen from his father when he killed him. His mother was always dirty; he is ineradicably soiled, and yet quirkily finical, squeamishly fastidious.

Even as a boy, a sullen, cunning, unaffectionate, ungrateful child, he is intelligent beyond his education—corrosively clever, a deviser of rationalistic sophistries challenging Scripture: If God created light on the first day and the sun on the fourth, where did that first light come from? And that's the end of Grigory's scripture lessons.

A week after this piece of misbegotten brilliance, Smerdyakov develops epilepsy. At crucial moments, it turns out, he can fake attacks—a true and a false sufferer from the holy "falling disease." He fakes falling down the stairs from a really bad attack as an alibi for the murder.

He also displays a trait that complements the epileptic's loss of awareness. The Russians call people so afflicted "contemplators" or "contemplatives." They undergo a sudden thoughtless abstraction without memory.* However, the author says

> Its thoughtful Greek counterparts are Socrates' episodes of abstraction from the world (Plato, *Symposium*).

of Smerdyakov that he is greedily but purposelessly hoarding the impressions gathered in these episodes.

His looks are anti-attractive: oily hair, a yellow old-baby face, shrunk stature (from his mother). He can't, when adult, quite bring off the soigné youth; he's a faux-gentleman. He carries about him a mephitic air*; even his suicide after his

> He's got a pitiably disgusting full brother in Parlabane of Robertson Davies' *Cornish Trilogy* (*The Rebel Angels*), similarly a suicide; also in Melville's Babo, the anti-hero of *Benito Cereno*. (See Essay 27, "Clueless Wisdom.")

confession to Ivan has a malignant element to it, since it prevents Ivan's exoneration of Dmitri in open court; now he can't produce the murderer.

Nevertheless, I want to claim that this unlovely individual has the stuff of a hero: he has a culpably neglected grief which calls forth some sympathy; he has a deep connection to the other middle brother, Ivan, that legitimizes him as a Karamazov, and above all, he dominates Ivan completely. Thus he arouses deserved compassion, displays human feeling, and evinces effective superiority.

I have a model from a novel earlier than *The Brothers* (1880): *The Demons* (1872). The hero of the latter, Stavrogin, a complex figure,* attracts the adoration of the meanly

His name is composed of the Greek word for the Cross, *stauros*, and (I'm told) a form of the word for "horn"—so "Christ-Devil."

devilish main agitator of the novel, Pyotr Verkhovensky. This coldly cunning son of a blatherer wants a word of acceptance from the reserved Stavrogin, a gesture of reciprocal love; it's hopeless.

So also to imagine Ivan's arm around Smerdyakov, calling him Pavel—it's impossible. Ivan positively dislikes even his half-brother Dimitri, "Mitya," who is a lovable man; he abhors Smerdyakov.

Let me take a moment here to remind the reader of Smerdyakov's prospects after the murder. He is believed by the Karamazovs to be the murderer, but the prosecutor, to convict Dimitri, paints an absurd but plausible picture of Smerdyakov, exonerating him completely.

Smerdyakov is an excellent cook, particularly of fish soup; his insulting epithet is "soup-maker." Old Karamazov had sent him to Moscow for culinary training. He is learning French vocabulary. Significantly, nothing is said of grammar; he is described as being psychically ungrammatical—temperamentally chaotic, confused emotionally. But he has a perfectly sensible plan, to go to Paris and become the chef of his own café-restaurant. He has Karamazov's three thousand rubles to start up his business. It is a fine, philistine dream, sane, sound, and achievable. There is, however, also more to him. We learn that he is reading in a yellow book, which turns out to be a volume we had heard of earlier as belonging to Grigory: the sermons of "The God-fearing Father Isaac the Syrian." So he'll be a chef-theologian, a Parisian celebrity. He has a future. Why does he hang himself? It's practically inexplicable.

I think it is because his faith in Ivan has collapsed—Ivan who, though he has persistently underestimated, misunderstood, and disrespected "the lackey," this half-brother, is *his*, Smerdyakov's, hero. I think this unloved and unloving youth wants above all to be acknowledged by the other middle brother. They are the same age, both twenty-four, thus—though born of different mothers—oddly twin-like, as only a scion and a by-blow are able to be. But it's hopeless.

When Ivan first comes home, Smerdyakov, waiting at the table, displays an extraordinary bit of bravura rationalization for a betrayal of faith. He does it, as old Karamazov perceives, to impress Ivan, who is, however, contemptuous: "He's a lackey and a mean soul." In the last interviews between this pair, Smerdyakov does, to be sure, several times evince a "frenzied hatred" of Ivan—the hellish fury, I think, of scorned love.

To flesh this conjecture out, I'll ask and answer four questions:

1) Whence comes the deep connection between these brothers?
2) What grief and grievance most deeply burden Smerdyakov?
3) How does he achieve dominance over Ivan and therewith hero-status?
4) Why, I'll ask once again and finally, does he hang himself?

1) Whence comes the particular, close connection between these half-brothers, Ivan and Smerdyakov? Well, as I said, they are the middle brothers,* of the same age and by their father

There is probably much research on the special position of middle siblings. It might be a condition Dostoevsky had in mind.

neither best loved—that is Alyosha the youngest—nor most disliked—that is Mitya, the eldest. To father Karamazov,

Smerdyakov's involvement with Ivan is obvious: "What have you done to fascinate him?" he asks Ivan; he himself thinks it's Ivan's superciliousness that's done it, and that Smerdyakov, himself secretly conceited, wants Ivan's praise. But until a day before the end, Ivan underrates and despises his brother. He thinks of him as an ineffectual closet rebel who wants to but will never succeed among the peasants as a social agitator. He goes much further in his obtuse contempt. He offers to beat him, to kill him. Smerdyakov thinks that he is a fly to his divinity Ivan.*

> As flies to wanton boys are we to the gods,
> They kill us for their sport. (*King Lear* IV 1, 38)

On his part, Smerdyakov assiduously insinuates himself into familiarity with Ivan. Proud Ivan is helpless before this scattered emotionality and single-minded will, and so Smerdyakov gains a surreptitious dominance over him.

The insight that belatedly arouses Ivan's respect for Smerdyakov's intelligence is the latter's observation that Ivan is the most of the four brothers like old Karamazov: a love of money, women, comfort—a sensualist; "You are not a fool," Ivan finally admits.

A sensualist is what Smerdyakov himself is surely not. In fact, he is physically emasculated; when his father offers to get him a wife, he grows furious. He is a eunuch of the soul; as I've said, scatty emotionally (but not without one deep longing). But he also thinks that he and Ivan are alike, surely in their skepticism, which is morose in Smerdyakov and labyrinthine in Ivan. It is corrosive in both, yet pure and simple for the former while doubt-beset and complex for the latter.

Smerdyakov claims, ironically, to have learned from Ivan the unbeliever's mantra: If there is no God "all is lawful [permitted]." His irony is confirmed by a saying he repeats on at least two occasions: "It's always worthwhile [interesting] speaking to a clever [intelligent] man." He utters it when jumping up into the carriage that is taking Ivan to Chermashnya so as to straighten the rug around him, and Ivan is troubled by its meaning. For this trip is Smerdyakov's machination (see 3, below), and his sentence is terminally ambiguous: Which clever man does Smerdyakov actually mean—himself or Ivan?

So they're involved with each other in bad business. But behind that is the Stavrogin-Pyotr analogy, a base man's one humanizing, even ennobling pathos—the longing for recognition and love. Smerdyakov says to Ivan, who has rightly accused him, "the lackey," of playing with him: "Why should I play with you, sir, when I put my whole trust in you as in God almighty?"* And he explains what he thought Ivan

> So says Caliban, the slavish, yet pathetic, monster, to unworthy Trinculo: "I prithee, be my god." (*Tempest* II 2)

would have understood: that he sent Ivan away to spare him, out of affection and devotion, but secretly hoping that he'd stay home to protect their father. And again, shortly after: "I liked [loved] you so much then and was open-hearted with you." It's a unilateral cri de coeur—to a deaf idol, and it makes the Shit-son weightier than the Theodor-son.

2) What is the deep grief whence springs Smerdyakov's general aggrievedness? It's the question of his origins, twice questionable: his father-perpetrated bastardy and his mother-caused degradation. Even the author colludes: he feels obliged to apologize for involving the reader in these affairs of common menials.

Actually, old Karamazov is quite kind to the boy Smerdyakov; he forbids Grigory, his parent in effect, to punish him corporeally. He sends him to Moscow to develop his talent for cookery. (It's not clear, however, that Smerdyakov even likes to eat.) Karamazov gets a doctor for Smerdyakov's increasingly serious epileptic seizures. And he speaks kindly to him—and trusts him for his proven honesty.

So it is Grigory whom Smerdyakov can never forgive. Grigory had called him a monster for his lack of love and said to him: "You grew from mildew in the bathhouse." ["You're not a human being, you were begotten of bathhouse slime."] It is evidently a proverbial expression for "you sprang from nowhere." The immediate occasion was that Grigory caught him at his habit of hanging cats and then burying them with mock-Christian ceremony. He is a sullen, unfriendly, mistrustful, and even savage boy, given to that ultimately dreadful wit: sarcastic actions, such as this derisory rite, through which the boy expresses his faithless love.

So everything about the youngster's being is questionable. His parentage is unacknowledged while taken for granted; his social status is menial as Smerdyakov but respectable as Pavel Fyodorovich; his family standing is denigrated as servile bastard and accepted as trusty cook. It is a life made problematic by murky beginnings, carrying the burden of unacknowledged secular original sin.* The rest is aggrieved resentment,

Whereas spiritual original sin becomes, so to speak, socially acceptable through the scriptural parentage of the "original pair," the real, originating cause of our original sin.

defensive conceit—and a heroic resolution to prevail.

3) How does Pavel Fyodorovich achieve dominance over Ivan Fyodorovich in particular and as a whole over the Karamazov clan's fate, so that he may well be called the nether-hero of the novel? I'll try to make it plausible that Ivan, the "genius," the respected intellectual, the sophisticated doubter, is entirely in the power of, dominated by, Pavel, the shit, the chef, the scoffer—in soul and in action. Smerdyakov plays Ivan like a fish until he hooks, lands, and brings him on the board of his purpose, with its clever double intention: He means to obtain Ivan's colluding approval of the patricidal plan as signified by his self-removal from the scene, and also,

of course, to prevent any last-minute intervention and eye-witnessing. Perhaps, above all, he hopes to implant more self-doubt in his shakily arrogant brother, so that with Ivan's loss of self-esteem Pavel will gain in his bestowed esteem.

As are all of Smerdyakov's proceedings, so this one is carried out with terrifying cleverness, malicious intensity, some emotional scattiness—and a certain noble pathos: All three legitimate brothers may eventually be better off materially, and the world the better humanly, by the removal of this rich but repellent specimen of a pater familias—but actually not the perpetrator's world, not Pavel himself. For Smerdyakov will not by his act become the fourth brother, nor will he gain materially, since he has already secured his patrimony by stealing.

Smerdyakov, then, in his malignant daring, does not want to involve Ivan actively but passively, not as indictable perpetrator but as enabler who is to be held harmless; Pavel's dominance has the base nobility or noble baseness that describes his cleft character.

His chief means for making Ivan a sleeping partner in patricide are creepy: He insinuates himself into familiarity (of course, he *is* family) by a half-arrogant, half-cringing lackey's flattery and a half-intimating, half-withdrawing co-conspirator's confidentiality. He speaks enigmatically and expresses veiledly insulting surprise at Ivan's slowness to unriddle the plan. Thus he creepingly establishes at once his mental superiority and Ivan's cravenness. It gains him only a grim, because self-lacerating, satisfaction. He is, after all, undermining his own earthly faith, his admiration of his twin brother. Ivan treats him always with nose-holding condescension; he's ever the "lackey." And yet, Ivan himself is almost Pavel's marionette.

The dominance goes way past Ivan's action, which is mainly that of fleeing, fleeing even farther than Smerdyakov had suggested, which was nearby Chermashnya; Ivan

goes to far-off Moscow. In his oblivion, Ivan has let Smerdyakov invade his soul and, it will turn out, his imagination in
particular.

The definitive episode occurs to—or in—Ivan, just after he
has had his "third and last interview with Smerdyakov." Ivan
had visited him in his new home with Marya Kondratyevna,
on the way nearly murdering a peasant, just incidentally. He
is, once again, alone with a physically declining Smerdyakov,
who again looks at him with "frenzied hatred [a wildly hateful look]." Smerdyakov wants to be left alone, contemptuously, tormentedly, and longingly. Ivan mutters, "I'm afraid
that you are a dream, a phantom sitting before me." Smerdyakov answers that there's just the two of them and a third, God,
who is not findable. At that moment he pulls the incriminating three thousand rubles from his stocking and hands them
to Ivan. It is a confession; Ivan goes white as a handkerchief.
"Can you really, can you really not have known till now?"
Smerdyakov asks. If he didn't, this brilliant Ivan, I must think,
is plain stupid. Smerdyakov ironically quotes Ivan's teaching—
more his own, for he has known it since his boyhood: "You
said 'everything is lawful,' and how frightened you are now."
Smerdyakov describes the manner of the murder, and cites
the evidence for Ivan's tacit sanctioning of it. Ivan appears
appalled: "Well, it was the devil who helped you," he says.

Then Ivan, ever Smerdyakov's fool, asks why he's giving
him the money, when he murdered for it. He *really* doesn't
know his amorally honest brother. At this point the reader
knows that Smerdyakov has renounced his bourgeois dream
of a new life in Moscow as a restaurant owner. But Ivan wonders cluelessly if Smerdyakov now believes in God, to be giving back the money: "'No, sir, I don't believe,' whispered
Smerdyakov." Ivan leaves, and Smerdyakov calls to him a last
"goodbye." Of course, he is telling Ivan that he, the patricide,
will now become a suicide. Ivan takes it in, but, in his false
contempt, not consciously.

Instead he goes home and has a "nightmare," a learnedly grounded conception turned into a vision, an extruded image. The devil comes to him.* And behold, this devil, a low-status

> It's the same devil to whom Faust, the magician, sells his soul, at whom Luther, the theologian, shies his inkstand, and of whom Ivan, the intellectual, flings his glass of tea (which the devil recognizes as Luther's inkstand), and who visits Leverkühn, the composer, in Thomas Mann's *Doctor Faustus*. Or maybe not the same, for the two sixteenth-century visitants, though anecdotal to us, may have been objective enough to their hosts and so resistible, while the devils of the nineteenth and twentieth century are possibly emanations of those entertaining them and, being subjective, excruciatingly possessive.

demon, is Smerdyakov in bourgeois costume, the Smerdyakov ensconced in his soul, emerging from Ivan's fevered brain in "falsetto" dress. The main message this shriveled devil gives him—all else the devil says is old news to Ivan, his own prior knowledge—is that Smerdyakov will kill himself. Of course, that too is old, but hitherto unacknowledged, news.

"How could my soul beget such a lackey like you?" Ivan asks the devil, the very Pavel-lackey he's got on his brain; so he's asking himself—the clueless intellectual. Then there's a knocking.* Ivan already knows that it's Alyosha to tell him

> Like in ominousness to the knocking in *Macbeth* (II 3) and its "Devil-porter." Here it's Angel-Alyosha who's knocking on the gate.

yet a third time the news of which his devil has apprised him: "An hour ago Smerdyakov hanged himself." Ivan responds: He already knows this from the visiting devil.

There are multiple signals that this emissary from Ivan's hell is impersonating Ivan's half-brother and is recognized as such by Ivan: He calls him "you lackey," his address for Smerdyakov; he offers to kick him as he did Smerdyakov; he calls him "stupid and vulgar"; he is driven by him into a cascade of Smerdyakov-like sophisms, and he allows this menial devil to present himself as one without whom "there would be no events." He makes his devil speak of himself as Ivan thinks of Smerdyakov: "How could such a vulgar devil visit such a great man as you!" He even offers to kill the devil, as he had offered to kill Smerdyakov. Perhaps he has actually already done just that by depriving his brother of his one faith.

Finally, the Smerdyakov-devil speaks of something, one thing, we've never heard of before: his theological, or rather, spiritual dream, in glowing detail. The reader already knows that Smerdyakov has a spiritual interest: It's after all Grigory's yellow volume of the sayings of the Holy Father Isaac the Syrian that he uses to cover up the fortune of rubles he has pulled out of his stocking for Ivan. If Ivan's subjugated soul has a watchword, it is "All is lawful." And that has gotten into him via Smerdyakov's devilry, which, in the ardent, visionary purity of its atheism, far surpasses Ivan's intellectual agonies, as he realizes in his "nightmare." So Smerdyakov is Ivan's worthy mentor. Accordingly, he takes the money that Pavel hands him—who knows with what in mind?

In their last interview Smerdyakov had half-convinced Ivan that he, Ivan, was the murderer and "I am only the instrument." That meant, however, that the lackey had Ivan in his secular as well as his spiritual power, and moreover, for life is now able, if not ready, to extract unceasing tribute.

To conclude with Ivan's near-identification of his brother with his devil: Ivan tells Alyosha that the devil called him a coward—"And Smerdyakov said the same."

4) Why does Pavel Fyodorovich, why does this Smerdyakov, hang himself? He's had sensible plans and the means to achieve them; in France he'd be a new man, rid of this bastardy, of his brothers' denial of the fraternity, even of his deficiency in Russian faith: "'No, Smerdyakov has not the Russian faith at all,' said Alyosha firmly and gravely." Thus does the kindest of the three exclude the fourth even from

his country, though Smerdyakov himself, in his usual mode of preemptive rejection when he does not hope for inclusion, has said that he hates Russia.

He isn't even in danger of being arrested for the murder, since, if Ivan succeeds in taking him in, it will be understood as a brotherly diversion for Mitya's benefit, and if Ivan accuses himself, incriminating Smerdyakov as a mere instrument, it will be taken for grandstanding or as a sign of madness. Nor has Smerdyakov acquired faith and with it a contrite conscience. Moreover, ill though he looks, he isn't dying. So he has no concrete reason to kill himself. There's just no obvious motive.

He is calm and composed before Ivan and reminds him— ironically, I think, for it's not really true—that he learned with Ivan's guidance, learned from his talk and his teaching, that if there's no God, there's no virtue and all things are lawful. And when Ivan once again expresses his wish to kill him, he says, I imagine with the calm of final despair for the loss of his own faith: "You won't dare do even that!" And he adds with a bitter smile: "You won't dare do anything, you, sir, who used to be so bold!" Then he haughtily dismisses Ivan, to recall him, hopelessly, for that last goodbye. He's killed his somewhat protective father, he's won no brother, and he's lost his human divinity, *his* hero. He, the only doer of real deeds among the four, has plotted cleverly, acted effectually, and is left with nothing, certainly with no loving recognition, *from* his brother, and what is worse, no admiring love *for* his brother. So this despised fourth brother, the one who has a hero's exploits to his discreditable credit and a hero's pathos about his unnatural nature, hangs himself.*

> And, thus, I think, sucks the life out of Dostoevsky's plan, told us in the preface "From the Author." In the "main novel . . . the second one," Alyosha, "my hero," will be, or rather, would have been, shown acting, out in the world. Dostoyevsky calls the first, the extant novel, his hero's "life story" [biography]. It is, however,

only the account of Alyosha's preparation for the stage of action, while it is Pavel who is born, acts to affect the world, and dies in the novel we have. This fourth brother is the only one who actually has a complete life story.

Annapolis, 2017

29

*Effi Briest**
A Personal Note

"Effi" is probably for Eva (Chapter 4); my brother called me "Eff."

Theodor Fontane's *Effi Briest* is an altogether wonderful novel—wonderful in the two ways that word encompasses for me: giving me delight and causing me perplexity. The delight stems, in some part, from its North German diction (Berlin-Pomerania),* the perplexity from its Prussian

> The Oxford World's Classics translation is Anglo-idiomatic, thus flavorless.

portraiture (military nobility), both from both, really.

I think of my native tongue as klutzy when grand (Luther), domineering when official (*verboten*-notices), and stuffy when *gründlich*, "thorough" (professors). Those auxiliary verb accumulations at the end of league-long sentences seem to me models of stylistic wrong-doing.*

> Truth to tell, I do take to the word-concatenations, *Wortverbindungen*, which invite spaces or hyphens—who knows which?—in English but are true meldings in German, "complexity-bearing-capable," *verflechtungstragfähig*.

Fontane wrote in the dialect, or better, cadence, of the region of my birth: Berlin, whose dialect is yet in my ear and whose wit still gets to me;* Berlin is the main city of Mark

> Example, main memory from my one and only visit to Berlin (1990s) since emigration (1941): On a bus, which used to (still does?) carry, besides the driver, a *Schaffner*, a conductor, who collected fares and kept order. Our driver was woolgathering at a traffic light; *Schaffner, berlinert*, "in Berlin's dialect": *Na, jriener wirt's nich.* "Come on, it won't get much greener." It made my otherwise somewhat bereft week.

Brandenburg, which was in turn the central region of Prussia.*

> In my childhood we vacationed (I think) on the beaches of the Pomeranian Baltic and visited my paternal grandmother, the widow of a *Gymnasialdirektor* in Deutschkrone, an East Prussian town. My father's family seems to have been secular-humanist (or, at least, he was), my mother's was orthodox Jewish, I went pagan.
> Among Fontane's local nobility, whose names he adapted from actual families, there is a noble lady, a "von Padden." My father, a physician, had a patient, Frau von Tadden. When he was already in America, unable to return to us because of the Crystal Night event (November 1938), which resulted in the first mass transport of Jewish men to concentration camps, she came to visit us—as I later understood at considerable risk to herself. At the opposite end of the social scale was our young and much beloved nanny, the daughter of a laborer. By the Nuremberg laws, she, an Aryan, was ejected from our family, but, again, at real risk to herself (the more so since her father had been a Communist), she came to visit us often and read to us. It became a ritual to enter on the margin of the story where she'd left off her habitual words: "*Kinder, ich muss gehen.*" "Children, I have to go."

I used to think of Fontane as the German Jane Austen, because of the pregnant elegance of his idiom and the idiosyncratic typicality of his characters. That parallelism, however, turns out to fail a little, for a surprising reason: She's more given to principle than he is.

Yet the two aspects I've just noted, Fontane's idiom and his characters, are central both to my delight and my perplexity. First the delight: The pleasure is in part the recognition that something really difficult is being accomplished. Effi, the un-

questionable heroine of the book named for her, is fated to
live a sad life and to die young. I think "fated," a word from
the vocabulary of tragedy, is right; from the first idyllic page,
I have a sense of lurking doom. And now comes the engaging oddity. *This girl, this very young woman, is absolutely
without tragic format.* She is in every dimension nice; she is
charmingly wild, readily loving, innocently carefree, laxly ac-
commodating, susceptibly temperamental. Just compare Antigone, a girl-woman of truly monstrous self-certainty, fully
capable of sustaining, indeed inviting, tragedy. Effi is perhaps
above average in what is now called "emotional intelligence,"
but below in intellectual endowments, in practical judgment,
energetic initiative, warranted self-assertion, and certainly in
*gravitas.** The pointillist art that has gone into making such a

A bearing of which late adolescents are in fact eminently capable.
  Here is an aspect of novel writing that never ceases to beguile
and puzzle me: when characters cast loose from their authors and
evince characteristics quite on their own and contrary to the writer's explicit or hinted prescriptions. American examples: Maggie
Verver of Henry James's *The Golden Bowl* is, I think, surreptitiously quite nasty, though James does not mean us to view her
thus, and Melville's Captain Delano, who is wiser than his author
avers (see Essay 27, "Clueless Wisdom").

lightweight plausible in her suffering, interesting in her reflections, but, above all, sympathetic in her diminishing vitality,
of bestowing pathos on such a mediocrity, is simply wonderful. It is not that I think Jane Austen incapable of depicting
girlish spontaneity, but that her leading young women are
all strong in character—principled, even when error-prone. I
think she wouldn't have invested her chief attention in any
other.

  And then the perplexity: This North German idiom is the
perfect medium, indeed is shaped for, the conveyance of a
Prussian trait not well known among Americans—terminal
skepticism, expressed through a disparaging, downgrading,

doubting, but not inelegant wit, delivered with pursed mouth, raised eyebrows, and a good shot of *Süffisance*, "self-complacency." Whereas Berlin dialect is of sturdy cockney caliber, the North German high diction is delicately derisive, snootily choice, self-consciously well-bred, gracefully piercing in Fontane's handling: *leiser Spott*, "delicate mockery," sometimes morphing into mordant irony.*

> *Effi Briest* seems to me to have a neat complement in Rose Macaulay's *The Towers of Trebizond*, whose key word is "odd"—Anglo-Saxon eccentricity raised to an ethnic universal, the counterpart to Prussian skepticism. There's the same fugitive wit, mordant in the Prussian, snobbish in the English book. The latter, however, is seriously theological (perhaps excessively so, to compensate for sidelined faith), while the former is seriously religious (though doctrinally reticent, probably because nobody in the book is up to it). Visions play a role in both books, but the dream of the court of Trebizond, induced by a green elixir, rises to imaginative magic.

But then there is rock-bottom conventionality and terminal conformism as the other side of this curious coin. The following sayings by the two characters, eminently respectable, who might nonetheless be thought of as the villains in a censorious reading of *Effi Briest*, are notorious. Frau von Briest, Effi's mother, refuses to receive her child on the family estate near Berlin, once Effi's adultery—long time-expired—has come to light. She is, in effect, totally ostracized, even by this mother, who writes to her that they will not receive her, not because they cannot bear to be absolutely cut off from society—a fate they have, however, no intention of suffering—but because they need to "show our colors," and because before all the world,

> I can't spare you the word—we want to express our condemnation of your conduct, the conduct of our only child and one so much beloved by us (Ch. 31).

It's a merging of hard-hearted self-pity and shameless hypocrisy, at least to my taste. The right message would surely have been these two words: "Come home."* And that the more so

> What about von Briest, the father? He is, in his ineffectual resignation, close to Mr. Bennet of *Pride and Prejudice*. The novel ends with his frequent formula for staving off serious engagement: Oh, Luise, leave it. . . . that's too wide a field.

since Luise von Briest has used her child as a surrogate for her missed marriage to Innstetten, who had courted her unsuccessfully over a score of years earlier. But all in all, the spirit of this letter is one of conformism—at once craven and zestful. As is that of a pronouncement, by Innstetten, now the very young Effi's husband, older by twenty-two years:

> One isn't just an isolated human being. One belongs to a whole, and to that whole we have constantly to pay regard; we are through and through dependent on it (Ch. 27).

On this faith he, in effect, murders Crampas, Effi's lover, in a duel. Crampas is an unreliable, irresponsible philanderer, yet a man of some—inconsequential—self-knowledge and of some—distractible—humane decency. Innstetten kills this lightweight from a rigidified, fear-ridden sense of honor, forgoing all independent judgment, any ultimate selfhood. His second for the duel says agitatedly but colludingly:

> That about "God's Judgment," as some pompously assure us, is, of course, nonsense—forget it—on the contrary, our cult of honor is idolatry, but we have to submit to him, as long as the idol has currency.

Innstetten is in full agreement. At the same time this ramrod-stiff man of honor is wafflingly ambiguous about the ghostly presences in his house and not averse to exploiting them to control his young wife.

These Prussian officers and officials are a sophisticated lot—and even, in their pungent ethnicity, somehow engaging, certainly to Fontane. So why "must" they submit? It is to me *the* perplexity behind the novel because it carries into the event of my youth, the Nazis. Was it this strange, even piquant, combination of skepticism and conformism that caused the descendants of these overbred folks, half a century after the dramatic time of the novel (1878–88), to stay loyal to a leader they despised?*

My friend, neighbor, and colleague, Beate Ruhm von Oppen, was engrossed by questions concerning the German resistance to the Nazis—its sparsity and its pathos. Thus one impediment lay in the Protestant Kantianism of the Prussian Officer Corps that esteemed duty and abhorred oath-breaking: Hitler had cleverly ordered the officers to swear fealty to him personally. (When Putin came into power in 1999, he had his former KGB colleagues swear personal allegiance to him as to a tsar, though I doubt that these functionaries were then similarly inhibited by morality.) The German resistance was largely Christian and in part Lutheran, but the officer who came nearest to dispatching Hitler, Claus von Stauffenberg, was Catholic. So in *Effi Briest*, the figure who most effectively sympathizes with Effi, Roswitha, is Catholic, a servant whom Effi has saved from destitution, a woman of limited intellect and large morality, who gauges rightly the disproportion of the societal punishment to the transient deed.

I remember Beate telling me this unforgettable fact about the nucleus of the "White Rose," the band of student resisters in Munich, drawn from the Catholic youth movement, who were all caught and hanged. They evidently met at a Bach choir directed by their anti-Nazi professor; Bach, of course, was a Protestant, though of the high sort. I think she did not know what they sang—chorales, motets, cantatas, magnificats, passions?—but the fact that they came together singing Bach seems to me somewhat to redeem history's prevailing incoherence.

Annapolis, 2017

30

Time Bounces
Skipping Through Tenses

I. We were conducting an oral examination with one of our seminar freshmen, a young woman from whom we wished we'd heard more in class (Elsa Ordahl, '21AN). She had chosen to talk to us about what she called "Herodotus bouncing around in time." Of course, she'd caught on to something highly characteristic: Like Homer, his rival, Herodotus leaps into the past, into the past's past, to work forward "chronologically," that is, linearly, to the culmination, that is, the grand Now of his "Inquiry" (Greek *historia*). Or he overleaps that present to land in the future and even in the future's future.* In terms of the order-imposing abstraction from real

> When he tells of an earthquake that occurs at Delos during the events he is then recounting, namely the first Persian invasion in 490 B.C.E. (VI 98), as portending in effect the fall of Athens at the end of Thucydides' war, the Peloponnesian War, nearly a hundred years later. Herodotus saw it coming, though he had died, perhaps still writing, about two decades before the utter finish.

language called "verbal syntax," I discern these *tense forms* in their relation to a *temporal* crux, namely *the present and its speaker, the author*:

Pluperfect—occurred even before all's gone and done
　　with, past of the past, as seen from a terminal stand-
　　point, the author's, or a past to which a more recent
　　past is future;
perfect—done with, completed in itself;
simple past—plain over with, complete or not;
imperfect—going on during the past, perhaps incomplete
　　up to now;
present—right now, "now" taken curtly, "momentously,"
　　the author's present;
progressive present—going on through an extended, a so-
　　called "specious present";
future—will happen, hasn't yet, nothing to be seen, every-
　　thing to be imagined;
future perfect—will have happened from a future stand-
　　point, so, past-in-future, or a future to which a more
　　recent future is past.

As far as Herodotus, the ever-lovable, is concerned, our
conversation was ditheringly inconclusive. Nonetheless it was
one sort of testing in which I have faith as producing some
good—not scattily brilliant but traipsingly engaged, not
memorably productive but hopefully thought-provoking—
not least to the examiners.

Here's a first result: Like all the "great" ancients—I mean
the adjective to bear significance as an attribution consequent to acquaintance rather than a pre-assumed category—
Herodotus seems to be what I'm driven to call "naturally
sophisticated." I mean by this contradiction in terms that he
seems both gullibly childlike and foxily canny: He appreciates
with relish everything he hears and sees, be it elicited by him
or proffered to him, *and* he critiques it all with the disengagement of his very own judgment. Otherwise put: His complexity is not due to his artfulness, but his artfulness results from
his giving its due to his object.

II. His object, clearly (but not so distinctly) announced in his proem, is to prevent the great and wondrous works of both Greeks and Barbarians from going gloryless, and, in general, to keep "the things that human beings have brought about from becoming *extinct in time*" (*exitela*—"going out [of memory]," *toi chronoi*—"in time").

Herodotus puts no preposition with "time," just the article in the dative case. Does he mean, as the dative allows, *in? with? by? time*:

"In" time would be "locative"; it would simply locate the extinction "in some time," date it;

"with" time would mean "in the course of time, as time went on";

"by time" would be instrumental, would make time a cause.

Some translations circumvent the question by just omitting the phrase; no one, in my reading, regards it even as problematic. For my part, I think there is to be found in the *History* a "phenomenology," a description of the appearances time makes in our consciousness, but no theory of time.*

Herodotus's work shows him as comfortably encompassing many opposites. Besides the above-mentioned amalgamation of skepticism *and* receptivity, he is a lover of factual details *and* of storied myths; a user of informants *and* of "autopsy" (Greek: "seeing-for-oneself"); he writes in a spirit of sober humanism *and* of respect for the gods; he is a man of wide tolerance *and* of decided judgment; a stylist of linear narrative *and* episodic rhapsodies; a memorialist of homely detail *and* of great grandeur (this latter sort of history, which Nietzsche, in *The Use and Abuse of History II*, called "monumental," and has little use for, Herodotus announces in his proem as his intended type); but above all, he is an inquirer of cosmopolitan scope *and* of centered devotion—focused on Athens.

Here is a brief survey of the ways Herodotus speaks of time:* He quanti- and qualifies it adjectivally as long/short,

The very long entry under *chronos*, "time," in J. E. Powell's *Lexicon to Herodotus* helpfully supplies the Greek phrase for each set of occurrences. Context, of course, requires recourse to the *History* itself.

much/little, more/less; as foregoing (before)/succeeding (after-wards); as happening/having happened; going forward/passing off; perpetual/brief; later/earlier—and more. So too time occurs with these prepositions: in, during, after, for—and more. To us Herodotus's word *historie* (his Ionic dialect) has come to mean an account of things past. History, now an academic discipline, is largely an accumulation of published inquiries that tend to descend into minute mundanity. I recall reading a report on night soil from colonial privies in Annapolis. I don't think that's Herodotus's main interest, although in his Egyptian book (II) he reports the micturating position of men and women, which are inverses of the Greek way (as is everything Egyptian). He writes by preference in the service of wonders,* that they may not go out of memory. Memories,

And only secondarily to explain the present.

however, as retrieved by historians, are practically convertible with psychic time—as are the strata scraped up by archaeologists with worldly time. So, of course, Herodotus must mention time often and multifariously.

But must he really? No, not really. He could have written, since he assigns no substantial power explicitly to time, "through the years" or "in a few days" or "for successive months." You might object that these are all time terms. Not so; our temporal language is etymologically tied to motions, events, weather; thus "week" is related to a motion of [life] turning around (as in *vici*ssitude), "month" to the moon's revolution, "day" to the sun's dawning, and both hour and year to seasons, both as in Greek *hora*. "Time" itself is related both to a natural event, tide, and is, way back, derived from a—presumably—human activity, *dividing*.*

As in Greek: *daiesthai*, "to divide, apportion"; another time word, *kairos*, "the right moment," may be related to *kerein*, "to cut off." Greek *chronos*, "time," has no assignable etymology in my etymological dictionaries.

III. Nonetheless our student was right. Like Homer, Herodotus loves flashbacks. In fact, the *History* ends with a flashback, a mytho-historic tale that is told of Cyrus, and set perhaps three-score years before the end of Herodotus's war, the Persian War.* No one knows whether the *History* is a

> The *History*, commonly called *The Persian Wars*, ends, with some of the aftermath, in 479, the year after Xerxes fled from mainland Greece.

finished, that is, a completed work. I think so, because the final story is a cautionary tale in which Cyrus warns the Persians, who want to take a crop-rich land from others to live in, that they'll end up soft and enslaved. So I think this is the kind of back-bounce that is also forward-leaping to episodes even beyond the culminating event of the work. As so often, Herodotus is right about the danger he foresaw: utter, enslaving defeat for the Athenians as told in Thucydides' *Peloponnesian War*. But he's wrong about the *particular* degeneration that caused the defeat: not loosening tautness through comfort but losing self-restraint from over-reaching.

In order to do flashbacks, you have to have an underlying, forward-driving timeline. Thus Herodotus starts his account of the Persian invasion of mainland Greece in prehistory's dateless time, with reciprocal depredations, particularly abductions of women. From the eighth century B.C.E. onwards Herodotus actually has a chronology constructed from lines of kingship and lengths of reigns, and so he begins to write what *we* call history (Bk. I). As I said, the work's timeline is leading to 480, the Great King's flight from Greece after his naval defeat at Salamis (Bk. VIII). There is yet one more great battle in Greece proper before the last Persians march home, and operations shift to Asia Minor (Bk. IX).

That is the underlying stream of time on which Herodotus imposes his variously motivated bouncings. But this little at-

tempt to think about temporal loops, so variously related to
the uniform chronological progress and its punctuations by
scenes of selected presents, the excogitated crux of the story
and its proposed denouement, the narrator's overt intrusions
and, behind that, the author's implicit disposition—that meditation on time bounces is probably best done in abstraction
from any one particular author, even Herodotus,* though he be

For whom, as for only one other, I might be tempted to give up
my American life, of course only if I could be sure of an appointment to some female priesthood or other, which would permit
me to hobnob conversationally with the men. From Herodotus I
could hear what is the positive effect on the soul of knowing the
world in its concrete detail and its national types. From Socrates
I would learn what deleterious effects occur when you immerse
yourself ardently in the worldly motions people call time and its
eventuations. In short: I would get to know what Socrates thought
about the *History*. I doubt that Herodotus would reciprocate with
a critique of philosophy; Socrates' defense is extant. Here is one
way a conversation might run between Herodotus, a decade or so
the elder, and Socrates—both, therefore, in the prime of life—
if held, say, in 430 B.C.E. Herodotus might point out that he too
introduces stable thinking into the variety of material, earthly
life, namely by way of ethnic schematisms and factual agnosti-
cism tempered by firm ethical preferences. Socrates might reply
that these interesting results of the kind of inquiry later ages call
"research" are, again in latter-day terms, valuations and, so, subjective and that his own notion of inquiry is that it ought not to
survey what is temporal and external but what is atemporal and
interior, not *of* the world but *for* the soul. It is precisely there, he
might say, that are found the inherently objective beings that are
stably and in themselves what things are (example: "itself the
equal," *auto to ison*). I am saying that Herodotus is Socrates' ideal
partner because he has the most acute knowledge of the world *as it
appears.*
    One more observation, pertinent here: Herodotus's chronologi-
cal timeline is huge. In the Egyptian book (II 142) he reports that
the priests have a list of royal succession going back 341 pharaohs,
which does not even bring the lineage into Herodotus's present.
Since the priests reckon three pharaohs to a century, by his figuring this comes to 11340 years. So, one way or another, the *History* stretches in thought over eleven thousand years back from its
event-reporting end in 479 B.C.E. Then, as I mentioned, it reaches

a century forward, even beyond events occurring while Herodotus was composing the *History*, to his conjectures about the catastrophic final outcome for Athens of the Peloponnesian War. He died, circa 425, at about fifty-five, in Italian Thurii, Pericles' Panhellenic foundation, during that war.

the master of flashbacks, of time-retrievals, inserted into the ample chronological time (set out in the note above) of the *History*.

IV. Now to the purpose of these time bounces. It is not possible here to escape the ever-roiled issue of particular causation and causality in general, to which Herodotus, full of actual causes, pays no systematic attention. Sometimes his reprises tell the story of the start of a still-functioning dynasty, for example, the Lydian one, but with no clear implication other than this: Nothing can exist on earth without an earthly beginning. Sometimes he gives the pre-historic antecedents. For the great Persian War, these are the reciprocal abductions of women by Europe and Asia Minor, whose precise effect on Darius's and Xerxes' invasion—the historical event in question—is hard to discern.* Sometimes an old story, an ancient

> And what a doctoral thesis it would be that made a plausible case! For the Greeks, *the* great abduction was, of course, that of Spartan Helen by Trojan Paris. The consequences are told in the *Iliad*. There was a little problem attached to this event: Everything points to Helen actually having run off from wimpy Menelaus with the Asian pretty boy.

wisdom, throws a bright light on a clueless present. Now and then a myth whose origins are lost has the more explanatory value for being currently believed than would the mere ascertained fact of the matter. So Herodotus's causality is not a stable idea but a grab bag of different—what word would there be? I can think of nothing more definitive than bearings—so, different bearings, a bundle of them, that time past may have on time present through the times passing in-between. I'll try to specify that more in my circumstance-abstracted* descriptions of time bounces.

> The Greeks have the perfect word for my six-syllable composite: *psilos*, "naked, bare, stripped, mere, abstracted." My highly practical notion of a grand new American dictionary: It would include, in transcription, a lot of really helpful words, from Yiddish to Chinese, green-card words, so to speak. I'm dying to be on the usage panel.

V. Down to business now. The presupposition of time leaping is evidently time traipsing; I mean chronological ("time-accounting"), calendrical, clocked time that steps, runs, flies, but mostly plods steadily onward. The accounting seems to work this way: Human beings in the pure waiting mode may beat out moments of passing time; One, one, one . . . , perhaps guided from within by their heartbeat. If they can count, they can sum the beats as they go: one, two, three. The naming system allows for the generation of indefinitely many names: *ten*, *elev*en (etymology: one left over [after ten]), *twel*ve, *thir*teen (three-ten), *four*teen, . . . *twen*ty (two tens), twenty-one, -two, -three, and so on. Each last number counted gives the how-many-eth beat, thus it bears in it the memory of all the foregone beats. Strictly speaking this has nothing to do with time, this keeping the beat and naming the count. Yet it brings about a *sense* of time: mobile-less passage, a motion without a movable thing but with regular, arbitrary divisions, elements that are both, ever and always the same *and* meaning-bearing; ever-diverse accumulating memories summed up in a denotable but insubstantial last, itself as insignificant as was each mere beat. In fact, remove all the interesting, purely arithmetical features of numbers, and turn the whole series from cardinal into ordinal, so that it accounts for *nothing but* sequence: first, second, third, fourth; then whatever the value connotation of ordinal placement might be in human contexts,* it is not evident in the beat accumulation—and yet it

> Example: being John Smith III is a little grander than J. S. II, though sometimes J. S. I is the grandest—the founder.

is its bearer.

Then there's the calendar, which combines the natural, re-entrant cycles—[minute], hour, day, [week], month, year.*

> Hour and year: the same derivation as Greek *hora*, "season"; day: one rotation of the earth; month: one completion of the moon's phases; minute and week are conventions.

Finally, the clock, ordinarily used in two modes: *analogue*, when the dial mirrors the earth's equatorial plane geometrically or the moving heavens Ptolemaically,* while the hands

> A witty colleague, asked why he preferred his analogue watch: "Because it shows time as 'the moving image of eternity'" (a reference of Plato's *Timaeus* 37d, see Essay 31, "Where, Then, Is Time?"). A witty friend, to the same question: "Because I don't want to know only what time it is, but also what time it isn't."

show the local hours, minutes, and seconds, and *digital*, when the same units are ticked off numerically. In all these accounting devices time shows itself as a division-demanding continuum, in accordance with its etymology.*

> "Time" is, as I've said, related to the Greek verb *daiesthai*, "to divide."

VI. This, then, is the runway from which and onto which the time leaps take place. Among the poets, Homer is a great flashback artist. Herodotus, his conscious rival for gaining a rapt audience,* outmatches him, I think. That is because in

> Herodotus gave live recitals of his *History* in Athens.

the art of fiction, though background adds, besides the suspense of a deliberate slowdown before a climax,* the charm

> Example: The two sons of goddesses, Achilles and Aeneas, meet on the field (*Iliad* XX). This promises to be the fight of fights, between the hero before Troy and (Homer didn't actually know this, of course) the founder of Rome. It is an aborted event, though it starts terrifically. But before its non-occurrence, time stands still while Aeneas recites his lineage over eight generations, and its glories. Why? To give gravity, I suppose, to his divinely directed sur-

vival, perhaps to insert a stillness before the wild event, perhaps to show the heroes as equal, as both descended from Zeus—none of it strictly necessary. But that is the soul of epic poetry: strict necessity yielding to fulfilling circumstantiality.

of subtly implied complexity, such diversions are often discretionary embellishments, while in the expositions of inquiry they are mostly required techniques, as I'll claim when I speak of causality below. Some Homeric leaps into the past are, it seems to me, largely enhancements of the poem's background; all Herodotean bounces are explanations of the *History*'s present.*

Once Homer looks into the future to explain the historical destruction of Agamemnon's Mycenae by Hera's handing the city over to Zeus's discretion (IV 52), an eerie temporal transgression.

While the time loops that lead Herodotus up to his glorious Persian Wars keep him close to his rival, Homer, they distinguish him from his successor, the historian of the catastrophic consequent Peloponnesian War, Thucydides, who is not given to flashbacks. The reason is that he is an annalistic reporter, a chronicler of successive years; his work could be called "The Annals of Campaigns and Their Politics." His explanatory interruptions of the temporal flow tend to be speeches, which are not transcripts but compositions making "the speakers say what was, in my opinion, demanded of them by the various occasions" (I 22). Herodotus and Thucydides are strikingly opposite in their interest in the past, their notion of what we call history. This antithesis seems to me well encapsulated in the former's more unloosed and the latter's more constrained treatment of time.*

One invigorating element in the study of the ancients is the opportunely antithetical pairings they seem to fall into; for example: Heraclitus/Parmenides—tension/unity, Herodotus/Thucydides—wonders/facts, Plato/Aristotle—idea/reality.

The one-lane timeway along with its more sightly byways, is unidirectional and runs through many "unsightly" areas,

like residential districts that are ordinary in their peaceableness or dreary in their utilitarianism—just as an American
highway that passes through residential and commercial
areas. By "unsightly" I mean that there's no return in looking,
you just make it through. That is how historians mostly deal
with every-dailiness: They subvert it.

Here is what I mean by such dailiness: Today three hundred
and near-thirty million plus people got up, mostly brushed
their teeth, scarfed up something, swooped up their stuff and
went to kindergarten, workshop, or office. There, especially
in the last, they daydream, authors of their own novels; then
they go home and to bed to be visited by nether muses bringing nightdreams made from their own lives—by visitors from
realms unknown, but not by themselves, who have neither the
talent nor the art. Nor by historians whose very profession
precludes the purview that would bring dailiness into their
sight.

So it's real life taking place, but it's not historian's history,*

> And God help us when it becomes sociology, the most politicizable
> of disciplines. Better by far anthropology, the study of humanity
> in its earthly setting. Until fairly recently, anthropology was what
> was done to—now recalcitrant—primitive outlanders (who proved
> to be hellishly complicated). Then the profession panicked because
> it was running out of "first contact" people, the crème de la crème
> of subjects, and turned to the people, in Greek, "the *anthropoi*,"
> back home (who were quite strange enough).
>
> One way to describe Herodotus's charm is that he really is an
> anthropologist, enchanted by the various ways of human life.

except for the first man to mount an inquiry into *both* ethnic
schematisms* and human variation.

> Actually, Herodotus was preceded in such typologies by Homer,
> except that the latter's tribes are imaginatively transmuted:
> Lotus-eaters, Cyclopses, Phaeacians, etc.: druggies, primitives,
> artists.

But even the most humanly engaged of historians can't
write out a continuum like linear time. So the chronological,

the straight time-account, of the past will, perforce, consist mostly of empty, unwritable time; thus a poet speaks of "the short and simple annals of the poor."* Here it's hard not to

> Thomas Gray, "Elegy Written in a Country Churchyard," l. 33—a poem that appeals to my populist but not my poetic sensibilities. Here's a personal confession. "Our time" is very much my own time—its populism, as a high regard for the "common" in its dual meaning from universal humanity to vulgar ordinariness: public permissiveness and private prejudice; intended eccentricity and achieved conformity; leaving each other be and righteous messing with minds. All that has its appeal as my private predilection—as social movements not so much.

conflate "unknown" with "uninteresting"; the missing time left nothing behind, so one assumes nothing happened.* But

> What used to be known as the "Dark Ages" was the victim of this fusion until research showed otherwise.

Gray's poem shows that all that matters humanly happened within and was done by his plowman, "inglorious" only in the sense of being without his Herodotus. And so it is now. Not that we are without annals, and not so short or simple either, of the poor, but that these seem to me, at least, to lack the Herodotean typological talent: they conceptualize rather than envision.

VII. But back to the underlying linear flow, both smooth and inexorable, emollient and irresistible: Truth is, we never actually experience the steady flux as flowing at an even tempo, except through the abstraction worked in us by emptying ourselves of all other experience or by attending closely to instruments of chronology, natural or artificial, heartbeat or clock.*

> If this residual steady flux is finally the work of the counting soul, as Aristotle says (*Physics* IV 14), one might say that a clicking clock is an external soul surrogate.

What we do experience are *congestions* of time when the

throng of events in fact overlays the sense of time. Then no *time* often seems to have passed during the experience while a long *time content* has dilated memory in a short clocked span. Happenings thicken and experience densifies, while time is occulted and its flow seeps away. The occasions might be personal: the soul being at work in the right way (Aristotle, *Nicomachean Ethics* I 7, my paraphrase for his understanding of happiness), the heart being engaged in a reciprocal affair. Or it might be public: performances, celebrations.* Of course,

Performances: say of music by students I know. Amusements: used to be time-without-end miseries, like cocktail parties: now I know ways out—be absent.

so-called "emergencies," catastrophes that emerge out of nowhere, are the negative time condensers.* Their time-revealing

Greek has the word *chronos* for the straight-running time continuum and *kairos* for critical condensed moments, though the term is mostly positive: opportunity.

counterpart is the above-mentioned panic-gripped waiting that drives all but bare passage out of the mind; even the imagination is too stricken to produce more than one fixed image—of the worst.

Besides these large-scale eventuations, there are small-scale discontinuities of the temporal continuum, the seasonings of the life-diet: the prospects of pleasure that give dull days an edge of expectancy or the spots of annoyance that arouse complacency to moral and practical ingenuity.

I think that these concretions of time are the occasions, the markers and termini for temporal bouncing; they are its landings.

VIII. Whence does a time-bouncer take off? From a present. In any narration there are, it seems, *three* distinguishable presents.

1. One is the present to which the story has just then come for me—the reader's now. Say I'm reading William Prescott's *History of the Conquest of Mexico*.* The year is 1519. Cortés

1843. To me Prescott is to Herodotus as Milton is to Homer—both late discovered and—almost—equally admired. (See Essay 7, "The Empires of the Sun.")

has just discovered that one of the slaves given him by a local chief, a woman who later became his secretary, mistress, and mother of a highly honored son, was a competent translator of the Mexican tongue. At this moment Prescott halts my reading to outline in brief the life of this woman, Malinche, going both into her lowly past and her illustrious future. This is the time bounce, a "time-out" in *my* narrative presence, my present as a participant in the story, the *reader's* present.

2. A second such present, *in medias res*, is the present of the author, where the narrator finds himself just then, just now in the story. It is, of course, the same chronological present as the reader's, but the consciousness is very different; the reader is between known and unknown while the author is in the midst of a project presumably already sketched out. He knows that Cortés will conquer Tenochtitlan-Mexico City with Malinche-Marina at his side. He knows of the great emperor Montezuma, whose death is the occasion of another time-out, a retrospective encomium for a complex and troubled man. He knows of the consequent *noche triste* when the Spaniards were driven out of Mexico City, and of its reconquest and dreadful sacking (1521). That's the *author's* present.

3. This is where the narrative essentially ends—in a kind of *nunc stans*, a "standing now" or a permanent present, the tragic low point after which the world's most beautiful city in a short span loses its simple Aztec brilliance to elaborate Spanish baroque. That is the third, the memory-dominating present. Thereafter Prescott's *History* turns into the mode of

the sequel of subsequence—Cortés's afterlife. That's the completion of the eventuation, the *work's* presentation.

So a time bounce begins when the historian thinks that his and the reader's present situation and the ever-present denouement call for a backstory.* The springboard is one of

> It's somewhat different for the novelist, whose management of the base narrative is not, as is the historian's, constrained by facts discovered from research and controlled by selectivity geared to clarity. The author of fiction conceives the story from its very beginning for telling, so that backstories are introduced for novelistic effect.
>
> For example, Ann Patchett's enchanting *Bel Canto* (2001) has a very explicit flashback on page 4. The main action, the miscarried takeover of a party by a bunch of quite human terrorists of the house of the vice-president of a small, Peru-like country in South America, takes place in 1993. The attraction of the party is a lyric soprano, whom Katsumi Hosokawa, a Japanese business tycoon, would go anywhere to hear. We learn in the flashback that he discovered opera at age eleven (he's now fifty-three). And, though he's now the hardest-working Japanese of any, he believes (as I do) that "true life was something that was stored in music." Since the long following siege is under the dominance of Roxane Coss's *bel canto*, the long early flashback serves a necessary narrative purpose, to drive on the housebound tragicomedy that has a very spare explanatory backdrop: when we've learned of Mr. Hosokawa's childhood epiphany we've got all the deep backstory we need.

the several discernible presents of a story.

IX. Where does it land? Where the author discerns a subsidiary beginning. The discernment of beginnings is, I think, the historian's true expertise.* It requires, to be sure, information

> As well as the novelist's first art and the philosopher's deepest insight: "Then let us try to take thoroughly good care in positing the beginning," says Socrates (*Philebus* 23b). As is his mode, it is uttered as a throwaway, but it's all-important: What's the true *arche*, "the beginning or ruling principle" of this event?

(that essentially superficial cognition of inherently dull mere so-ness), but what it really takes, more deeply, is judgment.

For example, on November 19, 1863, these words were uttered
at Gettysburg:

> Four score and seven years ago, our fathers brought forth on this
> continent, a new nation, conceived in Liberty, and dedicated to
> the proposition that all men are created equal.

Do your math; the leap is back to 1776. Thus the birth cer-
tificate of the nation engendered on the maternal land by
the founding fathers is the Declaration of Independence, as
is confirmed by the quotation from the document that ends
the sentence: "that all men are created equal." 1776 is a date
the more fraught for *not* being named, although it is *implied*,
being the year of the Revolution. Lincoln is referring the birth
of the nation to the Declaration rather than, as did others, to
the Constitution, adopted in 1787. Apply some civic imagination, and Lincoln's depth will appear: America was born
devoted to inalienable human rights belonging to its people through their creation by God rather than by amendable
civil rights granted them by a legal instrument. So this leap
over nearly a century chooses a landing, a beginning, that
grounds us in God and Nature rather than in human convention. I think that whatever beliefs we may confess to before
our inner court of conviction, the attachment to our country
under the first description has the grander format.*

> The Gettysburg Address ends with a balancing bounce into the
> future: Our government (here's the Constitution after all) "will not
> perish from the earth"—it began at a date certain but will survive
> indefinitely. That, one might say, defines a successful Founding:
> July 2, 1776–. This dash is the one with which the dates of the yet
> living are listed in dictionaries. Their death is at a date uncertain;
> for the immortals among them, be they people or institutions, it is
> not within sight.

Lincoln's was a primary landing, but in thought, in language, and so in grammar, secondary time destinations are
more frequent. Here is an example, a dreaded possibility: By
the time my much nudged senior essay advisee will have dis-

gorged a draft, the due date will have passed (future perfect). Here I leap in imagination to worse—to the young nudnik who will have been essayless as the midnight bell of celebration rings and will appear next morning at my door with an outline. Or (past perfect) I daydream my way back into childhood to the day I had stolen money from my mother's purse and provided myself with my soul's longing, the miniature Silver Shadow (Rolls Royce) on display at the local kiosk. I was, of course, caught, and my world collapsed. And then I bounced, once more, further back by yet another day, the (pluperfect— more than perfect) when I had had my last day of innocence. My main point here is that it takes memory, be it internal (got by reminiscence) or external (got by research), and really purposeful imagination, to find the landing place and to develop the disposition to dwell in the past or the future so found, and to go backward or forward, after having once landed, to the time before or the time after the time of such landing. These secondary leaps make a lot of sense: If the landings come down on significant moments, then the same explanatory impulse that looked for remote reasons, will also carry us on, into the reasons for the reasons.*

There is a conventional universal pluperfect introduced by our division of all historical time into B.C. (before Christ) and A.D. (*anno Domini*, "in the year of our Lord"). Two little notes to show how inconsequential fungible factual dates can be: 1. Just as Independence was declared not on July 4, but July 2, so Jesus was not born in 1 A.D. but 4 B.C. 2. Instead of B.C., the accepted era is now B.C.E., "Before the Common Era." Just as "secretary" is a greater title than the now obligatory "administrative assistant" (for example, Secretary of State), so "before Christ" is less oppressive than the crypto-Christian "Common Era." Why "common"? Whenever the tin-eared, meaning-proof language rectifiers prevail, there's a little shift downwards. (The same for movement title-devisers: How did an attempt to empower women get to be called "Me too," an expression of followership?) Anyhow, "B.C." is the era, the time, of the *Old*, the *Hebrew Bible*—to Christians the explanatory text, the backstory, for the eventuation of "A.D.," the time of the *New Testament*. My point is: The displaced designations had discernible

meanings that you could accept or reject; the new ones have the
vagueness that is characteristic of the iron fist in the velvet glove.

X. "Before" and "after" are, each of them, in turn, temporal,
spatial, and sequential prepositions, and even, ambiguously,
all of them at once.* How does that work? Time becomes most

> Temporal: devils speaking to Jesus, "Art thou come hither to tor-
> ment us before the time?" (Matthew 8:29); spatial: soldiers mock-
> ing him, "They bowed the knee before him" (Matthew 27:29);
> sequential: Jesus to disciples, "If any man will come after me . . ."
> (Matthew 16:24); ambiguous: to John the Baptist who "shall pre-
> pare the way before [Jesus]" (Mark 1:2).

concretely apprehensible as a measure of motion. The mea-
sured motion is that of a mobile, a movable object pursuing
a path through space, and its measuring device is the same: a
mobile moving through space, but one that is trusted to move
regularly.* Since time is merely one capacity of spatial distance,

> Thus, watch a car go from here to there while looking at the hand
> moving over the numbered dial of a watch face; the number you
> read at any point on the car's path is the time of the motion, and
> it is time simply as well. This understanding of time as *nothing but*
> the measure of motion is adapted from Aristotle's *Physics* IV 11.
>   This watch is an analogue device; its hands are the mobiles,
> whose motion is cyclical and reentrant; it is, among other things, a
> miniature model of the earth's diurnal revolution.
>   Aristotle regards the soul as the primary counter of time. Digi-
> tal watches produce a steady and numerable beat, analogous, as I
> said above, to the soul. What makes the perennial world's motion
> countable is a system of symbolization which easily generates a
> unique, new name for every beat; thus the last count memorializes
> all of the preceding ones, again as I said above.

that of countability by reason of being divisible into equal
units of length, it makes every sense that the same prepositions should govern time and space. Time bounces can land in
the same *space* from which they took off (though it's apt to be
a different *place*).* Or they can travel far in space as they leap

> Place being a containing environment, space a mere location.
> Space is uniform, place variable in space and over time. Thus in
> "time-warp" fantasies, of which there are multitudes, people go to

sleep in hermetic rooms or board time machines or are teletrans-
ported into the past and future. Usually they end up in the same
location but in a different place, their hometown a hundred years
before or after.

long in time, both all but instantaneously.

Since worldly time is insubstantial, a mere measure of motion, while space is real—and place even realer—the visual
laminations of imaginative memory, which produce the real,
the internal time, and which guide time leaps, will be more
topological (*topos*, "place") than chronological (*chronos*,
"time"); a great historian will paint from that treasure of
time-ordering visualizations convincing places, including the
frames of mind that imbue them.* There seems to me to be a

> The grandest such time leap of which I know, scandalous and deli-
> cious, is Edward Gibbon's insertion of a chapter on the rise of
> Christianity in his *Decline and Fall of the Roman Empire* (1788),
> a book conceived among the ruins of ancient Rome. This chap-
> ter (XV) reaches back, as it must, beyond the advent of Christians
> to the preceding Jews. Gibbon is an equal-opportunity despiser
> of religion, and his portrait of the Jews has nothing of latter-day
> racial antisemitism about it. It is, rather, about Judaism as a rela-
> tion to God and mankind, and it bristles with admiring distaste:
> ". . . when the tides of the ocean and the course of the planets were
> suspended for the convenience of the Israelites, . . . they perpet-
> ually relapsed into rebellion against the visible majesty of their
> Divine King . . ."—a very recognizable picture of a stubbornly
> unsubjugatable spirit, the explanatory backdrop for the fact that
> a truculent and ethnocentric people had, as if in atonement,
> spawned a soft-tempered and universalist faith, Christianity.

serious problem showing up in this way of thinking about
time loops: How can history, kept basically on track by the
numerically advancing chronology of dates, be explanatory of
anything, when the disruption of the linear flux by loops and
bounces, and thus its cancellation of time as a linear ordering
principle, is a necessity of its sense-making narrative?

XI. Here I am, at the crux: causation. What kind of causality is it that jump-starts temporal causation, that finds the
moment whence explanation originates? Time is empty, but

the world's flux is full, full of mud and murk when slow, flash-flooded and boulder-strewn when fast. What are the discernible discontinuities? Well, there are the life-changing natural catastrophes: eruptions, quakes, tsunamis, droughts—and some serendipity-prone prosperities.

But, I think, the chief discontinuities are due to human "spontaneity," to human free will. "Free" means outwardly unpredictable,* inwardly reason-bound. "Will" means readiness

> Except sometimes by those fellow humans who are equally engaged in thinking things through. I mean by "reason-bound" not "thoughtlessly rational" but "mindfully reasonable."
>
> It's possible—the enigma of character—to be free, that is, thoughtful, but not to have the will, that is, the executive impulse, to act. Of course, sometimes not-doing *is* the action.

to execute.

Is individual spontaneity clubbable, sociable enough for membership in a "movement"? Is a self-organizing tendency, a trending of human beings in the thinking mode thinkable? Only, it seems, if "movement" misdescribes it; call it instead a political party, or an organization, or, best, a community— to *that* a human being with free will* can attach herself as a

> Which in the great tradition, for example, in Thomas Aquinas's treatment, consists of a time-extended sequence: thinking, deciding, doing—not the "movement" mode, which is impulsive and more given to exhibiting righteousness by "demonstrating," "standing in the corners of the street" (Matthew 6:5) rather than entering into the closet and shutting the door to pray in secret (6:6), as I said. Lately it's been called "virtue-signalling."

member—and, of course, to certain fellow humans.

Movements, conglomerations of people, sweep free will away, and its constituents tend to be flabbily robotic (both soft and stiff), while persons, in-dividuals, the least, the undividable elements of humanity are recalcitrantly unprogrammable—as I think. If it's true, then eventuation, the coming about of a discernible event, becomes severely problematic: Was it determined by a "what," a crowd, or a "who," a human being? Otherwise put: Was the essential unpredictability of the happening the result of human unfreedom (its fixed but indiscernible necessity) or of human freedom (its unfettered, thus elusive, spontaneity)?—For that the future is unpredictable seems to me a fact—in fact, a fact of life: "There is no prophet of what's ordained for mortals."*

Sophocles, *Antigone* 1160. Yet, I hasten to add, that's no reason to stop trying to shape it. A colleague of my early days, an archaeologist, though he was, as then was I, professionally invested in the past, used to cite the wisdom of (I think it was) an economist: "Prediction is always difficult, especially of the future." My colleague meant: What will we find digging down? He might have emended: ". . . especially of the past." Any reader of revisionist history knows that: The past is unpredictable as well; the goodies of the ages are exposed and the baddies redeemed, and vice versa, every decade. And in a dig, no one except the director knows for sure what will come up.

A global proof of unpredictability: the twenty-first century was going to initiate the millennium of millennia. Looks more like much of a muchness, only a little more.

Causality, causation, cause—I find this trio* helpful in

Though my uses are not really supported by my dictionary (the *American Heritage*).

thinking about causes in history. Causality is the general notion, the meaning of being a cause; besides saying, unhelpfully, that it's whatever follows the conjunction "because," I leave causality aside as too deep for this essay, or perhaps too iffy: I'm not sure that everything that eventuates has à—temporal—cause.

Causation pertains to the modes in which causality appears; examples are the two just mentioned, individual decision and crowd tendency. Add natural and circumstantial necessity. *Causes* are the specification of causation, particular examples.

Here's a question about causes: I asked my freshmen, who'd just read Herodotus's account of the battle at Thermopylae (VII 201 ff.), what we would look like and be doing if two-hundred and ninety-eight Spartans had not died to prevent or at least slow down King Xerxes' march to the south. I was thinking: Would we women be veiled, wearing something like the hijab, would we be reading a Persian Herodotus, would there be liberal education? The response was skimpy; they probably thought it was a fatuous demand on their fantasy: "We" wouldn't be us. Anyhow, it made me think again: Is causation perennial or does it fade out?* How is the chain

Although it is a fantastic notion that an identifiable "we" might exist if the Persians had, as Xerxes planned, conquered the known world (VII 18), still there would be people here. Might they be immigrants from a Persian-dominated Europe (or Asia), and thus perhaps worshippers rather than masters of nature? Would they be subjects of an—often lenient—political absolutism; would they have the technology and democracy we live with?

The historians with the longest range and greatest scope are those dealing with the development of living beings, the evolutionists. For them causation is everlasting. One may read, for instance, that modern mothers are lovingly solicitous of their young because our arboreal primate ancestors had to worry about babies falling out of trees. I don't get it: If that ape mother protected its baby just because it was her child, why wouldn't a latter-day human be solicitously maternal just because she was a mother?

modified when there occurs a time loop not in history the account, but in History the Event? Is a *renovatio*, revival, renascence (such as *the* Renaissance), a disruption in the causal chain to return to a previous link or a likely progression, or, perhaps, a dual happening in which past and present are interpenetrative rather than sequential? Are singularities, symbolized in graphs as points of inflection, where conditions flip their mode of trending, or cusps when things come to a catastrophic or cathartic climax—are these discontinuities or realizations of causation?*

For example, was the Second World War, my war, a forfendable disaster or a necessary clearing out? Or is so long a view, which historians of the next century are bound to take, even humanly permissible so soon?

And ever and always: Is individual human action mostly an expression of antic license (willfulness) or disciplined thoughtfulness (will)? Is concerted human behavior mostly an expression of a common sheep nature* or of a common spirit?

> Sheep nature: say, a *Zeitgeist* acting in each and all of us or in some leader while we contribute biddable stupidity. Here's my opinion: first souls, then society; souls are substances, hence primary; society is a set of relationships, hence secondary. If it seems the other way around—that society determines us—it's because smart (meant derogatorily) people love to animate abstractions, which, being inventions, are grander to opine about than mere human singularities and more amenable to quantification than obstinate human ultimacies. What could be a more knock-down, drag-out argument than numbers? 77.8% of us believe in God, but only 21.4% of us attend services. The intervening 56.4.% go in, each for his/her own style of "spirituality." So that's supposed to be society, a venue of "life styles." Sensible people don't credit such computed exactitudes; they want the artless backstory.

To summarize a null result: How one occurrence, one event, makes another happen seems to me a many-faceted and ultimate perplexity: How do we discern an *event*, a "coming-out," an occurrence, a happening? Are causes in their essence discernible phenomena or invisible pseudo-connections* or

> See Hume, *An Enquiry Concerning Human Understanding* VII 1. Can we, in the case of human causation, find plausible Hume's substitute for the rejected "necessary connection," namely "constant conjunction" (VII 1), since human actions are not, in my experience, ever completely constant, that is, identical?

ideal powers? How do we frame the cause? Clytemnestra killed Agamemnon, no doubt. Was the cause of his death an axe wielded by the killer, or an assassination by a disloyal queen, or the revenge of a two-timed wife, or the family payback for ancient wrongs, or a punishment exacted for a recent child sacrifice? Was the agent a handy tool, an adulterous usurper, an insulted consort, a fated avenger of an old Atreid outrage or the executioner of a child-killer? (Aeschylus, *Agamemnon*.) Is the agent always responsible? Is Oedipus to be blamed for his patricide,* his incest, his incestuous

He himself finally disclaims responsibility (Sophocles, *Oedipus at Colonus* 960 ff.; see Essay 20, "Athens").

procreations?

And once again, is there a law of the conservation of causality through time in the following sense? It seems to me indubitable that a founding story, be it a bedroom tale (the kind the French call a *histoire*) in Sardis, Lydia, such as was thought to explain the origin of Croesus's dynasty (Herodotus, *History* I 7 ff.), or a Constitution framed by a solemn convention in Philadelphia, Pennsylvania, which legitimates the first as well as the forty-fifth in the line of presidents, is certainly causal, each acting as an instituting account, but in different modes of causation.

So by what sort of action? Do causes produce effects day *to* day and year *to* year or day *through* day and year *through* year? I mean: Once an effect has been caused, is it now *itself* a new sufficient cause or does the same old cause need again to work over all the following happenings? Suppose my genetic make-up really determined my conduct,* and that of my

Without disrespect to my excellent, even venerable, lineage—Ben Rabbi Akiba Nachman Nemowitzer—not if I can help it.

(non-existent) progeny, and so on and on: Is each generation a new or an old, perhaps incrementally modified, cause? Or if I had free will (which I think I do and thereby call it forth), then am I a—somewhat—originary, that is, spontaneous, element in the temporal chain, hence a disrupter of causation?

XII. Here is a little special attention to the real time of our life: the present. Rationally defined, it is an infinitesimal of time, the one unextended temporal phase: a point, dividing—

or connecting—the past pushing from behind and the future fleeing away up front.* Historically, it is a viewpoint, that of

> Or alternatively, the past loosing itself in a receding rear and the future impending on a present position. These metaphors are culturally determined; the Andean Aymara construe the future as coming up on them from behind. (See Essay 31, "Where, Then, Is Time?")

the inquirer, from which the beginning of the past is chosen and flashbacks are inserted into the past.* Journalistically, the

> Of course, a whole history (that is, an inquiry) can be regarded as a flashback, insofar as its findings are intended to be brought to bear on the historian's present. That raises the engrossing question whether, when "a history" has been read, and the reader leaps back into the author's present, that is still the same present, not because time has passed in reading the flashback but because, returning from the time loop, the present really has changed, where it counts—in the reader's consciousness. You might call that the psychological Rip Van Winkle effect. Washington Irving's Rip goes into a twenty years' hibernation as a subject of King George III and wakes up as an actual citizen of the United States, but not as a participant in the Revolution. Hence he's neither a truly insurgent subject nor a truly actual citizen. For if history is largely memory, what changes memory changes the past—all the past we have, and if the past is changed, so is the present, at least under the hypothesis under which the historian worked, that the past explains the present.
>
> Here is a counterargument: It is a curious, humbling fact that things outlast people. A nasty, charred cooking pot has a mite more eternity than a spruce, smooth youth. So there are always surviving witnesses, from scullery sweepings to great structures; the latter give their name to Nietzsche's "monumental history." Thus, since artifacts are surely embodiments of human consciousness, history can be produced even when memory, be it oral or written, is disrupted. That's the task of archaeology.
>
> So then is the past irretrievably fixed, as something in us believes with Lady Macbeth: "What's done cannot be undone"? Or is it ever-revisable and revised by forgetting and remembering, ever suppressible and revivable as says Jay Gatsby: "Can't repeat the past? . . . Why of course you can!"? Stranger yet: was what has now passed away so totally determinate even when it was still present? When a historian proposes to write history that tells it "as it really was" (von Ranke), is that asking too much of the past

that, after all, eventuates as passage? Was when? Was what? How, really?

present has passed into the past with today's deadline. Psychologically, the present, the specious, the only livable present is Janus-faced. It is the phase both of diagnosis—casting the mind into the still-relevant past to discern from its events the causes of a present condition, and of prognosis—projecting the imagination into the not-yet-emerged future, to form in the mind's eye a visual construct of things yet to be.*

> There is also bare, visionless prognosis by rational inference, usually involving number crunching. In my experience it's unrealistic. You have to visualize or somehow imagine in order to spot missed factors, unintended consequences, and, above all, human relevance.

XIII.   The future, to be perceptible at all, requires imaginative activity. From that thought it is a short way to fictions, both epic and novelistic,* which have some temporal similarities

> Epic: from *epos*, the word that tells tales; novelistic: from novel or *novella*, "new[s]," that is, fictions telling *realistic* news, as distinct, from *real* news such as is, we hope, reported in newspapers.

with our artless experience of the future. Fictions, especially fairy tales, take place in an unreal time, "time out of mind, once upon a time," which means a time specific to this tale yet indeterminable chronologically. Thus it is at once particular and vague, and that ill-assorted conjunction is acceptable because the past is inexistent, bygone, and so temporally inaccessible except by the often scrambled laminations of memory in the soul or the strata of burial in the earth.* Everyone,

> I've told this before but can't resist. In the excavations of the Athenian marketplace where I worked, excitement spread: a Neolithic deposit had been found, taking the site back some three millennia! A couple of hours later: deflation. At the bottom of the deposit a metal button bearing the legend "Army of the Hellenes." The Neolithic sherds were not *in situ*, not in their original site, not chronologically exploitable. Conclusion: Fiction is fixed; what critic would

dare literally tamper with a novel? History, however, is variable, editable by further fact—not to mention the historian's deep satisfaction in cutting-edge revisionism. Curious! Fiction demands: *Noli me tangere,* "Don't touch me." Reality solicits: "Keep working on me, hands on!"

as I think, believes that the past is linearly chronological even though many of our perceptions of it yield temporal loops, parallels, lacunae. What the past lacks in "straight-forwardness" it gains in malleability; *it's* the perfect base for fictions. Yet, on the face of it, the future should be even more so, at least for the wilder sort of invention. Except for the very iffy conjectures of futurology and the prognostications and predictions which concern the foretelling of trends and catastrophes, the future is, once again, a blank canvas to be painted over by the imagination. In other words, the perceptible future is a fiction waiting to become fact or fallacy.

If the past holds the matter of the imagination, the future has a back way to come into its imaginative own, to have its own past. It is a tense that is antisymmetrical with the pluperfect: "I had already figured this out," namely the future perfect: "Soon I will have figured this out." In order to say that, I've taken a position from which some of the future is past.*

The antisymmetry: the pluperfect (also called past perfect) is to the future perfect as the past's future is to the future's past (a-b/ b-a). All this is a bit too fungible to enthrall anyone not deep in figuring it out.

(See Section I.)

One of the greatest novels of the last century, to my taste, is Thomas Mann's *Joseph and His Brothers,* which, in one hundred and ninety-five fairly long chapters, fleshes out, backstories and all, twenty-five short chapters in Genesis. This novel begins, so to speak, in the pluperfect tense, with an extended pre-history of the human race on earth, and even, leaving terrestrial territory, transcends into heaven, for a pluperfect, a prophetic, that is, foretelling prelude—all told with verbal pomp and psychic circumstance. Some of this pluperfect time, this predictive pre-history, is framed as Joseph's own reminiscing over six hundred Babylonian years (short ones).

The affair in heaven is, however, reported, with characteristic irony, by Mann himself, God's, the Author's, author: The moralistic angels up there are not pleased by their God's benevolent involvement with sinning humans (particularly not, I imagine, with these rambunctious Israelis*), and with

Oops! Israelites.

his call on them, his recalcitrant minions, to honor these mortals. This heavenly discord takes place not in time out of mind, but in time out of time.

In short, the Joseph story itself begins "at a point of time . . . a pretty arbitrary point . . . since we've got to start somewhere and leave the rest behind." That's the "*once* upon a time," which Mann explicates thus:

What occupies us is not numerable time. It is rather its suspension [*Aufhebung*] through the mystery of the exchange of tradition with prophecy, which lends the word "once" its double sense of past and future, and thus its charge of potential present.

Thus past and future are antisymmetrical in several ways. 1) In their discernibility: the past runs back, behind us into more and more unfathomable depth;* the future runs forward,

Second sentence of the Joseph novel, on the well of the past: "*Sollte man ihn nicht unergründlich nennen?* Shouldn't one call it unfathomable?" (See Section XII.)

before us, into an ever less conjecturable blank. 2) In their contents: The past, being full, resides in memory, which supplies to the reality-based imagination its matter, some drawn from history,* most invented, but so as to abide by the requirements

When imaginative fiction gives green cards to real figures or facts, they become documented residents of the fiction and are referred to as "immigrant objects" (Terence Parsons, *Nonexistent Objects*, 1980).

of a possible reality. The future, however, being empty, is the venue of fantasy, which allows itself great latitude with respect to possibility; hence, lacking the tensions of reality, it is often mind-slackening. 3) In their tense structure: The pluperfect is a leap backwards from the occupied past that turns this past into the future; the future perfect is a leap forwards that turns the future into the past. Thus futuristic fantasy has its own "once upon a time."

XIV. A last thought about endings. They might be by solution, resolution, irresolution, dissolution. Examples are myriad.*

> Mine: *Solution*—mysteries, as a genre, end in solutions. "Who done it?" has its answer: problem done away with, solved. *Resolution*—classical novels (paradigm: Jane Austen) end in disentanglements and proper pairing; dissonance turns to consonance; tension is released, resolved. *Irresolution*—mostly contemporary short stories, but one great novelistic case, *Villette*, Charlotte Brontë's greatest, which ends in the middle of a storm, making it uncertain whether the heroine's fiancé will come home; reader hangs suspended and irresolute (to my mind a meretricious trick for enhancing a romance with a penumbra of tragedy). *Dissolution*—a story that doesn't culminate but fades out; the great exemplar, Mann's *Buddenbrooks*, subtitled "The Decline of a Family," ends in a dismal, albeit ironicized, family gathering; Hanno, the young heir, is dead and the family's bonds are dissolved; perhaps also the *Odyssey*, which fades away in a frustrated stand-off. Oddly enough, it's perfectly satisfying, because we know that Odysseus is off to one more adventure—his sloughing-off of his sea-life when he plants his oar on an island funeral mound, symbolizing his demise as a sailor (XI 121).

Now a few final observations on end-of-the-novel time leaps, for here too they show up. At solution, mysteries generally come to a full stop. Since they are about problems, not people, once the cleverly devised "mystery" has found its solution, we all go home, separately. Novels of resolution often run into the future or leap into the future-perfect: We see quondam Jane Eyre and her Edward Rochester *en famille* years later; there's even a baby; it worked out. Irresoluble plot

lines—did Paul Emanuel get home and is Lucy married?—
can have no single future perfect retrospective since the last
present of the story is indeterminate, and so the conjectur-
ally imagined future would run on at least two opposite lines
for the heroine: either wife and mother or old maid and di-
rectrix of a boarding school—who knows which is the happier ending? Neither do novels of dissolution have a bouncing
relation to either past or future; to bounce back into bygone
glories would be plain melancholy and to leap ahead would
be to set down in a no-man's land; thus eight-year-old Hanno,
in fact the last male Buddenbrook, ominously jinxes, puts
paid, to the family history by indolently picking up a pen and
carefully underscoring his name in the family portfolio with
a double line running horizontally across the whole page.
When his father has him on the carpet, slaps him, and demands furiously to know what's got into him, Hanno stam-
mers: "I thought . . . I thought . . . nothing more was coming"
(Pt. 8, Ch. 7).

Well, he's—cluelessly—clairvoyant, but why confirm it?

Annapolis, 2018

31

Where, Then, Is Time?

Not in the World

Let me first explain my odd-sounding title. It is a variation on the most famous question-and-answer about time ever posed. It comes from the eleventh book of Augustine's *Confessions*, published about 400 C.E.: This is his question: "What, then, is time?" And this is his preliminary answer: "If nobody asks me, I know; if I want to explain it to him who asks me, I don't know." But that's only the beginning. What follows is, to my mind, the deepest and most persuasive positive solution to the perplexity.

I. In modern times the most sophisticated and detailed answer is given by Edmund Husserl in his lectures on *The Phenomenology of Internal Time-Consciousness* (1928). It is essentially an elaborated version of Augustine's solution. Its title tells why I have substituted "where" for "what" in Augustine's famous question: Time is, in both works, understood primarily as an event *within* our soul (or, as it is called for the sake of scientific respectability, the *psyche*). I might say here

---

Talk at the U.S. Naval Observatory, 2015.

by way of clarification that "soul" is traditionally used for the power from which emanate all the activities of life, from sense perception through all kinds of thinking to the intuition of supra-sensory being, while "consciousness" applies only to the part of life that is aware or self-aware.

Now I hope you'll forgive me if I do some more name-dropping. It's for distinguishing a second answer to the question "Where is time," namely outside, in the world, in nature. Three great names stand for this location: Plato, Newton, and Einstein.

Plato's dialogue called *Timaeus* (circa 360 B.C.E.) is, into modern times, the classical astronomer's very own work. It provides one set of conditions under which it is plausible to make finite models of the world. That condition is that there be a *uni*-verse, a well-ordered cosmos consisting of an encompassing starry sphere, an inner array of closed, non-intersecting planetary orbits, including that of the sun, and a stable center for the human observer, the earth. Of this world it is possible to produce a moving mathematical model called an orrery. And the reason we can model the world is that it is itself the incarnation of a timeless ideal model, a mathematical paradigm for an incarnation that is the work of a divine craftsman.

Time is built into this cosmic universe by the god, who, upon having "thought of making a certain movable image of eternity," at once so ordered the heavens that they were "an eternal image going according to number, which we have given the name Time." In other words, the whole cosmos is a clock, whose starry sphere is a moving dial at night and the tip of whose hand is the planet Sun, marking out the hours of the day by its positions in the sky or by the shadows it causes the style of a sundial to cast.

Next, Newton, who states very definitively in his *Mathematical Principles of Natural Philosophy* of 1687, his *Principia*, that there is an "Absolute, true and mathematical time," an equable, independent flux, distinct from that relative time which is only the measure of some, presumably reliable, even motion.

And finally, in his introduction of special relativity, the 1905 paper "On the Electrodynamics of Moving Bodies," Einstein says boldly that for local time, the definition of time can simply be "the position of the small hand of my watch" (I, para 1). In other words, time is what the clock tells.

These three understandings of time seem certainly to place it squarely outside of consciousness, into nature, namely as the divinely made heavens themselves, or as a universal stream within them, or as a humanly made artifact, a clock.

However, the externality really only works for Einstein, for whom time, local or astronomical, is operationally defined in terms of a theory of measurement based on the postulates of relativity, a measurement by which astronomically remote clock time can be compared with local time. But even in that case it isn't clear whether time so defined is established as external or rather abolished altogether, being a mere designation for locations on an analogue dial or a digital register.

One more name here, actually the earliest to do away with time: Aristotle, in the fourth book of his *Physics* (after 335 B.C.E.), defines time as the counted number of a locomotion according to before and after. In other words, time is no visible or sensed something, such as a designated heavenly appearance or a pervasive flux, but just an activity of counting passages. And, as I said, it seems to me that Einstein's positivist, boldly practical understanding has the same effect: It's not time but stations of movement, the position of mobiles like clock hands, that is real. So if time is outside, it's just one unit of motion measuring out or counting up another motion.—What's more, counting is ultimately a psychic activity; if we didn't have the experience of counting up moments internally, we couldn't interpret a digitally displayed aggregate as time that has passed.

It's even worse with Plato's and Newton's view of time. Consider this: Some of the greatest works at the beginning of the sciences of nature are theologies. Certainly the *Timaeus* introduces a divinity, a divine artificer. But above all, so does Newton's *Principia*. He devotes its final pages to an exposition of God in Nature which ends with the words: "And thus much concerning God; to discourse of whom from the appearances of things, does certainly belong to Natural Philosophy."

In his *Optics* Newton says, moreover, that these appearances betoken an incorporeal Being "who in infinite Space, as it were in his *sensorium*, sees the things themselves intimately." He means that space is that part of God's soul in which he receives sensory impressions—presumably including primarily the temporal flux, which could, perhaps, be understood *as his stream of consciousness*!

So also does Plato in the *Timaeus* ultimately put time inside the soul, an encompassing world soul: For his divine craftsman wraps the cosmos with bands of soul-stuff, structured by musical ratios so as to impart rationality and beautifully proportioned motion to the world within. In this strange and wonderful cosmology, the soul is the cincture, the sash of the world's body.

The point I'm making is that if you ask the question: "Is time internal or external?", there appear to be some great scientists who believe the latter, but if you ask it differently: "Is time in the world or in consciousness?", the number of such believers is reduced, because they think that the world itself is comprehended, activated, by a sort of soul. And, as I said, there are those who reduce going time to the counting of passage and told time to the number pointed at on a dial (which is itself a motionless imitation of a celestial circuit) or displayed on a screen (which is a lifeless imitation of a soul seen counting). In effect, they too do away with time as a distinctive "something." It is nothing but one motion used to measure another.

II. The questions "What or where is time" now seem to need to become ultimate, to demand: "Is there time at all?" Perhaps a version of more immediate interest to you is: Is the dimension "t" really needed in formulas of physics? I have tried to read books like Barbour's *The End of Time* (2000), whose high-level arguments for the abolition of time from physics I am not competent to understand. But there is a very elementary consideration along the same lines: Diagrams in elementary kinematics tend to get loci of paths by plotting distance against time, but time itself is represented by distance, the t-axis (Galileo, *Two New Sciences*, Book IV, Th. 1). Now most objects we symbolize, we re-present in the dimension in which they actually exist, be they visual, that is spatial, or auditory or tactile. For example, the eight-sided sign that verbally says Stop, or crosses out motion with the cross-symbol X, is itself in the plane, the second dimension of space, and that, in turn, is the dimensionality of the viewing plane of our vision—for the third dimension is an experiential inference from the two-dimensional picture plane onto which sight-lines from the depths of space are projected—ultimately our retina. But when an item is not representable in its own physical dimension (because it has none), be it an idea, an angel, or infinity, we are alerted that something about it is not, so to speak, kosher. And all the images of time I know of are indeed either spatial extensions marked by selected now-points or registered counts of sensory pulses from heartbeats down to atomic periods.

And if that's the only way to get hold of time, then time has, as I said, been nullified: It's just a way of measuring something, say, life lived or ground covered, by means of the continuous motion of some uniformly moving mobile or the continual accumulation of some equably occurring events.

Are these notions a scientist needs to worry about? Well, no, the realm in which questions of Being or Nonbeing are at home is not a venue for result-oriented research. It's a place to park questions that need to be bypassed when you have

engaging and preoccupying research to do. They'll keep there
for the time when you can't help yourself because you really
want to understand the postulated conditions of science,
which cannot themselves be science.

The American psychologist William James knew as much
about the human soul as about the scientific psyche. I mentioned "Phenomenology" before, when I cited Husserl's work
on internal time. Phenomenology is the careful description of
the constitution of consciousness. I believe that James was actually the transatlantic founder of this European movement,
because I cannot think of a more acute analysis of our internal life than the one he presents in his short *Psychology*
of 1892. In the *Epilogue* to this classic he says plainly and
candidly what we all need to hear. He regards himself as a
natural scientist and takes that to involve two postulates:
1. Determinism—that all events are rigidly constrained by the
laws of nature, and 2. Atomism—that the stuff participating
in these events consists of massy elementary particles, which
are in force relations to each other. These claims applied to
psychology make it a science and the psyche a naturally constrained entity. In effect this means that our physiology determines our psychology.

Ethics, James then says, makes a counterclaim: Our wills
are free. Scientists do not concern themselves with spontaneity
and freedom. Then he goes on: "The forum where they hold
[such] discussions is metaphysics. Metaphysics means only an
unusually obstinate attempt to think clearly and consistently."
He continues: A specialized scientist's "purposes fall short of
understanding Time itself . . . and as soon as one's purpose is
the attainment of the maximum of insight into the world, the
metaphysical puzzles become the most urgent of all." There's
greatness, homegrown.

III. So let me launch into one account of time that I find both
in accord with experience and elegant in its presentation. It is

that of Augustine, with which I began. I am not quite sure if his understanding is metaphysical or theological. I've never read a great theologian about whom I was clear whether he was more metaphysician or more believer—probably each for the sake of the other: "I believe so I may understand" says Anselm in his *Proslogion* of the later eleventh century—and, though he denies it, perhaps the converse is true as well. Allow me to point out that scientists do just the same: They accept postulates on faith so that they may do research, and they do research so that they may find a truth.

If it is the case that time never makes its appearance out in the world where only motion is in evidence, then either time *is not* or it is in the only other venue of which I can think, *inside* our soul. As one of our seniors (Maxwell Dakin) put it to me when I took him to lunch: "We aren't in time, but time is in us." For Augustine time is internal psychologically but also external theologically. When physical time has been shown to lack all physical evidence and therefore to be scientifically void, it might still be theologically real.

Augustine's manuscripts contain no diagrams, as far as I know. Yet his exposition of time seems eminently diagrammable, and that's how I'll present it—to be internally imagined rather than externally projected.

Inscribe, then, in the mental field of your imagination an upright line. Make it finite in length, for it is to stand for your mortal soul, but also indefinite, for it is to represent that expansible storage, the part of the soul called the memory—and also those forward-projected images termed expectations. That is to say, points on it are moments of memory, long ago or recent, and also hopes and fears, near or far off.

Now set this perpendicular across a horizontal straight line. That line will be quite definitely finite, for it represents the world moving from the week of its creation to the last judgment and the somewhat less well-defined end-time: *Solvet saeclum in favilla*, "Secular time will dissolve into ashes," as goes the sacred text, the Dies irae of the Requiem Mass. The crossing (it would be the "origin," the zero point, if we were to think of this picture anachronistically as a diagram of Cartesian x and y axes) represents the location where we, our aware soul or consciousness, take place, so to speak; where we are actually *present in and to the ongoing* world as its participating eye-witnesses. The part of the psychic upright below the world-line represents *the past, all the memories left by the passing presents* that have been pushed down, point by memory-point, into the deeper past, way back to earliest childhood. The part of the upright above the world-line represents what we might call *"future-memory" or expectations*, our projection of images, drawn from modified memory, onto the future motions of the world. The closer to the origin, *the* present, the sooner and more likely are our predictions to come about and the more effective are our anticipatory decisions.

So far this is a plane figure, but there is also a line through the origin into the third dimension. Augustine calls this z-axis *extensio*, which means roughly "outreach." It represents the access we have to unmoving timeless realms, such as mathematics, eternal verities, and, above all, to the Divinity, whose time is the so-called "standing now" (*nunc stans*) of theology, within which our moving world is an infinitesimal interlude. "Extension" is thus our stretching toward immortality, and it has no definable extent.

The upright soul-axis, on the other hand, he calls "distention." By the z-axis we reach out beyond ourselves; by the x-axis, our consciousness, we are distended, prolonged, so to speak, within ourselves. Though we live in zero-time, within the present moment, on the cusp of now, we carry above and below this crossing of world and awareness all our past in memory and our future in expectant imagination. Though pointillistic beings in actual world-presence, we are all there in temporally ordered memory and expectation. We contain all the time there is for us individually, all our past and all our future, present within us. So I will quote Augustine's famous formulation of exclusively internal time. He says:

> Such three [past, present, future] are indeed in our soul, and elsewhere I do not see them. The present of what has gone by is memory, the present of what is present, eyewitness, the present of what is future, expectation. (XI 20)
> The future, therefore, is not a long time, for it is not, but the long future is merely a long expectation of the future. Nor is the time past a long time, for it is not, but a long time past is merely a long memory of past time. (XI 28)

In my youth I was an archaeologist, digging up the past in Greece. You astronomers are, similarly, the archaeologists of the universe, the experts of experts in pastness.—Nothing comes to your eyes but what is aeons in the past.

How then can Augustine say to us that the past that is not specifically ours as memory has passed away? Well, if I dig up, say, an Attic cooking pot, rough, undecorated, and with a blackened bottom, that pot is not past but present. The same for the stars of which you capture evidence in your observatory. What makes the pot a survival of the past, the kind called "historical evidence," is what might be called external memory. The fact that the pot was deep beneath the earth's surface, buried in strata that are analogous to the soul's memory stratification doesn't help to make it past; its thereness is still *now*. But the fact that there are written epics and histories and other transmitted memories of the "glory that was Greece," together with some common sense which tells me that they too boiled their beans—those circumstances make me infer a past beyond my own birth, a past-pot, so to speak, made 2,500 years before I was born.

I think it must be the same for you: You have ways of calculating the distance of the starry objects you focus on, and you know the traveling speed of the signals they emit, and so you calculate your way back into a past that is, in fact, over: That past is *now* for you or it is not at all. There is an argument that world time must be real because it has different configurations: The orbital times of classical Newtonian dynamics are cyclical and reversible. You can run the heavenly clock backwards without damage to the laws of nature. Also there is the so-called "arrow of time" for a thermodynamic understanding of the world as progressing, or rather deteriorating, into disorder in the absence of shots of energy. And there is the theological view I just referred to, in which the universe occupies a stretch of time inserted into an atemporal eternity with a dramatic first week and a less clear-cut, but possibly catastrophic, end. This theological time-line is countered in cosmology by the claim that time has a spectacular beginning but a fizzling end, if any. I should add here quickly that I am not pretending to understand these temporal possibilities. I just read about them. But this I do see: All these theories are actually about the measurements of motions and in them time may be a convenient symbolic dimension, but it's not a substantial being; the present alone, our *being there*, is real. It is not time that displays diverse qualities but particles of matter that obey different laws of motion. Augustine, it seems to me, saves our sense that we ourselves are temporal in the absence of any evidence that nature, the world of bodies in motion, is so.

Let me, finally, speak of a culminating clarification Augustine has accomplished. He has explained why time is naturally thought of as having three phases. The explanation is in terms of three psychic capacities: In our *memory* we store away in a time-generating order reproducible moments of the world's motions and events that have come to our attention. Those observations yield a *past* with a chronological structure. Through *sensory awareness* we live now, in an actual presence. That is our *present*, our *now*. And in our *imagination*, which is memory in its transfiguring mode, we prefigure, expectantly, in hope, fear, or resignation, things that might come to be. That's the *future*.

IV. Allow me to end with a particular preoccupation of mine. When I say that only the now is real, I may seem to claim that life in the "just now" is the life there is. The Latin word for "just now" is *modo*, from which comes our word "modernity." Living in the "just now," in expectation of the next "just now," does seem to be a primary feature of modern life with its obsession with the short term, with speed and novelty. In fact, the adverb "now" is etymologically related to "new" (Indo-European: *newo*). I'm all for making the most of our moments, but not so much insofar as they confront us with that hard-edged brash factuality, called *reality*. I have more faith in *actuality*, which I think of as bringing vibrant significance to our lives. However, that's a long story not for this essay (but see Essay 17, "The Actuality of Fictions"). So let me dwell instead for a moment on the comparative residual powers of the past and the future.

The past has passed away; we say "it was." But the verb *was* is a tensed form of *is*. For my part, I do not believe that anyone can succeed in recalling the past into the present, as a German historian (Leopold von Ranke) famously demanded of history: It should render the past "as it really, effectively had been" (*wie es wirklich* [or *eigentlich*] *gewesen ist*). That is impossible for two reasons: First, because an adequately real history would have to take account of and pass judgment on every one of the 86,400 seconds in a human day (called "specious presents," meaning lived moments), each of these psychic and physical minimals, of every dead human being as well as every resultant group activity—it would be a practically infinite task even if the material were actually accessible. And second, it seems impossible insofar as I believe that a thoughtful person coming to grips with the past will have to go schizophrenic, that is, "split-minded," in order to entertain the following, unavoidable dual persuasion: On the one hand, it is simply not determinable that there is *a* past that has really happened, because the conduct of human individuals, like the behaviors of electrons, may be terminally uncertain for an observer in a way analogous to the Uncertainty Principle of physics: The historian's observational perspective cannot help but suppress one feature of a situation in focusing on another. Or even worse: Perhaps human life is just not ultimately determinable because of our incurable inability to penetrate people's interior or, yet worse, because human beings are in themselves indeterminable, perhaps more radically than electrons.

On the other hand—and here's what splits the mind—who can avoid believing that there really was one way it had actually been in the past, that some things were the case and others not? Thus when some revisionists were arguing that the Germans had not indisputably initiated the First World War, the French statesman Clemenceau said something to this effect: "At least no one will claim that on the night of August 3, 1914, the Belgians invaded Germany."

So, all that said, whether the established past is always a tiny selection of the real past, or the real past is itself in principle uncertain, either within clear limits or with large latitude, it seems extreme to say that the past is totally not. There *is* a roughly recoverable past, especially by means of written works. And—I want to say this briefly but emphatically—the depth and coherence of the present depends on being mindful of this past. That too is a subject for a different inquiry.

So I come to my concluding expression of personal opinion. Just as it seems to me essential to coherent living to ascribe actuality to the past, so *it seems to me essential to effective action to deny it to the future:* The future is far more *not* than is the past. In fact it is a big Nothing—at least the *human* future is just a nonbeing.

I am an amateur reader of anthropology, and here's a pertinent anthropological discovery from the Andes (Rafael Núñez *et al.*, "With the Future Behind Them . . . ," *Cognitive Science* 30 [2006]). In most cultures the future is thought of as confronting us, coming toward us, existing ahead of us. In the Andes of South America there is, however, a language, Ayamaran, and its speakers for whom the future comes up from behind. These people use the Ayamaran word for "back" to refer to future events and gesture behind them to indicate its coming. This way is highly unusual, but to me it makes perfect sense. There *is* a future that is fixed from the past, that future which is predictable because past events are determinately causative. Thus having a bad drought in the summer just behind you makes a poor harvest in fall to come a practical certainty. Above all, celestial motions, which are fixed by natural law, are highly predictable; thus an *ephemeris* gives the coordinates of celestial bodies way into the future. That's a way of saying that the future is determined from behind us, since prior causes determine posterior effects—certainly in large-scale nature.

There's a huge "however." Determinists will argue that we human beings are also bits of nature and entirely determined by brain action. If we only knew the brain's condition in every detail we could entirely predict a human being's action. Never mind the practical impossibility of complete information; if we *are* altogether parts of nature, absolute prediction is *in logical principle* possible, and impracticable only in mere fact. Then there is indeed *a* future, though not one coming *at* us but one issuing *from* our circumstances, from behind.

But it is possible that we have a capacity for spontaneity of action based on liberty of choice and freedom of decision. If that is the case, then the human aspect of the future is indeed a great big Nothing until we, here and now, decide to give it the shape we choose. It may be that the antecedent causes of choice, which are trains of thought, are even more exigently binding than the laws of nature, since they are constrained by rules of reasoning and demands of truth-telling. Yet they include an ultimate element of weighing and judging that is inviolably ours. If there *is* this parallel track of free choice, then this is what those future-gurus who undertake to tell us what the future holds and sends at us, "like it or not," deserve—the ones who advise us to prepare for and adapt to these futuristic advents, even if we judge them to be bad, on pain of being overrun by them. They deserve to be told that they are trying to invade the realm of our expectations and intending to hijack our imaginations. In other words, they are attempting to curtail our freedom, and their bid to have us bow to their inevitabilities should be met with a counter-bid for them to butt out. For to the question "Where is time?" the answer is: For sure not in the future; the human future, the meaningful future, is nonexistent until we imagine it and act accordingly—and by then it's already the present.

Let me hasten to say as my final point: Our free choice, which is, as I've said, sure to be ultimately quite constrained by the demands of truth-seeking thought, has at least an *initial* moment of spontaneity, when we choose to focus our attention on a subject and commit ourselves to thinking it through—on *its* terms. This spontaneity, this freedom, seems to me to be anchored in two, somewhat iffy, facts. One is the powerful, personal experience of being *my*self, my own mistress, *unavoidably* in charge.* The other is the powerful public

Meaning that not to be free is a dereliction of duty.

sense of not belonging entirely to myself but of *willingly* surrendering* part of me to my community—and that this is a

Meaning that the abrogation of my will is my free choice.

particularly telling practice of freedom.

32

Studying the Imagination
Musing Introspection

This is my fourth or fifth visit to the University of Dallas, and I cannot think of a university I'd rather revisit. So I must warmly thank the Braniff Graduate Student Association for inviting me, especially to an occasion on a subject close to my heart.

Similarly, I cannot think of a more interesting constituent of our being than the imagination—initially engaging, terminally mystifying, and in between full of thought-inducing perplexities. It might even be that this is itself a primary puzzle: what it means to think about one capacity or faculty of the soul with another, or, more particularly, to try to apprehend what is, to be sure, not an a-rational element but equally surely a partly non-rational one, with the resources of thinking, which is surely in essence rational, meaning logic-constrained and word-reliant.

Since most of you are students, you presumably study, and since you are graduate students you probably think of study as including a lot of so-called secondary literature—second-

For the Graduate Students, University of Dallas, 2018.

ary meaning both derivative from, parasitic upon, primary texts and not so prime in itself.

I'm thinking of the choice of my lecture title, "Studying the Imagination," as giving myself a brief to dispense unasked-for advice. So here's the first bit: Don't do it. Don't approach this magnificent ability that preempts divinity by making worlds galore and confounds the devil by snatching truth from the teeth of deceit—don't first come to this inquiry by reading articles, or indeed by study at all.

So it's: always one more primary text rather than yet another secondary article, always one more experience rather than yet another study. There are, I hasten to add, exceptions. Your own Professor Sepper has written a truly fundamental book on the imagination, aptly entitled *Understanding the Imagination* and subtitled *The Reason of Images*. Thus the work is concerned with the very problem of image study I mentioned, namely how we can capture the imagination in understanding, that is, by thinking. It suggests one enabling hypothesis, that the imagination's images are actively imbued with reason. It has other excellences. The book actually asks you to stop reading and start imagining. It proposes a theory of imagining that involves playing with the appearances of one field of inquiry and projecting their possibilities upon another, a version of the imagination as a sort of dual vision that I embrace.

In order not to leave this formal description imaginatively empty, let me give one, my, version of it. Linger over a sentence of the *Song of Songs*; here is an abbreviated rendering of the man singing:

Thou . . . art comely as Jerusalem (6:4).

It is the poetic figure called a "simile," a likeness. I think actualizing the verbal claim means making an imaginative projection of the holy city's cherished appearance upon, behind, around the beloved woman, a projection that activates her specific appeal by setting her in a longed-for venue, placing her before a well-loved background, and enveloping her with an aura of desire.

But to get back to my point—such scholarly books are exceptions to my advice, which I will now put in an even more antinomian way: First write your thesis, then stick in oodles of references.

So begin instead of study with introspection. I've read the arguments that mean to skewer claims for looking within. They seem to me hard-hitting, but with a double-edged sword. By the same impossibility of our monitoring each other's internalities, it is also impossible to claim that we haven't got them—haven't got that psychic duality that makes *self-*consciousness possible. (So see Essay 14, "Self-Address.") After all, "self-conscious" has two meanings; one is apperception as Kant uses it, my introspective unifying awareness of all my cognitive functions; the other is the external sense of being myself critically inspected. Neither of these events is really visible, unless you admit a hermeneutic of subtle signs, an interpretational art of reading small indices.

In fact, until the discovery of mirrors, human beings rarely caught a glimpse, certainly not a sharp-edged, true-colored one, of themselves, insofar as our face is most ourself; then our condition was exactly the one implied by introspection-deniers, that others know us better than we know ourselves. I say "the discovery of mirrors" because, of course, they exist in nature. I will cite the most spectacular such self-discovery by means of a natural mirror, which I love. It comes from Milton's *Paradise Lost*. Eve has just issued from her male birth as Adam's rib. She wakes up and immediately discovers a liquid plane, a lake, that she looks into:

As I bent down to look, just opposite,
A shape within the wat'ry gleam appeared
Bending to look on me. I started back,

It started back, but pleased I soon returned,
Pleased it returned as soon with answering looks
Of sympathy and love; there I had fixed
Mine eyes till now, and pined with vain desire. (IV 460 ff.)

So her first act and affect is to fall in love with her so responsive self. And *thence*, from this self-love,* follows the whole

> Whose original model is, I think significantly, pagan Narcissus; the prelapsarian pair, or at least its female half, is pretty pagan, that is to say, all too natural, youthfully narcissistic.

sacred history of the human race, according to Milton, beginning with its ejection from the earthly paradise to its final reception into the heavenly home—Eve's *felix culpa*, her happy fault.*

> For this self-pleasing desirousness and responsive impulsiveness of Eve will later open her to Satan's temptation, and her lapse will, in turn, enter humanity on a history of salvation ending in heaven—paradise lost, heaven gained. (See Essay 24, "Eve Separate.")

I can't pretend to have defeated all arguments against the legitimacy of introspection as the beginning of this particular—and perhaps of any—philosophical inquiry. Nonetheless, my advice is to use most secondary reading only post-positively—to corroborate and elaborate what you already know, not to give you ideas, particularly since I doubt that it is either possible or good to "have" ideas, or true charity to be "given" them. We have settled thought-moments, to be sure, but though no one knows how we get them, it is a matter of experience to know that we have them, usually, because we've made a persistent effort. Perhaps we sometimes have a thought-product, an idea, but if we do, we should probably pack it away in mothballs.

Here's a second unasked-for piece of advice, crucial, I think, to any preoccupation with the imagination; this time not a "don't" but a "do." Do engage with works of the imagination, be they expressions of passion as is much lyric poetry, or narrations of mythical events ("mythical" in the sense of stories ante-dating their telling) as are epics, or narrations of new-made tales as are novels. And, of course, look at visual works like paintings and listen to works that affect the soul directly by physically embodied numbers, namely music. The reason for this injunction is obvious: How can you study analytically experiences that you haven't integrally experienced?

Let me be particular by connecting the two bits of advice: "Don't begin by reading up but by self-observation" and "Do begin with taking in works of the imagination, and not scholarly articles," and I'll add, "Don't do it as a dull duty but as a labor of love." The first thing you'll discover—not be told but experience, as does Eve in that supreme work of the theological imagination, *Paradise Lost*—might be that there are external images as well as internal ones. What's an example of an internal image? Well, the vision of herself as an aboriginal, non-pagan, female Narcissus—that image itself occurs to Eve in a watery mirror. Thus it is an external image, but when she tells Adam about it, it surely has become a mental image, thus internal. Moreover the incident "takes place," so to speak, in an English epic. "Epic" is a term from the Greek adjective *epikos*, pertaining to *epos*, "word." Epic is the poetry of many words, and the image of Eve seeing herself as a Greek myth in a fictive pond occurs in a long English poem of words, a Homer-rival. So here's a first experience of images: they can be somatic or psychic, external or internal—and their expression can be very complex.

And that is a second discovery: Images are, as we might say, intermodal. Visions turn into words, words into sights. The *Iliad* offers the first, unsurpassable example: Hephaestus's replacement for Achilles' armor that Hector has stripped from dead Patroclus, whom Achilles had sent into battle as his surrogate. Recall that Patroclus, the mildest, least self-assertive man before Troy, being encased in Achilles' armor, morphs, in a sort of ecstasy, into an Achilles-replica that displays a fatal Achillean aggression.

Achilles' new shield, a work of what scholars call "iconic poetry," is a magical artifact. It is round and around its rim flows—actually *flows*—Ocean, the river that bounds the world. Within it is depicted—this picture is a movie—the world that is carrying on while the Achaeans are locked in a stand-off before Troy. It is the ultimate visually specific artifact, with this small additional feature: it is a work of words. So words can image sights, visions can be verbalized.

The shield of Achilles takes Homer 910 words to depict, as I figure it (Book XVIII, lines 478–608 at seven words a line). But then think of the number of people who've read the *Iliad* and envisioned the shield. I have no idea what the number is, but say a million through the last 2700 years, and there'll be that many mental images from this less-than-a-thousand words: One picture is worth a thousand words, to be sure, but a thousand words generate a million pictures.

As an aside: Sometimes Homer—as many true artists after him—says nothing and so speaks volumes: Achilles, searching for a point of vulnerability in the all-covering armor of Hector, finally sticks his deadly spear into him. Visualize, form a mental image; Homer is silent, but we see: It's Achilles' own armor; he's taking his own life, killing Patroclus incidentally, a hair-raising sight. Thus the "Plan" of Zeus is fulfilled. Visualization is the key to reading Homer (see Essay 15, "Tips on Reading Homer"). It's also one element in *the* outstanding question concerning what is called "mental imagery," to my mind the crux of all thinking about imagining. A first aspect of this question is: How is this eyeless seeing properly described in all its elusiveness? What would be a truly satisfying phenomenology of mental imagery? A second aspect is: What is the difference between such images as are reproduced from memory and those produced originally by the imagination? Third: How do intermodal imitations work, such as for touch the deceptive cuddliness of visually cute comfort robots, or for hearing the duck-fooling duckless quacks of duck call devices,* or for smell, the scent that is applied from a bottle but

Such as made the Duck Dynasty fortune in the TV show—gross and subtle, both.

seems to be exuded by a body?

And a fourth aspect: Is the memorial imagination unintentionally yet deceptively transformative? Is the original imagination an organ for lying fictions or a conduit for revelatory illuminations? How do we explain those images that are apparently not imitations, don't have their origin in verifiable originals or in collections of reality-bits? Do all images have, *ipso facto*, by the very fact of being *images*, originals? For example, when Homer paints word pictures of gods, should we infer, a stunning thought, that there *are* gods in some mode of actual being?

To these four sets of questions not a soul knows the answer—which to seriously philosophical spirits is not an inhibiting but an inciting fact. And then there is a fifth, of first importance, closest to us and most perplexing: How do words generate germane images and visions invest themselves in words?—when the two modes have *no* discernible similarities of structure. Again, nobody knows.

That brings me to my third and last preachment. My first two said: Primarily, attend to internal and external experience. Now the complement, which says: Be uncompromisingly ontological. First and last, before even going into mental imagery, attend to an account of the *being* of images, their features insofar as they justify approaching the imagination with the intellect. Thus the ontological inquiry will direct you not only to the essence of images, but to that ultimate problem of thinking about imagining that I mentioned at the beginning: How do our distinct psychic capacities come to bear on each other?

Back to the shield: Just as Achilles, the Warrior Incarnate, goes into battle carrying before him the living world, *his* world, which he enlivens and endangers, and which, in turn, both protects him and is vulnerable to the piercings of hostile weapons, so the writers who have, to my mind, written most primally and originally about the imagination are fully in possession of the external world before them and the realm behind its experiential surface. Think of Plato's Socrates in the *Republic*, of Augustine in the *Confessions* and *Of the Trinity*, think of Kant in the "Schematism" of the First Critique, and of Hegel's worldly pageantry in the *Phenomenology of the Spirit*. I'm not name-dropping here, because, talking to graduate students, I know you can supply the particular matter, the way each author seizes the world and slips beneath its apperances. And even people without this know-how may take heart: Some writers, the great ones, know things.

For the ontology of images there is, I think, an indisputable prime text: Plato's *Sophist*, which my translating colleagues and I took a wicked pleasure in subtitling "The Professor of Wisdom." Its problem is not the definition of a sophist— only lexicographers get satisfaction from definitions—but the delineation of the essence of sophistry as embodied in a practitioner. On the face of it the dialogue seems to be an exercise in the only "method" of which Socrates can be said to be guilty: the so-called "method of division and collection." This method, imaginatively applied, does itself in: Socrates, or rather a visitor from Italy, develops seven specifications of the Sophist-type, so it must eventually come home to the participating reader of the dialogue that, at the least, this method vehemently over-determines the sophist or, at the worst, befuddles his being. In any case, it is clearly not a method at all, if by a method is meant a learnable jigged procedure. For it turns out that to do significant dividing, you have to know beforehand the whole universe of discourse, including the fea-

tures of the being you are seeking to delimit. Else how will
you know what you must posit, and why you may reject its
negation?

So the visitor gives up on division in general and attends
to the particular division which introduces the insight that a
sophist is an image-maker, a circumventer of genuine originals in his profession of wisdom. At that juncture it becomes
necessary to understand what an image is in its very being.
And that is the high point of the dialogue. The final collection of the specifications of sophistical image-making is only
a bit of clean-up; it is packed into an eminently forgettable
last paragraph (268c–d). But who can forget the analysis of
image-essence?

It requires a drastic deed, which is the imaginative paradigm
for our dialectical West, where "dialectical" means absorp-
tive overcoming, preservational undoing. It requires a patricide, in which the parent* to be undone is Father Parmenides.

> The intellectual parent both of the visitor from Elea, Parmenides'
> hometown, and of Socrates in his youth (see the dialogue *Par-
> menides*). Thus, these two are brothers.

It had been revealed to Parmenides by Aletheia, the Truth-
divinity—which is to say that he had received the gift of really
hearing what human beings say—that we can utter things
which we cannot think. We can mouth "is not," but we cannot *objectively* think what it is that is not. We can say "nothing" but we cannot *directly** think it. I might say here that

> We can think some vague thing and then mentally cancel it out.
> Then there it sits, a thing crossed out.

much later Aristotle gives, incidentally, one explanation of
this fact when he says in *On the Soul* that even for *theoria*, for
contemplative intellection, we need a mental image, a *phan-
tasma* (III 8). And of course such an internal appearance is

more a something than a nothing; hence there is no thoughtful concern with genuine nothing.

The Parmenidean progeny, the stranger from Elea, who carries out this patricide for Socrates' most thoughtful youngster, Theaetetus, does it in an exemplary dialectical fashion. He accepts from Parmenides that "true," "real," "genuine" nothing, *not*-being (*ouk on*), *is not* and, if spoken, conveys no thought. But he claims—a tremendous novelty—that there is a second kind of negated being, a *non*-being (*me on*). It has a roving sort of negativity that does not claim to annihilate, to produce an unthinkable, only spuriously sayable, nothing, a not-being, which "is not" (*ouk esti*). Rather, as it runs through the world and through speech, it produces difference and diversity. Motion is not rest, but that does not make it a not-thing, a nothing. It makes it *other* than rest, different from rest, a non-rest-being. Thus real-world opposition is not negating annihilation; it is acknowledging *diversity*, a potent Platonic form.

Its name in the *Sophist* is "Otherness." I'll just add here that besides introducing the principle of diversity among the Socratic forms, a principle that all but dominates our current political discourse, this mighty dialogue says more than any other about the forms or ideas themselves and the community (*koinonia*) by which they are connected.

But all I've said so far of the dialogue was prelude to the point: The sophist-type has been identified as a master of spuriousness, who substitutes images for original beings. (Incidentally, in his own dialogues Socrates speaks appreciatively of and respectfully with particular human sophists; it's the type that he derides.) The reinterpretation of not-being, a conceptual thicket in which the Sophist threatens to hide, was undertaken by the Elean stranger for the sake of an ontological analysis of an image. As Otherness, Nonbeing, now elevated into a form, does not subject world and speech to the white-out of Parmenidean truth-extremism. That demanded a world of absolutely undifferentiated, completely compact unity, and an impossible speech that cannot deny or falsify anything.* So non-being, newly Nonbeing, is now available to

Nor—this is crucial—even forbid, as Parmenides in fact attempts to do, the thought that non-beings are.

explain the being of an image. Any image, be it internal or external, made or natural, revealing or deceiving—every image is, particularity apart, a communion of opposite forms. Or, if the Platonic framework bothers you, say, a conjunction of antithetical concepts. An image is always *not* what it is; it *is* a being in the mode of a non-being. Try this: Next time a friend shows you a picture of his baby and says: "That's my child," say: "No, it isn't." If the friend is a graduate student in philosophy, he will look at you aghast for a moment, then get it and laugh. "You're so right," he'll say, "but it's something—better than nothing." So what is it?

The baby picture is what most images are: an imitative image. It may have been intentionally diddled so as to be in some aspect false (on the false hypothesis that babies benefit from beautification), or it may be as candid as is an artless snapshot; the subject imaged is recognizable to those who know or can surmise the look of the original. This imitative essence of imagery distinguishes images from symbols, which never did or no longer do signify by similarity.* For example,

Greek *symbola*, "things thrust together," were rectangular strips of pottery, cut apart in zigzag shapes. A citizen of an Athenian tribe received a half and the other was put in a vessel, from which an official drew a piece. The citizen whose counterpart could be "thrust together" with it was allotted a tribal office. This original symbol worked not by *similarity* but by *complementarity*.

there's the sign for a ladies' restroom, a skirted figure. It used to be an image, but since most women no longer wear skirts, it's now a symbol.

Let me say here that I'll be talking from now on about sights mostly, sights and their magical relation to words. The reason is that, although there are lots of auditory, tactile, gustatory imitations, visual images, imagery, and imagination seem to prevail over other kinds in complexity of detail and profusion of sorts. Thus the problems of visuality seem to me more gripping, particularly as they relate not to morphing into another sensory mode but to translation into speech, that is, a transmutation from spatiality (for visuality involves extension) into ideality (for speech reaches into the meta-physical realm). Moreover, there is a deep theory of the most poignant kind of audibility (except weeping), namely music. Schopenhauer claims that it is imageless in its very being, since it is a direct, non-representational expression—thus not a representation—of the human will in its vital immediacy (*The World as Will and Representation* II, Supplement, Ch. 39). My point is that this withdrawal from the imaginative realm of music, the most moving of artifacts, and therewith of audibility, leaves the field to visuality and its imagery.*

> Of course, his theory is wildly counter-experiential, since—I'm guessing—most listeners generate not entirely random imagery.

So what is an image, a being that is not what it is? I could flatten the inquiry by asking: What is an image such that it's not what it is *of*? That would make the question into a pseudo-question—one that dictates the answer. "Of" is here a preposition of derivation; it signifies dependent belonging. Thus "the United States of America" are contained by, united by the continent, America, that underlies them and on which they depend; as Lincoln says: they were "brought forth *upon* this continent" (First Draft, *Gettysburg Address*). So the question would encapsulate the derivative, dependent feature of an image, whereas the point of an image ontology might well be to give the being of an image an independent essence *of its own*. It would be the more desirable if it turned out, after all, that some images have no originals. That, surely, is what we mean when we babble so incessantly and admiringly of a human ability (!)—here I've put an exclamation point—called "creativity," a power once attributed to God alone, most relevantly that of making something out of nothing.

Here is the ontology of the *Sophist* in brief. In Plato's dialogue it goes both for images and for the human case that has turned itself into an image, a being that is, in this case, a poor but plausible imitation of its genuine original, the philosopher. Incidentally, here is yet another image perplexity: Why is the plausibility of an imitative image, its very rhetorical persuasiveness, absolutely no guarantee of its accuracy—and yet possibly a mark of its truthfulness? I'm thinking, for instance, of portraits that deform every proportion and distort every coloration and thereby produce a true likeness, once it's become familiar.*

> Recall the anecdote about Picasso's portrait of Gertrude Stein. She complained that it didn't look like her. He replied: "But it will."

Our common experience is that things may be genuine or they may be fake, and words can be true or they can be deceitful. Forgeries are perfectly real as things and that's what makes them hard to discern as forgeries, as counterfeits. False rhetoric is often perfectly good, even especially persuasive as language, and that is what makes it seductive. Thing-imitations are not nothing simply; word-falsifications are not nonsense simply: On the contrary, they are potently not what they pretend to be. The Elean stranger, Parmenides' true progeny, in following the way of thought, can be understood as setting before himself this double "im-passe," this *a-poria*: How to hold fast to the real but yet specious human purveyor of imitations by saving his mere and sometimes false images as *somehow* real beings? Put ontologically: How to understand images as being even less than derivative dependencies, as being mere yet potent nothings? And how to preserve the false character of the sophist-type as an indictable reality? Again, put ontologically: How to understand a deceiver (be he personally innocent by reason of ignorance or deliberately bad because of corruptness) as doing something effective and even crucial to the very being of a world?

Here is the answer: The not-being proscribed by Father Parmenides was rescued from utter nothingness by being understood as that aforesaid principle which relates all beings to each other *as* other, the form of Otherness, the principle of ontological relativity (255c ff.). It is "scattered" through the whole realm of thought, and, as *the* principle of relation, it holds its world together in a communion. Yet as a principle of opposition—and that's the practical application—it is the "source," the *arche*, of diversity: Any "this" is not a "that," but not, for all that, a nothing. Rather, once more, it is an *other*. Every negation is an assertion of something that is otherwise. Thus Parmenides' utter Not-being has turned into qualified Nonbeing, responsible for all worldly variety, from personal to political, including that diversity which is indeed America's current preoccupation, racial, ethnic, gender diversity (whose excluding inverse is "identity politics").

And, almost incidentally, an image is now explained as well. It is not nothing but an original's other, related to this original by that intensely peculiar relation called "likeness" or "similarity." Similarity, then, has this ensuing analysis: One being is similar to another when its perceptual looks, its appearance, is near-identical, while its thought-look, its form (*eidos*) is other. That Otherness, however, is *also* Nonbeing, so that the difference between original and image is also a *drop-off* in being: An image is a lesser being than its original. And so any proud father will agree: the baby's picture is not *the* baby, it's *of* the baby but is much *less* a baby than the infant itself. Here, incidentally, is another fascinating problem about these lesser beings: For all their affliction with secondariness, be it as quick electronic snapshots or time-consuming artful portraits or silhouettes outlining a natural shadow, all these mechanically achieved derivations, such material images, tend to be longer-lived than their flesh-and-blood originals. For example, I own a cut-out of a full-size portrait of my grandmother; once I looked liked it, like her—now she looks like me; she's been dead four-score and seven years or so. Or, I own a version of Plato's *Sophist* which has had countless reiterations since its words originally issued from Plato's mouth, and a servant first entered them into a scroll. (Isn't it remarkable that twenty-four hundred centuries on we're back to scrolling!) This account, however, bypasses the most wonderful of imaging questions: What about those images that are poetic ("made"), but from no producible original*—the Odysseuses, the Natashas?

> Notwithstanding the fact that characters are often known to have, perhaps always do have, portraitistic features.—If they're recognizable imitations, it's probably actionable.

Let me now top off these observations of image-study with another great text, not on the ontology of images but on the phenomenology of the imagination, Augustine's *Confessions*, Book X. I think I'm justified in calling it a phenomenology, an "account of appearances," because it precedes and prepares, by way of a vivid description of the inner experiences of remembering and recollecting, what is, to my mind, Augustine's unsurpassed contribution to time-studies, and, indeed, the basis of Husserl's canonical *Phenomenology of Internal Time-Consciousness*. Thus both Augustine and Husserl derive their understanding of time from a description of memory. But this Augustinian image of memory is also an image of the imagination, which he locates within memory, as its workshop, so to speak.

Contemporary memory studies speak drily of memory as a storage space. That is a very shrunken terminology. Augustine speaks of the "huge court," the "immense capaciousness" of "its fields and vast palaces." To me, memory, as he observes it in himself, has four capabilities.

First, much that is within it is time-affected, but some items are atemporal, for example, the "learnables" (*mathematika*). Second, memory itself is the source of temporality, recapitulating briefly, in this way: Perception is always now; past and future are made possible by remembrance and expectation, by image-recall and image-projection, both time-marked by the thickness and sequence of the intervening images. Much that is within memory is, in the lingo of memory studies, "reproduced," that is, memory renders sensory intake as a matterless reproduction, an imitation abstracted from stuff. Third, some of what is within memory, however, for example, what goes to make possible expectation, the hope or fear of things yet to be, and above all what is responsible for imaginative fictions, is produced—no one knows exactly how—in the memory that is depicted in Augustine's expansive view. This memory is thus not merely a place for laying up memories, a storage space speaking drily or a treasury speaking enthusiastically, but also, speaking operationally, a laboratory, a workshop for imaginative novelties; whence come its models, its originals, is the perplexity broached above. Fourth and finally, not to omit what matters most to the inquiring monk, the memory has in its recesses, way back, a path out and up, toward God.

To sum up the effect of what I've tried to express: Not a soul knows how imagination is possible or, least of all, putting it in broad contemporary terms, how any of the brain's functions become consciousness's activities. For example, no one really knows whence come poems, whether, as in Homer's experience, they are of the Muses who dwell on Olympus or, as in Wallace Stevens's doctrine, they are

> . . . of the [scriptless] mind in the act of finding
> What will suffice. ("Of Modern Poetry")

This general un-knowing is not at all caused by a lack of effort but is, in fact, the laboriously achieved result, not so much of diligent study as of *musing introspection*. It is also, once more, a telling test of a student's worthiness to be called a "lover of wisdom," a *philosopher* rather than a doctoral candidate. If you're that much the more eager to engage in the inquiry *because* it's bound to be inconclusive, you're the one—if not, the *other*.

33

Difficult Desire
Laborious Introspection

I. PRELIMINARY: PERTINENT INQUIRY

There is a very laborious and highly respectable way to do an end run around philosophy as a never quite satisfied, never quite fulfilled desire for wisdom—the defense against any definitive touchdown. This mode of inquiry is scholarly research. It begins with a clearly framed project, collects relevant arguments from respectable sources and forges outcomes that have at the least a slight edge of novelty, of so-called originality. It is sometimes more the labor of duty or ambition than the work of love or interest.

Here is why this approach is minimally helpful when the inquiry concerns our soul or psyche or *nous* or mind or reason or understanding or consciousness or subject or whatever term hard-headed people, unwilling to get entangled in invisibilities, are willing to utter. The expectation of progress is the underlying justification of scholarship that drives honest research, but it is by no means clear that with respect to the human constitution its direction hasn't been regressive. One way to put it is that in order to master consciousness intellectually and to treat the psyche therapeutically, they've been cut down to the size of our understanding. Or that what was once

515

an experience of grandeur—Heraclitus says, "Setting out for the bounds of the soul, you would not find them out, so deep a definition (*logos*) does it have" (Diels/Kranz 45)—has become a puzzlement about minutiae. Another, more positive, apprehension is that inquiries about the passions, emotions, feelings, or affects deal with internal processes often least known to those who harbor them and only minimally and unreliably open to public inspection.* But what is not physically

Perhaps the chief among these obstructions is the "mixed motive," suspicion of which leads to endless psychic second guessing, much like those "turtles all the way down" that appear in the answer to the man who demanded to know what supported the turtle that supported the world. Well, perhaps, deep in the bottomless, scarcely delimitable human soul, there *is* the turtle that treads the air and is yet the stay of our soul—our absolute, propless, bootstrapping moral self.

evidential is thought to be irremediably private, and what is private is non-contributory to the advance of secured knowledge.

Which brings me to that unamenableness to research of questions about the affects which I want to emphasize: Knowledge about affects must come, I think, primarily from direct experience, from a primary search rather than from a secondary research. And that means from *introspection*, not a path of inquiry congenial to everyone or easily brought under the protocols of the academy. Can you imagine an accepted proposal for a doctoral dissertation entitled "Me and my feelings"?

I think, therefore, that this search, which delves into interiority, has certain features I ought to try to set out. First, originality is out of it. A search whose written testimonials are two-and-a-half thousand years old will not yield novelties, and a human being of moderate endowments will not produce originalities. What matters is not that the inquiry yield new items to the store of knowledge but new understanding to the inquirer. One such seriously respectable understanding might be that the affect you are inquiring about is a mystery, a secular mystery—an uncircumventable fact that just won't yield to rational elucidation. Perhaps it may even appear that such a psychological mystery is ultimately a theological mystery. Accept, I would say, that there are certain conditions for inquiring into the affects, in the present case, into desire. For example, I think that a human being who has not seriously loved a being, be it animate or inanimate, or an activity, be it an attained fulfillment or an approach to a finality, is not prepared for thinking about desire. Nor is someone without the verbal copiousness to discern and give utterance to psychic subtleties, nor a person uncultivated by the fictional delineations and artful representations of psychic phenomena. Thus, for example, the bibliographical requirements for philosophy students should include the major novels of those languages not linguistically alien to them, for example the novels of Jane Austen and of Leo Tolstoy, of Charlotte Brontë and of Fyodor Dostoevsky. And, of course, the great epics, the *Iliad*-and-*Odyssey* (to be regarded as one) and *Paradise Lost*. And lyric poetry beginning with Sappho. But enough of preliminaries, except to say that I'll obey my own preachment in the manner of Frost's deceased old lady in his poignantly patriotic poem, "The Black Cottage." Her minister says of her, a widow with convictions, that

> She had some art of hearing *and yet not*
> *Hearing* the latter wisdom of the world. (My italics.)

I'll have her in mind when I launch into our subject without being much moved by, though not entirely ignorant of, current opinions upon it.

II. ETYMOLOGIES: SUGGESTIVE INCITEMENTS

I'm zeroing in on desire then, and I'll begin with some etymologies. I have no faith in etymologies as *revealing truths*, but only as *suggesting possibilities*. Etymology means, literally, the truth about words. It says nothing about primality, and it is not obvious that the oldest known meaning must be the truest—it might be simply primitive. To be sure, once linguistics had been established as a discipline, truth was indeed taken to lie in primordial meanings. The Greeks, however, had extracted significance from witty misconstruals. And even the Germans profited from plausible errors about homonyms; for example, Hegel etymologizes *Wahrnehmung*, "perception," as "taking for true," although the *wahr* here is not "true" but "aware" (*Phenomenology*, "Consciousness," II).

Now it is a truth, discovered by this same linguistic research, that the early meanings for items now considered nonsensory, that is, transcending the appearances that we take in by our sense-organs, do all—at least all that I've looked up—refer to events that come to us from the concrete stuff called material and the motions of things made of material. So the etymology of *nous* and *noein*, the capacity and action of taking in, of receiving idealities, is conjectural; however, one linguistically acceptable supposition relates it—hilariously—to "sn*uff*le," that is, to "sagaciously following the scent."* *Logos*

I'm repeating myself—from sheer glee.

and *legein* are more definitively related to "a collection," a gathering, and to the verb for "collecting" things dispersed. Concept, German *Begriff*, is traced back to "a seizing grasp"; soul, *psyche*, is originally "a cool breath."

But desire is the most surprising. It is close relative to "consider," which means originally "to take into account the stars (*sidera*)," your fate written into the heavens. Thus *desiderare* means something like "[to long for something to come] down from the stars." The verb "to long" itself is cognate with "to yearn and to lunge for" what is far beyond one's reach. So in German "desire" is *Verlangen* [*lang*/long], which also means "demand."

What's the point? The etymology underwrites one half of what I think is our common understanding of desire: It goes out from me to an object, not to confront or consider it but to snaffle it, to pull it in, to claim it, in imagination or in reality. There *is* another half.

III. EXCURSUS: RELEVANT TERMS

Before going on to desire in its wholeness, I'll take a—long—moment to list once more the human capacities and faculties responsible for (or standing aside from) and the internal states and events involved in (or left out of) desire. These brief delineations will not be news to you, but let them function as reminders. Each of them could be associated with certain particular thinkers as its prime sponsors.

Soul: the whole complex that animates the human body, including all mentation and every affect. I'll list under "soul" also its Greek name, *psyche*, latterly substituted for soul in the soul-aversive terminology of experts in soul-accounting ("psychology" in Grecized English), be it theory or therapy.—Plato.

Nous: the receptive capacity for direct insight into beings, that is, idealities, and the ability to attain such intuitions, stabilized thoughts, upon traversing the linear thinking called *dianoia* or "thinking-through," *dia* being, as ever in matters mental, a spatial preposition, indicating the two termini "from here to there." Also direct sensing.—Aristotle.

Mind: the latter-day successor of *nous*, a set of functions or operations rather than receptivities, which eventually shapes beings to its own requirements of certainty.—Locke.

Reason: *logos*, the faculty for thinking according to articulable rules called logic; also the ensuing accounts and

definitions, *logoi*; also the relation of things similar to
each other in qualities, such as analogies: *analogiai*;
ratio-relations of quantities: *logoi*.—Heraclitus.

Consciousness: a latter-day displacement of the now
largely proscribed soul. As *nous* is part of a *soul*, consciousness belongs to a *self* that is self-conscious in
both senses—self-aware and often ill at ease. Consciousness, apperception, belongs to a subject that confronts or harbors or constructs objects.—Kant.

Let me pass right on to some terms for human interiority that
are *not* mentation, that is, thoughts (ideas) or thinkings (reasonings).

Appetite: literally, "seeking toward"; directional seekings
are part active, part passive stretchings-out toward an
object, aware hunger, be it for physical satisfactions or
for non-physical objects of attraction.

Affect: literally, "done-to-ness," the most comprehensive
term. I think of our capacity for being affected as a
great human-centered mystery. It's my conclusion *after*
having produced 500-plus printed pages of research
on, and search into, the *feelings*. Its direct opposite is
spontaneity, the self-generated aspect of mind and its
apprehension, its "seizing hold of."

Passion: *pathos* in Greek, a "suffering" in both senses, a
painful affect but, more neutrally, a passive, done-to,
submissive condition.

Emotion: a mode and term that gradually takes the place
of *passion* in modernity. The term signifies an internal commotion or upheaval together with the expression of the internal motion—"emotion" is derived from
ex-movere, "to move out." If it's done dramatically, it's
called "emoting."—Hume.

Feeling: the most all-overish kind of affect, as its etymology suggests—it is related to "palpitate," to explor-
atory touch, to feeling out gently. Such tactile feeling
is our basic, most extended sense, whose organ is the
whole skin (Aristotle, *On the Soul* 413b). When transferred from the sensory to the affective realm, "feeling"
betokens the most mood-like, pervasive aroma-absor-
bent inner condition, melding into that diffuse kind of
thinking signified in our locution for an undeliberated
opinion: "I feel that . . ."

Mood: the most philosophically consequential affect:
our basic modality, our psychic condition. In German, mood is *Stimmung* as in the tuning, *stimmen*,
of an instrument. In the last century the mood of
most philosophical interest was anxiety (Latin *angor*,
"choking"), our constricting confrontation with
nothingness.—Heidegger.

The point of these listings is to help frame the questions
that will find the territory within which to locate desire. First,
then, in which of our non-physical capacities does desire
arise? I am bypassing here the strictly somatic answer implied
in the stimulus and response theories, the lusting and lunging,
such as Schiller attributes to worms in the "Ode to Joy."

Wollust ward dem Wurm gegeben,
Voluptuousness was bestowed on the worm,

and then he adds, to right the balance:

Und der Cherub steht vor Gott.
And the cherub stands before God.

(Incidentally but perhaps not altogether inconsequentially,
the "Ode to Joy" is, in Beethoven's setting [last movement of
his last symphony], the anthem of the European Union. But
back to business.)

So, first, on the hypothesis that desire is not explicable in purely bodily terms, is it a receptivity of *nous, intellect*? Or an operation of the *mind*, a mode of rationality? Or a condition of the conscious *self*, an aspect of subjectivity? I mention last what I think of first: Is it a capacity of the *soul*, the non-somatic principle most immediately involved with the body? I think so (Plato, *Philebus* 35b–c).

And second, on the hypothesis that desire is probably primarily, if not exclusively, an affect, a *done-to* rather than a *doing*, is it a *passion*, an *emotion*, a *feeling*, a *mood*? Again, I leave to last what I had listed first: Is it *appetite*? That's what I opt for because desire has a bodily side, but also because of what I learned from the two giants of the tradition concerning desire, who were not distractible by academic scholasticisms. They taught me, the one, namely Aristotle, that *a human being is appetitive from beginning to end*, and the other, namely Thomas Aquinas, that *all the passions are appetitive, however specified*.

Let me say right away to what I'm referring. Aristotle's *Metaphysics* begins with the assertion that all human beings by their very nature reach for, hunger for, desire, to know. And the text culminates in the delineation of a divinity that is at once so terminally interesting and so utterly self-sufficient as to be the most absolute, that is, the most *irresponsibly irresistible* object of the attraction, the hunger, the desire, with which this treatise on the theology of thought began and now comes to its climax. It is *Nous, Mind, Thought* itself (XII vii, ix).

On a smaller scale, Thomas, in the "Treatise on the Passions" of the *Summa Theologiae* (Questions 22–48 of the Second Part of the First Part) places the passions in the sensitive, body-related *appetitive* part of the soul, under two rubrics: *concupiscible* and *irascible*, that is, "desirous" and "vehement" (Part I, Qu. 81, 2). These categories distinguish passions according to their way of attaining their object: whether the effort is smooth or rough, advances in peace or requires a struggle, hence a certain aggression, to attain its goal. But with all respect for Thomas's huge powers of discernment, I think that his—so faithfully reported—objectors ("Treatise of the Passions," Qu. 23, 1) have a point. They say that all the passions are fundamentally desirous, and that both the recalcitrance against the object and the arduousness of the irascible passions serve as, and I quote Thomas's own admission, "the champion and defender of the concupiscible" (Qu. 81, 2); thus the vehement passions too are in the service of desire, the desirous passions. For both kinds, the desirous and the vehement passions, are appetites.

So far, then, I've said that desire is one half a non-somatic longing or a non-physical lunging. Now I owe you the other half. But first, recall that I assigned desire its seat in the soul, that conception of our transcendent nature which is, during our life, most inextricably involved with the body.

I might recall to you here that Plato makes Socrates the most vivid myth-teller in behalf of this involvement of soul and body. I am thinking of the *Phaedrus*. Precisely one half of this dialogue, the second half, is devoted to the notion that genuinely seductive speech, rhetoric, has to be based both on psychological insights and logical distinctions, while the first half gives an example of such an insight into the soul and its descriptive image, its visual analogy. The visual depiction of the soul shows it as tripartite; a chariot, representing the body, is pulled by a self-indulgent black horse coupled with a self-respecting white horse and driven by a rational human charioteer. This soul-image as an *external appearance* enfolds (literally, for it includes the figure within its description) the *internal feel* of it as a great male member, a phallus in the process of erection. The seductive message—it ought to pierce the awareness of all philosophy students—is that *the soul is as capable of arousal as the body.* The teaching of the *Phaedrus* is that the love of wisdom properly begins with the love of ensouled bodies—to be precise, in "enthusiasm," a Greek-derived word for having "the god (*theos*) within (*en*)," or for seeing the divinity in a human body.

IV. INWARDNESS: FIRST AROUSAL

It is this arousal that is the other, really the first, half of desire. That assertion is a claim about desire and therefore problematic. Here is a more concrete way to inquire: What is the relation of love to desire? The most explicit treatment of this question that I know of in non-fiction is again that of Thomas in the "Treatise on the Passions." It is set out in the yet more precise question "Whether love is the first of the concupiscible passions?" (Qu. 25, 2). The question itself suggests the answer, for it asks: "Is love the beginning of desire?" and the answer to Thomas's "yes or no" *quaestiones* is normally "yes," as far as I know. I'm about to quote extensively from the question. But first I want to say, I hope unnecessarily, that there's no point in reading Thomas, the master of human experience, unless you let it resonate—I mean, take it as a real perplexity not to be muted by the neat complexity of his response.

Thus the first objector (I like attributing the so-called objections to a person, as I may, since they are as much Thomas speaking, though for another, as the "I answer that . . ." which follows)—this first objector immediately picks up my problem: Thomas says that concupiscence is the same as the passion of desire, and since the whole faculty is named from its chief characteristic, namely the concupiscible or desiring power, desire *precedes* love in significance and exceeds it in scope. For love is but a member of that concupiscible class. Nonetheless, among the concupiscible passions, love is first. So here, then, is Thomas's answer to the question: "Is love the first of the concupiscible passions?," somewhat abbreviated, yet long; forgive that—it *is* the best treatment of our topic that I know:

> Augustine says that all the passions are caused by love since *love yearning for the beloved object, is desire; and, having and enjoying it, is joy.* Therefore love is the first of the concupiscible passions.
>
> Good and evil are the object of the concupiscible faculty. Now good has the aspect of an end, and the end is indeed first in the order of intention, but last in the order of execution. Consequently the order of the concupiscible passions can be considered either in the order of intention or in the order of execution. In the order of execution, the first place belongs to that which takes place first in the thing that tends to the end. Now it is evident that whatever tends to an end, has, in the first place, an aptitude or proportion to that end, for nothing tends to a disproportionate end; secondly, it is moved to that end; thirdly, it rests in the end, after having attained it. And this very aptitude or proportion of the appetite to good is love, which is complacency in good; while movement towards good is desire or concupiscence; and rest in good is joy or pleasure. Accordingly in this order, love precedes desire, and desire precedes pleasure.—But in the order of intention, it is the reverse: because the pleasure intended causes desire and love. For pleasure is the enjoyment of the good, which enjoyment is, in a way, the end, just as the good itself is, as stated above.
>
> [T]he effect of love, when the beloved object is possessed, is pleasure: when it is not possessed, it is desire or concupiscence: and, as Augustine says, *we are more sensible to love, when we lack that which we love.* Consequently of all the concupiscible passions, concupiscence is felt most; and for this reason the power is named after it. ("Treatise on the Passions," Qu. 23, 2)

I think it follows that there is a perspective from which love is a pre-desirous desire. I don't think this is the passionless love attributed to God and the angels, but it delineates a familiar phase of *human love*.

See if this description isn't true to your experience. You're now in the throes of the most yearning longing, a hungry attraction, probably to a human being, but by no means necessarily so. It could be a work of imagining or understanding or an event of action or contemplation. Wasn't there a moment or a span, depending on the sturdiness of your temperament, when the love was pure delighted contemplation, utterly devoid of cupidity—when love was without longing, lackless love? Perhaps it was, after all, what Schiller meant with the line from the "Ode to Joy" that follows on the voluptuous worm: "And the cherub stands before God." It doesn't last long, the "I want" in its triple sense asserts itself: I lack, I need, I choose—"I choose," because the Latin *voluptas* refers to the desirous wish, which is cognate with *voluntas*, the choosing will.* In sum, the direction is from hands-off

German *Woll-ust* may possibly bear a dual meaning: carnal delight and willful choice. But if read as *Wol-lust*, "well-lust," that duality collapses into one sense: ultimate pleasure.

quasi-stupefied looking to the urgent will to possess. Thus Satan, before beginning the willful seduction of Eve, stands for a moment, within sight of her innocence, "Stupidly good" (*Paradise Lost* IX 463). Incidentally, Milton's Eve is never innocent, not from the beginning when, at first consciousness, she falls in love with herself (*Paradise Lost* IV 449; see Essay 24, "Eve Separate").

So the first half of desire, often much briefer in time, but equal in significance with the longing part, is the love that is as yet mere delighting but also already a tending. Perhaps one way to put it is that there is *desire yet potential*, the pull of the object, attraction, and there is *desire now actual*, the push of the subject, longing.

So much for what I'll call, somewhat gracelessly, the structure of desire. It's bivalvic: early arousal of attention hinged to the consequent pursuit of the object.

V. CONSEQUENCES: AFTER DESIRE

Now comes a real problem in theory, and, heaven knows, in experience: What's next? Suppose the object, him-, her-, itself, is unwilling. William Thackeray's *Vanity Fair* tells the story of William Dobbin, who, through much of his adult life, longs for Amelia; she, in turn, quite willfully denies herself to him. When she finally wakes up, he's still willing but the other parts of wanting have been worn out. Desire is deflated. It happens. It also happens that the object is easily captured but not long kept: "I'll have her but will not keep her long" says the eerie soon-to-be King Richard III (I ii 230) of his wife-to-be, Lady Anne.

These are unfoldings good for fiction, but the case to put to philosophy is that of desire prosperously fulfilled. For it, the most head-on yet subtle treatment that I know of is in Plato's *Philebus* (34 ff., 44 ff.). Here is the setting of the problem: If desire implies a lack and a longing, two dual elements must be involved: pain/pleasure and memory/imagination.

The Greek word for desire is *epithymia*. *Thymos* as self-respect is the classical forerunner of will, so *epithymia* can be pretty faithfully rendered as "willing-toward," somewhat as my earlier analysis of desire suggested. Will and willing, however, always have a futural aspect; they are directed toward what is expectantly hoped for but is not yet, what *will* be, if we have our way.

Socrates develops these consequences for desire. Desire originates in a lack, which gives pain, and tends towards a fulfillment that is expected to give pleasure. Such expectant hope can never arise in the body because it requires imagination. Imagination, in turn, is a function of memory, for we can—or so I am persuaded—form mental images only of what we have seen in the past, either by eying terrestrial appearances or by receiving other-worldly visions, that is, by the deliverances of reality or by messages from the Muses. Consequently, although the body undergoes the deficiency, the lack that is psychic longing, and so desire, is never experienced there; physical needs, of course, are.

Now in the *Philebus*, Socrates reports that there are people who speak to this effect: If desire is the painful longing to fill a lack, then, when the lack is filled, the longing and its pain cease (also *Gorgias* 494a–b). They imply that there supervenes a pain-relieved state. I'll interject here that, as we all know, this relief can be intensely pleasant—for a moment. But we also know that very soon both pain and its relief have slipped out of awareness, and we find ourselves in the state of normality, which is a condition of awareness-neutrality. In fact, any additional fulfillment, for example, yet another serving of even the most delectable of foods, such as meatloaf with mashed potatoes, becomes painful when you're stuffed. Or perhaps a more refined case, from, say, Jane Austen: When the two who were destined for each other finally find each other willing, the story is over. The ensuing marriage lacks the tension of longing. If it's tellable at all, it's a comedy; all her major married couples that I can think of, be they quite contented or merely resigned, are more than faintly funny, often hilarious. Jane Austen's novels are fictional realizations of the *Philebus* problem.

This problem of desire has, it seems to me, two versions. One is this: Is ardent desire sustainable under conditions of availability? The other is: Can active love be maintained under conditions of normality? Perhaps there is a third and best way to put the question, in Thomas's own term: Is there *fruition*, "enjoyment," the ever-delightful union with the desired object—once it is attained? His affirmation of that possibility, his faith-driven answer "yes" to the problem of desire, makes a huge difference to the tenor of life: Is it, external conditions being favorable, inherently disappointing, or at best a-pathically contented? Is there secure delight? When Thomas opts for "fruition," he is saying that earthly happiness is, in principle, possible.

There might be, however, a take on life outside these three possibilities, the ones that I might call the classical cases, since ancient schools are nameable for each: Stoic, for the damping, Epicurean, for the maintaining, and Aristotelian, for the fruition of desire. This new possibility is the Romantic one, which, of course, like any way of thinking, may happen at any time, but also has its period of dominance. I take the canonical Romantic mantra from Keats's "Ode on a Grecian Urn":

> More happy love! more happy, happy love!
> For ever warm and *still to be enjoy'd*,
> For ever panting, and for ever young; . . .

I've emphasized "still to be enjoy'd." I take "still" here to mean "yet to come." Romantic desire is fixed as "for ever" futural, fruition-removed, and *that* is called happy love. It is love in the mode of indefinite increase: "*more* happy love! *more* happy, happy love!" Thus it is an example of the very pleasure that Socrates refuses to accept in the *Philebus* as the human good, partly because, as measurelessly and illimitably formless (31a), it is soul-destroying and partly because, as deliberately and willfully incomplete, it is self-incoherent. One might say that open-endedness, the lack of finality and limit, is the feature of romantic desire that distinguishes it from classical desire—as more excitation-fraught and less satisfaction-laden.

VI. COMPLETION: WHAT ENDS?

What might be a good way into the question whether the fulfillment of desire is, all in all, a fruition or a let-down? Is attainment a joy or should we, adapting a famous Aristotelian dictum to the contrary, *tristum omne animale post coitum*, "every animal is depressed after intercourse," say instead, in my made-up Latin, *laetus omnis homo post consummatio-nem*, "every human being is joyful upon fulfillment?"

I think this inquiry, if we engage in it for real (by "for real" I mean only secondarily to contribute to the advancement of knowledge and primarily to clarify our life), should probably begin with thinking about *pleasure*. Where does it arise, in the nervous system or in the soul? What kind of affect is it, a passion or a mood, or what? Aristotle's most memorably apt description of pleasure is also a dead end; he says that it completes an activity by being a certain supervening perfection, like the moment of bloom on things in their prime (*Nicomachean Ethics* 1174b 35). "The bloom of things in their prime" is the loveliest, the most telling figure of speech, but what does it tell? Not under what conception of our humanity pleasure is to be classified, nor what sort of affect it may be said to be. In fact, a bloom, a perfection, is perhaps not an affect at all.

Think of all the questions to be asked about pleasure, and you will, I imagine, end up realizing just why an inquiry about desire calls for an early analysis of pleasure and why, just as studying jokes is terminally unhilarious, so investigating pleasure is unavoidably unexhilarating. But it is, I think, the necessary beginning.

Here are my questions: Is there pleasure in anything for which longing desire has been extinguished by reason of fulfillment? To put it another way: Is fulfilled desire, desire sans longing, a contradiction in terms, or a nameless affect, or is its name perhaps pleasure itself? Is the motive, the "end"—ambiguously so named, since end means both termination and consummation—is this "end" of desire an object, the goal of an attraction, thus a present being, or is it rather a prospect, the hope of pleasure, and so a future condition? Why is desire bivalvic—a state of arousal within, hinged to a motion toward an object without? Can love, the inner arousal, be actually satisfied without any pleasure drawn in from an object beyond, can love be, so to speak, monopolar? Or can it rest content with inner images—or external simulacra? Can longing, the outward reach, arise in a soul quite unmoved by anticipation of pleasure? Can there be entirely objectless desire, pure vagrant longing? And finally, what are we to make of that complexly inverted desire, that attractive aversion for what is engrossingly ugly or even captivatingly bad, bad for us and bad in itself—and what is the nature of the beckoning pleasure? *Can* evil be our good?

I could go on: there are, concerning pleasure, questions of terminology, of classification, of causality, of valuation, and these are, I think, deeper, more primary and thus antecedent to the apprehension of desire. Let me frame my last question, the one that is as real as it gets, by returning to Thomas's classification of the passions. Although they are all desirous and long for the good, yet they are divided into a concupiscible and an irascible kind—those that simply seek what is good and goes down easy and those that are embattled for what is difficult to attain and demands a fighting spirit.

The Greeks have a saying: *chalepa ta kala*: "good things are hard." They mean, I think, thereby preempting and undermining Thomas's authority, that *everything* that is good is difficult, including pleasure. For example, to go for it directly is to forestall it terminally. I'm with the pagans here, and so I ask: Why is our desirous soul so in need of obliquity, of obliqueness, of slantwise and creeping approaches, when candor and naïvety seem to be its native, its Adamic virtues?*

"[E]rect and tall/ . . . with native honor clad . . ." (*Paradise Lost* IV 288).

Why are pleasure and its desire so beset by uneasiness?* This

For example: I think I've done pretty well with these essays and am pleased. And yet, here's the dis-ease: I don't think I could do better—hit my limit. Well, it's deflating, though sort of salutary.

question confronts, I think, a great mystery that envelops our affective nature: the mystery of ontological negation, the cognate opposition that confronts all positive being (see Essays 2 and 32, "Secular Original Sin" and "Studying the Imagination"). Here begins real thinking: How is the duality of our intellectual/affective nature related to the duplicity of the world's affirming/negating being? Somehow it must be.

School of Philosophy, The Catholic University, 2017

34

A Dispassionate Study
Of the Passions

Plato's dialogue *Gorgias* ends with a long speech culminating in a rousing cry by an aroused Socrates. He is speaking to Gorgias's student Callicles about his swaggering opinionatedness and their common—his and Socrates'—uneducatedness. The words he uses are *neanieusthai*, "to act like a youth," to behave like a kid, and *apaideusia*, "lack of education," ignorance. And then he concludes with a rejection of Callicles's whole "way of life" (*tropos tou biou*) "to which you call me, trusting it; for it is worth nothing, Callicles!" (*hoi su pisteuon eme parakaleis; esti gar oudenos axios, o Kallikleis*). My fine 1922 edition of the *Gorgias* by the classicist Otto Apelt rightly translates the address O *Kallikleis*, jingling in the Gorgian manner with *parakaleis* ("call me"), as "My Callicles," for there is a curious, straining intimacy in Socrates' peroration. The rest is silence, inviting us to imagine consequences. It is a favorite question of mine to ask our freshmen at St. John's College, who all read this dialogue, what Callicles resolved

---

A presentation to a conference on the emotions called by the Graduate Students in Philosophy of The Catholic University, 2012.

that night at home in bed when he was, perhaps, by himself. For that he, self-assertive though he was, remained altogether unmoved—that's not imaginable.

Now some of you may have heard of the late Seth Bernardete, a student of Leo Strauss and a brilliant classicist at New York University. In our youth we traveled together, and Seth once imparted to me the following wild conjecture.* "Plato"

> We were sitting on Epipolae above Syracuse, a place that figures largely in the Peloponnesian War (Thucydides, Bk. VI). Seth had, unwisely, grasped the fruit of the cacti that covered the high chaparral so fateful to the Athenians, and we spent a miserable morning de-spiking him.

was a nickname given to the author of the *Gorgias* because of his broad shoulders (Nails, *The People of Plato*, 243). His real name was Aristocles: *Call*icles, *Aristo*cles—"he of noble fame," "he of best fame"*; *kalos k'agathos*, "noble and good,"

> -kles, from *kleos*, "glory, fame."

was the Greek way of denominating what Chaucer calls "a verray parfit gentil knyght," a good and noble knight (Prologue, 72), a perfect gentleman. So Plato represents himself in this dialogue as a fundamentally well-bred yet rudely unregenerate youth in his moment before conversion, a conversion accomplished by a usually imperturbable Socrates impassioned to speak, for once, extendedly and hotly.

Do I believe this clever combination of clues? Not really. Plato was, after all, of good family and a writer of tragedies before Socrates captivated him, and the swaggering surly youth Callicles has little of the suave poet Plato about him, who, moreover, had probably already been philosophically involved when he met Socrates (Diogenes Laertius, "Plato" II 5).

Nonetheless, this anecdote of a conjecture seems to me thought-provoking. Here, for once, Plato permits us to see the spectacle of serene Socrates in a passion, unironic, touched to the quick—surely he is not merely in a high dudgeon at being dissed by a Gorgiastic know-it-all.

Many of you are already teachers, though perhaps young in comparison with Plato (b. 427 B.C.E.) when he wrote the *Gorgias* (c. 387). He was probably forty, and his Socrates was about the same age (b. 470) at the dramatic date of this dialogue (shortly after 429, the year of Pericles' death, mentioned as recent in 503c). You will have experienced the unbalancing sense that the stakes are high, and souls are to be pierced, and that passion, or an exhibition of it, is in order.

It is, to be sure, a wonderful question about the nature of passion whether deliberate demonstrativeness or disciplined reticence does more to damp or nourish it, be it in the speaker or in the listener, and how spontaneity and artfulness play into the effect. But we do know that Aristotle believed that Socrates' display in the *Gorgias* was effective, even if not for Callicles. He tells of a Corinthian farmer who was inspired by his reading of the dialogue to leave his vineyard to its own devices, to join the Platonic circle, and henceforth to make his soul the "seedbed," that is, the seminar, of Plato's philosophy.

The *Gorgias* is, therefore, a good reference for beginning to talk about the affects as an object of study. Not merely because it documents, so to speak, that people concerned with the soul have in fact plenty of temperament, be it sober Socrates or meek Jesus (for example, Matthew 21:12, Jesus wreaking havoc in the temple) and that they don't leave their affect at the entrance to their inquiries or preachings. I don't—of course—mean the little negative furies which Socrates calls "eristic," the contentious desire to win arguments, but I'm thinking of a large positive passion.

So this is where I zero in on my particular problem for this talk. I have read my way through a tiny fraction of the huge mass of contemporary writing on the emotions. I've come away with the cumulative—documentable—impression that there is a thoroughgoing misapprehension about a putative pagan rationalism and a supposed Western tradition for which it is held responsible and which breaks out with insidious virulence in the Enlightenment. This view owes something, I suppose, to Nietzsche's brilliantly skewed portrait of the "despotic logician," Socrates, the monster with the "one, great Cyclopean eye, in whom the lovely madness of artistic enthusiasm never glowed" (*The Birth of Tragedy*, 14). The attribution of monocular Cyclopeanism means vision without depth, and the charge of despotic sobriety implies thought unravished by beauty. All this of a man who thought that our soul contained a world that we could recover by going within and that true poetry requires a Dionysiac frenzy inspired by the Muses, one cognate in kind to the philosophical longing for beauty! All this of a man who, for once bathed and wearing shoes, slyly draws a picture of Eros, which is in fact a self-portrait—an unwontedly groomed Socrates looking at himself from a distance and recognizing the unwashed and unshod god of *love*! (*Meno* 81 c; *Phaedrus* 245a, 249d; *Symposium* 203d).

So much for the picture of Socrates the rationalist. And something similar holds for Aristotle the intellectualist. His great work, the founding book of institutionalizable philosophy (since it pre-sets the problems to be solved, *Metaphysics* III), *begins* with an *appetite*, a root passion, which, in the form of the desire to know, is humanly universal and culminates in a passionate portrait of the ultimate object of appetition. It is a divinity that attracts, without returning, love—an object that satisfies, that fulfills, by its mere actuality, by its own fulfillment (*energeia*, *ibid*. I 1, XII 7), unadultered by matter, as do those in Shakespeare's Sonnet 94,

> Who, moving others, are themselves as stone,
> Unmoved . . .

—except that the pure *energeia* of the divinity is the very opposite of the practically complete inertia of those unaffectable human objects of attraction, these beautiful but material lumps of mere resistance, that the speaker of the poem is excoriating.*

> Who was probably himself unmutually in love, so that one person's "a little too much" was the other's "much too little."

Would it be too much to claim that this is *the* difference between the philosophical Greeks and the God-regarding Hebrews, more significant than Homer's anthropomorphic polytheism, which is in any case more characteristic of the poets and the people than of the philosophers? I mean the lack of reciprocity between adoring human and worshipped divinity: The Socratic forms are great powers (*Sophist* 247e), but even when they come on the comic stage in visible shape—which they do in Aristophanes' *Clouds*, where they appear as wordily nebulous beings, as shaped mists—they don't do a thing for their summoning worshipper, Socrates. In fact they abandon him to possible suffocation in his thinkaterion—the play leaves this uncomic outcome open—and exit satisfied with their "temperate" performance (269, 1509). The Aristotelian divinity, *Nous*, is similarly unresponsive, an object of uninvolved attraction. The God of the Jews, on the other hand, is beneficently or banefully involved with his people, and when a certain Jewish sect grows into a great religion, He becomes caring outreach itself, Love impersoned (for example, Exodus 20:1–6, I John 4:8, 16).

Why am I dwelling first on the pagans and on the Christians in talking to you about the study of the passions, when the contemporary writers on the emotions simply drown out these earlier voices by their volume? It's not that I have much faith in the explanatory power of chronology or in those longitudinal studies by which a genetic history is attributed to ideas; these tend to develop more arcane information than illuminating depth. I can think of half a dozen reasons for my distrust, which there is no time to set out at the podium, though we might talk about the implied historicism of such studies over the next days of your conference. Moreover, it is probably less necessary at a Catholic university than at any other to try to induce respect for the tradition. There is, however, a particular way in which I think that emotion studies should begin with, or pick up at some point, the great ancient and medieval works—of the latter, above all, Thomas's "Treatise on the Passions," which he placed in the very center of the *Summa Theologiae*. For this monk knew—God knows how—everything about human passion.

I think these pre-modern works should be studied for their *shock value*, for the *news* they contain for us. Such a reading, a reading that places them not in the bygone superseded past but in a recalcitrantly unfashionable present, requires a difficult and never quite achievable art, one that graduate students should certainly be eager to acquire: first, the art of summing up, with some credibility, what a philosopher is really and at bottom about (I don't mean "all about," a hand-waving locution, but the compact gist of his intention); and second, the art of discerning how the particular part on which you mean to focus is, or fails to be, properly derivative from that central intention. Then, opposing gist to gist and consequence to consequence, there will emerge a coherent and discussable schema both of the general notions that preoccupy the denizens of modernity willy-nilly, and of the sophisticated twists that studious scholars and trendy intellectual elites have given them. Approached in this way, emotion studies seem to me as necessary to our self-understanding as any subject can be—necessary to us, as human beings with a contemporary affectivity.

So now let me give you some, perhaps vulnerably sweeping, observations about more recent emotion studies, particularly in English-speaking lands. The groundbreaking works for us were English; I will name Errol Bedford (1956) and Anthony Kenny (1963). But the American father of this field is Robert Solomon with his book *The Passions* (1976).

The Solomonic beginning and its consequences are full of oddities. (I am avoiding the harsher term "self-contradictions.") The thesis of the book is "to return the passions to the central and defining role," snatched from them by Socrates, and "to limit the pretensions of 'objectivity' and self-demeaning reason that have exclusively ruled Western philosophy, religion, and science" since his day (xiv). Well, I guess we've read different works of Western philosophy. But now comes a surprise. How will this salvation from two and a half millennia of despotic rationalism be achieved? We must recognize that "an emotion is a *judgment*" (185). Of course, this dictum runs into difficulties concerning the meaning of non-rational judgments. Indeed, Solomon eventually accepted that his claim is actually a cognitive theory. As such, he says rightly, it has "become the touch-stone of all philosophical theorizing about emotions." He could, in any case, hardly escape this cognitivist denomination, since it turns out that we become responsible for our emotions by adopting this very theory of cognitive emotion. For as the theory works its way into our unconscious volitions, it will become true, and our emotions will indeed be as much in our control as our judgments (188 ff.); so control is what it's—after all—about. Cure dominating rationalism with a strong dose of insidious rationalism!

The Stoics are the moderns among the ancients. Their cognitive theories, the first truly representational theories, are more future-fraught than any others in antiquity that I know of; they dominate modernity until Heidegger's *Being and Time*. The Stoics are hard to study, because the deepest of them, belonging to the so-called Early Stoa, exist only in fragments. But we do have an extended text on Stoic passion theory, the third and fourth books of Cicero's *Tusculan Disputations*. Some of you, who have read the work, will recognize that the modern dictum "an emotion is a judgment" is pure Neostoicism. Neostoicism has, in fact, dominated modern emotion studies. One major work in this vein is Martha Nussbaum's *Upheavals of Thought: The Intelligence of Emotions* (2001).

But how strange! The Stoics meant to reduce emotions to *mistakes*, to diseases, to pathologies, of judgment. An emotion is a false appraisal, a perturbed opinion about what matters: an "upheaval of thought." It is a deep and complex theory underwritten by the Stoics' fearless physicalism, their notion of a material substratum, the *pneuma*, "spirit," on whose ground the psychic capacities can morph into one another. But there is no question, that, taken summarily, rationality trumps affect. How odd, then, that, as I've said, modern theories so largely save the emotions from rationalism by rationalizing them. And I'll list associated oddities.

First is the pervasive fear *for* the emotions, the sense that we moderns have suppressed and demeaned them so that they *need* saving. What teacher of the young (as scholars by and large are) or observers of the world (as some of them may be) could possibly think that *that* was what was troubling our nations, cities, neighborhoods!

Second is a curtailed sense of the vitality of thought in the West. I think I've given some prime examples of the interpenetration of thought and affect, even of the primacy of appetition in the human soul in antiquity. When the ancients fight the passions it is because they are so alive, experientially alive, to the meaning of the word *pathos*, "suffering," and to the effect of its licensed reign, its invited tyranny. It is really, I think, a modern idea of emotion that is at work here, among our contemporaries, one which pits its vapidity against the verve of hard reason.

Inherited Enlightenment terminology indeed conveys this sense that our passions are attenuated, all but quelled by reason. The pivotal figure here is Hume. In his *Treatise of Human Nature*, the term "passion" begins to be displaced by "emotion." He uses both, mostly interchangeably. But emotion is the word of the future. Solomon's book is entitled "The Passions," but the key word inside is "emotions." Your own conference called for papers on "Emotion."

"Emotion" derives from *ex-movere*, Latin for "to move out." The significance of this substitution of emotion for passion is powerful. Ancient *pathos*, passion, was an affect emanating from an object; the object elicited the responsive affect, from the *outside in*. Modern emotion comes from *inside out*; it emphasizes expression; subject prevails over object. It is the Romantic worm eating its way out of the Enlightened apple.

At the same time, the non-affective, the rational part of the subject becomes *mere* reason. Hume, famously, says: "Reason is, and *ought* [my italics] only to be the slave of passions, and can never pretend to any other office than to serve and obey them" (II iii 3). He can say that because Humean and enlightened reason is not deeply affective, not driven by love, and so its relation to emotion may indeed be one of subservience, stand-off, or finally, enmity. I need hardly add: *With this transformation of the appetitive, longing, loving intellect into manipulative, instrumental, willful rationality, philosophy loses its proper meaning and becomes a profession.* My brush here is broad but, I think, it has some good overlap with the case. So my second oddity is the severely foreshortened view of the capabilities of passionate thought.

Now a third curious notion, the oddest one of all: the unreflective launching of an enterprise which is, on the face of it, like embarking on a destroyer with the idea of going swimming. The vessel of war displaces, cleaves, churns up the element, but, absent a shipwreck, the sailor stays dry. So the student of emotion banishes perturbations, analyzes wholes, whips up terminology, and, unless melancholy seizes him, sails high and dry over the billowing depths of feeling, with much solid bulkhead keeping him from immersion in the element to be apprehended. This not very elegant simile is just a way of expressing my surprise at the fact that emotion studies tend to precipitate themselves into the subject proposed without much thought about how the subject can even become one—how emotion *can* be subjected to thought without being denatured in the process.

Here, incidentally, lies, it seems to me, the best reason why cognitive scientists, and those philosophers who like to be on solid ground, are by and large physicalists and might well regard the Stoics as their avatars (for example, Damasio, *Looking for Spinoza*, 275). What matter and its motions has in its favor in emotion studies is that in this spatial form the different motions of the mind appear not to occlude each other; spatio-temporal events, laid out in extension and sequence, have patency. However, since cognitive brain studies, including the emotion research, depend on prior conceptualization and introspective protocols, it is hard to think of them as independent of a philosophical phenomenology.

Therefore, in the unavoidable preparatory philosophical exploration, the perplexity of thinking about feeling remains a vexing one, the more so since it appears to me to be a variant of the greatest quandary, now and always: How is thinking about any form of our consciousness even conceivable? How is it—or is it indeed—that thought about awareness does not collapse into a union, as does "thinking of thinking," the *noesis noesios* of the *Nous* (*Metaphysics* XII 9)? How can we know that thought about itself or its fellow internalities does not transform its object out of its true being? (See Essays 14 and 32, "Self-Address" and "Studying the Imagination.")

Just this latter eventuality makes emotion studies problematic. Study does have its own affect, one of the most interesting in the list of feelings, namely *interest* itself. The word—from *interesse*, "to be in the midst of"—signifies what student parlance calls "being into it" (Silvan Tomkins, *Affect Imagery Consciousness*, I 337; see Essay 19, "On Being Interested").

To study is to bring to bear received learning and native analytic and combinatory capacities on a determinate object. If it is of a high quality, it is preceded and accompanied by its opposite, leisure—free time for meditating or musing, during which original questions rise up and take shape. But the business itself focuses on problems such as Aristotle first set for himself and left for his successors; nowadays it's the dissertation advisor's job. Now all the questions become formulated as demands for reasoning, and under reasoning all things turn to reason—as under studious production all thinking turns to footnoted paper-writing.—For a hammer, everything's a nail.

It is indeed curious that this fact is not more of a perplexity to students of the emotions. Yet on second thought, it is perhaps not so surprising that emotion studies seem so desiccated—perhaps they are not really more so than serious scholarship ever must be. Robert Browning has his lovingly respectful students sing at the Grammarian's Funeral:

> Learned we found him.
> Yea, but we found him bald, too, eyes like lead,
> Accents uncertain:
> "Time to taste life," another would have said,
> "Up with the curtain!"
> This man said rather, "Actual life comes next?
> Patience a moment!
> Grant I have mastered learning's crabbed text,
> Still there's the comment . . ."

Here is the picture of interest raised to the pitch of passion. There *is* this pure dry professional love—Browning's grammarian's passion was for Greek syntax, those little particles in particular—that *can* capture the loving admiration of students. (I know this from my own student days.) But I doubt that it suits philosophy, and, in particular, philosophizing about the emotions. Here another poem expresses our condition more aptly, Wordsworth's "The Tables Turned." It begins:

Up! up! my Friend and quit your books;

and this is its seventh verse:

Sweet is the lore which Nature brings;
Our meddling intellect
Mis-shapes the beauteous forms of things:—
We murder to dissect. (My italics.)

To be sure, there are now less intrusive ways of getting inside Nature. Yet the conceptualizing of feeling will ever and always be abstraction in the basic sense—a removal, a drawing away, from life—in respect to the affects doubly dubious. For in ordinary abstraction, the concept incarnate in concrete things is, by a specifically human cognitive operation, separated off from them. But it is simply a premature, a prejudicial notion that the affects "stand under" (to use Kantian diction) abstractable concepts in the same way as do things.

It might follow that to view the dispassionate, the studious study of the affects—be they impositions from without or stirrings from within—as problematic is a *sine qua non* for beginning rightly. I think it *does* follow.

There are early bonuses. I'll give you in turn a suspicion, a conjecture, and a figure. The *suspicion* is that we really are partite beings, so that our affective and our thinking capacities are terminally distinct, structurally and dynamically *heterogeneous*. The *conjecture* is that it is this very *dis*junction in their being which makes possible their *con*junction in thought and action, their effective complementarity. Here I've written a sentence that I don't even quite understand as I'm reading it to you, and yet I have some faith in it. Finally, my *figure* is that our affective capacities *lie deeper* in our nature than our reflective powers.

To be sure, neuroscientists also say that certain brain structures especially subserving the emotions are deeper within the brain and so, evolutionarily early, but that is not dispositive: What is biologically primitive might, after all, *not* be humanly primary. What I rather mean is that affectivity has a certain abysmal, incomprehensible character that makes it—I don't know how else to put it—*feel* submersed; affects touch us ("to feel" is related to Latin *palpare*) in intimate, that is, "innermost" regions, while articulable thought-activity *intends*, "stretches toward" emergence, towards comprehension of objects. We might be constitutionally bipolar, extended between emotional depth and thoughtful height. Perhaps an original question might be formulated from this figure; it is something to talk about later.

Wordsworth's lines imply that the murderous dissection is performed on a lovely, living object. I must tell you that emotion studies sometimes—too often—read as if they were carried out on a latex-injected corpse which suffers every cut with supine springiness. It is, as I've tried to show, a partly inevitable result of making affectivity a "subject," a thing lying still under thought, literally "thrown under" (*subjectum*) its wheels.

Nonetheless, I feel tempted, by way of an ending, to say how I think we can mitigate the dilemma, for if we can't think about our feelings, we'll come apart. I'll try to be practical.

First, then, you can't study emotions at even the kindliest advisor's prompting. They are a subject that requires experiential urgency, some pressure for the relief of confusion. In brief, you not only have to be a feeling being—so are we all—but a being enticingly oppressed by the enigma of emotionality, the arcanum of affectivity. Some topics are well approached in the brisk spirit of pleasurable problem-solving. Not this one, I think.

Second, listen to what Socrates says in the *Apology*. It is not, as often reported, that "the unexamined life is not worth living." What he really says is, I think, something stronger: Such a life is *"not livable* for a human being" (*ou biotos anthropoi* 38 a). He means: not a *possible* life, not a *lived* life. That is what the *tos* ending of *biotos* signifies: "livable or lived." He means, I think, that experiences, passions among them, that are not internally re-viewed, introspectively re-lived, are in effect un-lived—an unexamined experience is not *yours*. A nice corroborating illustration comes in Thomas Mann's *Magic Mountain*, whose hero—meant to be a paradigm of simple humanity—engages in an introspective discipline he calls *regieren*, "ruling, regulating," in short digesting, appropriating his affects and images (Ch. 6, "Of the City of God and Evil Deliverance"). For as experimental emotion research requires protocols drawn from inner experience, so conceptual emotion studies cannot do without introspection. And, unlike egocentric self-analysis, which is a spontaneous sport, disciplined self-inspection is an art learned by practice. So now I seem to have contravened everything I've just said, which was that feeling is choked by thinking.

Here, then, is my last attempt at being practical about our problem as students: how to keep feeling before ourselves while bringing thought to bear on it. Or, more learnedly put: how to turn what is, regarded in itself, the most subjective element of our being, perhaps our very subjectivity itself, into an object.*

> I might get myself into a word muddle here, unless I remind you that before the eighteenth century, "subject" meant just what we now call an "object," for example, the being that arouses passion; we still use it in this way, as in "the subject to be studied." But by an only partially complete inversion, "subject" is now used also for the host of the emotion rather than for the object affecting it, and "subjective" signifies a feature of that emotional affect.

Deliverance from the quandary of objectifying the essentially subjective seems to me to come from our great representational faculty, *the imagination*. Mental images are summoned by feeling, arouse feeling and are, famously, affect-fraught, feeling-laden. There are those who deny that we have analogue images before our inner eye, but they are in retreat. The cognitive scientist Kosslyn (the prime defender of mental analogue images), lay persons in general, and most students of the imagination are convinced by their own inner experience of imaginative vision and its affectivity—and what claim could possibly override such personal, one might say, eye-witness knowledge?*

I might add here that the very latest neuroscience seems, though incidentally, to clinch the argument for mental visuality; mental images are directly machine-retrievable: Francisco Pereira *et al.*, "Generating text from functional brain images," *Frontiers in Human Neuroscience*, Aug. 23, 2011.

These affect-laden sights can indeed be held in mind, and thinking can turn to them, play over them, study them. So, it seems to me, emotion studies require an imaginative life. Here is a practical consequence: Your profession requires you to read scholarly articles, but your mission needs you to read works of fiction, particularly novels. For these not only stock your minds with visualizable scenes of passion on which to dwell while you think, they also school you in the adequately expressive diction with which to articulate what you discovered. For, my fellow students, if you speak of feeling either in flabbily pretentious or technically formalizing diction, your papers will be worth—well, next to nothing.

35

Parmenidean Identity
Thinking and Being*

With thanks to the Summer Classics seminar on Heraclitus and Parmenides, held at St. John's College in Santa Fe, 2017. The insights developed by this group of amateurs reinforced my conviction that it is preferable to think one more thought than to read one more article. But then don't, in all fairness, expect to be yourself referenced. Writing should fulfill an inner exigency, not an external expectation.

Text: *Parmenides of Elea, Fragments: A Text and Translation with an Introduction* by David Gallop. University of Toronto Press (1984).

Parmenides says in his poem—it is the whole of Fragment 3 and could not be more curtly blunt:

1. For it is the same: to think and also to be.
   To gar auto estin noein te kai einai.

Rearranging the Greek in English word order:

gar	*estin*	*to auto*	*noein*	*te kai*	*einai*
For	it is	the same:	to think	and also	to be.

Here is the prevalent English rendering:

". . . because the same thing is there for thinking and for being."

That is scandalous. Translating should be the self-denying effort to transfer meaning from one language to another. If the original is a text apparently of stature, but its meaning is not evident to you, blame yourself in the first instance, and translate *just what you see.*

So why the blatant creativity? Because these scholars can't believe that, more than two dozen centuries before the fact, this poet-philosopher managed to sound like a German idealist, one who believes that the thinking mind makes all Being in its own image, so that Being *thinks*, has (or is) ideas, and, reciprocally, Thinking *is*, has Being. But since the love of wisdom and its search for the way things are is not a progressively advancing science (perhaps even the opposite), why shouldn't that be possible? To be sure, Parmenides' version, since it is at the very recorded origin of the philosophical enterprise, is not hung about with the bells and whistles, the metaphysical technicalities of the later version, nor constrained by demands of latter-day logic; possibly this early simplicity, its apparent naïvety, intrinsically affects the insight. So there is nothing left to do but to try to see meaning on our own—to look at the saying directly and, supposing that Parmenides means just what he says, to clue it out.

Of the eight words only one is problematic; the rest are fairly fixed, not univocal in meaning, to be sure, but without divergent synonyms; there is not an alternative vocabulary. *Noein*, "to think" or "thinking," however, has two aspects to consider. One is the meaning: Is "think" right? The verb is derived from *noos*, contracted to *nous*,* usually translated as

> All terms dealing with ideality that I've followed out etymologically are sensory or quasi-sensory. "Mind" appears originally to refer to memory, as in "mindful." *Nous* may, as I reported before, be related to "snuffling," sniffing-out. Note that Heraclitus says that souls in murky hell use their sense of smell (Fr. 98). In any case, these sensory origins remind us that human speech can lead us *up to* but not *into* the supersensory realm.

"mind," the agent of *noein*, "to think." The question is this: Does this mind "think" in the sense of *following out* or *through* a line of reasoning, or does it "intuit" in the Latin sense of *gazing at*, of insight not in the common sense of a penetrating look but of a contemplative beholding—or is there, perhaps, yet a third, stranger mode? *There is*, so let me articulate it up front prematurely, in all its mystery: It is the self-seeing performed by a vibrantly solid thoughtspace. The other aspect is its syntax, as an infinitive that has become a substantive by means of its implied Greek neuter article *to* ("the").* Does it retain its verbal character, its activity?

It is a confusing coincidence that the English indicator that turns an infinitive into a noun is the preposition "to." Anyhow, the "to think" = "thinking," a participle that's used as a noun.

If it is the same "to think and to be," then perhaps Being is as active as Thinking and Thinking as stable as Being. Does Parmenides provide help?

But first, to reinforce that he means what he says, I'll point out that he says it once more, from a somewhat different aspect:

2. It is the same: thinking (?, *noein*) and also that for the sake of which there is Thought [*noema*]. (Fr. 8, 34)

(I am now putting a question mark after "thinking" because I will soon reject it as the meaning of *noein*.)

So the first says simply: Thinking and Being are the same.

The second is a little more complex. Here Thinking seems to differ from Thought; the former might be an activity, the latter its product. But that is not possible, since then the Parmenidean stillness would be perturbed. I must conclude that Thinking is not what *to noein* means. This infinitive has lost its verbal mode; it is identical with its derivative noun—surely an intended linguistic imposition. More: Its agent-noun, *nous*, is assimilated to the one meaning as well: *Thought*. Parmenides avers that the *one permissible Thought is of Being, and that it is identical with Being itself.* The claim is clear, its meaning submerged.

So arises the desire to find help in the fragments remaining to us of Parmenides' work.* It can be found in the longest

It is usually said to have been called "On Nature" [*Peri Physeos*], a highly unlikely title. For whatever *physis* means, it has to do with motion. Now the part of the poem that is "about truth" (Fr. 8, 50) never mentions *physis*, being about the "un-moved" (Fr. 8, 38).

surviving one, Fragment 8, where Parmenides offers a figure for Being (8, 14). Being is:

Every-whence rather like the bulk of a well-rounded sphere.

This sole, this unique Thought, then, whether it be uttered or just visualized, is much like a sphere, be it ideal, matterless like that defined by Euclid* or real, immattered like a beach

Elements (IX, Def. 14), generated by carrying a semicircle about its diameter, so ultimately defined in terms of equal radii from a center (I, Def. 15).

ball or a planet. "Rather like" [*enalingkion*] is exactly what my first note picked up on: the realm of Thought is accessible to us only in moderately figurative speech, here in a simile ("like"). Later in the life of thinking these concrete similes turn into very dead metaphors. Thus it is imaginable that the word "sphere" might have come—it didn't—to mean "idea-world," the way that "breath" came to mean "spirit" and "gathering" turned into "reasoning" (see Essay 33, "Difficult Desire").

So the sphere is a simile for Being.* Hence its several explicit

A spatial simile is most apt here for representing cohesion; I recall a philosopher—was it Schopenhauer?—saying, very pertinently, that "space connects, time divides."

features should be paired with the many characteristics of Being to help us see *and say* how Being is like enough to Thought to *be* Thought, and *ipso facto*, the converse: Thought is like enough to Being to *be* Being.

This Thought, however, cannot, as I've said, be the concluding product of the thinking we're familiar with*—an

Socrates will name it, descriptively, *dia-noia*, "through-thought." He means that it is the utterance of internal conversation, a progression into a topic through time. (See Essay 14, "Self-Address.")

"idea" evolved in our mind. Nor can it be the less ordinary, yet not unfamiliar receptive activity enabling contemplative absorption.* Nor can it be the ordinary human thrusting

Aristotle will call it *theoria*, "viewing," and its agent, *Nous*, "Mind."

power for penetrating a proposed perplexity.* So, once again,

We call it "problem-solving."

the effort will be to examine this figurative sphere for clues about the one, the unique Thought that is also Being—and is consequently its own object.

Here, then, is a list of all the features Parmenides attributes to this sphere, this Being-simile. They are, to be sure, mentioned before the sphere comes on the scene (8, 2 ff.). But it is quite clear that, as they are "signs" [*semata*] on the only way, the way of "[It] Is," so they are also marks of its simile, its likeness, the sphere, which is introduced immediately after the feature-list.

But one more preliminary item. One might be tempted to think of the Being-sphere as a mini-mind writ large, a Thought-globe, so to speak. That particular mind could belong to young Parmenides before the goddess Truth (*Alethea*) has received him into her heart (Fr. 7, 29); thereafter he has, in his human mind, Being and nothing else—no proscribed non-being. Nonetheless he is not the Sphere writ small, since there is not a number of minds as there are a multitude of human heads. I think we should regard this possibility: Once the youth has foresworn all kinds of "non," he merges into Thought; in terms of its Sphere we might locate

him in a locationless place: one of the Sphere's densely innu-
merable centers, each of which is equally distant from its
indeterminable circumference. This is not in Truth's text, but
I propose that each of these centers represents a point whence
emanates Thought, an origin of that thoughtful vibrancy
which permeates Being and constitutes it.

But first, let me say plainly what my claim will be: The
sphere, with all the features attributed to it, will represent
Being both as *nothing but Thought* and *what Thought is of,*
which is, in turn, Being. Thus it will be a mind writ large.
Then, conversely, the knowing human being, the youth whom
the goddess, Truth, receives into her heart (Fr. 1, 29), has, in
his particular human mind, Being and nothing else (Fr. 2, 5).
Indeed, Mind and Being are identical in sphere and man, for
Being is Thought *and* that of which Thought is, and Mind
is what is *and* what it is mindful of. I want to claim that the
above is less of an oracular muddle than an unsympathetic
reader might aver. I am futzing my way to some specificity;
whence would it arise but from some initial mental mush?

So here is the ensuing list of features in the order of their
mention in the poem (Fr. 8, 2 ff.). The sphere of Being [*eon*]
is really *all* there is. For nothing else *is* since only Being can
be. Thus Nothing, Nonbeing, *is absolutely not.* This Being is:

1. unborn and indestructible;
2. whole, single-limbed;
3. untrembling, fulfilled;
4. such as never "was" nor "will be," but is all at once,
   "now";
5. one, holding together [continuously];
   [explanation and exhortation (8, 6–20)];
6. not divisible but all-homogenous;
7. beyond extinction and destruction;
8. not more here [than there];
9. nor any worse [here] but everywhere all full-up with
   Being;

10. all held together, connected, since Being neighbors Being;
11. unmovable, held in place by the limits of great chains;
12. un-beginning, un-stoppable;
    [explanation (8, 27–32)];
13. not lacking [anything];
    [explanation (8, 33)];

Then: "It is the same thing—to think (*noein*) and that whereof there is Thought (*noema*)."

[explanation (8, 35–41)];
14. encompassed by an outermost limit and completed, while *nothing other is* outside.

Then: Thus Being is "everywhere much like the bulk of a well-rounded sphere" (8, 43). The sphere itself is described as:

15. bulky but not massy, i.e., immaterial;
16. everywhere from the middle equally matched, i.e., spherical;
17. neither denser nor slighter here or there, i.e., homogeneous;
18. containing no "not being" to keep it from reaching its like, i.e., continuous;
19. not such as to have here more, there less of Being, i.e., uniform;
20. inviolable, i.e., impenetrable;
21. every-whence equal, reaching out alike to its bounds, i.e., every location is a center so that the sphere is indeterminately bounded.

Here is a way to sum up these items. The Greeks have, as do we, a number of terms to denote ultimacies: whole (*holon*), all (*pan*), everything (*panta*), complete (*teleion*). The sphere is all of these, except "everything." *It is not a collection.*

Then: "With this I stop my trusty speech [*logos*] to you and Thought/About Truth. Learn from here on mortal opin-

ions, listening to the deceitful world [*kosmos*] of my words"
(8, 50–2).

Three observations: First, the goddess herself has often
taken the proscribed way, against which she repeatedly
warns young Parmenides, the way of saying and thinking the
non-being asserted in negation (7, 1 ff.; 8, 1–2). Indeed, her
description of both Being and the sphere are largely negative.
Second, in making Being rich in descriptive properties, she
is undermining its uniformity, its self-identity; in particular,
nos. 16 and 21 countermand each other; this sphere is at once
determinate and indeterminate. And third, she now embarks
on a lengthy account, not well preserved, of false opinions
and the false world they construct—an account that ought,
by her own injunction, to be unsayable.

In respect to the last, the false physics, the untrue nature
of this second part of Parmenides poem, I have little to say
except this. It presages the necessity pursued in Plato's dialogue, *The Sophist*, by a stranger from Elea, an intellectual
descendant of Parmenides, to commit a sort of thought-patri-
cide on his "Father Parmenides." He must do so in order, first,
to secure the very thinkability of falsehood and then to hunt
down that incarnation—sometimes personally innocent—
of deception, the Sophist (241 d; see Essay 32, "Studying the
Imagination"). For if nay-thinking and -saying is prohibited,
falsity is unreachable in thought and inarticulable in speech.
And all agree that true speech must mirror Thought, which
would seem to require the naming and negation of falsehood.
Recall as well the self-contradictions delineated above, those
following on the descriptive multifariousness of the supposedly homogenous simplicity of Being. Thus, ultimately, divine
Truth's teaching is not viable—ultimately, but not before her
spectacular news is given its full due of awe.

To say it succinctly: When we deny the "is," the "copula"
of a sentence, and therewith deprive its subject of any preten-
sion to substance (by saying: this being is not, or doesn't exist,

or is a nonbeing), or to truth (by saying: this being is not genuine, or this saying is false), or to a property (by saying: this being is not such and such)—when we engage in this kind of speaking we are saying more than thinking can keep up with. "Is not," be it the denial of existence, or truth, or being-so, is not ever quite intelligible, for where, what, how is this item that *is* not? Perhaps he—we—must be "nothing himself" to behold the

> Nothing that is not there and the nothing that is.
>
> (Wallace Stevens, "The Snow Man")

Such nothingness is not Parmenides' condition, so he accepts Truth's restriction:

> For neither could you know non-being, for that is not to be
>   accomplished,
> Nor could you intend it (*phrasais*, 2, 7–8)

But of course, you *could* say it, as the goddess has indeed just done. So here speaking and thinking diverge, and the goddess, divinely untroubled by the fine-tuned demands of a latter-day logic, enjoins her pupil just to avoid the way of no, not, and non-. And that is hard, since even some two and a half millennia later, I defy a listener to language to claim that a fellow citizen who says "There's nothing there" doesn't— somehow—believe that there's something spooky there that's a nothing, a being that is not, a non-being, though Truth herself has said: "For never shall this prevail: 'non-beings are'" (7, 1)—and some rational rectitude in us prompts us to agree with her. Yet there are soul-shaking imaginative experiences of Nothingness such as the one that dominates E. M. Forster's *A Passage to India*: the Marabar Caves (I vii, II xii, xiv).

Now to my attempt to show that the Sphere is indeed the model of the Being which is the same as Thought—hence also the same with what Thought is (I'll try this): Thought-ing, meaning *a non-progressive vibrancy of awareness*. Thus

Being, Thought, Thing are identical, each the same with the other two. Moreover, this triple identity obeys Truth's injunction against the positive affirmation of negative being (7, 1) and the negating assertion of positive Being (2, 5). Succinctly put: The sphere as a figure for Being might, after all, yield a delineation of a grandly primeval *noesis*, an intuition or direct knowing in which mind and object become one, as opposed to dianoetic, sequential, temporal object-thinking. If that worked out, it would not be surprising if some of the features of the Being-sphere resembled those of Mind, *Nous*, set out by Aristotle in *On the Soul*. Let me list the latter. Aristotelian *Nous*, mind, is:

1. potentially identical with the object of its thought; this capability, to be identifyingly receptive to beings, is its one chief feature (429a);
2. nothing, blank, before it is fulfilled in thought (429b);
3. itself thinkable as one thought (430a);
4. what becomes all things and makes all things (430a);
5. impassible [affectless] and unmixed (430a);
6. what does not know in or through time or think at one time but not another (430a);
7. what [truly] is only when by itself, immortal and everlasting (430a);
8. not predicative in its thinking [thus incapable of false attribution], and so always true (430b);
9. such that its "motion" is not the kinetic sort as understood by Aristotle, the temporal fulfillment of a goal, but that of an already complete, perfect being, a kind of non-physical vibration (431a) [hence incapable of dianoetic, linear thinking];
10. ultimately a god, whose non-kinetic activity and defining actuality is thought (*noesis*, thought-activity in the non-kinetic mode) of his own thought, so that

He and his Thought and its Object are all identical
(*Metaphysics* XII 7).

To avoid the absurdity of being about to argue that Parmenides' Being-sphere prefigures Aristotle's mind (well, perhaps it's not so absurd), I want to insist on a distinction:
Notions with the same name are apt to be descriptively similar, but that does not mean they are identical in their connotations, in the ground from which they spring and the end
into which they debouch. In particular, Aristotelian *Nous* is
"separable" and emerges as a god beyond, separated from the
world and also separated from stuff, *hyle*, which is *worldly
capability incarnate* waiting to be "actualized." Parmenidean
Being, on the other hand, is *not* separable, since it is all that
there is.

So now I finally come to the Being-sphere as identical with
Thought through the features I have listed, all found in Parmenides' Fragment 8. Once more, I'll try to show that this
Being-simile's attributes are also those of a kind of mentation
that it makes sense to call *noein*, "looking at," "intuition"
(recall that "in-" here is Latin "at," not "into"), that is, direct,
immediate knowing in which the agent and the object become
identical—or "intellectual perception," such as Kant particularly denies to human reason. In short, the sphere is a figure
for both identities, that of Fragment 3: "For it is the same to
think [*noein*] and to be [*einai*]" and that of Fragment 8, 34:
"It is the same: Thinking [*noein*] and that whereof there is a
Thought [*noema*]."*

Vocabulary, once again: On the one hand, "think" is better used for
that sequential reasoning called by Plato and Socrates *dianoia* than
for *noein*, but, on the other, the verb "think" has, conveniently, the
substantive, its product, the past participle "thought," roughly parallel with *noein* and *noema*. Thinking leads up to but neither conditions nor really produces Thought. A mysterious culminating
leap or connecting transformation must supervene. So: sequen-

tial thinking leads up to the noetic insight, and in that insight *noesis*, the thought-activity and *noema*, its product, are melded into one. Otherwise put: Ultimately, Thinking *is* Thought—and the converse. Where's the original object, a substance, say *this* human being? It has given up its particularizing material and become purely essential, noetic, a *noema*.

1. The sphere is self-same, self-transparent, "the same in the same" (Fr. 8, 29), self-contiguous and continuous, as is the thinking of insight: all self-identical, homogeneous; "reflective" without actual "bending back," everywhere surface, patent and unhidden, without inside, so to speak (10, 5; these features derive from the list above from *On the Soul*; the references are to Parmenides' poem).

2. It is unmovable, as is a thought [as distinct from penultimate thinking], all in place, given neither to locomotion nor qualitative change; at once an action without being kinetic, and a passion without being expressively moved by "e-motion" (11, 3).

3. It neither arises nor fades out, but is there, all at once or not at all; it is without genesis or decline, just as is intuitive thinking: sudden (1).

4. Thus it is atemporal; its "time" is a "standing now," it has in it neither incipience and consequent history nor expectancy and implied inevitability; this is the timelessness of intuitive thinking (4, 12).

5. It has no outside, no delimitation by any negating non-being; it is beyond any destruction, as is unmediated thought, which has no expugnable intermediate steps. What is beyond and might determine this Being-sphere *is not* in an even more absolute sense than is a negated being (6).

6. Its center—the seat of awareness—is everywhere and yet its circumference is one and the same; thus the sphere,

like a thought, is, as I've pointed out, at once definite, well-rounded, and yet indefinite in extent, undetermined (21, 16).

7. The sphere is homogenous, without differential density, without otherness, be it gaps, cracks, divisions in its quasi-spatiality: no negations to disrupt the simplicity of concentrated thought (18, 19).

8. Hence it has no exigencies, no protrusions, no snags, but is figuratively smooth, well-rounded, repellent to apps and adhesions (2).

9. The sphere is unshaken, dispassionate, desireless, since it lacks nothing, it has the very feel of an achieved insight (3).

10. The sphere is inviolable, being closed in its completeness, having no oppositional externality. So is Thought only of what is (14, 20).

11. It is unreachable by disruption, having, like Thought, no *locus minoris resistentiae*, as physicians used to say, no "points of vulnerability" (5).

12. The sphere has, like Thought, the bulk [*ogkos*] of gravity but not the massiness of matter: weightless gravity (15).

13. Thus, as displayed in the figure for Being, the Sphere, Being is indeed thought-like; the Thought of Being, by Truth's injunction the one and only permissible thought (2), is not to be differentiated from Being itself (7, 8, 10, 13, 14, 17). Being is both a single Thought and its Object, and so it must be ultimately the Thought of Itself.

If philosophy has an originating scripture, it is Parmenides' poem conveying to an ardently receptive youth the words of *Aletheia*, "Truth."* That's, however easy it is to say, gravely

---

Science has its originating text in Heraclitus's sayings channeling to a rare fellow listener the words of the Logos, the "Relater."

consequential. For it means that Truth is desirable, even if her first utterance is, for all its grandeur, untenable. Thus, in that descending ascent from depth which masquerades as progress, the early *possession* of wisdom (*sophia*) must recede into a later *love* of wisdom (*philosophia*), where truth becomes a hoped-for futurity—vernacularly, a pig in a poke. Those who think philosophizing is nonetheless a happy pursuit owe this clairvoyant perplexity to these founding sages.

Annapolis, 2017

36

Three Platonic Places
Or Better, Spots

Our students come to us from a world in which there isn't much time given to the snuggly world-removed scarfing-up of nice novels,* much less to the effortfully attentive assimilating

> I mean those time-without-end reading sessions spent on a rainy vacation day in a nook of an old village library, with shelves unculled to make room for multiple copies of current best-sellers and full of those competently produced middle-brow romances.

of books way over one's head. Hence, there's a problem* for

> To be sure, probably a lesser problem for us at St. John's College; our students come to us in order to read.

us teachers, a pre-learning problem. Its usual formulation is "how to excite students." But consider that in ordinary life "I'm so excited" often means "Leave me alone already." So our proto-mission is not to cause excitation in an overstimulated world, but to induce some quiet faith: "There might be more to this than I expected." So: how to induce faith in a book?

Well, the answer is: every which way. That does need specification. Here's one way. It's not really good but it's a resort:

Point to a *topos*, Greek for "place," the word from which
we get "topic."* Or better, call it a *spot*, a sudden definitive

> The title of an Aristotelian treatise, *Topics*. He meant by a topic a
> "commonplace," a platitude, that guides probabilistic reasoning as
> common notions, postulates, guide scientific argument.

maxim. Like a gold flake in a creek, floating in the flux of
exposition, it goes by unnoticed until the umpteenth reading. In singling out such nuggets for students, you're short-cir-
cuiting the hoped-for re-reading, but sometimes something is
gained—a flicker of incipient faith: "What if I myself found
such spots?"* So sometimes just telling is just right. Here are

> The great ancients, the Greeks of the sixth, fifth, fourth, third
> century, were full of hermeneutically exploitable tricks: large
> structures like the "ring composition" of Plato's *Republic* (when
> successive topics leading to the climactic center of a work—here
> the philosopher kings—are repeated inversely in the second half,
> leading to the grand exit), pregnant silences, suggestive puns,
> etc. Jacob Klein, our dean in the fifties, himself the expositor of
> such devices, used to worry about students who reveled in what
> he called "hochmatism"—from Hebrew *chochmah*, as in the so-
> called "Wisdom" books of the Bible: "Hochmatism" is to *chochmah*
> as *sophistry*, "plausibly fallacious cleverness," is to *sophia*, "wisdom"
> in Greek, and it's the bright student's pitfall—lots of smart revela-
> tions and little simple depth.

three such spots in Platonic dialogues, Socrates speaking. The
first, in the *Phaedo*, I'd like to come to believe, if only on the
last day of my life; the second, in the *Phaedrus*, is an illumination plain and simple; and the last, from the *Republic*, is to
me *the* key to that unsurpassable masterpiece of philosophical writing.

First, *Phaedo* 69c:

> *The truth, in its very being, might be a sort of cleansing from all
> such things, and soundmindedness and justice and courage and
> mindfulness itself might be a sort of clean-up.**

> The truth: *to alethes*, "the true thing"; soundmindedness: *sophrosyne*
> from "safe," *sos* and "mind," *phren*, the deep mind that's still close to

the affects; justice: *dikaiosyne*; courage: *andreia*, literally "manliness"; mindfulness: *phronesis*, the thinking that's insightful and heartfelt, from the bosom as much as from the brain; cleansing: *katharsis*, and "clean-up": *katharmos*, which seem to have the same meaning, though perhaps the latter, in the plural, goes more toward practical rituals, such as fumigations and sprinklings (*Cratylus* 405b).

So the excellence (*arete*) that the four virtues, those accepted by Socrates from ordinary talk, have in common, is *cleansing*. The four are 1. sound- or safemindedness, moderation, the self-control that keeps the faculties of the soul in balance; 2. justice, the self-acceptance which makes us stick to and accomplish our own business that we are born to do; 3. courage, the ability to make out what is really to be feared; and 4. wisdom, discernment without which we will not purify ourselves of "all such things."

What things are they, the ones that need a catharsis and its practices?* They are all that goes with the mindless notion

Aristotle and Plato's Socrates seem to me both initially (beginning with the world of the senses) and ultimately (ending with transcendence) much closer than textbooks make out. Aristotle too speaks of catharsis, in relation to tragedy, which effects a purification of pity and fear. Yet here, in the middle realm betwixt sensation and truth, in the realm of the arts, the two come far apart. For Aristotle psychic purgation, catharsis, is to be found in the theatrical spectacles *we should attend to* (*Poetics*), for Socrates these are part of what *we must purify ourselves from* (*Republic*).

that human goodness is bought with the common coin of pleasure and terror; that we are good because we fear postmortem punishment or hope for trans-worldly reward. This is excellence without true virtue, without wisdom or mindfulness (*phronesis*). Thus *that* virtue, *phronesis*, is the master virtue, the virtue of virtues. But all the good attributes of the popular virtues are, if guided by wisdom—here's the news— properly *cleansings*.

So what is the purification that is the very essence of virtue and is later said to be a function, no, *the* work, of philosophy, namely "the release and clean-up" it effects (82d)?

"Pure" means free of every element but that belonging to the being itself, to its very being. So "pure" focuses concentration on what is true in the sense of "genuine," not-fake. It also implies that the unmixed being is fully in being on its own. Moreover it intimates that its admixtures are less valuable than the simplicities.

Purity is the mantra that ghosts through Socrates' last day, though it comes to aphoristic expression only in the passage quoted. (Of course, it turns up in other dialogues.)

I think it is exactly what excellence/virtue (*arete*), the human goodness that combines outstanding competence with unfailing decency, looks like on the day whose evening is death's dawn for Socrates. What has presented itself to him through life as deep, soul-involving thinking, be it about the soul's proper disposition or the body's right doing, now looks like Socrates' single-minded, concentrated preparation for the impending loss of the body's sensory frauds and desirous misdirections; it now appears as the soul's readiness, through philosophy, the "love of wisdom" (that is, *mindfulness as a semi-affect*), to be itself by itself. The effort to reduce all goodness to knowledge proves finally to be exactly what Socrates had said it was: the present practice of, and future-bound preparation for, death (67e), a final this-worldly catharsis from sensory attachments that readies the soul for life in the realm of knowability. In sum: what in the continuum of this life appeared as an *inquiry into being*, on the last day turns out to have been *a simplification of the mind*, the adoption of a sort of mood.

There's one more thing to be said. This vigor-abounding, enjoyment-prone, excess-invulnerable phenomenon of a man has not given up his irony in his last hours. This irony is not, as it is sometimes taken, a stand-offish, supercilious pretense of ignorance, but a terminal, chuckling double-mindedness. The abnegation of the senses and their body was always an unsettled problem for Plato's Socrates. To my mind, the *Pha-*

edo, the account of his last day, is, all in all, a very precise record, for future use, of unsettled Socratic problems, sensory enjoyment being not the least of them.

Accordingly he dies—not with a joke on his lips, he's no joker—but with a chuckle in the soul expressed in his last words, when somatic self-cleansing is no longer an option. "Crito," he says to his simplest, and so his closest, friend, "We owe a cock to Asclepius. So pay the debt and don't be careless." Debt for what? Well, the god has now taken over the somatic catharsis; Socrates can take a rest—it's the way to die, the end for which the philosophic life is a preparation.

Second, *Phaedrus* 250d:

> *Now beauty alone has this portion, to be outstanding in visibility, and most beloved.**

> Beauty: *kallos*; portion: *moira*; to be outstanding in visibility: *ekphanestaton einai*, the verb *phainein* means "to appear, to shine out," (and yields *phaos*, "light"); *eis* is "out"; the -*taton* ending signifies the superlative; the infinitive *einai*, "to be," indicates that the characteristic of a Socratic form, a Platonic idea, is meant.

Aesthetics is the modern theory of beauty. One would expect its study to be relatively thrilling; instead it tends to be absolutely boring—perpetually disappointing. Sometimes a canon, that is, a set of objective rules (such as harmony or symmetry, that is, proportionality of parts), is proposed, sometimes subjective conditions (such as the interaction of parts of the soul, say of understanding and imagination), sometimes an inspiration from models*—all, to my mind,

> Of these last, the most daring is the notion, found in Plotinus and Schopenhauer, that works of fine art imitate Platonic ideas directly.

either too formal or too intricate or too high-reaching.

A first appeal of the passage quoted is that it lends meaning to Keats'—or rather his urn's—fancy nonsense. That pot says, when it finally utters:

"Beauty is truth, truth beauty,"—that is all
Ye know on earth, and all ye need to know.*

It doesn't seem quite enough, really.

If, however, beauty is just visibility, strong inner illumination and high external reflectance, then it is indeed convertible with truth, which might be understood as rendering
lucid, making clear, that of which it is the truth.

A stronger second appeal is that the understanding of
beauty as visibility is confirmed in experience: "This being
appears beautiful to me" really does seem to be redundant; it
can be adequately expressed more succinctly: "This being appears to me." I see it and can't get enough of seeing it; I can't
take my eyes off it or surfeit my ears with it.*

> Well, actually, the bodily senses, being subject to—not always
> unwelcome—weariness, I can't, and actually don't, in some recalci-
> trant part of my soul, want to be forever rapt in a longing distance.
> I go with Duke Orsino:
>
> > If music be the food of love, play on
> > Give me excess of it, that, surfeiting,
> > The appetite may sicken, and so die (*Twelfth Night*).

Visibility can, from the disengaged onlooker's point of
view, settle on anybody or anything. Not so, I imagine, from
the side of the vision-seeing viewer, or, to talk a little strangely,
from the side of visibility itself: Is everything in the visible (or
audible) world capable in its very being of becoming visible
(or audible) so as to seem beautiful to someone among us?*

> A colleague to whom I posed this question said right off: Well,
> babies form such a class. They are indeed all adorable; hence the
> Christian divinity entered earthly life in that age group.

My presupposition is that beauty is a form *whose very
being is visibility*, the power to bestow looks, the capability of being seen, of *thereness* to a sense. As such, it is the
form of forms, the form-enabler which brings out the Socratic
thought-shapes' shapeliness, the aspect that empowers them

to be visions* not only to those mortals, if any, who have

Phasmata, "things taken as appearances, even as apparitions" (*Phaedrus* 250c).

risen up to the outskirts of the realm of "looks,"* but also

Eide, the Socratic name for the forms; note the root *id*, as in "[v]ideo," the visual part of a telecast.

shapes apparent to everybody's senses on earth to be looked at: good looks, of which the opposite is the "unsightly."

On earth, however (all this comes from the paragraph leading up to the passage quoted), there is so little light in or over these likenesses of, say, the virtues, because our sensory organs are dim. They are dim not by reason of our needing reading glasses, but because, as the very senses they are, they are constitutionally incapable of beholding the a-sensual being whence shapeliness descends to terrestrial appearances. Still, of all the sensations, vision is the clearest, and so it is primarily through it that there is sometimes beauty on earth.

Hence I speculate that, while from the point of view of earthlings observing what humans are capable of finding beautiful, any ordinary dull thing would seem to have a chance of becoming outstandingly luminous to someone, yet it might also be true that visibility discriminates and would not settle on just anything.* If visibility is a form, it is not

Consider also that Socrates regards the "things" around us, to begin with, as "appearances" (*phainomena*), in the denigrating sense of "mere" appearances, not true beings. That complicates this line of inquiry: How does the shapeliness of the forms, their aspectual, "intuitable, "at-sight-able" character, differ from the phenomenal irreality of sense-objects?

only a thought-*object*, but, to permit myself an anachronism, a thoughtful *subject*, not only knowable in the highest degree but also powerfully knowing.* The forms possess a strange

See Plato, *Sophist* 248e ff., for the forms not only as knowable but as knowing.

power to be at work in a remote realm as semblances which they emanate, images that imitate the inimitable, because intrinsically viewless, originals. Forms can, moreover, conjoin communities of ideas. And they are able to serve as ideal models for practices that operate in an entirely different mode of existence.from the paradigm.* In sum, why wouldn't the

> Such as politics. Each such capability needs more words to become plausible than are desirable here.

form of visibility, which so spotlights terrestrial things that you can't stop looking, have discernment enough to abstain from settling on an item with just too little intrinsicality, with too perfect a dreariness, to warrant illumination? There might be some things or people that are terminally unsightly.*

> Or animals: manatees? But they're said to have been the original mermaids. There is an apt German word: *unscheinbar,* "homely," literally, "not-lustre-supporting." Note well: Perfect ugliness is absolutely receptive to visibility, since it is arresting.

Third, *Republic* Bk. IX, end, 592b:

*"But," I said, "perhaps in heaven a model is deposited for him who wishes to see it, and seeing it, to found himself."**

> Heaven: *ouranos;* model: *paradigm;* to found himself: *heauton katoikizein, heauton* is a reflexive pronoun, *katoik-izein* means "to settle down in the manner of a home," so to colonize.

The Greek words for "to found himself" signify a self-colonization. When a mother-city (*metropolis*) sent out a colony, it often supplied a civic constitution, a *politeia* such as would be realized in a regime (also *politeia*), a political way of life. *Politeia* is the Greek title of the book we call *Republic.* So the reader is, near the end of the work, bidden "to realize within himself the "fair city" (*kallipolis*) built in the body of the book.*

> Recall that the city began as a magnification of the soul *into* a city (Book II). Hence the founding of the soul is in accordance

with the book's structure, the ring composition mentioned above. To repeat: In it each major incident (such as the building of the city caste by caste and the program for the arts within it) going into the pivotal center (Books V-VIII: the philosopher kings, the world's ontology, the philosophers' education) is repeated inversely with some modification on the way out, to the end. So symmetry requires that Socrates should *gather the city back into the soul*, from which and for the sake of which his "fair city" was constructed (Bk. IX).

Socrates continues:

And it makes no difference whether it exists or will exist anywhere. For he would engage only in the practices of this city and of none other.

And so, nine-tenths through the *Republic*, all the standard complaints about Plato's totalitarian state and closed society are nullified: It's not a model constitution for a dystopian community but a real psychology for a sound human being.*

The major attack on Plato as anti-democratic was mounted by Popper (1966). A preceding defense comes from Rousseau, who says of the *Republic* at the beginning of his *Émile*: "Those who mainly judge a book by its cover take this for a treatise on politics, but it is the finest treatise on education ever written."

And so it is; its seventh book is the founding document of the liberal arts as the matter of liberal education, for which the sixth book has provided both the ontological ground and the metaphysical culmination. It is a philosophical introduction to a philosophical life, the free life not of corrosive "questioning" but of respectful question-asking. It is also the preparations for wise statesmen.

These three spots all seem to me to be located at extreme moments in summit situations. In the *Phaedo* Socrates speaks as one in the extremity of impending death; in the *Phaedrus* he goes to such heights, touches such extremes as philosophy permits in its imaging mode; in the *Republic*, having reached the limits of his proof that justice is an intrinsic good apart from external rewards, Socrates now confronts the denouement of many a philosophical conversation: What is the practical consequence?

But why must these golden nuggets wash by, spin out of sight, so quickly? Otherwise put: why are they so imbedded in the conversation as to be effectively secreted? Plato's Socrates is not the man to fear persecution—he's already its serene victim. Nor is he the teacher willing to hide his wisdom—his problem in each dialogue is rather how to make himself understood.*

> Besides, artful diversion doesn't stave off suspicion, it only diffuses it; folks smell a rat but can't spot it, and so they become the more vigilant. That's why esotericism is so futile.

Well, I've noticed a trait in people who have matters of consequence to tell: a certain bashfulness about apothegmatic (maxim-like) revelations. They want, sometimes, to be summary, but they also wish hardly anyone would notice these too concentrated, inadequate exposures of long care. So they go fleetingly transient.

Annapolis, 2017

37

Is Philosophy a Subject?
Love of Wisdom

Of course, it *isn't*. How could it be, considering that, according to its name, it is an affect, a passion, a love* and its object

> From *philos*, "loving" or "fond of" and *sophia*, "sagacity" or "wisdom."

is the arousal of the soul by an inquiry into, the pursuit of, the kind of knowledge that satisfies our humanity. Thus "philosopher" is said not of one who *is* sage* but who *would be* wise.

> Socrates says of a person in pursuit of truth: "To call him 'wise,' Phaedrus, seems to me to be big talk and to suit god alone, but 'wisdom-loving' or something like that would befit him and keep more in tune" (*Phaedrus* 278d).

But again, of course, it *is* a subject. It appears as one in the catalogues of colleges and universities that I've checked out, in course sequences of advancing expertise, usually beginning with introductory courses numbered from 100 upwards.* The

> Thus Philosophy 105: "Historical Introduction to Philosophy"— perhaps an initially paradoxical self-contravening project, for if it's history, it's not exactly philosophy, the two being, to my mind, antithetical inquiries. But there is this saving implication: the students enrolled in these courses must have been prepared by 104 previous propaedeutic study occasions.

course titles and descriptions tell what subject matter is being "offered"—to take or leave: the thinking life as an option.

Before going on, I should think about "subject." What is meant by a subject as the term appears in my title? First, what is it *not*? 1) It's not meant in the sense in which my friend Anne in London is the Queen's subject, rather than my country's citizen—a purely formal relation in which she feels not a hint of subjection.* 2) It's not the object of a suspecting

> Though she takes, privily, some pride, pride mitigated by a dash of Scots distance, in her father's service with his sovereign's Hundred Rifles (as I recollect the name of this choice band).

regard, such as we've recently learned to distinguish from a target: A "subject" is a person of interest under some scrutiny by authorities, while a "target" is the human object of a criminal investigation. 3) It is not an underlying basis (*hypokeimenon*), a substrate, to which accidents are attached, a receptacle (*dektikon*) receiving descriptive attributes, not a "subject" in its literal sense, a thing "thrust under" to give a unifying stability to the swarm of adjectives hanging about it, 4) nor a subject of a sentence, whose function it is to bear the burden of a predicate, a term said of, modifying, the subject.* 5) Nor

> It is a classical question whether our particular language consists mostly of subject-copula-predicate sentences because that's how things are constituted or whether the inverse holds: that the world is (re)constructed for us by our language. I think—as do, I'm pretty sure, most people who don't think professionally— that the language given us is, first and last, *about* the things we speak of. (I'm leaving aside the question *how* words can intend things, since, except for onomatopoeia, word-imitation, they have no relation of similarity or other evident bond to connect them to things. On this hypothesis, that of aboutness, the semantic realm of meaning follows the ontic realm of being: As things *are*, so we *speak*.)

do I mean the subject that is a person, an ego, a self, a being terminally "subjective," such as is self-involved to the point of regarding itself as the world-constituting center by whom and for whom all that is, is made. There is a vitiated version of this subjectivity (reduced to a less pure level than that of Kant*)

> Whose *Critiques* are the grand exposition of this philosophical subject: world-constituting, world-interpreting, and world-valuing.

with reference to whose bruisable ego all is to be evaluated: How am I feeling? Is my world, that owes me its existence, enhancing me properly? Here subjectivity is ultimate reflexivity, self-mirroring. In philosophy this subject appears particularly in epistemology, the knowledge of knowledge. It is regarded with suspicion for its tyrannical implications in at least one ancient work and rejected as the basis of a falsely framed initial inquiry in a masterwork of modern philosophy.* 6) Nor

> Ancient: Plato's *Charmides* (and David Levine's exposition, *Profound Ignorance*). Modern: Hegel's Introduction to his *Phenomenology of Spirit*.

am I thinking of the "subjectivity" found in literature and music, emotionality artfully expressed, which is the primary characteristic of Romanticism (capitalized, a particular, actual movement) and romanticism (lower case, a universally possible mode).

7) Finally, there is the subject in the material, the "subject matter" sense, the sense of the question "Is philosophy a subject?" It is not a liege to a sovereign, nor an object of suspicion, nor a leading noun of a sentence, nor an ego in its selfishness, nor an emitter of emotion. It is none of these actually, yet perhaps it resonates in each of them.

What then is a subject as learning matter? Ordinarily that's simple. It's a body of accumulated knowledge which a professor thereof commands and conveys with more or less aptitude to the students.

The order of delivery goes in two directions. In introductory courses it is from basics up, if the subject has formulable beginnings such as definitions, axioms, and postulates in mathematics or vocabulary, paradigms, and syntax in language. A talented teacher will initiate students into these elementary beginnings so cunningly that they consider even them as deeply, as humanly, interesting.

The second way is the inverse. Some subjects are actually progressive; what comes last is more powerful and more comprehensive than the early stages and versions. Mathematics and science are progressive in this way. The humanities are faux-progressives: Sophisticated conceptions, clever concepts are devised, captivate the profession for a while, and give way to other novelties*; they come into vogue and fade out. They

> In fact, faux-novelties, for, setting aside that such inquiries are probably as old as humanity, they became self-conscious, received names, and were written down as long ago as over two and a half millennia (taking 600 B.C.E. as a rough date of inception).

may leave traces in the subject-matter or they may not. But except for veiling works of primary quality with accretions of secondary texts they don't do much beyond consigning themselves and their subjects to the black hole of out-of-dateness, and to cycles of resurrection whose length has, I'm sure, been researched. Advance in wisdom isn't in it, but there may be, as I've noted, some vestigial conceptual vocabulary. For apt students, to learn of cutting-edge mathematics or science is exciting and confirming, for inept students it is, albeit unforgettable, also deflating. But to fill students' heads with the parasitical conceptualizing rife in the humanities is plain wrong. Tell them instead, "When you're tempted to seek relief from cluelessness about a primary work in a simplifying introduction or a sophisticating article, just read the work once more."

So the presentation of a subject can be, might be, from the first foundations up* or from the last discovery inward.

> If it has them; history, for example, doesn't seem to have any accepted axiom-analogues. Nor do social studies, whose foundational categories seem to me to be high-level interpretative generalizations. Exhibits nos. 1 and 2: "Society" and "Culture."

I've started with firsts and lasts, because they show something crucial to my question, whether philosophy is, can be,
or ought to be a subject: A subject, to be taught, requires of
its teacher *expertise*, a thorough knowledge, from its foundations to its cutting-edge condition, even if it's by nature topical or ephemeral.*

Topical: of a "place" (Greek: *topos*), that is, local; ephemeral: of the
"day" (Greek: *hemera*), that is, temporal.

However, as I indicated before, there is a Socratic watchword, mindful of the literal meaning of this subject (if it is
a subject). It is not the expert's "I know my own subject,"
but the amateur's "I know my own ignorance"—a mantra of
many implications. With it, philosophy's pivotal plier boldly
denies having any expertise. But he slyly insinuates that he
knows a great deal. He is the wisest of all for knowing his
ignorance, for knowing—somehow—the "nothing" that is
the matter of his non-knowing.* I'll give a summary of the

For example, *Apology* 21b ff.: "So I saw for and within myself that
I knew nothing." To be sure, this is taking a manner of speech,
meaning "to know *not one thing*," literally: "to know *no-thing[ness]*."
Irony, Socratic irony, is meaning-fraught double talk.

points just made overtly or intendedly, reconciledly mindful
that they amount more to an asserted claim than to an argued
doctrine.

First then, a subject-matter ought to bear a direct connection to its titular name. The *love* of *wisdom*, of the title in
question, consists of two problematic terms. For love, be it a
friendly inclination or an erotic possession, is longing attraction. And longing betokens a lack, albeit an image-filled emp-
tiness, or alternatively, it is an imposed passion, an affect.
And a passion is a sort of suffering—to be sure, a welcome
suffering. In any case it is unsettling, as desire-driven longing
or as pathological excitement.

Next, wisdom is distinct from expertise, as different as extracting meaning from a flute score is from playing it off flawlessly: making music versus displaying know-how. Wisdom inhabits a psychic universe of stably accreting significance; its principle of growth is truth rather than novelty, its temporality is leisure rather than haste, its talent is receptivity rather than efficiency.*

> Of course, freshness, vitality, and effective action are intended concomitants of sagacious wisdom.

Furthermore, a philosopher or a philosophy, as the case may be, is not of course (at least as I, an avid amateur rather than a proud professional,* think of it) a submitter to arbitrary

> In my own terms, I'm effectively quite unmusical and affectively very musical.

rule by a fellow human being, nor the legitimate focus of official suspicion, nor a substrate supporting attributes, nor a noun governing a sentence's copula, nor a self-involved ego.

So on the somewhat iffy hypothesis that this collection nearly covers the meaning-territory of the term "subject," here's the completing piece of the picture-puzzle: A subject *is*—metaphorically—an "area" of knowledge, demarcated from the outside by pretty well understood boundaries and divided internally by knowledgeable distinctions.*

> It is significant that the most exhaustive such "division" (*diairesis*), or set of divisions, of which I know, in fact deals with the divisions and collections of the activities that constitute the realm of expert knowledge itself. They are presented in Socrates' presence but *without* his participation in Plato's *Sophist*. Expertise is the fitting field for division in this dialogue because it is enabled by the great genus of Otherness introduced there (257c).
>
> The modern, antithetical counterpart, initiating the project of empirical scientific inquiry, is announced by Bacon in *The New Organon*, which concludes with a prescient catalogue of future subjects. To my delight, its number 103 is a "History of Pottery," the very subject I worked at for several years as an archaeologist in Athens, the properly productive prelude to my defection to philosophy.

Clearly, the above is not a description of philosophizing true to its name; to grind that in I'll quote Socrates against Descartes:

> So this especially is the affect [*pathos*] of a philosopher: to wonder (Plato, *Theaetetus* 155d).

versus

> [Wonder] can entirely eradicate or pervert the use of reason. That is why, although it is good to be born with some inclination to this passion, since it disposes us to the acquisition of the sciences, we should try afterwards to emancipate ourselves from it as much as possible. . . . But to prevent excessive wonder there is no remedy but to acquire the knowledge of many things . . . (Descartes, *The Passions of the Soul*, Article 76).

The one speaks as a lover of wisdom, the other writes not ". . . as a moral philosopher but as a physicist," that is, a scientist, from Latin *scire*, "to know."* These then are two ways,

> I'm not making this up: *Scire*, "to split," shares its derivation with "shit." (In view of my final recommendation below, this citation will not be imputed to me as prejudicial.)

one subject-resistant, the other subject-constituting. The first way is to *long* to know under the hopeful learning-hypothesis that knowledge is approachable asymptotically as we converge on death; the second is to *expect* to know under the confident postulate that knowledge is attainable directly as we* advance in research—*conjecture* versus *certainty*. To me

> "We" here is a courtesy-plural; in fact, not all of us have the talent and the taste. When speaking of philosophy, "we" is more warranted. Everyone is up to and desirous of wisdom—at some time in life. And yet, even mathematics and science are "humanities," humanly engaging subjects, when humanely taught. Fun example: Take (so to speak) a square and squeeze it (without deforming its sides). First it will look like a diamond, a rhombus; then it will collapse onto itself, forming a line half the length of its former circumference. Now try the same on a triangle. It won't budge. Why on earth (so to speak) not?

it seems that almost everyone should learn and come to relish some elementary mathematics and some mathematical
science. And absolutely everyone should at some right time
actually do what we all really want to do, to cultivate and
pursue the inborn longing for insight and its sagacity.

A final summary thought: Who's capable of philosophy?
Any human being endowed with humanity. And what is that?
It is the roiled melding in us of what is intensely personal and
what is comprehensively common; as I put it to myself, a little
more academically: it's to know that ontological and theological conversation is the ultimate intimacy. And who's human?
Nearly everyone.

So is philosophy a subject? Not really.

Annapolis, 2019

38

[The Idea of] The Good
The Ultimate Interest

I don't know whether I'm right to do this: I'm off to collect
a compendium, delineate a description, of a notion that occurs in just one spot in Plato's thirty-six dialogues (as far as I
can tell) and is their high point, the sort of high point that is
a basis as well, and thus diffused throughout. In fancy terms,
it is *transcendent, foundational,* and *immanent,* all of these.
The notion is *the Idea of the Good,* the more localized place
is the *Republic,* Books VI–VII, 503–516. At 509b appears the
most interesting, most thought-arousing feature of this or any
notion I can think of: this Idea of the Good is said to be "beyond [the farthest] being" (*epekeina tes ousias; ekeino* points
to the more remote of two things). Gently put, it not only
doesn't *exist* here and now, it even *isn't*—neither on earth nor
in the realm of ideas.*

> *Existence:* here and now; *Being:* space- and time-lessness.
> I keeping saying "notion" to avoid the latter-day term "concept."
> There are no concepts, meaning mental constructs abstracted,
> that is, pulled off, from perceptions, in the Dialogues that I know
> of; there are *opinions* (*doxai*), unthought-out thoughts, often false.
> The ideas or forms (*eide*) are not poorer but richer in substance
> than sensory perceptions, not "abstract" but "concrete," that is,
> dense in content.

It is a characteristic of Plato's writing to embed crucial notions in the literal middle of the text; thus the thought of a philosopher-king comes up in the almost exact center of the *Republic* (473; the text runs from marginal Stephanus pages 327 to 621).

Another feature is a by-the-way, vanishingly brief formulation of absolutely central matters. The best example I know is the sentence at the end of Book IX which announces that the city they've been founding is not intended for political realization but as a model of the well-adjusted soul (592c). Compare 443c–d: "[J]ustice is not concerned with the external but the internal doings of anyone, as being truly about himself and his concerns." Thus the *Republic*, in Greek *Politeia* (Constitution), contains not a political but a psychological prescription—of a well-constituted soul. (See Essay 36, "Three Platonic Places.")

Why does Plato do that? I have two intimations: He might be driven by a sort of bashfulness about announcing the notions that really matter. Or more likely, he is thinking of his fugitive presentations as a reward reserved for readers with a noticing mind.

For my delineation I mean to stick with the exposition of the pages cited from the center of the *Republic*, except for four helpful supporting references, which I'll report up front, then to go to the *Republic* pages alone.

1) At the end of the *Republic* a myth is told, commonly called the Myth of Er. It contains a vision of the cosmos, the well-formed universe (616b–c). Four of its encompassing features are A. a pillar or shaft (*kion*) of light which, so to speak, skewers the heavens, B. eight nested spindle whorls which are pierced by this pole, each bearing one of the known planets, with the earth also transfixed by the pole and static at the center, C. beams of light-radii radiating from the center of this light pole outward through the cosmos (or in the reverse direction). And D. straps of light issuing from the pole's poles (the shaft's tips) like the "undergirding" (*hypozomata*) of warships, enchaining the whole, meridian-like, in cables.*

I've seen a picture of a ship's hull tied up in ropes: James Adam, Editor, *The Republic of Plato II*, opp. p. 442.

The understandings of this passage are my own and debatable. They are driven by the larger interpretation I wish to give it, which is equally assailable. I might refer to Plotinus's Neoplatonic systematization of the *Dialogues* to corroborate my vision of the Myth of Er, but that would involve me in more detail than this essay can bear.

If this envisioning of the universe, sensory and beyond, is accurate, it fits the three features of the Idea of the Good with which I began: The light radii correspond to its *immanence* (its cohesive diffusion throughout being and appearance); the pole of light corresponds to its *foundation* (its supporting, albeit vertical, basis); and the *undergirding* by light strips corresponds to *transcendence* and *externality* (its being above and beyond both the heavenly and earthly world itself). Thus the concluding myth of the *Republic* contains a visualization of the Idea of the Good, a light structure—brilliantly imaginable, but only allusively and negatively articulable.

2) Plato wrote letters to various people in the Greek world, mostly in Italy. Some of them are thought to be spurious, not so the *Seventh Letter*, the longest and most philosophically interesting one. This letter sets out very baldly the elements of knowledge in ascending order: what ways we have of getting hold of appearances, what are our modes of cognition and what is the true object of knowledge (342). Among these objects Plato names the good, the beautiful, the just, all on the same level, probably the level of the forms that are *within* the realm of Being. This letter was written late in Plato's life, and might be regarded as a summation. Therefore the absence of the Idea of the Good that is beyond the forms is to me significant: This Good really is unique to the *Republic*. That is a rousingly mysterious fact: Why should so spectacularly interesting a notion, and so fruitful a one, be a singleton, a unicorn-idea?*

> Fruitful: Plotinus again. This ultimate Good that is "beyond being" comes into Christian theology through the *via negativa*, the way of approaching God in negative terms, his No-thingness. Plotinus provides a waystation on this road. On this and other matters the work of Werner Beierwaltes has proved unfailingly helpful

to understanding Plotinus's *Enneads*, as has Plotinus, in turn, to thinking about Plato's *Dialogues*.

The *Seventh Letter* has one salient word in common with the *Republic*: "suddenly" (*exaiphnes*), for the first turn into the light in the latter (515c) and for the light flashing in the soul in the former (341c). On the other hand, the Platonic letter is more curmudgeonly than the Socratic dialogue, evincing what we nowadays call elitism, Plato's insistence that true philosophy is for the few, whereas in the *Republic* Socrates says plainly that there is "an inherent power each one [of us] has in the soul, and that is the organ by which each one learns. . . ." We can only be turned to the light by the whole soul being brought around to see Being and then what is even brighter than Being, The Good (518c–d). Moreover, the *Republic* actually presents a written version of the Good, while the letter says that no one who is inquiring into really serious matters—and what could be more so than The Good—will ever write about them for the general public (344c).

3) Aristotle mounts strong critiques of the Idea of the Good: *Metaphysics* III ii ff., *Nicomachean Ethics* I vi, and *Eudemian Ethics* I viii. He is touchingly reluctant, because those who introduced the forms (*eide*) are "men dear to him" (*N.E.*). I will take a chance and here simply set his objections aside, because of a circumstance for which Plato himself is to blame. It is his naming of this notion an "idea" (*idea*) that justifies Aristotle in treating the idea of the Good as one of the whole group of "separable" beings, those forms that Plato refers to by that intensive neuter pronoun *auto*, "itself," such as "the Beautiful *Itself* or the Just *Itself*."*

> The Platonic "itself" is sometimes translated "absolute," meaning that the intensive is turned in on itself, absolved from all external dependence.

Aristotle objects to these because they seem to him terminally divorced from the sensory particulars for which they are meant to be responsible. In his criticism he ignores the fact that the Good is *not* an idea* or form. So his objections

> Plato's *idea* doesn't, in any case, mean an idea *in* the mind but an intelligible object *for* thought (*noesis*). In *E.E.* I viii 17 he does, in fact, speak of "the *eidos* of the good"; *eidos* is the more ordinary term for the ideal beings.

miss the aim. Nor is he well placed to mount an attack on the Idea of the Good as being beyond, on the other side of, a natural cosmic or a thinkable ideal place, since his own high point, the divinity called *Nous*, "Mind," is also beyond all the beings Aristotle recognizes—certainly beyond the moving cosmos (*Metaphysics* XII vii).

4) Aristoxenus records in his *Elements of Harmonics* (¶ 30) an anecdote often related by his teacher, Aristotle. People came to hear Plato lecture on the Good because they expected to be told something about worldly goods, such as health and wealth. Instead, to their disappointment, the lecture was entirely about mathematics and said, in short, that "The Good is unifying" (*agathon estin hen*).* I cite Aristoxenus

> I'm taking *hen* as adjectival here. With the article, *to hen*, it would be a noun, "unity." So: neither "the Good is *the* One," that is, is the "principle called unity," nor "the Good is one," that is, "the Good is a unit" are the right reading, but: "The Good is uni-fying, one-ing." Both Heraclitus (D 10) and Plotinus (VI vi 14) indirectly point to this understanding: "One" is active in *unifying*.

because the story is in line with my interpretation.

One last preliminary. I think that all great philosophy, the kind that is not absorbed in devising and then cluing out puzzlements, is theological. That's as true of the great moderns as of the ancients, but I'll here stick with the latter. Both Plato's and Aristotle's high points are divinities that are grand in their aspect, plenary in their efficacy, and ultimate in their rule.*

> Socrates calls the approach to his high point the "greatest learning"; Aristotle calls it "prime philosophy" (*Republic* 503e, *Metaphysics* 1026a). My first mention of this highest study is the place to emphasize that Socrates is far from introducing some handwaving idealism. He insists that the way up to and the study itself demand perfection, not sketchiness; and exactitude, precision (both *akribeia*), purity, not laxness (*rathymia*, 504c–e). Under The Good of the *Republic*, the romantic elevation of the *Phaedrus* and the *Symposium* turns into heavy lifting, effortful attention—learning.

Neither "The [neuter] Good" (*to agathon*) of Plato/Socrates' nor "The [masc.] Mind" (*Nous*) of Aristotle is a *Person* or a *Creator*,* and both are *external* to the sensory universe though

> I do not really know what a *person* is. Perhaps these three attempts will do, the one very loose, the second paradoxical, and the third otiose; 1. a person is a being *pretty much* like me; 2. a person is a being who is highly individual *by reason* of belonging to a common humanity; 3. a person is a being whose right-sounding relative pronoun is not "which" or "that" but "who." No. 2 actually says something.
>
> *Creator:* meant in the most radical sense, not as a maker (*poietes*) of things out of given material, according to a given model (such as the "Craftsman" [*demiourgos*] of the dialogue *Timaeus*), but as one who creates a world out of nothing according to his own will, contingently (like the God of the Bible, in some interpretations). But see the "Exit" to this essay.

both function within it. The *Nous* moves the world by exercising an—unreciprocated—attraction at a distance, by raising a hunger toward it in all mobiles, all beings capable of motion, in the world; thus Aristotle's nature is *pervaded by hunger*, appetitiveness, traceable ultimately to the desire to know. His greatest work begins with the claim that all human beings hunger (*oregontai*) to know and culminates in the claim that the divine Mind attracts all movables; it attracts them both as being itself knowable and as "hungered for" (*orekton*; *Metaphysics* I i, VII vii 2).

The Good works differently—somewhat. It is neither a "demiurge"—a craftsman, artificer, literally a "worker for the people," nor a maker of any sort, probably least of all a creator; nor has it any aspect of personhood such as humanity or personal divinity—and yet it enlivens the cosmos and its people with purposeful activity.*

> Activity is an Aristotelian term (*energeia*), and so I use it hesitantly. Yet Socrates/Plato are in crucial respects Aristotle-precursors. More below.

Now for a sort of Index of the topic, the Idea of the Good (*he idea tou agathou*), not alphabetical but as its features appear in the *Republic*.

INDEX: THE IDEA OF THE GOOD
Plato, *Republic*

Here begins my explication of the Idea of the Good itself, from its one text. Plato's mode of composition is circular. I mean not only that the whole *Republic* is structured to be envisioned as a nest of concentric circles,* with, as I said, the

Like the nested spindle whorls of the Myth of Er.

announcement of the philosopher-rulers at the exact center and a critique of poetry going in and passing out of the work along its diameter. But I also mean that his arguments tend to begin and end on the same note.* This fact is not overt but

E.B., *The Music of the Republic*, Paul Dry Books (2004).

implied. From the first introduction of the Idea of the Good, to the first step of the education that is under its aegis, oneness, uni-fication, is on the scene. Recall Aristoxenus's report on Plato's own lecture on the Good as having "one," here an adjective, as a predicate. In this vein, the philosophers' philosophical education begins with the unit of mathematics, the small-scale, stand-alone one that is the principle and constituent of number, of multiplicity. Socrates thinks that as such it is a "winch," a levering device, into Being. He means, I believe, that it is the beginning of philosophy to study arithmetic, that is, number, not for computational competence but as an incitement to thinking about the one-over-many character of forms.* And the *Republic* ends with the image of a

Because a number *differs* from a form in the way that it presides over what it collects. Take the form Courage; every individual it imbues is courageous. Not so a number; the items it collects do not borrow its character, since those, say, under Three are not threeish but remain ones. Socrates thinks that to find this remarkable is to be about to philosophize.

unified world, a cosmos, undergirded by the light-bonds. (See number 1 above.)

Socrates takes care of some peripheral circumstantials before focusing on The Good itself, or rather precisely, not on it "itself," but on its image, its analogue, and its myth. His two main conversational partners are Plato's two brothers; surely that humanly significant fact has some bearing on the unique appearance of what must have been a notion deeply important to Socrates—a man of greatest reticence about his most cherished positive opinions (see Essay 36, "Three Platonic Places"). I do not mean that he never speaks of them (how would I know?) but that he does it explicitly only on rare and highly fraught occasions, consequently in moments of memorable pathos.*

The two brothers are present together in one other dialogue, significantly the dialogue on the One, the *Parmenides*.

Of the two, it is Adeimantus who is the partner at the beginning. He is the brother apparently less gifted for the higher studies that lead up to The Good, partly because he is impatient. Socrates begins by setting out the context. The "highest study" or "learning" (*mathema*) marks the completion of the philosopher kings' education. He sketches out briefly the sort of soul, rarely manifest,* that has the aptitude for just these

Though potentially universal (*Republic* 518c).

studies: large-minded *and* orderly, sharp *and* stable. He has already said that there is no quick way to this culmination, but a long effort is necessary. Since I take the long way to be that very education, Socrates is about to contradict himself and to offer an outline of the way.

Adeimantus is now pushing Socrates just to tell his own opinion of The Good; he even frames the terms: Is it knowledge or pleasure? Socrates becomes evasive, and seems about to veer away from the topic. Glaucon, in a brotherly way, jumps in to save the conversation. He is the one for the long way; he and Socrates have that teacher-student reciprocity which is the *methodos*, the "way to be followed," in the higher studies delineated in the *Seventh Letter* (341c, 344b). He will be Socrates' partner for a long time.*

> Adeimantus reenters the conversation when they are speaking of the falling away from the philosopher king's polity in Book VII (548d). His first contribution is some well-meant but slightly obtuse praise for his brother; Socrates sets him right. He's the sociable brother (*Parmenides* 126a), but perhaps not so alert to his own speech. He likens Glaucon to the first type to fall away from the rule by philosophy to the power of honor, because his brother is a lover of victory; Socrates quickly points out that this timocratic type has some unadmirable features. Yet Adeimantus is also, unwittingly, elevating his brother, since the philosophers have all had to be warriors, hence surely lovers of victory.

Socrates sets aside fairly curtly Adeimantus's two suggestions. The Good is not knowledge because no one has gotten further when asked what this knowledge is than to say that it's "knowledge of the *good*," which advances nothing. And The Good is not pleasure because there are bad pleasures. But this much can be positively said: The Good is useful and beneficial and, whereas we might want what *seems* just and beautiful, when it comes to good, everyone wants what *is* good, not what just seems so. And as I've said, Socrates will soon set his own requirement of a long and "circuitous way" (*periodos*, 504b) to a sort of knowledge of The Good.

The preliminary circumstances done with, Socrates responds to Glaucon with a tsunami of likeness types: punning simile (Offspring), visual image (Sun), analogic diagram (Divided Line), picturable myth (Cave). In the world superintended by The Good imaging is the primary activity, and this is the second half of the double question I'll have to address concerning The Good: What is its function from *beyond* Being, and so from beyond both the cosmos of nature and even the realm of forms? And what is its work *within* these two realms? Otherwise put: How does the good act transcendently *and* how immanently?

But one more preliminary. I've been writing "The Good"

rather than "The Idea of the Good" now for quite a while. Why does Plato's Socrates say "Idea"? *Idea* and *eidos*, two interchangeable terms in the *Dialogues*, both have the same root: [v]id, as in our *vid*eo, signifying what has to do with vision, seeing, having an aspect, a look.* But The Good is far

> At *Republic* 596a–b, for example, *eidos* and *idea* occur in tandem, also in *Phaedo* 103e, 104b. In the *Republic* both are applied to artifacts, beds, and tables. That fact bears on the vexed question whether there are forms of crafted things. To me it seems a partial answer that in certain contexts a divine Craftsman is said to have made both the cosmos and, presumably, the ideal model from which he works (*Republic* 507c, 530a; *Timaeus* 29 a); in that case *everything* that exists is an artifact and so the forms are all of artifacts.
>
> I have a sense that in fact *idea* is a mite more visual than *eidos*. Thus my favorite translator of the *Republic*, Raymond Larson, says "shape" for *idea*, "form" for *eidos*. And Ast's *Lexicon Platonicum* defines *eidos* as *species vel forma*, but *idea* as *species vel forma sub oculos cadens:* "a kind or form falling under the eyes' observation."

removed from the intellectual mode called *intuition*. That is because in "being" beyond Being it is outside of *all* vision, sensory and hypersensory, ocular or mental. As the *source* of knowability and of knowing—see below—it is itself beyond intelligibility. So I think that Plato wrote "Idea" of the Good for a mundane reason: He did not have our printed symbols for signifying its extraordinary status—neither capitals nor italics; he couldn't write *The Good* (as I now shall), so he gave it a title, *Idea*.

And yet. Socrates' first response is to withdraw from the long circuit to a verbal duplicity, a pun. He begins: "Then won't our polity (*politeia*, "constitution," the book's Greek title) be perfectly ordered [*kosmesetai*, literally "made a cosmos"] when its guardian who oversees it is such a one as knows these things?" "These things" are the just and the beautiful—the city is called *kallipolis*, "city beauteous" (457b)*—

> Which is pretty nearly how my city, Annapolis, advertises itself.

and its guardian-ruler has to know "how ever they are good."*

> Jacob Howland, in *Glaucon's Fate* (2018), mounts the very convinc-
> ing claim that the City Beauteous of the *Republic* is deliberately
> modeled on the terrifying deformation of Sparta's Lycurgan polity
> imposed by the Thirty, a gang of Athenian proto-fascists, includ-
> ing Plato's relatives Critias and Charmides. This group was put in
> charge of Athens by the Spartans after her total defeat by them
> at the end of the century that had begun with the victory of the
> Greeks over the invading Persians. It was a victory achieved under
> Athenian leadership. From a golden glow to a dank miasma in less
> than a hundred years!
> Anyhow, Jacob Howland's thesis shows that the soul-to-city
> magnification is flawed: What works well for a sound soul—self-
> submission to thoughtfulness, self-control over one's psychic
> elements, ascent by learning to an ideology-preventive highest
> principle—all these can be devastatingly tyrannical as a political
> instauration.
> Here's corroboration: Socrates himself clearly preferred to live
> in a chaotic democracy, because "it contains every kind of consti-
> tution on account of its resources, and so it befalls him who wants
> to construct a city—which we just did—that he must of necessity
> enter a democratically governed city" to select the mode he likes
> (as in a department store for constitutions) and then "found it
> accordingly" (557d).
> Moreover, we know from the *Crito* that Socrates preferred to die
> in a democracy as well.

Then Socrates, having reiterated his own inability to expound and theirs to receive "*Th'Good*" (*tagathon*, now without "idea of"), gives a thumbnail review of the "itselves," the
forms, here called ideas, and their one-over-many function.*

> I mean their ability both to bring particular appearances into
> being and to collect their inherent multifariousness under one
> word, their name.

Among them he names the good. So there is an ideal good
among the beings, especially in this context of the knowledge useful and beneficial to the governance of Callipolis.
He emphasizes that these "ideas" are there for thought but
not eye.

The more immediate point, however, is that the Craftsman of the senses made sight the most extravagantly valuable

(*polytelestaten*) of all, because it alone (he thinks) needs a "third" to mediate between object and sense. In other words, and this is all-important, Socrates values *distance*, which makes looking *at* and *panoramic* seeing possible and which requires that third, both to distinguish and to connect the knowables and their knowers as well as things and their place (*topos*)—to illuminate and bring them out: light, the "most honored yoke."*

> In the language of the profession this passage founds "light-meta-physics," in which the non-sensory analogue to seeing is taken so seriously—think of Plotinus—as to develop vitalities of its own—a metaphor morphed into an experience.
>
> I think that the gravity of this vision, with which Plato credits his Socrates, is not only in the luminousness of the world of thought, but more far-reaching, in the distantiality (to coin a term) of human existence; we live *in*, love *through*, think *over* real and ideal distance—this by way of an *obiter dictum*, central, however, to me.

The light section is the occasion for the pun. Socrates will not, cannot, speak of *The Good* directly, so he will speak of its "offspring" (*ekgonos tou agathou*). Who is the most lordly of the gods in the sky? Glaucon gets it right away: the Sun. The Sun is the *tokos* of *The Good*. *Tokos* means both "son-by-birth" and "interest-borne-by-a-principal." So this sun-son is the filial image of the paternal ancestor, hence its fitting representative. This Sun is also, as is monetary interest, a benefaction self-generated by an apparently quiescent capital, *The Good*. So we have a first figure (of speech) to start us on a delineation of *The Good*, whose first instance is an *image*, a (visual) likeness—in words.

And immediately there is also a derivative likeness: The eye is "most sun-sortish" (*helieidestaton*) as from an "overflow" (*epirryton*) emanating from the Sun, as the Sun did from *The Good*. This by-the-way word, "emanating," is as much as we get about the likeness-making power, its cosmos-immanent effect. I think, as fast as it goes by, it is not to be taken as a

mere figure of speech but as an indication: *The Good* emanates likenesses by reason of its constitutional generosity.
Overflow, however, is neither a mode of operation (because
its action is unclear) nor a way of being (because *The Good*
is beyond being). Emanation rather names for us, who have
sight derived from *The Good* at two removes, a way to assim-
ilate our insight to something we cannot make positive, cannot set out dispositively, for ourselves.*

> I'm sketching a receptive position, neither gabble nor sound sense;
> it's being *in medias res*, in the middle of things; it's *inter-esse*, to be
> interested, drawn into interest.

Socrates has, moreover, enunciated an analogy; *The Good*
generates the Sun as its analogue (*analogon*).
Symbolically put—

Good : Thought and thoughts in the thought-place ::
Sun : Sight and sights in the visible place.

To be articulated—

As the Good is to both the organ and the objects of thought
    in the ideal realm,
So the Sun is to both vision and visibles in the sensory world.

I think we have been told of two very significant aspects
of *The Good*: First, it *is at once* the source of knowing and
of knowables, of the activity and of its objects, though it *is
neither* of these, but beyond them; they are, to be sure, of
a "good sort" (*agathoeides*). Human vision images at two
removes these complementary powers; it both discerns and
constitutes. It initiates knowing *and* envisions its objects.*

> It's Socrates who mentions these connected powers in this appar-
> ently inverse order: knowledge precedes knowables. I think this
> order prefigures that of the Sun Image about to be set out: first the
> illuminating Sun, then its generated world. In any case, the com-
> plementary duality cascades from the highest to the lowest realm.

So now Socrates looks further at the image (*eikon*) of the

Sun. The Sun doesn't only illuminate visibiles by "shining down" on them; as I've intimated, it also bestows on them generation, growth and nourishment—although it is not itself "generation" (*genesis*). And he paraphrases with emphasis: *The Good* not only makes "being known" to be present to things "knowable," but also Being* itself and Beingness (*to*

> I take Being to signify the—false "accidental"—attribution that would place *The Good* among the forms, which are all Beings by participating in Being. Then Beingness is the—here falsely attributed—inherent constitution that would make such placement correct.

einai, ousia) are present to things through that famous (*ekeinou*) Good—though *The Good* is not Beingness but is rather yet beyond Beingness, surpassing it in seniority and power. Glaucon cries out, laughingly: "By Apollo [the Sun-god], what a divine excessiveness (*hyperboles*)!"*

> I think no one else really laughs merrily in this book; Glaucon is sensitive to, startled by, the salience of the passage. It's a discombobulatingly singular high moment.

So we have been told that *The Good* acts within our world through its offspring and likeness, the Sun, which provides the yoking light that joins known and knowing,* and through

> An intra-mundane presage of *The Good's* all-encompassing unification; see below.

its warmth (I suppose) engenders the births that people the world as well as the nourishment that supports their growth.

Thus the "useful and beneficial" aspect of *The Good* mentioned a while ago (505a) appears to be justified. But on turning back, it seems that the crucial sentence is not quite determinate. It says quite clearly that this topic is well known to both brothers—though probably in a pedagogical-practical rather than in an ontological context. The puzzling part of the sentence, however, says: ". . . it is the Idea of the Good, the highest study, by putting which to use, the just and other such become useful and profitable." Here's the question: Is this highest study that of *The Good* or of the *Idea* of the Good?*

> I forbear to say "The Good 'Itself,'" for *The Good* is beyond Being-ness and has no "itself," self-identity being presumably involved in Beingness (*ousia*).

In a note above I gave a somewhat piddling, typograph-ical, reason for Plato's reference to *The Good* in terms of an *idea*. Here now is a more significant one: Insofar as *The Good* is a study, an object of learning, it is still an idea, a thought of an object. But once attained, it becomes an expe-rience as in the *Seventh Letter*—the difference between, I might say, thoughtful *at*-sight and mystic *in*-sight or even, to coin a term, "*in*-being." Socrates is about to pass from the Sun Image, a visualization, to the Divided Line, a diagrammatic representation. As presiding over this bare-line ascent, *The Good* is, perhaps, no longer an *idea* "for us," but a beyond-being, somewhat contradictorily "in itself"—so to speak. In any case, it is off the diagram with which Socrates wants to complement the Sun Image.

So he now divides the visual image into its two parts. Or better, he brings together its parts, intelligible original and sensory image, in a more perspicuous collocation. Now the ideal and the natural world are attached to the segments of a line divided into unequal parts. The position of the line and the ratio of this first division is not given; we may sup-pose that the line is upright to depict an ascent, and that the upper part is longer to signify its thicker substance.* The two

> Though not a larger multitude.

segments are then subdivided in the same ratio, so that an extended proportion of the four segments, a, b, c, d, arises: a + b : c + d :: a : b :: c : d—three ratios, a + b : c + d and a : b and c : d, all included in the proportion.* The most significant

> The Greek for "ratio" is *logos*, "expressible relation," for proportion, *analogia*, "ratio carried through."

peculiarity of this diagram is that the middle two of the four sections can be proved to be equal under this division (Jacob Klein, *A Commentary on Plato's* Meno, p. 119).

In the diagram below, the six segments (0–5) stand for the following objects of knowledge and their cognitive powers (in italics), going upward, ascending in thought (though reading down on the page).

The equality of the second and third segment signifies the applicability of mathematics to the natural realm and of

---

OUT OF THE INFINITE DOUBLE

0. The Human Cave: Deceitful artifacts (a *Hades aeides*,* a "sightless underworld").

   Phaedo, Republic 515

   UNDER THE SUN

1. Images natural (shadows and mirrorings) and artificial (metaphors and pictures): "*Image-recognition*" (*eikasia*).
2. Things natural and artificial: *Trust* (*pistis*).

   UNDER THE GOOD

3. Mathematical and logical objects: "*Thinking things through*" (*dianoia*).
4. Forms, the "itselves": *Thought** (*noesis*) or

   Thought is the past participle of the action verb "to think," of which *thinking* is the continuative present participle. Thus: Thought : thinking :: *noesis* : *dianoia*.

   knowledge (*episteme*), working by "*the power of dialectic*."

   BEYOND BEING

5. The Good: *Negative Analogy* (*via negativa*).

Going upward

logic to the rational dwellers therein. The two kinds of cognition are complementary, coextensive. *"Trust"* is the usually unmindful faith we have that the sun will rise and the table not topple, a belief in so-called facts. *"Thinking-through"* supplies the rational hypotheses that modify our trust in the natural and artificial environment.

So, reading the Divided Line as described above, we are presented with the stages of the ascent into the highest study (532b, 534e), a "climb," an "upwards road" (*epanodos*). Below the line of learning and off it is a zero world of Nonbeing and its deceits, the human cave of ignorance. The first and lowest of the line's cognitive rungs is occupied by images natural and artificial, governed by the ability to recognize images as images. It is *least* substantial but *most* influential, since all the subsequent rungs or stages involve recognizing the objects there studied as images, as copies of the rung above, of the things that are thought to be more themselves, such as the real sun-lit world rather than its shadows. Actually thinking here overleaps itself in each section by thoughtlessly borrowing as "sub-positions" (*hypotheseis*, 510c) the contents of the rung above. For example, arithmeticians blithely assume that there are units and what a unit is (Euclid, Bk. VII, Def. 1). Finally thought comes within "sight" of the ultimate, the hyperbeing, the "*un*hypothesizable beginning" (*arche anhypothetos*, 510b*), "the source of the Whole" (*tou pantos arche*,

Verbal adjectives ending in *tos* denote what is possible or impossible.

511b), *The Good*; it is no longer referable to a higher ground.*

"Assumptionless" or "un-assumed" means colloquially: the buck stops here. There is no further Beyond to what is already "beyond Being," no attainable determination to backstop the "source of the whole," no supporting sub-position (*hypo-thesis*) to supply the cause of the Cause or to explain why the Origin rules.

Even in the upper two segments, image recognition is still

the task. Thus mathematicians, as I've just reported, suppose, *assume*; they devise definitions, axioms, and postulates, and they use these, once more, as those "hypo-theses," literally "sub-positions," ungrounded props, of which they even make sensory diagrams. From these they reason downwards to conclusions. But the philosophers, at home in the uppermost segment, try to give actual accounts, for example, of the unit, by asking "What is Unity?" and of the circle: "What is Circularity?" So they climb, by means of dialectic,* above sensory aids

> It is the art of dealing, never with abstractions, but with concrete idealities (*noeta*), using both dianoetic logic and noetic insight. Glaucon felicitously introduces the term "theorizing" (*theoroumonon*)—viewing, beholding (as in a theater)—for one who is engaging in dialectic (511c): A dialectician turns vision (*theoria*) into words (*logoi*), sight (*eidos*) into logic (*logike*).

and hypotheses, perhaps to attain sight of the "unhypothesizable beginning": *The Good*.

But then again, the Divided Line can be read from the top down. Now we begin with the power of "dialectic," by which I understand (put otherwise than in the note just above) what is technically termed "onto-logy," the study of Being. It is, when pure, an imageless "way to follow" (a *methodos*, not a jigged method) by means of forms and through them, a way, Socrates thinks, no longer communicable at this nocturnal moment and to this unprepared company.

From this highest segment (remarkably a merely one-dimensional representation invoking the image of the most substantial, the ideal realm), there issues a cascade of ever more being-removed images occupying the lower segments. Thus, read in a downward direction, the Divided Line is, so to speak, a directory of a cosmic polity, hosting the Callipolis Socrates has depicted, including its castes and its competences—with this great difference: The political polity is unachievable in practice and not even meant to be realized (592b, see Essay 36, "Three Platonic Places"), while, as the unidimensional representation of the whole, the Divided Line represents a serious physical and metaphysical ontology and is meant to be actual.

Socrates packs one more grand image into this image-riot: "Make a copy," he asks Glaucon, meaning a mental image, of our human nature with respect to education (*paideias*, really "upbringing," 514a) and the lack of it. There follows the Myth of the Cave.* It is a picture of people chained to, presumably

Numbered zero in the listing of the Divided Line's segments.

comfortable, couches in an underworld grotto. They sit with their backs to the entrance, watching through night and day a shadow show thrown on the screen-like back of the cave by people walking on a road running along a low wall located behind the prisoners' backs. These people are carrying puppets of all kinds, whose talking shadows are projected on the screen by a fire in back of the puppeteers.* Now a savior

Scarce a soul of us who hasn't been one of them. Glaucon observes how strange the image is; Socrates says: "Like us." Current designation: couch potatoes.

appears and unshackles one of the prisoners, who is suddenly forced to stand up, turn around, and walk up to exit into the day's sunlight. This turn-around is a literal conversion (*periagoge*, 518c). Now, dragged up into real nature, he has a hard time, being blinded by the sun's light. But he has a yet worse time when he returns to the cave; down there they would, if they could, kill him.* "This image," says Socrates to Glaucon,

Plato is writing after Socrates' execution in 399 B.C.E., perhaps some twenty years later, not long after he founded the Academy in 385; the date is speculative.

"must be attached to all the foregoing."

Fine, but how, where? Socrates intimates that this might be an image of the soul's ascent to what is truly knowable and of its "finally" but "scarcely" (*mogis*, 516c) coming within sight of the Idea of the Good. If so, the picture of the released prisoner's issuing into nature should be laid alongside the upper part of the line, and the cave along the lower. It's simple, just a humanized, fleshed-out version of the theoretically skeletal diagram. But there are two little details in the way. First is the grotto, the manmade cave whence the freed prisoners enter into the natural world. It's not on the Divided Line. And then there is the Sun's position in the scheme. The Sun is not beyond but *in* the sensory cosmos, which we moderns call nature, though our natural universe is a *space* of motions governed by binding laws of motion, while this ancient cosmos is a *place* ordered by a beautiful geometry of figures.

So I propose an expansion of the diagram's theoretical layout, whose pervasive defect is that it contains no account of the deficiencies, shortcomings, negativities, in short, of the badness of Being. Attach the Myth of the Cave, the human story, to the Line below "Under the Sun" and its two lower segments, nos. 1 and 2 in the diagram, as no. 0. Thus the subterranean dwelling falls into an additional segment below these—a cavernous realm not so far thus imaged: as a *Hades*, an underworld of deceit rife in the social and political polity.*

> There is support for this alignment in a figure of speech Socrates himself uses. This conversion that brings the prisoner from a night-like day in the Cave to a sunny one in the Cosmos is analogous to someone leading certain people "from Hades [to be] among the gods" (521c). Also, at 516d, Socrates quotes Achilles, who famously says that he'd rather live the life of a serf than his present one, which Socrates has him describe like that of the Cave; Achilles is speaking from Hades. Other cases of turning Hades into a "speaking name": Aides/aeides, "Hades the Sightless," see *Phaedo* 81c, *Cratylus* 404b.
>
> There is a hint early on in the *Republic* that there must be a second cause: "So the good isn't responsible for everything, . . . it is not responsible for bad things" (379b).

For what are the puppeteers but entertainers and, if need be, spin doctors, addicting us to artificial make-belief? Thus there appears an element of ethics, connecting the *Republic*'s central books of ontology to the two serious ethical critiques of poets and painters, the people who devise the puppet plays— critiques that occur symmetrically on the way into and out of the book.*

Book I is often regarded as a preface; in that case Books II and X, where these critiques are located, become the ingress and egress, and Book VI is the nuclear center.

Socrates segues into the intended consequence, the actual upbringing, really the higher education of those by nature fit for it:

Our job as founders is to force (*anagkasai*) the best natures to arrive at the learning that we've said before is the greatest: to see *The Good* and to ascend this ascent (519c–d).

I pointed out before that rule by philosophers is proposed at the almost exact middle of the whole *Republic*. But if, again, Book I is set aside as a preface, the middle shifts to round about 491d, where Socrates is discussing with Adeimantus, his conversational partner when things go wrong, the greater danger of corruption facing the best natures. Socrates avers that "bad" (*kakon*) is more opposite to "good" (*agathon*) than to "the [merely] non-good" (*to me agathon*). I think this might be the first reference to *The Good* that is a sentential assertion, not merely a description by an adjective or a relation to a form. But though it would be nice, I wouldn't swear to its actually placing The Good—a deep ontological decision—in opposition to Evil rather than Nonbeing.*

A great distinction for medieval philosophical theology.

These true philosophers will not, however, be allowed to remain up there when they've seen enough for practical purposes, certainly not just because they don't want to leave: "They must go *down*" (*katabateon*, 520c).*

My italics. The *Republic*, significantly, begins with Socrates' own report: "I *went down* (*kateben*) yesterday into Piraeus . . ." Piraeus

was the port of Athens and a working-class district. It is possible
to connect the properly transliterated name *Peiraieus* to a noun, *he
peraia*, "the country beyond [the river]." Thus the Piraeus stands
for the land below and beyond, like Hades, across the River Styx,
distantly opposite to the heaven of the Good.

So Socrates has gone down into the terrestrial underworld, the
earthly Hades, to discharge his obligations. Moreover his Plato
employs for him the narrative style of the first-person account,
which in this very book explicitly escapes Socrates' own strictures
against that fictional make-believe in which the narrator responsible, the tragic poet, disappears behind his characters (393 ff.).
Socrates' first-personal account is completely candid insofar as he
takes responsibility for what he reports. And again, it's delivered
down below; "I went down." Diogenes Laertius (III 37) reports that
on Plato's death a tablet was found with his various transpositions
of this first sentence.

For these philosophers-to-be Socrates now prescribes, in
outline, a curriculum, the initial program of what came to
be called the liberal arts. From the first, this course has a culmination, a conclusion: the end (*telos*, 532b) of the knowable
realm, *The Good*, as well as a purpose, a practical application: the education of the community's leaders.

Thus this program was and is, as long as it still seeks to
be coherent and vigorous, afflicted with two inherent problems: 1. Can there be such an education which is not directed
toward and pervaded by a finality, that is to say, shaped at
least implicitly as a theology or as a metaphysics? And if so,
shaped by whom? And 2. Can this learning, which is altogether liberal, here meaning "for its own sake,"* so much so

Liberal in this sense comes from Aristotle's *Politics* (1338a).

that its participants think they live in the Isles of the Blessed
(519c), be reconciled with their obligation to return to the
mundane realm and rule it?* And if not, why would they?

Here, too, is introduced the extraordinary and completely true
notion that a test for fit rulers is their reluctance to rule—because
they've got better things, not to do, but to think about.

Insofar as liberal learning is taken seriously these issues remain alive both as problems to be practically resolved and questions to be theoretically pondered.*

> Hence genuine institutions of learning may advertise utility, but they offer happiness (not pleasure).

The actual curriculum introduces what will later be called the *quadrivium*, the "four-way," three kinds of mathematics plus physics.* Socrates begins with arithmetic, not primarily

> Thus Boethius, translating the *tesseres methodoi*, "four ways to pursue," of Nicomachus in his *Introduction to Arithmetic* I iv.

as an art of calculation but as an inquiry into the nature of one and many, unit and number (see above). For in sensation one is also always many, and that invites thought. It is a winch (*holkos*, 521a), fit for "truly hauling us up toward Beingness." This upward path starts in the small, in the one, the unit, which is the origin of, and whose multitude constitutes, numbers, to end in the greatest, in *The Good* which is *the One*, the unifier.*

> As imaged in the Myth of Er of Book X, it is, I've claimed, *at once* the piercing pole, its penetrating radii, and the cincturing understrapping.

For the rest, the philosopher kings-to-be study geometry insofar as it generates, from unidimensional elements, lines, mathematical two- and three-dimensional objects, planes and solids; the resulting mathematical bodies are set in motion, and a rational astronomy is achieved, the first condition for the earliest of the physical sciences. These rational heavens, by being set in motion, produce a mathematical music (*harmonia*, a musical scale "fitted together," compounded from consonances), and finally, as a result, a world-picture, a "cosmology"—a "well-ordered rational whole." Neither of these, this astronomy or this cosmology, are experimental sciences, but pure theory. The imaged result, as I've claimed, is incorporated into the culminating Myth of Er (see 1, above).

The desired end of this way (*methodos*) is that it arrive at the *community* and *kinship* (*koinonia, synggeneia*, 531d) these studies have with each other. In other words, the very coherence of the arts curriculum is intended to imprint a sense for commonality and unity in the future leaders.

It was, however, only the "prelude" to the strain, the song.*

> Why "song" (*nomos*, 532a; this word also means usage, custom, law)? How is dialectic a musical usage? One guess: dialectic moves over a non-sensory panorama of forms; perhaps Socrates is saying that it does so in a non-sensory passion for harmony, supplementing the visual figure for knowing with an auditory figure for desiring to know.

The aspirants now must become "terrific dialecticians." Dialectic is the activity of the uppermost segment of the Divided Line below The Good, where thought as insight prevails. It deals, as I said, with questions and problems of individual beings, ideal Being, and their essential Beingness (*onta, on, ousia*), in sum, with ontology.*

> There are the two dialogues I think of as immediately dialectical: the *Phaedo*, where, on his last day, Socrates, in an Athenian prison, lays out unresolved dialectical issues as his legacy for the youngsters with him and, perhaps, for the non-Greek world yet to be and far away (78a). And the *Sophist*, where he instigates a conversation but only listens, as a visitor from Italy, an intellectual child of Parmenides, solves the dialectical problem concerning Nonbeing (the second-most interesting piece of ontology I know of), thereby doing away with his "Father," while setting in train the dialectical tradition of the West. This is Plato saying very discreetly that the day of Socrates' death is only the end of the beginning, and that Socrates' listening sets the scene for something new.
>
> There is much, much more to this dialectical realm than I've tried to make explicit with respect to the Good as a uni-fying One. Two examples:
>
> 1) There is a plausible argument that the form (*eidos*) of Being is a Second to the presiding One, the Good, and thus an "eidetic Two." The background is a theory concerning the quasi-arithmetical structure of "genera," relatable assemblages of forms. These are number-like collections which have this strange feature: Instead of consisting of homogenous units, they are constituted of substan-

tial monads, which, though *together* the same, say "Virtues," are *each* irreducibly different, even opposites of each other. (It is actually possible to show that some Socratic excellences are in mutual opposition, such as courage and moderation.) Thus Being is an eidetic number consisting of the *two* very primal apposite units, "standstill" and "motion" (Klein, *Greek Mathematical Thought and the Origin of Algebra* 79–99, esp. 94). This Being-number is beyond linear thinking (*dianoia*) or articulate speech (*logos*), just as The Good is beyond Beingness. *So The Good is, in fact, two levels away from daily mentation: non-rational and non-ideal.*

2) In his "Unwritten Teachings" Plato spoke of an *aoristos dyas* (Aristotle, *Metaphysics*, esp. Bk. XIII; its published counterpart plays a central role in the dialogue *Philebus*). Translations of *aoristos dyas* are: "Indeterminate Dyad" or "Indefinite Duplicity" or "Infinite Double." It denotes the ultimate source of all the doubling that pervades the world—yes/no; same/other; image-making/faking; excess/deficiency; shapeless stuff/ultimate matter. All these terms are correlative; most pairs have a primary and a secondary term, and a few couples are "duplicitous" in the derogatory sense, that is, cognitively or morally corrupt, evil.

We may imagine that, as *The Good* is enthroned on top of the Divided Line, so the Indeterminate Dyad sits below its lowest segment, as the inherently oppositional principle, sucking the world downwards, attenuating its being, while increasing its multiplicity. So this second, secondary, principle would provide the duplicating pull that draws images out of and down from originals. Thus it is, like Mephistopheles, "a part of that force / Which constantly wills evil and constantly effects good" (Goethe, *Faust* I 1336–37). As sitting below the realms represented on the Divided Line, the Indeterminate Dyad is the counterpole to the Good above—these are the ontologically opposite and ethically opposing principles that between them encompass all there is and hold it together as a variegated whole.

Just as there is a tradition, deriving from the Good beyond Being, of God as Nothingness, so there is a tradition of the two-ended infinity, "the Great and the Small," that is one description of the Infinite Dyad. Hegel alludes to it: a *bad* infinity of mere unending More and Less—as opposed to a good infinity that, though unbounded (having neither beginning nor end), is self-enclosed (has a finite periphery) and thus encompasses finitude; the circle is an example. I cite these cases as examples of Platonic resonances in the Western tradition.

Although Plotinus does not admit a principle antithetical to the One, because everything has to fall out smoothly from that prime principle, he might, I think, have appreciated my version as a congenial fallacy.

Socrates, finally, attaches the ages of life at which the guardians of the community are to reach the successive stages both of study and of service in their lifelong education. At fifty the most apt at these begin their final ascent "toward the end" (*telos*, 540a). Just as the bodily eye has been said to be sun-like, so the soul's eye is "good-like" (508b, 540a) insofar as the organ of vision shares in illuminating its realm.*

> But how, I do not understand. Does the eye beam *bestow* visibility? Apparently.

Therefore they must

> bend upwards the beam of the soul, to look towards that itself which supplies light to all. And seeing *The Good Itself*, they must use that as a model, and must spend the rest of their lives, each in turn, ordering (*kosmein*) the city, private citizens, and *themselves* (my italics; recall that this dialogue is really about the sound founding of the soul [592b]).

Socrates ends by reminding Glaucon that women with apt natures too will be rulers and receive their education. Glaucon agrees: they'll have everything in common with the men. It's said at a prominent juncture, yet by-the-way; it's obvious to *these* Athenians.

Here, then, once more is what seems to me the first and last question: How close do these learners come to *The Good*?*

> For that matter, what of Socrates himself? Are the times he appears lost in thought (for example, *Symposium* 175a, 220c) just intense bouts of problem solving or ascents *to* the forms or *into* or even *beyond* them? What did Plato, what should we think?

Socrates says that no learning can be placed higher than dialectic (534e) and that "the greatest learning is the Idea of the Good" (505a). The word for learning, *mathema*, is the same in both contexts. I think I'm justified in concluding that dialectic is the learning or study of the *Idea* of the Good. The terms used with *The Good* supports this. It is most often

spoken of as an *idea*, so also, just above, as an "itself," as of
a form, and only sometimes just as *The Good* (505a, 508e,
534c, 532b, 540a, 519c, 534b). There seems to be no progression, though to me it makes sense that the titles, which belong
to ontology, would be dropped as the learners "come within
sight" (*idontas*, 540a) of *The Good*. For it is *not* a Being (*on*).
Yet the very word "seeing," that is, mental vision, contradicts
the beyond-being—literally the placement of *The Good* "on
the side yonder of Beingness" (*epekeina tes ousias*, 509b).*

Ep-ekeina, once more: "parts beyond," further off even than Being.

Indeed, we're told early on (508e) that as the cause (*aitia*) of
knowledge, which bestows truth on things known and the
power to know on the knower, the Idea of the Good is beyond
these in seniority and power. Knowledge and truth are good-
like, but they are not features of *The Good* (509a). It follows
that *The Good* does not, after all, fall under dialectic, which,
I claimed, is ontological. Indeed, once more, how could it be
known by ontology, the "account of Being," since it is not
a *thing* (a being) nor a form (Being), nor the form's nature
(Beingness) at all, but beyond all three? Neither can any
knowing get to it—neither rational thinking-through (*dianoia*) nor intuitive directness (*noesis*). Yet there are, I hope
to have shown, this-worldly *approaches*, way short of mystic
transiting.*

Here is a suspicion I mention hesitantly. Is it possible that Plato's
treatment of *The Good* as idea-like and imageable is a gentle deflec-
tion of a Socratic tendency (never, indeed, put directly in words)
to mysticism, to ecstatic rapture? Is he discreetly rebuking the
hero of his life by asserting that the push past verbal articulation
does not need to issue in mysticism? It might just further entrench
wonder, the "*initial source*" of philosophy (*Theaetetus* 155d).—Now
I've said it, I can't any longer believe it.

Notice that Socrates speaks of the "greatest learning" *before* he introduces its matter, *The Good*. To me that says that
the *upward* way, the *methodos* itself, points to the necessity

for a, so to speak, off-the-charts hyper-*telos*, some preceding intimation of indefinable beyondness. He himself applies the term "cornice," coping-stone (*thrigkos*, 534e) to dialectic; there is "rightly, no longer any other learning higher than it"—though there *is* the roof.

So, yes and no—we are to think about The Good. It's like the truncated Cathedral of Santa Fe, where will or means failed for putting steeples on its towers—meant to have them, and so somehow there. Without transcending transcendence, without placing a Beyond yet above the highest, the "intelligible place" (*noetos topos*, 509d) on the Divided Line, the journey upward would hit a ceiling of brute unintelligibility. And going up the Line by studies, there would be nothing to ensure that it was the joyful experience Socrates intends it to be, that the cascade of images among which we live, being traced back and up to ever fuller originality, is in fact a rise, an increasing closeness to genuine goodness.*

> A rise in which the lowest rung remains infused with the interest of inquiry into the nature of images and the highest is alight with actual knowledge. This is what I call to myself "Socrates' *philosophical optimism.*"

Moreover, without the goodness-emanating *Good* working immanently, this curriculum would not be, along with being philosophical, eminently practical, a sort of management training for "leadership"—the philosopher kings are also called leaders (*hegemones*, for example, 489b)—which taught "best practices" that actually *were* good.* It should go

> In what I might call the pre-ontological first half of the *Republic*, the guardians' community of women and children had been called "the cause of the city's greatest good" (464b). Here is a practical instance of the unifying effect later to be achieved through the philosopher-kings' "greatest learning," when they study "The Idea of the Good."

without saying that this thought-demanding, problem-loaded course, whose connection to action in the world is itself continually put in question, is anything but an indoctrination: It is the ultimate *ideology-preventive* learning.*

> Here's what I take as corroboration of my disinclination to believe in the old arguments about Plato's totalitarianism. Not only is Socrates, the question-asker, a truly implausible protagonist of this or any ideology. But also Plato himself devised, through Critias in his own dialogue, the *Critias*, an intendedly horrid dystopia, Atlantis, a totalitarian realm under a technological ideology.

The chief contribution of the Idea of the Good is, however, its doubly transcendent, extra-ideal and extra-sensory "being." As such it is a uniting, unifying understrapping, the Unit, the *One* holding together all that is thinkable and visible, making it a Whole.* As such it is, as I've said, envisioned

> The Whole is identified with the One in a Parmenidean context (*Sophist* 244d ff.; see Essay 35, "Parmenidean Identity").

in the final image, the Myth of Er.* Who is there that knows

> Where, in fact, the "greatest study" is indirectly but unmistakably mentioned, along with my aforementioned favorite fact about the *Republic*: It's *not* the Constitution, the *Politeia* of cities but of souls (618b–e; recall that *Politeia* is the name of the book).

how the unthinkable comes to be imaginable or how the mind comes to have an eye? But not knowing *how* need not prevent believing *that*.

Exit: One last question about *The Good*, which, be it as an aspect-idea* or as a beyond-being, is surely of ultimate

> Recall that an idea, a form, is accessible to us as an *eidos*, a mental look or aspect—as a cognitive act, a nonesuch, a hybrid of thinking and imagining.

interest—a question not within the *Republic* but beyond it. Can *The Good* of the *Republic* be understood as a creator, not so unlike the Creator of the Bible? I'm reluctant even to note the perplexity, having been brought up to regard Creation—not the mythical making from pre-existent matter according to a given model by a Craftsman, the Greek mode, but the real mystery of genesis from Nothing, contingent on a divinely spontaneous will—as a Judeo-Christian prerogative.

Other differences are certainly powerful. The Good of *Republic* is impersonal, ungendered, somehow thinkable as an idea. The God of the Bible is a person, gendered, even a triune personality, best apprehended through faith. The Good is, at worst, ignored; God is crucified.

Yet here are similarities: Both the Good and the God have offspring. The Good is imaged by the Sun, God is incarnate in the Son. Both sustain the world, the Good in letting the Sun emanate its goodness to make the world flourish, God in sending his Son to mankind on a mission of salvation. Thus both act immanently, within the world, yet from a place of transcendence. Both have a complementing antagonist; the Good has its counter-principle, the Indefinite Dyad, a source of variation, God has a fallen angel, the Adversary, Satan, a mover of apostasy.

And finally, the Good and God are each known in the same two ways, to put it curtly: through the hard-edged way of negation and the fuzzy insights of intimations.*

A while after writing this essay I learned of the formulas through which the members of the Middle Platonist Academy and its school (2nd century B.C.E.) approached the Idea of the Good: 1. the *via negationis*—the apprehension of the Good by way of positing what it is not, 2. the *via eminentiae*—the comprehension of the Good by way of intimations drawing on something beyond the mere definition, 3. The *via analogiae*—the imagining of the Good by way of a relatable likeness, be it picture or myth. See Zeke Mazur, *Introduction and Commentary to Plotinus' Treatise 33 (II.9) Against the Gnostics and Related Studies* (2019), p. 54.

Had I known of these formulas I might have, animated by Zeke's account, conceived this essay as an "Academic" exercise, quite literally so. Then, however, it would not have been the culmination of, indeed it could not have had a place in, these, my Pursuits of Happiness.

So while the *Republic* appears to me as centrally theological and *The Good* is—as it were—its divinity, Socrates never calls it a god.* *The Good*, then, has a missed relation to divinity.

> In 508a the Sun is, to be sure, called a god, not so its ancestral *Good*. In 597b–c a maker-god (*theos*), probably identical with the Craftsman (for example, 507c), turns up, but again no connection to *The Good* is made.

Is this intentional? Does it signify that the connection is too obvious for words or too dangerous for emphasis? Perhaps I can call a poet to aid for a picture Socrates paints but leaves untitled—Milton in *Paradise Lost* (VII 225 ff.). Recall that the *Good*, as I've delineated it, is first and last a circumscribing *arche*, a "ruling principle"* of encircling, of unification,

> Perhaps, finally, the best rendering of *arche*.

and of cohesive community, and thus, to be sure, an immanent but primarily an *encompassing* principle. So Milton:

> He [the Son] took the golden compasses, prepared
> In God's eternal store, to circumscribe
> This universe and all created things:
> One foot he centered, and the other turned
> Round through the vast profundity obscure,
> And said, "Thus far extend, thus far thy bounds,
> This be thy just circumference, O world."
>
> (*Paradise Lost*, VII 225)

> *Explicit* (abbreviation for *Explicitus est liber*, "The Scroll's Unrolled").

> Annapolis, 2019